INTERNATIONAL HANDBOOK ON THE PREPARATION AND DEVELOPMENT OF SCHOOL LEADERS

Sponsored by the University Council for Educational Administration (UCEA), the British Educational Leadership, Management and Administration Society (BELMAS), and the Commonwealth Council for Educational Administration and Management (CCEAM), this is the first book to provide a comprehensive and comparative review of what is known about the preparation and development of primary and secondary school leaders across the globe. It describes current issues and debates and examines where the field of leadership and development is headed. Key features include the following:

- Global Focus — This book provides the first comprehensive look at leadership preparation and development across the globe. The chapter authors, all of whom are well known scholars, are drawn from the following countries: USA 7, UK 5, Europe 6, Asia 3, Canada 3, Australia/New Zealand 6, Middle East 2 and Africa 6.

- Topical & Geographical Focus — Provides researchers and policymakers with critical descriptions and assessments of both topical and geographical areas.

- International Expertise — Chapter contributors are drawn from a variety of theoretical perspectives and represent all major continents.

Jacky Lumby is a Professor of Education at the University of Southampton, England.

Gary Crow is Professor in the Department of Educational Leadership and Policy Studies at Indiana University.

Petros Pashiardis is Professor at the Open University of Cyprus. He is also the President of the Commonwealth Council for Educational Administration and Management.

INTERNATIONAL HANDBOOK ON THE PREPARATION AND DEVELOPMENT OF SCHOOL LEADERS

Edited by

Jacky Lumby
University of Southampton, U.K.

Gary Crow
Indiana University, U.S.A.

Petros Pashiardis
Open University of Cyprus, Cyprus

Routledge
Taylor & Francis Group

NEW YORK AND LONDON

First published 2008
by Routledge
270 Madison Ave, New York, NY 10016

Simultaneously published in the UK
by Routledge
2 Park Square, Milton Park, Abingdon, Oxon OX14 4RN

Routledge is an imprint of the Taylor & Francis Group, an informa business

Typeset in Times and Helvetica by EvS Communication Networx, Inc.
Printed and bound in the United States of America on acid-free paper by Edwards Brothers, Inc.

Library of Congress Cataloging-in-Publication Data
International Handbook on the Preparation and Development of School Leaders / edited by Jacky Lumby, Gary Crow, and Petros Pashiardis.
p. cm.
1. Educational leadership—Handbooks, manuals, etc. 2. School management and organization—Handbooks, manuals, etc. I. Lumby, Jacky. II. Crow, Gary. III. Pashiardis, Petros.
LB2805.I4544 2008
371.20071'1—dc22
2007052145

ISBN10: 0-415-98847-0 (hbk)
ISBN10: 0-8058-6387-7 (pbk)
ISBN10: 1-4106-1847-1 (ebk)

ISBN13: 978-0-415-98847-6 (hbk)
ISBN13: 978-0-8058-6387-1 (pbk)
ISBN13: 978-1-4106-1847-4 (ebk)

CONTENTS

III. INTERNATIONAL REFLECTIONS

CONTRIBUTORS

Michelle Anderson, B.Ed (Rusden), M.Ed (Melbourne), is a Senior Research Fellow in the Teaching and Leadership program area at ACER. She joined the organization in 2005 after two years abroad as a researcher with the National College for School Leadership in England. Recent work includes, reviewing co-principal models of leadership for the South Australian Voices of Women Board, research for The Smith Family on the post school plans of young people. Currently, Michelle is doing her Ph.D. with the University of London, Institute of Education, examining Leading Teacher leadership in multi-campus schools. Her research interests are inclusive education, school leadership, professional learning and change.

Linda Barallon, a former B.Ed. (Honours) Science Education graduate from Sussex University, has worked for several years as a Science teacher, head of Science department, and for five years as deputy head for curriculum in secondary schools. She graduated from Reading University with an MA in Organisation, Planning and Management (OPM) in Education, and took up headship in 2004. Linda is currently working as an Education Coordinator (support provider) for Secondary Schools in the Schools Division of the Ministry of Education in the Seychelles, and is also a Warwick University Ph.D. student, researching on School Leadership Development in the Seychelles.

Bruce G. Barnett is a Professor in the Educational Leadership and Policy Studies Department at the University of Texas at San Antonio, having entered the professorate in 1987. He has held similar faculty positions at Indiana University and the University of Northern Colorado. Besides developing and delivering master's, doctoral, and certification programs, his research interests include leadership preparation programs, particularly cohort-based learning; mentoring and coaching; reflective practice; leadership for school improvement; school-university partnerships; realities of beginning principals; and team learning and development. Recently, Bruce has become involved in international research and program development, authoring books on school improvement with Australian colleagues; researching mentoring and coaching programs operating around the world; and presenting workshops in Australia, New Zealand, England, Ireland, and Canada.

Brenda R. Beatty is designer and Director of the highly regarded *Monash Master in School Leadership*, *Mentoring for First Time Principals* and *Human Leadership: Developing People* programs. Born in Canada, she studied at OISE University of Toronto with Andy Hargreaves. Her doctoral dissertation *Emotion Matters in Educational Leadership: Examining the Unexamined*, won the Thomas B. Greenfield award for best Canadian doctoral dissertation. Dr. Beatty lectures and conducts research about the emotions of leadership, leadership development, and school improvement. Her work has been well received in China, Ireland, England, New Zealand, the United States, Canada, Australia, and Italy. Recent publications include a book co-authored with Ken Leithwood: *Leading with Teacher Emotions in Mind*.

Paul T. Begley is Professor of Educational Leadership at Pennsylvania State University and Director of the Willower Centre for the Study of Leadership and Ethics. This centre is affiliated with the University Council for Educational Administration (UCEA). His current teaching and research interests focus on all aspects of school leadership including: the influence of values and ethics on school leadership practices, socializing influences experienced by aspiring principals, international images of effective school leadership, the ethics and procedures of performance appraisal, the administrator's role in school improvement, and state of the art pre-service and in-service practices for school leadership development (including online education). Because of his extensive field development experience in Ontario and the Northwest Territories of Canada, Sweden, Hong Kong and Australia, his work reflects a strong practitioner orientation. Recent publications include three books: *The Ethical Dimensions of School Leadership* (2003) published by Kluwer Press, *The Values of Educational Administration* (1999) published by the Falmer Press, and *Values and Educational Leadership* (1999) published by SUNY Press.

Christopher Bezzina is a member of the Faculty of Education, University of Malta. He is mainly responsible for co-ordinating the B.Ed. (Hons) and PGCE teaching practicum. He runs courses and seminars on classroom management issues. Christopher is course leader of the Masters program in Educational Leadership. He is involved with a wide range of school development and school improvement initiatives. He has taught and done consultancy work both locally and abroad in the areas of teacher education and the professional development of teachers and educational leaders. He is a board member of various educational journals and also involved in various European bodies. In 2004 he was a Fulbright Scholar at the State University of New York at Buffalo.

Stefan Brauckmann is a research scientist at the Center for Planning and Financing in Education of the German Institute for International Educational Research, a member of the Leibniz Association. His main academic fields and interests are governance strategies of education systems, school management and educational policy analysis. Dr. Brauckmann participated as a researcher and assistant of project coordination in several international comparative studies, such as *Education systems in Canada and Germany — An In-depth Comparison of System Governance and Educational Attainment* and *Education systems in Europe*. For the spring term 2007, he was a visiting scholar at the Institute PACE (Policy Analysis for California Education) of U.C. Berkeley and Stanford University.

Tony Bush is Professor of Educational Leadership at the University of Warwick and previously held similar posts at the universities of Leicester, Reading and Lincoln. He has published more than 100 books and refereed journal articles and chapters on many aspects of educational leadership. He has been an external examiner, visiting professor, invited keynote speaker or consultant in Australia, China, Germany, Greece, Hong Kong, New Zealand, Norway, Portugal, the Seychelles, Singapore, and South Africa and is currently leading the research strategy for the new national qualification for school principals in South Africa. He has directed many research and evaluation projects for the English National College for School Leadership and has been the editor of the leading international journal, *Educational Management, Administration and Leadership*, since 2002.

Shuanye Chen received her undergraduate education in Peking University and her Ph.D. from The Chinese University of Hong Kong. Now she is an instructor in the Department of Educational Administration and Policy, The Chinese University of Hong Kong. Her current research interests include educational leadership, education policy, education marketization and higher education in China.

Marianne Coleman is a Reader in educational leadership and management and Assistant Dean of Research at the Institute of Education, University of London. Her working life has been spent in education, in universities, schools and working for a local education authority. Present teaching responsibilities focus on doctoral supervision but she has recently developed and established an on-line distance-learning course for an MA in Applied Educational Leadership and Management. She is an experienced researcher on leadership in schools, particularly focusing on gender issues in leadership. Her most recent work in this area has been funded by the National College for School Leadership in England.

Jorge Adelino Costa is an Associate Professor at the Department of Education Sciences of the University of Aveiro, Portugal. He earned his Ph.D. in 1995 in the area of School Management. He is the author of several books and has published various papers in national and international journals. His field of teaching and research is educational management and his latest projects are in the subject of school leadership. He has collaborated throughout the years with several Portuguese universities and with the Inter-University Institute of Macau in Masters and Ph.D. programs.

Gary Crow is Professor in the Department of Educational Leadership and Policy Studies at Indiana University. He received his Ph.D. from the University of Chicago. His research focuses on the school principalship and school reform and in particular the work socialization of principals in reform contexts. He has conducted research on U.S. principals and U.K. head teachers. His work is published in numerous journals including, *Educational Administration Quarterly*, *Educational Management, Administration and Leadership* (U.K.), *Journal of School Leadership* and *Journal of Educational Administration*. His books focus on the principalship, mentoring and leadership. He is past president of the University Council for Educational Administration.

Tanya Fitzgerald is Professor of Education at Unitec Institute of Technology, Auckland, New Zealand, and in 2007 was Visiting Research Fellow at the University of Nottingham. Her research interests include gender and educational leadership, social justice and education policy and the history of women's higher education. Tanya is currently working on a book on women professors that will be published by Peter Lang.

Nick Foskett is Professor of Education and Dean of the Faculty of Law, Arts and Social Sciences at the University of Southampton in the U.K. He has held senior posts in schools and in HE, has worked as a consultant to government and to a wide range of educational institutions both in the U.K. and internationally. His expertise is in educational policy and management, with a particular focus on education 14–19 and higher education. His research in recent years in this field has included: the nature of education markets and institutional and individual responses to markets policy and reform in 14–19 education/training and its implications for institutional management international comparisons of education policy and management in education. Nick has published extensively with eight books and over 100 academic papers since 1989.

Margaret Grogan is currently Professor and Chair, Department of Educational Leadership and Policy Analysis, University of Missouri-Columbia. She taught high school in Australia, and was a teacher and an administrator at an international school in Japan. A past president of the University Council of Educational Administration (UCEA), she has taught and researched educational leadership preparation and development at the University of Virginia as well as at the University of Missouri-Columbia. She also researches women in leadership, the superintendency, the moral and ethical dimensions of leadership, and leadership for social justice. Together with Cryss Brunner, she has just published a new book, *Women Leading School Systems: Uncommon roads to fullfillment*, 2007, Rowman & Littlefield Education. Other recent publications include a book chapter in *The Handbook of Doctoral Programs in Educational Leadership*, 2007, Disrupting the status quo: The action research dissertation as a transformative strategy with Joe Donaldson and Juanita Simmons.

David Gurr has a background in secondary teaching, psychology, school supervision, and educational leadership research, in a career spanning nearly 30 years. Currently David is Senior Lecturer in Educational Leadership in the Centre for Organisational Learning and Leadership, Faculty of Education, the University of Melbourne. He coordinates the Master of School Leadership and has research interests in school review, educational leadership, and technology and leadership. He is a member of the International Successful School Principalship Project (ISSPP), and is a Fellow and past Vice-President of the Australian Council for Educational Leaders.

Stephan Gerhard Huber is Head of the Institute for the Management and Economics of Education (IBB) of the Teacher Training University of Central Switzerland (PHZ), a co-opted member of the Centre for Research on Education at the University of Erfurt, and honorary research fellow in the School of Education within the Faculty of Humanities, University of Manchester, England. His fields of interest are system counseling, education management, school effectiveness, school improvement, the professionalization of teachers and school leaders, and professional learning communities. He publishes in international book series and journals, and he gives keynote speeches at international symposia and congresses. He is also chairing various academic networks and also some school and practitioner networks.

Stephen L. Jacobson is Professor of Educational Administration and the Associate Dean of Academic Affairs for the Graduate School of Education at the University at Buffalo/State University of New York. His extensive publications have examined teacher compensation, school finance, the reform of leadership preparation and effective leadership in challenging schools. He is the 2007/08 President of the University Council for Educational Administration (UCEA) and, in 1994, received UCEA's Jack Culbertson Award for outstanding contributions by a junior professor. He is the lead editor of *Leadership and Policy in Schools* and co-director (with Kenneth Leithwood) of the UCEA Center for the Study of School-Site Leadership. In 1999 he was President of the American Education Finance Association.

Jonah Nyaga Kindiki began his teaching career in 1984. He worked as a classroom teacher, deputy principal and later a principal. He studied his BD degree and taught at Kenya Methodist University (KEMU). He did his M.Ed. and Ph.D. degrees in International Management and Policy in Education at the University of Birmingham in the U.K. His major interest is on policy issues in school effectiveness and improvement. He joined Moi University in 2005 as a lecturer in the School of Education, Department of Educational Management and Policy studies. He is also the time table coordinator of the School of Education. He has written a number of forthcoming papers and textbooks.

Elizabeth Kleinhenz, an ACER Senior Research Fellow, has led and worked on many projects of national and international significance. With Dr. Lawrence Ingvarson she has provided reports and advice to state government education agencies across Australia and in New Zealand in areas of teacher education, teaching standards, teacher evaluation and teacher workload. Dr. Kleinhenz's recent book, *Towards a Moving School*, written in conjunction with a school principal, is about to be published. She has published other work in professional journals, and presented at education conferences in Australia and overseas.

Kenneth Leithwood is Professor of Educational Leadership and Policy at OISE/University of Toronto. His research and writing concerns school leadership, educational policy and organizational change. Dr. Leithwood is the senior editor of both the first and second *International Handbooks on Educational Leadership and Administration* (Kluwer Publishers, 1996, 2003). His most recent books (all with Corwin Press) include *Leading with Teacher Emotions In Mind* (in press),

Making Schools Smarter (3rd edition, 2006) and *Teaching for Deep Understanding* (2006). Dr. Leithwood is the recipient of the University of Toronto's *Impact on Public Policy* award and Fellow of the Royal Society of Canada.

Ben Levin is Professor and Canada Research Chair in Education Leadership and Policy at the Ontario Institute for Studies in Education. His academic work includes four books and more than 150 other publications. His main current interests are in research-practice links, large scale change, and poverty-equity issues. He has also served as a senior manager in government, including as chief civil servant for education in two Canadian provinces. More information is available at http://www.home.oise.utoronto.ca/~blevin.

Jacky Lumby is a Professor of Education at the University of Southampton, England. She has researched and published widely on leadership and management in schools and colleges in the U.K., Republic of Ireland, China, Hong Kong, and South Africa. She is interested in adopting an international perspective, challenging the appropriateness of Western-derived concepts, theories and suggested practice to diverse cultures. She is co-editor of *International Studies in Educational Administration*, and a member of the Council of the British Educational Leadership, Management and Administration Society. Her most recent book (with Marianne Coleman) considers diversity and leadership.

Reynold Macpherson has just completed an assignment as the foundation Chancellor and CEO of Abu Dhabi University. He is currently researching a political philosophy of educative leadership and has a portfolio of commitments in Australasian universities. Professor Macpherson has advised Ministerial Commissions in New Zealand and New South Wales, served as Visiting Professor at a number of North American universities, and edited 17 editions of scholarly journals. He has served on leading editorial boards and published extensively. In his spare time he reads biographies of leaders and geo-political analyses, and tries to imagine how educative leaders around the world in knowledge organizations might help people learn in ways consistent with the ideals of the European Enlightenment.

Jorunn Møller is Professor at the Department of Teacher Education and School Development, University of Oslo. Her professional interests are in the areas of educational administration and leadership, supervision, action research, and school evaluation. She has been involved in a range of research projects on educational leadership and policy change. Her teaching is connected to doctoral programs and a Master program in Educational Leadership at the University of Oslo. In addition, she is involved in the design, provision, and evaluation of a broad range of in-service education and workshops for school principals and superintendents.

Kholeka Moloi is an Associate Professor of Educational Management at the University of Johannesburg. She is in the Faculty of education but presently seconded to the position of Executive Director: Student Affairs in the same University. She is currently involved in working with nonperforming schools and school districts in Gauteng and Mpumalanga Provinces of Education. Her specialization is in Schools as Learning Organisations. She has published in this area during the past ten years. She has also worked with Professor Tony Bush, University of Warwick, on numerous research projects and has published with him.

Bill Mulford researches and publishes in educational leadership and change and school effectiveness and improvement. He is editor for the Leadership and Management Section of the *International Encyclopaedia of Education*. His most recent book is *Leadership for Organisational Learning and Student outcomes*. A former teacher, school principal, Assistant Director of Education and Faculty Dean, he continues as an adviser to numerous state and national Departments of Education and international organizations OECD and UNESCO. Among his awards, the Australian Council for Educational Leadership Gold Medal — for academic attainment, successful practice and an outstanding record of contributing to the field.

Gary R. O'Mahony was formerly a Project Director at the Australian Principals Centre where he was instrumental in the development of a range of professional career development programs for novice and experienced principals. He also has been a primary school principal, a state Government senior project manager for state principal professional development, and has worked as a consultant with a range of professional business consultancy groups. Gary is a Director of his own consultancy company, O'Mahony & Associates Consulting, which provides state based and regional programs in leadership for aspirant leaders, principals and school teams. Gary is currently involved in international research and program development, co-authoring books on school improvement; researching mentoring and coaching programs operating around the world; and presenting workshops in Australia, United States, New Zealand, and Canada.

Ruth Otunga began her professional career working as a high school teacher for five years after qualifying with a B.Ed. degree from University of Nairobi in 1980. She proceeded to do her M.Ed. at Kenyatta University after which she taught as a middle level college lecturer for a number of years. She joined Moi University as a tutorial fellow in 1988 and registered for her D.Phil in 1990. She was the first woman D.Phil graduate of the University in 1993. She has attended and presented academic papers in learned conferences and workshops. She has risen through the ranks to become an Associate Professor of Education with 20 publications to her credit. She is a teacher educator with vast experience of lecturing at both undergraduate and postgraduate levels. She has served as Head, Department of Educational Administration, Planning and Curriculum Development. In 2005 she became the first elected Dean of the School of Education, Moi University.

Petros Pashiardis is Professor at the Open University of Cyprus. He is also the President of the Commonwealth Council for Educational Administration and Management. He has been a Fulbright Scholar during his doctoral studies in the United States. He has conducted research and lectured in many countries around the world. Over the last 20 years Professor Pashiardis has researched and published in a variety of areas of education management, leadership, and policy making at institutional, local, national and international levels. On his own or with others, he has authored well over 80 articles in scholarly and professional journals. He has also authored or co-authored eight books in the area of educational management and leadership.

Marie-Therese Purvis is currently the co-ordinator for higher education in the Seychelles Ministry of Education, and she also teaches on an education management and leadership course at the National Institute of Education. As part of a team developing a National Qualifications Framework for the Seychelles, she is involved with the development of curricula at post secondary level. Prior to this she was director of the National Institute of Education and director of the Ministry's Curriculum Development Section and has just completed a doctoral thesis on school improvement initiatives in Seychelles secondary schools. It has been accepted by Warwick University.

Haiyan Qian is a Ph.D, candidate in the Department of Educational Administration and Policy at The Chinese University of Hong Kong. She has degrees from Nanjing University in China and Cambridge University in the U.K. She is currently studying the roles of Chinese principals.

Peter Ribbins is Professor of Educational Leadership at Lincoln University and Emeritus Professor of Educational Management at Birmingham University. He has been Chairperson of BELMAS, is a Vice-President, and received its Distinguished Service Award. He is a Fellow of CCEAM and has been a member of its Council. He was a long serving editor of *Pastoral Care in Education* and of *Educational Management and Administration*, and has edited special editions of other journals and two book series. He is a member of the RAE Education Panel in the U.K. He has been researching headship for over 30 years and in many countries. He has published 25 books and 110 articles.

Edith A. Rusch is an Associate Professor of Educational Leadership at the University of Nevada Las Vegas. Dr. Rusch researches educational settings engaged in profound cultural change, searching specifically for evidence of equity in action and the developmental traits of educational leaders who practice their craft in democratic ways. She also examines the intractability of gender and race as an issue in educational settings. Her recent work has appeared in the *Review of Higher Education*, *Educational Administration Quarterly*, and the *International Journal of Leadership in Education*. She currently serves as the editor of UCEA's *Journal of Research on Leadership Education*.

Terezinha Monteiro dos Santos is a Professor at the Federal University of Pará (UFPA), Brazil. She earned her Ph.D. in 1999 in the field of Education with a grant from the CAPES (Coordination for the Enrichment of Higher Education Staff). She participated in various research projects and has several published papers, and is the coordinator of the Postgraduate Program in Education of the Federal University of Pará.

Michael Schratz is Professor and Director of Teacher Education and School Research at the University of Innsbruck. His professional interests are in educational innovation and change with a particular focus on leadership, quality development and self-evaluation. He is an Austrian representative for the European Union, for ENTEP (European Network of Teacher Education Policies) and for the OECD (School Leadership Development). He is also (with W. Schley, University of Zürich) the scientific director of the Austrian Leadership Academy. He has been involved in research projects on educational leadership and policy development, and his publications have been translated into several languages.

David K. Serem earned his Doctorate degree in Educational Administration from the University of Wyoming in 1985. He returned to Kenya and was employed as a lecturer at Kenyatta University. He relocated to Moi University in 1988, and was among those who started a new University College at Maseno where he became its first Dean of Education and first Deputy Principal. Professor Serem later became the Acting Principal, who saw the transition of the college to a fully-fledged university in 2001. He was promoted through the ranks to become an Associate Professor of Education. He was the first Deputy Vice Chancellor of Maseno University, in Charge of Finance and Administration. Professor Serem has attended many national and international conferences and workshops on Educational Leadership. Currently, he is the chairman, Department of Educational Management & Policy Studies.

Omid Tofighian is currently a Ph.D. researcher in philosophy at Leiden University, The Netherlands. He has taught at Abu Dhabi University for about two years and has lived and worked in the UAE for three years. He has traveled extensively throughout Australia, Asia and Europe for the past four years and has been involved in the promotion of art, culture and education by conducting and managing a number of art exhibitions and festivals which have mainly focused on Middle-Eastern artists from various genres. He has had two journal publications with a third one forthcoming and has participated in three conferences.

Alexandre Ventura is Deputy Chief Inspector of the Portuguese General Inspectorate of Education. He is also a Researcher at the Research Unit *Pedagogical Knowledge in the Systems of Formation* of the Department of Educational Sciences at the University of Aveiro, Portugal. He is the author of several books and papers in different journals and a speaker at National and International Public Lectures and Conferences. He was awarded a Ph.D. in the area of Educational Sciences. His field of teaching and research is Educational Sciences and most of his projects are in the scope of Institutional Evaluation.

Allan Walker is Professor of Educational Administration and Policy and department chair at The Chinese University of Hong Kong. He has worked extensively with school leaders throughout Asia for over 20 years. His current research interests include the influence of culture on school leadership and organization; leader development; the principalship in Chinese societies; leadership and student learning; and leadership in international/intercultural settings.

Michelle D. Young is the Executive Director of the University Council for Educational Administration and an Associate Professor at the University of Texas. Dr. Young's scholarship focuses on how school leaders and school policies can ensure equitable and quality experiences for all students and adults learning and working in schools. She is the recipient of the William J. Davis award for the most outstanding article published in a volume of the *Educational Administration Quarterly*. Her work has also been published in the *Review of Educational Research,* the *Educational Researcher*, the *American Educational Research Journal*, the *Journal of School Leadership,* the *International Journal of Qualitative Studies in Education*, and *Leadership and Policy in Schools*, among other publications.

PREFACE

There are many areas of education which are contested, where practitioners, policy makers, parents and the wider community disagree on what are the right aims and the right ways to achieve them. In the melee of debate and divergence, one of the few points of general agreement is that the quality of leadership of schools matters to how children mature, develop and achieve, and to their future life chances. This handbook is intended as a rich resource for those who contribute to such quality by supporting the preparation of leaders for their role and their continuing development. This includes policy makers who may decide what resources and systems are needed, members of government sponsored and of private organisations who provide programs, aspiring and current leaders, and academic faculty who create and share relevant knowledge.

The handbook is sponsored by three professional organizations, the University Council for Educational Administration, based in the United States, the British Educational Leadership, Management, and Administration Society, and the Commonwealth Council for Educational Administration and Management. As such it evidences an international collaboration reflecting a world wide membership of practitioners and academics. The handbook adopts an international perspective. What the latter might mean and why it might be important is a central concern of the volume. At the commencement of the project the editors were clear what it did not mean; the handbook is not a descriptive tour of policy and practice covering all parts of the globe. It is not intended to offer knowledge related to every aspect of leadership preparation and development in all geographic locations. Such an ambition would be futile. It offers rather a means of engaging with the values, knowledge and practical wisdom that has emerged variously in differing cultures. It is intended to stimulate reflection on patterns of thinking, feeling and doing which will help readers understand better their own practice and its connection to others in a globalised world.

The editors were also clear that inclusion was a foundational principle. The handbook consequently is written both by internationally recognised distinguished researchers and by emerging researchers, sometimes writing together. The handbook was intended not just to write about inclusion and social justice but to embody it. Equally, insights and perspectives from all inhabited continents find a place.

The handbook is structured into three broad sections: Concepts of Leadership Preparation and Development, The Practice of Leadership Preparation and Development and finally, International Reflections. The first section provides a conceptual framework mapping the theoretical terrain related to leadership in the belief that leadership development is intimately connected to how leadership is understood and enacted. It considers the purposes of leadership, the relevance of culture, how a leadership career may be understood, why race/ethnicity and gender still matter, what effect leaders may have on students and on learning and finally the theories of learning which may underpin programs. The first section therefore provides the groundwork for considering, in section two, the various approaches to the practice of preparing and developing leaders, including the recruitment and selection of leaders, provider and delivery modes, curriculum and pedagogy, mentoring and coaching, the evaluation of principals and how the impact of leadership development might be assessed.

All chapters of the handbook adopt an international perspective. However, in the final section, the international focus takes center stage as writers consider the current context, achievements and emerging research issues in North and South America, Europe, Africa, the Middle East, Chinese Societies, Australia and Small Island States. This section offers information, insights and stimulation which considerably enlarge our understanding of how leadership preparation and development are variously practiced and challenges the reader to reconsider context and practice close to home in the light of the different histories, value bases, priorities and practice revealed by the contributors.

Assembling an international handbook exposes the strengths and frailties of the current field. It is intended to build on the picture which emerges by offering an agenda for future research priorities and by cementing cross cultural and intercultural bonds. While the handbook may help us understand better the nature and completeness of current answers to critical issues, the questions that remain, and the importance of the learning journey towards addressing them, emerges strongly. The handbook offers a view back and a path forward to all those who aspire to lead or to support leaders of schools and of children.

Jacky Lumby, Gary Crow, Petros Pashiardis

ACKNOWLEDGEMENTS

A project of this magnitude is dependant on the help and support of very many people. We wish to acknowledge the part many individuals and organizations have played. The University Council for Educational Administration (UCEA), the British Educational Leadership, Management and Administration Society (BELMAS) and the Commonwealth Council for Educational Administration and Management (CCEAM) have been supportive throughout and provided resources to underpin the final production of the manuscript. Lane Akers of Routledge was an enthusiastic, positive and responsive link to the publisher. Michelle Young and Tony Bush contributed to conceiving the original idea. Our thanks go to the authors who had many other projects to which they could give their time, but chose to contribute to this endeavor from commitment to the field and to the three sponsoring organizations. Many individuals also contributed their expertise by reviewing chapters:

Professor R. K. Aula, University of Namibia; Professor Johan Beckmann, University of Pretoria, South Africa; Dr Christopher Bezzina, University of Malta; Lars Bjork, University of Kentucky, USA; Dr Allison M. Borden, University of New Mexico; Professor Ann R. J. Briggs, Newcastle University, UK; Professor Miles T. Bryant, University of Nebraska-Lincoln, USA; Dr Linda Chisholm, Human Science Research Council, South Africa; Dr John Collard, University of Canberra, Australia; Professor Michael Crossley, University of Bristol, UK; Professor Clive Dimmock, University of Leicester, UK; Dr Lisa Ehrich, Australia; Dr Fenwick English, Robert Wendell Eaves Sr. Distinguished Professor of Educational Leadership, University of North Carolina, USA; Professor J. Tim Goddard, University of Calgary, Canada; Professor Stephen Gorard, University of Birmingham, UK; Professor Helen Gunter, University of Manchester, UK; Professor Philip Hallinger, Mahidol University, Thailand; Professor Clive Harber, University of Birmingham, UK; Dr Abrar Hassan, IIEP, UNESCO; Professor Olof Johansson, University of Umea, Sweden; Dr Khaula Murtadha, University of Indiana, USA; Professor Frances Kochan, Auburn University, USA; Associate Professor Leonidas Kyriakides, University of Cyprus; Jenny Lewis, Australian Council for Educational Administration, Australia; Associate Professor Gerardo Lopez, University of Indiana, USA; Professor Daniel Muijs, University of Manchester, UK; Dr Izhar Oplatka, Ben Gurion University of the Negev, Israel; Margaret Terry Orr, Bank Street College, New York, USA; Associate Professor Bradley Portin, University of Washington, USA; Professor Viviane Robinson, University of Auckland, New Zealand; Dr Helen C. Sobehart, Duquesne University, USA; Professor Emerita Angela Thody, University of Lincoln, UK; and Professor Charles F. Webber, Faculty of Education, University of Calgary, Canada.

Alison Williamson cheerfully undertook the considerable task of turning the chapters submitted into a coherent manuscript. Finally, we salute each other as editors, for weathering the difficulties of working together over eighteen months with few opportunities to meet and many challenges to overcome.

Jacky Lumby, Gary Crow and Petros Pashiardis

1

Introduction: Why an International Handbook on the Preparation and Development of School Leaders?

Gary Crow, Jacky Lumby and Petros Pashiardis

RATIONALE FOR AN INTERNATIONAL HANDBOOK

The *International Handbook on the Preparation and Development of School Leaders* meets a growing need to identify, describe, critique and enrich the international literature on school leaders' preparation and development. We believe the rationale for such a volume is strong and is based on the evolving recognition of both the importance of leadership, and leadership development and preparation, as well as the value of an international perspective.

IMPORTANCE OF SCHOOL LEADERSHIP IN CONTEMPORARY SCHOOLS AND REFORM

During the last few years we have observed numerous economic, scientific and technological advancements, as well as demographic shifts, the advent of state interdependence, and globalization. Many educational organizations are faced with large-scale reforms initiated as a response to strong accountability pressures for increased performance. Educational leaders need to act as the "torchbearers of educational change" (Pashiardis, 2001), initiating and sustaining school transformation: the responsibility for providing direction and support for the implementation of planned change lies with the leader.

However, as Marcoulides, Larsen and Heck (1995) point out, leadership is a necessary but insufficient condition for learner achievement as principals and other leaders may not have direct control over the elements which contribute to school improvement (Usdan, McCloud, & Podmostko, 2000)

Another relevant issue regarding the importance of leadership is the question of "who should be the leader". Should there be only one person at the top? Or could there be others as well? According to Harris (2004) multiple leadership models have been developed, most of which focus on formal-institutionalized forms of leadership, neglecting the value of the alternative non-formal ways of leading. Gronn (2002) also maintains that the past model of the "heroic leader" has not been sufficiently responsive to the complexity of contemporary leadership demands (cited in Hatcher, 2005). Consequently, new models of school leadership involving lateral forms of leadership are enriching the existing diversity of practice throughout the world (Harris, 2006).

As these examples and others later in this chapter demonstrate, the nature of leadership itself is a contested idea. We acknowledge in beginning this handbook and emphasize, particularly in the chapter by Paul Begley, that leadership in general, and school leadership in particular, is not a uniformly defined nor understood idea. However, the diversity and complexity of leadership theory and practice provides a rich terrain with which our discussion of leadership development as an international phenomenon exists and can be extended.

EVOLVING RECOGNITION OF IMPORTANCE OF SCHOOL LEADERSHIP AS AN INTERNATIONAL PHENOMENON

School leadership issues have been increasingly debated and explored in an international and comparative context. The priorities of many countries revolve around developing leaders as essential to improve school performance. For example, inspection evidence produced by The Office for Standards in Education (OFSTED) in England has guided the UK government's work on identifying and preparing prospective heads, developing experienced ones and establishing the National College for School Leadership (Southworth, 2002). The latter has introduced the National Professional Qualification for Headship (NPQH) for prospective principals and the National Professional Qualification for Serving Headteachers (NPQSH) for the development of existing principals (Weindling & Dimmock, 2006; Briggs, Bush & Middlewood, 2006). In the United States, a Master's degree in Educational Administration remains a common requirement in most states in applying for a leadership position (Hillman, 1992 cited in Wong, 2004). Additionally, in Hong-Kong prospective principals should acquire a Certification for Principalship (CFP) in order to meet requirements for the specific position, while serving principals are required to undergo a continuous development program for about 50 hours per year during a three-year cycle. In Ontario, Canada prospective school leaders have to follow the Principal Qualification Program (PQP) offered by ten universities in Ontario (Huber & West, 2002).

Furthermore, international organizations are beginning to realize the key role of school leaders. Education ministers of the countries participating in organizations such as the Organization for Economic Cooperation and Development (OECD) have emphasized the need to improve school leadership. The OECD in particular, in the context of the Program for International Student Achievement (PISA), is planning to collect data in relation to school leadership dimensions so as to identify leadership practices in various contexts and to relate these to student achievement.

IMPORTANCE OF THE PREPARATION AND DEVELOPMENT OF SCHOOL LEADERS

It is relatively recent that the growing evidence of the importance of school leadership for school improvement, student learning, and other outcomes has led to recognition that the preparation and development of school leaders might make a difference to their leadership practices (Crow, 2006). If school leaders and leadership are important, then perhaps we should be deeply concerned with how leaders learn to do their jobs and, more importantly, how they learn to do them in ways that contribute to these outcomes.

The focus on leadership development and preparation, however, is far from an uncontested debate. At times, the attention on leadership development avoids the most obvious question of "preparation for what?" Obviously this reflects larger debates on leadership itself, including models of leadership such as distributed leadership, sustainable leadership, and turn-around leadership and the desired outcomes of leadership. The broader debates about leadership percolate into questions regarding leadership development and preparation. For example, if we should avoid thinking of leadership in simplistic de-contextualized ways, should we not also think of leadership development and preparation as contextualized? Also, there are questions about preparing school leaders for specific types of school structures or circumstances, e.g., leading challenging schools or leading professional learning communities (Coles & Southworth, 2005). The call by researchers and policy makers for innovative leadership highlights the need to think of preparation for leadership in the future rather than simply current challenges and circumstances (Fink, 2005). Although much of the leadership literature focuses on student learning, as we will see there are national contexts in which state political purposes are emphasized. These situations raise other issues of preparation and development as a political process.

Although the attention on leadership preparation and development has increased recently, the quality of this attention varies. Reports and articles, primarily in the UK, Australia, New Zealand, Sweden, Canada, and the US, have acknowledged the importance of understanding how school leaders prepare for and develop in their roles. Frequently, however, these reports have been critiques of preparation by universities (in the case of the US) rather than exhaustive descriptions of the range of preparation and development processes and providers. The rise of new managerialism and neo-conservative critiques of public education have also influenced the literature on leadership preparation forms, institutions, and processes, adding a further politicized element to the debate.

The acknowledgement of the importance of preparation and development has not always been followed by rigorous empirical research of preparation/development delivery modes and outcomes (Murphy & Vriesenga, 2004). Research on leadership development practices is still largely descriptive. The literature for some time has focused on descriptive accounts of, in some cases, idiosyncratic programs and modes of delivery with evaluations largely based on participants' satisfaction. Only recently have there been directed, rigorous efforts to document the implementation and effects of leadership development and preparation over time (Orr, 2005). This dearth of published research on leader preparation and development provides a large part of the impetus for this handbook, so that researchers can be encouraged to look for and fill gaps in our research knowledge.

The editors recognize that leadership preparation and development is by no means uniform in definition or practice throughout the world. As the valuable range of chapters in this volume emphasizes, the global landscape of leadership preparation reflects a wide assortment of definitions and practices, as does the meaning of school leadership itself. But merely establishing the variety of practices like some type of leadership development museum is hardly sufficient justification for a handbook. What is much more valuable is to identify the patterns and implications of this rich and complex variety.

We have also tried to be inclusive by acknowledging that learning to be a school leader is not a one-time process but a career-long process (Earley & Weindling, 2004). Preparation prior to becoming a school leader is emphasized in some parts of the world, while developing after one becomes a leader receives much more attention in other areas. We believe, as Peter Ribbins' chapter appropriately emphasizes, that learning to be a leader is a career-long process and have thus emphasized both preparation and development as a school leader. Even in those countries where preparation has received the greater attention, development after one becomes a school leader has recently been emphasized (Kelley & Shaw, in press).

IMPORTANCE OF AN INTERNATIONAL PERSPECTIVE

In spite of the decreasing travel and communication barriers in our world (Friedman, 2005), very little attention has been given to larger international perspectives on school leadership development and preparation. The three professional organizations, the University Council for Educational Administration the British Educational Leadership, Management, and Administration Society, and the Commonwealth Council for Educational Administration and Management, have acknowledged the lack of a sufficiently international dimension in leadership development research and have taken significant steps to remedy it. This handbook, the development of which they have supported, is certainly one method for mapping the terrain of leadership preparation and development and encouraging researchers, policy makers, and other educators to further extend international perspectives.

As we will note in the next section, the concept of "international" is contested and that fact argues for care in not only defining but in using an international perspective on leadership development and preparation. While acknowledging the pitfalls of misusing such a perspective, we believe that a sensitive use of an international perspective on leadership preparation and development has the potential to contribute to research, policy, and practice in multiple ways.

The Meaning of 'International'

The terms comparative, global and international are used liberally in texts related to educational leadership, sometimes interchangeably as synonymous and sometimes as distinctive. Each carries a weight of contested and variable meaning, reflecting the time period, the political and cultural context of their use, and the individual values of the writer. Communicating a clear framework of how we understand the terms and how they have been selectively applied in practice to the handbook is a critical underpinning to support the reader. Our intention is both to distinguish and clarify uses of the terms and also to identify the implications of such uses for an orientation to a body of research from many parts of the world. The discussion reflects the analytical journey we have undertaken as editors, as our understanding developed through engagement with the literature and with the authors, scholars and practitioners who supported the endeavor. Addressing the ontological, epistemological and axiological fractures, confusions and nuances are more than an intellectual enterprise. Rather, the differing orientations signaled by the use of different terms reflect a changing ethical engagement with those leading or researching schools, particularly those who may be deemed 'other' from the perspective of the reader.

A Comparative Approach

Looking back to the nineteenth century and the majority of the twentieth century, a comparative approach to educational research was based on a firm sense of one's own location and traditions as the intellectual point of departure. Higginson (1979) lists the intended benefits, to:

- gain a better understanding of one's own education system;
- satisfy intellectual and theoretical curiosity about other cultures and their education sys-

tems; and better understand the relationship between education and the wider society;
- identify similarities and differences in educational systems, processes and outcomes as a way of documenting and understanding problems in education, and contributing to the improvement of educational policy and practice;
- promote improved international understanding and co-operation through increased sensitivity to differing world views and cultures. (p.19)

While points three and four assert a determination to engage with other systems, there is a rather lofty tone. Rather as the eighteenth/nineteenth century European Grand Tour was the essential finishing school for aristocrats, supplying the desired knowledge of and sensitivity to art deemed in the aesthetic top drawer, so comparative research as described here has a sense of supporting the education of the superior by viewing what is worthy elsewhere. The stance has been variously depicted, those straying outside their own nation, or even the dominant voice in their nation, reporting 'travelers' tales' of curiosities (Crossley & Watson, 2003, p. 12) and, magpie like, indulging in 'cultural borrowing' (Kay & Watson, 1982, p. 23) or 'a process of *bricolage*' (Ball, 1998, p. 126). Lumby, Walker, Bryant, Bush and Bjork (in press) describe the outcome as a 'typology of the alien', fascinating and occasionally of practical use. While the stated intention was to increase knowledge, understanding and links across the world, the result may have been the contrary, embedding ethnocentricity, a hierarchy of value and disconnectedness. As Paige and Mestenhauser (1999) point out, the danger is that a comparative approach leads to 'international' becoming every country other than one's own. Differential value was ascribed to the ideas and practices of different nations; rhetorically all nations potentially had something to teach. In practice, some appeared to have more to offer than others. Hallinger (1995) highlights the resulting 'ritualistic transfer' (p. 4) of largely Western knowledge to other parts of the globe with little attention to its cultural validity. Rather than equality and solidarity, the outcome of the dominant version of a comparative approach, as it was conceived, is an intensification of disconnectedness and inequity.

Globalization

The concept of globalization has produced ideological flows which have mutated orientations to the comparative study of policy and practice. Global is sometimes used as a relatively neutral adjective, for example, global change indicating similar changes evident in many parts of the world. Globalization, the outcome of the verb to globalize, is far from neutral, conceptually contested and value laden. Globalization as a phenomenon is subject to multiple and contradictory analyses. Its goals, enactment and outcomes are disputed. Some deny its very existence (Giddens, 1999). Others assert not only the reality of the phenomenon but also its defining influence on the late twentieth and early twenty-first centuries (Rosenberg, 2000). Farrell (2006) distinguishes its core as 'strategies of predatory mobility' (p. 237), as nations, corporations and individuals seek to facilitate the maximization of economic opportunity. Jones (2006) suggests that while the inception of globalizing forces may have been primarily related to economic goals, the achievement of the latter swiftly implied cultural and political change, by challenging the geographical and governance grip of nation states. Whether mobility is seen as predatory or otherwise, globalization has resulted in changes which have profound impact on the goals, communities and processes of education (Bottery, 1999; Brown & Lauder, 1997; Ohmae, 2000; Parsons, 1995; Waters, 1995).

The communities to which schools relate increasingly include immigrant and diverse peoples, resulting in what Scholte (2000, p. 170) terms 'ethno-nations' and diasporas of 'global tribes'. Not only the people have changed. As the means of travel becomes more inclusive and communication links the geographically far distant as easily as the close, the connection between time and space has altered. It is no longer a dauntingly lengthy endeavor to speak to learners several thousand miles away, or even to visit them. The boundaries and identity of the school community are less certain, less homogenous and less secure. Bryan and Vavrus (2005) suggest any discussion of globalization is 'replete with ambiguity and paradox' (p. 184), one such being the degree to which globalization has torn apart local communities in powering the virtual and real dispersal of people who, nevertheless, determine to remain powerfully tied to far distant people and places by those factors which create their identity, ethnicity, religion, tribe, language, and culture.

The social and ontological changes bring epistemological shifts. Bryan and Varvus (2005) see the result of globalization as a move 'beyond an ethnography of location to an ethnography of circulation' (p. 184). Such is the strength of the latter that writers are able to analyze education policy reflected, not in all nation states, but in a sufficient number to amount to a global orthodoxy (Ball, 1998). Research informed preparation and development of educational leaders reflects the paradoxes and ambiguities. While the local defined as the geographically close remains critical to school leaders, the far distant may be as or more relevant in terms of particular issues, policies or the character of a particular section of the community. Profound change sits alongside entrenched 'sameness'. Some communities do not change significantly, and the potential for connectivity enjoyed by the wealthy remains, as ever, but a dream to poor communities.

Schools and their leaders have no choice but to position themselves in relation to global inequalities and global pressures. The moral stance they take, for example, in the face of what Ball suggests to be one global orthodoxy 'tightening the connection between schooling, employment, productivity and trade' (p.122), places them as supporters or creators of 'counter narratives' (Cambron-McCabe & McCarthy, 2005, p. 208). As such, their leadership functions in both a single local and multiple global arenas.

One of the effects of globalization may be therefore to paradoxically increase and decrease the sense of 'otherness'. The traditional detached stance of comparative study seems not only inappropriate but absurd given the increasingly worldwide arena for addressing educational issues and the rapid flows of knowledge across unstable real and epistemological boundaries (Hallinger & Leithwood, 1998; Hallinger, 2003). An 'international' perspective takes on a new meaning and new resonance.

International

If, as we have argued, globalization has fundamentally shifted the context in which research of educational leadership takes place, then how we perceive our orientation within this volume must also transform. We must move from the previous traditional stance which dichotomized study of one's own nation and study of 'other' reflected in terms like 'international' (Rosenberg, 2000). Engagement is different in quality, in mindset. Various commentators have struggled to express the difference. Kay and Watson, as long ago as 1982 encouraged a different kind of approach to learning across territorial boundaries. Rather than a detached view leading to pragmatic, piece-meal borrowing:

> We must get inside the skin of other people as nearly as we can. We must learn 'the language of life' as far as possible. We must 'make sense' of their conditioning and concerns in their idiom… a holistic contemplation of a national education system could be compared with the aesthetic appreciation of a work of art: the complete experience is of more value than the discussion of the parts which compose it. (p. 33)

Cambron-McCabe and McCarthy (2005) stress not only the journey to get to know other systems in depth and close up, but also the purpose of the journey, which as 'transformative intellectuals, public intellectuals' (p. 203) is to increase social justice. How this concept is to be understood is of course as contested as the concept of globalization. Many Western writers such as Cambron-McCabe and McCarthy stress links with democracy. The latter is not perceived as desirable in many parts of the world and is therefore not, as is sometimes assumed, a universal goal. Nevertheless, the two strictures of Watson and Cambron-McCabe and McCarthy hold true; in a globalized world, those who engage with research from many parts of the world increasingly strive to deepen their cultural understanding to avoid superficial conclusions (Walker & Dimmock, 2004), and position their engagement as part of a socially critical endeavor in concert with others (Caldwell, 2003) calling on world efforts to solve problems which are both locally specific and globally present (Heck, 1996).

Following on from such shifts in orientation, writers such as Ball (1998) point out the absurdity of the long-standing belief that, to be credible in educational research in developing economies, one must study in the US or Europe; as a result, importing theory based on US/European culture to the different environment on return. Rather, increasingly, preparation and development of educational leaders is suggested to be more appropriately constructed and delivered within a knowledge base and understanding which embraces both the local and the global (Walker, Bridges & Chan, 1996) There are impassioned arguments for founding development on local moral and spiritual beliefs such as Islam (Bajunid, 1996; Shah, 2006) or the Indian philosophers, Vivekananda, Tagore and Ghandi (Sapre & Ranade, 2001). Simultaneously, all educational leaders may need to be aware of the largely Western dominant theories and practice with a world wide presence, in order to knowingly accept, reject or adapt them.

In summary, leadership programs are no longer necessarily preparing leaders for the more homogenous communities and theoretical context that predated globalization. Rather they are supporting leaders as part of global epistemic communities to take their place as, to use Foster's (2004) phrase, 'public intellectuals' (p. 184) critically marrying their commitment to local cultures, issues and practice with global flows of problems and potential solutions. More than this, to 'get inside the skin of other people' (Rosenberg, 2000, p. 33) the engagement is emotional as well as intellectual, connecting with others engaged in education as well as learning from and with them. An international perspective on educational leadership preparation and development can therefore be defined as a foundational stance of intercultural competence which uses engagement with the culture and practice of colleagues who are geographically and may be ideologically distant to increase awareness of one's own accultured parameters. The increased awareness is the intellectual and moral frame in which to search for ways to address issues which are local, global or, increasingly, both; it shapes this handbook.

Adopting an International Perspective

How then, in practice, can we learn with and from each other in the 'transnational epistemic community' (Stone, 2004, p. 548)? How do we respond to the simultaneous homogenizing and diversifying of knowledge which is the result of globalization and use the process to improve the experience of school for learners (Lumby et al., in press)?

Globalism implies both positive and negative forms of isomorphism. Negative isomorphism equates to changes which are unconscious or enforced, but in either case may be inappropriate to the environment in which change takes place. Stone (2004) describes a process where 'policy percolates or diffuses; something that is contagious rather than chosen' (p. 546). The increasing emphasis on accountability is one illustration of a global flow of policy which appears to have been caught as a quasi disease. Enforced change is often linked to funding, where amongst others, national governments, non-governmental organizations and the World Bank make funding dependant on specified actions. For example, African universities reliant on donor aid must comply with a Western model of strategic planning as 'recommended' by the World Bank Working Group on Higher Education (Farrant & Afonso, 1997). Pay rises for teachers are unofficially linked to 'efficiency' improvements in the UK.

Positive isomorphism is evident when change reflects policy makers' and practitioners' response to similar global pressures, utilizing knowledge from elsewhere to adjust to the pressures in a way which is conscious, critical and mindful of local conditions (Welch & Wong, 1998). The latter reflects a knowledge base which has the potential to capitalize on international communities of researchers and practitioners aiding each other to search for local solutions to global problems. DiMaggio and Powell (1983) summarize the forms of isomorphism as coercive, mimetic and normative, all of which are widely evident.

Rose (1993) categorizes five different types of learning: 'copying, adaptation, creating a hybrid, synthesis, inspiration' (p. 30). All of these, including copying, are potentially beneficial to schools and to learners. The degree to which they are beneficial or otherwise is dependant on the way knowledge is managed. The role of researchers and those who prepare leaders is ambivalent. On the one hand they may spread norms and theory which are dangerously hegemonic. Numerous commentators have deplored such inappropriate transmission of idea (Gronn, 2001; Foskett & Lumby, 2003; Walker, Bridges & Chan, 1996). On the other hand, researchers have the potential to contribute to international transformation through constructing and communicating knowledge in a way which is creative and sensitive; this is easy to write, difficult to achieve. Heck (1996) analyses the range of difficulties facing those who research internationally. He argues that most of the research on educational leadership is based on Western models and assumptions 'about the structure of knowledge, the nature of reality and the appropriate methods of investigation' (p. 76). Additionally it is largely focused on principals rather than the multilevel process which reflects the input to leadership of various others within and beyond the school. There are also methodological difficulties in addressing conceptual equivalence across national boundaries, problems of metric accuracy, issues of translation and language. Samples are problematic, related to doubtful generalizations even within nations, let alone transnationally. While Heck sees some advances in methodological sophistication as hopeful, the lack of any 'universal theory or paradigm' of leadership (p. 76) is a fundamental constraint on international research. But, then, is it? Is it a universal theory or the "holy grail" that we are all searching for?

APPROACHES TO RESEARCHING EDUCATIONAL LEADERSHIP

Researchers have used a variety of strategies to attempt the creation of knowledge across national boundaries. Comparative studies apply the same method to more than one national or cultural setting. Heck's (1996) study of principals in the US and the Marshall Islands is an instructive example. The research was primarily to investigate construct validity. While Heck concluded that the construct was valid, a range of limitations were also raised, so that the study provided only 'hints' for the future of comparative study. The difficulties and limitations of such an approach are both explicitly discussed and emerge powerfully from the analysis of data. Almost ten years on, Heck and Hallinger (2005) reiterate concerns about the lack of methodologies which are sufficiently sophisticated to investigate leadership, including transnational studies. Nevertheless much of the body of research on school effectiveness adopts such an approach, using statistical analysis to identify elements of leadership which appear to lead to positive results (Silins & Mulford, 2004;

Sun, Creemers & De Jong, 2007; Wikeley, Stoll & Murillo, 2005). Such work has value though it may tempt the reader to simplify the results and discover solutions rather than create them.

Alternatively a study may juxtapose a similar investigation in different national settings. An example is Billot, Goddard and Cranston (2007) where researchers from three countries (Canada, Australia and New Zealand) each investigate a principal's orientation to diversity in their school. The intent is not to suggest a generalizable set of values, policy or practice, but to stimulate, relating more strongly to the inspiration end of the spectrum 'copying, adaptation, creating a hybrid, synthesis, inspiration' (Rose, 1993, p. 30).

A third approach is to use research to investigate global issues and how practitioners have responded in their own context. Bottery, Ngai, Wong, P. M. & Wong P. H. (2007) consider how principals in the UK and in Hong Kong experience increasing workload and inspection regimes. The similarities and differences are illuminating of how principals in very different contexts are responding to globally experienced change. Rather than aiding the reader to learn from what is happening elsewhere, the article has the effect of focusing on the effects of context, directing the reader to consider more deeply the way in which local conditions interact with global change.

Finally, there are single studies; that is studies undertaken in one cultural or national context. For example, Bryant's (1998) study of Native American leadership, Shah's (2006) consideration of the relationship of Islam and educational leadership in the UK, Ribbins and Jun's (2004) investigation of principals in rural China. Each of these, focused as they are on one national or cultural context, may seem to be the least qualified for the appellation 'international'. Yet all, and of course many more, challenge leaders and those that prepare them to question the assumptions of their own practice. They make strange the familiar, to those who work within the nation which is the setting of the study, but they may also demand attention be paid to the differences within nations. As such they offer a powerful leverage to understand and respond to the plurality of peoples and culture within, as much as across, national boundaries, and the necessity to continuously renew practice in the light of changing and diversifying communities.

All these kinds of research are reflected in the handbook as writers explore what, if anything, may be in some sense universal and what is distinctive in the preparation and development of leaders. Paige and Mestenhauser's (1999) depiction of internationalization may serve to summarize the elements of an international perspective intended within the handbook. They suggest 'a complex, multidimensional learning process' (p. 504) which involves a number of elements:

- Integrative: the field incorporates knowledge from diverse settings, culture and languages into the curriculum and integrates (i.e. translates, synthesizes and connects);
- Intercultural: the field reflects a profound understanding of culture;
- Interdisciplinary: the field draws on the knowledge found within other disciplines to construct new and more holistic ways of understanding social phenomena;
- Comparative: the field demonstrates the ability to compare and contrast education in diverse cultural contexts;
- Transfer of knowledge technology: professionals in the field can take knowledge from one setting and apply it in another in a manner that respects both the origins of the idea and the setting into which it is being transferred;
- Contextual: professionals in the field know how to analyze context;
- Global: professionals in the field are aware of how global trends influence global practice. (Adapted from Paige and Mestenhauser, 1999, pp. 504–505)

The handbook incorporates all of these. Its orientation is to decenter currently hegemonic notions of leadership and preparation. The value base of an international perspective is to strive for 'new solidarities' (Lipman, 2005, p.142) in exploring 'the meaning of education and what it means to be educated and what it means to learn' (Ball, 1998, p. 128). The aspiration is that this volume will support 'a community of practitioners who encourage virtuous activity in each other' (Foster, 2004, p. 184), but where the multiple, contested and mutable nature of 'virtue' is fully embraced.

Implications for the Handbook

The implications for the structure and scope of this volume are significant. Authors have been requested to make their ontological, epistemological and axiological assumptions explicit, and to adopt a perspective which reflects the multiple dimensions set out by Paige and Mestenhauser (1999). Inevitably they have faced tensions in how to encompass the variation within practice world wide or even within a defined area of the world, with sufficient depth to allow the reader to understand the context of the policy or practice they are exploring. Consequently, 'international' does not mean referring to every country or cultural group in the world. It is understood as using research reflecting different strategies, comparative, juxtaposing, global and single studies, to illuminate the diversity of preparation and practice. The aim is to allow the reader critically to copy, reject, adapt, hybridize, synthesize and be inspired by research and practice from many parts of the globe (Rose, 1993) in order to deepen reflection on how they can contribute to the work of preparing and developing leaders of education who will function in both local and global contexts.

OVERVIEW OF THE HANDBOOK

Purpose and Scope

Within these overarching aims, the main purpose of the *International Handbook on the Preparation and Development of School Leaders* is to focus on global scholarship on educational leadership preparation and development at the primary and secondary education levels, thus, providing a valid and current account of empirical studies, conceptual analyses, and critical interpretations of trends, challenges, and opportunities across the globe in the field of educational leadership. We are confident that the handbook has identified both a critical description of the current debates and issues in this area and an assessment of where the discipline of leadership preparation and development is headed. Thus, the scope of this volume is truly international and highly informative to the field, given the global awareness of the importance of leadership in education and the increasing globalization of education in which, borrowing of leadership development strategies and perspectives across national and regional borders is occurring. Chapter authors are from a variety of national, cultural, and ideological perspectives and describe these issues and trends in educational leadership preparation and development from a multi-perspective approach.

Based on the above, the audience for the *International Handbook on the Preparation and Development of School Leaders* consists of four primary constituencies: (1) academics who will use the volume in their teaching, research, program development and improvement; (2) professional development providers who will use the volume in their professional development activities; (3) practitioners who serve in primary and secondary education settings who would use the volume to inform their practice; and (4) policy makers who participate in the accreditation, program approval, licensure/certification, and development of preparation systems.

Organization

The volume is organized into three broad sections, as follows:

- Concepts of Leadership Preparation and Development
- The Practice of Leadership Preparation and Development
- International Reflections

Concepts of Leadership Preparation and Development

This section consists of seven chapters and identifies a number of theoretical frames through which leadership and its preparation and development could be understood, drawing on a range of debates reflecting the highly problematic concept of leadership. Defining its contested nature and purposes, this section provides a springboard from which leadership preparation and development can be explored. Overall, this section maps the current theoretical field which supports leadership preparation and development across the globe.

The chapter on *The Nature and Specialized Purposes of Educational Leadership*, written by Paul Begley, focuses on general concepts about leadership and examines the contested nature of leadership in terms of its purposes. For example, although leadership for instructional purposes has been claimed by scholars and policy makers from many national contexts, alternative aims, including political purposes, are evident in other contexts. Moreover, the instructional purposes of leadership are far from uncontested. Ethical and political purposes have been argued as the ultimate aim of instructional leadership. Therefore, in this chapter the author has tried to identify the various goals and aims of leadership in a number of national contexts, in addition to providing a critical, international review of substantive, empirical and conceptual literature on this topic.

Jacky Lumby and Nick Foskett's chapter, *Leadership and Culture*, considers key conceptualizations of culture and explores the impact of culture on leadership preparation and development in the major cultural traditions of the west, the Islamic world, Africa, and the great eastern cultures of China, Japan and southern Asia. As the authors mention, while national culture may influence preparation and development systems, culture cannot be assumed to be unified or uncontested within any domain. Multiple indigenous alternatives, sub- and counter-cultures may interplay; imported culture, particularly from the west, may be both adopted and resisted. Furthermore, this chapter recognizes that culture is a complex and unstable construct which strongly shapes the patterns that emerge in leadership and its development.

The chapter on *A Life and Career Based Framework for the Study of Leaders in Education: Problems, Possibilities and Prescriptions,* written by Peter Ribbins focuses on the developmental nature of leadership and provides frames to suggest how we might understand entry to and progress throughout a leadership career. The chapter further considers how 'progress' may be conceptualized and how this relates to preparation and development programs and reviews empirical and conceptual literature on such issues as the stages of leadership, the application of adult development theory to leadership, and gender and racial differences in leadership careers. The chapter also relates leadership emergence and leadership persistence to a holistic view of life patterns as they relate to men and women in different contexts. As with other chapters in this volume, the foci are on important international similarities and contrasts.

The chapter on the *Effects of Leadership on Student Academic and Affective Achievement*, written by Stephen Jacobson and Christopher Bezzina, focuses on an issue that has become critical in several national contexts, namely, the role of leaders and leadership in influencing student outcomes. As with the other foundational chapters, this chapter prepares the reader for an understanding of how leadership development is affected by the larger leadership context, in this case the relationship with student outcomes. In the last few years, an increasing number of empirical studies have been conducted especially on the direct and indirect effects of leadership on student achievement. This chapter reviews this pertinent literature but also the contested nature of student outcomes, for example, the various ways student outcomes are defined and measured, including achievement test scores, well-being, and citizenship.

Tony Bush and Konstanze Moloi's chapter on *Race and Racism in Leadership Development* examines issues of ethnicity in South Africa and other parts of the world where affirmative action has created a need for the development of large numbers of those Black educators previously excluded from leadership positions and still experiencing the effects of a different education system. Furthermore, this chapter explores the different ways in which ethnicity influences recruitment to preparation and development programs and the interplay of program curriculum, delivery and ethnicity, as well as critically reviewing the work which has been undertaken and suggesting ways in which researchers might address the issues related to ethnicity within preparation and development programs.

The chapter on *Gender and Leadership Development*, written by Marianne Coleman and Tanya Fitzgerald, argues that gender influences recruitment to, and progress within, leadership careers. Gender effects the construction and enactment of leadership and this is embedded within leadership preparation and development programs, generally to the disadvantage of women. Furthermore, this chapter critically reviews research to date on how gender is differently conceptualized in various parts of the world, and how this relates to the recruitment of men and women to leadership positions.

Finally, in the chapter of *Theories of Learning*, Brenda Beatty considers theories of learning in association with current trends and issues in leadership preparation and development. The chapter provides the opportunity to revisit many ideas that are familiar to readers and some less so, with a view to reflection upon the field. Through the lens of understandings of mind, knowledge, and learning, the reader is invited to consider some directions for the future of school leadership practice, preparation and development. Following a review of some current issues, and underlying assumptions and visions for school leadership in the future, the author introduces some historical background and influential schools of thought about human mind and learning. Thereafter, a review of specific individual and collective learning theories is complemented by key concepts from adult learning and adult development theory. These gleanings are then considered in light of emerging trends from empirical studies of promising practices in leadership preparation and development.

The Practice of Leadership Development

This section consists of six chapters and adopts an inclusive approach to considering how preparation and development are provided in varying contexts. Providers range from formal, long-standing institutions such as universities, to non-governmental organizations operating more short-term. Similarly, formal processes to recruit and select candidates for preparation and development exist, but in many countries, the issue is rather one of access, when 'selection' may be more a matter of economic filtering of those who can find funds for fees and travel and those who cannot. Within these varied contexts, the different curricula and the pedagogies which follow are outlined, including modes of development. These varied perspectives together provide a map of the history, advance and current issues in the practice of leadership preparation and development.

The chapter on *Leadership Development and School Development: Enhancing the Leadership Capacity in Schools*, written by Stephan Huber, suggests that international contexts vary considerably in term of the types of providers of leadership education and development. Providers can include universities, government agencies, not-for profit leadership academies, for-profit training agencies, and other groups. These external and internal providers use a variety of modes to deliver leadership preparation and development. For instance, distance modes have grown world wide in response to leaders' needs, offering alternative means to support development. Therefore, this chapter identifies and describes the different types of external and internal providers and delivery modes of leadership development, and empirical and conceptual literature that examines the influences on these providers and the effects/outcomes of the different types of providers and delivery modes.

Stephan Huber and Petros Pashiardis's chapter on *Recruitment and Selection* focuses on the important issue of the selection of educational leaders (primarily principals and assistant principals) for our schools, an issue which has always been given a degree of importance. Moreover, as the authors argue, the importance of this process has been underscored by recent findings which indicate that a school's leadership is critical to its success. Therefore, the issue of who is allowed into formal educational leadership positions is indeed of fundamental importance for educational systems around the globe. Selection for preparation and development programs is a precursor and so shaper of this process. Recruitment and selection to programs in effect construct the pool from which leaders are drawn. Therefore, this chapter describes and critically presents and analyzes different issues of leader recruitment and selection for preparation and development programs.

The chapter on *Curriculum and Pedagogy*, written by Edie Rusch, examines the content and instructional methods of leadership development used in the variety of leadership preparation and development programs discussed in other chapters in the handbook. In addition, the chapter examines literature on field or clinical experiences, such as internships, designed to bridge coursework and school practice and provides a critical, international review of substantive, empirical and conceptual literature on this topic.

Bruce Barnett and Gary O'Mahony's chapter, *Mentoring and Coaching Programs for the Professional Development of School Leaders*, demonstrates the increasing evidence that school leaders, throughout all stages of their careers, can benefit from a mentoring system in which an experienced leader helps the intern or protégé place theory and praxis in the context of experience. Usually, school leaders identify other school leaders as their primary source of help in becoming a school leader themselves, and they confirm that these mentoring relationships serve them throughout their careers, not just initially. As the authors note, the need for mentoring relationships has become even more evident than the provision of formal pre-service education in leadership and management. Therefore, this chapter critically reviews major issues of planning, mentor selection, matching, training, and evaluation.

The chapter on *Evaluation of School Principals*, written by Petros Pashiardis and Stefan Brauckmann, argues that the progress of potential and current leaders may be formally and informally assessed at a variety of points during a leader's career. Evaluation may comprise a formally mandated entry point to a leadership role. Alternatively, other points of evaluation, such as those undertaken in postgraduate study may not formally relate to progress, but may impact nevertheless on access to career steps and to remuneration systems. Evaluation therefore relates strongly to career frames as discussed in Ribbins' chapter. The method of assessment is also subject to critical debate. A wide range of means are adopted in various parts of the world, incorporating not only examination of knowledge and understanding in written form, but also evaluation of competence through the observation of real and simulated practice and peer evaluation. Furthermore, this chapter critically reviews the relationship of evaluation to career frame and to career progress and critically reviews the methods adopted to reach an assessment judgment, reflecting on the relationship between context and method.

Finally, the chapter on *Understanding and Assessing the Impact of Leadership Development*, written by Ken Leithwood and Ben Levin, argues that national governments, organizations involved with leader preparation and development, and individual leaders continue to be concerned with the refinement of methods to assess the impact of development. As the authors explain, the substantial resource invested and the importance attached to the efficacy of leadership in schools render assessment of impact a high priority. However, the multiple variables which influence individual performance and the impact of school context have an effect on results. This chapter critically reviews the research to date and considers the assessment models currently in operation or evolving.

International Reflections

This section consists of eight chapters and provides the detail of leadership preparation and development in practice in a number of contexts throughout the globe. Its intention is not only to provide a description of the very varied systems in existence, but also the differing ontological and epistemological foundations of various approaches in Western, Arab, Asian and African thinking. As the world increasingly becomes smaller and smaller — indeed an ecumenical village — the topic of international or comparative perspectives in educational leadership, management and administration becomes increasingly current. It is within this context that the chapters in this section have been written. More specifically, each chapter includes some of the following elements with variations for specific circumstances: a brief historical account of educational leadership in their respective area; philosophical issues that have emerged over the years; dilemmas facing educational leadership; current approaches to school leaders' preparation and development; and views for the future in the respective areas of the world.

This section includes the following chapters: *Leadership Preparation and Development in North America* written by Michelle Young and Margaret Grogan; *Leadership Development in Latin America* written by José Alexandre da Rocha Ventura Silva, Jorge Adelino Rodrigues da Costa, and Terezinha Fatima Andrade Monteiro dos Santos; *Leadership Development in Europe* written by Jorunn Møller and Michael Schratz; *School Leadership Development in Africa*, written by Ruth Otunga, David Serem and Jonah Kindiki; *Preparing and Developing School Leaders in the Middle East* written by Reynold Macpherson and Omid Tofighian; *Leader Development across Three Chinese Societies* written by Allan Walker, Chen Shuangye, and Qian Haiyan; *Professional Learning of School Leaders in Australia* written by Michelle Anderson, Elizabeth Kleinhenz, Bill Mulford, and David Gurr; and *Leadership Development in Small Island States* written by Tony Bush, Marie-Therese Purvis, and Linda Barallon.

REFERENCES

Bajunid, I. A. (1996). Preliminary explorations of indigenous perspectives of educational management. *Journal of Educational Administration, 34*(5), 50–73.

Ball, S. (1998). Big policies/small world; an introduction to international perspectives in education policy. *Comparative Education, 34*(2), 119–130.

Billot, J. Goddard, T. & Cranston, N. (2007). How principals manage ethnocultural diversity: Learnings from three countries. *International Studies in Educational Administration, 35*(2), 3–19.

Bottery, M. (1999). Global forces, national mediations and the management of educational institutions. *Educational Management and Administration, 27*(3), 299–312.

Bottery, M., Ngai, G., Wong, P. M. & Wong P. H. (2007). Leaders and contexts: comparing English and Hong Kong perceptions of educational challenges, *International Studies in Educational Administration, 36*(10, 56–71.

Briggs, A. R. J., Bush, T. & Middlewood, D. (2006). From immersion to establishment. The challenges facing new school heads and the role of "New Visions" in resolving them. *Cambridge Journal of Education, 36*(2), 257–276.

Brown, P. & Lauder, H. (1997). Education, globalization and economic development.,I In A. H. Halsey, H., Lauder, P., Brown, and A.S. Wells. (Eds.), *Education, Economy and Society* (pp. 172–192).Oxford: Oxford University Press.

Bryan, A. & Vavrus, S. (2005). The promise and peril of education; the teaching of in/tolerance in an era of globalization. *Globalization, Societies and Education, 3*(2), 183–202.

Bryant, M. (1998). Cross-cultural understandings of leadership: Themes from Native American interviews. *Educational Management & Administration, 26*(1), 7–20.

Caldwell, B. (2003) Successful leadership and globalization of learning. In P. Hallinger (Ed) *Reshaping the Landscape of School Leadership Development: A Global Perspective* (pp. 23–40). Lisse: Swets and Zeitlinger.

Cambron-McCabe, N. & McCarthy, M. (2005). Educating school leaders for social justice, *Educational Administration Quarterly, 19*(1), 201–222.

Coles, M. J. & Southworth, G. (2005). *Developing Leadership. Creating the Schools of Tomorrow*. Maidenhead, England: Open University Press.

Crossley, M. & Watson, K. (2003). *Comparative and International Research in Education*. London, Routledge Falmer.

Crow, G. M. (2006). Complexity and the beginning principal in the United States: perspectives on Socialization. *Journal of Educational Administration, 44*(4), 310–325.

DiMaggio, P. J. & Powell, W. P. (1983). The iron cage revisited: Institutional isomorphism and collective rationality in organizational fields. *American Sociological Review, 48*(2), 147–160.

Dimmock, C. & Walker, A. (2002). Connecting school leadership with teaching, learning, and parenting in diverse cultural contexts: Western and Asian perspectives. In K. Leithwood & P. Hallinger (Eds), *Second International Handbook of Educational Leadership and Administration* (pp. 395–426). Dordrecht: Kluwer.

Dimmock, C. & Walker, A. (2004). The international role of the NCSL: Tourist, colporteur or confrere, *Educational Management, Administration and Leadership, 32*(3), 269–287.

Earley, P. & Weindling, D. (2004). *Understanding School Leadership*. London: Paul Chapman.

Farrant, J. & Afonso, L. (1997). Strategic planning in African universities. *Higher Education Policy, 10*(1), 23–30.

Farrell, L. (2006). Labouring in the knowledge fields; researching knowledge in globalising workspaces. *Globalization, Societies and Education, 4*(2), 237–248.

Fink, D. (2005). Developing leaders for their future not our past. In M. J. Coles & G. Southworth, G. (Eds.), *Developing Leadership. Creating the Schools of Tomorrow*, (pp. 1–20). Maidenhead, England: Open University Press.

Foskett, N. & Lumby, J. (2003). *Leading and Managing Education: International Dimensions*. London: Paul Chapman.

Foster, W. P. (2004). The decline of the local: A challenge to educational leadership, *Educational Administration Quarterly, 40*(2), 176–191.

Friedman, T. L. (2005). *The World is Flat: A Brief History of the Twenty-first Century*. New York: Farrar, Strauss, and Giroux.

Giddens, A. (1999). *Runaway World*. London: Profile Books.

Gronn, P. (2001). Commentary. Crossing the great divides: problems of cultural diffusion for leadership in education, *International Journal for Leadership in Education, 4*(4), 401–414.

Gronn, P. (2002). Distributed leadership as a unit of analysis. *The Leadership Quarterly, 13*, 423–451.

Hallinger, P. & Leithwood, K. (1998). Editors' Introduction. In P. Hallinger & K. Leithwood (Eds.), Leading schools in global era. *Peabody Journal of Education, 73*(2), 1–10.

Hallinger, P. (2003). The emergence of school leadership development in an era of globalization: 1980–2002. In P. Hallinger (Ed.), *Reshaping the Landscape of School Leadership Development: A global perspective.,* Lisse: Swets and Zeitlinger.

Hallinger, P. (1995). Culture and leadership: developing an international perspective in educational demonstration. *UCEA Review,* Spring, 1995, *46*(2), 1–13.

Harris, A. (2004). Distributed leadership and school improvement. Leading or misleading? *Educational Management, Administration and Leadership, 32*(1), 11–24.

Harris, A. (2006). Opening up the "Black Box" of leadership practice: taking a distributed leadership perspective. *International Studies in Educational Administration, 34*(2), 37–45.

Hatcher, R. (2005). The distribution of leadership and power in schools. *British Journal of Sociology of Education, 26*(2), 253–267.

Heck, R. (1996). Leadership and culture: Conceptual and methodological issues in comparing models across cultural settings. *Journal of Educational Administration, 34*(5), 74–97.

Heck, R. & Hallinger, P (2005). The study of educational leadership and management: Where does the field stand today? *Educational Management Administration & Leadership, 33*(1), 229–244.

Higginson, H. K. (1979). *Selections from Michael Sadler: studies in world citizenship.* Liverpool: Dejall & Meyorre.

Huber, S. G. & West, M. (2002). Developing school leaders: a critical review of current practices, approaches, and issues, and some directions for the iuture. In K. Leithwood & P. Hallinger (Eds.), *Second International Handbook of Educational Leadership and Administration* (pp.1071–1102). Dordrecht: Kluwer.

Jones, A. (2006). Developing what? An anthropological look at the leadership development process across cultures. *Leadership, 2*(4), 481–498.

Kay, W. K. & Watson, J. K. (1982). Comparative education: the need for dangerous ambition. *Educational Research, 24*(2),129–139.

Kelley, C. & Shaw, J. J. (in press). Comprehensive school leadership development: a portrait of programs. In Young, M., Crow, G. Murphy, J. & Ogawa, R. (Eds.), *Handbook of Research on the Education of School Leaders.* Mahwah, NJ: Erlbaum.

Lipman, P. (2005). Metropolitan regions – new geographies of inequality in education: the Chicago metro region case. *Globalization, Societies and Education, 3*(2), 141–163.

Lumby, J., Walker, A., Bryant, M., Bush, T. & Bjork, L. (in press). An international perspective on leadership preparation. In Young, M., Crow, G. Murphy, J. Ogawa, R. (Eds.), *Handbook of Research on the Education of School Leaders.* Mahwah, NJ: Erlbaum.

Marcoulides, G. A., Larsen, T. J. & Heck, R. H. (1995). Examining the generalizability of a leadership model: issues for assessing administrator performance. *International Journal of Educational Management, 9*(6), 4–9.

Murphy, J. & Vriesenga, M. (2004). *Research on Preparation Program in Educational Administration: An Analysis.* Columbia, MO: University Council for Educational Administration.

Ohmae, K. (2000). *The invisible continent; four strategic imperatives of the new economy.* London: Nicholas Brealey.

Orr, M. T. (2005). Comparing leadership development from pipeline, to preparation and practice. A paper presented at the annual meeting of the University Council for Educational Administration, Nashville, TN.

Paige, R. M. & Mestenhauser, J. A. (1999). Internationalizing educational administration, *Educational Administration Quarterly, 35*(4), 500–517.

Parsons, W. (1995). *Public policy.* Cheltenham: Edward Elgar.

Pashiardis, P. (2001). *International perspectives on educational leadership.* Hong- Kong: Centre for Educational leadership, The University of Hong-Kong.

Ribbins, P. & Jun, H. Z. (2004). Headteachers in rural China: aspects of ambition. *International Journal for Leadership in Education, 7*(2), 127–146.

Rose, R. (1993). *Lesson Drawing in Public Policy.* Chatham, NJ. Chatham House.

Rosenberg J. (2000). *The Follies of Globalization Theory.* London, Verso.

Sapre, P. & Ranade, M. (2001). Moral leadership in education: an Indian perspective. *International Journal for Leadership in Education*, *4*(4), 367–381.

Scholte, J. A. (2000) *Globalization: a critical introduction*. Basingstoke: Palgrave.

Shah, S. (2006). Educational leadership: An Islamic perspective. *British Educational Research Journal*, *32*(3), 363–386.

Silins, H. & Mulford, B. (2004). Schools as learning organizations — effects on teacher leadership and student outcomes. *School Effectiveness and School Improvement: An International Journal of Research, Policy and Practice*, *15*(3 & 4), 443–466.

Southworth, G. (2002). Lessons from successful leadership in small schools. In K. Leithwood & P. Hallinger (Eds.), *Second International Handbook of Educational Leadership and Administration* (pp. 451–484). Dordrecht: Kluwer.

Stone, D. (2004). Transfer agents and global networks in the 'transnationalization' of policy. *Journal of European Public Policy*, *11*(3), 545–566.

Sun, H., Creemers, B. P. & De Jong, R. (2007). Contextual factors and effective school improvement. *School Effectiveness and School Improvement*, *18* (1), 93–122.

Usdan, M., McCloud, B. & Podmostko, M. (2000). Leadership for Student Learning: Reinventing the Principalship. *School Leadership for the 21st Century Initiative. A Report of the Task Force on the Principalship.* Washington, DC: Institute for Educational Leadership.

Walker, A. & Dimmock, C. (2004). The international role of the NCSL: Tourist, colporteur or confrere? *Educational Management Administration & Leadership, 32*(3), 269–287.

Walker, A., Bridges, E. & Chan, B. (1996). Wisdom gained, wisdom given: instituting PBL in a Chinese culture. *Journal of Educational Administration*, *334*(5), 12–31.

Waters, M. (1995). *Globalization*. London: Routledge.

Weindling, D. & Dimmock, C. (2006). Sitting in the "Hot Seat". New headteachers in the UK. *Journal of Educational Administration, 44*(4), 326–340.

Welch, E. & Wong, W. (1998). Public administration in a global context: bridging gaps of theory and practice between Western and non-Western nations. *Public Administration Review*, 58, 40–49.

Wikeley, F., Stoll, L. & Murillo, J. (2005). Evaluating effective school improvement: Case studies of programmes in eight European countries and their contribution to the effective school improvement model. *School Effectiveness and School Improvement, 16*(4), 387–405.

Wong, P. (2004). The professional development of school principals: Insights from evaluating a programme in Hong-Kong. *School leadership and Management, 24*(2), 139–162.

I

CONCEPTS OF LEADERSHIP AND ITS DEVELOPMENT

2

The Nature and Specialized Purposes of Educational Leadership

Paul T. Begley

All professions have their meta-values. These are the transcending purposes that give meaning and direction to the work of people in those professions. For example, a soldier's priority is commonly understood to be a focus on mission (Griggs, 2005). This is an example of a meta-value or transcending purpose for that profession. In this case, a deceptively simple statement of purpose drives decision making in the profession and underlies all training for individuals being prepared for that profession. Other professions and organizations adopt different meta-values and core purposes — some more complex and multi-dimensional. Corporate meta-values typically focus on growth, profit, maintenance and survival (Hodgkinson, 1991). Their influence can be readily detected in the decision making processes of people working in those sectors, be it a bank, brewery, insurance company, oil company or automobile manufacturer. When one experiences the life-style advertising on television used to promote the products from these companies, the operation of these underlying meta-values and economic purposes may be veiled but still very much apparent. While the themes of the advertising may be focused on a consumer's wants and needs, the driving motivation is still selling the product to the consumer. This illustrates how meta-values that reflect the fundamental purposes of an organization or profession are sometimes veiled or obscured within the context of an environment or the culture of a community.

Education as a profession also has its fundamental purposes. It is no exception as a profession. Indeed, although it has become popular in North America to impose corporate values on education, this profession already has a very special set of purposes. Three broad and relatively transcending purposes have been traditionally associated with education. Although various terms may be used to describe these purposes, they generally focus on three areas — aesthetic purposes, economic purposes and ideological purposes (Hodgkinson, 1991). In the same way that infantry officers would be lost without a primary focus on mission, educational leaders should keep the fundamental purposes of education in mind as they make decisions, manage people or resources, and generally provide leadership within their organizations. Otherwise they will be tossed about like a rudderless ship in a storm by the competing agendas and interest groups that make up any community. In application these fundamental and context-stripped statements of purpose often take on more specific forms as they are interpreted for particular educational contexts, such as a concern for the best interests of students (Stefkovich & Begley, 2007) or accountability (Begley,

2006). However, the underlying purposes remain the same and are generally recognized as the traditional and enduring purposes of education.

The three purposes of education just introduced will be used to structure the discussion in this chapter. The nature of these specialized purposes also leads to a clarification of the key functions of school leadership, the identification of particular skills and capacities required by school leaders, and bodies of knowledge relevant to expert school leadership practices across multiple national contexts.

CONCEPTUALIZING THE PURPOSES OF EDUCATIONAL LEADERSHIP

Hodgkinson (1991) provides an insightful and comprehensive exploration of the special purposes of education. He does so by examining the historical roots of each category of educational purpose. He traces aesthetic purposes back to the humanistic traditions of Greece — a focus on the formation of character and the subsequent notions of a classic liberal education. Applied to modern education practices in many countries in recent decades, a concern with aesthetic purposes has become associated with progressive education and focused by notions like student self-esteem, personal fulfillment of the individual, and life-long learning. There is also a curricular tradition that most clearly associates with aesthetic purposes. It is that of transformational learning with its emphasis on synthesis and reapplication of learning and personal transcendence (Miller & Seller, 1985).

The economic purposes of education, according to Hodgkinson (1991), can be traced back to the influence of the Romans. Learning to earn is a simple but accurate way to conceptualize the economic purposes in education. The Romans were apparently the first to promote the notion of professional accreditation in the sense that has become so common to our societies today. For example, a centurion might have been expected to successfully complete particular training to become qualified for that military role in the same way we do today with aircraft pilots, doctors, lawyers, yoga instructors, and perhaps even kindergarten graduates. The curricular tradition that aligns best with the economic purposes of education is a transactional orientation to learning. If it is accurate to say that teachers have a bias towards the aesthetic purposes of education, then it is parents, the media, and business leaders that tend to champion the primacy of economic purposes in education today. Yet economic purposes, as much as aesthetic purposes, remain an important priority for school leadership.

The ideological or socialization functions of education represent perhaps the most basic of educational purposes. This third broad purpose is normally associated with notions of citizenship and social skills. During the early days of North American settlement, or any new settled region of the world, it is not hard to imagine parents being highly motivated to quickly establish schools so their children can learn what they need to know to function in society, comply with the norms of society, and contribute to the well-being of their communities. Moreover, this is one of the most powerful ways for a society to pass on its norms and standards of conduct to succeeding generations of citizens. For example, at the time of Hong Kong's reunification with China in 1997 an immediate and much increased emphasis was put on a civic education curriculum for all students attending Hong Kong schools. Similarly, in Pakistan, the centralized state curriculum developed during the last decade includes a heavy emphasis on political ideology consistent with the civic needs of the national government. Other smaller scale manifestations of ideological purposes in modern schooling might include an anti-racism curriculum, the promotion of tolerance for cultural diversity, and notions of environmental responsibility. The curricular tradition that most closely aligns with ideological purposes of education is the transmission mode of curriculum — the direct transfer of knowledge and skill to the learner, the filling of the empty vessel.

Examining the educational mission statements produced by many school districts typically reveals the implicit if not explicit presence of all three of these purposes of education, albeit with the usual culturally driven ebb and flow of emphasis from district to district and region to region across time. To this extent the purposes of educational leadership can become codified and made accessible to professional educators as a mandate. However, a balanced education can be defined in terms of how well all three purposes have been accommodated as part of the educational experience of each child. Too much emphasis on one purpose can compromise the overall educational experience of learners. For example, consider the current preoccupation in many countries, but especially the United States, with standardized testing. These circumstances are widely understood as having narrowed the curriculum to a transactional relationship between learner and educator. In particular, the arts have been discounted in favor of the sciences. This illustrates a disturbing trend in a diverse range of countries, including nations like the United States, China, Mauritius, and Korea, towards an over-emphasis on economic purposes and trans-actional curriculum at the expense of the more transformational agendas of aesthetic learning, and the social interaction skills associated with ideological literacy. Nevertheless, even under ideal circumstances, the purposes of education are somewhat fluid and dynamic, the emphasis and balance shifting with time and circumstances, yet they require a balanced presence. Other-wise educational purposes can be skewed by loud, persistent or powerful voices as the emphasis among purposes cycles through alternating periods of conservatism and liberalism.

It is proposed that a balanced attendance to all three of these fundamental purposes of edu-cation is critical to the educational leadership process. They represent the special purposes of education. In that sense they constitute the meta-values of educational leadership, or at least they should. Also implied are particular skills and categories of knowledge that school leaders must possess if they are to be professionally effective.

THE RELATIONSHIP OF EDUCATIONAL PURPOSES TO SCHOOL LEADERSHIP

People working in professional roles require purposes and goals every bit as much as they do in their personal lives. Without purpose educational leaders are, at a minimum, vulnerable to directing their energy to inappropriate or wasteful tasks, and at worse, subject to manipulation and exploitation by individuals, organizations and special interest groups bent on pursuing their self-interests. The importance of keeping a robust and socially defensible set of fundamental edu-cation purposes at the forefront of educational leadership practices is pretty much self-evident. However, one of the persistent dilemmas we encounter among educational leaders today is a failure to adequately distinguish between means and ends.

Should national regulations relating to education, like the U.S. Federal *No Child Left Behind* (NCLB) legislation, a current preoccupation for most American educators, be best considered a means or an end of education? Are standardized test scores a means or an end? When leaders manage the operation of educational programs in their schools — a traditional notion of in-structional leadership in many countries, is this attending to a means or an end? Even venerable and seemingly inviolate notions like child-centered or learner-centered education might be best thought of as a means to an educational end rather than some sort of absolute objective if the educational focus is on the individual child rather than children in the more global sense. In the practitioner world it often seems that every educational innovation that comes along is touted as some sort of unquestioned end of education. Obviously, they cannot all be that important, and one of the best ways for educational leaders to navigate these perennial challenges is to keep their professional goals and purposes at the forefront of their administrative practices. But, it does not stop there. As leaders they must also develop an awareness of the goals and motivations of the individuals, groups and organizations that share their space in the organization and society. And once identified these goals and needs must be monitored because they tend to evolve and change over time, and it is the duty of professional educators to be responsive to the needs of the communities they serve.

Before school leaders attempt to sort out and respond to the quagmire of curricular innovations characteristic of modern education, and the dynamics of social expectations for schools, it makes sense for them to take the time to identify the fundamental purposes of education — as they exist traditionally, in the recent past, and currently. Identifying these transcending meta-values for educational leadership and doing some careful thinking about how they can be applied in specific contexts is good preparation for effective administrative practice. It will enable school leaders to critically deconstruct edu-babble, respond effectively to trendy initiatives, and perhaps even help to defuse those assaults on the teaching profession that have become so common to education. Developing this capacity can happen in a number of quite specific ways. Furthermore, these relationships between purpose and strategic action have important implications for the nature of leadership development processes.

HOW PURPOSES INFLUENCE THE NATURE OF LEADERSHIP ACTION

Perhaps the most fundamental way in which educational purposes relate to leadership is as an influence on the cognitive processes of individuals and groups of individuals. It is important, perhaps essential, for persons in leadership roles to understand how their values and professional goals reflect underlying human motivations and shape the subsequent attitudes, speech, and actions of personnel (Kohlberg & Turiel, 1971; Hodgkinson, 1978; Begley, 2006). Begley's conception of authentic forms of leadership (2006), discussed in further detail in this chapter, emphasizes this capacity as something that begins with self-knowledge and then becomes extended as sensitivity to the perspectives of others. Genuine forms of leadership begin with the understanding and thoughtful interpretation of observed or experienced processes by individuals. This implies the appropriateness of a focus on the perceptions of individuals in the context of school leadership situations and the culture of the community as both a starting point and as a priority. Although organizational theories, the policy arena, and other macro perspectives are relevant as elements of the context in which a school leader works, they cannot be the primary locus of concern. Leaders need to focus on people as a priority. This is an important consideration for university teaching in the educational leadership area because such courses have traditionally adopted a strong organizational focus and relied on texts that reflect these largely organizational postures and orientations. A more appropriate starting point for culturally and socially sensitive school leadership in an increasingly globalized world is the perceptions, goals and belief systems of the individuals. The rest is working in the local professional context.

A second way in which educational goals relate to leadership practices is as a guide to action, particularly as supports to resolving educational problems and ethical dilemmas. A clear conception of educational purposes is highly relevant to school leadership in that the purposes become the rubrics, benchmarks, socially justified standards of practice, and templates for morally justified professional action. The individual leader may use these as they process situations in their minds or employ educational purposes in more collective ways with groups of people. Langlois (2004), to name one scholar, has conducted much research on the ethical dilemma analysis processes of principals and superintendents that illustrate empirically how these processes occur. A typical application for professional goals or educational purposes in this administrative context is as a personal guide to action, particularly as supports to resolving ethical dilemmas. True dilemmas are situations where one is faced with a choice between equally unsatisfactory alternatives. These are fortunately not everyday occurrences in most schools, but they do occur from time to time and can generate very difficult circumstances for school leaders. A number of other scholars have also conducted research and published in this area. These include Begley and Johansson (1998), Stefkovich (2006), and Branson (2006). These scholars have each subsequently developed well-documented processes for the analysis of dilemma situations and development of ethical responses.

A third and perhaps the most commonly observable application for purposes of educational leaders is strategic in intent and collective in process. It is common in a school or district setting for goals and/or ethical postures to be adopted with a strategic organizational intent — for example, as a focus for building consensus around a shared social or organizational objective. To illustrate, a school district superintendent might choose "ethic of community" (Furman, 2003) as a rallying meta-value to focus the energies of personnel on collective action aimed at meeting and promoting the best interests of a community. Or, ethical notions such as "due process" (Strike, Haller & Soltis, 1988) or "social justice" (Shapiro & Stefkovich, 2005) might be used as the objective for focusing the reform of school district processes in support of students with special needs, or social imbalances relating to gender, race or class. In this sense leaders literally use statements of educational purpose or ethical postures as leadership tools to support actions taken, model ideal practice, and/or promote particular kinds of organizational or societal activity.

THE EVOLVING NATURE OF SCHOOL LEADERSHIP

In 1984, Clark, Lotto, and Astuto published in *Educational Administration Quarterly* a useful comparison and analysis of the Effective Schools and School Improvement modes of inquiry. The vocabulary and ideas associated with that body of research have since become comfortably familiar to the thinking and the practices of many school administrators. Many of the interventionist and planned change notions described in that seminal article persist today in discussions on educational leadership; reinforced through the content of formal preparation courses, critically debated at conferences focused on administrative practice such as the annual meeting of the *University Council for Educational Administration*, and very much evident in the professional literature on school leadership. In many respects these notions became the foundation of professional knowledge for school administrators. Thus, leadership practices have come to be viewed as uni-dimensional (e.g. Cuban, 1986) or multi-dimensional (e.g. Sergiovanni, 1984). Prescriptions for effective administration are often proposed in terms of typical practices (e.g. Kingdon, 1985) or effective practices (e.g. Larsen, 1987), or as actual roles versus preferred roles (e.g. Gousha, 1986). Other researchers, preferring a more contextualized view of school leadership, described patterns of practice or leadership styles (e.g. Hall et al., 1986 or Leithwood & Montgomery, 1986). However, from a scholarly perspective virtually all these images of effective practice have shared one persistent limitation. They were founded on empirical research findings that are basically descriptive or correlational in nature. As a result, practices have often been espoused in the educational leadership literature when they have not had a good fit in communities or leadership contexts other than the urban American communities in which the research was originally conducted. To that extent these studies have been allowed to exercise an undeserved degree of influence on leadership practices as the content of leadership preparation programs.

Often schools and school leaders have been described as effective without saying much about how they became effective. The focus has been on the empirical and technical, and the bulk of the literature has been blind to what Barnard (1938) proposes as the moral dimension of leadership. At least this was the case until scholars of educational leadership began to incorporate additional and important perspectives as components of their models of school leadership.

Partially in response to these inherent limitations, during the late eighties and early nineties a number of North American researchers (e.g. Prestine & LeGrand, 1991; Leithwood, Begley & Cousins, 1992; Leithwood & Hallinger, 1993) shifted their attention to theories of human cognition as a better way of explaining the nature of expert leadership and justifying particular organizational configurations. As a result, a more contextualized view of the thinking and learning process has gained prominence and greater emphasis is accorded to the internal and external influences on the principalship.

Extending these notions to the design and development of administrator preparation programs implies important changes for the content and process associated with the development of expert school leaders. Solutions became available, or at least implied, for several persistent problems that confound the efforts of those committed to the development of expert school leadership practices. For example, several scholars began experimenting with problem-based instructional approaches as one response to the challenge of situating administrative learning experiences within relevant contexts (see Bridges, 1992; Leithwood, Begley & Cousins, 1992; Hart, 1993). Another approach complementary to the cognitively focused, problem-based instructional strategy that developed during the same era was the development and use of role profiles of leadership practices as a way of fostering and supporting the development of expert school leadership practices (e.g. Begley, 1995; Begley & Slater, 2001; Walker, Begley & Dimmock, 2000). In many respects these approaches remain the mainstays of many university based principal preparation programs.

CROSS-CULTURAL DESCRIPTIONS OF SCHOOL LEADERSHIP

In societies where curriculum is centralized nationally or where one cultural group predominates in terms of political power or access to resources, distinctive, unique, or minority-based social conditions often become obscured, veiled, or blurred by the perspectives and language adopted to describe social processes. In many respects this is a natural outcome and limitation of language as a means of assigning meaning to concepts and events, or the bounded rationality that occurs when models and frameworks are applied to complex social situations. It is also an outcome of general human inclinations to generalize processes across contexts to the point that they become automated as a cognitive schema or a set of abstract principles (Begley, 1996). A number of scholars, notably Allan Walker and Clive Dimmock, believe the field of educational administration has developed along ethnocentric lines, dominated by Western perspectives emanating mostly from the United States and United Kingdom (Dimmock & Walker, 1998; Walker & Dimmock, 1999; Walker, 2003). The consequences are a risk that the generalized experiences of one country may be inappropriately assumed to be instructive to practices in radically different contexts. Examples of this phenomenon have been documented by Walker and Dimmock as part of the Hong Kong experience. As societies become more globalized, and as the exchange of information among international scholars becomes more widespread, the implications become more urgent. Many administrators are discovering that they must consider carefully before adopting the ideas and educational ideas from other cultures. Conversely, they may also discover that some of their own society's most cherished ethical foundations must be carefully re-examined in terms of how they are interpreted and their appropriateness to more globalized social circumstances. As our communities and societies become more diversified, school administrators have by necessity become more sophisticated in their leadership, and more sensitive to the value orientations of others. For their part, researchers have gradually confronted the need to move beyond their traditional orientation towards generalization and description to consider the deeper matters of intent and motivational base. What emerges as the critical implication is the need for dialogue and negotiation of meaning among stakeholders in professional educational settings.

KEY FUNCTIONS OF LEADERSHIP IMPLIED BY THE PURPOSES OF EDUCATION

Given the purposes and scope of this chapter, it is appropriate to examine some comprehensive and current images of what is considered effective school leadership practices in several countries. The discussion begins with a brief introduction to the conceptual underpinnings and procedures of a methodology employed to produce comprehensive and multi-dimensional descriptions of school leadership practices, or leadership profiles, as they are usually termed. This is followed by brief descriptions and comparisons of several recently developed profiles of school leadership. Within this discussion, examples are provided of how these resources may be employed as supports to cognitive apprenticeship experiences within formal and informal preparation programs.

Eight or more such profiles of school leadership have been developed by the author since 1990 with writing teams from a variety of regions of the world including: Western Australia in 1989; the Canadian Province of Ontario in 1993, with updated editions in 2000, 2002, and 2006; the Canadian Northwest Territories in 1993; Hong Kong during 2000; Karelia in 2000; Belarus in 2003; Pennsylvania in the United States during 2005; and Sweden in 2005. The basic utility of these role profiles as supports to leadership development conforms to what Prestine and LeGrand (1991) describe as cognitive apprenticeship processes. Specifically, profiles can operate as support resources by providing structures for courses and workshops that are grounded in three important ways: a comprehensive image of effective leadership, the identification of key functions, and the promotion of reflective practice and critical deliberation by aspiring and incumbent school administrators.

The profiles that were developed are essentially two dimensional matrices that describe developmental stages of growth in professional performance within selected dimensions of professional practice. Applied to the school leadership role, the profile development process produces situationally specific, multi-dimensional descriptions of action consistent with the findings of research on effective professional practice, and as espoused by experienced, exemplary practitioners from a given region. The creation of a profile typically begins with a writing team of ten or more individuals establishing a goal statement, followed by a series of decisions about which categories of professional action are most relevant to the achievement of the desired state described in the profile goal statement. In a profile these categories are called dimensions or key functions. Each of these dimensions is also usually broken down into a set of sub-dimensions. To accomplish this, various facilitative and consensus building strategies are employed to blend research findings with local craft knowledge.

In application, the role profile user is able to benefit from the wisdom and experience of local expert school leaders by comparing the specific descriptions of administrative action contained in a profile to situations and problems with which the novice principal, or experienced but challenged administrator, is grappling. Abstract knowledge is situated in locally relevant contexts of practice using locally relevant vocabulary. Also, the profile user is presented with a range of acceptable responses, thereby emphasizing the notion of differentiated response and providing an element of choice that holds considerable appeal for many adult learners.

In the sections that follow several of the more recently developed leadership profiles from several countries are discussed and contrasted. Important distinctions in school leadership practices become apparent from country to country. At the same time, a common core also emerges as characteristic of school leadership practices in several countries.

When three of the more recently developed profiles are compared, those produced in Ontario (2001), Belarus (Begley & Johansson, 2003) and Hong Kong (Walker, Begley & Dimmock, 2000), it becomes evident that school administration in the three locales has much in common. With semantic differences, all three profiles incorporate descriptors of effective practice relating to three common key dimensions; school culture management, instructional leadership, and organizational management. In some ways this is a remarkable outcome given the far-flung distances and the variations in culture involved. It suggests that there are important similarities in the principalship in many countries. In these three countries principals apparently see their contemporary roles as extending much beyond traditional building management to include instructional and cultural leadership responsibilities; something which the school leadership literature has been promoting since the early 1980s (e.g. Leithwood & Montgomery, 1982). Admittedly each of the profile writing teams reviewed much the same school improvement literature as part of the profiling process. However, they may be assumed to accurately represent current school leadership practices, in a range from typical to ideal, espoused by experienced school leaders currently working in those regions since each of the three profiles has received extensive validation within their respective regions.

GROWTH STRANDS FOR SCHOOL LEADERSHIP

The preceding section focused on the key functions of practice identified by the writing teams to describe school leadership practices in their respective countries. In this section attention is shifted to the developmental growth described in the profiles, moving from the descriptions of lower levels of competent practices to the ideals described at the highest level of the profiles. A comparison and analysis of these descriptive statements reveals the implicit *growth strands* that the writing teams have incorporated within their profiles. Some intriguing images of professional growth emerge. What follows is a sampling of the growth strands common to profiles produced in several countries:

From a Tendency Towards Reactive Responses to Proactive Responses

The "management" dimensions of leadership profiles invariably illustrate this growth strand. For example, at the lowest level of practice the principal might be said to devote available administrative time to immediate administrative tasks and daily occurrences, whereas at a more ideal level the principal might develop and use a time management plan to focus the use of personal time, as well as staff resources, towards the achievement of short and long term goals. This illustrates what is for administrators the ubiquitous trap of reactively responding to day to day events, using up valuable time doing administrivia, or letting crises shape the role (Leithwood & Montgomery, 1986).

From Reliance on Personal Preferences in Decision Making, to a Focus on Consensus, to an Outcomes-based or Consequences Focus, to a Sensitivity to and Accommodation of Multiple Environmental Influences

This growth strand is evident particularly in the school and community culture management dimensions of most profiles we have developed. It reflects a movement from inwardness or personal preference to a more collaborative and empowering perspective on leadership. What is illustrated, as one proceeds along the stages of growth, is an increased awareness and responsiveness to educational stakeholders, or educational influences derived from the broader school community. At lower levels the principal might only be aware of parental, staff and student impact on the culture of the school, but rely on personal preferences as a guide to decision making. At an ideal level the principal is more likely to collaborate with students, staff and community to create and promote a culture in which unique needs and cultural diversity are respected. This growth strand may very well constitute one of the prerequisites to becoming an empowering transformational leader (Leithwood, 1992).

From Rigid Adherence to Fixed Procedures, to Procedural Flexibility, to Philosophical or Conceptual Fidelity

The instructional leadership dimensions in all profiles produced to date illustrate this growth strand within such sub-dimensions as evaluation. At lower levels of competence, a principal might rigidly conform to district policy and use established procedures to evaluate staff or participate in mandated program reviews. A more skilful instructional leader would monitor progress toward attainment of school goals through program and staff evaluation procedures and work with teachers to develop self-evaluation procedures and professional reflection. This represents an integration of effort towards the attainment of multiple goals. Also reflected is the capacity for cognitive flexibility that Leithwood, Begley & Cousins propose as a characteristic of ideal leadership practice (1992).

From In-school Focus, to Inter-school Focus, to School within the Greater Community Focus

All of the leadership profiles incorporate this growth strand, particularly within the school and community culture management sub-dimensions. At one time it was enough for principals to maintain a span of awareness that was limited to the immediate school community. For example, a competent principal would be sensitive to the need for incorporating local cultural activities in the school and invite the community to attend special school events. However, a principal who employs the cultures of the community to enhance individual and collective self-esteem and to promote learning in a multilingual educational system would demonstrate more ideal practice. This notion is reminiscent of Barth's (1990) conception of a community of leaders.

From a Limited Repertoire to a Broad Repertoire of Strategies

The highest levels of practice across several dimensions of the leadership profiles, but especially the sub-dimensions of instructional leadership, manifest this notion. At lower levels of effectiveness principals might employ a limited number of broadly accepted strategies to manage instructional affairs (e.g. inform staff of professional development opportunities), whereas at more exemplary levels principals might recognize and encourage the development of curricular expertise among teachers and resource staff and promote sharing among staff to encourage skill development and reflection about teaching practices (e.g. collaborative peer coaching). This notion of associating a broader repertoire of strategies with leadership expertise is consistent with Leithwood and Stager's (1989) findings on the problem solving processes employed by expert principals.

MOVING BEYOND PRESCRIPTIVE GUIDES FOR SCHOOL LEADERSHIP

Developing and using resources such as the integrated images of leadership practice just discussed often generates a situation where people become tempted to use these images of practice as prescriptive models. However, this temptation must be resisted because the conditions of social ferment and diversity characteristic of our times confound any notion that we might develop a prescriptive guide to ethical or value-added leadership — a catalogue of correct values that school administrators ought to adopt without question. This will disappoint those who might hope that such frameworks can be used as some sort of silver bullet solution for the dilemmas of administration and ultimate curriculum for leadership development programs. Unfortunately, the processes of leadership in most school situations are much too context-bound to permit this kind of quick fix. It is not enough for school leaders to merely emulate the practices of other principals currently viewed as experts. Leaders in schools must become reflective practitioners and authentic towards local needs in their leadership practices. The first step towards achieving this state is, predictably enough, to engage in personal reflection (see Coombs, 2004). However, once a degree of improved self-knowledge has been achieved through personal reflection, administrators must then take the next step towards authentic leadership. That is, they must strive to develop sensitivity to the values orientations of others in order to give meaning to the actions of the students, teachers, parents and community members with whom they interact. The pay-off to these more sophisticated forms of leadership occurs when understanding the value orientations of others provides leaders with information on how they might best influence the practices of others towards the achievement of broadly justifiable social objectives.

As appealing and practical as theories, models, frameworks and procedural guides may be to people working in professional settings, they must be employed as initial organizers, not as prescriptions or recipes. The complexity of social and administrative situations makes it attractive for school leaders to employ processes to aid their interpretation and structuring of situations, but this must be done in socially and culturally sensitive ways. For example, Americans or Canadians might very well derive useful insights from studying the educational protocols of Australia, New Zealand and Sweden, just as the converse is also true. However, they should never expect to adopt practices without careful consideration of the cultural adaptations necessary and the appropriateness of fit. Educational practices in any given country are the outcome of a complex set of intersecting social variables and history. The intersection of circumstances that makes a practice sensible in one country is relatively unlikely to be matched by the conditions in other countries. Indeed, although it seldom happens, a sounder strategy for policy makers might be a comparative consideration of practices and protocols in several countries.

THE IMPACT OF SOCIAL EXPECTATIONS ON SCHOOL LEADERSHIP

A preceding section of this chapter addressed academic and scholarly influences on the formation of images of effective school leadership practices. However, there are other influences on school leadership that are more direct and even more important than research scholarship and the leadership literature. These are the cultural influences derived from the community and the greater society. These influences evolve in response to changing social trends and manifest themselves as expectations for school leaders.

In recent decades, school leaders have learned how important it is to lead and manage with proper reference to the broader environmental context of their community. The influences on leadership and education can be thought of as coming from multiple social sources. Some of these influences can take on the status of personal or social values when they are perceived as conceptions of the desirable with motivating force (Hodgkinson, 1991). Unfortunately, our personal values as well of those of the profession, organization, community and society are not necessarily consistent or compatible with each other. As a result these influences and values derived from the various arenas of our environment can generate inconsistencies and conflicts. Current social circumstances in many countries could be safely characterized as conflicted. In North America, for example, these circumstances include a persisting absence of consensus on educational purposes; an intensified emphasis on individual rights and concerns for equity; greater cultural diversity, especially in urban centers; the presence of more pressure and special interest groups; skepticism and an absence of trust towards leaders and authority figures; and a general mistrust of bureaucracy and bureaucratic process.

To trace the source and influence of these social circumstances on school leadership it can be helpful to think in terms of multiple arenas of leadership practice. The author has frequently employed a simple onion figure (see Figure 2.1) to show these relationships.

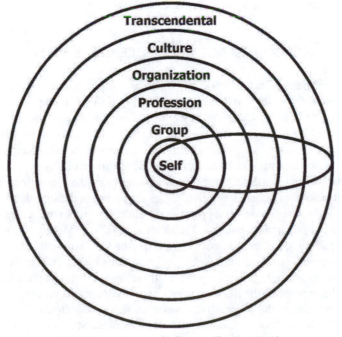

FIGURE 2.1 Arenas of influence (Begley, 2006).

There are seven interactive environments portrayed within this graphic. These arenas can be thought of as the school leader's source of personal, professional and social values, as well as the source of many of the conflicts encountered in a professional role. Within the figure, the individual is represented within the center ring and extending through all the rings. Their character is the outcome of many transient influences as well as relatively more enduring values acquired from multiple arenas. The second ring from the center represents the arena of groups, and other collective entities including family, peers, friends and acquaintances. The third ring, profession, represents a more formal arena of administration that is closely related to the second ring, but is given special emphasis here because of its relevance to the professional context that is the focus of this article.

The fourth ring represents the arena traditionally of most concern to academics and practitioners in the field of educational administration, the organization. Much of the literature of educational administration and most of the corporate literature are grounded within the organizational perspective, adopting it as a primary reference point for administrative activity. Moving further outwards in the figure, one encounters the arenas representing the greater community, society, and culture. Within recent decades, school administrators have learned that it is necessary to pay a lot more attention to the community as a relevant administrative arena and source of influence on school leadership (Leithwood, Begley, & Cousins, 1992). The increasing diversity of our societies and a general trend towards globalization has highlighted society and culture as relevant arenas of administrative activity. A final, seventh ring is included to accommodate notions of the transcendental — God, faith, spirituality, even extra-sensory perception. Spirituality is of considerable importance to many individuals, and has begun to attract the attention of more scholars as an important influence on educational leadership (e.g. Dalia, 2005). Even school leaders who do not subscribe to a spiritual dimension as a source of influence on their own daily lives are well advised to keep this arena in mind, if only because others associated with their professional role do. A leader who wants to understand the motivations of those they are supposed to lead will be sensitive to all potentially significant categories of influence.

THE MORAL CONTEXT OF SCHOOL LEADERSHIP SITUATIONS

Ethical postures and frameworks are often presented as abstract concepts stripped of the contextual details that would give them relevance and specificity in particular settings and in support of particular roles. Yet the application of any ethic occurs within a normative and cultural context. This can generate a number of problems in school leadership situations. The most obvious problem is that an ethic stripped of context requires interpretation as it is applied to a particular social or cultural context. This can be a serious challenge in culturally diverse societies where, for example, headgear (e.g. the Sikh turban) is sometimes more than just a hat, or daggers may be religious symbols and not so much a weapon. Or, as suggested in the introduction to this chapter, consider how a "focus on mission" as a professional ethical posture would mean radically different things to a school principal as compared to an infantry officer. Moreover, human nature being what it is, individuals, groups and societies are more often than not inclined to interpret ethics in ways that are appropriate to their preferences and traditions rather than any commitment to the social inclusion of minorities. In extreme forms, these interpretations can extend to preserving self-interests at the expense of the freedom of others. If a person in a professional role is carrying out the moral deliberation, the process becomes even more complicated because professionals are also expected to be agents of society or of their profession. So, their pursuit of moral literacy must involve more than addressing their own belief systems.

The sheer austerity and abstractness of many ethical frameworks poses a second challenge for school leaders. Practitioners tend to be attracted to practicality and relevance. Philosophically based discussions about ethics and valuation processes by their nature often are not very appealing in terms of relevance because of the context-stripped manner in which they are often portrayed. For example, the ethics of administration, as proposed by Strike, Haller, and Soltis (1988), identify maximizing benefits and respecting individual rights through protocols of due process. These are key notions associated with an ethic of justice perspective. However, the task of clarifying the inherent benefits associated with a situation, and the fair distribution of resources among an *a priori* identified set of potential recipients, sorted according to degree of entitlement and need, is something that requires a good deal of contextual information as well as skill. This is one of the reasons why the use of context-rich case problems, critical incidents and dilemmas of practice is such a successful way to teach and study ethical analysis and valuation processes with practitioners.

For these reasons there is a lot of merit in speaking of ethical actions within a specific professional context or through the use of heuristic applications of ethical postures appropriate to a professional or personal context. There are several examples of this that can be used as illustrations. Furman (2003) uses the "ethic of community" as a focus point for ethical educational practice in North American schools. Stefkovich (2006; Stefkovich & Shapiro, 2003) adopts the notion of "best interests of students" as a focus for her professional ethics in education. Begley (2006) speaks of "authentic leadership" as an approach to presenting ethical leadership practices and moral literacy in a manner that has relevance for people working in school leadership situations. However, even these context grounded heuristic applications require definition and the establishment of consensus on meaning. Fortunately, there is literature that can be helpful in this regard. For example, Stefkovich and Begley (2007) and Stefkovich and O'Brien (2004) have identified and explored the various meanings associated with the concept of "best interests." Leithwood, Edge and Jantzi (1999) have done much the same for the concept of educational accountability. The innovative dimension being proposed here is the advisability of careful selection and adoption of professionally and contextually relevant metaphors to make the goals of moral leadership more understandable, compelling, and achievable. It is in this context that Begley proposes authentic leadership as a relevant way of conceptualizing educational leadership development processes. It is a way of thinking about ethical and effective leadership that is grounded in professional practices and orientations that have meaning for school administrators.

Several scholars, beyond the author, have in recent years explored authentic leadership as a way to conceptualize ideal leadership practice that goes beyond the description of practices to include a consideration of the intentional and moral aspects of leadership. These scholars include Taylor (1991), Duignan and Bhindi (1997) and Starratt (2004). Begley defines authentic leadership as the outcome of self-knowledge, sensitivity to the orientations of others, and a technical sophistication that leads to a synergy of leadership action (2001; 2003; 2006). It is the incorporation of the third component that integrates the management and leadership functions of educational administration.

In order to lead effectively, individuals in any leadership role need to understand human nature and the motivations of individuals in particular. In the practical professional context of educational administration, school leaders need more than just the normative ideology of ethics, as relevant as that may be to some educational situations and as responses to the dilemmas of practice. Individuals in school leadership roles require frameworks and ways of thinking that will encompass the full range of human motivations and valuation processes encountered in school settings. To do this one must think in terms of *values* and *valuation processes* where ethics are one category or component within a broader spectrum of value types. Furthermore, a full appreciation of ethics should include more than just a concern for the high ground of ethics-motivated action. The study of ethics should be as much about the life-long personal struggle to be ethical, about failures to be ethical, the inconsistencies of ethical postures, the masquerading of self-interest and personal preference as ethical action, and the dilemmas which occur in everyday and professional life when one ethic trumps another. These and other matters related to purpose-driven school leadership practices are explored in further detail in succeeding sections of this chapter.

THE ROLE PLAYED BY ETHICS AND VALUES IN SCHOOL LEADERSHIP

As discussed in a preceding section of this chapter, goals, values and ethics are an important influence on the cognitive processes of individuals and groups of individuals whether or not they are consciously employed as guides to decision making by individuals. Values can be formally defined as conceptions of the desirable with motivating force characteristic of individuals, groups, organizations, and societies that influence choices made from available resources and means (Hodgkinson, 1978). Begley (2006) describes the influence of values within individuals as the internal psychological reflections of more intrinsic levels of motivation (e.g. a concern for personal interests, consequences, or consensus) that become tangible to an observer in the form of attitudes, speech, and actions. Thus, values in their various forms, including ethics, can be thought of as conscious or unconscious influences on attitudes, actions, and speech. However, it is important to note that valuation processes can involve more than ethics. This is a distinction important to leadership practices that is not often made in the literature. Values can take different forms and can be best categorized according to their motivational grounding. Ethics, as a particular form of values, as opposed to Ethics, the scholarly discipline, are normative social ideals or codes of conduct usually grounded in the cultural experience of particular societies. In that sense they are an *uber* form of social consensus. Most societies have core ethics equivalent to the American notions of democracy, freedom of speech, and the priority of individual rights. Those of us steeped in the traditions of such classic Western philosophical thought can easily make the mistake of assuming that these most cherished of ethical postures are universal. However, they seldom are, especially as interpreted from culture to culture. Ethics in their purest forms tend to be expressed in a relatively context-stripped form that conveys the essence of the normative behavior. Indeed, in some forms and social applications they are treated as absolute values. This inclination to view ethics as some sort of absolute value is sometimes exacerbated by evidence of consensus across cultures on certain ethics like respect for human rights, honesty, and democracy. And, indeed there are probably some ethics of the human condition that approach a condition of universal relevance. However, the devil is literally in the details when it comes to ethical postures in the real world of school leadership. The interpretation of meaning associated with an ethic can vary greatly from society to society. Simply pondering the contrasting notions of what constitutes democracy in countries like Sweden, the United States, and China illustrates this point. Using ethical postures as a basis for making social choices requires the inclusion of a dialogic component, except perhaps in the most culturally homogeneous of contexts. This is largely because of our increasingly culturally diverse societies and a much more globalized world. This is not to argue against the relevance and importance of ethics to leadership actions. It is more a caveat to their proper use.

There is another issue when it comes to considering ethics and their relevance to leadership development processes. Human behavior can and does frequently involve a range of motivational bases, only a few of which can be associated with ethical postures. These other motivational bases can range from self-interest to a concern for rationalized positions grounded in consensus or consequences, in addition to the trans-rational groundings of ethical postures (Hodgkinson, 1978; Begley, 2006). The point is that because ethical postures are usually associated with ideal states, they do not necessarily accommodate the full range of motivations of typical human behavior. This circumstance may not matter that much to academics and philosophers focused on the description and promotion of ideal moral conditions, but it is critical to individuals in leadership positions seeking to understand their own motivational bases as well as those of others. It hardly needs to be said that not all individuals encountered in organizational settings act in ethical ways. Ethics based postures are highly relevant for guiding appropriate responses to complex organizational situations, but they may not be sufficient in themselves for a comprehensive analysis and understanding of human motivations. There is some evidence for this assertion.

As argued earlier, in order to lead effectively, individuals in any leadership role need to understand human nature and the motivations of individuals in particular. Leadership is essentially focused on people and relationships. In the practical professional context of educational administration, school leaders need more than just normative ideology, as relevant as that may be to educational situations. They require frameworks and ways of thinking that will encompass the full range of human motivations and valuation processes encountered in school settings. As indicated above, these can range from the more primitive forms of self-interest all the way to the most altruistic and inspiring trans-rational values inspired motivations of saints and heroes. To understand and accommodate the full range of human motivations, which are understood to be an important influence on the adoption of particular values (Begley, 2006), one must think in terms of *values* and *valuation processes* where ethics (as opposed to the field of inquiry called Ethics) are one category or component within a broader spectrum of value types. Furthermore, as previously implied, a full appreciation of ethics should include more than just a concern for the high ground of ethics-motivated action.

To summarize the points made in this section, most current leadership development programs in the United States, Canada, and Australia, university-based and otherwise, emphasize the importance of ethics based decision making. This is admirable and well advised. However, it is not sufficient. Research on principal valuation processes (Begley & Johansson, 1998) and earlier research on administrative problem solving processes (Leithwood & Steinbach, 1995) demonstrate that administrators tend to consciously employ ethics as a guide to action relatively infrequently and under particular conditions — in situations of high stakes urgency, when consensus is impossible, when responding to unprecedented situations, and for certain hot-button social issues which tend to quickly escalate debate to a point where people seek refuge within an ethical posture. This is so for a number of reasons. Ethics are culturally derived norms and if the context for leadership action is multi-cultural there can be issues associated with shared interpretations of ethical postures grounded in the experience of one culture and not another.

A MULTI-ETHICAL APPROACH TO INTERPRETING
AND RESPONDING TO DILEMMAS

Shapiro and Stefkovich (2005) espouse the application of a multi-ethical analytical approach to the interpretation of ethical dilemmas by people working in professional leadership roles. The key ethical orientations suggested by these scholars include the ethic of justice, the ethic of critique, the ethic of care, and a hybrid multi-dimensional model, the ethic of profession. Strike (Strike, Haller & Soltis, 1988; Strike 2003) is well known for his work grounded in the ethic of justice with its familiar dualistic tension between maximizing benefits and respecting individual rights. Bates (1980) and Giroux and Purpel (1983) are good arch-types for an ethic of critique orientation. Nodding's (1984) writing is a good representation of the ethic of care orientation. And finally, Starratt (2003), and Shapiro and Stefkovich (2005) are proponents of a multi-dimensional model that subsumes the ethics care, critique and justice into one ethic of profession.

Although Shapiro and Stefkovich (2005) propose the use of multiple ethical lenses as a basis for responding to the dilemmas of school leadership, they stop short of proposing any particular sequence for applying those ethics. Their research suggests that individuals vary in their preferred ethical postures and are thus satisfied with espousing that administrators adopt a multi-ethical analysis of problems and situations, rather than a rigidly fixed sequence of application. For example, a school principal or head teacher responding to an ethical dilemma might prefer, in the sense of a *personal* inclination that is the outcome of their social formation, to gravitate towards the application of an ethic of care perspective.

This author, however, contends that in the *professional* context of school leadership, where the individual is essentially an agent of society and accountable to the community for actions taken in the execution of his or her duties, there is probably an implied sequence for the appropriate application of these classic ethical lenses. A professionally appropriate sequence for the application of ethical lenses in a school leadership situation might be: ethic of critique, followed by the ethic of care, and then ethic of justice. Beginning with the ethic of critique is necessary in order to name and understand all perspectives applicable to a situation, especially those of minorities and individuals otherwise without voice or representation. To do otherwise is to risk gravitation to the preferred cultural orientations of the leader or the mainstream orientations of a given cultural group. The ethic of care naturally follows next in the sequence as a way to keep the focus of the process on people rather than on organizations or policies. Using the ethic of care, one can also assess the capacity and responsibility of stakeholders to a situation in a humane way. Finally, once the ethics of critique and care have been used to carefully interpret a situation, the ethic of justice can be applied as a basis for deciding on the actual actions that will maximize benefits for all while respecting the rights of individual.

However, as Shapiro and Stefkovich (2005) advise, this is not to promote the notion of a dogmatic adherence to a prescriptive sequence of application for ethics derived from Western philosophy. In all cases, the sequencing and application of ethical perspectives needs to be very fluid and dynamic as an initial organizer, not a recipe, and as a stimulus for reflection, not a prescription. The application of any lens to a situation, including ethics, begins the process of highlighting some information as relevant and diminishing or veiling the relevance of other information. School leaders accountable to their communities must take care to interpret situations in a sensitive way. Most school administrators do not consciously adopt ethical perspectives as specific guides to problem solving and the few that do often use just one posture (justice, care or critique) as some sort of absolute moral rubric.

HOW SCHOOL LEADERS RESPOND TO MORAL DILEMMAS

The achievement of consensus on educational issues among even traditional educational stakeholders has become more difficult in many communities. School administrators increasingly encounter dilemmas or value conflict situations where consensus cannot be achieved, rendering obsolete the traditional rational notions of problem *solving*. Administrators must now often be satisfied with *responding* to a situation since there may be no solution possible that will satisfy all. Such value dilemmas can occur within a single arena of administration or among two or more arenas. The most difficult dilemmas occur when one ethic literally trumps another.

A pilot study conducted by the author during 2004 examined principals' perceptions of and responses to the moral dilemmas encountered in the professional context of their roles. While the data were collected from a sample of principals from Ontario, Canada and Pennsylvania, USA using a survey instrument and follow-up interviews, the general findings are illustrative of school leadership practices in other countries. The data were interpreted through a values framework (Begley, 2006) that is the outcome of an interdisciplinary integration of administrative theory about valuation processes with information processing theory derived from the field of cognitive psychology. An overview of the findings from this project provides insights into how school leaders respond to the ethical dilemmas encountered in their professional work.

Theme or Context of Dilemmas

The dilemmas identified by the principals in this study could be readily grouped according to a number of themes or topics. A surprising number of the dilemmas focused on various forms of educational system policies that were alternately perceived as overly punitive, procedurally rigid, and/or negatively influencing a principal's professional autonomy or expertise and discretion. Another common theme was the principals' overarching desire to do what they perceived to be in the best interests of students. Other themes included: conflicts with parents or other community members, dealing with abusive or incompetent professional staff, and risking career or job in the defense of personal moral beliefs.

Sources of Dilemma

Begley's (2004) graphic portrayal of the arenas or domains of administration was employed as a guide to determining the source or sources of the dilemmas presented by the participants. Many of the dilemmas reported by the participants could be readily connected to conflicts between organizational policies (e.g. zero tolerance policies, required reporting of alleged abuse) that reduced the professional discretion of the administrator to make decisions in the best interest of students or the school. The most difficult of the situations occurs when the policies are perceived as inappropriately punitive or when the student in question had no intention to break a rule or violate policy. Several participants also reported dilemmas that clearly revealed conflicts between personal moral positions and those of the profession, school district or community (i.e. persistent racial discrimination by administrative colleagues).

Interpersonal/Intra-personal Dilemmas

The notion of arenas as a guide for identifying the source of the dilemmas was also useful for assessing whether the dilemmas were inter-personal or intra-personal; that is, whether the dilemma explicitly involved more than one person or was an essentially internal struggle experienced by one person. In a surprising number of cases, most of the cases actually, clear evidence suggests that the dilemmas were intra-personal. School administrators seem much inclined to sort out the dilemmas on their own, without seeking the opinions and support of others. For the school administrators participating in this study, the dilemmas of practice seem to be private and internal mental processes. Only one principal made reference to actively involving other staff or colleagues in the moral deliberation of the dilemmas encountered in the school.

Guiding Meta-Values

Prior work by the author has regularly proposed accountability as a dominant meta-value employed by school administrators in their assessment and interpretation of situations. This apparently strong inclination and quite consistent pattern of response across cultures has also been described as a natural inclination for school administrators to gravitate towards the rational motivational bases of consequences and consensus, again because of their preoccupation with accountability issues. The previously discussed notion of ritualized rationality is a closely related aspect of these patterns of action. This phenomenon has also been used to explain in part why school administrators often avoid ethics as an explicit guide to decision making, in preference of more rationally defensible decision processes grounded in consequences or consensus.

The data collected in support of this study both confirm and challenge the pre-eminence of accountability as a meta-value for school principals. Many of the dilemmas submitted by the participants do indeed make explicit and/or implicit reference to accountability as an over-riding concern. However, there is another equally strong and frequently articulated meta-value that becomes apparent as an outcome of these dilemmas; that is, "doing what is best for kids" or "the best interests of students". As much as accountability may be a primary influence on the general decision-making processes of school administrators, when situations are perceived by administrators to be dilemmas, there appears to be a strong inclination to adopt "students' best interests" as the meta-value of choice.

Strategies for Interpretation

The strategies employed by the participants to interpret and respond to the dilemmas of practice they perceived conform fairly well to Roche's (1999) earlier research findings based on the practices of principals in Queensland, Australia. He found that school administrators routinely confront moral and ethical dilemmas that demand a response. His inquiry focused on how school administrators actually respond to moral and ethical dilemmas, the most difficult value conflicts they encounter.

He identified four primary ways in which principals respond to moral dilemmas. The press for accountability appears to heavily influence such processes. Listed in order of frequency of use by the administrators in Roche's study, the strategies principals used in response to the professional dilemmas they encounter are: avoidance, suspended morality, creative insubordination, and taking a personal moral stand. Avoidance (re-interpreting the situation so it no longer involves an ethical dimension) is the most frequently employed response among the administrators in this study. Suspended morality, the second most common strategy, illustrates the ability of administrators to set aside some of their personal value orientations and consciously respond to situations from a professional or organizational perspective. Campbell (2003) identifies the same phenomena as common administrative practice and condemns it as immoral when student needs are subordinated to organizational imperatives. The third category of response identified by Roche is creative insubordination. As a strategy it is an opposite response to suspended morality. In this case organizational dictates are set aside, or creative approaches to compliance are found, that favor more humane concerns. The taking of a personal moral stand was the least frequently employed response, usually adopted only when the administrator assessed a high likelihood of successfully challenging the competing demands of the profession, organization or society.

There is evidence of all four of Roche's identified strategies being used by the respondents in the study. Appeals to policy as a basis for responding equate with the avoidance strategy. Many of the dilemmas submitted by the principals conveyed the angst encountered when they felt compelled to suspend their own morality in favor of a professional or organizational position. A few of the reported dilemmas reveal the intent of the principal to take a public moral stand.

Effect of Prior Training or Experience with Axiological Models

It must be acknowledged that most, but not all, of the participants in this study are, or have been, engaged in advanced graduate or doctoral studies. In terms of the influence of prior learning, one participant in the study wrote extensively about the influence of prior exposure to axiological models and the study of valuation processes as a powerful influence on her response to and interpretation of dilemma situations. She asserts that consciously and explicitly applying internalized approaches to moral interpretation has the effect of converting the situations from "dilemmas" to "tensions". She also states a perception that the speed, certainty, and quality of her responses to challenging school situations has significantly improved through the application of these models. She further admits to encouraging and demonstrating these processes to members of her staff and colleagues as a strategy for improving the quality of decision making in her school and school district.

CONCLUSION: EDUCATION IS SPECIAL

This chapter explored the special nature and purposes of school leadership as a profession, the evolving expectations for the role in response to social trends, the dynamics and variety of influences on the practices of individuals in those roles, and some of the generic functions of the role across cultural settings. What stands out as characteristic of the role is complexity, human interaction, and the dynamics of continually evolving social expectations. School leadership involves management, but management skills are not enough. The mediation of competing interests and fair allocation of scarce resources in support of an increasingly complex educational process necessitates that school administrators have a clear sense of educational purposes. They need to be able to lead, to navigate through multiple and competing interests.

Fortunately, there are historically clear purposes of education. They are multi-faceted and therefore complex to manage, but they are nevertheless the socially justified objectives of education in our societies. The mandate is clear and it is an educational one, not a corporate agenda or economic agenda. The challenge for school leaders is to keep the aesthetic, economic and ideological purposes of education in the forefront as guides to decision making and as the meta-values of their profession. This is nothing less than a purpose-driven approach to educational leadership.

In support of this argument, a number of related concepts and issues have been explored. The purposes of leadership and the formation of leadership roles were described as the dynamic outcome of influences from several arenas or social domains. Authentic leadership was proposed as an educationally appropriate approach to school administration and the outcome of self-knowledge, sensitivity to the perspectives of others, and the technical skills of organization management and personnel leadership.

The importance of focusing on leadership intentions, not just the description of practices, was also demonstrated. And the need to be aware of intercultural variations in perceptions and interpretation of leadership purposes was also argued as necessary in a world made up of increasingly diverse populations and communities. These are the specialized purposes and nature of educational leadership.

ACKNOWLEDGEMENT

Portions of this chapter were based on material taken from several previously published journal articles with the permission of the publishers. These include: Begley, P. T. & Stefkovich, J. (2007). Integrating values and ethics into postsecondary teaching for leadership development: Principles, concepts, and strategies. *Journal of Educational Administration, 45*(4); Stefkovich, J. & Begley, P. T. (2007). Conceptualizing ethical school leadership and defining the best interests of students. Special issue of *Educational Management and Leadership, 35*(2), 205–226; Begley, P. T. (2006). Self-knowledge, capacity and sensitivity: Prerequisites to authentic leadership by school principals. *Journal of Educational Administration. 44*(6), 570–589; Begley, P. T. & Slater, C. (Eds.). (2001). *School leadership in Canada* (3rd ed.). Mt. St. Louis, Ontario: Paul Begley & Associates.

REFERENCES

Barnard, C. I. (1938). *The functions of the executive.* Cambridge, MA: Harvard University Press

Bates, R. (1980). Educational administration, the science of sociology and the management of knowledge. *Educational Administration Quarterly, 16*(2), 1–20.

Barth, R. S. (1990). *Improving schools from within.* San Franisco, CA: Jossey-Bass.

Begley, P. T. (1995). Using profiles of school leadership as supports to cognitive apprenticeship. *Educational Administration Quarterly, 31*(2), 176–202.

Begley, P. T. (1996). Cognitive perspectives on values in administration: A quest for coherence and relevance. *Educational Administration Quarterly, 32*(3), 403–426.

Begley, P. T. (2004). Understanding valuation processes: Exploring the linkage between motivation and action. *International Studies in Educational Administration, 32*(2), 4–17.

Begley, P. T. (2006). Self-knowledge, capacity and sensitivity: Prerequisites to authentic leadership by school principals. *Journal of Educational Administration, 44*(6), 570–589

Begley, P. T. & Johansson, O. (1998). The values of school administration: Preferences, ethics and conflicts. *The Journal of School Leadership, 8*(4), 399–422.

Begley, P. T. & Johansson, O. (Eds.). (2003). *School leadership in Belarus* (2nd ed.). Umea, Sweden: Umea Universitet. Published in Russian and English editions.

Begley, P. T. & Slater, C. (Eds.). (2001) .*School leadership in Canada* (3rd ed.). Mt. St. Louis, Ontario: Paul Begley & Associates.

Branson, C. (2006). Effects of structured self-reflection on the development of authentic leadership practices among Queensland primary school principals. *Educational Management Administration and Leadership, 35*(2), 227–248.

Bridges, E. M. (1992). *Problem based learning.* Eugene, OR: ERIC

Campbell, E. (2003). Let right be done: Trying to put ethical standards into practice. In Begley, P. T. & Johansson, O. (Eds.), *The ethical dimensions of school leadership.* Dordrecht: Kluwer, pp. 107–125.

Clark, D. L., Lotto, L. S. & Astuto, T. A. (1984) Effective schools and school improvement: A comparative analysis of two lines of inquiry. *Educational Administration Quarterly, 20*(3), 41–68.

Coombs, C. P. (2004). Developing reflective habits of mind. *Values and Ethics in Educational Administration, 1*(4), 1–8.

Cuban, L. (1986). Principaling. *Peabody Journal of Education, 63*(1),107–119.

Dalia, D. (2005). *The relationship of spirituality to leadership in schools.* Unpublished doctoral thesis, University of Toronto, Toronto, Ont.

Dimmock, C. & Walker, A. (1998). Comparative educational administration: Developing a cross-cultural conceptual framework. *Educational Administration Quarterly, 34*(4), 558–595.

Duignan, P. & Bhindi, N. (1997). Authentic leadership: An emerging perspective. *Journal of Educational Administration, 35*(3), 195–209.

Furman, G. (2003). Moral leadership and the ethic of community. *Values and Ethics in Educational Administration, 2*(1), 1–8.

Giroux, H. A. & Purpel, D. (Eds.). (1983). *The hidden curriculum and moral education: deception or discovery?* Berkeley, CA: McCutchan Publishing.

Gousha, R. P. (1986). *The Indiana school principalship: the role of the Indiana principal as defined by the principal.* Bloomington: Indiana University School of Education.

Griggs, R. F. (2005) *Applying military leadership principles in the development of educational leaders.* Unpublished master's research paper, The Pennsylvania State University, University Park.

Hall, G., Rutherford, W. L., Hord, S. M. & Huling, L. L. (1986). Effects of three principal styles on school improvement. *Educational Leadership, 41*(5) 22–31.

Hart, A. W. (1993). An instructional strategy in educational administration. *Educational Administration Quarterly, 29*(3), 339–363.

Hodgkinson, C. (1978). *Towards a philosophy of administration.* Oxford: Basil Blackwell.

Hodgkinson, C. (1991). *Educational leadership: the moral art.* Albany, NY: SUNY Press.

Kingdon, H. D. (1985). The role of the teaching elementary school principal. *Principal Issues, 4,* 20–23.

Kohlberg, L. & Turiel, E. (1971). Moral development and moral education. In Lesser, G. (Ed.), *Psychology and educational practice.* New York: Scott Foresman, pp. 530–550.

Langlois, L. (2004). Making the tough calls: Complex decision-making in light of ethical considerations. *International Studies in Educational Administration, 32*(2), 78–93.

Larsen, T. J. (1987, April). *Identification of instructional leadership behaviours and the impact of their implementation on academic achievement.* Paper presented at the Annual Meeting of the American Educational Research Association, Washington, D.C.

Leithwood, K. A. (1992). The move towards transformational leadership. *Educational Leadership, 49*(5), 8–12.

Leithwood, K. A., Begley, P. T. & Cousins, J. B. (1992). *Developing expert leadership for future schools.* London: Falmer Press.

Leithwood, K., Edge, K. & Jantzi, D. (1999). *Educational accountability: The state of the art.* Gutersloh: Bertelsmann Foundation Publishers.

Leithwood, K. A. &Hallinger, P (1993). Cognitive perspectives on educational administration. *Educational Administration Quarterly, 29*(3), 296–301.

Leithwood, K. A. & Montgomery, D. G. (1982). The role of the elementary school principal in program improvement. *Review of Educational Research, 52*(3), 309–339.

Leithwood, K. A. & Montgomery, D. G. (1986). *Improving principal effectiveness: the principal profile.* Toronto: OISE Press.

Leithwood, K. A. & Stager, M. (1989). Components of expertise in principals' problem solving. *Educational Administration Quarterly, 25*(1), 126–161.

Leithwood, K. A. & Steinbach, R. (1995). *Expert problem solving.* Albany, NY: SUNY Press.

Miller, J. & Seller, W. (1985). *Curriculum: Perspectives and practice.* New York: Longman.

Prestine, N. A. & LeGrand, B. F. (1991). Cognitive learning theory and the preparation of educational administrators: Implications for practice and policy. *Educational Administration Quarterly, 27*(1), 61–89.

Roche, K (1999). Moral and ethical dilemmas in Catholic school settings. In Begley, P. T. (Ed.), *Values and educational leadership.* Albany, NY: SUNY Press, pp. 255–272.

Sergiovanni, T. J. (1984). Leadership and excellence in schooling, *Educational Leadership, 41*(5), 4–13.

Shapiro, J. & Stefkovich, J. (2005). *Ethical leadership and decision making in education.* Mahwah, NJ: Erlbaum.

Starratt, R. J. (2003). Democratic leadership theory in late modernity: An oxymoron or ironic possibility? In Begley, P. T. & Johansson, O. (Eds.), *The ethical dimensions of school leadership.* Dordrecht: Kluwer, pp. 13–31.

Starratt, R. J. (2004). *Ethical leadership.* San Francisco, CA: Jossey-Bass.

Stefkovich, J. A. (2006). *Best interests of the student: applying ethical constructs to legal cases in education.* Mahwah, NJ: Erlbaum.

Stefkovich, J. & Begley, P. T. (2007). Conceptualizing ethical school leadership and defining the best interests of students. Special issue of *Educational Management and Leadership, 35*(2), 205–226

Stefkovich, J .A. & O'Brien, G. M. (2004). Best interests of the student: An ethical model. *Journal of Educational Administration, 42*(2), 197–214.

Stefkovich, J. & Shapiro, J (2003). Deconstructing communities: Educational leaders and their ethical decision-making processes. In Begley, P. T. & Johansson, O. (Eds.), *The ethical dimensions of school leadership* Dordrecht: Kluwer, pp. 89–106.

Strike, K. A. (2003). Community, coherence, and inclusiveness. In Begley, P. T. & Johansson, O. (Eds.), *The ethical dimensions of school leadership.* Dordrecht: Kluwer, pp. 69–87.

Strike, K. A., Haller, E. J., Soltis, J. F. (1988). *The ethics of school administration.* New York: Teachers College Press.

Taylor, C. (1991). *The ethics of authenticity.* Cambridge, MA: Harvard University Press.

Walker, A. (2003). Developing cross-cultural perspectives on education and community. In Begley, P. T. & O. Johansson (Eds.), *The ethical dimensions of school leadership.* Dordrecht: Kluwer, pp. 145–160.

Walker, A., Begley, P. T. & Dimmock, C. (Eds.). (2000). *School leadership in Hong Kong.* Hong Kong: Chinese University of Hong Kong.

Walker, A. & Dimmock, C. (1999). A cross-cultural approach to the study of educational leadership: an emerging framework. *Journal of School Leadership, 9*(4), 321–348.

3

Leadership and Culture

Jacky Lumby and Nick Foskett

The interrelationship of culture with leadership and its development is the focus of this chapter. The concept of culture has appeared frequently in analyses of both. However culture is often defined in broad general terms as, for example, 'the way we do things around here' (Deal & Kennedy, 1982), obscuring complex and contested conceptualizations. What we mean by the term culture is both argued to be generally understood (Lumby, Walker, Bryant, Bush & Bjork, forthcoming) and suggested not to be understood, misunderstood or so variously understood as to be verging on meaningless. Archer (1996, p. 1) contends that 'the notion of culture remains inordinately vague' to the extent that 'poverty of conceptualization' leads to culture being 'grasped' rather than 'analysed'.

Despite the difficulties of establishing the meaning of the concept of culture, it is used ubiquitously as a key variable, Janus-like, suggested both to influence and be influenced by a range of factors which impact on education. For example, culture is suggested to both shape and reflect values (Begley & Wong, 2001), philosophy (Ribbins & Zhang, 2004), gender (Celikten, 2005), religion (Sapre & Ranade, 2001), politics (Hwang, 2001), ethnicity (Bryant, 1998) and history (Wong, 2001). Culture is so rooted in all aspects of human activity that its all encompassing nature may limit its usefulness in practice to conceptualizing leadership and shaping the development of leaders. Metaphorically culture is like the air we breathe; all around us, vital, and yet difficult to discern and to change.

In relation to leader preparation and development culture has been framed largely as an issue of *diffusion,* particularly of Western values and practice applied to the development of leaders in all parts of the globe (Leithwood & Duke, 1998). The mechanics of diffusion and the appropriateness of the results have been subject to unequal research interest. The former has received very little and the latter a good deal more attention (Gronn, 2001; Heck, 1996). Consequently, although there is relatively little empirical data on which to draw, the issue of *fit* between culture and the conception, development and enactment of leadership has become a key concern. In part this reflects a revolt against the perceived global homogenization of leadership. It is also a response to the greater sensitivity brought about by the increasing diversity within many societies and the insistence that a perspective based on a single dominant culture risks sustaining a hegemonic, ineffective and excluding approach.

A primary aim of the chapter therefore is to explore how we understand culture in its infinitely variable expressions, and how it relates to the design and implementation of leadership preparation and development programs. The chapter aims to avoid becoming ensnared in the complexity of culture by confining its discussion to a sample of illustrative examples of both simple and complex conceptualizations.

The focus on culture at the macro or societal level is matched by concern with the micro or organizational level, the school level. Preparing leaders involves considering the nature and impact of culture on the crafting of their development (for example, the curriculum or mode of delivery). It involves consideration of fit to the culture of each individual school but also the necessity to equip leaders to engage with their own organization's culture, to sustain, develop or challenge it. The school leader is therefore at the fulcrum point, subject to exogenous effects of culture, refracted in part through his or her leadership development and personal cultural 'locus', and in turn engaging with endogenous culture in the school and its community. At the interface with exogenous and endogenous cultures, preparation and development reflect choices which are more than technical. Decisions to encourage acceptance or critique of the dominant culture and its effect lie at the moral heart of supporting the education of leaders. Such decisions will be founded on a concept of leadership that embraces far more than a capacity to competently manage the technical aspects of instruction. No one theory of leadership is implied. Rather, cultural competency, the ability to recognize, analyze and engage purposefully with culture at the macro and micro levels is a foundational skill, which positions educational leadership as critical contributors to shaping society and not just the school.

The chapter considers five main themes. Firstly, it examines key theoretical models and perspectives on culture. Secondly, it considers the important issue of the macro relationship of culture and globalization. Thirdly, it offers an international perspective by looking at the micro relationship of culture to the multiple identities and cultures of individuals and organizations. The fourth theme addresses a key concern for both policy and practice which is the connection between culture and leaders' preparation and development. (Throughout, the term 'development' is used to indicate both pre-appointment preparation and the post-appointment on-going development of leaders.) Finally, we identify key issues and areas for future research.

CULTURE — CONCEPTS AND PERSPECTIVES

Despite the recognition that culture is an elusive and diverse concept, identifying some of the existing intellectual paradigms of 'culture' is an important starting point. There exists a considerable literature on culture, which provides a range of conceptualizations. None is universally applicable nor comprehensive in its utility, yet they provide a range of perspectives to assist in clarifying this miasmic concept. Here we shall consider three of these perspectives which we believe provide diverse insights — reflections on the tangible components of culture and a number of models of those components in action; consideration of the organizational scales at which culture is important in educational contexts; and a systems view of 'culture' which enables the areas of potential management influence of culture in schools to be identified

The Components of Culture

Culture is the set of beliefs, values and behaviors, both explicit and implicit, which underpin an organization and provide the basis of action and decision making, and is neatly summarized as 'the way we do things around here'. In a strict sense we might argue that the culture of every educational institution is unique, derived from the context in which the school operates and the values of those who have led or been part of the organization over time. This unique culture will reveal itself through a number of institutional characteristics:

a. conceptually, through the ideas that are valued and promoted
b. verbally, through the language, terminology and discourses in use
c. behaviorally, through the activities, social interactions and rituals that occur
d. visually, through the designs and styles adopted by the organization in its physical and material components

While these representations are identifiable and mostly tangible, the illusiveness of the concept of culture lies in the fact that it is an holistic concept which is more than the sum of these component parts. These elements are but the tangible appearance of the underpinning set of values and beliefs, which shape the intended outcomes of the educational enterprise within a school. A number of summative frameworks for analyzing culture have therefore been developed which seek to reduce the complexity of culture to simplified 'types' which can be labeled for ease of comprehension. We present here a small number of examples in order to illustrate a range of typologies.

Sarason (1971, 1996), writing of US schools, was one of the earliest to insist that improving schools was primarily a question of changing culture. He created a series of descriptors of the culture of schooling with a particular focus on how key cultural characteristics equate to the absence of a productive learning environment. He also insisted that the complex creation of culture was the result of multiple inputs from staff, learners and the wider community. His ideas were widely influential. A second early example from the US of a description of a cultural type was 'the shopping mall school'. Powell, Farrar and Cohen (1985) used research from fifteen high schools to depict a culture of easy and uncritical acceptance of underachievement. In the period since the 1970s many commentators have created sometimes a single description of school culture, and sometimes typologies providing alternate descriptions. One of the best known is that applied to schools by Handy and Aitken (1986), which draws on observations across diverse organizations. Their typology distinguishes club, role, task and person cultures in organizations, and enables a simple analysis of the dominant cultural themes within a school or a team. Hargreaves (1995) developed a different typological model in which he distinguishes formal, welfarist, hothouse, and survivalist school cultures based on the educational priorities of the school in the context of external 'market' environments. Hothouse culture exists where the pressure is to high academic achievement, typically in response to government or parental pressure to deliver high quality examination results. A welfarist culture, alternatively, emphasizes the individual needs of pupils. Stoll and Fink (1996) created a typology of five types of school culture: moving (dynamic and successful determination to keep developing), cruising (rather complacent, often with privileged learners who achieve despite little school dynamism), strolling (neither particularly effective or ineffective, but long term not keeping pace with change), struggling (ineffective but trying to address issues), and finally sinking (ineffective and not improving). Their description of each provides significant detail of the culture of the type.

There have, of course, been many more attempts to categorize school cultures, each offering a particular perspective to illuminate the nature and effects of culture. Such simple categorizations provide briefly interesting analytical tools to assist school leaders in gaining an initial understanding of their school culture, but are of limited wider utility. None is universally applicable or comprehensive, but all can serve to support an educational leader's reflection on the culture of a specific school.

More helpful is the model of Schein (1990), which, in contrast, has provided a generic and analytical model of culture. Schein's model provides a greater level of sophistication by focusing on a challenging interrogation of the culture of the school and linking culture more strongly to underpinning values and beliefs. The model identifies seven dimensions of organizational context that shape resultant culture, based on a series of key questions:

1. The organization's relationship to its environment. Does it perceive itself as dominant, submissive, harmonizing or searching out a niche within its operational environment?
2. Its view of the nature of human activity — does it believe that people behave in a dominant/proactive mode or a passive/fatalistic mode?
3. Its view of the nature of truth and reality — how does it define what is true and what is not and how is truth defined in the context of the social or natural world?
4. What is the significance of time — is the organization most oriented towards the past, the present or the future?
5. Its view of human nature — is there a belief that people are essentially good, neutral or evil?
6. Its view of the nature of human relationships — are people essentially collaborative or competitive, do they function best in groups or as individuals?
7. Homogeneity or diversity — is the organization more effective when it is characterized by diversity or homogeneity?

These questions provide a helpful analytical framework, which can be applied in most educational contexts, and which seeks to identify the underlying values and beliefs within a school. As we shall demonstrate later in the chapter, it is getting to understand these values and beliefs that is a critical first step for educational leaders in developing the skills to 'manage', develop and evolve culture in their school.

Scales and Contexts of Analysis

Cultural differences can be observed at a range of organizational scales. Prosser (1998) has shown how culture is expressed at different levels within an organization, ranging from the individual classroom, to teams of teachers, to the whole school. While there may be commonalities within a whole school, in practice each of these levels will differ in the detail of its culture. The product will be a mosaic of sub-cultures, which may reinforce the cultural objectives of the whole school or, in some cases, appear as counter cultures that challenge the organizational hegemony. The extent of this range of sub-cultures and counter-cultures and their positive or negative interactions will be a key issue for those in leadership within the school and may cause cultural management issues to be significant or insignificant within the whole management task.

Beyond the school, though, lies a range of contextual cultures extending from the community within which the school lies to regional, national and international cultural contexts. Each of these contexts has a culture that expresses itself conceptually, verbally, behaviorally and visually, and which is a product of the complex interaction of communities, socio-economic contexts and contrasts, ethnic and faith-based values and beliefs, and the history of that community as a whole and of the individuals within it. At the international scale, for example, the work of Hofstede (1991), has sought to provide a broad general analysis of national organizational cultures.

The key dimension of cultural scales is that they all exist synchronously, and they all interact upwards and downwards. Each of the cultures influences and is influenced by each of the others. The challenge for educational leaders is to recognize and conceptualize each of these cultural realms and understand how it impacts on and provides implications for their own school.

Cultural Systems and School Leaders

In recognizing that culture has dimensions at a wide range of scales of analysis, we explicitly acknowledge that it raises challenges for school leaders in relation to each of these scales. We consider later in this chapter the implications of this for the professional development of 'leaders' within educational institutions. However, a model which merely identifies cultural elements doesn't take account of the dynamic nature of culture and it is useful therefore to consider culture in the context of a systems perspective on organizations. Systems theory enables us to conceptualize every school and educational organization as being characterized 1) by a range of inputs, 2) by the processes in operation within the school, and 3) by a set of outputs — and in each of these three elements of the system we can identify culture as a key component.

Cultural inputs have many facets — these will include the external cultural context (society, community and economy at local, regional and national scales), and the cultures brought to the school by all those engaging with it (teachers, parents, pupils, for example). At first sight these components of culture may be thought to be significantly outside the control of schools themselves. Every school, for example, has a specific geographical and social location which will strongly shape its cultural context — the inner city school serving a diverse multi-ethnic community will inherit a diversity of cultures that may be quite different to those of the suburban middle class school. However, such a perspective ignores the ability of schools to select many of the cultural inputs. Where there is any element of selectivity of pupils, whether by ability/prior achievement or by geography or by capacity to pay, then the school will be involved in processes of cultural selection. These may be through processes of exclusion or processes of inclusion, resulting in a relatively homogeneous or diverse student body, but in either case the outcome will be a pupil profile which reflects a particular set of cultural characteristics. Similarly, the selection of teaching staff provides at least an implicit and possibly an explicit mechanism of shaping a key cultural input into the school. And, of course, the selection of principals by governors, education boards or regional/national education authorities is a key mechanism through which the cultural inputs to a school will be strongly controlled

Cultural processes, the second element of a systems perspective, will be reflected in almost every dimension of the operation of the school. These are the cultural, verbal, visual and behavioral components of the school in action through which a wide range of cultural messages and aims will be delivered. From the approach adopted for teaching and learning, to the cultural values espoused in the pastoral and ethical functions of the school, to the relative value ascribed to possible destinations for pupils beyond school, the fabric of school life will be imbued by these cultural processes.

The third element of the system is the cultural output of the school. In many ways this is the summation of the school and reflects its overall purpose and aims, which have two distinct dimensions. The first relates to the ways the day-to-day operations of the school interact with the outside world. Pupils, staff and school leaders have an on-going engagement with external stakeholders, from parents, to neighbors, to employers, to the media, and every one of those interactions conveys a message about the culture of the school and its underpinning values. These can have negative or positive dimensions — the media report of the school's excellent examination results will convey a different message about the school's culture than a local reputation for rowdy behavior by the school's pupils during lunchtime breaks.

Another output lies in the cultural characteristics and values of the young people who are the product of the school once they have completed their time there. The values they espouse or eschew, the aspirations and achievements they have, and their contribution to communities (local, regional, national), whether positive or negative are the cultural product of the school. Ultimately, it is the cultural product/output of the school by which it will be judged, for it will be benchmarked against the cultural expectations that government, society and community have for "their" schools.

Conceptualizing the school's culture through such a systems approach helps clarify the challenges for school leaders in relation to culture. In terms of cultural inputs it is important that leaders within a school have the skills and knowledge to read the cultural landscape of the school, to recognize those aspects of it which can be controlled or manipulated, and decide which *should* be influenced and in what ways. In terms of cultural outputs school leaders need to understand both what the external societies expect from the school and what they wish to achieve themselves — this will require an integration of their personal and professional values, their vision of the purpose of schooling, and the visions and values of the key external stakeholders. Once the inputs are understood and the intended outputs identified, the major challenge for the school leader is then to organize and operationalize the processes within the school to enable pupils to travel from their cultural starting point to the output position the school seeks to achieve. All this is set within a strongly performative macro context in many countries. Many leaders are constrained to varying degrees by the pressing demands of accountability and competition which in themselves create a dominant cultural context. This is but one element of the interplay of competing values, priorities and hierarchies of power which influence culture. Leaders navigate cultural choices which are always constrained.

We have looked at three 'theoretical' aspects of culture here. While the analytical models described are helpful in conceptualizing the nature of culture, there are a number of key issues for leaders to recognize in reflecting on their own organizations. The first is that culture is 'neither unitary nor static' (Collard & Wang, 2005), and while change may be evolutionary rather than revolutionary, trends and developments in internal and external influences will move the culture forward. The challenge for leaders, therefore, is to manage that change in terms of speed, direction or nature to support the organization's goals.

The second is that cultural plurality is the norm in many educational systems and within most individual schools and colleges. For most leaders this provides perhaps the most challenging dimension of leadership, for it is necessary to understand what those cultures are, why they exist and what aspects of them can or cannot, or should and should not, be subject to change to achieve the school's goals. Research in such contexts is still not extensive, although Billot, Goddard and Cranston (2007) report the findings of an international study which explores how leadership in successful multi-cultural schools is exercised in three different national settings (Canada, New Zealand and Australia). The study identifies how cultural 'literacy' amongst the principals of the schools is a key element of the positive achievements they report. Training and educating principals for such cultural literacy is the focus of later sections in this chapter.

MACRO RELATIONS: CULTURE AND GLOBALIZATION

A key influence on culture within and beyond schools has been globalization. The processes of globalization have been a significant feature of all dimensions of society and economy over the last three decades. Waters (1995) has identified three interwoven strands to globalization — political globalization, economic globalization and cultural globalization. Cultural globalization is the international transfer of values and beliefs, and while strictly it is multi-directional it is typically perceived as dominated by the spread of western, particularly American, values and symbols across the globe. In the context of education this is seen through the promotion of policies and practices around the globe that have been initially developed in the west, based often on western approaches to educational management and the key concept of economic rationalism. Bottery (1999) has described this as managerial globalization, in which the adoption of western managerialist approaches and business-based forms of accountability underpins educational reform and development. Bottery asserts that there is a risk through this that there may be emerging a perspective that 'defines what looks increasingly like a global picture of management practice'. As Foskett and Lumby (2003, p. 8) indicate:

> We must be aware that the spread of 'good practice' internationally through the educational management literature, through the actions of international organisations such as UNESCO, and through the impact of professional development programmes, all of which are dominated by the perspectives of western educational management practitioners and academics, is in danger of presenting such a global picture of 'good practice'.

There have been strong responses to the lack of critical awareness of these processes. Collard (2006), for example, contends that much of the global level educational development through programs of agencies such as UNESCO and the World Bank is based on an import model which he portrays as a tidal wave of western values, sweeping away existing cultural environments. His critique suggests that there is insufficient time given in such an approach to understanding existing cultures, both at a general level and in terms of the underpinning key components and variables, and the consequence is cultural imperialism.

An example of the cultural challenges that emerge from this has been described by Hallinger and Kantamara (2001) in the context of Thailand. The government of Thailand sought to introduce the western concept of school-based management, but found this problematic in the context of an existing societal culture, typical amongst the staff of Thai schools, in which deference to senior management and leadership made the introduction of collaborative and distributed approaches to leadership very difficult.

Two other approaches might be more desirable ethically and politically. The first is the blending of western (or, more correctly, exogenous) cultural values with existing cultures to generate a new cultural environment, a model sometimes described as the 'melting pot' perspective. The second has a similar perspective but rather than losing the identities of existing cultures in the melting pot sees the retention of plural cultures within education which can enrich and reinforce each other — what is sometimes described as the 'salad bowl' approach to cultural change.

The key issue, of course, arising from globalization is that educational leaders will be faced increasingly with challenges to manage cultural change within their institution. Cultural isolation is difficult, even in societies which seek strongly to conserve traditional cultural values within their educational systems. Preparing head teachers to respond to these challenges will be a significant challenge, therefore, and this is a focus later in the chapter.

CULTURE AND LEADERSHIP — GLOBAL PERSPECTIVES

Cultural Contrasts and Commonalities

Following our examination of globalization and culture in the previous section, we consider here the picture of culture within educational leadership internationally. At the exogenous level, there appears to be widespread cultural homogeneity implicit in leadership development; that is, whether explicitly acknowledged or not, development is underpinned by some degree of belief in leadership as an invariable activity (Walker & Walker, 1998; Bhindi & Duignan, 1997): this despite recognition that even the word 'leader' has very different connotations in different cultures (House, 2004). A major international study, The Global Leadership and Organizational Effectiveness (GLOBE) project, aimed to establish which leadership behavior was 'universally' viewed as 'contributing to leadership effectiveness' (House, Paul, Hanges, Ruiz-Quintanilla, Dorfman & Mansour 2004, p. 3). The project established 21 common perceived effective leadership attributes and behaviors within the 57 participating nations, providing evidence of widespread assumptions about leadership. For example, being dynamic and dependable, encouraging and displaying integrity were agreed to be positive leader attributes across all the nations involved. Education researchers have also assumed such common attributes, for example, integrity (Begley, 2004; Bhindi & Duignan, 1997). However House et al. (2004) also found evidence of 35 aspects of leadership which are culturally specific, for example, the degree to which compassion, status-consciousness, autonomy and domination are perceived to contribute to effective leadership is culturally contingent. The GLOBE project was undertaken in a business context. In the absence of a similarly complex or authoritative study of the cultural factors in educational leadership, the design of much preparation and development seems to adhere to an assumed commonality and to avoid detailed engagement with the culturally contingent (Lumby et al., forthcoming), resulting in 'an international curriculum for school leadership preparation' (Bush & Jackson, 2002, pp. 420–421).

The assumed commonality in attributes and behaviors may also be evident in axiological assumptions. All leadership development has embedded cultural values. However, these may be taken-for-granted, and only apparent to those designing and delivering development when a lack of fit is pointed out by specific groups. For example, Bryant (1998), researching the leadership culture of Native Americans in the United States, suggests a number of cultural assumptions embedded in American leadership:

- leadership is vital
- every organization must have a person in charge
- a focus on instrumental ends
- acute awareness of the expenditure of time
- encouragement of individual initiative
- an obligation to accommodate other's right to participate

The result is a simultaneous requirement for a task and people orientation. Bryant (1998) suggests that as a consequence school leadership as conceived in the US is unlikely to be appropriate to Native American educational leaders whose culture and consequent conception of leadership is very different. A person in charge is not required. Rather, in leadership 'every person has a role to play' (Bryant, 1998, p. 12) undertaking a leadership act as need and personal understanding or skill require. Leadership is therefore a community property shaped by a complex interrelationship between individuals and context, rather than resulting from individual intent and competition. Similarly, Louque (2002) challenges the appropriateness of the culture embedded in the selection and development of educational leaders to Hispanic and African American Women. Rejection of the cultural assumptions in preparation and development programs abound on the grounds of gender (Brunner, 2002; Coleman, 2005; Louque, 2002; Rusch, 2004), ethnicity (Bryant, 1998; Tippeconic, 2006), national culture (Bjerke & Al-Meer, 1993; Hallinger, Walker. & Bajunid., 2005; Sapre & Ranade, 2001; Walker, 2006; Wong, 2001), and faith (Shah, 2006). The cacophony of objections highlights the failure of development programs to accommodate the diversity of culture within one geographic area as much as across widely distant locations.

Identity and Essentialism

The notions of cultural diffusion and cultural fit assume that programs designed to take account of the cultural expectations and preferences of participants are more likely to lead to effective learning and resulting practice. The identification of the relevant culture and the group to which it is appropriate is predicated on the notion that humans can be classified, that a specific culture can be assigned to those in a particular geographic area or sharing a particular characteristic such as gender, language, ethnic background or religion.

Litvin (1997) attacks such essentialism, ascribing the taxonomy of groups to a Western Platonic purportedly scientific paradigm. She challenges whether any classification of humans is tenable in the light of increasing certainty deriving from advances in natural science that whatever taxonomy is adopted, the complexity of human beings, biologically, linguistically and culturally, cannot be placed into easily described categories:

> There are no essential, innate and immutable characteristics of race, age, gender, disability or other demographic categories. Instead there are history, context, process, interactivity, power relations and change. (Litvin, 1997, pp. 206–207)

Categorization of groups which might be assumed to hold a culture in common is therefore problematic. For example, 'the East' or 'the West' continue to be used as descriptive terms for cultural groups in the context of considering leadership. (See, for example, Buruma and Margalit's book, *Occidentalism: The west in the eyes of its enemies*.) Hofstede (2003) has argued strongly that there are measurable differences between the cultures of nations. However, his analysis of national culture has been abused to support stereotypical views and crude dichotomies, such as between Western cultures and those of Asia. In fact, Hofstede's work shows very great variation within regions. For example, '86% of the worldwide variance on individualism-collectivism and 70% of variance across power-distance are found in Europe' (Sparrow & Hiltrop, 1998, p. 73).

As within continents or regions, within each nation, a common culture cannot be assumed, the differences between the culture of Native Americans, Hispanic and African American women and that of white males within the United States being an example given above. Developing the argument further, Litvin's point is that even within an apparently homogeneous group there will be wide variation in culture related to the multiple characteristics, history and context of each individual.

The implication is that if leadership preparation and development is to aspire to cultural fit, a high degree of sophistication is required. Curricula and delivery which are founded on a set of cultural assumptions, even those which are dominant within the region or country, are likely to miss the mark for many. A more flexible and subtle shaping will be needed. Matching culture to preparation and development engages with what is perceived to be universal, what appears to be distinctive to the region or nation or group of people, and what is unique to the individual.

Lack of uniformity of culture is therefore an issue even among small, apparently homogeneous groups Distinguishing rhetoric from practice is a second challenge. Analysis of culture embedded in preparation and development programs will involve discriminating between what is rhetorical and what is evidenced. For example, North American and European development assert a cultural commitment to inclusion and equality for all. Analysis of the content of programs might suggest that such commitment is largely camouflage for neglect of such values (Lopez, 2003; Rusch, 2004). Discernment of the publicly espoused culture, the culture implicit in practice and the desired culture will inevitably comprise a kaleidoscope of differing opinions and wishes reflecting the perspectives of the individuals responsible for the design and delivery of development.

Culture and Power

If culture embeds, among other things, power relations, then the issue of programs matching or challenging dominant cultures becomes a matter of negotiating competing notions of appropriate power relations, political and social structures.

Two distinctive views of this connection can be identified (Collard, 2006). The first is that leaders are passive ambassadors of culture. This suggests that they are prepared, appointed and developed to reflect a specific set of values and beliefs and are expected to simply transmit those imposed and inherited values to staff and to pupils within their institution. Hallinger (2001, p. 65) suggests that the primary purpose of schooling is the onward transmission of established culture and values between generations. He suggests that schools are 'bastions of conservatism, not centers of social experimentation'. Such a perspective suggests that the dominant culture, were it to be discerned with any certainty, would be embedded, unexamined and therefore unchallenged, in preparation and development programs.

A second view, though, is that of leaders as agents of cultural change, as discussed earlier in the chapter. This may be interpreted in several ways ranging from the operational to the political. The political perspective would see educational leaders as seeking to generate in their pupils and staff a critical view of society, to challenge existing orthodoxies and to become citizens able to participate in social and cultural change. At the operational scale, the leader may focus on the culture within the institution in order to facilitate the achievement of institutional improvement, with culture conceptualized as an agent of change.

Such an approach to cultural change is, of course, a key component of western approaches to educational leadership, and has been criticized for representing a fundamental misunderstanding of what culture is and can be. Essentially it makes a questionable assumption. It takes the view that culture can be unified and that 'dissent, anomaly, conflicts of interest or ambiguity are viewed.... as aberrations instead of being endemic to organizations' (Hoyle & Wallace, 2005, p. 116). If leaders believe that a dominant culture is identifiable or achievable, and that it is a single, stable and unifying phenomenon, then changing it becomes a matter of choice, but relatively straightforward and without any moral ramifications. Changing the culture becomes merely a question of technical fit, of shaping leadership development to align it to local culture. If alternatively, culture is viewed as multiple, unstable, persistently contested, reflecting the differing perspectives and power of individuals and groups, changing the culture of a school is a different kind of endeavor. The attempt to mould culture in any direction involves alignment with some and challenge to others. It will therefore involve engagement with the moral choices which lie at the heart of leadership. Choices will continue as culture evolves and the perspectives of all players mutate over time. Changing the culture of a school or of a leadership development program is therefore not a finite endeavor. Nor is it amoral.

Preparation and development programs therefore face a twofold challenge:

- Deciding which cultural assumptions to attempt to embed in the design and delivery of development, including the degree to which they will replicate or challenge dominant cultures;
- Deciding how best to equip leaders with intercultural competence, so that they in their turn can decide which cultural assumptions to attempt to embed in their school leadership, including the degree to which they will replicate or challenge dominant cultures.

In the next section we shall examine the issues of culture and leadership preparation and development.

CULTURE AND LEADERSHIP PREPARATION

Despite the widespread acknowledgement that culture varies considerably and that leadership preparation and development could be adjusted in relation to the culturally embedded ontological, epistemological and axiological differences between cultures, the content, method of delivery and assessment of preparation and development shows relatively little variation throughout the world (Bush & Jackson, 2002). The adoption of similar sets of competences, for example, reflects to some degree airbrushing out the influence of local culture (Davis, 2001; Macpherson, Kachelhoffer & El Nemr, 2007).

This may be due in part to the fact that understanding culture and its connection to leadership in education is a poorly researched field. It is characterized by very limited research at the within school subunit scale, and by the adoption of generalized models of culture from business and management disciplines at whole-school or national/international scales of analysis.

One consequence is that there is currently no precise means of assessing dimensions variously labeled as 'cultural distance' or 'degree of diversity' (Iles & Kaur Hayers, 1997, p. 107) or diversity amount and diversity degree (Thomas, 1999; Taras & Rowney, 2007); that is the differences between the culture of one location of leader development and another, or the extent of cultural differences within a leader development group. The design of curriculum and delivery is therefore to an extent a cultural guessing game requiring those responsible for preparation and development to hold a high level of cultural fluency themselves and to support the development of cultural fluency in others.

Designing Curriculum and Delivery

Culture can then be viewed in shorthand as:

> a set of shared values and preferred actions among members of a society that largely determines among other things, the boundaries within which leader development is possible. (Hoppe, 2004, p. 333)

However, boundaries are permeable. Inevitably therefore, design of the curriculum and its delivery will involve judgments not only about the relevant local culture and the degree of diversity, but also how far global or international cultural assumptions may be relevant. Hallinger (2001) notes the changing aims of Asian education and specifically the global standards applied to assessing the quality of education in Hong Kong. As a consequence, leaders must be equipped to work with both imported as well as indigenous culture. Dorfman and House (2004) suggest three competing propositions: that cultural congruence in development and leadership is more effective; that cultural difference can be stimulating and bring about positive change; that leadership is universal activity. Notwithstanding these different positions, knowledge of how leadership is conceptualized and enacted locally is a sine qua non of successful design.

Very many illustrations could be offered of the different expectations and practice of leadership throughout the world. Two examples will suffice to illustrate this, though. In Saudi Arabia a command system is accepted by culture and tradition and schools have, in any case, little power to take decisions. Bjerke and Al-Meer (1993, p. 31) suggest that in the Arab world:

Subordinates expect superiors to act autocratically. Everyone expects superiors to enjoy privileges, and status symbols are very important.

Not only may there be particular cultural assumptions about the relationship between staff and principal, the principal and regional/national authorities, but underpinning ontological assumptions may be distinctive. Ali (1996, p. 7) argues that the Jabria school of Muslim thought, influential in the Arab world, might rule out systematic planning as to plan is 'in conflict with pre-destination'. As a second exemplar, in China the millennia long influence of Confucianism has led to a 'compliance culture', the impact of this cultural norm being a tendency to see 'change as an event rather than a process' (Hallinger, 2001, p. 67). A more extensive discussion of the variation in culture and practice internationally is offered by Foskett & Lumby (2003) and Lumby et al. (forthcoming). For the purposes of this chapter, these two snapshots highlight issues that result from consideration of culture, such as who are the primary leaders and how might the leadership theory used in their development be shaped in response to differing ontological, epistemological and axiological assumptions? Clearly in these two instances, Western derived theories of autonomy, planning and change management are all thrown into question.

Who Are the Leaders?

Internationally leader preparation and development tends to focus on the principal. There is relatively little attention paid to middle leaders such as department heads and teacher leaders (Bush & Jackson, 2002). In many countries the principal may indeed be key. In others, variation is considerable and the primary drive to develop teaching and learning, attainment and achievement may be located elsewhere. In China the relatively low contact hours enjoyed by teachers combined with a culture of comfort with peer critique has resulted in teacher groups working together for a considerable proportion of their time to achieve change (Bush & Qiang, 2000), while principals spend much of their time on operational administration (Washington, 1991). A similar situation is the case in Norway and in Japan (Moller, 2000). Leader and leadership development may therefore be as effectively focused on teacher leaders as on principals in these two countries. In another region of China, Hong Kong, teacher contact hours are considerably higher and leadership is more firmly placed with the principal. Research has shown the principal to be a significant factor in school effectiveness (Hallinger & Heck, 1999). However, the findings which result from research in one location may lead to indiscriminate transfer of assumptions, such as the primary location of leadership in the principal. Cultural sensitivity demands consideration of how leadership is dispersed amongst the players within schools and the regional administration in a specific context before designing national and local systems in response.

Leaders' Values

Those undertaking preparation for development may have differing value priorities which are culturally shaped. For example, the balance of time given to study of the legislation relevant to schooling or to the implications of a particular faith, whether Islam, Christianity, or any other, will embed values within the curriculum through the choice of priority reflected in the time allocated. Sapre and Ranade (2001, p. 379) deplore the fact that 'there is very little in 'modern' Indian education that is truly rooted in the culture, tradition and genius of its people'. They suggest the spiritual values embedded in the teaching of Vivekananda, Tagore and Ghandi would provide a more culturally appropriate basis for the leadership of education than the currently 'Western' values which relate in part to the colonial history of the nation.

Similarly, Bajunid (1996, p. 56) argues that the richness of Islamic teaching is absent from concepts of leadership. Consequently 'mid-forged manacles of Western generated categories' hinder the development of leaders in Malaysia where Islam is deeply embedded in culture.

Theoretical Underpinning

Much leadership theory reflects Anglophone and particularly US culture which Hoppe (2004, p. 335) suggests 'is consistently described as being individualistic, egalitarian, performance derived, comfortable with change, and action-and-data-oriented'. There is also a preference to 'face facts' whether positive or negative. The result is that most preparation and development takes egalitarian participation and transformational leadership as key (Bush & Jackson, 2002). Transactional leadership, often viewed negatively in many Anglophone countries, may be a more appropriate theoretical basis in many contexts. Hallinger (2001) also points to the ubiquitous use of theories such as Learning Organization and School Based Management, which are firmly embedded in similar cultural norms. While awareness of and reflection on hegemonic theory may be of use, its global dominance in preparation and development seems inappropriate on a number of grounds. It may be limiting, ineffective and ethically dubious, particularly in those countries with a history of previous colonization and suppression of indigenous cultures.

Delivery of Preparation and Leadership

Culture also impacts on delivery. Lumby et al. (forthcoming) distinguish transmission models, where experts pass on theoretical knowledge (often indiscriminately, as discussed earlier), and process models which use more community based styles of learning. While the former classroom and lecture based model is widespread, they suggest that the process model of problem solving, mentoring and internship holds more hope of reflecting indigenous cultures. However, process models may not mesh with some cultures. Hoppe (2004) suggests that experiential learning proves enjoyable and effective for US leaders while French and German leaders often view this approach as time-wasting 'child's play' (p. 353). Cultures which are comfortable with hierarchy or with the co-creation of knowledge may find affinities with process modes. Hoppe asserts that US leaders find difficulty with accepting supportive relationships. By contrast Singaporean culture's emphasis on collective action and respect for seniority underpins acceptance and effective use of mentoring as an important mode of development, defined as 'a process whereby an expert or senior person guides a less experienced leader (Tin, 2001). However, Lumby et al. (forthcoming) provide a strong warning that collective cultures as well as honoring hierarchical superiority may also have an acute need to maintain self-esteem. Mentoring is therefore flavored by ease and acceptance of the views of seniors but sensitivity to negative feedback. However, Cardno (2007) argues that the dilemma created by the need to give negative feedback and to save face, for example in appraisal, often emphasized as a cultural context in Chinese societies, is in fact universal. Cultural complexity offers only multiple complications in assessing fit, not safe generalized conclusions.

Assessment

Just as there is an interplay between culture and modes of delivery, assessment may also be rendered more or less effective by the degree of cultural fit. One dimension of fit may relate to ease with receiving positive and negative feedback and from whom. Hoppe (2004) believes US leaders have little difficulty in receiving negative feedback. Lumby et al. (forthcoming) point up the greater sensitivity within some cultures where responsibility for success is group owned and/

or where maintaining face is a high priority. Assessment is also increasingly against competences which are exported internationally (MacPherson et al., 2007). While there is extensive research on the implications of assessment modes on school learners, including the relationship of assessment to variables such as gender and ethnicity, no similar body of research informs how we understand the assessment of leaders. Educators would be extremely concerned to consider fully the implications of assessing school students against standards imported from another nation. In contrast the assessment of educational leaders often assumes that consideration of cultural fit is unnecessary in relation to standards which are uncritically accepted as 'international'.

Preparing Leaders for Cultural Fluency

Leaders interact with culture at the organizational level both in terms of efforts to include the multiple cultures which may be present and also to sustain, adapt or change the dominant culture. Fullan (2001) has suggested that recognizing the need for, and understanding the processes involved in, cultural change are essential tools of leadership development, for it is in establishing a culture of change in school that successful school development can occur. Such 'reculturing' (Fullan, 2001) is perhaps the biggest challenge to school leaders, though, for it will certainly generate conflict, contradiction and destabilization as part of the process — as DiPaola (2003, p. 153) has indicated:

> Creating this culture of change by constantly challenging the status quo is a contact sport involving hard, labor-intensive work and a lot of time.

The processes of cultural change in schools have been considered extensively in the literature (e.g. Prosser, 1998). The implications of these strategies for leadership training and development have been analyzed by DiPaola (2003) who outlines a number of key components of principal preparation programs.

In parallel, preparation and development sometimes include an element of raising awareness of cultures deemed to be 'other' than that of the majority or the dominant group, what Stier (2003, p. 84) refers to as 'content-competencies', generally targeted at increasing knowledge of minority groups within the region or nation. They may also tackle the issue of how culture can be 'managed'. While these are different aims, they both involve intercultural fluency. Stier insists that the latter cannot be achieved by content competencies alone. 'Processual competencies', comprising 'intrapersonal competencies' and 'cognitive competencies' (2003, p.84), are also needed. As in the acquisition of any language, fluency can only be achieved by practice and not just by theory (Taras & Rowney, 2007). Accultured, automatic, emotional responses preclude awareness of internalized culture. Consequently, a tendency to stereotype or discount alternative cultures must be halted by conscious, persistent effort (Lumby with Coleman, 2007). The aim is to encourage leaders to address obliviousness to their own culture and challenge approaches which may inappropriately embed a single culture and/or a culture alien to some participants. Research concerning leadership in multinational corporations defines three components of cultural fluency, 'cognitive complexity, emotional energy and psychological maturity' (Iles & Kaur Hayers, 1997, p. 105). Cultural fluency will be predicated on more than cognitive effort (Lakomski, 2001). Lumby with Coleman (2007) identifies the emotional dimensions of rage, confusion, and anxiety in engaging with alternate cultures (DiTomaso & Hooijberg, 1996; Osler, 2004; Prasad & Mills, 1997; Rusch, 2004). Where preparation and development engage at all with culture, the current prevalence of 'content-competencies' (Stier, 2003, p. 84) does not begin to equip leaders with the skills needed to relate to exogenous and endogenous cultures.

CULTURE AND LEADERSHIP — ISSUES AND FUTURE RESEARCH

Bajunid (1996, p. 52) argued over a decade ago that in Malaysia 'there is an urgent need to inspire, motivate and work with relevant and meaningful concepts that the locals are at home and familiar with' and to free educational leadership and management from the intellectual domination of 'Greco-Roman, Christian, Western intellectual traditions' (1996, p. 63). Despite some advances since that time, understanding of culture and its relationship to leadership and its development remains empirically underdeveloped. A number of research areas seem indicated as urgently required.

Understanding international differences in culture would provide a basis for planning cultural fit in preparation and development programs. Any research which attempts to map such differences in concept and practice will face severe methodological challenges. However, over a decade ago, Heck (1996) suggested that advances in statistical methods held some hope of achieving conceptual and metric equivalence in investigating theoretical models across nations and within organizations. Certainly it would be helpful to undertake an educational equivalent of the GLOBE project (House et al., 2004) and to establish the education leadership attributes and behaviors that are held in common across a large number of nations and those elements that are culturally contingent. As in the GLOBE project, subgroups within nations might be also identified for inclusion. Such a knowledge base would allow theory to be developed in a more culturally aware way.

Secondly, investigations of the cultural fit of transmission and process models of learning would support those responsible for design in making more appropriate choices. For example, Walker, Bridges and Chan (1996) provide a rare example of research into the fit of a particular learning approach, problem-based-learning, to a specific cultural context, Hong Kong. More research of this kind, exploring fit not only to the dominant culture of the nation/region, but also fit to the multiple cultures within the nation or region would provide a potentially powerful antidote to programs which are currently not culturally inclusive.

Hodgkinson (2001) argues that culture 'is always determining, subliminally and subconsciously, our value orientation and judgments'. Those attempting to loosen the bonds of dominant cultures implicit in preparation and development programs research and write within the very dominant orientations they are trying to question (Gronn, 2001). School leaders work within pressing cultures which sustain themselves by multiple conscious and unconscious mechanisms (Lumby with Coleman, 2007). The capacity of any individual or group to engineer culture is questionable (Adler, 1997; Morgan, 1986). A challenge to dominant cultures and the evolution of cultures which are seen as fitting will be achieved only by persistent efforts to increase the intercultural fluency of all involved, in part by increasing the evidence base, and in part through detailed translation of such evidence to impact the design and delivery of the development of leaders.

REFERENCES

Adler, N. (1997).*Organizational behaviour* (3rd ed.). Cincinnati: South Western.

Ali, A. (1996). Organizational development in the Arab world. *Journal of Management Development*, *15*(5), 4–21.

Archer, M. (1996). *Culture and Agency. The Place of Culture in Social Theory*. Cambridge: Cambridge University Press.

Bajunid, I. A. (1996). Preliminary explorations of indigenous perspectives of educational management, *Journal of Educational Administration*, *34*(5), 50–73.

Begley, P. (2004), Understanding valuation processes; exploring the linkage between motivation and action. *International Studies in Educational Administration, 32*(2), 4–17.

Begley, P. & Wong, K-C. (2001, October). Multiple perspectives on values and ethical leadership. *International Journal of Leadership in Education, 4*(4), 293–296.

Bhindi & Duignan, P. (1997). Leadership for a new century; authenticity, intentionality, spirituality and sensibility. *Educational Management & Administration, 25*(1), 117– 132.

Billot, J., Goddard, T. & Cranston, N. (2007). How principals manage ethnocultural diversity: Learnings from three countries. *International Studies in Educational Administration, 35*(3) 3–19.

Bjerke, B. & Al-Meer, A. (1993). Culture's consequences: management in Saudi Arabia. *Leadership and Organization Development Journal, 14*(1), 30–35.

Bottery, M. (1999). Global forces, national mediations and the management of educational institutions. *Educational Management and Administration, 27*(3), 299–312.

Brunner C. (2002). Professing educational leadership: conceptions of power. *Journal of School Leadership, 12*(2), 693–720.

Bryant, M. (1998). Cross-cultural understandings of leadership: themes from Native American interviews. *Educational Management & Administration, 26*(1), 7–20.

Bush, T. & Jackson, D. (2002). A preparation for school leadership: International perspectives. *Educational Management & Administration, 30*(4), 417–430.

Bush, T. & Qiang, H. (2000) Leadership and Culture in Chinese Education. *Asia Pacific Journal of Education, 20*(2), 58–67.

Cardno, C. (2007). Leadership learning – the praxis of dilemma management. *International Studies in Educational Administration, 35*(3) 33–50.

Celikten, M. (2005). A perspective on women principals in Turkey. *International Journal of Leadership in Education, 8*(3), 207–221.

Collard, J. (2006). Towards a framework of investigating leadership praxis in intercultural. Paper presented to the Conference of the Commonwealth Council for Educational Administration and Management. *Recreating Linkages between Theory and Praxis in Educational Leadership*, 12–17 October 2006 Lefkosia, Cyprus.

Collard, J. & Wang, H. (2005). Leadership and intercultural dynamics. *Journal of School Leadership, 15*(2), 178–195.

Coleman, M. (2005). Women and leadership: The views of women who are '*Leading from the Middle*' paper presented at the BELMAS conference, Milton Keynes, 23 September.

Davis, (2001). The Australian Principals Centre: A model for the accreditation and professional development of the principalship. *International Journal for Leadership in Education, 4*(4), 20–29.

Deal, T. & Kennedy, A. (1982). *Corporate rituals: The rites and fituals of corporate life*. Reading, MA: Addison Wesley.

DiPaola, M.F. (2003). Conflict and change. Daily challenges for school leaders.I In N. Bennett, M. Crawford, & M. Cartwright, M. (Eds.), *Effective educational leadership* (pp. 143–158). London: Paul Chapman.

DiTomaso, N. & Hooijberg, R. (1996). Diversity and the demands of leadership. *The Leadership Quarterly, 7*(2), 163–187.

Dorfman, P. W. & House, R. J. (2004). Cultural influences on organizational leadership. In R. J. House, P.J. Hanges, M. Javidan, P. W. Dorfman & V. Gupta (Eds.), *Culture, Leadership, and Organizations: the GLOBE study of 62 Societies* (pp. 51–67). London: Sage.

Foskett, N. & Lumby, J. (2003). *Leading and Managing Education: International Dimensions*. London: Paul Chapman.

Fullan, M. (2001). *The New Meaning of Educational Change* (3rd ed.). New York: Teachers College Press

Gronn, P. (2001). Commentary. Crossing the great divides: problems of cultural diffusion for leadership in education. *International Journal for Leadership in Education, 4*(4), 401–414.

Hallinger, P. (2001). Leading educational change in East Asian schools. *International Studies in Educational Administration, 29*(2), 61–72.

Hallinger, P. & Heck, R. (1999). Can leadership enhance school effectiveness? In T. Bush, L. Bell, R. Bolam, P., Glatter, & P. Ribbins (Eds.), *Educational management: Redefining theory, policy and practice* (pp. 178–190). London: Sage.

Hallinger, P. & Kantamara, P. (2001). Exploring the cultural context of school improvement in Thailand. *School Effectiveness and School Improvement, 12*(4), 385–408.

Hallinger, P., Walker, A. & Bajunid, I. A. (2005). Educational leadership in East Asia: implications of education in global society. *UCEA, 45*(1), 1–5.

Handy, C. & Aitken, R. (1986). *Understanding Schools as Organisations* London: Penguin.

Hargreaves, D. H. (1995). School culture, school effectiveness and school improvement. *School Effectiveness and School Improvement, 6*(1), 23–46.

Heck, R. (1996). Leadership and culture: Conceptual and methodological issues in comparing models across cultural settings. *Journal of Educational Administration, 34*(5), 74–97.

Hodgkinson, C. (2001). Tomorrow, and tomorrow and tomorrow: a post-postmodern purview. *International Journal of Leadership In Education, 4*(4),297–307.

Hofstede, G. (2003). *Culture's Consequences, Comparing Values, Behaviors, Institutions, and Organizations Across Nations* (2nd ed.). Newbury Park, CA: Sage.

Hofstede, G. (1991). *Cultures and Organisations: Software of the Mind.* London: McGraw-Hill.

Hoppe, M. H. (2004). Cross-cultural issues in development of leaders. In C. D. McCauley & E. V. Velsor, E. V. (Eds.), *Handbook of Leadership Development* (pp. 331–360). San Francisco, CA: Jossey-Bass.

House, R., Paul, J., Hanges, S. Ruiz-Quintanilla, A., Dorfman, P. W., & Mansour, J. M. (2004). Cultural Influences on Leadership and Organizations: Project Globe. Accessed online 16.2.07. http://www.thunderbird.edu/wwwfiles/ms/globe/Links/process.pdf

House, R. J. (2004). Introduction. In R. J. House, P. J. Hanges, M. Javidan, P. W. Dorfman & V. Gupta (Eds.), *Culture, Leadership, and Organizations: the GLOBE study of 62 Societies* (pp. 1–7). London: Sage.

Hoyle, E. & Wallace, M. (2005). *Educational Leadership: Ambiguity, Professionals and Managerialism.* London: Sage.

Hwang, K. K. (2001). Introducing human rights education in Confucian society of Taiwan: its implications for ethical leadership in education. *International Journal for Leadership in Education, 4*(4), 321–332.

Iles, P. & Kaur Hayers, P. (1997). Managing diversity in transnational project teams. A tentative model and case study. *Journal of Managerial Psychology, 1*(2), 95–117.

Lakomski, G. (2001). Organizational change, leadership and learning: culture as cognitive process. *The International Journal of Educational Management, 15*(2), 68–77.

Leithwood, K. & Duke, D. L. (1998). Mapping the conceptual terrain of leadership: a critical point for departure for cross-cultural studies. In P. Hallinger & K. Leithwood. (Eds.), *Leading Schools in a Global Era: A Cultural Perspective, Peabody Journal of Education, 73*(2), 81–105.

Litvin, D. R. (1997). The discourse of diversity: from biology to management. *Discourse and Organization, 4*(2), 187–209.

Lopez, G. R. (2003). The (racially neutral) politics of education: a critical race Theory perspective. *Educational Administration Quarterly, 39*(1), 68–94.

Louque, A. (2002). Spicing it op: Blending perspectives of leadership and cultural values from Hispanic American and African American women scholars. *Education Leadership Review, 3*(2), 28–31.

Lumby, J., Walker, A., Bryant, M., Bush, T., & Bjork, L. (Forthcoming). An international perspective on leadership preparation. In M. D. Young, G, Crow, J. Murphy, & R. Ogawa (Eds.), *The University Council for Educational Administration: Handbook of Research on the Education of School Leaders.* Mahwah, NJ: Erlbaum.

Lumby, J. with Coleman, C. (2007). *Leadership and Diversity; Challenging Theory and Practice in Education.* London, Sage.

Macpherson, R., Kachelhoffer, P., & El Nemr, M. (2007). The radical modernization of school and education system leadership in the United Arab Emirates: towards indigenized and educative leadership. *International Studies in Educational Administration, 35*(1) 60–77.

Moller, J. (2000). School principals in transition. Conflicting expectations, demands and desires. In C. Day, A. Fernandez, E. Trond & J. Møller (Eds.), *The Life and Work of Teachers* (pp. 210–223). London: Falmer.

Morgan, G. (1986). *Images of Organization.* London: Sage

Osler, A. (2004). Changing leadership and schools: diversity, equality and citizenship. *Race Equality Teaching*, 22(3), 22–28.

Powell, A. G., Farrar, E. & Cohen, D. K. (1985). *The Shopping Mall High School: Winners and Losers in the Educational Marketplace; National Association of Secondary School Principals (U.S.); National Association of Independent Schools. Commission on Educational Issues,* Boston, Houghton Mifflin.

Prasad, P. & Mills, M. (1997). From showcase to shadow: understanding dilemmas of managing workplace diversity. In P. Prasad, M. Mills, M. Elmes & A. Prasad (Eds.), *Managing the Organizational Melting Pot: Dilemmas of Workplace Diversity* (pp. 3–30). London: Sage.

Prosser, J. (Ed.). (1998). *School Culture.* London: Paul Chapman.

Ribbins, P. & Zhang, J. H. (2004). Head teachers in rural China: aspects of ambition. *International Journal for Leadership in Education,* 7(2),127–146.

Rusch, E. (2004). Gender and race in leadership preparation: a constrained discourse. In *Educational Administration Quarterly,* 40(1), 16–48.

Sapre, P. & Ranade, M. (2001). Moral leadership in education: an Indian perspective. *International Journal for Leadership in Education,* 4(4), 367–381.

Sarason, S. (1971). *The Culture of the School and the Problem of Change.* Boston: Allyn and Bacon.

Sarason, S. (1996). *Revisiting "the Culture of the School and the Problem of Change".* Boston: Allyn and Bacon.

Schein, E. H. (1990). *Organisational Culture and Leadership.* San Francisco: Jossey-Bass.

Shah, S. (2006). Educational leadership: an Islamic perspective. *British Educational Research Journal,* 32(3), 363–386.

Sparrow, P. & Hiltrop, J. (1998). Redefining the field of European human resource management: a battle between national mindsets and forces of business transition? In C. Mabey, G. Salaman & J. Story (Eds.), *Strategic Human Resource Management* (pp. 68–86). London: Sage.

Stier, J. (2003). Internationalisation, ethnic diversity and the acquisition of intercultural competencies. *Intercultural Education,* 14(1), 77–91.

Stoll, L. & Fink, D. (1996). *Changing Our Schools: Linking School Effectiveness and School Improvement.* Buckingham: Open University Press.

Tippeconic, J. (2006). Identity based and reputational leadership: an American Indian approach to leadership. *Journal of Research in Leader Education.* Accessed online 22.5.06 http://www.ucea.org/JRLE/pdf/vol1/issue1/Tippeconic.pdf

Taras, V. & Rowney, J. (2007). Effects of cultural diversity on in-class communication and student project team dynamics: Creating synergy in the diverse classroom. *International Studies in Educational Administration,* 35(2), 66–81.

Thomas, D. C. (1999). Cultural diversity and group work effectiveness. *Journal of Cross-Cultural Psychology,* 30(2), 242–263.

Tin, L. (2001). Preparation of aspiring principals in Singapore: a partnership model. *International Studies in Educational Administration,* 29(2) 30–37.

Walker, A. (2006). Leader development across cultures. *Journal of Research in Leader Education.* Accessed online 22.5.06 http://www.ucea.org/JRLE/pdf/vol1/issue1/Walker.pdf

Walker, A. & Walker, J. (1998). Challenging the boundaries of sameness: leadership through valuing difference. *Journal of Educational Administration,* 36(1), 8–28.

Walker, A., Bridges, E. & Chan, B. (1996). Wisdom gained, wisdom given: instituting PBL in a Chinese culture. *Journal of Educational Administration,* 334(5), 12–31.

Washington, K. (1991). School administration in China: a look at the principal's role. *International Journal of Educational Management,* 5(3), 4–5.

Waters, M. (1995). *Globalization.* London: Routledge

Wong, K. (2001). Chinese culture and leadership. *International Journal for Leadership in Education,* 4(4), 309–319.

4

A Life and Career Based Framework for the Study of Leaders in Education: Problems, Possibilities and Prescriptions

Peter Ribbins

Meeting the developmental needs of leaders in education has in recent times become big business. Increasingly elaborate and expensive programs of training, assessment and certification, especially for school principals,[1] have mushroomed in many parts of the world.[2] Whatever its merits, as an innovation this has too often been implemented as an 'act of faith' rather than as the outcome of a systematic and critical examination of the available evidence and theory. This chapter considers this claim and relates it to what is known of the lives of principals and their need for support and development at different phases of their careers. It will seek international similarities and contrasts in the way such leaders are formed, selected, developed and supported.[3] It will take a broadly life story and career history approach.[4] Drawing heavily on a series of portrait-based studies involving over 100 principals in eight countries, on which since the late 1980s I have worked with indigenous researchers, the chapter will examine how this approach can be interpreted, its strengths and limitations, and the knowledge it can draw on. The chapter is constructed of three parts. Part one is methodological and takes the form of an introduction to issues of how we know. Part two is primarily empirical and offers a much fuller account of aspects of what is known. Part three is broadly prescriptive and offers some ideas on what should be done.

HOW WE KNOW?

This topic warrants a chapter in its own right; what follows only outlines key issues. My approach is biographically orientated. English (2006) identifies 12 forms of life writing and discusses the contribution each can make to "understanding the meaning of the decisions and actions of leaders" (p. 141). In a helpful table (pp. 146–147) he defines and gives exemplars of each form. They are divided into two types (first and third person) and positioned on two axes (lifespan scope and contextual density) (p. 148). My work, he lists as portrayals ("a…detailed account of a specific episode or event in a person's or persons' life/lives") (p. 146) and prosopographies ("a form of group biography usually identified within a specific time period…") (p. 147). Whilst *prosopography* aptly classifies the studies from China, Cyprus, Hong Kong, Malaysia, Malta, and Singapore (the principals are not named but are described as a group and not as individuals), I am less persuaded that *portrayal* appropriately describes the studies from England and Wales (the principals are named and their stories, which cover much of their lives, are reported individually). For such reasons I have described these as *portraits*. I have studied educational leaders ethnographically (Ribbins 1999, 2007a), but the work reported in this chapter depended on face-to-face interviews[5]. The reliability of this method is much contested. For Sanders and Pinhey (1983) "people tell others what they think others want to hear or what they want them to know…What they tell researchers is even less candid…As Goffman (notes) 'I rarely believe what people say…in an interview situation, I hardly believe them at all'" (p. 224). Similarly Shamir, Dayan-Horesh and Aldler (2005) suggest autobiographies should not be seen as "windows to the leaders' actual lives or history but as texts that operate at the time of their telling. We make no assumption that the events and experiences related in leaders' development stories are the actual factors that contributed to their development, although this is possible, but rather that the events and experiences chosen by leaders to appear in their life stories reflect the leaders' self concepts and their concept of leadership, and allow or enable them to enact their leadership role" (pp. 16–17). Gronn (2005) disagrees "if a leader' story is a version of leadership in itself and a source of influence…then I see it as a dubious claim to try to accept as valid whatever learning about leadership may be obtained solely from freestanding textual sources…any consideration of leaders' writing (and speaking) exclusively within their own terms is problematic. The implication of this skepticism…is not that autobiographical sources have no place in leadership learning but that they need to be treated critically" (p. 482 and p. 483). Even when this occurs, as sources of leadership knowledge, biography is still likely to be preferable to autobiography since "biographers desirous of being taken seriously normally justify their claims by reference to information sources. This means there is at least some possibility of public verification and/or disputation when new sources of evidence come to light" (p. 483). Reflecting on his long experience, Gronn (2007, p. 193) concludes that whilst "interviews can be powerful and compelling in their verisimilitude and convey the sense that one is…succeeding in penetrating the consciousness of an informant, the difficulties I canvass (regarding high profile leaders and informants about them) suggest that use of interviews as a sole data source should be treated with skepticism".

For three reasons I found these ideas disconcerting: (1) because Gronn was involved in four of the interview-based projects on which this chapter rests; (2) because although I regarded such research as biographic in nature, it might be better categorized as producing 'assisted autobiographies'; and (3) because I recognize the temptation to romanticize when talking to educational leaders which he identifies. On this I accept there is a strong case for believing the findings of studies employing more than one method and involving more than one kind of respondent (Ribbins 1997b, pp. 9–11) are likely to more reliable than those that use only interviews and talks only to principals. But it does not follow the latter must necessarily be untrustworthy. On this Gronn has frequently, and rightly, stressed the need to contextualize. I suggest that, applied to those we research, there is a *prima facia* case for believing some are far more likely to misinform, evade and lie than others. Those likely to be unreliable will usually have something serious to hide or a major public reputation to protect. I doubt if many principals come into these categories.[6] Concluding his critique Gronn (2005, p. 489) argues that "textualism promises nothing more… than inadequate social science and a grossly undernourished reading of history". Whilst I would not go as far as this, I do agree that if the study of leadership in education is to progress it must emancipate itself from a contemporary tendency to privilege the instrumental and evaluative and to underplay knowledge that is conceptual, axiological, descriptive, aesthetic, humanistic and critical, and in doing so build on a fuller understanding of how knowledge is produced than has been available to date (Gunter & Ribbins 2003a, 2003b). In doing so, the field will also need to take history much more seriously (Ribbins 2006, 2007b).

WHAT WE KNOW?

The literature contains strong claims on the theoretical and practical importance of developing an understanding of the career stages of headteachers. Oplatka (2004), for example, drawing on his research, argues "theories of educational leadership are not applicable to novice, established and mid-career principals alike…that the assumptions underlying different leadership styles are more likely to be appropriate for a principal's particular career stage, rather than any career stage. Principals should be expected…to adopt a leadership style which is more compatible with the unique context of a certain career stage, and to refrain from employing a leadership style which is in contrast with those features and context. For example…instructional leadership appears more suitable for established principals rather than for those in the induction and disenchantment stages" (p. 44). My conclusions are more modest. Thus Gronn and I (Gronn & Ribbins 1996) identify three ways in which biographies (and autobiographies) can facilitate theorizing on leadership. (1) They can, as case histories, be inspected for evidence of the development of leadership attributes. (2) They can provide analytical balance sheets on the ends to which leaders direct such attributes during their careers given the demands on, and options available to, them. (p. 3) They can, as comparative analyses of the career paths of leaders, offer answers to system level questions such as do "particular sets of leaders, sanctioned by their societies and organizations as worthy to lead them, share common attributes?" and do they "screen their leadership cohorts to guarantee conformity to preferred cultural types or models?" (p. 464).

In all this the concept of 'career' is central. Following Goffman (1976), we take this to refer "to any social strand of any person's course through life" (p. 119). Applied to leaders, for Gronn (1999) it "has usually signaled the idea of a…sequenced and planned movement, and therefore, some sense of anticipated trajectory…" (p. 25). As such "career progression is (to be) understood generally as a desired, vertical, ladder-like movement through age-related and time-phased stages. The…locations occupied by individuals at any one time generate corresponding expectations and perspectives of career trajectories" (p. 27). What, then, do we know of the careers of leaders in education?

The Careers of Educational Leaders

Until comparatively recently there has been "an absence of any systematic understanding in the literature of how individuals get to be leaders, an ignorance of culturally diverse patterns of defining leadership and of knowledge of the culturally different ways prospective leaders learn their leadership remains in its infancy" (Gronn & Ribbins, 1996, p. 465). Without this there seems little chance of a worthwhile answer to Kets de Vries' (1993) question "What determines who will become a leader and who will not?" (p. 3). One response would be to devise a framework for ordering the biographical details of their lives thus enabling a comparative analysis of individuals set against the systems or cultural traditions of leadership that nurture a career. It would also allow a longitudinal, comparative analysis of leaders' careers in a variety of cultural and national settings that would go some way to answering Kets de Vries' challenge. In what follows, various frameworks are examined and a preferred model outlined.

Weindling (1999) reviews the large body of work on stage theories of socialization from the United States to study headship transition. Like Hart (1993) he notes three stages of organizational socialization through which leaders commonly pass. In Stage one the arriving leader, meeting the organization and its people, faces steep learning. Stage two involves "trying to fit in (reaching) accommodation with the work role, the people… and the…culture (of the institution). They look for role clarity …and may face resistance from established…members". By Stage three "stable patterns emerge but this is only visible in data from longitudinal studies" (p. 91). Before achieving this some move on. From a longitudinal study with Earley[7] and drawing on research by Gabarro (1987), Hall and Parkey (1992), Day and Bakioğlu (1996), Gronn (1993) and Ribbins (1997a), Weindling (1999) proposes a six stage model mapping the transitions: preparation; entry and encounter (first months); taking hold (3 to 12 months); reshaping (year 2); refinement (years 3 to 4); consolidation (years 5 to 7); and, plateau (year 8 and more).

Most models, especially those attributing a time dimension, are underpinned by various shared assumptions. Parkay and Hall (1992) identify four. First, principals can begin at different stages and not all do so at Stage one. This is especially the case with those taking up a second or subsequent principalship. Second, principals can pass through the stages at different rates. In particular, principals taking up a new principalship can, but by no means always do, pass through the early stages very quickly. Third, no single factor (personal characteristics at time of succession or the condition of the school at the point of take over) determines a principal's stage of development. Fourth, principals may operate at more than one stage at the same time. In such a case, the attribution of a particular stage can mean little more than identifying a predominant orientation. I would propose three further assumptions. First, principals can operate at more than one stage in different aspects of their role and also with regard to their relationships with relevant others. Second, it is possible for a principal to slip back one or more stages or progress more than one stage. Third, some principals never progress to the final stage described above. In searching for a career map, and in studying the careers of over 100 principals, I have found cases in which each of these assumptions was relevant (Pascal & Ribbins, 1998; Rayner & Ribbins, 1999; Ribbins, 1997b; Ribbins & Zhang, 2005).

Principal Portraits: Career Maps of Stages and Phases

My research is shaped by two models: (1) Gronn's (1999) "four sequential phases" (p. 32) (Formation, Accession, Incumbency, Divestiture) in the *lives of leaders*; and, (2) Day and Bakioğlu's (1996) four successive phases (Initiation, Development, Autonomy, and Disenchantment) in the *careers of headteachers*. The latter opt for 'phase', arguing that "Stage" implies distinct periods of time that differ quantitatively from both the preceding and succeeding stages, whereas a phase may include behavior across several domains. Karmiloff-Smith (1986) summarizes the difference: "The phase concept is focused on the underlying similarity of process, whereas the stage concept usually refers to similarity of structure" (p. 207). My field work leads me to combine and revise these models into a framework of two ideal typical leadership pathways as follows:

- *Making* (Formation), *Becoming* (Accession), *Being* (Incumbency as initiation, development, and autonomy), *Moving Out* (disenchantment and divestiture)
- *Making* (Formation), *Becoming* (Accession), *Being* (Incumbency as initiation, development, and autonomy), *Moving On* (enchantment and reinvention)

In describing these stages/phases, I will outline what is involved in the making of and being a principal and in leaving principalship, but will focus mainly on becoming a principal, not least because this stage has arguably attracted the greatest attention world wide in recent times.

1. Making a Principal

   The process of formation is made up of all the influences which shape the kinds of people prospective principals become. In this, the future principal is socialized into deep-rooted norms and values by the action and interaction of such key agencies as family (notably parents), school and teachers, peer groups, and local community. These agencies, especially those exerting their greatest influence in early childhood (Gardner 1995; Kets de Vries, 1995), shape personality and in doing so generate a conception of self, with the rudiments of work style, attitude and outlook. My research has led me to qualify these finding in a number of respects, most significantly insofar as they emphasize the primacy of *micro* (parents, particular teachers, etc) and *meso* (peer groups, schools, local community etc) level variables, they tend to underplay, in some contexts at least, the sway of *macro* level factors. In a case in point, from a recent study of secondary school principals in rural China, Zhang and I argue "the impact of societal and cultural influences on the formation of headteachers…seems to have been as great, and may even have been greater, than that of family, school or college, peer group and local community" (Ribbins & Zhang, 2006, p. 85). From our conversations with these principals we identify five influences: Confucianism, the Paternalist Culture, the Cultural Revolution, Communist Education, and the New Economic Culture. This research echoes the findings of similar studies conducted in mainland China by Bush and Qiang (2000) and in Singapore by Chew, Stott and Boon (2003). Summarizing, Zhang and I conclude that these findings represent "a significant reversal of the order as normally seen from the perspective of Western and Western orientated studies of the lives and careers of principals. This may reflect an important reality: alternatively it could be that…the significance of such macro level influences had simply not been given the attention they deserve in such Western studies" (Ribbins & Zhang 2006, p. 85).

2. Becoming a Principal

   Following formation future candidates for principalship become teachers. They then seek advancement, looking for experience in one or more leadership roles and in due course prepare for promotion to principalship. This means developing capacity and testing readiness in comparison with existing principals and likely rivals. In doing so they develop networks of peers, mentors and patrons, learn to present themselves, and jockey for position in the competition for preferment. This is the standard model but in at least four ways things can be very different.

First, the idea that to be a candidate a principal must have been an accredited and experienced teacher has not been universally accepted, and may indeed be on the way out in some parts of the world. In saying this it is necessary to stress that in most countries some teaching experiences has been and remains the norm. In a recent study on *Selecting and Developing Heads of Schools: Twenty Three European Perspectives* its editor, commenting on the prerequisites for appointment, concludes that "almost all systems require the headteacher to be a trained and (to some extent) experienced teacher" (Watson, 2003, p. 7). Whilst he identifies Sweden as the only exception, Derks (2003), reporting on the Netherlands, claims "a School Board can appoint anyone to be their new head teacher" (p. 170). However, he recognizes "In practice heads in compulsory education have almost always started their careers as a teacher" (p. 70). Much the same is true of the United States. In a wide ranging study Gates et al. (2003) point out that although it is possible to become a principal without such experience, in practice teaching is the common gateway, and this is demonstrated by the fact that "over 99 percent of public school principals…

have some teaching experience" (p. xv). However, they also note on this that in response to grow-ing, and in their view largely unjustified fears, "many states are contemplating changes to their requirements…routes because they are concerned about a shortage of people qualified" (p. xv) to hold such positions. Finally, as Male (2007) notes, although it is widely believed in England that "to be a headteacher in the (state) school system you had to have Qualified Teacher Status (QTS)" (p. 12), this is incorrect since under existing legislation a 'school teacher' is defined "either as someone who has QTS status *or*…who serves as a headteacher" (p. 12, my italics). However, as in the United States and the Netherlands, very few principals have not had some teaching experi-ence. This may be about to change with PricewaterhouseCoopers (2007), in a study sponsored by the Department for Education and Skills (DfES), questioning whether the person who is to lead a school (or rather the multi-agency integrated child services bodies envisaged for the future) must be a teacher. It is suggested "there should be no barriers for individuals with the relevant skills to take on the leadership role as long as there is always a senior qualified teacher on the team to act as the 'lead learner' and direct teaching and learning within the institution" (p. 111). For Gunter and Forrester (2007) this proposal should be seen, in part, as a means of tackling perceived prob-lems in recruiting future headteachers, claiming that if it is implemented it will mean "the status of teaching is downgraded in comparison to generic leadership skills and attributes" (p. 6).

Although many reports in Watson (2003) note how stressful principalship has become, few suggest this has led to serious recruitment difficulties; those that do include France, Hungary, Norway, Scotland and Sweden. To this list can be added China and the United States. In Eng-land, as pointed out in a recent report on *Leadership Succession* from the NCSL (2006), "We have better headteachers than ever…but they are in increasingly short supply. Almost one-third of primary and secondary headships are re-advertised because no suitable candidates come for-ward. Nearly a quarter of heads are aged over 55, and as they retire over the next five years…too few new candidates are putting themselves forward" (p. 3). Explaining this it is argued that whilst "some are discouraged by what they see as the overwhelming demands of modern headship" others are put off because "it takes a long time to become a head — 20 years on average — off-putting to the young and ambitious" (p. 3). Two broad 'market' type solutions to these problems can be identified. First, by increasing supply in various ways (by extending the available pool by making it possible for non-teachers to become principals); by appointing younger principals (by fast tracking); and keeping them in post longer (by making it harder to retire early and supporting them better whilst in post). Second, by making the role less stressful (via co-headship in which "two heads either job-share a single headship or work as full time joint head teachers [offering] a better work-life balance…By making the head teacher role less demanding in day-to-day terms and more varied, it can aid recruitment and retention" (NCSL 2006, p. 8) and/or more attractive in status and/or remuneration. Similarly it is possible to diminish demand, for example, by reduc-ing the number of schools (creating fewer and bigger schools) or by setting up a federation ("a federation is a group of two or more schools that formally agree to work together…One head-teacher may oversee a number of schools within the federation, again challenging the tradition of every school having its own headteacher" (NCSL, 2006, p. 8).

Second, the notion, if this is implied by the standard model, that principals normally choose eagerly to be teachers is highly debatable. In my studies many rejected this view. This was so for 13 of the 34 British principals. As Valerie Bragg recalls "teaching was the last thing I wanted to do" and Sue Benton remembers leaving school "not intending to go anywhere near a school ever again in my life" (Ribbins & Marland, 1994, p. 16). The 25 principals from rural China (Rib-bins & Zhang, 2004) were more dismissive still with only one describing becoming a teacher as a personal commitment to a desirable vocation. The rest saw it as an occupation which was low on their list of preferences: "I did not wish to be a teacher but I did not have other choices…If I had another choice I would have given up teaching, but in China at the time you couldn't choose the job you wanted" (p. 140). Most readily acknowledged that they had been forced into teaching because they had done poorly in the public examinations — "I did not achieve a high score in the exam (and) had…to go to teachers' college because the other colleges required higher scores… If I had other choices, I would have changed my career" (p. 140). Cyprus represents a case at the other end of the spectrum. There teaching, especially in secondary schools, has long been regarded as a highly desirable profession and after graduating prospective teachers are willing to endure many years on a waiting list before being called up (Pashiardis & Ribbins, 2003). As one, reflecting a view expressed by several, put it, "I cannot remember a time which I did not want to be a teacher". Even so, not even in Cyprus did all the principals regard teaching as their occupation of first choice. Thus amongst the women we talked to, one had failed to get a post in industry ("I was a woman. I was looked at as if I had come from Mars") and another would have preferred to continue her studies but family problems meant "I became a teacher because I had to earn a living" (p. 25).

Third, insofar as the standard model presumes those who become principals proactively seek promotion it can be far from the truth. What seems the case is that accounts of teacher promotion in much of the Western world, notably in English-speaking areas, are inclined to assume within structures of selection characterized by open competition, it is individual teachers who, other things being equal, take the initiative in presenting themselves as candidates for advancement. It is also taken for granted that, unless there are compelling reasons to the contrary, teachers will take a positive view of promotion and, at appropriate stages in their careers, seek it actively. Indeed, those who have the capacity and experience for promotion but choose not to pursue this can be seen as curious or even undesirable on the grounds that they are depriving themselves, schools and the system of something worthwhile. In exploring such issues with principals I have found it helpful to differentiate according to the part they see themselves as having played in achieving promotion at the various points, especially principalship, at which they seek this (whether and to what extent this had been active or passive) and how they see such promotion (whether and to what extent their attitudes to such a promotion had been positive or negative).

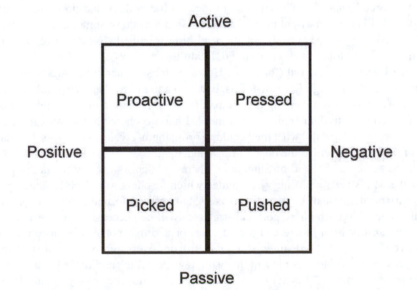

FIGURE 4.1   Principals and their role in and attitude to promotion.

My research has thrown up many examples of three of these types; the exception being the 'pressed' — it is hard to see why a prospective candidate, who does not wish to be a principal, should take this initiative. It could be those pressed reluctantly into applying qualify. One, for example, spoke of his local authority inspector coming "to see me...and said 'Have you applied for Blaengwrach?' 'No I haven't applied...', 'Why haven't you?', '...I don't think I want to work there.' 'Yes you do, apply.', 'I am not applying'" (Rayner & Ribbins, 1999, p. 98). But he changed his mind, applied and was successful. In passing there are many reasons for wishing to be a principal, some less worthy than others. Whilst many, with Tomlinson, claim "I had to...to achieve the things I felt I ought to achieve. I could help children and teachers" (Ribbins & Marland, 1994, p. 18), others offered different reasons: "Whilst I was teaching I was telling myself I am meant for better things...I looked around and compared myself with other heads and said I am as good as them, if not better" (Malaysian principal); "I decided to apply for prestige. You see other people being promoted and you feel you are being left behind" and "there is an increase in salary, which is important" (Cyprus principals). Similar justifications were made by British heads: "I decided I had seen a number of people who I didn't respect professionally doing the job and I thought I could do it as well if not better ...the underlying motivation...was that I'm competitive and I wanted to prove I was better than some of the people for whom I had worked"; and, "I had a family...and wanted more money. Teachers don't get paid that much money...." One admitted frankly to wishing for the power: "I like being in charge; I am sure this is one of the seven deadly sins".

Principals from the UK were almost always 'proactive'. Most saw themselves as taking the initiative in putting themselves forward for promotion. The great majority were positive about achieving this with only a few talking of regretting leaving the classroom or having enjoyed other roles (notably subject department leadership) more.[8] In contrast, the great majority of the principals from China saw themselves as playing little or no active role in the processes by which they were promoted. Those taking a positive view of this can be described as 'picked' but another term is needed for the significant minority who claim to have done their best to avoid promotion. The latter might better described as 'pushed'. As one put it, "When I was appointed to be a head of a rural secondary school I tried to refuse...I went because the director of the county educational committee insisted" and "The Party talked to me...in the end...I had no choice" (Ribbins & Zhang, 2004, p. 141). To an extent much the same could be said of some of the Malaysian principals. One, asked if she had actively sought headship exclaimed, "Never, never, never — right from the minute I was told I would have to go, I didn't want to accept it...I never wanted to be a head — I felt I was never cut out (for this)". However, most of her colleagues were classifiable as the 'picked' since although few saw themselves as having played an active role in the process ("I began to work towards becoming a principal. But our system is that teachers are appointed to principal according to their seniority and merit. I had no choice but to wait my turn") most wished to be promoted and did what they could to bring themselves more or less discretely to the attention of decision makers in the hope of this happening.

Much the same can be said of Singapore where "educators...apply for nothing once employed by the Ministry...the Ministry...decides which teachers to promote. They can bring... themselves to the attention of key decision makers, but unlike a formal application system, there are no guarantees that such micro political strategies will be successful" (Chew et al., 2003, p. 63). Given this proposition, there could be a case for adding another dimension to the model set out above (Figure 4.1) — distinguishing covert from overt micro political strategies in the ways that prospective principals present themselves as possible candidates for promotion. As a Malaysian principal put it, "it is not normal practice...for a teacher to say openly 'I want to be a headteacher. They may think this but it is not usual to say it". Singapore might be regarded as another case in which a covert approach stands a better chance of resulting in a successful outcome. As Chew et al. (2003) explain, "It is an Asian cultural phenomenon that it is seen as wrong to put oneself forward. One should be reticent, indicate one's unworthiness, and express the view that others are more capable" (p. 64). But things might be changing since "such false modesty — some might call it dishonesty — is not as prevalent as it was a decade ago. Some respondents, for instance, were prepared to say at their career planning interviews that they were ready to head schools or at least expressed the wish that they would like to be trained for such a posting" (p. 64).

Fourth, in so far as the standard model assumes that principals typically plan their careers and in doing so have prepared for principalship, it has, hitherto at least, been largely honored in the breach. In the cases of the pressed, and even more so the pushed, this is hardly surprising given that they did not wish for this. As the principals from China said "I did not want to be a head, so did not have any plans for this"; "I did not plan to be a head at all", and even the very few classifiable as picked, tended to say things like "I wanted to be a head, but I did not have a specific plan for this" (Ribbins & Zhang, 2004, p. 141). It was largely true even of the proactive, like Harry Tomlinson, who told me "in preparing for this interview I have tried to look back on my career — it is easy to impose an *ex post facto* rationale which was less evident at the time" (p. 19).

Such views need to be contextualized. They represent conversations with principals mostly appointed more than a decade ago. Since then as a study reporting on 23 countries in Europe makes clear "virtually all systems of schooling now recognize the importance for the headteacher of training and development. In almost all countries there are significant training opportunities for headteachers and for those who wish to be considered for such promotion" (Watson, 2003). Even so, "a continuing problem…is the identification of 'development' with 'training' (in which) the development of headteachers is seen as being met through training courses alone, and little emphasis is given to other forms of professional development" such as reflection on experience, job enrichment, and job rotation (p. 9). He also stresses that "experience of the leadership of subject or other teams, and the holding of subordinate leadership roles, provides valuable developmental opportunities. In some systems, however, these opportunities are virtually absent given the lack of 'middle management' levels, or even deputy headship, within all but the largest schools" (p. 9).

Things could be different now, but amongst all the principals I have been involved in studying, few anywhere admitted to having prepared in any substantial pro-active or systematic way for principalship. This usually meant their initial experience was deeply stressful. Four quotes, typical of many others, must suffice. The first two are from principals given little or no training; the second two from those who had some training but found this unhelpful. "I did not have any training before I was appointed… I found I was spending all my time and energy on trivialities… I worked hard (but) was only just about able to fulfill my obvious responsibilities (China); "I didn't have any. Unfortunately the Ministry of Education deals with this….They give you a file and notices and send you to your school and let you swim on your own. You have to develop what you need to know to survive on your own" (Cyprus); and, "I don't think training in management helped me very much…in the first years. If a mentor had been available this would have been better…In the difficult time in my early days I really wanted someone to ask" (Hong Kong); "I did go on a 'Preparing for Headship' course which was run for deputies in the year I applied for headship…I don't remember much about it. I don't remember who took it" (England). Some did prepare for principalship and found this helpful. In Singapore, as Chew et al. (2003) explain, "all the principals received some kind of formal training to prepare them for their leadership roles (usually) full time…at the National Institute of Education (on) a program of nine months' duration for vice-principals who had been selected by the Ministry to train for principalship" (p. 65). Reflecting on this, one principal said she had "found lectures on organizational structures particularly useful, since they explained how organizations worked and what the lines of authority mean". Others found the chance to work with an experienced mentor helpful, but most felt there was no substitute for the "learning derived from time spent doing the real job, which formed part of the attachment period…by encountering the daily grind, the rough and tumble of day-to-day responsibilities". I recall just one principal who wondered what the fuss was about; "I do not think school affairs are too difficult to deal with. I am confident with this…I motivate myself using the following steps: first learn to be a man, then learn to do business, finally learn to lead" (China).

So much for the view of a man; of the principals I have studied, 40 per cent and more were women in Cyprus, England, Malaysia and Singapore, but only one in Hong Kong (of nine) and in China (of 25). Indeed the last was the sole woman principal in the 158 junior secondary schools of Chuxiong. Similarly, Coleman, Qiang and Li (1998) in a study in Shaanxi found that although some 2,000 women teachers worked in them there were no women principals in its 89 secondary schools (p. 145). In Chuxiong we found complacency, even hostility, on this issue among male principals and education officers who variously claimed: gender discrimination no longer existed; women could be good teachers but professionally and physically not as good as men and so were unfit for higher level posts; and, it was not worth fostering women cadres, because women were trouble makers (Ribbins & Zhang, 2006, p. 83). The women principal believed calls for the appointment of more woman cadres were mainly propaganda, claiming "the Government does not pay serious attention to this" (p. 83). She felt unsupported and stressed; we later heard from a local official that she had retired prematurely to be replaced, to his patent satisfaction, by a man. Such findings support Bush and Qiang's (2000, p. 65) view both that "China …may be slower than most to acknowledge the issue and to seek remedies" and also that it "is by no means alone in experiencing an under-representation of women in management positions within and outside education" (p. 65).

There is a great deal of evidence for this last claim. A statement from the Eurostat Press Office (Dunne 2003) shows that in the European Union in 2001 whilst there were more female than male teachers in Upper Secondary Education in 21 of the 29 countries, in the 13 for which data are available male headteachers were more numerous than female in all except Bulgaria and Slovenia. Even in Slovenia, Erčulj (2003) points out that although "most classroom teachers in the basic school are women (around 90 per cent) headteachers are predominantly male (around 64 per cent)" (p. 226). Sweden was amongst the very few of the 23 countries reported in Watson (2003) in which men were in a minority with at the time "over 60 per cent of all principals are woman" (Johansson 2003, p. 243). But even there the bad news was that the salary level of headteachers is now "lower in real terms than it was 20 years ago" (p. 243). Conversely the Swedish case shows how quickly things can be turned around when a Government is determined that this should happen — thus the numbers of female principals have risen "from 7 per cent in 1989, to 24 per cent in 1990 and to more than 60 per cent in…2000" (p. 243). Other countries in which similar progress has been made include Singapore (Chew et al., 2003) and Cyprus (Pashiardis & Ribbins, 2003). All are all highly centralized: Pashiardis and Ribbins (2003) suggest an advantage of such systems "is that once political weight is put behind a policy, it can be implemented far more rapidly than is normally possible in a decentralized system" (p. 15). This can be illustrated with reference to England where, despite much effort to increase the number of women principals, Government figures (see NCSL, 2005) reveal a modest outcome: between 1997 and 2002 those heading secondary schools rose from 26 to 31 per cent (where 55 per cent of teachers were women), nursery and primary rose from 56 to

62 per cent (85 per cent of teachers were women), and special schools rose from 41 to 47 per cent (almost 70 per cent of teachers were women). Given the problems many other countries are having in recruiting and retaining sufficient able and experienced principals, there are good practical, as well as ethical, reasons for encouraging more women to seek principalship and to support them during incumbency.

Adler, Laney and Packer (1993) warn of the dangers of treating women in educational management as a homogenous group. There is much evidence that in the competition for place and promotion with men for a first principalship women are commonly treated unequally, but it is also clear that some women are treated more unequally than are others. From a study of ten Black people (six women) holding senior positions (six as principals) in education in Britain, Osler (1997), having asked if "Black senior educators, female and male, might have some similar experiences to White woman teachers", concludes "the narratives of all the senior managers (indicate) that Black and ethnic minorities need to make twice the effort of their White counterparts" (p. 125). This resonates with my research. Thus if Hall (1996), in her ground breaking study of the careers of six White women principals in England, describes this as 'dancing on the ceiling', and later as 'skating on thin ice', for Black and ethnic minority women principals in my study in England, their experience in achieving and enacting headship was described as 'overcoming granite barriers'. Elaine Foster, whilst accepting White women seeking appointment to senior management positions may meet real problems, argues there are others whose difficulties are far greater. In three years in post, several Black women had already come to talk to her as a Black women principal, "about ways into management...I do think this is a big issue for Black women and Black people in general, I don't think there are enough of us and I don't think the channels and the opportunities are there for Black people, and let me say Black women in particular, to map out the path they wish to take" (Ribbins & Marland, 1994, p. 22). For Sudarshan Abrol, principal of a special school, "it's three times the battle being a woman, an Asian woman in a male dominated society, and then in a racialist community" (Rayner & Ribbins, 1999, p. 65).

Bush and Moloi (2007) report similar findings from parallel research projects in England and South Africa that aimed, using in part a life history approach, to "establish how Black and ethnic minority (education) leaders are identified, developed and supported" (p. 41). From this they conclude "there is widespread evidence of covert or indirect discrimination in England... this was blatant and statutory in apartheid South Africa. Following the election of the first majority government in 1994... (the) Human Rights Commission stated 'the State may not discriminate directly or indirectly against anyone on [any] grounds, including race'. However, attitudes change more slowly than the law, as the authors' research findings in both countries demonstrate" (p. 48). I have talked to principals from minority communities in a number of countries who share this view. In Malaysia, for example, there was a feeling that although national policy was broadly opposed to such discrimination, in the search for promotion the dice were in practice heavily loaded against Chinese and Indian candidates. Furthermore, whilst the English principals quoted above were ready to talk, even on the record, minority ethnic principals in Malaysia would only discuss such matters with me outside formal interview settings and only after repeated assurances that anything they said would be off the record. So much then for becoming a principal: what of being one?

3. Being a Principal
   Incumbency runs from when a principal is first appointed to the time he/she finally leaves. Many will experience two or more principalships: and in doing so face starting again on the first phase of incumbency and moving through the following phases. My research suggests incumbency can take one of two routes, each with four successive sub-phases.

Following the Day and Bakioğlu (1996) model, the first three sub-phases common to both routes involve *initiation*, *development* and *autonomy*. The fourth, which can take one or other of two directions, one negative (*disenchantment*) the other positive (*enchantment*), I will deal with as an aspect of the final stage in the life of a principal which I will refer to as moving out (*divestiture*) or moving on (*reinvention*).

Initiation

Following appointment there is an immediate period of initiation. During this time new principals become familiar with the organizational and workplace norms of their new school and community and the roles they are expected to fulfill. The evidence suggests that this first phase normally takes at least three years before a new principal feels fully initiated in post. During this phase most experience a broadly similar range of emotions — beginning with feelings of elation and enthusiasm quickly followed by a growing sense of realism and adjustment to what the real parameters of the job are. In general new principals felt uncertain about what was expected of them; unsurprisingly most view these years as exhausting. Some claim to have had a relatively smooth transition; others faced great difficulties. The quality of this transition is shaped by contextual variables (see above) and also by factors such as self-belief; depth, breadth and relevance of previous experience and an ability to transfer this; the depth, breadth and relevance of prior-preparation and training and an ability to transfer this; learning from working with appropriate and inappropriate role models; ability to learn on the job; and the quality of institutional and local support structures.

Development

This phase, characterized by enthusiasm and growth, normally takes four to eight years. By this time the principal feels in control, has the measure of the job and has made good progress in developing the range of capacities and competencies it requires. Such principals have developed confidence in their ability to manage their schools. This allows them to maintain self-belief in the face of the stress that is their lot today. A growing sense of assurance is often expressed in a new vision for the school and/or the development of new ways of working. This tends to be the phase principals recall as the period of their careers in which they were most effective and made the most progress.

Autonomy

This phase usually comes after eight years or more in post. By this time principals are generally very confident and competent. A combination of experience and survival has given them a sense of control, knowing they have largely mastered the demands of principalship. They have devised strategies to cope with its stresses and can take a more open and longer perspective on the problems they face. Some believe this makes them more effective as leaders. Their day to day professional life is usually much easier than it was. They see themselves as "management experts". Having put in place appropriate posts and teams and delegated responsibilities to them, the school seems to run smoothly without much hands-on management from them. They tend to advocate a collegial approach to managing the school. Of course not all principals in post for eight years and more achieve all this. And there is evidence that even some of those who do can view the final phase negatively (termed 'disenchantment' by Day and Bakioğlu, 1996) and that this has significant consequences for how they regard leaving principalship.

Before turning to this theme, I will consider an associated issue. In 'Do school leaders have a shelf life?' Earley and Weindling (2007) explore the relationship between length of tenure and school leadership performance and consider what can be done to ensure long serving headteachers remain as effective as possible. Interviewing newly appointed heads in 1982, many saw seven years as about the optimum length for headship in any one school. Returning to these heads many years later they found 70 per cent were still in the same school after ten years and five per cent after 20 years (p. 79). They conclude "something needs to be done as it is not in the long-term interests of school, or headteachers themselves, to be in the same post for long periods" (p. 87) and explore the attractions of various solutions such as secondments and, after Fidler and Atton (2004), fixed-term contracts. My studies in China and Malaysia focused on the question 'Can principals have too short a shelf life?' In Malaysia few had spent much time as the principal of any one school; most being moved to a new post every two or three years, sometimes shuttling between the primary and secondary sector. One had been the principal of five schools in ten years. Several from China spoke of being given too short a time in any school to make a worthwhile impact — "I could not change the teaching attitude of the teachers and the learning attitude of the students...mainly because I did not have sufficient time to do so" (Ribbins & Zhang, 2005, p. 80). This echoes the findings of other research in China. Xiao (2000), for example, argues "It takes time to achieve results...if the tenure is too short...it is not helpful to master educational rule; it is not helpful to form the characteristics of a headteacher" (p. 102). I believe it is possible to have too short a shelf life. Many of the principals to whom I have spoken have suggested that it takes at least three years to really develop the kind of full understanding of a school and its people which allows them to begin to take things forward with confidence and several more years to implement their vision for it. I suppose it is possible to have too long a shelf life although I am not sure what this is. Much depends on the individual principal and the particular school. As I have noted above, conversations with a number of principals early in their term of office indicated that many of them thought at the time that to remain effective they would need to move on after seven or eight years. In practice many were still in post several years later; of these few believed that their ability to lead 'their' school had diminished. However, such differences have been little researched. Even the lesser question of why principals in some systems tend to remain in post for much shorter periods than those in other systems has been little studied. I suspect such differences are to be explained in part in terms of context. Thus in decentralized systems like the UK (however circumscribed of late) headteachers are expected to exercise significant levels of discretion in determining key aspects of the aims and operation of their schools, whereas in more centralized systems such as China and Malaysia their authority is far more narrowly delineated: as such if the former are seen as 'professionals' and therefore needing time to grow into their complex roles, the latter are regarded as 'technicians' and therefore much more readily interchangeable.

4. Leaving Principalship
This phase focuses on how principals anticipate and divest themselves of office. How they view this transition depends largely on their experience of the final phase of incumbency. I have examined this transition in several countries, most fully in China (Ribbins & Zhang, 2006) and so most of my examples come from this study.

Moving Out

The final phase of incumbency as described by Day and Bakioğlu (1996) is a transitional time for highly experienced principals. Some face the prospect of *disenchantment*; the seeds of disillusion and loss of commitment may stem back to the previous phase of autonomy. They seem at the height of their power and authority, but it is at just such a time that feelings of stagnation and loss of enthusiasm can set in. This can be a point they reassess their life goals. Failure to achieve what they wished can leave them feeling trapped and facing a downwardly spiraling process leading to disillusion and, in Gronn's term, 'divestiture'. Gronn (1999), responding to this account, claims if "Day and Bakioğlu's notion of disenchantment does imply 'a pattern of creeping negativism' the same cannot be said for divestiture". I cannot see what positive meaning can be given to disenchantment. On divestiture, he suggests that "At some point in their lives, due to factors associated with ageing, illness, lack of fulfillment or incapacity, leaders have to divest themselves of leadership by releasing their psychological grip". Whilst he distinguishes between voluntary and involuntary departure and their different meanings for those involved; I struggle to see these factors in any but negative terms.

Ribbins and Zhang (2006) identify three reasons for moving out as disenchantment and divestiture. (1) Being demoted or even dismissed, for perceived incompetence.[9] This was the fate of two Chuxiong principals. As one put it, "I lack authority, which influenced my image...I was negative in the latter period of my headship, so I did not do my job well. I was hurt and misunderstood, but did not hear the rumors so just ignored them...I left headship mature but negative... My headship is full of sweet, sour, bitter and spicy feelings" (p. 76). (2) By being demoted or even sacked, for corruption. Within a year of appointment to a first headship, 'Su' found he had to manage a major building project at the school. Competition was brisk and a bidder sent him a large sum. He kept the money, but the project was not awarded to this company. Its angry boss wrote a letter to the authorities disclosing the bribery. Su was arrested, confessed, returned the money, and demoted to a rural school as a classroom teacher. An interviewee who knew him felt he was lucky to escape imprisonment. But Su felt hard done by: "I suffered a disastrous impact on my life. My glorious history had been blackened. I fell into an economic trap set by others. I lost my headship and was dismissed by the party... I failed because I was careless" (p. 77). (3) It is possible to be disillusioned for more conventional reasons. 'Qiang', the only woman principal, felt "it is too difficult to be a head. I do not have confidence and want to step down. My work is too trivial and too boring...my energy does not allow me to work so hard. I am 52. I spend my time dealing with all kinds of inspections at all levels when I should be in classrooms discussing important teaching issues with teachers". Shortly afterwards she resigned.

Moving On

Several of the long serving principals I studied seemed still enchanted, appearing at least as optimistic as some in the earlier phase. Happy with their lives as principals, they voiced feelings of much to do, and saw their work as focusing on children. Hubermann (1993) lists four conditions for sustaining high levels of professional satisfaction: enduring commitment; good relations with colleagues; manageable job expectations; and a balanced home and school life. I would add two more: a balance between leisure and work activities; and good opportunities for continuing professional development.

Not all such principals enjoy all these conditions. Some who continue to enjoy the post are not content with every aspect of principalship today. John Evans, for example, told us "Some of my best headteacher friends have retired because of illness or stress... To survive you've got to be much tougher than in the past. I am diabetic with serious stomach problems and think this is stress related; it is part of the job". But he, like several others, still claimed "It's still the most rewarding job there is" (Rayner & Ribbins, 1999, p. 184). Perhaps the best expressions of enchantment leading to reinvention and moving on came from Michael Asford who said "Last year I started to think about what I would do when 55... I ought to move on and let somebody else have a go at this job. But there is so much to do still…when I am 55 I will say 'Thank you, I have got 30-odd years in…a reasonable pension, a nice home, things are OK.' I'll go into some form of management training, if anybody wants me. If they don't I'll be a gardener. Can you think of a better second occupation for an educator?" (Pascal & Ribbins, 1998, p. 69).

As noted earlier, there are ways of leaving principalship that do not involve retirement or resignation: there is demotion, dismissal or promotion. Most British principals regard this as the top of the career ladder, with the only promotion possibility being a move to a more prestigious and/or better paid principalship. This is not so in China, or in much of the world, where principalship is seen as a form of middle management with many ambitious for further promotion, and others having little choice in the matter, within the educational system. Ribbins and Zhang (2005) discuss the careers of five such principals. None were given much say in the decision to move on from principalship and one claimed not to miss it. The others offered various reasons for doing so including regretting not being able to work closely with students and teachers and in doing so playing a day-to-day role in enabling them to achieve their potential. However, four became education officers: whilst regretting moving on from headship, they did so at a time when they had still felt stimulated by its challenges and had transferred to work which they found worthwhile — in other words they had been enchanted and were in process of re-invention. Even so their experience points up problems in the way that principals are managed in China and elsewhere. In explaining why, I will relate this to the issue of what should be done?

WHAT TO DO?

This chapter focuses on how the study of life histories can enable understanding of the lives and careers of school leaders. It examines the merits of various theoretical approaches and analytical models, including my own. These characteristically seek to identify key stages and phases and illustrate this drawing on the findings of studies which, in my case, have usually involved research with others internationally. This has found that career patterns can vary substantially from country to country and culture to culture. Thus major differences can be found in terms of the experiences of men and women, of different ethnic groups, and of young and old. Given the weight widely accorded to the role of the principal in determining school quality and student achievement,[10] these and related issues merit far more research drawing on a fuller range of knowledge sources, over longer time periods, and employing a wider range of methods than has tended to be the norm to date. Reflecting on the contents of this chapter and what it can tell us of school principals and how they might be produced and retained in numbers and quality sufficient to meet the needs of school systems, leads me to propose a research agenda informed by three main themes.

1. Preparing and Promoting
   Since almost everywhere principals are drawn overwhelmingly from the teaching profession, the quality of those recruited to the latter will be crucial in determining that of the former. This can be a problem. For example, most of the Chuxiong principals became teachers because their school leaving grades were too poor to allow them to pursue better options. Most felt little had changed. If the quality of principalship is to be improved in line with stated national policy it would be "necessary to attract far more teachers of above average ability and train them better. For this to happen, it will be necessary to make teaching a much more attractive occupation than it is" (Ribbins & Zhang, 2004, p. 142). But as Cyprus shows, it is not enough to make teaching desirable to ensure a high

quality profession. Here, although many graduates fervently wish to be teachers, the system entailed most languished on a waiting list for over ten years; at which point, usually with little or no up-dating or professional training, they were appointed. This has undesirable implications for the quality of the teaching profession and also means that older teachers lead to older principals, with a few years only to make a mark. Without denigrating the benefits experience outside education can bring to first time teachers, there does seem a strong case for appointing younger teachers thus enabling some to be promoted at an earlier age. Conversely, it is hard to see what benefit of rigidly applying leaving age regulations which mean that able and experienced principals are forced to leave whilst still capable of serving with distinction.

2. Supplying and Supporting

   Providing future principals, means ensuring candidates in sufficient numbers and quality are available and developed. Achieving this means attracting enough good candidates to teaching and preparing them. Various frameworks have been designed to achieve this usually with mixed success. Levine (2005), reviewing preparation programs for educational leaders in the United States, of whom there are currently some 250,000, describes most as inadequate or poor.[11] Almost all this provision is decentralized; provided in over 600 programs in universities. Since 2001 the authorities in England have pioneered a centralized approach in which the NCSL has overall responsibility for the development of school leaders. To organize this it employs a model of five stages: emergent leadership, established leadership, entry to headship, advanced leadership, and consultant leadership. Given the increasing control that the college exerts over research (Weindling, 2004)[12] and training, independent evaluation of how this is interpreted in practice and with what outcomes is surely both overdue and essential.

The quality of leadership training and development is likely to be a significant factor in ensuring the provision of school leaders in sufficient numbers and quality but there are other considerations which are at least as important. Critical amongst these is ensuring that the pool from which prospective principals are drawn is appropriate in character and sufficient in size. As principalship has come to be seen as increasingly stressful and its rewards diminishingly small, a growing number of countries have experienced supply side problems. Attempts to overcome such difficulties have relied on a variety of strategies, with mixed success, including: making principalship less demanding; making it more rewarding; appointing non-teachers; appointing principals younger; encouraging them to remain in post older; and, appointing more women and more from minority ethnic communities. In reflecting on such strategies, particularly the last, it should be stressed that the problem is not just to do with the dynamics of supply. It would be possible to meet the demand for principals but in doing so to fail to achieve other highly desirable goals. For example, the implementation of one or more of the above strategies could result in a flood of candidates whose appointment 'solves' the problem of supply but which does so at the cost of reinforcing the structural inequalities (which reflect the existence of discrimination, overt or covert, most commonly on grounds of gender and ethnicity) to be found in many systems. Considerations of social justice require that the problem be addressed in suitably disaggregated terms.

3. Retaining and Re-energizing

   If one way of sustaining the pool of available principals is to appoint them younger, another would be to encourage those in post to stay longer. In a number of countries the opposite seems to be happening. From his latest survey of the situation in England and Wales, Howson (2007) concludes that "head teachers…are, on average, spending fewer years in post than a decade ago" (p. 3). On this, evidence internationally, some noted above, suggests that the increasing stresses of principalship mean that more and more retire early. On this Howson (2007) concludes that "if past trends continue, a large number (of principals) will decide to retire before reaching the age of 60. We do not believe that the new pension rules (designed to make it harder to take early retirement) will have any effect on persuading head teachers to remain in post until they reach the age of 60" (p. 16). In some countries, for example Cyprus, this problem has been compounded by legislation which makes retirement mandatory at 60. European Union legislation came into force last year designed to prevent this. Given the growing pressures of principalship I doubt, in England and Wales at least, if it will on its own persuade many to remain in post much beyond 60. What else can be done?

One approach would be to re-energizing long serving principals. On this Earley and Weindling (2007) identify a number of ways in which they might be professionally refreshed. These included opportunities to work outside their schools for a period before returning to principalship. They quote Sammons, who suggests that "one way of helping would be for LEAs to provide sabbaticals of a term, or even a year, to [long serving] head teachers. Whilst out of their schools they could visit other schools, follow academic courses, or use the time to reflect on their aims and the changes that have taken place in education and in society, since they first became a head teacher When they returned to their school it is hoped they would have developed new ideas and enthusiasms" (p. 83). In my research in England and Wales I found very few principals who did this: those that did, one had a sabbatical of a year completing a doctoral study and another was away for the year as the president of the National Association of Headteachers, found this a deeply re-energizing experience. Other ways of achieving this include time spent working part-time outside their school as, for example, external advisers to governing bodies in school improvement partnerships (Crawford & Earley 2004), consultant leaders, and associate researchers for the NCSL. Or they could do so by taking on new responsibilities as executive principals (with responsibility for more than one school) or as leaders of federations (with responsibilities for several schools).

TOWARDS A RESEARCH AGENDA

The previous section of this chapter identifies three main themes in which further research is necessary. In summary, whilst a good deal more is known in some countries of the lives and careers of school principals than was the case in the past, this is far less true of others. Furthermore, in few countries has there been anything like the same attention given to other levels of school leaders. With regard to the ways in which system demands for able school leaders are met, partially met, or not met, whilst each of the three approaches identified above has been to some extent the subject of study, again in some countries much more than others, there is an urgent need everywhere for far more systematic and sophisticated research into what has been achieved and why and how, and with what outcomes intended and otherwise.

NOTES

1. In a few countries the term 'headteacher' persists. Although I prefer this, with its implication of 'educational leadership' not just leadership in education, I will mostly use 'principal'.

2. For example, in England the National College for School Leadership (NCSL) was set up in 2000 with a budget of £25m (Passmore 1998); by 2004–5 this was £111m (Gunter & Forrester 2007).

3. Although I focus on the school principal, I believe the model proposed is relevant to other kinds of leader within education and beyond. It has, for example, been used in the study of Ministers of Education (Ribbins & Sherratt 2004) and of Permanent Secretaries in the Ministry of Education in the United Kingdom (Sherratt, 2004).

4. There is a growing use of this approach in the study of leaders' lives (Biott, Moos & Møller, 2002).

5. Accounts of these studies and copies of the interview schedules are available in Pashiardis and Ribbins (2003, pp. 11–12) and Pascal and Ribbins (1998, pp. 44–46).

6. There are those, like Douglas (1976, p. 55), who take "for granted that many of the people one deals with, perhaps all the people to some extent, have good reason to hide from others what they are doing and even to lie to them". If, however, as he also argues we must interpret what people say in context, we should be clear on the settings of his own research. Thus whilst the study of nude beaches, massage parlors, drug pushers, and gangs may justify deep skepticism, and the resort to covert participant observation, I do not believe this is equally warranted whatever the setting (see Ribbins 1986, pp. 38–40).

7. For an updated report of their unique and on-going longitudinal study see Earley and Weindling (2007). I will comment on aspects of this paper later in the chapter.

8. Few spoke well of their time as deputies (Ribbins, 1997a). Even so, with principalship seen as increasingly demanding and its rewards diminishingly marginal, growing numbers of deputies are now settling for this (Fidler & Atton, 2004; Howson, 2005) causing problems in recruiting principals. For some this "has led policy makers to pursue the possibilities of having heads who had not been teachers" (Gunter & Forrester, 2007, p. 12).

9. Until recently heads in the UK were rarely dismissed for lack of competence. OFSTED inspections have each year encouraged several to quit. Similarly Beckett (2007) suggests that the average 'life expectancy' of principals in the City Academy initiative is six months (p. 127).

10. Given that the powers of principals vary greatly from country to country, the nature and extent of their contribution to school effectiveness and student achievement has become the subject of increasingly sceptical debate. Many years of researching, teaching and working with principals leads me to believe if in the past their influence may have been exaggerated in recent times the pendulum of academic opinion might be in danger of swinging back too far.

11. For a forceful refutation of this critique see Young et al. (2005).

12. It is, at least, questionable how appropriate this is in a liberal society.

REFERENCES

Adler, S., Laney, J. and Packer, M. (1993) *Managing Women*, Bucks: Open University Press.

Beckett, F. (2007) *The City Academy Fraud*, London: Continuum.

Biott, C., Moos, L. and Møller, J. (2001) Studying headteachers' professional lives: getting the life history, *Scandinavian Journal of Educational Research*, 45, 4, 395–410.

Bush, T. and Moloi, K. (2007) Race, racism and discrimination in school leadership: evidence from England and South Africa, *International Studies in Educational Administration*, 35, 1, 41–60.

Bush, T. and Qiang, H. (2000) Leadership and culture in Chinese education, *Asia Pacific Journal of Education*, 20, 2, 58–68.

Chew, J., Stott, K. and Boon, K. (2003) On Singapore: The making of secondary school principals, *International Studies in Educational Administration*, 31, 2, 54–75.

Coleman, M., Qiang, H. and Li, Y, (1998) Women in educational management in China, *Compare*, 28, 2, 133–140.

Crawford, M. and Earley, P. (2004) Headteachers' performance management, *School Leadership and management*, 24, 4, 377–389.

Day, C. and Bakioğlu, A. (1996) Development and disenchantment in the professional lives of headteachers, Goodson, I. and Hargreaves, A. (Eds) *Teachers' Professional Lives*, London: Falmer, 205–227.

Derks, J. (2003) The selection and development of headteachers in the Netherlands, Watson, L. (Ed) *Op Cit*, 167–175.

Douglas, J. (1976) *Investigative Social Research*, New York: Sage.

Dunne, M. (2003) *Education in Europe: Key Statistics 2000/01* (available from Eurostat Data Shop, Office for National Statistics, Newport NP10 8GX).

Earley, P. and Weindling, D. (2007) Do school leaders have a shelf life? *Educational Management Administration and Leadership*, 35, 1, 73–89.

English, F. (2006) Understanding leadership in education: life writing and its possibilities, *Journal of Educational Administration and History*, 38, 2, 141–155.

Erčulj, J. (2003) The selection and development of headteachers in Slovenia, Watson, L. (Ed) *Op cit*, 223–233.

Fidler, B. and Atton, T. (2004) *The Headship Game*, London: Routledge.

Gabarro, J. (1987), *The Dynamics of Taking Charge*, Boston: Harvard Business School.

Gardner, H. (1995) *Leading Minds: an anatomy of leadership*, New York: Basic Books.

Gates, S., Ringel, J., Santibanez, C., Chung, C. and Ross, K. (2003) *Who is Leading our Schools? An Overview of School Administrators and their Careers*, Santa Monica: RAND.

Goffman, E. (1976) *Asylums*, Harmondsworth: Penguin.

Gronn, P. (1993) Psychobiography on the couch, *Journal of Applied Behavioural Science*, 29, 3, 343–358.

Gronn, P. (1999) *The Making of Educational Leaders*, London: Cassell.

Gronn, P. (2005) Questions about autobiographical leadership, *Leadership*, 1, 4, 481–490.

Gronn, P. (2007) Interviewing leaders: penetrating the romance, Briggs, A. and Coleman, M. (Eds) *Research Methods in Educational Leadership*, London: Sage, 189–204.

Gronn, P. and Ribbins, P. (1996) Leaders in context, *Educational Administration Quarterly*, 32, 2, 452–472.

Gunter, H. and Forrester, G. (2007) New Labour education policy and the rise of school leadership in England, paper given to AERA, April in Chicago (unpublished).

Gunter, H. and Ribbins, P. (2003a) the field of educational leadership, *British Journal of Educational Studies*, 51, 3, 254–282.

Gunter, H. and Ribbins, P. (2003b) Challenging orthodoxy in school leadership studies, *School Leadership and Management*, 23, 3, 129–149.

Hall, G. and Parkey, F. (1992) Reflections on becoming a principal, Parkey, F. and Hall, G. (Eds) *Becoming a Principal*, Boston: Allyn and Bacon.

Hall, V. (1996) *Dancing on the Ceiling: A Study of Women Managers in Education*, London: Paul Chapman.

Hart, A. (1993) *Principal Succession: Establishing Leadership in Schools*, New York: SUNY.

Howson, J. (2005) *The State of the Labour Market for Senior Staff in Schools in England and Wales*, Haywards Heath: National Association of Head Teachers.

Howson, J. (2007) *22nd Annual Survey of Senior Staff Appointments in Schools in England and Wales*, Oxford: Education Data Surveys.

Hubermann, M (1993) *The Lives of Teachers*, London: Cassell.

Johansson, O. (2003) Leadership and compulsory schooling in Sweden, Watson, L. (Ed) *Op Cit*, 239–251.

Kets de Vries, M. (1993) *Leaders, Fools, and Impostors*, New York: iUniverse.

Kets de Vries (1995) *Leaders, Fools and Impostors*, New York: iUniverse.

Karmiloff-Smith, A. (1986) Stage/structure versus phase/process in modelling linguistic and cognitive development, Levin, I. (Ed) *Stage and Structure*, Norwood: Ablex, 164–190.

Levine, A. (2005) *Educating School Leaders*, Washington, DC: Education Schools Project.

Male, T. (2007) Whither headship, *Management in Education*, 20, 4, 11–14.

NCSL (2005) *Gender and Headship in the 21st Century*, Nottingham: NCSL.

NCSL (2006) *Go for it: Reasons to be a Headteacher*, Nottingham: NCSL.

Oplatka, I. (2004) The principal's career stage: an absent element in leadership perspectives, *International Journal of Leadership in Education*, 7, 1, 43–55.

Osler, A. (1997) *The Education and Careers of Black Teachers*, Bucks: Open University Press.

Parkay, F. and Hall, G. (1992) (Eds) *Becoming a Principal*, Boston: Allyn and Bacon.

Pascal, C. and Ribbins, P. (1998) *Understanding Primary Headteachers*, London: Cassell.

Pashiardis, P. and Ribbins, P. (2003) (Eds) The Making of Secondary School Principals on Selected Small Islands [Cyprus, Hong Kong, Malta and Singapore], *International Studies in Educational Administration*, 31, 2 (special edition).

Passmore, B. (1998) Headship novices learn the creed, *Times Educational Supplement*, 23rd October.

PriceWaterhouseCoopers (2007) *Independent Study into School Leadership*, London: DfES.

Rayner, S. and Ribbins, P. (1999) *Headteachers and Leadership in Special Education*, London: Cassell.

Ribbins, P. (1986) Qualitative perspectives in research in secondary education, Simkins, T. (Ed) *Research in the Management of Secondary Education*, Sheffield: Sheffield Hallam University, 3–55.

Ribbins, P. (1997a) Heads on deputy headship: impossible roles for invisible role holders? *Educational Management and Administration*, 4, 3, 295–308.

Ribbins, P. (1997b) (Ed) *Leaders and Leadership in the School, College and University*, London: Cassell.

Ribbins, P. (2003) Biography and the study of school leader careers, Brundrett, M., Burton, N. and Smith, R. (Eds) *Leadership in Education*, London: Sage, 53–74.

Ribbins, P. (2006) History and the study of administration and leadership in education, *Journal of Educational Administration and History*, 38, 2, 113–125 (Special edition on *Administration and Leadership in Education: A Case for History?*).

Ribbins, P. (1999) Context and praxis in the study of school leadership: a case of three? Begley, P and Leondard, P. (Eds) *The Values of Educational Administration*, London: Falmer, 125–140.

Ribbins, P. (2007a) Middle leadership in schools in the UK: improving design — a subject leader's history, *International Journal of Educational Leadership*, 10, 1, 13–31.

Ribbins, P. (2007b) Leadership and management in education: what's in a field? *South African Journal of Education*, 27, 3, 351–377.

Ribbins, P. and Gronn, P. (2000) Researching principals: context and culture in the study of leadership in schools, *Asia Pacific Journal of Education*, 20, 2, 34–46.

Ribbins, P. and Marland, M. (1994) *Headship Matters*, London: Longman.

Ribbins, P., Pashiardis, P. and Gronn, P. (2003) the making of principals on selected small islands: an introduction, Pashiardis, P. and Ribbins, P. (Eds) *Op cit*, 2–13.

Ribbins, P. and Sherratt, B. (2004) the role of the Chancellor of the Exchequer in the making of educational Policy, *Journal of Education Policy*, 19, 6, 715–733.

Ribbins, P. and Zhang, J. (2004) Headteachers in rural China: aspects of ambition, *International Journal of Leadership in Education*, 7, 2, 127–147.

Ribbins, P. and Zhang, J. (2005) Headteachers and their exits: moving on and moving out in Chuxiong in rural China and elsewhere, *International Studies in Educational Administration*, 33, 3, 74–89.

Ribbins, P. and Zhang, J. (2006) Culture, societal culture and school leadership: a study of selected headteachers in rural China, *International Studies in Educational Administration*, 34, 1, 71–89.

Sanders, W. and Pinhey, P. (1983) *The Conduct of Social Research*, New York: Holt.

Shamir, B., Dayan-Horesh, H. and Aldler, D. (2005) Leading by biography: towards a life-story approach to the study of leadership, *Leadership*, 1, 1, 13–29.

Sherratt, B. (2004) *Permanent Secretaries and Education Policy*, PhD Thesis, University of Birmingham (unpublished).

Watson, L. (2003) (Ed) *Selecting and Developing Heads of Schools: Twenty Three European Perspectives*, Sheffield: Sheffield Hallam University, 125–137.

Weindling, D. (1999) Stages of headship, Bush, T., Bell, L., Bolam, R., Glatter, R. and Ribbins, P. (Eds) *Educational Management: Refining Theory, Policy and Practice*, London: Paul Chapman, 99–101.

Weindling, D. (2004) Funding for Research on School Leadership. Accessed April 21, 2008 from: http://www.ncsl.uk/mediastore/imagez/randd_research_funding.pdf.

Young, M., Crow, G., Orr, M., Ogawa, R. and Creighton, C. (2005) An educative look at 'Educating School Leaders', *UCEA Review*, XLVI, 2, 1–5.

Xiao, Z. (2000) *Research in Educational Administration*, Wuhan: Central China Normal University Press.

5

Effects of Leadership on Student Academic/Affective Achievement

Stephen L. Jacobson and Christopher Bezzina

The focus of this chapter is on leadership and the role of school leaders, particularly principals and head teachers, in influencing student outcomes. In the chapter, we review what we believe are some of the most important empirical studies that have examined direct and indirect school effects on student achievement over the past forty years, from the 1966 Coleman Report on Equality of Educational Opportunity, through the Effective Schools and School Improvement literatures of the 1970s, 1980s and 1990s, and subsequent studies conducted through 2007. Much of the latter part of the chapter will review the International Successful School Principalship Project (ISSPP), an ongoing examination of successful school leaders in Australia, Canada, Denmark, England, Hong Kong, Norway, Sweden and the United States begun in 2001. Among other key sources, e.g., Day, Harris and Hadfield (2001) and Mulford, Silins and Leithwood (2004), the conceptual framework of the ISSPP drew upon the claim by Leithwood and Riehl (2005) that, regardless of context, when it comes to student achievement, successful school leadership requires the following core practices: (1) setting directions; (2) developing people; and, (3) redesigning the organization. The ISSPP examined the existence of these core practices across different national contexts, as well as similarities and differences in how these leadership practices were enacted to enable student performance to improve.

We preface this review with a brief consideration of the epistemological assumptions that underlie the methodological approaches to knowledge generation that we deemed appropriate for a study's inclusion in this chapter. In our conclusions, we also consider the limitations we believe exist in the studies presented, as well as the gaps that remain in the extant literature. We shall see that both the nature of student outcomes and how leadership is defined remain contested. For example, student performance has been alternatively defined and measured by standardized test scores, a child's personal sense of well-being, and/or the development of habits of good citizenship. Similarly, leadership has been conceptualized and defined as being both an individual and a collective construct, with examinations of distributed leadership prevalent in contemporary research. With these issues in mind, the chapter concludes with a discussion about the implications of this body of literature for the preparation of school leaders, as well as promising directions for future research.

UNDERLYING ASSUMPTIONS AND CAVEATS

As for our underlying assumptions, we recognize that our review of the school leadership literature is predominantly Western in its structural-functionalist orientation, and that industrial psychology, scientific management, human relations and the social sciences, particularly sociology, political science and economics, have had the greatest influence on our perspectives. We draw our accounts almost exclusively from leading peer-reviewed journals, mostly North American, European and Australian; journals that tend to privilege manuscripts written in English and structured on traditional experimental research methodologies, both quantitative and qualitative. We consciously chose to ignore informal case accounts, the personal testimonials of experienced administrators from education and elsewhere, journalistic stories and other anecdotal forms of evidence as they might appear in biographies, autobiographies, and oral histories and traditions. We acknowledge that by constraining our sources in this manner, the chapter is open to criticism as being too narrow in terms of thought and disciplines relative to the context of a post-modern world. We recognize our "positivistic" orientation and understand its limitations, however we believe that, as acceptable empirical evidence is accumulated in a systematic fashion, knowledge claims can be more readily asserted. Therefore, we feel that this well-traveled path deserved our primary attention. That said, it was also the reality of editorially imposed page constraints that limits our ability to report fully the alternative approaches and obstacles that the field has encountered over the years, although we will also try to fill in some of these gaps in our critique.

The framework underlying this chapter is essentially a production function model situated in a rationalist paradigm, as introduced in our analytic starting point, the 1966 Coleman report. We report studies that examined what leaders did in order to have influence on the technical processes within their schools and school systems that resulted in the accomplishment of intended goals, specifically improved student performance. We will see that, over time, research revealed the influence leaders exert is not situated exclusively within the school or school system, but in fact begins to permeate the non-school factors that earlier researchers (e.g., Coleman, 1966) found account for much of the variation in student performance, particularly parent and community involvement. Moreover, we will see that leadership, once viewed almost exclusively as a set of personal characteristics best exemplified by trait theory has morphed into a broader, collective conception that appears to be in its ascendancy under the broad, but often ill-defined, heading of distributed leadership.

A BRIEF ACCOUNT OF ALTERNATIVE PERSPECTIVES

While ours is primarily a traditionally scientific perspective on leadership, others have examined alternative sources for understanding leadership worthy of attention. Crow and Grogan (2005), for example, reference such classics from Western literature as Shakespeare's *Richard II, King John, Richard III, Julius Caesar, Macbeth,* and *King Lear,* Machiavelli's *The Prince,* Sophocles' *Oedipus the King,* and Aristotle's *Nicomachean Ethics* and *Politics.* Non-Western and indigenous political thought has also influenced the ways in which leadership is considered, including written and oral traditions from Africa, East Asia, North and South America. Crow and Grogan (2005) explored the influence of Confucianism, in which leaders are expected to exemplify humaneness, ritualism and morality. They suggest that in the Confucian ideal, morality and politics are inseparable and a leader is expected to personify the role model of moral order.

In contemporary popular culture, television and cinema provide some of the most pervasive images of leadership, especially the solitary "strong, silent" hero of the American West, best exemplified by Gary Cooper in *High Noon*, as a sheriff who must single-handedly take on a gang seeking revenge. That powerful image of righteous authority has given way to the morally ambiguous leadership styles of leaders who challenge traditional notions of right and wrong, such as *The Godfather* Don Corleone and mob boss, Tony Soprano, protagonist of one of America's most popular and controversial television shows, *The Sopranos*.

When Hollywood has turned its attention to leadership in schools, it tends to focus on the superhuman efforts of one individual overcoming seemingly overwhelming odds, such as in *Stand and Deliver*, a 1988 film about high school mathematics teacher Jaime Escalante who helped Hispanic students in East Los Angeles exceed everyone's expectations by passing Advanced Placement Calculus, or in *Lean on Me*, a 1989 movie about baseball bat wielding principal Joe Clark who turned around a chaotic New Jersey high school.

As powerful as these literary and visual images may be, they don't advance our understanding of the associational and causal relationships between leadership and learning that will most productively inform school leaders and policy makers. Therefore, we turn our attention to the scientific research base suggested in the introduction.

REVIEW OF THE LITERATURE

The literature reviewed in this section focuses on context — historical, social, political and philosophical. The aim is to review 'what works' to improve schools by focusing on strategies that seem to be effective across the varied and diverse situations in which schools operate, with specific attention paid to those facing challenging circumstances. We start by setting the literature into a historical context beginning with the U.S. report on Equality of Educational Opportunity (Coleman et al. 1966).

More commonly known nowadays as the Coleman Report (after lead researcher James S. Coleman), the report turned the educational establishment on its head due to its sheer size (data was gathered on some 4,000 schools, 60,000 teachers and 570,000 student test scores) and because its findings countered long held beliefs about education. Specifically, Coleman's team of researchers found that variation in student performance was accounted for more by out of school factors such as family background, socio-economic status and race — over which school leaders have little control, than in-school resources such as expenditures and facilities — which they presumably do control (Mosteller & Moynihan, 1972). So surprising and controversial were these findings that the data were reanalyzed and the findings reassessed numerous times (most notably by Jencks et al. 1972). Using a production function approach in which the dependent variable of student performance, as measured by standardized test scores, is considered to be a functionally related outcome of the independent input variables contributed by students, teachers and schools to the educational enterprise, one consistent interpretation of the data is that what schools contribute to the equality of student outcomes is more limited than educators had formerly assumed. Yet if that finding holds, i.e., the racial and socio-economic composition of a student body is a better predictor of student performance than a school's expenditures and resources, then why was it that students in some high poverty, predominantly African American inner city elementary schools were performing well above expectations based upon their demographics? These statistical outliers became the focus of effective schools research, because it appeared that at least in some cases, schools could make an important difference in the academic performance of children, especially those at risk of failure.

THE EFFECTIVE SCHOOLS LITERATURE

Studies that began to focus on schools performing at levels well beyond what the composition of their student body might otherwise suggest restored hope to school leaders that what they did mattered. Duke's (1987) analysis of this emerging body of effective schools literature contrasted it with earlier (pre-Coleman) conceptions of leadership effectiveness that focused almost exclusively on the skill sets that leaders had to acquire in order to do their job well. Duke argued that leadership skills in the absence of measurable student outcomes ring hollow if the primary goal of the principal or superintendent is simply to maintain organizational control and/or employer satisfaction:

> Unlike the preceding approach, outcome-based concepts of effectiveness take a relatively benign stance toward the training of school leaders. What counts is output. A school leader's effectiveness is based on how well students achieve. As long as student performance meets or exceeds expectations, school leaders are presumed to be doing their jobs well. (Duke, 1987: p. 23)

So, what are the leadership correlates of school effectiveness? Brookover and Lezotte (1979) compared six elementary schools that had improved student tests scores with two elementary schools that had declining scores. They found marked differences in school leadership, structure and climate. Specifically, principals in schools with improved performance focused more on instruction, making it the school's primary objective. This body of work gave rise to interest in instructional leadership as the linchpin between principals' practice and student achievement, yet as Duke (1987) points out, correlates of leadership effectiveness do not address causation, i.e., "the studies do not prove which came first, student achievement or able leadership" (p. 73). In other words, it is equally plausible to suggest that effective schools create effective leaders, as it is to argue that effective leaders create effective schools. This emphasis on the products of leadership behaviors, as opposed to pre-existing skills, led to subsequent research seeking to tie the two together by analyzing the processes used by successfully leaders to promote school improvement.

THE SCHOOL IMPROVEMENT LITERATURE

In contrast to effective schools research, which examined school characteristic correlates of relatively high student achievement, school improvement studies focused instead on the processes used to change and improve schools. The 'first phase' of school improvement started to take shape as a distinct body of approaches in the late 1970s and early 1980s (Potter, Reynolds & Chapman, 2002: p. 244). This phase was characterized by the Organization for Economic Cooperation and Development's International School Improvement Project (ISIP) (Hopkins, 1987) but, unfortunately, many of the initiatives associated with it were 'free floating, rather than representing a systematic, programmatic and coherent approach to school change' (Potter et al., 2002: p. 244). The emphasis was on organizational change, school self-evaluation and on how individual schools and teachers owned the change process. However, there was no significant conceptual or practical connection of these initiatives to student learning outcomes. Furthermore, they were variable and fragmented in conception and application and, consequently in the eyes of most school reformers and practitioners, struggled to have an impact on classroom practice (Reynolds, 1999). Despite this somewhat negative analysis, Hopkins does acknowledge that many of these studies initiated:

…widespread research into, and understanding of, the change process and the school as an organization… The studies highlighted the limitations of externally imposed changes, the importance of focusing on the school as the unit of change, and the need to take the change process seriously… Similarly, the research on schools as organizations, demonstrated the importance of linking curriculum innovation to organizational change. (2001a: p. 29)

The early 1990s gave rise to a 'second phase,' which was characterized by bringing together various contributions from the school improvement and school effectiveness communities. A number of effectiveness and improvement researchers and practitioners had called for such a fusion of approaches and insights (Reynolds, Hopkins & Stoll, 1993; Hopkins, Ainscow & West, 1994; Gray et al., 1996), and this led to a merged perspective (Hopkins, Reynolds & Stoll, 1996). The school effectiveness tradition made significant contributions to this merged intellectual enterprise, such as the value-added methodology for judging school effectiveness and for bringing about a large-scale, proven knowledge base about 'what works' at the school level to improve student outcomes (Teddlie & Reynolds, 2000).

The more recent 'third phase' of school improvement started during the mid 1990's with attempts to draw lessons from contemporary improvement projects and reforms in the U.K. such as Improving the Quality of Education for All (IQEA) (Hopkins, 2001a) and High Reliability Schools (HRS) (Stringfield, 1995). In Canada, it has been in evidence in work conducted by the Halton Board of Education (Stoll & Fink, 1996); in the Dutch National School Improvement Project in the Netherlands (Hopkins et al., 1994); and in the work of the Education Trust in North Carolina, U.S. (Education Trust, 2005).

Given that there are significant variations amongst these programs, if one were to draw conclusions from third phase improvement initiatives, it is clear that there has been an enhanced focus upon the importance of pupil outcomes. Instead of the earlier emphasis upon improving processes, now the focus is on whether these improvements are powerful enough to affect pupil outcomes. This is not to say that the importance of the 'process' of improvement had been shelved, instead there has been an adoption of a 'mixed' methodological orientation, in which bodies of quantitative 'outcome' data plus qualitative 'process' data are used to measure educational quality and variation in that quality. This includes an audit of existing classroom and school processes and outcomes, and comparisons with desired end states, in particular the educational experiences of different pupil groups (Potter et al., 2002: p. 245). There has also been an increasing awareness of the importance of 'capacity building' through sophisticated training, coaching and staff development (Crowther et al., 2002), as well as medium-term strategic planning, change strategies that utilize 'pressure and support' and the intelligent use of external support agencies (Stoll & Fink, 1996). This third phase brought with it an appreciation of the importance of cultural change in order to embed and sustain school improvement. The focus is now on a careful balance between 'vision building' and the adaptation of structures to support those aspirations. Next we examine some of these strategies.

STRATEGIES FOR IMPROVING SCHOOLS

Most of the works we have reviewed refer to a set of processes managed from within the school (Stoll & Fink, 1996), targeted at both pupil achievement and the school's ability to manage change (Ainscow et al., 1994); a simultaneous focus on outcome and process. In this context, an improving school is considered to be one that increases its effectiveness over time; i.e., the added value it generates for pupils increases for successive cohorts. These authors stress the self-managing nature of the improving schools and that schools are most effective when they are aided from time to time by external support, apparently taking control of an externally determined agenda; controlling, rather than the objects of change.

When schools are empowered with the right mix of autonomy and support, they have much better prospects for improvement. Researchers have been looking for similarities amongst schools that have been running successful school improvement programs in order to come up with lists of 'what works'. For example, Harris (2002: p. 29) conducted a comparative analysis of highly successful school improvement programs and found a number of shared features; specifically, they believe in the ability of all their students and teachers and are committed to them; focus closely on classroom improvement; utilize discrete instructional or pedagogical strategies, i.e., they are explicit in the models of teaching they prescribe; apply pressure at the implementation stage to ensure adherence to the program; collect systematic evaluative evidence about the impact upon schools and classrooms; mobilize change at a number of levels, e.g., classroom, department, teacher level; generate cultural as well as structural change; engage teachers in professional dialogue and development, and provide external agency and support.

Harris' study showed that while the improvement programs evaluated varied in content, nature and approach, they reflect a similar philosophy. Central to this philosophy is an adherence to the school as the centre of change and the teacher as the catalyst for classroom change and development. Within these highly effective programs the non-negotiable elements were a focus on teaching and learning, a commitment to professional development and diffused or devolved leadership (Harris, 2002; MacBeath, 1988, Wenger, 1998).

In an extensive analysis of school improvement literature and twenty-five successful programs world-wide, Potter, Reynolds and Chapman (2002: p. 246) found the following general features of effective improvement programs:

- *having a vision*: since without a concept of where we are trying to get to, the verb 'to improve' has no meaning;
- *monitoring:* we must know where we are now in relation to the vision;
- *planning*: how will we get from where we are, towards where we want to be?
- *using performance indicators*: to track progress over time in respect to the aspects we monitor.

Other researchers (Ainscow et al., 1994; Gray et al., 1999) show that, regardless of the type of school, there are certain internal preconditions for successful improvement, including a school-wide emphasis on teaching and learning, a commitment to staff development and training and the use of performance data to guide decisions, targets and tactics. In addition, they point out the importance of teamwork both within staff groups (collaborative planning, effective communication) and with stakeholders (involvement of teachers, pupils and parents in decision making) and the need for time and resources for reflection and research.

Many of the principles governing effective improvement in the literature reviewed thus far are treated as universals, with little evidence about 'context specificity' (Teddlie & Reynolds, 2000). However, there are certain principles that have been associated with improvement programs successfully implemented in schools facing challenging circumstances. Specifically, the literature indicates that schools that succeed 'against the odds,' i.e., against a background of significant pupil and community disadvantage (Education Trust, 2005; National Commission of Education, 1996), share the following characteristics:

- A leadership stance that embodies and builds a team approach;
- A vision of success that includes a view of how to improve;
- The careful use of targets;
- The improvement of the physical environment;
- High expectations about behavior and success;
- An investment in good relations with parents and the community.

Summarizing the literature surveyed so far, we can group the recurring features of successful school improvement programs into several sub-sections beginning with leadership, and then the mechanisms through which successful leaders operate, such as a focus on teaching and learning, capacity building, staff development and collective review, parental and community involvement, improving the learning environment, and a strong belief in students. Next we consider each in turn.

Leadership

Effective or purposeful leadership is generally accepted as a central component in implementing and sustaining school improvement. Evidence from school improvement literature, starting with seminal studies in the U.S. (Brookover et al., 1979; Edmonds, 1982) and the U.K. (Rutter et al., 1979), consistently highlight that effective leaders exercise a direct or indirect but powerful influence on a school's capacity to implement reforms and improve students' levels of achievement. Although quality of teaching strongly influences and determines the level of student motivation and achievement, quality of leadership matters in determining the motivation of teachers and the quality of their teaching (Fullan, 2001; Leithwood et al., 2004; Marzano, Waters & McNulty, 2005; Sergiovanni, 2001). Moreover, there is growing evidence that high quality leadership is especially important in schools serving low socio-economic youngsters who have often been at greatest risk for academic failure (Scheerens & Bosker, 1997), thus making leadership a variable of significant interest. Yet, there is some disagreement as to how powerful an effect leadership actually has on student performance. For example, while some have found that leadership effects on student achievement account for almost five per cent of the overall variation in pupil test scores in aggregate — or almost 25 per cent of the in-school variables over which educational policymakers have control (Hallinger & Heck, 1996), others place the figure at less than one per cent, and find that the effects appear to be stronger in the U.K. and U.S. than in countries such as the Netherlands (Creemers & Kyriakides, 2007; Witziers et al., 2003). We will discuss such contextual differences in greater detail when we report findings from the ISSPP.

Traditional views of leaders — as special people who set the direction, make the key decisions, and energize the troops — are deeply rooted in an individualistic and non-systemic worldview (Senge, 1990: p. 340). So long as such myths prevail, they reinforce a focus on short-term events and charismatic heroes rather than on systemic forces and collective learning. The contemporary view of effective school leaders has since moved on, and is summed up by Riley and MacBeath:

'Effective' school leaders are distinguished by their vision and passion and by their capacity to bring a critical spirit into the complex and demanding job of headship, whilst at the same time focusing on staff and pupil performance, and on classroom pedagogy. (1998: p. 151)

Contemporary leadership literature has produced further developments in the reconceptualization of successful school leadership. Leadership is now associated with empowerment, transformation and community, and no longer refers only to titular or officially designated leaders, but can be distributed within the school among members of teaching or support staff (Gronn & Hamilton, 2004; Spillane, Camburn & Pareja, 2007). The ability to lead is dependent upon others and the relationships or networks leaders cultivate (Fullan, 2001). Thus, teachers as leaders and teachers as supporters of leaders are beginning to play a central role in determining school reform (distributed leadership will be discussed in greater detain later in the chapter).

Teacher leadership is not a new concept in a number of countries, notably the U.S., Canada, and Australia, where for some time researchers have documented leadership roles and functions of teachers in processes of successful reform (Silins et al., 2000). More recently, researchers have begun exploring efforts that involve teacher leaders at various levels of school improvement in additional countries. This work examines teacher leadership as it relates to distributed leadership, sustainable leadership, teacher teaming and collective approaches to school improvement (Hollingsworth, 2004). An effective school leader, however, must be able to translate this shared vision into day-to-day practice through effective strategic planning and operational target setting (Davies & Ellison, 1999). Day et al. (2001) go further and argue that a school leaders' vision is continually tested by difficult day-to-day decisions:

> Continuing poor teaching by a member of staff, for example, creates a leadership dilemma, cutting across the head teachers' personal framework of values and beliefs, their ideological and educative commitments to the development of everyone in the school community. Engaging in dismissal procedures touches upon the culture of the school, staff morale, and the nature of the relationship between leader and led. (Day et al., 2001, p. 31)

The authors stress that successful head teachers do not shrink from taking 'tough decisions', illustrating the clear, if painful, boundary that must be drawn at times between personal and professional relationships, which are at the heart of the educational health of school communities.

Silins and Mulford (2002) further explored these relationships between leadership, organizational learning and student outcomes. They highlight the importance of teachers working together in collaboration for successful school restructuring and improvement to occur. They argue that teachers cannot create and sustain the conditions for the productive development of children if those conditions do not exist for teachers themselves. If schools are to become better at providing learning for students they must nurture opportunities for teachers to innovate, develop and learn together. Studies have shown that student outcomes are more likely to improve where leadership sources are distributed throughout the school and the school community and where teachers are empowered in areas of importance to them (e.g., Crowther et al., 2000; Silins & Mulford, 2002).

FOCUS ON TEACHING AND LEARNING

A recurring theme we find throughout the literature reviewed is that school leadership is essentially concerned with high quality learning and teaching. Hopkins' vision for authentic school improvement is of, "students engaged in compelling learning situations, created by skilful teachers in school settings designed to promote learning for both of them" (2001b: p. 90). Brighouse and Woods (1999: p. 83) reinforce the centrality of teaching and learning to the school improvement process when they contend that:

The quality of teaching and learning is at the heart of school improvement and real, lasting change can only come from what teachers and learning assistants do consistently in classrooms and other learning areas in the school.

Darling-Hammond and Ifill-Lynch (2006: p.13) take this point further by emphasizing that, "struggling learners benefit when learning goals and the desired quality of learning products are public and explicit."

Understandable as these statements may appear, what happens in schools does not always follow this logic. All too easily other pressing issues take over, which is why some leaders feel that they spend too much time on administration, budget, school site and plant problems. The urgent takes priority over the truly important (Southworth, 2003: p. 14). It is also curious that although schools in the U.K. have policies for almost everything, partly with an eye on the OF-STED inspection process, many schools still do not have policies on teaching and learning. Brighouse and Woods (1999: p. 83) argue that:

In successful schools, the staff have thought through together what constitutes effective teaching and learning in their particular context, based on a set of core values and beliefs, and they continue to speculate how they might improve their practice, involving pupils, parents and governors in the debate. They are aware that their central purpose and the focus of all their endeavors is raising the achievement of pupils and they engage in collaborative activity to ensure this.

CAPACITY BUILDING

A widely accepted definition of capacity building is "the collective competency of the school as an entity to bring about effective change" (Harvey, 2003: p. 21). This implies that schools need to adopt a "fully collaborative culture, which draws upon the full range of professional skills and expertise to be found among the members of the organization" (Fullan & Hargreaves, 1996). Such management cultures move us away from the individuality that characterized schools of the previous generation, heavily dependent on the principal or head teacher as the leader, towards the high-performing organization...distinguished by those teams in which each member is a 'self-led, growing and dynamic individual prepared to contribute to the greater good of the team and the organisation' (Sawatzki, 1997: p. 147). In other words, within the context of school improvement, capacity is the ability to enable all students to reach higher standards. Capacity may be built by improving the performance of teachers, adding more resources, materials or technology and by restructuring how tasks are undertaken (Harris, 2002: p. 51).

Research into capacity building (Hadfield et al., 2002) reveals divergent perspectives between theorists and practitioners. When describing their own approach to leadership and building capacity, head teachers found Stoll's 'action orientated principles' of challenging expectations, establishing a positive climate, working between and beyond schools, managing structures, broadening leadership and listening, especially to students (Stoll & Fink, 1996), among the most useful.

Another factor that increases a school's capacity for improvement is the relative stability within the Senior Leadership Team. Howson (2003) researched the relationship between head teachers' length of service in primary and secondary schools in the U.K. and selected PANDA grades.[1] The analysis revealed a definite association between the length of service of the head teacher and the PANDA grade for the school, whereby A and A* schools had the greatest

percentage of heads that had a length of service of over six years in the same post and E and E*
schools had the smallest percentage of schools with heads having a length of service of six years
plus in the same school.

Heads can sustain improvement through capacity building and equipping teachers to lead
innovation and development. The message is unequivocal: sustaining the impact of improvement
requires the leadership capability of many rather than of few, and improvements in learning are
more likely to be achieved when leadership is instructionally focused on teaching and learning.
It also implies that initiatives are undertaken in a systematic and sustainable manner within the
school setting. Schools continuously transform themselves through their own internal capacity
(Crowther et al., 2002; Wald & Castleberry, 2000). It occurs every day in activities such as sharing of good practices and model lessons, cross-disciplinary teaching, cross-grade activities, and
sharing of subject matter expertise (Aseltine, Faryniarz & Rigazio-DiGilio, 2006).

Staff Development and Collective Review

School improvement is ultimately about the enhancement of student progress, development and
achievements, so it not surprising that most research evidence points towards the importance of
teacher development in school development. It has been shown that schools that are successful
facilitate the learning of both students and teachers (Harris, 2002) and the quality of professional
development and learning consequently becomes an essential component of successful school
improvement interventions. Stoll and Fink (1996) argued that establishing relationships between
teachers helps to extend their morale and encourages the development of a clear and shared sense
of purpose, greater collaboration and collective responsibility for student learning. Collegial relations and collective learning are at the core of building the capacity for school improvement
(Bezzina, 2006). This implies a particular form of teacher development that extends teaching repertoires and engages teachers in changing their practice (Hopkins & Harris, 1997). Highly effective school improvement projects reflect a form of teacher development that concentrates upon,
and goes beyond enhancing teaching skills, knowledge and competency. It involves teachers in
an exploration of different approaches to teaching and learning, often based on fundamental educational principles that are being introduced, revisited or reviewed (Frost, 2003).

Despite these views, and the extent of comprehensive professional development programs
in the U.K. and elsewhere, the impact of such training upon classroom practice remains variable. There is evidence to show that many in-service training programs fail to change teaching
behaviors. Fullan (1992) contends that staff development will never have its intended impact as
long as it is grafted on to schools in the form of discrete, unconnected projects. "The closer one
gets to the culture of schools and the professional lives of teachers, the more complex and daunting the reform agenda becomes" (1992: p. 111). Furthermore, Harris (2002: p. 100) argues that
one of the limitations of traditional in-service training within schools largely resides in the lack
of ongoing support once the day is over. To improve this position implies changes to the way in
which staff development is organized in most schools. In particular, this means "establishing opportunities for immediate and sustained practice, classroom observation, collaboration and peer
coaching" (2002: p. 100).

Moreover, the literature points towards the centrality of collaborative enquiry and reflective practice in the school improvement process. Costa and Kallick (2000: p. 60) suggest that,
"every school's goal should be to habituate reflection throughout the organization individually
and collectively, with teachers, students, and the school community." Reflective organizations
are places where people can bring themselves fully to work. One powerful way in which teach-

ers are encouraged to reflect upon and improve their practice is through a process of enquiry, a means by which they can consider their work in a critical way. It has been suggested that engaging in school-based enquiry is an essential element of the teacher's role (York-Barr et al., 2001). Enquiry and reflection are expected of teachers as part of their professional learning and development.

If schools are serious about school improvement, the centrality of teacher development in that process needs to be recognized. For improvement to take place, all stakeholders need to be involved and engaged. School improvement is at heart a collective activity where organizational learning is a dynamic and systemic process (Harris 2002: p. 100). Schools that improve become learning communities that generate the capacity and capability to sustain that improvement. They are the "communities of practice" (Sergiovanni, 2000: p.140) that provide a context for collaboration and the generation of shared meaning.

Parental and Community Involvement

Challenging schools are often located in communities of extreme socio-economic disadvantage and as a consequence they have to deal with problems that are common by-products of such contexts: poor nutrition, high rates of transience, drug use and crime. The community may view the school with mistrust and suspicion; as having relatively little to do with their lives and aspirations (Louis & Miles, 1990). A main task facing leaders in schools facing challenging circumstances is to build bridges with their community and to form relationships with families that extended beyond just getting them into the school.

Harris and Chapman (2002: p. 15) established that head teachers believe that schools with solid and lasting links with the local community are more likely to gain their support and loyalty in difficult times. In their study, head teachers who implemented successful improvement programs had created opportunities for parents to come in to school, to talk to teachers, to use the facilities and to see the school as a resource for them and their children. They also tried to break down barriers by seeking ways to integrate and involve parents in school life. Social, sporting and charitable events offered points of entry for some parents, but evening classes and community meetings were also used to encourage parents to view the school as an important resource.

Landsman (2006) reports strategies that schools in Minneapolis, Minnesota introduced to find out about students' home lives and underlying needs, such as phoning parents and holding conferences in locations closer to their residences. Other teachers used staff release days to visit neighborhoods and talk to parents in their own homes, thus better understanding the contexts in which students live. Hargreaves (1995: p. 20) describes this as a 'cultural relationship' with the parent community. In his analysis of parent-school relationships, he suggested that there are four forms of relationship between parents and schools: 'market-based', 'managerial', 'personal' and 'cultural'.

'Market-based relationships' treat parents as clients and consumers who can send their children to the schools of their choice. The connection is a contractual one that tends to individualize and fracture collective social relationships between schools and parents, whereas the 'managerial relationship' approach is better at creating than building communities and is a poor solution for the permeable school. It diverts teachers' and head teachers' energies more to procedural accountability than to personal and emotional responsiveness, and has yet to show demonstrable benefits in terms of student outcomes (Fullan, 1993, in Hargreaves, 1995: p. 18). 'Personal relationships' between teachers and parents, by contrast, concentrate on the most important interest that parents have in school; the achievement and well-being of their children. This kind of relationship aims at bringing principles commonly advocated for collegial relationships among teachers, such as openness, trust, risk-taking and collaboration, to relationships among teachers, children and their parents.

'Cultural relationships' are founded on principles of openness and collaboration developed collectively with groups of parents and the community as a whole. When schools involve communities in the uncertainties of change, assistance, support and understanding are more likely to be forthcoming. Instead seeing community involvement as tantamount to displaying dirty linen, it is better for schools to see successful change as bringing the community into its 'beautiful launderette' — a communal place of work and conversation where all do their washing together. Involving parents more closely has the potential to develop new understandings by each party of the other's cultural practices and thus lead to the type of 'reciprocity,' which Harry (1992) argues is needed. Cairney (2000) states that schools need to respond to the diverse cultural resources of families in positive ways, rather than simply attempting to transmit school knowledge to them.

Improving the Learning Environment

Purkey, Novak and Schmidt (1996) and the Education Trust (2005) emphasize the importance of the 'welcoming' aspect of schools facing challenging circumstances and the positive effect it can have on students' self-esteem, especially those coming from disadvantaged backgrounds. The research they carried out in the U.S. and Canada showed that significant improvements to the learning environment may have positive effects on students' learning outcomes. The majority of schools in the U.K. study by Harris and Chapman (2002: p. 14) that implemented successful improvement programs were located in surroundings that were very poor. A number were located on council estates or in inner city contexts that presented run-down and hostile environments. The physical condition of these schools was initially very poor with leaking classrooms, broken windows, graffiti-covered furniture and litter-covered corridors. One of the first actions taken by head teachers in this study was to improve the immediate environment. Resources were allocated to painting and repair work, new furniture, new reception areas, display boards and refurbishing the staff room. Emphasis was placed on litter removal and students were given the task of sanding down desks to eradicate graffiti. This strategy had a symbolic and real purpose as it demonstrated to staff, students and parents that the school was changing and improving.

Harris and Chapman (2002) conclude that making significant improvements to the learning environment, especially at the initial stages of the school improvement process, could provide the psychological leverage needed to give the implementation of other improvement strategies a better prospect of succeeding.

Focus and Belief that All Students Can Learn

Scherer (2006: p. 7) talks about the need to support what she describes as 'silent strugglers,' "invisible strugglers, falling through the cracks and being written off ...." Landsman (2006) emphasizes the need for teachers to be "bearers of hope" in contexts that are full of depression and despair. Various studies, such as those cited, go a long way to show that when teachers work collaboratively; when they work together to identify the 'real' student(s) they are facing daily; when they create work which is doable, manageable and concrete (Darling-Hammond & Ifill-Lynch, 2006); when they are hopeful, compassionate, flexible, treat students with respect and at the same time create clear expectations and a sense of purpose and meaning (Cushman, 2006; Landsman, 2006); when students are held accountable (Miller, 2006); then improvements can be noted at various levels.

These recurring themes of successful school leadership practices also appeared in the work of the Task Force on Developing Research in Educational Leadership, commissioned by Division 'A' (Educational Administration) of the American Educational Research Association in 2001. In its report, *A New Agenda for Research in Educational Leadership* (Firestone & Riehl, 2005), Leithwood and Riehl (2005) provide a comprehensive synthesis of research about what is known about leadership practices linked to successful school improvement. The core practices they described helped to establish the analytic framework for the International Successful School Principalship Project (ISSPP), which along with a discussion of distributed leadership comprise the next sections of this chapter.

The reason the ISSPP is examined is that it is one of the few large scale studies to explore successful leadership practices across multiple contexts in order to get a better sense of how these common themes get mediated by the values and systems that structure education in different nations. In other words, are there practices of successful school leaders that are common regardless of context? Are there some that are context specific? And, even in the cases where commonalities exist, are they enabled differently in different locales?

CORE PRACTICES FOR SUCCESS IN DIVERSE CONTEXTS: THE ISSPP

Using selection criteria similar to those employed for this chapter (i.e., focusing exclusively on empirical studies in refereed journals), Leithwood and Riehl (2005) reviewed many of the articles that we have already discussed. These authors concluded that considered collectively, this body of work led them to make four strong claims about school leadership, the most pertinent in relation to the objectives of this chapter being that a core set of basic leadership practices is necessary, though insufficient, for achieving improved student success in almost all contexts. Specifically, these core leadership practices for success are:

1. *Setting directions* by identifying and articulating a vision, fostering the acceptance of group goals and creating high performance expectations.
2. *Developing people* by offering intellectual stimulation, providing individualized support and an appropriate role model.
3. *Redesigning the organization* by strengthening school cultures, modifying organizational structures and building collaborative processes (Leithwood & Riehl, 2005: pp. 19–22).

One can readily see how the earlier described themes of leadership focused on teaching and learning, capacity building, staff development and collective review, parental and community involvement, improving the learning environment, and a strong belief in students can be nested within these core practices. Indeed, it is this consistency in the research findings that led Leithwood, et al. (2004) to conclude that among school-related factors, leadership is second only to classroom instruction in contributing to what students learn. Moreover, this congruence in findings lends confidence to the use of these core practices as an analytic framework for examining the actions of successful principals and head teachers across a variety of national contexts, and as such leads us to the International Successful School Principalship Project (ISSPP).

Begun in 2001, the ISSPP has been an on-going, coordinated attempt by researchers in eight nations: Australia (examining schools in Victoria and Tasmania), Canada, China (examining schools in Shanghai), Denmark, England, Norway, Sweden and the United States (examining schools in Western New York), to create a rich database of case studies in the first phase that has been completed; survey responses in the second phase, which has begun; and school and leader observations in the third phase, to begin in 2008. The ultimate goal is to help researchers and practitioners better understand what successful school principals do across diverse contexts, and then apply these findings to the preparation of future school leaders.

As it evolved, the guiding framework and methodology for the ISSPP drew from several sources including leading schools in times of change (Day, Harris, Hadfield, Tolley & Beresford, 2000); successful school leadership (Gurr, Drysdale, DiNatale, Ford, Hardy, & Swann, 2003); leadership for school-community partnerships (Kilpatrick, Johns, Mulford, Falk & Prescott, 2002); leadership for organizational learning and improved student outcomes (Mulford, Silins & Leithwood, 2004); and the previously mentioned review of the literature on successful school leadership by Leithwood and Riehl (2005).

In the first phase, ISSPP case study sites were selected using a combination of evidence of improved student achievement on standardized tests, principals' exemplary reputations, and/or other indicators of site-specific success during a principal's tenure. The U.S. team added one additional requirement for site selection, i.e., the school had to be listed as 'high need' by New York State's Education Department, a categorization based upon the percentage of the student body eligible for free or reduced lunch. Therefore, the sites examined by the U.S. team were exclusively "challenging" contexts. While this was not a selection criterion for the other national teams, 'challenging' schools were also found in England and Australia, and to a much lesser extent in Norway, Denmark, Sweden and Shanghai.

This approach to case site selection, i.e., working backwards from trends in student outcome measures in relation to a principal's tenure, was based upon an *a priori* and circumstantial argument that if school improvement occurred during a principal's term, then he or she may have had something to do with the school's success. By collecting 'multiple-perspective' case data through interviews with each school's principal, its teachers, support staff, parents and students, we then tested this premise. These key school participants were asked if they believed the principal had played a key role in their school's success and, if so, what was it that the principal had done to make it happen. A common, semi-structured interview protocol was developed specifically for use by all ISSPP teams and, for the purpose of triangulation, secondary data were also obtained from official school documents, minutes of meetings, press reports, historical sources and ethnographic notes made during visits by the research teams.

Quite simply, the ISSPP sought answers to several overarching questions:

1. What practices do successful principals use?
2. Do these practices vary across contexts?
3. Under what conditions are the effects of such practices heightened or diminished?
4. What variables link principal's leadership to student achievement?

In essence, this study connects the school effectiveness research concern with outcomes to the school improvement concern with processes, focusing specifically on the practices of a school's formal leader and then expands this inquiry trans-nationally. Over the first six years of the ISSPP, more than sixty cases were developed across the different national contexts, making it one of the largest international studies of successful school leadership ever undertaken. Typical of qualitative research, findings from these cases were primarily descriptive and informative, therefore transference to other contexts must be undertaken with caution. Nevertheless, the scope and quantitative breadth of the ISSPP go some way in overcoming weaknesses typical of qualitative research (Leithwood, 2005).

INITIAL FINDINGS FROM THE ISSPP

In his analysis of the seven country reports first published collectively in the *Journal of Educational Administration,* 43(6), Leithwood (2005) concluded that the ISSPP has produced "progress on a broken front." He notes that, collectively, these national reports support the existence of a core set of leadership practices that are necessary for improved student achievement in almost any context, though insufficient by themselves. However, a careful examination and comparison of the reports reveals how the enactment of these core practices were adapted by principals to their specific contexts in order to achieve their anticipated effects. Leithwood (2005: pp. 621–22) contends that:

> From these data, it is reasonable to conclude that successful principal leadership practices are common across contexts in their general form but highly adaptable and contingent in their specific enactment. As Ray, Clegg, and Gordon (2004) explain, leadership is a "reflexively automatic" activity and such activity is never innocent of context.

More specifically, each of the core practices was enacted differently, but successfully, as a result of and in relation to differences in national context. For example, direction setting by principals in the U.S. cases (Jacobson et al., 2005) was effectively linked to national, state and local demands for greater accountability. These accountability pressures helped principals set a school's direction because of the relatively single-minded policy focus of standards and high stake testing. Principals capitalized on this clarity by shaping teachers' discourse around goals related to mastery of literacy and numeracy, and then they used state testing to leverage their high expectations for student and faculty performance. Test scores and other accountability data were used to determine school goals and improvement plans; to stimulate collaborative dialogue and recognition of the importance of professional development; and to monitor progress and overcome obstacles to improvement (Giles et al., 2007).

In contrast to the relatively short-term direction setting found in the U.S. cases, and to a lesser extent those in England (Day, 2005), the shared visions of successful Australian principals tended to focus more on learning over a lifetime (Gurr et al., 2005); and it was the development of democratic values that were the focus of discussions about school direction setting in Norway (Møller et al., 2005), Denmark (Moos et al., 2005) and Sweden (Hoog et al., 2005). In other words, direction setting was found in every case, but the actual directions set were context-specific and sensitive to policies and/or values prominent in each nation.

The country reports also provided examples of principals working successfully at developing people, such as principals in Shanghai (Wong, 2005) helping teachers develop skills of self-analysis, and Australian (Gurr et al., 2005) and Norwegian principals (Møller et al., 2005) engaging teachers in critical reflection and productive debate. In every national context, successful principals were highly visible and readily accessible to staff, students and parents, often modeling the type of professional practice and behaviors they expected of others. Although specific expectations of good practice were often contextually sensitive, the more general practice of helping others to reach that goal was common to all.

Finally, successful principals in most country reports redesigned their organizations by fostering cultures of collaboration through teamwork (in England), distributed leadership (particularly in the Scandinavian cases), the development of broad based governance structures (Australia) and de-privatizing teaching practice (U.S.). Most notably in the northern European cases, leadership as participation did not need to be developed, as it already existed as a traditional value. This was particularly the case in Norway, where the term 'team on top' was used to explain the preeminence of collective over individual leadership. In contrast, the cases from Shanghai illustrated a different meaning of leadership distribution — one more specific to cultures characterized by "high power distance" (Hofstede, 1980) such as China, in which people demonstrate considerable respect for hierarchy, position, age and formal authority. As a result, Chinese principals involved their staff more often in decisions about how things would be done than in deciding what it was that had to be done.

These diverse, culturally sensitive perspectives about how leadership is distributed and the meanings that different cultures ascribe to it was an unintended outcome of the ISSPP study. Distributed leadership has gained considerable currency of late, yet most studies have tended to focus on a limited number of sites, often within the same LEA or state/provincial jurisdiction (see, e.g., Gronn & Hamilton, 2004; Firestone & Martinez, 2007; Leithwood et al., 2005; Mayrowetz et al., 2007, and Spillane et al., 2007). Moreover, while some view 'distributed leadership' as a deliberate element of organizational work redesign having potential for school improvement (Firestone & Martinez, 2007, Leithwood et al., 2005; Mayrowetz et al., 2007) — and in some cases going so far as to design co-principalships (Gronn & Hamilton, 2004), others see it as just an alternative 'distributed' perspective that simply helps to explain regular leadership/management interactions between formal leaders and their subordinates, so that in any given moment it is often difficult to determine who is leading and who is following. Since the focus of the ISSPP was specifically on principals and the practices that seemed to facilitate success, the distribution of leadership functions, whether intentional or not, was a theme that emerged within the core practice of organizational redesign, but not as a focus in and of itself. Initial impressions, as noted above, suggest that collaboration with teachers and parents supported school success, but whether these types of collaboration can be construed as synonymous with distributed leadership remains debatable and a subject in need of further examination. At the very least, it may help to explain national differences in the aggregate direct and indirect effects of leadership on student achievement reported earlier.

SUCCESSFUL LEADERSHIP IN CHALLENGING SCHOOLS

One aspect of the ISSPP that intentionally sought to expand prior successful school research was on how leadership works in challenging contexts. When looking specifically at cases of successful leadership in challenging schools, principals seem to bring certain key dispositions to the task, most notably a passion for the socially just and equitable education of the children and the communities they serve (Jacobson et al., 2005; Day & Leithwood, 2007). Their enthusiasm was often accompanied by persistence and optimism in pursuit of those goals, and in the high accountability contexts of England, Australia and the United States, these principals used increasing external demands as a tool for overcoming resistance to change on the part of those teachers who questioned the innate academic abilities of their students. As Jacobson et al. (2005a: p. 35) noted in their examination of three high poverty inner city elementary schools, the principals would not tolerate teachers 'blaming the victims:'

> All three principals recognized the barriers to learning and academic achievement that poverty can produce, but none would allow these conditions to be used as excuses for poor performance. Poverty may be the current reality of many of these children's lives, but it need not be the final determinant of their futures.

Moreover, these ISSPP findings about successful leadership in challenging schools provide support for Harris and Chapman (2002) contention that upgrading the learning environment at the initial stages of a school improvement initiative is a prerequisite for the successful implementation of other important strategies. This was an absolute necessity in the schools studied by the U.S. team, where students and teachers had legitimate concerns about their physical safety. Jacobson et al. (2005a: p. 33) described this practice as, "closing the school to open it:"

> In all three cases, the principal began her tenure by physically securing the building. This included limiting access to the school and screening visitors. It also meant more careful scrutiny of who had access to classrooms and when it was appropriate to enter, so as not to disrupt instruction. These security initiatives were coupled with efforts to make the school more inviting to children and adults alike. In essence, while doors were being locked, the school was actually more open than in the past, so long as your purpose in coming to school passed the aforementioned test of being in the interest of children.

RECOMMENDATIONS FOR FUTURE RESEARCH

While ISSPP findings lend support for the contention that there exists a set of core leadership practices necessary for success in almost all contexts, the cases also reveal that each of these core practices was best realized in ways that were culturally sensitive. Attempts to enumerate lists of 'what works' seem to make little sense unless such lists are embedded in rich descriptions of where they have worked, especially in terms of cultural expectations and national and local policies and practices. If we are to better understand relationships between leadership and student achievement, then Leithwood et al.'s (2005) conclusion that the ISSPP findings represent 'progress on a broken front' can be applied quite appropriately not just for work still to be done by this project, but for research in school leadership more generally. For example, the schools examined in almost all of the studies referenced in this chapter are located in Western or Western-oriented national contexts. Expanding both the number and type of national contexts studied (e.g., public and private schools in Africa, Latin America and the Middle East), would help to fill existing gaps in what we know about how school leadership effects student academic and affective achievement, as well as the complexities that exist in the perspectives and practices of educators across the globe.

In addition, future research needs to further tease out the individual and combined influences of key classroom and school factors such as time on task; quality of instruction; the curricular and instructional climate; developing a safe and orderly climate; school culture; and teacher commitment, to name just a few, and how these factors are themselves influenced directly and indirectly by school leadership. Each of these factors emerged in the various studies reported as having the potential to enhance school success. Unfortunately, linkages between any and all of these variables with school and national contexts, and then to student success remain unclear.

Prior research and evidence from the ISSPP cases also suggest that certain demographic and personal characteristics, such as student background factors like wealth, prior achievement and family educational culture; or organizational characteristics such as governance (e.g., public, private), location (e.g., rural, urban), size (numbers of students and faculty) and level of instruction (elementary, middle, secondary); and even the dispositions of school leaders themselves (e.g., passion, persistence and a commitment to social justice) may effect a school's success in improving student achievement, but yet there remains insufficient evidence at this time to feel confident about making strong claims with regard to these factors.

The studies reported make it clear that effective schooling is a dynamic, ongoing process (see e.g., Creemers & Kyriakides, 2007; Slater & Teddlie, 1992); a process which suggests the need for more longitudinal studies to be built into this line of research. Almost all the studies reported are relatively short in duration, perhaps a few years at most. In other words, they are just snapshots of a period in a school's life when it achieved some measure of success. Unfortunately, the issue of sustainability has gone noticeably under-examined. We believe that this topic requires considerably more attention, especially as we come to understand that school improvement cannot be dependent upon one person. Some obvious questions worthy of further exploration include: What happens to schools after a successful leader leaves? How can distributed leadership and organizational learning sustain improvement over time? Can effective leaders bring their templates for success to subsequent schools? Can leadership succession planning help schools sustain improvement initiatives?

Finally, while appreciating that the need to link leadership with student academic achievement has been of primary importance given the pressures of current accountability measures, we recommend the need to further explore whether and how school leadership affects the affective outcomes of students, especially for students with special needs and those in challenging schools. This reveals the importance of expanding the current criteria of measuring effectiveness.

RECOMMENDATIONS FOR LEADERSHIP PREPARATION

The purpose of this chapter has been to report what peer-reviewed research reveals about the effects of school leadership on student achievement, and though we have some understanding of the core practices school leaders need to contribute to the improvement of student learning, we know far less about how school leaders actually acquire the knowledge of and ability to successfully utilize these practices. As subsequent chapters of this handbook will attest, many but not all school leaders receive some type of formal, prescribed preparation, either prior to their official service or as a part of their on-going professional development. Regardless of when such training occurs, the findings we have reported suggest several recommendations for leadership preparation, with the first being that aspiring leaders be introduced to the core practices of setting directions, developing people and redesigning the organization. Similar to an artist, scientist and/or craftsperson, the school administrator must have an awareness of the key practices needed to succeed in their work. Second, they need to understand that while these practices are necessary for success in terms of student achievement, there is no single template to guide their application. Instead, leaders must learn to recognize and appreciate the cultural, political and economic environments in which their schools reside. Aspiring school leaders need to understand the extent to which these essential practices are mediated by context, especially in those schools confronting the greatest challenges. Thus, we further recommend that in developing the understanding and application of core practices, preparation programs give particular consideration to how they apply in challenging, high poverty schools, where the creation of a safe, nurturing learning environment is a prerequisite to school improvement.

One component of preparation we would encourage is that all programs require at least two administrator internship placements including, whenever possible, at least some period of time in high poverty or otherwise challenged schools. Moreover, these clinical placements should be in schools with leaders who have proven records of successfully improving student achievement, so that aspiring administrators have an initial road map they can use in the future.

The idea of creating high quality clinical placements should not be reserved only for aspiring administrators. Mentoring programs should also be developed so that acting principals and head teachers have the opportunity to observe first-hand, the practice of exemplary school leaders, or by giving these exemplary leaders the chance to visit and consult in struggling schools.

CONCLUSIONS

In this foundational chapter we have attempted to provide a broad survey of the literature on school leadership, especially in terms of its effects on student academic and affective performance. We began with the 1966 Coleman Report on Equality of Educational Opportunity and then followed the evolution of this line of research from the Effective Schools and School Improvement literatures of the 1970s, 1980s and 1990s, through subsequent studies conducted in 2007, particularly the International Successful School Principalship Project (ISSPP). Several key themes echo through the years, specifically, that school success, as it relates to student achievement, depends upon leadership (whether formal and/or distributed) that focuses on teaching and learning; builds capacity, especially through staff development; involves parents and the community; works on improving the learning environment, particularly in terms of safety in challenging contexts; and finally, commits everyone to the belief that all children can learn.

Leithwood and Riehl (2005) distilled these themes into three core practices: setting directions, developing people, and redesigning the organization, which the ISSPP confirmed in seven different national contexts, but which also uncovered context specific differences in how these core leadership practices were enacted. Of particular note was the enactment of these core practices in challenging, high poverty schools, where students are at the greatest risk for failure.

The chapter concluded with recommendations for both future research and the preparation of aspiring and current school leaders. By providing empirically supported linkages between what school leaders do and the successful improvement of student performance, we hope to have laid a solid foundation for subsequent chapters that will go into greater detail about the preparation of educational leaders worldwide.

NOTE

1. PANDA reports provide an overview of each school's performance in relation to other schools using data from OFSTED, the Department for Education and Skills (DFES) and the Qualifications and Curriculum Authority (QCA). Throughout the PANDA, a school's performance is assessed against the national average, and, using the national benchmarks in the autumn package, in comparison with other schools in similar contexts as defined by free school meal statistics.

REFERENCES

Ainscow, M., Hopkins, D., Southworth, G. and West, M. (1994) *Creating the conditions for school improvement*, London: David Fulton.

Aseltine, J., Faryniarz, J. and Rigazio-DiGilio, A. (2006) *Supervision for learning*, Alexandria, VA: Association for Supervision and Curriculum Development.

Bezzina, C. (2006) "The road less traveled": Professional communities in secondary schools. *Theory Into Practice*, 45 (2): 159–167.

Brighouse, T. and Woods, D. (1999) *How to improve your school*, London: Routledge.

Brookover, W., Beady, C., Flood, P., Schweitzer, J. and Wisenbaker, J. (1979) *School social systems and student achievement: Schools make a difference*, New York: Praeger.

Brookover, W. and Lezotte, L. (1979) Changes in school characteristics coincident with changes in student achievement. East Lansing, MI: Institute for Research on Teaching.

Cairney, T. (2000) Beyond the classroom walls: The rediscovery of the family and community as partners in education. *Education Review*, 52 (2): 163–174.

Coleman, J. et al., (1966) 'Coleman Report', Equality of Educational Opportunity, Washington, DC: U.S. Government Printing Office

Costa, A. and Kallick, B. (2000) Getting into the habit of reflection. *Educational Leadership*, 57 (7): 60–62.

Creemers, B. and Kyriakides, L. (2007) *The dynamics of educational effectiveness: A contribution to policy, practice and theory in contemporary Schools*, London: Routledge Falmer.

Crow, G. and Grogan, M. (2005) The development of leadership thought and practice in the United States, in F. English (Ed.), Sage *handbook of educational leadership: Advances in theory, research, and practice*, Thousand Oaks, CA: Sage Publications.

Crowther, F., Hann, L., McMaster, J., and Ferguson, M. (2000) Leadership for successful school revitalization: Lessons from recent Australian research. Paper presented at the annual meeting of AERA, New Orleans, LA.

Crowther, F., Kaagan, S., Ferguson, M., and Hann, L. (2002) *Developing teacher leaders: How teacher leadership enhances school success*, Thousand Oaks, CA: Corwin Press.

Cushman, K. (2006) Help U.S. care enough to learn. *Educational Leadership*, 63 (5): 34–37.

Darling-Hammond, L. and Ifill-Lynch, O. (2006) If they'd only do their work! *Educational Leadership*, 63, 5, 8–13.

Davies, B., and Ellison, L., (1999) *Strategic direction and development of the school*, London: Routledge.

Day, C. (2005) Sustaining success in challenging contexts: Leadership in English schools. *Journal of Educational Administration*, 43 (6): 573–583.

Day, C., Harris, A. and Hadfield, M. (2001) Grounding knowledge of schools in stakeholder realities: A multi-perspective study of effective school leaders. *School Leadership & Management*, 21 (1): 19–42.

Day, C., Harris, A., Hadfield, M., Tolley, H., & Beresford, J., (2000) *Leading Schools in Times of Change*, Buckingham, UK: Open University Press.

Day, C. and Leithwood, K. (eds. 2007) *Successful principal leadership in times of change: An international perspective*. Dordrecht, The Netherlands, Springer.

Duke, D. (1987) *School Leadership and Instructional Improvement*, New York: Random House.

Edmonds, R.R. (1982) Programs of school improvement: an overview. *Educational Leadership*, 40 (3): 4–11.

Education Trust (2005). *Gaining traction, gaining ground: How some high schools accelerate learning for struggling students*. Education Trust, Washington, DC.

Firestone, W. and Martinez, C. (2007) Districts, teacher leaders, and distributed leadership: Changing instructional practice. *Leadership and Policy in Schools,* 6 (1): 3–35.

Firestone, W. and Riehl, C. (Eds.) (2005) *A new agenda for research in educational leadership*. New York: Teachers College Press.

Frost, D. (2003) Teacher leadership: Towards a leadership agenda. Paper presented within the symposium: 'Leadership for Learning: the Cambridge Network', 16th International Congress for School Effectiveness and Improvement, Sydney, Australia.

Fullan, M. (1992) *Successful school improvement – The implementation perspective and beyond*, Buckingham: Open University Press.

Fullan, M. (2001) *Leading in a culture of change*, San Francisco: Jossey-Bass.

Fullan, M. and Hargreaves, A. (1996) *What's worth fighting for in your school*, New York: Teachers College Press.

Giles, C., Jacobson, S., Johnson, L. and Ylimaki, R. (2007) Against the odds: Successful principals in challenging U.S. schools, In C. Day and K. Leithwood (Eds.). *Successful principal leadership in times of change: An international perspective* (pp. 155–168), Dordrecht, The Netherlands, Springer.

Giles, C., Johnson, L., Brooks, S. and Jacobson, S. (2005) Building bridges, building community: Transformational leadership in a challenging urban context. *Journal of School Leadership,* 15 (5): 519–545.

Gray, J., Reynolds, D., Fitz-Gibbon, C. and Jesson, D. (1996) *Merging traditions: The future of research on school effectiveness and school improvement,* London: Cassell.

Gray, J., Hopkins, D., Reynolds, D., Wilcox, B., Farrell, S. and Jesson, D. (1999) *Improving schools: Performance and potential,* Buckingham: Open University Press.

Gronn, P. and Hamilton, A. (2004) A bit more life in the leadership: Co-principalship as distributed leadership practice. *Leadership and Policy in Schools,* 3 (1): 3–35.

Gurr, D., Drysdale, L., Di Natale, E., Ford, P., Hardy, R. & Swann, R. (2003). Successful shool leadership in Victoria: Three case studies, leading and managing, 9(1): 18–37.

Gurr, D., Drysdale, L. and Mulford, B. (2005) Successful principal leadership: Australian case studies. *Journal of Educational Administration,* 43 (6): 539–551.

Hadfield, M., Chapman, C., Curryer, I. and Barrett, P. (2002) *Building capacity: Developing your school.* London: National College for School Leadership.

Hallinger, P. and Heck, R. (1996) Reassessing the principal's role in school effectiveness: A review of empirical research, 1980–1995. *Educational Administration Quarterly,* 32(1): 5–44.

Hargreaves, A. (1995) *Rethinking educational change,* invited keynote address to the ACEA International Conference, Sydney July 1995.

Harris, A. (2002) *School improvement – What's in it for schools?* London: Routledge Falmer.

Harris, A. and Chapman, C. (2002) *Effective leadership in schools facing challenging circumstances,* London: National College for School Leadership.

Harry, B. (1992) An ethnographic study of cross-cultural communication with Puerto Rican-American families in the special education system. *American Educational Research Journal,* 29: 471–494.

Harvey, S. (2003) Looking to the future in *Ldr,* London: National College for School Leadership, 1,7 (Feb), 21–23.

Hofstede, G. (1980) *Culture's consequences: International differences in work-related values,* Thousand Oaks, CA: Sage.

Hollingsworth, A. (2004) *The school as a professional learning community: Perspectives from Tasmanian and English Schools on the essentials for creating a community of learning in a school.* International Research Perspectives, National College for School Leadership, Spring.

Hoog, J., Johansson, O. and Olofsson, A. (2005) Successful principalship: The Swedish case. *Journal of Educational Administration,* 43 (6): 595–606.

Hopkins, D. (ed.1987) *Improving the quality of schooling,* London: Falmer Press.

Hopkins, D. and Harris, A. (1997) Understanding the school's capacity for development: Growth states and strategies. *School Leadership and Management,* 17 (3): 401–411.

Hopkins, D. (2001a) *School improvement for real.* London: Falmer Press.

Hopkins, D. (2001b) *Improving the quality of education for all.* London: David Fulton Publishers.

Hopkins, D., Ainscow, M. and West, M. (1994) *School improvement in an era of change,* London: Cassell.

Howson, J., (2003) The Relationship between Headteachers' Length of Service in Primary and Secondary Schools and Selected PANDA Grades, London: National College for School Leadership.

Jacobson, S., Brooks, S., Giles, C., Johnson, L. and Ylimaki, R. (2007) Successful leadership in three high poverty urban elementary schools, *Leadership and Policy in Schools,* 6 (4): 1–27.

Jacobson, S., Brooks, S., Giles, C., Johnson, L. and Ylimaki, R. (2005) *Leadership in high poverty schools: An examination of three urban elementary schools.* Albany, NY: The Education Finance Research Consortium. Retrieved December 2004 from: http://www.albany.edu/edfin

Jacobson, S., Johnson, L., Giles, C. and Ylimaki, R. (2005) Successful leadership in U.S. schools: Enabling principles, enabling schools. *Journal of Educational Administration,* 43 (6): 607–618.

Jencks, C. et al., (1972) *Inequality: A reassessment of the effect of family and schooling in America,* New York: Harper & Row.

Kilpatrick, S., Johns, S., Mulford, B., Falk, L., & Prescott, L. (2002) *More than Education: Leadership for rural school-community partnerships.* Retrieved June 2002 from: http://www.rirdc.gov.au/reports/HCC/02-055.pdf

Landsman, J. (2006) Bearers of hope, *Educational Leadership*, 63 (5): 26–32.

Leithwood, K. (2005) Understanding successful principal leadership: Progress on a broken front. *Journal of Educational Administration,* 43 (6): 619–629.

Leithwood, K., Mascall, B., Strauss, T., Sacks, R., Memon, N. and Yashkina, A. (2005) Distributing leadership to make schools smarter: Taking the ego out of the system, *Leadership and Policy in Schools,* 6 (1): 37–67.

Leithwood, K. and Riehl, C. (2005). What do we already know about educational leadership? In W. Firestone and C. Riehl (eds.) *A new agenda for research in educational leadership* (pp. 12–27), New York: Teachers College Press.

Leithwood, K., Seashore Louis, K., Anderson, S. and Wahlstrom, K. (2004) *How leadership influences student learning,* Learning from Leadership Project, University of Minnesota and University of Toronto, Commissioned by The Wallace Foundation.

Louis, K. and Miles, M. (1990) *Improving the urban high school: What works and why*, New York: Teachers College Press.

MacBeath, J. (ed. 1988) *Effective school leadership: Responding to change*, London: Paul Chapman.

Marzano, R. J., Waters, T. and McNulty, B. A. (2005) *School leadership that works: From research to results,* Alexandria, VA: Association for Supervision and Curriculum Development.

Mayrowetz, D., Murphy, J., Seashore Louis, K. and Smylie, M. (2007) Distributed leadership as work redesign: Retrofitting the job characteristics model. *Leadership and Policy in Schools,* 6 (1): 69–101.

Miller, M. (2006) Where they are: Working with marginalized students. *Educational Leadership*, 63 (5): 50–54.

Møller, J., Eggen, A., Fuglestad, O., Langfeldt, G., Presthus, A., Skrovset, S., Stjernstrom, E. and Vedoy, G. (2005) Successful school leadership: The Norwegian case. *Journal of Educational Administration,* 43 (6): 584–594.

Moos, L., Kresjsler, J., Koford, K. and Jensen, B. (2005) Successful school principalship in Danish schools, *Journal of Educational Administration,* 43 (6): 563–572.

Mosteller, F. and Moynihan, D. (1972) A pathbreaking report: Further studies of the Coleman Report, in F. Mosteller and D. Moynihan (ed.) *On equality of educational opportunity,* New York: Vintage.

Mulford, B., Silins, H. and Leithwood, K. (2004) *Educational leadership for organisational learning and improved student outcomes*. Dordrecht, The Netherlands: Kluwer.

National Commission of Education (1996). *Success against the odds*. London: Routledge.

Potter, D., Reynolds, D. and Chapman, C. (2002) School improvement for schools facing challenging circumstances: A review of research and practice. *School Leadership & Management*, 22 (1): 243–26.

Purkey, W., Novak, M., and Schmidt, J. (1996) *Inviting school success: A self-concept approach to teaching, learning, and democratic practice (3rd ed.),* Belmont, CA: Wadsworth.

Ray, T., Clegg, S. and Gordon, R. (2004) A new look at dispersed leadership, knowledge and context, in Storey, L. (ed.) *Leadership in organization: Current issues and key trends* (pp. 319–336). London: Routledge.

Reynolds, D., Hopkins, D. and Stoll, L. (1993) Linking school effectiveness knowledge and school improvement practice: Towards a synergy, *School Effectiveness & School Improvement*, 4 (1): 37–58.

Reynolds, D. (1999) School effectiveness, school improvement and contemporary educational policies, in J. Demaine (ed.) *Contemporary educational policy and politics*, London: MacMillan, pp. 150–162.

Riley, K. and MacBeath, J. (1998) Effective leaders and effective schools, in MacBeath J (Ed.) *Effective school leadership: Responding to change* London: Chapman.

Rutter, M., Maughan, B., Mortimore, P. and Ouston, J. (1979) *Fifteen thousand hours,* London: Open Books.

Sawatzki, M. (1997) Leading and managing staff for high performance, in B. Davies & L. Ellison, *School leadership for the 21st century*, London: Routledge.

Scheerens, J. and Bosker, R. (1997). *The foundations of educational effectiveness* New York: Elsevier.

Scherer, M. (2006) The silent strugglers, *Educational Leadership*, 63 (5): 7.

Senge, P. (1990) *The fifth discipline*, New York: Doubleday.

Sergiovanni, T. (2000) *The lifeworld of leadership*, London: Jossey-Bass.

Sergiovanni, T. (2001) *Leadership: What's in it for schools?* London: Routledge Falmer.

Silins, H. and Mulford, B. (2002) *Leadership and school results: Second international handbook of educational leadership and administration*, Dordrecht, The Netherlands: Kluwer.

Silins, H., Mulford, B., Zarins, S. and Bishop, P. (2000) Leadership for organisational learning in Australian secondary schools, in K. Leithwood (Ed.) *Understanding schools as intelligent systems*, Stamford, CT: JAI Press, pp. 267–292.

Slater, R., and Teddlie, C., (1992) Toward a theory of school effectiveness and leadership, *School Effectiveness and School Improvement*, 3 (4): 247–257.

Southworth, G. (2003) Balancing act – the Importance of Learning-Centred Leadership in *Ldr,* London: National College for School Leadership, 1,6 (Feb), 13–17.

Spillane, J., Camburn, E. and Pareja, A. (2007) Taking a distributed perspective to the school principal's workday. *Leadership and Policy in Schools,* 6(1): 103–125.

Stoll, L. and Fink, D. (1996) *Changing our schools: Linking school effectiveness and school improvement,* Buckingham: Open University Press.

Stringfield, S. (1995) Attempting to enhance students' learning through innovative programs: The case for schools evolving into high reliability organisations, *School Effectiveness and School Improvement,* 6(1): 67–96.

Teddlie, C. and Reynolds, D. (eds.) (2000) *The international handbook of school effectiveness research,* London: Falmer.

Wald, P. and Castleberry, M. (2000) *Educators as learners*: *Creating a professional learning community in your school*, Alexandria, VA: Association for Supervision and Curriculum Development.

Wenger, E. (1998) *Communities of practice*. Cambridge: Cambridge University Press.

Witziers, B., Bosker, J. and Kruger, L. (2003) Educational leadership and student achievement: The elusive search for an association. *Educational Administration Quarterly*, 39 (3): 398–425.

Wong, K (2005) Conditions and practices of successful principalship in Shanghai, *Journal of Educational Administration*, 43 (6): 552–562.

York-Barr, J., Sommers, W., Ghere, G. and Montie, J. (2001) *Reflective practice to improve schools: An action guide for educators*, Thousand Oaks, CA: Corwin Press.

6

Race and Racism in Leadership Development

Tony Bush and Kholeka Moloi

This chapter focuses on the place of race and racism in the preparation, development and practice of educational leaders. We explore conceptions of race and racism and examine the evidence relating to the role and development of Black leaders within education. Wherever possible, we adopt a comparative perspective, drawing on international research and literature on race, racism and leadership. However, the main empirical evidence underpinning the chapter is the authors' own research on Black and minority ethnic (BME) leaders in England (Bush et al., 2005; Bush, Glover and Sood, 2006; Bush et al., 2007a) and 'cross-boundary' leaders in South Africa (Bush and Moloi, 2007).

Livers and Caver (2007: p. 1) claim that addressing self-development, education and behavior can provide Black leaders with a starting place for thinking consciously, comprehensively and constructively about race and leadership. They caution that we should not be naïve about racism as many people, consciously or unconsciously, have racist notions and many organizations have subtle racist practices. Although these practices and beliefs are rarely articulated, they can and do affect how Black people are judged and their opportunities for career progress (Livers and Caver, 2007). Lumby and Coleman (2007: p. 59) cite King's (2004: p. 73) notion of 'dysconscious racism', a form of racism 'that tacitly accepts dominant White norms and privileges'. These concepts underpin the present authors' discussion of race and leadership development.

The rest of this chapter examines the statistical evidence about under-representation of Black leaders, explores notions of community and identity, and assesses the evidence on the relationship between race and the several stages of leadership preparation and development.

UNDER-REPRESENTATION OF BLACK LEADERS

In England, the statistics show that BME teachers are much less likely to be promoted to leadership positions than White teachers. Powney et al. (2003), drawing on a survey of 2,158 teachers, show that teachers from BME backgrounds enter the profession later, and have lower satisfaction levels. This seems to result in lower levels of participation in leadership roles (52 per cent BME remain as classroom teachers compared with 29 per cent of White women and 35 per cent of

White males). They add that this may be partly because BME teachers are concentrated in Inner London and are not geographically mobile for family reasons. There is evidence of hidden discrimination for teachers securing promotion.

Powney et al. (2003) cite six responding heads who identified barriers, including marginalization, indirect racist attitudes and post-ghettoization — all compounded by a female glass ceiling which is particularly serious for BME women. Harris et al. (2003), in a literature review of the career progress of deputy heads, note reliance on informal networks from which ethnic minorities are excluded. They also note that BME teachers are less likely to be encouraged to apply for promotion.

Bush et al.'s (2007a) study of BME participation in the English National Professional Qualification for Headship (NPQH) provides evidence of the patchy nature of ethnic leadership. In London, for example, there are significant numbers of BME heads and other leaders, although they are still under-represented compared to the communities they serve. In certain parts of England, however, BME leaders are rare, as one male Asian respondent to their survey explains:

> The geographical area I am based in does not have any heads or deputies from minority ethnic backgrounds. Having applied for some posts, I didn't even secure an interview. I am in the process of looking outside the North East. (p. 27)

These problems are not confined to education. Musterd's (2003) investigation shows that problems of access to educational opportunities and labor markets are enhanced in areas of moderate, as opposed to high, ethnic concentration.

Singh (2002) presents a full analysis of contemporary BME employment in England and Wales, pointing out that only 6 per cent of BME men and 4.6 per cent of BME women hold leadership positions. The barriers to progress arise from educational choices, gender issues, the lack of role models, and low self-esteem against societal expectations. There is also negative stereotyping by performance assessors, and misjudgment of potential and 'fit' by White leaders. We explore these issues in more detail later in the chapter.

Modood (1998) notes that Chinese and African Asians, of whom a greater proportion had university-level education, were more rapidly integrated while there was limited progress for Afro-Caribbean and Bangladeshi groups. He identifies covert discrimination, professional marginalization, religious intolerance, cultural stereotyping and group immobility as possible causes of differential enhancement.

South Africa provides a different picture linked to its unique history of brutal political, economic and ideological oppression (Shonhiwa, 2006). In the Apartheid era, teachers and leaders were required to live and work in their own communities, as defined by the minority White government. For example, Black Africans could teach only in those schools set aside for Black African learners. More than ten years after the election of a majority government, little has changed. In the Gauteng province, for example, 93.4 per cent of leaders in the former White schools are White, despite great diversity in the learner population in most of such schools. Most 'Black' schools remain mono-cultural, with almost all learners and 97.8 per cent of teachers being Black Africans (Bush and Moloi, 2007). This racial geography has a significant impact on the leadership development opportunities of Black leaders.

In the remainder of this chapter, we explore reasons for the racial stratification of school leadership and consider the role of leadership development in perpetuating or modifying the disadvantage experienced by many Black professionals.

COMMUNITY AND IDENTITY

In many countries, people tend to live where they feel comfortable. In England, this often leads to BME families forming their own communities and then relying on tight local social contacts that may inhibit community and cultural integration until the second or third generations. This may lead to a BME view that is fatalistic with limited aspirations (Papadopoulos, 1999).

Implicit in the discussion of cultural integration is the concept of identity. This has two aspects, the historical in terms of the 'roots' of the individual, and the geographical, in terms of the concentration of people of similar BME groups within an area. Shonhiwa (2006: p. 8) asserts that Africa is a complex cultural kaleidoscope as a result of its ethnic, racial and tribal distinctions, posing a puzzling picture of cultural dynamics. Malik (1996) distinguishes between the 'right to be equal' and the 'right to be different' within contemporary society.

Rassool (1999) examined student perceptions of their own ethnicity and considers that those who have recently arrived in England from the former colonies have been affected by 'discontinuity, differences and social displacement'. The problem that results is one of 'in-betweenness' with the potential for conflict, contradiction and ambiguity that have to be resolved before undertaking careers. Identity is then affected by the sense and perception of community, racism, culture and belonging, which are strengthened by geographical concentration. Osler (1997) suggests that there is a need to move from personal cultural identity, which may have racial connotations, to a personal social identity based upon membership of an organizational community.

The abolition of the previous statutory limitations on where South Africans could live has not produced a major change in the lifestyles of most people. While some middle class Black Africans have moved to the previously Whites-only cities, the great majority of Black people continue to live in the townships and rural areas. The reasons may be partly economic (it is expensive to live in the cities) but they also relate to the 'comfort' people experience in being with their extended families and their wider community (Bush and Moloi, 2007). Soudien (2002: p. 74), in his study of teacher professionalism, reports that there were 'several moments when racial realities were naturalized into people's explanations, where people rendered their stories as if they were living in worlds which were structured naturally, as opposed to deliberately and in racial terms'. Flores (1993: p. 1) adopts a more pragmatic perspective, arguing that effective school leaders, irrespective of race, culture and creed, are required to have cross-cultural skills to function effectively in twenty-first century South Africa. This requirement is also likely to apply in many other countries.

In the next section, we examine the relationship between race and leadership succession.

LEADERSHIP SUCCESSION: IDENTIFYING LEADERS FOR SENIOR POSTS

In principle, there are two main strategies available to identify potential school leaders. First, those interested in such positions may be able to 'self nominate' by applying for available posts and submitting themselves to the (stated or implicit) selection criteria. This approach is typically used by education systems with a high degree of decentralization. Candidates need a sufficient level of confidence to apply for leadership posts, and there is evidence that Black teachers and leaders may lack self-belief (Bush and Moloi 2007). One explanation for under-representation of Black leaders, then, may be a reluctance to apply for leadership posts when they become available.

Bush et al.'s (2005) research with English BME leaders shows the importance of confidence building. A typical response to their survey was, 'I am not particularly ambitious'. A Caribbean man says that 'Sometimes I have been reluctant to "sell" myself and push myself forward, not wanting to be seen as pushy and arrogant' (p. 27). Developing confidence depends on appropriate support. 'Those who have made progress have been supported by a range of people' (p. 19). They cite the experience of several of their respondents, including this Asian woman:

> For one year, I had a fantastic head of department. She became my mentor. Even after she left she continued to develop me … She encouraged me to apply for posts I would never consider. (Bush et al., 2005, pp. 19–20)

A related factor is the availability of suitable role models, who can help BME teachers to think that they could also progress. Several of Bush et al.'s (2005) respondents refer to this factor. One Caribbean woman praises 'dynamic Black headteachers who I worked for and their personal self-belief that anything is possible' (p. 21).

The second strategy, typically used by centralized systems, is a planned approach, leading to central determination of who should be considered for promotion. This approach reduces the 'chance' element and provides the potential for smooth leadership succession. However, it can be criticized on grounds of equal opportunity and it increases the prospect that the 'selectors' will appoint people with the 'appropriate' characteristics. This was shown in the progression of senior and middle leaders in banking and the public services in Zimbabwe in the late 1990s, where planned progression was linked to acceptability within the existing organizational culture (Manwa and Black, 2002). Gronn and Ribbins (2003) say that such 'ascriptive' systems tend to reproduce a leadership cohort (often predominantly male) from a narrow social base. It is only a small step from this stance to a process that discriminates against Black leaders.

The English system is decentralized but local authorities retain overall responsibility for succession planning and are often perceived by BME leaders to have an important role in 'climate setting' for leadership succession, as one Caribbean woman illustrates. 'My [local authority] needs to do more to promote equal opportunity for all' (Bush et al., 2005: p. 39). Local authority staff sometimes provide support; 'the … science adviser has encouraged me' (Ibid, p. 58). However, most BME leaders perceive negative attitudes and practices:

> The LEA does little in terms of tracking BME people and promoting them. They operate under a broad umbrella of equal opportunity but the reality is different . . . There are hardly any Asian or Black heads . . . diversity at the very top is non-existent.
> There is too much networking, nepotism, canvassing within the LEA and it is difficult for us to penetrate the networks our White colleagues have created in there. (Bush et al., 2005: p. 62)

Another of Bush et al's (2005) participants refers to the importance of Whites-only networks. 'There's more networking when you are White and, as a BME person, you can't really penetrate these networks' (p. 68).

Bush, Allen, Glover, Middlewood and Sood's (2007a) study of Diversity and the English National Professional Qualification for Headship (NPQH) shows that proactive local authorities can make a significant difference to the climate for BME leaders. One London borough, for example, 'is considered to be excellent at supporting BME teachers at all levels' (p. 49). However, Bush, Glover and Sood's (2006) earlier work shows that more LEAs are regarded as negative, or indifferent to these issues, as one of their interviewees illustrates:

The LEA is not supportive to Black teachers and leaders in its recruitment policy: it recruits White staff from Australia and Canada and never from Africa and the Caribbean. (p. 292)

Bush et al. (2005) conclude that 'negative discrimination is at its worst where the predominant ethnic group is White Caucasian, and to be most unfortunate in its effects on those who have not followed traditional UK educational paths ... British born BME teachers are more likely to become senior leaders while those born overseas are thinly spread' (pp. 31 & 72). This links to Lawrence et al's (2004: p. 11) notion of structural racism, a system of allocating social privilege. They discuss a 'privilege scale' that can be applied to leadership. The upper end of the scale gives access to opportunity, benefits and power and is associated with 'Whiteness'. The Bush et al. (2005) evidence fits this model in that White leaders are perceived to be at the upper end of the privilege scale, those born and educated outside Britain are at the lower end, with British born BME leaders scattered along this continuum according to variables such as accent, dress and modes of behavior.

The South African system has a degree of centralization with the provincial officials and the school governing bodies (SGBs) sharing responsibility for leadership succession. Despite the overthrow of Apartheid, Lawrence et al. (2004: p. 12) say that racism persists in national policies and institutional practices. Moorosi (2007) notes that Black African women suffer both racial and gender oppression, which create barriers to career progression.

Dee (2004), Mikatavage et al. (2002) and Parvis (2003) assess the shortage of BME teachers and health workers in the United States, and conclude that there is a need for inclusive language, cultural mediation and the development of mentoring role models.

Regardless of the type of education system, it is evident that the 'gatekeepers' play a vital role in supporting, or blocking, BME progression. Where these senior officials are predominantly White, there is a heightened risk that inappropriate policies or behavior will occur. What Blackmore (1999) describes as the 'monoculture of the powerful' serves to inhibit the development of BME leaders. Lawrence et al. (2004: p. 12) argue that structural racism means that White leadership and dominance are taken for granted. Historically accumulated White privilege shapes society's attitudes and judgments.

In the next section, we explore the leadership preparation opportunities available to Black leaders.

LEADERSHIP PREPARATION FOR BLACK LEADERS

The notion of preparation suggests a deliberate process of acquiring appropriate knowledge and skills before taking up the position of principal. In several countries, e.g. Canada, England and the United States, aspiring principals must complete an approved qualification before being considered for appointment. This focuses the attention of ambitious teachers who know what is required to progress towards senior leadership. In other countries, specific training and experience may not be prescribed and potential leaders must use their own judgment about how to prepare for senior posts, including headship. 'Throughout Africa, there is no formal requirement for principals to be trained managers. They are often appointed on the basis of a successful record as teachers with an implicit assumption that this provides a sufficient starting point for school leadership' (Bush and Oduro 2006: p. 362). South Africa may become the first African nation to require its principals to have a leadership qualification. The ACE: School Leadership is being piloted from 2007–09 and, depending on the outcome of the evaluation, it may become mandatory from 2011 (DoE, 2007, Bush et al., 2007b).

Access to Preparation

Black teachers may experience difficulties at the initial stage of accessing preparation opportunities. This may be because 'gatekeepers' are able to restrict or discourage access or because potential applicants lack the confidence to seek preparation. Bush et al.'s (2007a: p. 33) research in England shows that BME applicants, and Asian women and African men in particular, 'face considerable difficulties of selection for NPQH'. They report the experience of one Asian woman who says that 'from within the [local authority] advisory service, people had been openly making derogatory remarks about Asians within education' (p. 29).

Such remarks damage the fragile confidence of some Black leaders, but two access courses in England have helped in promoting self-belief. One of Bush et al's (2007a) respondents found the Investing in Diversity program in London to be invaluable. 'It boosted my confidence, I met many colleagues who have made it "big" in my profession and have learnt a lot from their experiences'. The Equal Access to Promotion course, led by the National Union of Teachers and the NCSL, was also influential in encouraging four of Bush et al's (2007a) survey respondents to move on to NPQH. However, even such programs may be subject to 'gatekeeper' restrictions. 'When I approached [my head] about the Equal Access to Promotion course, [she] said "Oh, I don't know about the budget at the moment" ... Nothing more was said and needless to say I didn't do the course' (Ibid, p. 13).

Many Black South African teachers and leaders also lack confidence. Luhabe (2007: p. 1) attributes this to the legal and structural discrimination of the Apartheid education system and advocates 'validation', an experience that builds self-confidence in a new and unknown environment.

Motivation to Access Preparation

A critical aspect is the level of motivation to access preparation. Bush et al's (2007a) survey shows seven different reasons, offered by BME leaders, for undertaking the NPQH program in England:

Challenge
 'I wanted to develop my understanding of what it is to be an effective leader'.

Professional Development
 'Professional development and gaining experience on current issues'.

Career development
 'My reading and conversations with other staff confirmed that NPQH would be needed to move onto headship'.

Leadership vision
 'To make a difference to the lives of young people'.

Advice and support
 'The headteacher advised me that she would support me on the NPQH course'.

Skills Acquisition
 'Wanted to know more about . . . how to be a head'.

Headship Requirement
    'I chose the NPQH because it has been clear to me for some time that I had aspirations to be a headteacher and, of course, NPQH is compulsory for this to occur'.

Bush et al. (2007a: p. 12) conclude that motivation varies from essentially instrumental strategies (NPQH has to be completed before applying for headships) to vocational approaches (the desire to become a head). These may combine to produce powerful imperatives to seek leadership preparation.

Experience of Preparation

Even when preparation opportunities are available, they may not be appropriate for Black leaders. Some of Bush et al.'s (2007a) respondents criticized the NPQH for its lack of attention to BME issues. 'Many interviewees note the low number of candidates from BME backgrounds and some criticize the program's lack of attention to issues relevant to BME leaders and to leading multi-ethnic schools' (p. 71). Some survey respondents and interviewees also refer to the disadvantages of a predominantly White male tutor force. One respondent reports a particularly unpleasant experience:

> As an ethnic minority and a woman, the tutors on this course did everything to attack my self-esteem. After this, I did learn that there are groups that do not want BME groups to move forward … Being shouted at during one night … destroyed all my confidence in the residential process. (p. 22)

The authors recommend the 'inclusion of current BME leaders in NPQH delivery … as a means of raising the profile of minority ethnic groups within the program' (p. 70).

Customized Preparation

Given the reported difficulties in accessing preparation opportunities, and the uncomfortable experience of some who manage to do so, there has been discussion in the literature about whether customized preparation, to meet the specific needs of Black leaders, should be available. This is a controversial issue with polarized views.
    Some of Bush, Glover and Sood's (2006) respondents favor customized support because:

- It could help to raise cultural issues in training.
- It helps to address barriers arising from family and cultural issues.

Others advocate preparing leaders for a particular ethnic context but they also caution that:

> If you are customizing for someone to be a BME leader in a particular context and take them out of that context they would probably be found wanting. (Bush, Glover and Sood 2006: p. 300)

Beyond this reservation, a majority of BME leaders dislike this approach 'because it is patronizing, inappropriate, or would be likely to cause further resentment within the profession' (Ibid: p. 299). Bush et al. (2007a: p. 49) add that many BME leaders 'are fiercely opposed to anything that appears to mean positive discrimination'. There is also a widespread belief that 'leadership transcends ethnicity issues' (Bush, Glover and Sood 2006: p. 300).

LEADERSHIP SELECTION

The recruitment and selection of school principals follows the 'succession' processes discussed above. In centralized systems, criteria are developed that inevitably reflect the values and beliefs of the senior Ministry personnel who are often responsible for selection. Gronn and Ribbins (2003: p. 91) point out that 'culturally grounded recruitment and selection regimes generate particular occupational profiles'. These are likely to be unhelpful for Black leaders, particularly where they are absent from, or under-represented on, selection panels.

Bhatt et al. (1988) note that 'the potential power and influence [of BME people] has often been neutralised'. They add that 'at all levels it is the White construction and interpretation of black reality that prevails' (p. 150) and this results in an alienating ethos where rules are not related to culture and where the use of diagnostic tools favors the English cultural heritage. These factors contribute to an atmosphere that makes for problems in securing career progression at all levels.

There is a growing body of American literature reporting on the problems of securing promotion once on the career ladder. Manuel and Slate (2003: p. 25) list a range of inhibitors for women in minority ethnic groups in the United States. These include lack of recruitment of women of all ethnic groups by school boards and failure at the hurdle of the mid-management career 'glass ceiling'. Their analysis links race and gender to suggest a 'double bind' for BME women leaders. Tallerico (2000: p. 37) reaches a similar conclusion that there are largely invisible criteria for selection:

> Because they do not appear … in advertisements of desired qualifications … Instead they manifest themselves behind the scenes…unwritten rules involve head hunters and school board members a. defining quality in terms of hierarchies of particular job titles, b. stereotyping by gender, c. showing complacency about acting affirmatively, and d. hypervaluing feelings of comfort and personal chemistry with the successful candidate. (Tallerico 2000: p. 37)

Ortiz (2000: p. 565) notes that 'the great majority of cases, however, show that succession is controlled by school board members and former superintendents holding search committee membership. Most of these individuals are White males'. Mason (1995) argues that being rejected on the grounds of so-called communication problems, and skill or experience deficiencies, may be a cover for deeper prejudice and employers' failure to understand cultural norms. Singh (2002) refers to biased negative stereotyping by performance assessors and misjudgment of potential and 'fit' by White leaders. Jones and Maguire (1997) point to tokenism in appointments, and prejudice against BME teachers, in predominantly White schools.

Lawrence et al. (2004: p. 11) point to structural racism as a system in which policies, institutional practices, cultural representations and other norms reinforce ways to perpetuate racial group inequalities. These dynamics work to maintain the existing racial hierarchy in South Africa.

Bariso (2001) distinguishes between external and internal exclusion. The former may affect employment and promotion prospects while the latter may impact on the experience and internal promotion of Black teachers and leaders after appointment. External exclusion occurs because of the lack of Black role models, evident racism, negative personal experiences, poor prospects and a lack of career advice. As a result, underachievement, stereotyping, poor employment prospects, low pay, and negative parental influence become embedded in institutional racism. Exclusion from promotion also operates through unrepresentative governing body selection panels, tokenistic approaches, and the complexity of the process of recognizing overseas qualifications.

In decentralized systems, recruitment and selection are usually the responsibility of local or site-level bodies. In England, these are the predominantly lay school governing bodies. Bush, Glover and Sood's (2006: p. 297) research with BME leaders provides a mixed picture of the appointments process. Fifty seven per cent of their interviewees comment that the process was 'smooth', 'fair' or 'very positive'. The other 43 per cent report negative experiences, including:

> Unlike Whites, I don't stand as many chances of being appointed to a senior management position.

Page (2003), referring to social work, concludes that time in a country is a significant factor reflecting acculturation and understanding of context and culture. Bush, Glover and Sood's (2006) research found several examples of BME leaders experiencing discrimination on grounds of nationality, dress and having a 'foreign accent'. 'When I told the head that I was from [country] … he was negative. Being a foreigner is an issue and that is sad. It is not openly said and blocks are created'.

Bush et al.'s (2007a) research with English NPQH candidates included 13 graduates who had been unsuccessful in their applications for headship. More than half of these (53.8 per cent) assert that diversity issues contributed to their problems:

> I … have not come across one Black governor at interview. One of the schools had about 70 per cent BME intake but did not have a member of staff, volunteer or governor that was Black. (p. 27)

These authors conclude that several candidates report racist experiences during the selection process: a significant number of leaders cite ethnicity as a factor in unsuccessful applications and several are concerned about unrepresentative selection panels ("a sea of White faces"). (p. 72).

Bush and Moloi's (2007: p. 52) research on 'cross-boundary' leaders in South Africa shows that all Black participants had a negative experience of the appointments process in the former White schools, describing it as: 'very bad' and characterized by 'racism' and 'bitterness'. The appointments process for the White leaders was 100 per cent positive in Black schools and overwhelmingly comfortable in the 'coloured' schools. Eight of the nine 'coloured' leaders had a good experience in Black schools. 'I was treated the same as other candidates'. The five Indian participants all reported a positive appointments process in Black schools: 'The appointment process was fair, not biased, not discriminating' (Indian).

This evidence supports the Apartheid era hierarchy with White leaders being regarded as 'superior' and both Indian and 'coloured' professionals being deemed as better than Black leaders, by all racial groups, including many Black Africans.

'Although the policy of "inclusion" is high on the agenda in South Africa, the deeply "ingrained" separation of the four predominant cultures (Black, White, "coloured" and Indian) has a strong influence on how individuals and groups perceive each other' (Bush and Moloi 2007: p. 55).

The recruitment and selection processes provide the starting points for discrimination in many countries. Developing and implementing appropriate and non-racist processes are essential if appointments and promotions are to be equitable.

INDUCTION FOR LEADERSHIP

Induction is the process by which new incumbents become familiar with the context in which they are leading, including the school culture. It may occur within the school and/or at the wider system level. Bush, Glover and Sood (2006) report that there is little evidence of specific formal induction for BME leaders in England but many have benefited from unofficial encouragement and mentoring. Several participants in their research refer to support and nurturing from heads, senior colleagues and local authority staff:

> Most support came from my general inspector who was very clear about issues of race — felt able to discuss issues with him that I would otherwise have kept to myself. This was very empowering.
> The head was very good at supporting my career. He believed in me. (p. 295)

As noted earlier, internal exclusion (Bariso, 2001) may operate to make life uncomfortable for new Black leaders. Bush et al. (2007a: p. 42) cite many examples of discomfort for new heads. One was called a 'Paki' by a parent who was 'rampaging through the school'. Another had problems with a teacher union official in her borough who was racist and sexist, and 'impugned my integrity'. There is bullying and intimidation and a 'total lack of respect'. A third experienced difficulties, including racist remarks, from parents with low literacy levels and poor life skills; 'you're Chinky, aren't you?' Taking on a new headship is challenging for anyone without the additional stresses of dealing with racists within the role set. There appears to be little if any induction to help leaders deal with such problems.

Bush and Moloi (2007) report that many Black leaders in South Africa have experienced racism in previously 'Whites only' schools. One middle manager had a very difficult experience in a primary school, including:

> The [White] principal would not take advice from a Black person. She was never invited to SMT meetings [which she was entitled to attend].
>
> The White educators [for whom she was responsible] defied her.
>
> White managers and educators 'displayed selfishness, racism and hatred.

Several other Black leaders described similar problems:

> Change is highly resisted by White educators.
>
> It will take a long way before White discrimination and racism are addressed.
>
> White educators are disrespectful because of race.
>
> There are enormous problems concerning racial issues in my school.

Bush and Moloi (2007: p. 53) conclude that 'such in-school "exclusion" 'is ... (particularly] damaging as it is an ongoing feature of the workplace rather than a single snub'.

LEADERSHIP DEVELOPMENT

Leadership development is often the generic term used to describe any form of preparation or training for leadership. In this section, we use it specifically to refer to activities undertaken following appointment to a particular post, for example that of principal. Such provision may be seen as complementary to pre-service preparation or as a substitute for it. In developing countries, pre-service training is rare and the limited resources are devoted to in-service support (Bush and Oduro, 2006).

A key factor is the process by which development opportunities are identified and accessed. This begins with the development 'culture' of the school, or the local or national education system, and whether it nurtures an enabling climate. Basit and McNamara (2004) suggest that, for ethnic minorities, there has to be more than an equal opportunities policy. They prefer the more positive notion of 'affirmative action'. Allen (1998) considers the ways in which being both Black and female imposes limitations on leadership potential:

> I have felt slighted to the point of being discouraged from sharing my ideas, which can be detrimental not only to my morale but also to the growth of my academic unit. (p. 583)

Bush et al. (2007) discuss the experience of the small number of participants who have withdrawn from the English NPQH program. A few people appear to have experienced unsupportive cultures that contributed to their withdrawal:

> I moved schools to give myself more opportunities but the head teacher of the school (who was appointed at the same time) was a bully. She did not want me in the position and made my life a living nightmare because she wanted someone else in the deputy's position. She was scornful of the NPQH and did not support me. I moved schools and found it difficult to continue with the NPQH because the school had different priorities and my school improvement work was not valid. The other Deputy head teacher at the school felt threatened by my presence and undermined my authority at every opportunity. I felt isolated, worn out after battling on all fronts for two years, and decided to take a break. I am a supply teacher now. (p. 25)

These authors also report the more positive experience of those BME participants who took the access courses (EAP and Investing in Diversity) discussed earlier. These programs gave them the confidence to plan their careers and to consider preparing for headship. This evidence suggests that development should be conceptualized as an ongoing process and not simply a specific course that must be completed to underpin career progression.

CONCLUSION — THE WAY FORWARD

Much of the literature refers to possible strategies and tactics for the enhancement of Black leaders. These occur at three levels — the generic gains from diversity, the gains to the community, and the enhancement of the individual. Bariso (2001: p. 180) points to the barriers of prejudice, underachievement, exclusion, stereotypes, low expectations and overt racism but contends that these cannot be overcome whilst:

> The voices of the Black communities and educators are rarely heard in educational debates and have had little influence on policies and practice.

This problem certainly exists in some former 'Whites only' schools in South Africa, where Black leaders are often excluded and feel great discomfort (Bush and Moloi, 2007). While discrimination has been outlawed by statute, these often subtle snubs continue for many professionals, leading some to 'retreat' to Black schools, or to leave teaching altogether. The view that Black teachers and leaders are less worthy than White ones is shared even by some Black parents (Bush and Moloi, 2007) and shows that there is a long way to go to overcome residual attitudes based on racial stereotypes.

The under-representation of BME teachers and leaders is also likely to be an ongoing problem in England and elsewhere unless clear and decisive action is taken to address the issue. Black children seeing few, if any, BME teachers, are unlikely to aspire to educational careers. Similarly, Black teachers who see all-White senior leadership teams are likely to conclude that leadership and management are the preserve of the majority group. Three strategies are required if balanced leadership teams, comprising members from all ethnic groups represented in the school's community, are to be achieved.

Confidence Building and Support

The literature shows that Black teachers and leaders often lack the confidence to seek promotion, or to sustain their engagement in development activity if they encounter setbacks. Succession planning needs to include specific strategies to prepare Black leaders. Alston (2000) suggests the identification of potential leaders, and then the fostering of abilities through intentional and supportive encouragement and the development of formal mentoring. Allen (1998) and Page (2003) point to the need for positive role models, and mentors who recognize the cultural and contextual issues involved for the mentee.

Targeted Preparation

The idea of customized leadership preparation for Black leaders is controversial, as we noted earlier. Some English BME teachers reject the notion completely while others are cautious about being prepared separately from other groups. In South Africa, it is unpopular because it is uncomfortably close to their previous Apartheid experience (Bush and Moloi, 2007). Elsewhere, most people say that leadership is not about race and that everyone should have the same preparation, regardless of ethnicity. Bush et al. (2007a) respond to this view by suggesting the provision of specific preparation opportunities that are available to, but not mandatory for, Black leaders aspiring to headship:

> Our recommendation is that NCSL should set up pilot BME specific NPQH programs in multi-ethnic regions such as London and the West Midlands. This would signal NCSL's determination to address under-representation of BME heads while allowing such leaders to make their own decisions about whether to attend a generic or BME specific NPQH group. (p. 77)

McKenley and Gordon (2002) make the similar but wider point that there should be enhanced leadership training, and enhanced monitoring, for all from BME backgrounds. While these strategies may not be appropriate for all countries and regions, they do underscore the need for a proactive approach to leadership preparation for this disadvantaged group. A 'do nothing' stance is likely to perpetuate the current unsatisfactory position.

Modified Recruitment and Selection Practices

Bush et al. (2007a) show that a proactive strategy increased the proportion of BME leaders in one London local authority and advocate the preparation of guidance to generalize such good practice. It is also important for selection panels to be representative of the community served by the school instead of the 'all-White' groups typical of such processes in many countries. 'Panels tend to appoint in their own likeness so it is unsurprising that all-White panels tend to appoint White candidates. All such panels should have sufficient representation from BME groups, particularly those present in the school community' (p. 78). Prejudice requires top-level commitment to change and equal opportunities training for all involved in staff selection.

In South Africa, local and provincial officials are usually committed to ending racist recruitment and selection practices but the school governing bodies (SGBs) also have a significant role in these processes. A major educative process is required to overcome deeply ingrained racial prejudice.

These three strategies offer the possibility of ameliorating the problems experienced by Black leaders but improving the current unsatisfactory position is likely to be a long-term process. Changes to the law, where necessary, and to national and local policies, are essential but they can only succeed if they are matched by changes in the attitudes and practices of all concerned with the leadership preparation and selection processes. Bush, Glover and Sood (2006) conclude that English BME leaders are exceptional people who succeed despite the barriers to progression. The drive for equality means that they should be no more, and no less, 'exceptional' than White leaders.

REFERENCES

Allen, B.J. (1998), Black womanhood and feminist standpoints, *Management Communication Quarterly 11*(4), 575–586.

Alston, J. (2000), Missing from action. Where are the black female school superintendents, *Urban Education 35*(5), 525–530.

Bariso, E.U. (2001), Code of professional practice at stake? Race, representation and professionalism in British education Race, *Ethnicity and Education 4*(2), 167–184.

Basit, T. and McNamara, O. (2004), Equal opportunities or affirmative action? The induction of minority ethnic teachers, *Journal of Education for Teaching 30*(2), 97–106.

Bhatt, A., Carr-Hill, R. and Ohri, S. (1988), *Britain's Black Population: a new perspective*. London: Gower; Radical Statistics Race Group.

Blackmore, J. (1999), *Troubling Women: Feminism, Leadership and Educational Change*. Buckingham: Open University Press.

Bush, T. and Moloi, K.C. (2007), Race, racism and discrimination in school leadership: evidence from England and South Africa, *International Studies in Educational Administration 35*(1), 41–59.

Bush, T. and Oduro, G. (2006), New principals in Africa: preparation, induction and practice, *Journal of Educational Administration, 44*(4), 259–375.

Bush, T. Glover, D. and Sood, K. (2006), Black and minority ethnic leaders in England: a portrait, *School Leadership and Management 26*(3), 289–305.

Bush, T., Glover, D., Sood, K. and Tangie, K. (2005), *Final Report on BMEL Leadership*. Nottingham: NCSL.

Bush, T., Allen, T., Glover, D., Middlewood, D. and Sood, K. (2007a), *Diversity and the National Professional Qualification for Headship*. Nottingham: NCSL.

Bush, T., Duku, N., Glover, D., Kiggundu, E, Kola, S., Msila, V. and Moorosi, P. (2007b), *The Zenex ACE School Leadership Research: First Interim Report*. Pretoria, Department of Education.

Dee, T. (2004), The race connection Education Next. Accessed August 13, 2007 from: http://www.educationnext.org

Department of Education (2007), *ACE: School Leadership Pilot Programme*. Pretoria: Department of Education.

Flores, E. (1993), Leadership Training as a Tool for Confronting Racial and Ethnic Conflicts, Conflict Consortium, Working Paper 93–24. Accessed August 13, 2007 from: http://www.colorado.edu/conflict/full_text_search/A11CRCDocs/93-24.htm

Gronn, P. and Ribbins, P. (2003), The making of secondary school principals on selected small islands, *International Studies in Educational Administration, 31*(2), 13–34.

Harris, A., Muijs, D. and Crawford, M. (2003), *Deputy and Assistant Heads: Building Leadership Potential.* Nottingham: NCSL.

Jones, C. and Maguire, M. (1997), *Before, during and after: being black and doing a PGCE*, Paper to British Educational Research Association Annual Conference, September, York.

King, J.A. (2004), Dysconscious racism: ideology, identity and the miseducation of teachers, in Ladson-Billings, G. and Gillborn, D. (Eds.), *Journal of Negro Education, 60*(2), 133–146.

Lawrence, K., Sutton, S., Kubisch, A., Susi, G. and Fulbright-Anderson, K. (2004), *The Aspen Institute Roundtable on Community Change, Structural Racism and Community Building*, Washington, DC, The Aspen Institute.

Livers, A. and Caver, K. (2007), What Black Managers can do to make the Organisation Work Better for them, Centre for Creative Leadership Inc. Accessed February 7, 2007 from: www.multiculturaladvantage.com

Luhabe, W (2007), Defining moments. UCT Graduate School of Business. The International Business School in South Africa. Accessed 19 June from: http://www.gsb.uct.ac.za/newsletter Article. ASP?intArticleID.

Lumby, J. and Coleman, M. (2007), *Leadership and Diversity: Challenging Theory and Practice in Education.* London: Sage.

Malik, K. (1996), *The Meaning of Race: Race, History and Culture in Western Society.* London: Macmillan.

Manuel, M.A. and Slate, J.R. (2003), Hispanic female superintendents in America: a profile From Advancing Women Network http://www.awnettech.advancingwomen.com, based upon: Manuel, M. C. (2001). Career pathways and perceived barriers of women superintendents. (Doctoral dissertation, University of Texas at El Paso). Dissertation Abstracts Online, AAT3023411, accessed August 13, 2006.

Manwa, H. and Black, N. (2002), Influence of organizational culture on female and male upward mobility into middle and senior managerial positions: Zimbabwean banks and hotels, *International Journal of Cross Cultural Management, 2*(3), 357–373.

Mason, D. (1995), *Race and Ethnicity in Modern Britain.* Oxford: Oxford University Press.

Mikatavage, R., Aldrich, J. and Ford, M. (2002), Immigration, ethnic cultures and achievement: working with communities, parents and teachers, *MultiCultural Review, 11*(3) 38–41.

McKenley, J. and Gordon, G. (2002), *Challenge Plus: The Experience of Black and Minority Ethnic School Leaders.* Nottingham: NCSL.

Modood, T. (1998), Ethnic diversity and racial disadvantage in employment, in Blackstone, T., Parekh, B. and Saunders, P., *Race Relations in Britain: a developing agenda.* London: Routledg, pp. 53–73.

Moorosi, P. (2007), Creating linkages between private and public: challenges facing women principals in South Africa, *South African Journal of Education, 27*(3): 507–522.

Musterd,S., (2003), Segregation and integration: a contested relationship, *Journal of Ethnic and Migration Studies, 29*(4), 623–641.

Ortiz, F.I. (2000), Who controls succession in the superintendency? A minority perspective, *Urban Education 35*(5), 557–565.

Osler, A. (1997), *The Education and Careers of Black Teachers: Changing Identities.* Buckingham: Open University Press.

Page, M. (2003), Race, culture and the supervisory relationship; a review of literature and a call to action, *Journal of Curriculum and Supervision 18*(2), 161–174.

Papadopoulos, I. (1999), Health and illness beliefs of Greek Cypriots living in London, *Journal of Advanced Nursing, 29*(5), 1097–1104.

Parvis, L. (2003), Diversity and effective leadership in multicultural workplaces, *Journal of Environmental Health, 65*(March), 37–38.

Powney, J., Wilson, V. and Hall, S. (2003), *Teachers Careers: the Impact of Age, Disability, Ethnicity, Gender and Sexual Orientation.* London: DfES.

Rassool, N. (1999), Flexible identities: exploring race and gender issues among a group of immigrant pupils in an inner city comprehensive school, *British Journal of Sociology of Education, 20*(1), 23–36.

Shonhiwa, (2006), *The Effective Cross-cultural Manager: A Guide for Business Leaders in Africa.* Cape Town: Zebra Press.

Singh, V. (2002), Managing diversity for strategic advantage Report to the Council for Excellence in Management and Leadership. Accessed February 7, 2007 from: www.cranfield.ac.uk.

Soudien, C. (2002), Notions of teacher professionalism in the context of a racially divided society: the case of South Africa, in Lewin, K., Samuel, M. and Sayed, Y. (Eds.), *Changing Patterns of Teacher Education in South Africa.* Cape Town: Heinemann, pp. 273–283.

Tallerico, M. (2000), Gaining access to the superintendency: headhunting, gender and colour, *Educational Administration Quarterly, 36*(1), 18–43.

7

Gender and Leadership Development

Marianne Coleman and Tanya Fitzgerald

The focus of this chapter is the relationship between gender and the development of school leaders. While we recognize that gender issues are the concern of women and men, our focus is mainly on women as leaders and managers and the extent to which leadership development programs and initiatives do/do not situate gender as a core concern. Although the rhetoric might suggest that equity and equitable practices are embedded in organizations, recent research has highlighted the extent to which trends and stereotypes regarding women and men as leaders in education remain (Coleman, 2007; Shakeshaft et al. 2007). Primarily, in this chapter we draw attention to the persistent and continuing 'problem' of women's under representation in educational leadership and the multiple cultural, social and structural barriers that exist for women relative to their male colleagues. In particular, we highlight that formal and informal leadership development programs reinforce these gendered barriers precisely because little attention is paid to women's ways of knowing and leading (Blackmore, 1999). What appears to be uncompromising is that models of leadership implicitly draw on hegemonic male images of what it means to be a leader and act in a leadership role (Fitzgerald, 2003). These hegemonic images and values may then be used to implicitly and explicitly judge all those who do not match up to them, both women and men.

Although there has been several decades of research and theorizing on women and educational leadership (see for example Blackmore, 1999; Hall, 1999; Schmuck, 1996; Shakeshaft, 1987), access to leadership positions and the exercise of leadership remains intensely gendered; a situation that is troubling to both authors. Despite awareness of inequities and attempts to address imbalances via the implementation of legislation for equal opportunities and, in some cases, affirmative action, official statistics from a range of countries are testimony to the fact that men occupy the majority of official leadership positions in education, particularly at senior levels. A review of national statistics is beyond the scope of this chapter, but to give one example, Shakeshaft et al. (2007) state that whilst 55.8 per cent of teachers in US secondary schools are women this is true for only 21.6 per cent of principals and 18 per cent of superintendents. Further relevant national statistics are given in Coleman (2002). We do recognize that it might well be the situation that women across the developed and developing worlds do not aspire to leadership for a variety of differing reasons (see for example Oplatka, 2006). This is not to suggest however that women 'lack' aspirations to be leaders; it might be the case that family, social and cultural demands preclude the active pursuit of career opportunities. Furthermore, as a number of professional and career development programs occur away from home and in non-teaching times, family and community obligations may take precedence. Long hours at work which is increasingly the norm for both women and men leave little time to pursue activities on either a professional or personal level outside of the school (Fitzgerald and Moore, 2005). For those women who do wish to be leaders and managers in education, there are significant barriers to be overcome that we would argue are essential for both women and men to confront in any program of leadership preparation and/or development.

There are a number of key assumptions that underlie this chapter, and they may not be equally shared by all readers. In the first instance, we are of the view that in the main, there are enduring elements of patriarchies and their traditions across a number of cultures. That is, economic, social, and political power operates in a homogenised environment that subtly reinforces inequalities (Christie and Limerick, 2004). One of the immediate repercussions is that women and women's work remain inextricably linked with the private domain of the home and family, and men with the public domains of work and the regulation of the wider society. Secondly, we are supportive of arguments that point to ways in which patriarchal traditions continue to privilege institutions, structures (political, economic, religious and cultural), individuals and societies that are closely aligned with hegemonic masculinities (Lingard and Douglas, 1999). Thirdly, it is our view that schools, particularly secondary schools, remain deeply connected with men's ways of leading and managing (Blackmore, 1999; Fitzgerald, 2003). Accordingly, the ideal leader is constructed in masculine ways and reinforced by leadership preparation and development programs that take for granted the concept of 'leadership', 'leading' and being a 'leader' commonly employing dominant discourses of masculinity that many men as well as women are unable to support. And finally, we would suggest therefore, that it is an enduring myth that several decades of affirmative polices and practices have resolved inequalities based on gender (Wacjman, 1998). Numerically women remain a permanent minority in the leadership of the majority of educational organizations in developed countries as the work of Oplatka (2006) pinpoints. In countries such as Turkey (Celikten, 2005) and Trinidad and Tobago (Morris, 1999), the majority of women teachers believed that a male principal was preferable. As Chisholm (2001), Schein (1994, 2001), Blackmore (1999), Sinclair (2004) and others have indicated, popular discourses and images of leaders and leadership draw on (white) male and masculine models that associate traits such as rationality, accountability, efficiency, line management styles and practices, entrepreneurship, requisite political and administrative expertise with the 'good' (male) leader (Collinson and Hearn, 1996; Fitzgerald, 2003).

Although men tend to dominate in educational leadership, there has been a slow growth in the proportions of women leaders in most cultures and contexts. In addition, in a number of situations, conditions exist that invariably position women as 'natural leaders (often based on [gendered] assumptions of their inherent caring and nurturing qualities). The first of these factors that has been identified is the age of the pupil. In the majority of countries women are less likely to be leaders in secondary/high schools than in primary schools. Women are more likely to be leaders in schools catering to the younger age groups; indeed in South Africa and in China it is virtually impossible for a man to be in such a role (Coleman, Bush and Thurlow 2003, Coleman, Qiang and Yanping, 1998). However, where it is possible for men to work with younger children, they tend to be disproportionately promoted to leadership positions (Cameron, 2001). Secondly it also seems to be the case that women are more likely to be leaders in urban than in rural settings, where a female leader may be very rare e.g. China (Coleman et al., 1998), New Zealand, (Fitzgerald, 2003), Ghana (Oduro, 2004). The same holds in England where at least half of the secondary school principals in London are women, but in most of the rest of the country the proportion is around one quarter (Coleman, 2002). The third factor that is relevant to the employment of women leaders is the perceived status of the role within education. In the Israeli system, the majority of schools are state controlled and open to the Jewish population. In these schools the status of teachers and principals is not considered particularly high and women dominate numerically. The dominance of women in leadership of the secondary/high schools may be accounted for by the fact that power has moved from the level of principal to the level of the local education authority which is male dominated (Goldring and Chen, 1994). However, within Israel there are also Arab schools where the status of teacher and principal is much higher. In these schools men predominate as teachers and particularly as principals (Addi-Raccah and Ayalon, 2002). What is evident however is that in schools where there are young children, children from predominantly low socio-economic backgrounds or children with high levels of special needs, it is highly likely that the majority of staff, including the principal/head, will be female (Fitzgerald, 2003). One reason that can be forwarded to explain this 'trend' is that, in the main, a significant degree of caring and nurturing of school and community is required in those areas where there is a social and economic deficit and it is this emotional labor that women are considered 'naturally' better at undertaking (Blackmore, 1996). Another circumstance where women obtain leadership in education is in countries and cultures where males and females are educated separately. In these cases women naturally hold leadership roles in female only institutions. Outside of these specific exceptions, the ideal norm of leadership remains male, employing masculine values.

The chapter focuses on gender and leadership development. Where possible, we have included perspectives from a range of countries and nations. However one of the difficulties is that there is an apparent dearth of research that examines the intersection of gender and leadership preparation and development, particularly in non-English speaking countries. Thus, Dimmock and Walker's (1998) conclusion that the knowledge base in educational administration reveals little information about the lives and careers of women in developing countries remains relevant. As Fitzgerald (2003) notes, it is critical that further research that contradicts taken-for-granted assumptions about gender and whiteness is undertaken.

We are duly aware of the inherent difficulty in focusing on gender which is just one aspect of diversity (Lumby with Coleman, 2007). We do recognize the complexities of multiple and overlapping identities, particularly the interplay of ethnicity with gender (Chisholm, 2001; Mirza, 2006). Individuals' identities derive from a range of loyalties and socialization dependent on their culture, language, religion and history. We begin this chapter with a brief understanding of the literature on gendered patterns and practices that impact on leadership in education in order to bring into sharp relief numerous implications for leadership and leadership development. The chapter concludes with recommendations for the future after considering existing leadership development programs and processes.

Conceptualizations of Leadership and Gender

The fact that women are under represented in leadership and management positions is nothing new and it is a moot theoretical point that arbitrary divisions between leadership as a public constituted activity is linked with immutable assumptions that the public world of work with its insistent focus on productivity, competitiveness, hierarchy, strategy and the inalienable logic of the market is both a male and masculine domain as Jill Blackmore (1999) has argued. What has become institutionalized across the past two decades of educational reform are leaders and leadership that draws on the male and masculine attributes that Blackmore highlights. In the main, therefore, authority is associated with certain types of masculinities, and further strengthens the discourse that men manage and women teach. As Coleman (2001) has pinpointed, it is qualities such as caring, nurturing, empathy, in essence, skills with which women are associated, that are linked with pastoral roles in schools and colleges. Career progression is more difficult from a pastoral rather than the more authoritative positions (Blackmore, Thomson and Barty, 2006) although what is encouraging to note is that in a survey of English principals in 2004, men and women deputies were almost equally likely to have experience of both pastoral care and the more prestigious management of curriculum (Coleman, 2005a).

Several previous studies have shown that organizations operate in gendered ways (for example Blackmore, 1999; Chase, 1995) and, consequently, women are less represented at higher levels of leadership and decision-making (Coleman, 2001). In a number of countries (for example England, Australia and the US) the under-representation of males in the teaching profession has caused considerable public concern and debate. This concern is twofold: the decline in numbers of men in classrooms and the complementary increase in the number of women in classrooms. However, there does not appear to be a similar disquiet surrounding the numerical dominance of men in leadership and management positions in schools. This apparent lack of concern may lie in the rhetoric of the authoritative masculine image (Lingard and Douglas, 1999; Shakeshaft, 1987; Schein, 1994, 2001) that is 'ideally' suited to the hierarchical organization of schools, schooling and educational leadership. It is reasonable to suggest therefore that the pedagogy of leadership is constructed as 'normally' the domain of men and the pedagogy of teaching as essentially the work of women. The resultant emphases on technical, task-oriented responsibilities and accountabilities have been pinpointed as one of the central reasons why women predominantly occupy the lower level of workforce hierarchies (Court, 1998; Strachan, 1999).

In essence, good (male) leaders are portrayed as visionary, multi-skilled, self-regulatory, facilitative, goal oriented, entrepreneurial and service oriented (Gronn, 2000). In a subliminal and subtle way the literature popularizes women's leadership in oppositional ways and suggests that they might exercise traits characteristically described as flexible, supportive, nurturing, collaborative, collegial, and socially just (Hall 1999; Ozga 1993). Values such as openness, trust, empowerment and compassion provide a relief map for charting ways in which women inevitably exercise leadership in schools (Hurty, 1995). That is, women as educational leaders have been theorized about as if they are a homogenous group and considerations of circumstances such as ethnicity/social class/location and beliefs have been discounted. Or, at the very least, distinctions between and among women have collapsed in the attempt to provide a meta-narrative that describes and defines women's experiences and practices as educational leaders (Fitzgerald, 2003).

What this all points to is the need for multiple understandings of leadership to surface and, more significantly, for those programs that aim to train, mentor and develop women and men for leadership to take into account that 'one size' does not 'fit all'. It is reasonable to suggest that educators are cognizant of the need to provide for a variety of learning styles in classrooms, this now needs to be extended to learning styles *for* leadership. Such an approach could take into account the manifold and differentiated experiences that women and men leaders bring to their role as well as the structures and realities of their daily personal and professional lives.

Structures and Realities

In terms of the profession of teaching, women and men enter with the same qualifications and similar skills, and career progression is based on assumptions that these qualifications and skills will be further developed particularly if teachers wish to obtain leadership and management posts/positions. Although on the surface it would appear that there is both equality and equity of opportunity to engage in professional development, the reality, we would suggest, is strikingly different for women and men. Yet one of the underlying difficulties is that assumptions regarding what makes a 'good' leader and what 'good' leadership constitutes remain. It is not a matter of women merely 'fitting in' to prescribed leadership models, or indeed 'giving in' to powerful yet constricting models but a recognition of the strategic value and importance of recognizing and merging a plethora of skills, attributes and abilities. And as we point out in the next section, formal leadership development programs can be premised on 'fitting in' or 'giving in' models. Leadership development however takes a number of forms that occurs prior to formal appointment and might involve mentoring, coaching, succession planning, feedback (both informal and formal in terms of performance appraisal) and opportunities to act temporarily in a leadership or management role. In addition, leadership preparation and development may involve successful completion of a relevant postgraduate qualification as in the United States or a mandated leadership program such as the National Professional Qualification for Headship in England.

While women are numerically dominant as teachers, they are in a significant minority as leaders (Coleman, 2002; Shakeshaft, 1987, 2007). It is not so much that women who aspire to leadership are prevented from applying for positions but that access is difficult. External barriers such as recruitment, selection and evaluation are in place that cast the male model of leadership as the 'norm' (Blackmore, 1999) as we have discussed above. These external barriers also include strong religious and cultural values about the respective roles and careers of women, for example in Islamic countries (Koshal, Gupta and Koshal, 1998). Although there have been systemic and measurable attempts in both western and developing countries to increase the numbers of girls attending school thereby increasing the potential for barriers to be dismantled, this has not necessarily translated into an increase in women in leadership and management positions (Oplatka, 2006). In addition, internal barriers exist such as the absence of role models, little or no opportunity for mentoring, lack of support and gendered assumptions regarding what is 'best' and, by inference, what is 'right' for the school. How then might these external and internal barriers be lessened?

External barriers are, arguably, more systemic and therefore increasingly more difficult to overcome than internal barriers. Part of the reason is that external barriers occur due to gendered assumptions about leaders and leadership that earlier sections of this chapter outlined. These assumptions exist at both the local and national level and pervade how schools are organized and led, inspected and described and the policy context in which schools, teachers and leaders exist and operate. Although it may appear an impossible task to initiate meaningful change at the local and national level, we cannot remain paralyzed by the scope of the problem and associated issues. Several suggestions can be forwarded here. It is important for employing authorities and policy makers (e.g. Governors, Boards and such) to recognize and challenge discriminatory policies, procedures and practices (Skrla, 2000) and that this might involve, at a primary level, professional development that directly focuses on understanding women and men's ways of leading and managing. Secondly, schools might usefully engage in a culture audit that pinpoints both inclusionary and exclusionary practices and which identifies strategies to eliminate gendered ways of operating. These strategies might then offer a platform for the dismantling of internal barriers.

In terms of internal barriers, in the first instance we advocate that a careful, systematic and critical examination of professional development programs offered to aspiring leaders occurs and that the strategic value of incorporating a variety of styles and perspectives is recognized. Secondly, to address the under representation of women as leaders and managers, particularly at the senior level, school policies, procedures and practices that might inhibit women's career progression be scrutinized. This would necessarily involve a high level of critical self reflection to identify inclusionary and exclusionary practices. Thirdly, an expansion in the range of opportunities for diverse leadership styles at all levels could promote and encourage non-traditional ways of leading and managing. And, finally, identifying potential women leaders and putting into place a cohesive and co-ordinated program of leadership development that would include coaching and mentoring within and across gender lines is imperative (Young and Mountford, 2006). One of the immediate challenges this presents is that there are frequently not enough women in senior roles to act as mentors and coaches and prepare other women for leadership and management. One way this might be addressed is for schools to look outside of its gates and seek the assistance of other professional women mentors. In this way a level of strategic value can be placed on nurturing and growing women leaders. Mentoring and coaching is, therefore, a form of strategic career development that actively targets potential women leaders and which reinforces the need for different and differing forms of leadership in 21st century schools.

While these suggestions appear feasible, it is more difficult to universalize and translate policies and practices to educational systems in developing countries. Despite rapid modernization that has occurred in recent years, there exists a range of levels of development from countries that have experienced swift economic development (for example China, South Korea, the Philippines, India, Malaysia) and those that remain in crisis (for example Bangladesh, Zambia, Uganda, Nepal). Universal schooling is far from guaranteed, particularly for girls, educational resources are limited, and civil unrest and the impact of HIV-AIDS has decimated education at all levels.

One of the immediate challenges in any context is that preparation for leadership in schools concentrates on the individual as a professional. Thus, the individual outside of the organization and how s/he might negotiate the personal dimensions of their lives with the professional is not fully considered. As indicated in the introduction, the realities of the construction and practices of leadership have also been influential in determining who may be considered leaders and who may lead. Western traditions have held that men lead and women administer first to family structure and then to organizational or extra familial structures (Doyle, 2000; Smulyan, 2000). In similar ways, Curry (2000) concurs in her assessment of women's primary role to administer to family whereas male leaders, on the other hand, are primarily concerned with administering the organization.

Previous studies have examined the tensions women leaders experience as they attempt to juggle the demands of their professional and personal lives (Chase, 1995; Smulyan, 2000). 'Balancing' the personal and professional has multi-dimensional challenges. In the first instance, women seek to manage the complex interactions between their daily personal and professional lives (Coleman, 2002). Secondly, women principals must manage the demands of school, staff and community; each with their own expectations as to how an effective school principal might act. Additionally, women principals juggle demands made on the basis of institutional structures that presuppose a male model of leadership that can influence how change can be initiated and implemented (Blackmore, 1999). As increasing numbers of women move into the paid workforce, expectations regarding mothering and caring do not necessarily decrease and, as Haas (1998) indicates 'even in households where both partners work, women are likely to do the bulk of household tasks' (p. 1). This has produced what Phipps, Burton and Osberg (2001) refer to as a double workday. That is, women complete a day of paid employment only to perform unpaid domestic chores at home; tasks which have traditionally been viewed as a woman's responsibility. Even though men might assist with these domestic tasks, in general women continue to complete the majority of the work at home (Court, 1998). As Bujaki and McKeen (1998) conclude, the burden of household tasks and responsibilities fall disproportionately on women.

The challenges of juggling paid and unpaid work has been commonly labeled the 'double burden' and this is exacerbated when the demands of professional work collide with domestic work. One of the ways in which the professional and domestic can collide is when extra burdens are placed on already busy leaders; and leadership development and training has the potential to be one of these rupture points as time away from school *and* family is often required to complete these programs.

LEADERSHIP DEVELOPMENT PROGRAMS AND GENDER

Formal leadership development programs have been adopted in a range of countries. In some cases, as in the United States, educational leadership courses are offered mainly through universities with the UCEA (Universities Council for Educational Administration) and the AASA (American Association of School Administrators) providing guidance and support. In other cases educational leadership programs are offered through national or state programs. Bush and Jackson (2002) reviewed the programs offered for principal preparation in two Australian states, Ontario, Canada, Hong Kong, New Zealand, Singapore, Sweden and four states in the USA in relation to the work of the National College of School Leadership (NCSL) in England. Unfortunately, literature on leadership preparation and development programs outside this range of countries is very sparse. However, Bush and Jackson comment in relation to the growing importance of the preparation courses they reviewed:

> The development of school leaders is a critical component in system building if schools are to be places in which teachers learn, teaching and learning are powerfully planned and delivered, students achieve and leadership is widely distributed. It is unsurprising then, that leadership preparation and development are on the agenda across the world. (p. 418)

Despite the importance credited to programs of leadership development, there is no specific mention in the Bush and Jackson (2002) review, or in the comparison of leadership preparation programs in England and the United States (Brundrett, 2001) or elsewhere of ensuring that programs are available equitably to all potential candidates and that gender and other equity issues are addressed within them.

Access to Leadership Courses

It is difficult to obtain detailed figures on gender and access to leadership development programs throughout the world, but theoretically equitable access may not be the problem. In the United States, Shakeshaft et al. (2007) estimate that women are now more likely to have degrees in education than men at all levels, with women earning 76.7 per cent of masters degrees and 66.1 per cent of doctoral degrees in education, with the female proportion of doctoral degrees increasing by 19 per cent over the last 25 years. With the national program in England 'Leading from the Middle' open to middle managers in schools, the proportion of women taking part is the same as the proportion of women in the teaching workforce, although the majority of tutors and mentors are male, in keeping with the majority of senior leaders in education (Coleman, 2005b). It is unlikely that suitably qualified women would be denied access to such programs. The difficulties are more likely to lie in the subtle complexities of indirect discrimination mentioned earlier which are likely to reduce the proportion of women who might put themselves forward for leadership development opportunities. Women are less likely than men to envisage themselves as leaders. In an early pilot of the English National Professional Qualification for Head teachers (NPQH), Cubillo (1998) noted that the candidates who gave themselves low scores on self-evaluation were all women. When interviewed afterwards their reasons included a lack of confidence, not wishing to show off and viewing the activity as a development exercise. Male candidates tended to believe that they could deal with challenges as a principal even if they had no evidence to back up their belief. Women are less likely to plan their careers than men (Coleman, 2002, 2005a). Those who become principals are likely to have been encouraged during their career particularly by their own principal, whether male or female, and to have benefited from mentoring and same sex role models (ibid). Women interviewed on the 'Leading from the Middle' program in England (Coleman, 2005b) were unlikely to have planned their career beyond the next immediate move. The older participants were also likely to have put off application for promotion until their children were safely established at school and required their immediate presence less (ibid).

As women face particular challenges in becoming and being leaders, women only courses might be appropriate. However, as gender issues have become less 'fashionable' and gender problems are thought to have been at least alleviated, programs specifically for women in leadership appear to have become less available. Although a pilot scheme was run by NCSL in England for 'Taking women's leadership forward', it has not become a regular feature of their suite of training courses. In a survey of principals in England in 2004, 17 per cent of women secondary school principals and 13 per cent of men mentioned promoting the career of women by sending them on women only courses, while half of the principals did not seek to develop the careers of their women teachers in any special way (Coleman, 2005a).

Depiction of Leadership Within Programs

Generally it does appear that within educational leadership programs there tends to be an implicit reversion to a male model of leadership. This therefore presents a gender-skewed view of leadership that reinforces notions of the 'good' (male) leader. One of the net effects is that leadership development programs might be a disincentive for women to undertake if they cannot foresee how their voices and perspectives might be recognized.

An examination of two forms of leadership preparation and induction, the NCSL in England (www.ncsl.org.uk; accessed July 2007) and the First-time Principals Programme in New Zealand (www.firstprincipals.ac.nz; accessed 24 January 2007) reveals the extent to which these programs are deeply embedded in gendered assumptions about school leadership. Four photographs were provided on the front page; in three of these photos either a male leader or male pupils dominate the imagery. The program states that its intention is to develop 'the knowledge, skills, and capabilities of first time principals' and while this objective espouses a neutral stance, questions surface as to whose knowledge, which skills and which capabilities? What is known is that women face a range of difficulties securing appointment at the head/principal level primarily due to gendered assumptions regarding what knowledge, skills and attributes an 'ideal' leader' might demonstrate (Reynolds, 2002; Schein, 1994). Programs such as those on offer in New Zealand do not appear to deeply question the underpinning gendered practices on which such a program rests. Both the New Zealand program and any one of the leadership programs that the NCSL offer in England are directly linked with government agendas for schools and school leadership. Neither program is wholly independent of government; they rely on government resources for their existence and are littered with terms that are directly imported from policy. Although not an exhaustive list, these terms include: effective schools, standards, accountability, improving outcomes for pupils, budgets, resources, property, and teacher performance management. In essence, these are public activities with public outcome and as Blackmore (1999) emphasizes, public knowledge, skills and abilities that are equated with the male and masculine. Getting to the glass ceiling (Hall, 1997) involves, it would seem, transcending barriers in place at the point of appointment (Blackmore et al., 2006), eliminating gendered assumptions with regards the qualities 'necessary' for an educational leader to display and confronting leadership preparation and development programs that uncritically reinforce the uniformity of leadership.

In a comparison of the leadership development programs of England and New Zealand, Brundrett, Fitzgerald and Sommefeldt (2006, p. 99) point to the 'underlying assumption of both the Hay Group's report and the NCSL's leadership programes [is] that principals act as one homogenous group, that their professional development needs can be homogenised and that a normative view of leadership is possible to simultaneously predict and develop.' Accordingly, the program in New Zealand has been scoped and devised based on the Hay Group's (2001) recommendation as to which skills, knowledge and competencies lead to highly effective performance. In not dissimilar ways to the program in England, the New Zealand program encompasses:

- Educational leadership;
- Strategic and operational planning, working with the Board of Trustees;
- Building community relationships;
- Staff management, finance property and administration.
- and the skills identified include:
    1. Conceptual thinking
    2. Leading others
    3. Transformational change
    4. Building community relationships
    5. Interpersonal insight
    6. Stakeholder awareness
    7. Influencing others
    8. Results orientation
    9. Analytical thinking
    10. Gathering information
    11. Holding people accountable
    12. Results orientation
    13. Self-management
    14. Self-assurance

Although leadership development is necessary in terms of the ongoing professional development of leaders and managers in education, what appears not to have been questioned are the assumptions in which any such program is based. For example, casting an eye over the above list provides the impression that the 'ideal' and high performing leader is individually motivated, highly results oriented with an aptitude for business skills and the requisite time to work within and beyond a school environment. We do not doubt that leaders embrace high standards but for women leaders in particular this presents a double burden: working for the school and working for the family. These can appear, at times, irreconcilable. That is, working for the school and demonstrating the high performance that the Hay Group identifies, demands a sacrifice of family needs or, alternatively a high performing woman principal may be seen to be 'lacking' as a mother. Conversely, those who take leave or have reduced schedules to attend to family and domestic matters may be seen to be 'lacking' as principals. This interplay of identities is freshly examined in a study of head teachers who are mothers:

> In taking up a position the women do not subvert one identity but use one to enable the other: headship can be used to support motherhood and vice versa. There seem to be multiple identities but the mother and head teacher identities are paramount, coexisting with the woman identity weaving through this. The commitment of the women to each of these identities is presented as total and passionate, where each of these identities defines the women in an apparently complete manner, and yet it became clear that the women could not be fully understood unless account was taken of each of the identities. (Bradbury and Gunter, 2006, p. 501)

Despite the apparent success of these women there is skepticism about the ability of women to combine leadership and parenthood (or indeed any domestic responsibility) and this may therefore affect decisions with regard to appointment, promotion and performance. This is not alleviated for women leaders who do not have children. While they might have the care of older relatives or family members, that there is an absence of children can also provoke negative images (Rhode, 2003). A resolution of these challenges is problematic as women can be accused of being insufficiently committed to the school, family or community.

Gender and Equity Issues in Leadership Programs

The content and learning opportunities of leadership development programs is as important as the ability to access the courses. As new educational leaders are trained it is vital that they are made aware of the importance of gender and other diversity issues since they will have the responsibility of ensuring that the schools that they lead develop a culture where diversity is valued and where gender issues are that have been reviewed and/or evaluated do not rule out consideration of gender and diversity, but neither do they ensure that these important areas are raised and considered as we indicate above. Addressing gender and other equity issues can be done through applying the lens of gender to the existing courses. For example the educational leadership program for aspiring principals in England (NPQH) contains modules on: strategic direction and development; leading and managing staff; teaching and learning; and resource management. Other programs reviewed by Bush and Jackson (2002) in Ontario and in North Carolina also include interpersonal skills, self knowledge and technology. Any of these named areas potentially involve issues of gender but there is no necessity for them to do so. For example leading and managing staff could include the scenario of a young woman manager leading a team including men who resent her promotion. Such practical scenarios are not addressed in the national program 'Leading from the Middle' in England despite the opportunity for participants to take part in an on-line 'Virtual School'. One of those leading this course commented, particularly in relation to young women managers: 'Now that I think about it, they [women] can be brow-beaten and there is nothing in the program that addresses 'stroppy' men' (Coleman, 2005b, p. 7).

As a specific example of an important leadership development program introduced for middle leaders in schools in England, 'Leading from the Middle' was subject to a gender audit (Coleman, 2005b). As mentioned above, there was an equitable gender balance amongst participants, although the tutors were predominantly male. The content was monitored through the review of hard copy and on-line materials used in the program and the experience of participants and tutors was investigated through questionnaires and interviews. The conclusion was that although the program was valued and provided excellent growth opportunities for all participants it was gender neutral. One aspect of this avoidance of gender issues is that work/life balance issues and the career disadvantages that having children may bring for women can be carefully ignored. This is an important gap in the coverage of the course for the participants, but it also means that they are less likely to bring understanding of family related social justice issues to their own leadership practice. There was an unspoken assumption that the program was directed at the mainstream of potential leaders so that gender and ethnicity and other equity issues are not directly addressed or discussed in this and other training programs. The recommendations that emerged from the audit were quite practical and if adopted would help to ensure that gender was embedded in such programs.

The first suggestion was to consider as an over-arching principle, the adoption of gender mainstreaming:

> Gender mainstreaming involves not restricting efforts to promote equality to the implementation of specific measures to help women, but mobilizing all general policies and measures specifically for the purpose of achieving equality by actively and openly taking into account at the planning stage their possible effects on the respective situation of men and women (gender perspective). This means systematically examining measures and policies and taking into account such possible effects when defining and implementing them. (EU, 2003)

Specific recommendations included the need to maintain good practice on the gender balance of participants and to increase the proportion of women as tutors; to ensure that in discussion of leadership theories there is discussion of gender stereotyping and that recommended reading includes literature about women in school leadership. Discussion addressing work/life balance issues for both women and men would be relevant and helpful to all future leaders, as would ensuring that senior women role models are involved. The training of tutors to employ a 'gender lens' would equip them to ensure that gender issues for women in leadership are addressed, for example, the difficulties that women may face in leading teams of men. Finally women in leadership courses will particularly benefit from support for career planning and where possible arrangements for mentoring and networking as adjunct components of leadership courses.

Literature in the United States (McClellan and Dominguez,, 2006; Rusch, 2004; Young and Mountford, 2006) and Australia (Cruikshank, 2004) confirms that gender and other equity and social justice issues are also generally not present in leadership preparation programs in these countries and moreover indicates that resistance that is encountered where it is. The research undertaken by Rusch (2004) involved all educational leadership faculty at UCEA affiliated institutions in the United States and included responses from half of all the professors of educational administration representing 85 per cent of the UCEA affiliated institutions. Although there were some encouraging signs of progress in recruitment and in the acceptance of research on gender and race, it was still largely true that there was 'fear of equity discourse' (p. 41). Rusch also makes the point that: The academic culture that prizes individual expertise also supports the privilege 'not to know' an area outside an individual's expertise' (p. 41). Thus it is possible for the majority of academics, however well-meaning, to avoid issues relating to equity which Rusch describes as 'not an easy subject' demanding 'debate about emotional and value-laden issues' (ibid).

Some of the same type of resistance was encountered in an experiment conducted by Young and Mountford (2006) who attempted to change the attitudes relating to gender in a course of educational leadership training in the United States. They introduced a feminist reader over a period of a year to the students who were aspiring to be educational leaders. At the end of the year their views had not drastically changed and in fact the students, both male and female were reported as being resistant to the feminist views that they had encountered. Young and Mountford have identified three types of resistance: distancing, where sexism (or racism) is believed to exist, but is not seen as relevant to the individual in question; opposition, where there is denial of any problem, and thirdly an intensely emotional reaction of, for example, guilt, or anger, reminiscent of the point made by Rusch above.

Both Young and Mountford (2006) and Capper, Theoharis and Sebastian (2006) have identified the necessity for discussion on such emotive topics to take place without time pressure. It is likely that insufficient time is made available to students to examine and potentially change their attitudes to gender and other contentious issues with equity and social justice issues being treated as an add-on at best. A reflective approach may be best suited to consideration of sensitive equity and social issues for both men and women and there is some evidence to suggest that women in educational leadership and management programs prefer group work and do not respond well to direct or adversarial approaches (Gold, 1993).

In relation to the formal leadership development courses offered in education, it would appear that little attention is paid to the more subtle issues of access that women may face, those attitudes that are built into the way that leadership is conceptualized and the messages that are given consciously and unconsciously labeling women leaders as outsiders. It also seems that the content of the courses does not prepare future leaders for gender dynamics in the workplace or for work life balance issues that will affect both men and women, but are likely to disproportionately affect women. When efforts are made to introduce topics related to gender discrimination and/or feminism into such courses, they are likely to be faced by resistance and denial. If gender is to be incorporated into the mainstream of school leadership development, it cannot be as an add-on, but if it is to be meaningful, will require the time and emotional space for reflective consideration.

CHALLENGES

In this chapter, we have avoided, where possible, suggesting 'solutions' to some of the challenges and issues we have presented. It has not been our intention from the outset to suggest universal solutions to the difficulties women face and the many challenges raised by gender issues for both women and men. We are in agreement however, that orthodox policy resolutions such as affirmative action do not, in essence, interrogate or rehabilitate the fundamental origins of the problem/issue. As Jill Blackmore (1999) cogently points out, uncertainties that have arisen as a result of radical restructuring of the state and its agencies (including schools and schooling) across a number of Western nations in the past two decades has produced almost insistent discourses that call for 'hard' leadership in hard times; leadership that is inevitably cast as male and masculine. Rather than problematizing leadership *per se*, unthinkingly women may be situated as the problem. Such underlying assumptions could be addressed thoughtfully through leadership development programs.

It is not uncommon for women to be 'blamed' for their apparent lack of aspiration and ambition. However, we acknowledge that socialization within a culture has tended to predispose women towards more domestic and supportive roles. Discrimination both direct and subtle, domestic responsibilities and cultural pressures affect women in all cultures, but there are differences. For example, women in leadership roles in Singapore (Morris, Coleman and Low., 1998) do not perceive the same difficulties related to domestic responsibilities, as women in Europe or the United States, since professional women in that setting are expected to have a high level of paid support, albeit from other women. Or, as reported by Fitzgerald and Moore (2005), women principals employed other women to undertake these domestic tasks that further involve them in the work of hiring of a housekeeper or cleaner, allocation of daily or weekly tasks, arranging payment for these services and dealing with any issues. Women may be limited in both opportunities and aspirations because they are expected to take the major responsibility for the home and for children. In a comparison of men and women secondary/high school principals in England, the vast majority of the wives of the male principals took most of the domestic responsibilities, but the women principals tended to either take major responsibility or at least share it equally with their partners (Coleman, 2005a).

Equal opportunities and the concept of diversity apply not just to gender, but also to ethnicity, disability, sexual orientation and age as well as a range of other factors. However, gender remains a significant and continuing factor that conditions our responses and attitudes. Gender is particularly significant in that it carries connotations of worth and it is continuing, despite the assumptions noted above that gender issues have been resolved and the real improvement that has occurred in many Western and developed countries throughout the twentieth century. The recent perceptions of young women in England reported in research carried out for the Equal Opportunities Commission (EOC) found clear evidence of continuing discrimination: 'The main concerns are a lack of support to combine work and family roles, and sexism — in their working, personal and social lives. Women may have less well paid jobs, or do much more domestic work, but people see this as a result of individual choice and natural gender differences, rather than bias in society as a whole' (Howard and Tibballs, 2003: p. 7). The work of Moller Okin (1999) and Nussbaum (1999) reminds us of the huge challenges that remain for women in some cultures that remain highly patriarchal.

It has been well argued that essentialist assumptions with regards to gendered differences between women and men create further barriers for women moving into leadership positions beyond the classroom (see for example Acker, 1989; Blackmore, 1999; Schmuck, 1996). However these essentialist views are too simplistic and theorizing in the field of educational leadership has developed a more sophisticated understanding of the interaction between gender and social contexts. To illustrate this point even further, Connell (1995) called for an abandonment of unitary typecasting and posited a theory of multiple femininities and masculinities that suggested that social variables such as gender, class, ethnicity, location, sexuality and culture contradicted simplistic explanations. This view supports research undertaken by Evetts (1994), Kruger (1996), Court (1998) and Coleman (2005a) that concluded that educational leaders drew on both feminine and masculine qualities.

Two fundamental questions remain. Firstly, how can women and men equally have access to leadership roles and posts? And, secondly how can educational organizations create equitable conditions in order for this to occur?

As we have outlined in this chapter, there are a number of formal and informal initiatives and programs for leadership preparation and development. Although the work of Bush and Jackson (2002), Brundrett et al. (2006) and Coleman (2005b) has examined the current suite of programs available across a number of countries, what has not been fully examined is the potential interaction between the gender of course developers and trainers and participants. Given too the translation of training and policies across westernized countries as Brundrett et al. (2006) emphasize, we are left to ponder the extent to which policies and practices travel across western and developing countries and the 'fit' given the unique settings. In line with the arguments expounded in this chapter, while leadership cannot be homogenized, neither should gender be subject to assumptions that 'women leaders' are a unitary group (Fitzgerald, 2003).

Our penultimate proposition is that there are a number of areas in which future research could be conducted. In the first instance, given the dearth about leadership and training for leadership in developing countries, future research should be undertaken to illuminate the numerous and complex ways in which women lead and manage. In particular, a focus on the career trajectories of women in countries where there is a significant emphasis on masculine dominance, would offer an important comparative contribution to the knowledge base.

Secondly, research concerning the inter-relationship between gender, the delivery content, and development of leadership programs should be carried out to investigate the links between the gender of the participants, course/program developers and course/program personnel. Strategies could then be devised to ensure that the present roles of women and men in the organization are not mirrored in the content and delivery of the program impacting on participant experiences and perspectives about leadership.

Thirdly, what appears as a significant silence in the generic educational leadership literature and the literature that pays attention to women's ways of knowing and leading, are ethnographic accounts that reveal the everyday realities of leaders' lives and practices and the complex circumstances in which leadership is exercised in a diverse settings. And finally, we would strongly conclude that this research agenda we have outlined should, as its central focus, give primacy to the multiple voices and agency of women leaders in a range of diverse settings.

CONCLUSION

Difficulties are experienced by women who wish to access and occupy leadership positions in education, but there are potential ways in which the situation might be improved. It is difficult to change the deep underlying assumptions which color our perceptions of gender and of leadership, but it is possible to break into the vicious circle which continues to equate leadership with the male through the education for tomorrow's leaders. This might be done within formal national programs or in the structures and processes of individual schools.

Capper et al. (2006) have undertaken a review of social justice literature in the United States from which they have extracted a framework for preparing leaders for social justice in education. Such a framework might not just be used in the training of leaders, but could be adapted by them in their own leadership role to extend knowledge and understanding of social justice issues to their staff. Their framework identified what is referred to as 'critical consciousness' the examination and identification of the values of the individual. The framework also includes knowledge, e.g. of relevant legislation and practical skills such as the use of data for monitoring, and of hiring and supervising appropriate staff with a focus on social justice. What is also a key to the application of the framework is that those preparing for leadership are in an environment and conditions where they 'experience a sense of emotional safety that will help them take risks toward social justice ends' (Capper et al., 2006: p. 212).

If school leadership is to reflect values of equity and social justice, it is essential that gender issues are mainstreamed through school structures and processes. In order for this to happen, it will be necessary for new generations of school leaders to develop critical consciousness, and the most efficient way of doing that is through ensuring that content and approach of formal leadership and management programs/courses take full account of the gender issues that have been outlined in this chapter.

REFERENCES

Acker, S. (1989) *Teachers, genders and careers.* New York: Falmer Press.

Addi-Raccah, A. and Ayalon, H. (2002) Gender inequality in leadership positions of teachers. *British Journal of Sociology of Education,* 23(2): 157–177.

Blackmore, J. (1996) Doing emotional labour in the educational marketplace: Stories from the field of women in management. *Discourse,* 17(3): 337–350.

Blackmore, J. (1999) *Troubling women: Feminism, leadership and educational change.* Buckingham: Open University Press.

Blackmore, J, Thomson, P. and Barty, K. (2006) Principal selection: Homosociability, the search for security and the production of normalized principal identities. *Educational Management Administration & Leadership,* 34(3): 297–317.

Bradbury, L. and Gunter, H. (2006) Dialogic identities: the experiences of women who are headteachers and mothers in English primary schools, in *School Leadership and Management,* 26(5): pp. 489–504.

Brundrett, M. (2001) The development of school leadership preparation programmes in England and the USA: A comparative analysis. *Educational Management and Administration,* 29(2): 229–245.

Brundrett, M., Fitzgerald, T. and Sommefeldt, D. (2006) The creation of national programmes of school leadership development in England and New Zealand: A comparative study. *International Studies in Educational Administration,* 34(1): 89–105.

Bujaki, M. L. and McKeen, C. A. (1998) Hours spent on household tasks by business school graduates. *Women in Management Review,* 13(3): 1–10.

Bush, T. and Jackson, D. (2002) A preparation for school Leadership: International perspectives. *Educational Management and Administration,* 30(4): 417–430.

Cameron, C. (2001) Promise or problem? A review of the literature on men working in early childhood services. *Gender Work and Organization,* 8(4): 430–453

Celikten, M. (2005) A perspective on women principals in Turkey. *International Journal of Leadership in Education,* 8(3): 207–221.

Capper, C., Theoharis, G. and Sebastian, J., (2006) Toward a framework for preparing leaders for Social Justice. *Journal of Educational Administration,* 44(3): 209–224.

Chase, S. (1995) *Ambiguous empowerment: The work narratives of women school superintendents.* Amherst: Massachusetts University Press.

Chisholm, L. (2001) Gender and leadership in South African educational administration, *Gender and Education,* 13(4): 387–399.

Christie, P. and Limerick, B. (2004) Leadership as a field of study. *Discourse,* 25(1): 1–3.

Coleman, M. (2002) *Women as headteachers: Striking the balance.* Stoke on Trent: Trentham Books.

Coleman, M. (2001) Achievement against the odds the female secondary headteachers in England and Wales. *School Leadership and Management,* 21(1): 75–100.

Coleman, M. (2005a) *Gender and headship in the twenty-first century,* Nottingham, NCSL. http://www.ncsl.org.uk/mediastore/image2/twlf-gender-full.pdf

Coleman, M. (2005b) Women and leadership: The views of women who are 'Leading from the Middle'. Paper presented at the BELMAS conference, Milton Keynes, 23 September.

Coleman, M. (2007) Gender and educational leadership in England: A comparison of secondary head teachers' views over time. *School Leadership & Management,* 27(4): 383–399.

Coleman, M., Qiang, H. and Yanping, L. (1998) Women in educational management in China: Experience in Shaanxi Province. *Compare,* 28(2): 141–154.

Coleman, M., Bush, T., and Thurlow, M. (2003) Managing Schools in South Africa: Leadership and Strategic Management, London, Commonwealth Association.

Collinson, D. and Hearn, J. (1996) *Men as managers, managers as men: Critical perspectives on men, masculinities and managements.* London: Sage.

Connell, R.W. (1995) *Masculinities.* St Leonards, NSW: Allen and Unwin.

Court, M. (1998) Women challenging managerialism: Devolution dilemmas in the establishment of co-principalship in primary school in Aotearoa/New Zealand. *School Leadership and Management,* 18(1): 35–57.

Cruikshank, K. (2004) Towards diversity in teacher education: teacher preparation of immigrant teachers. *International Journal of Teacher Education,* 27(2): 125–138.

Cubillo, L. (1998) Women and NPQH - An appropriate leadership model? Paper presented at the BERA conference at Queen's University, Belfast, August.

Curry, B. (2000) *Women in power: Pathways to leadership in education.* New York: Teachers College Press.

Dimmock, C. and Walker, A. (1998) Comparative educational administration: Developing a cross-cultural conceptual framework. *Educational Administration Quarterly,* 34(4): 558–595.

Doyle, J. (2000) *New community or new slavery: The emotional division of labour.* London: The Industrial Society.

European Union, (2003) Gender Mainstreaming Briefing. Accessed 13 April 2008 from: http://europa. eu.int/comm/employment_social/equ_opp/gms_en.html

Evetts, J. (1994) *Becoming a secondary head teacher.* London: Cassell.

Fitzgerald, T. (2003) Interrogating orthodox voices: Gender, ethnicity and educational leadership. *School Leadership and Management,* 23(4): 431–444.

Fitzgerald, T. and Moore, W. (2005) Balancing or juggling: The challenges of professional and domestic work for women principals. *New Zealand Journal of Educational Leadership,* 20(2): 59–69

Gold, A. (1993) Women-friendly' management development programmes', in J. Ouston, (ed.) *Women in Education Management* (pp. 81–96). Harlow: Longman.

Goldring, E, and Chen, M (1994) The feminization of the principalship in Israel: the trade-off between political power and cooperative leadership, in C. Marshall (ed.), *The new politics of race and gender.* London: Falmer Press.

Gronn, P. (2000) Distributed properties: A new architecture of leadership. *Educational Management and Administration,* 28(3): 317–338.

Haas, B. (1998) Waged domestic help: Chances and risks for whom?, *Equal Opportunities International,* 17(7): 1–15.

Hall, V. (1997) Dusting off the phoenix: gender and educational leadership revisited, *Educational Management and Administration,* 25(3): 309–324.

Hall, V. (1999) Gender and educational management: Duel or dialogue? In T. Bush, L. Bell, R. Bolam, R. Glatter and P. Ribbins (eds.) *Educational management: Redefining theory, policy and practice.* (pp. 155–165). London: Paul Chapma.

Hay Group (2001) *Identifying the skills, knowledge, attributes and competencies for first-time principals: Shaping the next generation of principals: Report to the Ministry of Education,* Hay Acquisitions Inc.

Howard, M., Tibballs, S. (2003) *Talking inequality* London, Future Foundation

Hurty, K. (1995) Women principals - leading with power. In D. Dunlap & P. Schmuck (eds.) *Women leading in education* (pp. 380–406). Albany: State University of New York Press.

Koshal, K., Gupta, A.K. and Koshal, R. (1998) Women in management: A Malaysian perspective. *Women in Management Review,* 13(1): 11–18.

Kruger, M.L. (1996) Gender issues in school leadership: Quality versus power? *European Journal of Education,* 31(4): 447–461.

Lingard, B. and Douglas, P. (1999) *Men engaging feminisms: Pro-feminism, backlashes and schooling.* Buckingham: Open University Press.

Lumby, J. with Coleman, M. (2007) *Leadership and diversity: challenging theory and practice in education.* London: Sage.

McClellan, R. and Dominguez, R. (2006) The uneven march toward social justice: Diversity, conflict, and complexity in educational administration programs. *Journal of Educational Administration*, 44(3): 225–238.

Mirza, H. (2006) Transcendence over Diversity: black women in the academy, in *Policy Futures in Education*, 4(2): 101–113.

Moller Okin, S. (1999) *Is multiculturalism bad for women?* Princeton, NJ: Princeton University Press.

Morris, J. (1999) Managing women: Secondary school principals in Trinidad and Tobago. *Gender and Education*, 11(3): 343–355.

Morris, S. B., Coleman, M., and Low, G. T. (1998) Leadership Stereotypes and female Singaporean Principals in *Compare*, 29(2): 191–202.

Nussbaum, M. (1999) *Women and human development: The capabilities approach*, Cambridge, Cambridge University Press.

Oduro, G. (2004) Unpublished PhD thesis, University of Cambridge.

Oplatka, I. (2006) Women in educational administration within developing countries: towards a new international research agenda. *Journal of Educational Administration*, 44(6): 604–624.

Ozga, J. (1993) *Women in educational management*. Buckingham: Open University Press.

Phipps, S., Burton, P. and Osberg, L. (2001) Time as a source of inequality within marriage: Are husbands more satisfied with time for themselves than wives?. *Feminist Economics*, 7(2): 1–21

Reynolds, C (2002) *Women and school leadership: International perspectives*. Albany: State University of New York Press.

Rhode, D. (2003) (ed.) *Difference 'difference' makes: Women and leadership*. Palo Alto, CA: Stanford University Press.

Rusch, E. A. (2004) Gender and race in leadership preparation: A constrained discourse. *Educational Administration Quarterly*, 40(1): 14–46.

Schein, V.E. (1994) Managerial sex typing: a persistent and pervasive barrier to women's opportunities, in M. Davidson and R. Burke, (eds.) *Women in management: Current research issues* (pp. 41–54). London: Paul Chapman.

Schein, V.E. (2001) A global look at psychological barriers to women's progress in management. *Journal of Social Issues*, 67: 675–688.

Schmuck, P. (1996) Women's place in educational administration: past present and future, in K. Leithwood (ed) *International handbook of school leadership and administration* (pp. 337–368). Dordrecht: Kluwer.

Shakeshaft, C. (1987) *Women in educational administration*. Newbury: Sage.

Shakeshaft, C., Brown, G., Irby, B., Grogan M. and Ballenger, J. (2007) Increasing gender equity in educational leadership, in S. Klein, B. Richardson, D.A. Grayson, L.H. Fox, C. Kramarae, D. Pollard, and C.A. Dwyer, (eds.) *Handbook for achieving gender equity through education* (2nd ed.) (pp. 103–129). Florence, KY: Erlbaum.

Sinclair, A. (2004) *Discourse*, 25(1), pp. 7–19.

Skrla, L. (2000) The social construction of gender in the superintendency. *Journal of Education Policy*, 15(3): 296–316.

Smulyan, L. (2000) *Balancing acts: Women principals at work*. Albany: State University of New York.

Strachan, J. (1999) Feminist educational leadership: locating the concepts in practice. *Gender and Education*, 11(3): 309–322.

Wacjman, J. (1998) *Managing like a man*. Sydney: Allen & Unwin.

Young, M. and Mountford (2006) Infusing gender and diversity issues into educational leadership programs. *Journal of Educational Administration*, 44(3): 264–277.

8

Theories of Learning

Brenda R. Beatty

This chapter considers theories of learning in association with current trends and issues in leadership preparation and development. It provides the opportunity to revisit many ideas that will be familiar to readers and some less so, with a view to reflection upon the field. Through the lens of understandings of mind, knowledge, and learning, the reader is invited to consider some directions for the future of school leadership practice, preparation and development.

Leadership for the future presupposes there will be a future for human life on earth, a supposition that may depend more than we know upon leaders in general and the quality of leadership in schools in particular. In today's complex and rapidly changing world, fraught with challenges to our very existence, questions arise about how school leaders are best to prepare for their critical roles. While licensure protocols, policies and performance review processes are setting more comprehensive criteria for successful leadership of educational change and school improvement, mandates cannot in and of themselves create the learning conditions necessary to support leaders in developing these capabilities.

International understandings of leadership and leadership preparation and development represent a truly moveable feast. A consideration of these multiple perspectives raises perplexing issues and frames some key questions for the field: What are the purposes of school leaders? Are they instructional leaders, financial managers, moral models, developers of social capital and social cohesion, or learning community catalysts? If they are perhaps all of these, how do school leaders learn to do justice to these complex roles? How can leadership preparation and development programs and organizational processes best assist school leaders in becoming all that they can be, while retaining their wellbeing and providing living models of self-actualization and learning in communities of practice?

Following a review of some current issues, and underlying assumptions and visions for school leadership in the future, the reader is introduced to some historical background and influential schools of thought about human mind and learning. Thereafter, a review of specific individual and collective learning theories is complemented by key concepts from adult learning and adult development theory. These gleanings are then considered in light of emerging trends from empirical studies of promising practices in leadership preparation and development.

SOME ISSUES AND ASSUMPTIONS

Schools and school systems worldwide are facing a crisis in leadership succession. The complexities of the work of school leadership present a daunting picture of overwork and early death (Saulwick, 2004). At the same time, the stakes could not be higher for getting education right. Generation Y individuals, in contrast to their martyr-like outgoing Boomer predecessors (Hurley, 2007) are choosing "Not" in droves. Even committed educationist lifers are sticking to the more manageable domain of the classroom. While leadership in schools is often idealized as a widely distributed phenomenon, still the ultimate responsibility for school success falls to the principal. If the position of principal is unappealing from the outside, and almost impossible to perform with balance and sustainability from the inside, who is going to guide the schools of the future and how are preparation pathways to be designed? We need answers to these questions, now, more than ever before.

Even with sufficient numbers of aspirant school leaders, the challenges of preparing people for sustainable professional lives in official roles as head of school or school principal, present difficulties that send us back to the drawing board. It is time to rethink. How do we facilitate the learning of leadership? How do we foster wellbeing and sustainability along with a welcome embrace of the challenges in leading learning in schools? What is leadership development? For that matter, what is school leadership?

From among 121 articles in four representative English-language educational administration journals as far back as 1988, Leithwood, Jantzi and Steinbach (1999: p. 8) sorted the concepts of educational leadership into six categories or models: "instructional, transformational, moral, participative, managerial and contingent leadership". For the first three categories, these authors report that instructional leadership presupposes a focus on teaching, transformational leadership features building capacities, and moral leadership invites the consideration of values and ethics in the context of relationship and implies the image of community. Distributed, shared, or, participative leadership involves a focus on the ways decisions are made. Discussions of participation by stakeholders and various lines of communication characterize this category. Managerial leadership places the emphasis on "functions, tasks, or behaviours" and "contingent leadership" emphasizes context; in all of these approaches, *influence* plays a central role as it is evident even within the transformational models where individualized support is noted as a way of ensuring influence (Leithwood et al., 1999: pp. 12–17). Yet, no matter what models are *out there*, leadership comes from *in here*, from who we are as persons. Thus, the argument follows that "leadership of reform is as much a matter of discovering self as discovering strategy" (Caldwell, 1997: p. x).

Learning about leadership begins early and involves the inseparable blend of formal and informal experiences. We have all been exposed to a myriad of leadership models: our care givers, teachers, and a range of significant others and authority figures who have influenced us personally and professionally. From all of our experiences, we gather impressions, consciously and subconsciously, about how life is and how to be in the world. We can observe our own beliefs and some would call them implicit theories of leadership in our very thoughts, feelings, words and behaviors. Whether we consider them beliefs or actual theories, we also acquire our implicit assumptions and operating theories about learning in various ways.

While economic viability continues to dominate national educational outcomes agendas, the balance among featured facets of educational reform remains highly contested. For instance, it is argued that the intense emphasis on schools as instrumental to the workplace can overshadow their potential to foster a focus on other values, including the public good in general and social justice issues in particular (Shields, 2005). As Kumashiro notes (cited in Shields, 2005: p. 85) schooling is not "unimplicated in the dynamics of oppression"; Shields (2005: p. 87) argues further that, "We will need to bring new moral purposes, broader conceptual frameworks, and more deliberate action into the uncharted and difficult territory of holistic and purposeful educational leadership for the 21st century". This, she suggests, will require some soul searching, self knowledge and purposeful envisionment of answers to Max DePree's invocation, "Who do we intend to be?" (Shields, 2005).

If we are to accept DePree's question as worthy of consideration, we would wisely also engage in an active comparison between what we have intended our schools and their leaders to be and what they have become. After all, the road to hell is paved with good intentions. Indeed, the research tells us that many school leaders discover that their intended selves have become all but lost due to the pressures of performativity (Ball, 2000; Beatty, 2002; Blackmore, 2004). Leaders regularly report that their leadership vision is constantly eclipsed by the drain of bureaucratic compliance demonstrations and inescapable administrative minutiae. The job would appear to be simply too large and too complex to go it alone.

A FOCUS ON IMPROVING SCHOOL LEADERSHIP

Sixteen years ago Mulkeen and Cooper (1992: pp. 17 & 22) argued that:

> [t]he limits of the bureaucratic regulatory model have been reached.... Schools will need to flatten out the hierarchies [and principals will need to be] prepared to create the conditions for a professional teaching force by sharing planning and decision-making responsibilities with staff.... The idea that answers to school problems cannot be fixed from the top requires a fundamental reordering of the very fabric of the relationship between administrators and teachers.

Similar calls for a more distributed perspective on school leadership have followed (e.g., Murphy & Adams, 1998; Spillane, Halverson & Diamond, 2001; Knapp, Copland & Talbert, 2003). More recently, the Organisation for Economic Co-operation and Development's (OECD) *Improving School Leadership* project (2005), grounded in the notion that school leadership is most effective when it is widely distributed, has gathered models of innovative distributed leadership from 22 participating countries based on the following understanding:

> Effective school leadership may reside not exclusively in formal offices or positions, but instead be distributed across a range of individuals in the school. Principals, managers, academic leaders, department chairs, and teachers can contribute as leaders to the goal of learning-centered schooling....Principals can act not only as managers but also as leaders of the school as a learning organization. Together with teachers, they interact to constitute a productive, cohesive community (OECD, 2005, p. 18).

In later phases The OECD *Improving School Leadership* project will also involve developed and developing nations in a knowledge exchange. The acknowledgment that school leadership needs to be, first and foremost, a cooperative learning endeavor that involves the pursuit of partnerships and innovative collaborations is gaining global acceptance. Learning leadership means learning to collaborate, something that is not innate or even normative in traditional models of school leadership.

Whatever the balance of factors in one's vision of desirable educational outcomes, part of the personal learning challenge for today's school leaders is developing a predisposition to share control and knowledge authority with others in the creation of dynamic new partnerships. This is a professionally and personally confronting imperative, one with complex emotional demands that need to be addressed. Correspondingly, the challenge of creating conditions for the learning of leadership defined in this way rests with those who would be leadership developers.

Theories of Learning

We are located in a time and place that has social, psychological, philosophical and historical moment and meaning, and it is within this array of knowings that we know. Thus theories of learning may be considered epistemic, but not epistemological. Splitting hairs? Perhaps. But the take home message for me is that we wisely seek to acknowledge these influences upon our ways of thinking, knowing, perceiving and believing, and theorizing, as well as theorizing about theories.

As educators, our theories of learning, explicit and implicit, espoused and in use (Argyris & Schon, 1974, 1978, 1996; Argyris, Putnam & McLain- Smith, 1985) are foundational to our very *raisons d'etres*, our professional reasons for being. In schools, the assumption that learning can and does occur in situations created to foster it, underpins professional identities and daily labors of love. But the full potential in our love's labors can be diminished if not lost, when the theories that are implicit in our teaching and leadership development practices remain unexamined and unquestioned.

UNDERSTANDING MIND

We seem to have been grappling for a very long time with trying to understand just how the mind works, how learning occurs and how to optimize learning. Given the sheer quantity of theoretical perspectives on learning already produced and pondered over (Moon, 2004), one could be forgiven for perceiving that what there is to be known about learning and learning potential, is now mainly in hand. Yet in the larger scheme of things, our understanding of human mind and human potential is more likely in its infancy. In traversing some selections from this extensive terrain, we wisely continue to consult our own knowledge and beliefs about how we as individuals learn, and how our experiences of learning, teaching, leading and creating learning opportunities for leaders have shaped our understandings. All learning, even learning about learning, is contextual, shaped and reflected in cultural factors. Incidental learning about survival within our own particular cultural domains is a powerful part of the process throughout our lives.

Leading for life long learning is a philosophical and theoretical proposition that acknowledges both individuals' and society's needs. More recent scholars such as Sharan Merriam and colleagues (2001: p. 5) have proposed that present demands for learning are distinct from earlier times:

> It can be argued that the nature of society at any particular point in time determines the relative emphasis placed on adult learning. In pre-industrial societies, the rate of change was such that what a person needed to know to function as an adult could be learned in childhood. In societies hurrying to catch up, however, and in our own society with its accelerated rate of change, the urgency of dealing with social realities is felt by adults. Society no longer has the luxury of waiting for its youth.

So it is that the philosophy of the day is an influential social factor in what is valued and what is learned. In terms of the school leader as a model of life long collaborative professional learning, our understandings of adult learning and development are particularly pertinent to leadership preparation and development, a theme to which I return later in this chapter.

Disconnectedness is dangerous. The philosophical holism that is required to embrace connectedness among our inner faculties of mind may be essential to our ability to fully experience interconnectedness in its most comprehensive sense. Globally, economic rationalism which contrasts with more environmentally holistic perspectives may be endangering life itself. Correspondingly, models of leadership that position groups as warring factions and perpetuate the adherence to win-lose scenarios are not serving the species well. What evolutionary and cultural historian Riane Eisler (1987, 2007) argues would be a *return* to the main road of social evolution — that is to the ways of partnership and cooperation — may be more ably explored in our schools and school systems than in many other sectors of society. This makes the leadership of schools and schooling strategically critical.

Theories that address the human side of school leadership have emerged (e.g. Sergiovanni, 1992; Evans, 1996; Hargreaves, 1998; Fullan, 1999, 2001; Gronn, 1999; Leithwood, Jantzi & Steinbach, 1999). Yet they are largely outwardly directed in their conceptualizations of leadership defined as influence upon others. Furthermore, in practice, rationalist managerial bureaucratic approaches to school leadership continue, despite their obvious limitations as noted above by Mulkeen and Cooper (1992). The conceptualization of leadership development as the preparation for using one's fully dimensional capabilities requires focused reflection and deep learning about the subtle yet powerful blend between intellectual and lived inner experiences in emotional ways of knowing (Beatty, 2005). Yet a focus on emotion has only begun to emerge in the leadership discourse. More robust theories of leadership and leadership development need to integrate these understandings and address the complexities of learning for inner leadership given that connectedness to others relies upon the living relationships one has with one's socially situated self.

As we consider theories of learning, we wisely consider theories of mind that have underpinned their emergence. Our appreciation of learning and our ability to theorize it, continue to labor under the influence of a contrived disjuncture between reason and emotion. As I have argued elsewhere, it is unwise to treat emotions as pesky interlopers, as if they can be excluded, since emotions are not optional (Beatty, 2000a, 2000b). This is particularly pertinent to our understanding of leadership and leadership development. Like Galileo's banished truth regarding the position of the earth in the cosmos, the systemic prohibition of emotion in educational professionalism and professional discourses flies in the face of lived experience. Furthermore, it is becoming clear that the theoretical separation of emotion and reason is a contrivance that has simply outgrown its usefulness and its claim to scientific validity (Damasio, 1997). For leaders, rationalization and objectification of the other as a means to the end of managing anxiety, is all too likely when the emotions are numbed and banished from view (Hochschild, 1983). If we were to return to the road not taken in the age of reason, we might be able to explore alternative more integrative pathways and perspectives on learning and leadership that have remained inaccessible until now. By embracing the reunification of the human mind as a multi-dimensional whole that continuously experiences reason and emotion, of what better things may we discover we are capable? This is a critical question for leadership preparation and development.

UNDERSTANDING EMOTION

We are our emotions. They are the lenses through which we experience the world. To understand emotions is to understand ourselves. As Hochschild argues:

> Emotion functions as a prism through which we may reconstruct what is often invisible or unconscious — what we must have wished, must have expected, must have seen or imagined to be true in the situation. From the colors of the prism we infer back what must have been behind and within it. (Hochschild, 1983: p. 246)

The acknowledgment of the presence of emotion in all human endeavors makes intuitive sense. As Macmurray (1962: p. 75) argues, "The emotional life is not simply a part or an aspect of human life. It is not, as we so often think, subordinate, or subsidiary to the mind. It is the core and the essence of human life". Recognizing the place of motivation, attitudes and feelings at the core of everything we do, Macmurray maintains:

> Any personal activity must have a motive and all motives are in the large sense, emotional. Indeed, an attitude of mind is simply an emotional state. The attitude of a scientist pursuing his vocation is, therefore, an emotional state....[If] the scientific state of mind were completely free of emotions, scientific enquiry could not be carried out. Further, if we identify this objective attitude with rationality, then it follows that rationality is itself an emotional state. (Macmurray, 1962: pp. 31–32)

According to Macmurray, emotion has a foundational role in the scientific state of mind, such that rationality itself may need to be reconceptualized. This has important implications for understanding all knowledge and thus all learning and leadership along with the learning of leadership.

Silence on Emotion

In educational administration, professionalism is often considered synonymous with being (or at least seeming) unemotional. While self control and composure under stress remain critical capabilities, an attendant loss of connectedness with one's inner emotional meaning making processes can result from continuously engaging in the emotional labor of masking real feelings and projecting others, resulting in emotional numbness (Hochschild, 1983). In this way the rich resource of emotional meaning making can be rendered inaccessible. What we are left with is a divided self, fragmented and barred from its ethical centre which is accessed through the emotions. The adage that power corrupts may be misleading. Perhaps it is the unquestioning acceptance of a dehumanized/de-emotionalized definition of leadership that tears the fabric of the self (Margolis, 1998). Without deliberate intervention to prevent it, the leader's integrated (albeit socially situated) self is subtly but decidedly compromised.

How has this tradition of detachment and even shame (Scheff & Retzinger, 2001) about our emotional selves evolved? Historically the ubiquitous processes of emotional inferencing have been denied and/or denigrated, despite their intrinsic relationship to the whole of human mind. Boler (1999) charts the history of this dichotomized relationship, claiming that reason and emotion have been separated in response to a deep seated distrust of the receptive, intuitive dimension that is part of all human beings regardless of gender (see also Bem et al.,1976). Boler treats the artificial separation of reason and emotion generally, as a multi-faceted manifestation of social control. Tracing its beginnings, she cites Bordo's (1987: p. 58) contention that the rejection of emotion is associated with the rejection of the feminine, resulting from the lost comfort of maternal "symbiosis and cosmic unity" that was enjoyed before the discovery that the Earth is not the centre of the universe. In Bordo's view, the resultant masculinization of thought was a collective psychological response to separation anxiety and an attempt to regain control. As a consequence Boler (1999: p. 10) argues that today, "one finds the powerful Western confluence of femininity and subjectivity as a corruption to be transcended". This is a disturbing possibility, but one to be considered seriously if the beginnings of the separation of reason and emotion are themselves emotionally rooted and it is actually (emotional) denial that keeps the inherent importance of emotion's role unacknowledged and unconsidered. In this case a reinforcing spiral of cause and effect can be envisioned. Emotional reasons may have been responsible for emotion's relegation to the sidelines, then and now.

Woodward (1990: p. 3) reminds us that "our vocabularies for the emotions are impoverished" and asks, "If our language is so bizarrely truncated, what of our experience both in and out of the academy?" Further, what of our experiences in leading, theorizing it and preparing people to lead? With little practice in using language to describe our emotional lives, it is small wonder our understanding of its role in learning and leading remains limited.

Ellis and Flaherty (1992) admonish the social science community for hierarchically positioning reason and objectivity above emotion and subjectivity. They argue that this has created a distorted view of what we have and have not searched for and correspondingly, what we have and have not found. The repositioning of emotion as the complement of reason and a key ingredient in a different kind of meaning making, challenges us to acknowledge the inner realities of our experiences and to deliberately develop a legitimate place for the language of emotion in the educational leadership discourse, both in theory and in practice. Emotions in the end are epistemological, even if our institutions regularly filter out the acknowledgment of this way of knowing (Boler, 1999).

The denigration of emotion as feminine and/or inferior to, as well as separate from reason and/or masculinity, is also biologically misrepresentative. Recent brain research points to neurobiological evidence of an inherent error in the Cartesian dichotomizing of reason and emotion. For Descartes, emotions happened to our souls, not to our thinking parts. His expression, '*cogito ergo sum*' or 'I think therefore I am', depicted a separation of mind and body that has held the modern world in its grasp for centuries. Descartes error lay in "the separation of the most refined operations of mind from the structure and operation of a biological organism" (Damasio, 1997: p. 250).

In contrast to Descartes' separation of body and mind, reason and emotion, Damasio (1997: p. 144) describes the mind in terms of dynamic and interactive emotional processes, as "ceaseless change [in the] landscape of our bodies.... There are many maps coordinated by mutually interactive neuron connections". In effect, one might just as appropriately declare, "I feel, therefore I am". Damasio's sequential, interactive model of emotion is a novel depiction of what goes on inside the 'black box' of the human psyche:

> ...emotions and feelings may not be intruders in the bastion of reason at all: they may be enmeshed in its networks for better and worse.... feelings may be just as cognitive as other precepts. (Damasio, 1997: p. xv)

No longer a question of mind or body: from this post-Cartesian perspective, even Western minds can begin to consider the body and mind as one. While the Western consciousness of this fact may be in its infancy, the wholeness of mind and body is foundational to Eastern philosophies and many indigenous peoples' perspectives.

Research on human psychological and social processes including theories of learning that acknowledge the importance of emotion are ultimately not less, but more scientific. With tangible evidence that human consciousness is a seamless simultaneous blend of thinking and feeling, perhaps now alternative pathways to understanding and exploring the lived experience of learning can take their place in formal schooling contexts.

This precept holds true in particular for the development of new theories of ideal learning conditions for leaders. Leadership is an inescapably emotionally challenging endeavor; good leadership, even more so. It is important to accomplish a non-anxious presence (Friedman, 1985) from which to listen deeply to and appreciate others' perspectives, without being thrown into defensive shut down modes of coping. Instead of the emotional numbness that is associated with habitual emotional labor (Hochschild, 1983), the 'noise' of the leader's own inner emotional turmoil can be quieted and at the same time, fully engaged through reflective learning. The key is acknowledging and attending to it. The learning of this counterintuitive approach to managing inner conflict and tension is supported through experience in collaborative reflection with trusted others. However, given the supreme pressure and personal isolation that most school leaders face every day such opportunities are not normatively occurring. However, well designed leadership preparation programs can provide valuable exceptions to this rule, and thereby help leaders to redefine their professional selves in connection with their professional contexts.

Theories of learning and theories of leadership have only relatively recently begun to integrate emotion's place. The field of educational leadership is beginning to appreciate that leader self-awareness is foundational to best practices in leadership (Gronn, 1996; Caldwell, 1997; Fullan, 2001 Beatty & Brew, 2004; Beatty, 2005; Beatty, 2006). Correspondingly, we are gradually beginning to develop a respectable and generative place for emotions in the lexicon of leadership. Beyond an instrumental view such as that inherent in much of the discourse surrounding emotional intelligence (Goleman, 1995), we are beginning to appreciate the inevitability of leaders becoming wounded (Ackerman & Maslin-Ostrowski, 2002) and the dangers in the cycle of mistreatment of themselves and others that can be associated with untended wounds (Blase & Blase, 2003; Beatty, 2004).

Deep understanding and self-acceptance extend far beyond skill sets and behaviors and well into a philosophical commitment to connectedness. Connectedness in relationship with others requires at the least, emotional connectedness with oneself. Arguably then, a first step in leader preparation and development involves reflective self-study in collaboration with others and engagement with a complex, interconnected emotionally loaded web of experiences.

PERSPECTIVES ON KNOWING

As Marshall and Greenfield (1987) noted, aspirant leaders are expected to demonstrate their ability to deny and silence their actual feelings and beliefs in order to qualify for membership in the leadership class. Meanwhile, the detrimental impact of self-silencing on learning has been studied in some depth by Belenky et al., 1986/1997). Perry (1970), Belenky et al. (ibid.) and Baxter Magolda (1992) have contributed to the understanding of shifts in adult epistemological perspectives by proposing various frameworks, which have important concepts in common. In the context of adult education, Brew (2001) provides a reconsideration and synthesis among concepts from all of these frameworks that is helpful for understanding the transformational power of the changing role of peers. This is particularly pertinent to the concept of knowledge authority, which shifts from being experienced as relatively external to increasingly internal through the sharing with others of experiences in personal meaning making. Part of the process of learning to lead involves learning to believe in one's internal knowledge authority, one's exercise of good judgment. If internal knowledge authority is fostered by meaningful learning exchanges and problem solving with peers, but such collaborative learning is counter to the dominant norms of school leadership culture, a paradox emerges: the dichotomy between the way leaders and teachers believe they must seem and the ways as highly functioning fully dimensional people, they need to be. Emotional control is one thing. Emotional numbness is quite another.

Yet, the sharing with professional colleagues about problematic experiences is anything but typical. Again the theme of safe spaces emerges. Blackmore (1996) has cautioned that fiscal reform jeopardizes local schools' principals' sense of safety for discussing their foibles and school concerns with each other, especially in an educational market economy. Webber and Robertson (1998), Beatty and Robertson (2001) and Crawford (2001), have argued for the learning potential for educational leaders who participate in electronically supported discussion groups. These views are consistent with Belenky et al.'s (1986) argument for the transformational power of connecting with peers. In their ability to bring peers together for shared meaning making, online educational administrator discussion groups have also supported emotional epistemological shifts (Beatty, 2002, 2005).

While online environments can be powerful catalysts, if leaders are to re-culture their schools with the people they encounter there, they also need successful face to face experiences in generating new collaborative learning communities. Leadership preparation programs can provide the structure and impetus for fostering these new ways of leading by *learning with* others (Beatty, 2006).

The concept of a safe space within which to come to terms with one's unfinishedness is particularly relevant to leaders, leadership and leadership preparation and development. A leader who believes s/he must appear fully formed and certain, cannot afford to provide openings for new learning and genuine inquiry with others. Conversely, the leader and for that matter, the teacher, and student who learn to safeguard the entitlement to being a work in progress, can also afford to share their fears, hopes and dreams and wonder aloud as they ask questions to which they do not yet know the answers.

A critical role for school leaders then, is the establishment of a culture of inquiry within which one is entitled to imperfection and therefore safe to engage in critical self-reflection and collaborative explorations in the generation of new knowledge. If they have not yet embraced this perspective nor experienced it in their own professional lives, leaders are sorely challenged in attempts to model such a view and create such safe learning spaces. The provision of opportunities for learning to re-culture is a responsibility that leadership preparation and development would wisely embrace.

LEARNING TO RE-ENVISION SCHOOL LEADERSHIP
IN TERMS OF CONNECTEDNESS

Huberman (1993: p. 219) suggests that a "necessary distance" between teachers and leaders arises from a sense of the need to remain in control. Teachers enjoy a sense of belonging to a professional peer group (ibid.) yet express a fervent desire for more interpersonal contact and professional collaboration with their leaders (Beatty, 2002). All educational leaders have the entitlement to invite new ways of connecting with teachers. Leaders can learn to refuse to be controlled by outdated norms and correspondingly, can choose to reject the imperative to control others in deference to a more respectful, caring and empowering approach (Leithwood & Beatty, 2008). Connectedness and trust among adults within schools is predictive of students' academic success (Bryk & Schneider, 2002) and is foundational to successful outreach to the community.

Despite the anticipated difficulties of doing so, Grogan calls for reconceiving educational administration and changing professional practice toward a culture of greater connectedness for social change:

> Connectedness to the wider community, not separation from it, must be encouraged in order that the education of students is achieved in the cultural context of the societies from which they emerge. If leadership is informed by an ethic of care and commitment to social change, school communities can model the kind of interdependent relationship feminist perspectives advocate. (Grogan, 1996: p. 189)

Consistent with theories of cooperative and collaborative learning, the recognition of interdependence at all levels is a vital lesson for all educational leaders and those who prepare them.

COMPETING OR COMPLEMENTARY CONCEPTUALIZATIONS? THE LEARNING CHALLENGE

The most pressing challenge remains to understand our behavior and our minds, in time. The competition among conceptualizations of human mind, human potential, the purpose of learning, and theories of learning, especially those to be applied in institutions such as schools, while enriching and fascinating, may also inadvertently inhibit the actualization of a coherent sustainable way of being. The relatively young discipline of psychology which gave birth to our theories of learning is a perfect example of the power of paradigm wars.

The search for universal patterns of mind gave rise to the organismic school of psychology which looked to essentialist, universal traits and behaviors in human nature, predictable and understandable as drives. Freud's (1935) model of psychology proposed tensions between the id, the ego and the superego. While acknowledging the role of culture in creating the superego that oversees the acceptability of behavior and engenders conscience, it was the libidinous drive for pleasure and avoidance of pain that captured Freud's imagination. Freud's influence on thinking about parents and children is important to our understanding of some of the assumptions about adult child relationships that influenced many parents in the early part of the century. Freud (cited in Blum, 2002: p. 7) disdained parental love: "Parental love, which is so touching and at bottom so childish, is nothing but parental narcissism born and, transformed though it be into object-love, it reveals its former character infallibly." Until the mid 20th century, in most Western societies, parental display of affection was frowned upon for fear that children would become spoiled. Freud was equally dismissive of children's love for the parent, believing it to be a simple pursuit of drive reduction in search of relief from hunger. While Freud's ideas were challenged in Benjamin Spock's popular theories of parenting with affection, the residue of de-emotionalized relationships between parents and children can be found in some outmoded ideas about schools and schooling.

We are beginning to appreciate the critical role of the relational factor inherent in later theories of social learning. Student sense of belonging at school depends on the solvency of their relationships with both peers and teachers (Osterman, 2000). The sense of belonging with their peers is linked to their trust in teachers and leaders (Beatty & Brew, 2005). Conversely, as we have learned with horror through children's violent sprees over the past 20 years, the alienation children suffer at school can have dire consequences for themselves and others. Theories of learning that evolved from studies of early conditioning helped to change the picture of ideal relationships between adults and children.

Learning Theories Evolve

Attempts to explain learning exclusively in terms of conditioning have their beginnings in experiments with Pavlov's dogs. The power of classical and operant conditioning and positive and negative reinforcement have become widely understood concepts. The positivism of the 1930s gave rise to an emphasis on predictability and behaviorism which continued to blossom. The notion of learning theory is itself, often associated with the behavioral view such that conditioning can be considered synonymous with learning. Behaviorism per se has it roots in the work of J. Watson and B.F. Skinner who were interested in studying only observable behaviors, as responses to stimuli, dismissing what could not be observed as irrelevant or non-existent. However, behaviorism was contentious as it purported that consciousness was irrelevant to scientific inquiry:

> ...behaviorism leaves a vacuum at the heart of our moral and practical life. It makes us out to be hollow men in a wasteland. It tells us that we are machines — enormously complicated machines, but in the end nothing more. (Blanshard & Skinner, 1967: pp. 317, 318 & 322)

Purist behaviorism's reductionistic conceptualizations of mental processes met their match in Noam Chomsky. The theorization that language is acquired or learned strictly as a result of verbal operant conditioning (a complex set of reinforcement processes whereby acceptable words and expressions are rewarded and unacceptable expressions and errors unrewarded or negatively reinforced) was insufficient to explain the phenomenon of language learning structures as Chomsky knew them (Chomsky, 1959). Such challenges began to be aimed at behaviorism more broadly for its inability to address the complexities of inner mental processes. This served to limit behaviorism's position as sufficiently robust, and other psychological theories began to emerge.

Thinkers and schools of thought are products of their times. In the 20th century, congruent with images of industrialization, the view of people as mechanisms that could be understood and thereby rendered as predictable captured the imagination of psychologists, learning theorists, teachers and leaders. One of the earliest learning theorists from this time, Edward Thorndyke (1861–1947), sought the formula to predict outcomes in learning, in order to have an impact on children's minds and bodies. He focused on cause and effect relationships in order to gain control of the learning process.

By the late 1950s, even affection, which had been dismissed as unworthy of scientific study, came under scrutiny (Blum, 2002). To explore the relationship between bonds among parents and offspring Harry Harlow's famous wire mother experiments in which he tested baby monkeys' preference for warmth against the drive to reduce hunger, revealed the critical role of emotion in early learning.

Paradoxically, his darkest experiments may have the brightest legacy: By studying neglect and its life altering consequences, Harlow confirmed love's central role in shaping not only how we feel but also how we think. The more children experience affection, he discovered, the more curious they become about the world. Love, it turns out, makes people smarter (Blum 2002; http://library.primate.wisc.edu/collections/books/love.html).

In the Harlow and Harlow (1965) experiments, the ability of monkeys to apply prior knowledge upon new learning seemed a revelation. However, his willingness to inflict harm upon monkeys and his apparent neglect of his wife and children stand in sharp contrast to the positive legacy of his work (Blum, 2002). Ironies abound in the contrast between theories espoused and those put to use for this brilliant, troubled, lonely man. Such dissonance is sobering if, as has been suggested, some educators are drawn into teaching as a way of addressing deficits in their own childhoods (Riley, personal communication. May, 2007). The same psychodynamic yearnings could arguably be operating among some teachers who seek positions as school leaders. Harlow would later connect his willingness to undertake such grueling monkey experiments with his own childhood sense of having been deprived of sufficient maternal affection due to an older brother's illness. Alice Miller's (1991) *The Untouched Key,* points to early childhood deprivation as having a powerful influence in adulthood. She explores case studies of gifted adults such as Picasso, Neitzsche and others who played out their childhood psychodynamic constructs in later life.

The need for a psychologically and emotionally secure base may indeed be a biological fact, and attachment behavior a biologically rooted and socially conditioned phenomenon resulting from learning experiences in a range of relationships (Bowlby 1969/1988). Bowlby's prize student, Mary Ainsworth observed children and mothers in Uganda and conducted some cross cultural research, which indicated that separation anxiety seems to occur between six and nine months. She studied mothers and children in various settings and at different ages and stages of development, concluding that there were four attachment styles: securely attached, insecurely attached, anxious/resistant (Ainsworth, Blehar, Waters & Wall, 1978). The connection between childhood attachment issues and adult psychodynamic working models is a space that leaders and teachers need structure and support to consider. Riley (forthcoming) explores the role of attachment theory in remediating teacher attitudes and behaviors associated with recidivist dysfunctional approaches to classroom management. As leaders seek to improve student learning by providing professional development opportunities for teachers, the deeper learning about self again appears on the horizon. Teachers' need for security to support their own learning is foundational to their ability to optimize the learning conditions for students including the behavior management strategies and social climate in their classrooms. Children's needs for a secure base are becoming foundational to our understanding of success in schools especially those whose children come from socially and economically challenged family situations (e.g., Dean 2001; Beatty & Brew 2005; Dean, Beatty, & Brew, 2007). The theory is that the learning that we try to facilitate in our schools is dependent upon the fulfillment of needs for security in all learners, including teachers and leaders themselves.

The focus on the acknowledgement of emotional needs as antecedent to higher order endeavors echoes the familiar hierarchy of human needs proposed by Abraham Maslow (1954), Harlow's assistant in the Madison monkey experiments. He is credited with having founded humanistic psychology, which continues to influence educational practices today. Like Husserl, Rogers and others in this school of theories of mind, and learning to be, Maslow positioned the phenomenological lived experience as well worthy of scientific inquiry. This perspective is reflected in the ascendance of constructivism as a theory of learning which advocates that learning occurs through connections that individuals construct between themselves and their existing inner knowledge and new understandings.

Constructivism was founded in reaction to behaviorism due to Edward Tolman's (1949) experiments with rats which showed that they had a way of building on prior learning with the use of a kind of cognitive map. This concept was applied by Jean Piaget (1958), who studied his own children and introduced the concept of schemas/schemata, or working models of the environments within which children were experimenting to learn. Discovery learning grew out of his work. Piaget's concepts of assimilation and accommodation were built on the notion of networked schemas. Assimilation positions learning as the integration of new learning within existing schemas, while accommodation requires the modification of old schemas for the integration of new learning.

Many who began in other schools of learning gravitated to a social learning theoretical approach in later stages of their careers. For example, Albert Bandura shifted from behaviorism (1965) to social learning and developed the theory of self-efficacy (1986); Jerome Bruner moved from early behavioral perspectives to cognitive psychology (1957) and on to education and learning theory that located learning as culturally contextualized and individually constructed through motivation or mental sets that affect perception. His and Vygotsky's ideas of scaffolding for learning that builds from one understanding to the next is much applied today:

> It is surely the case that schooling is only one small part of how a culture inducts the young into its canonical ways. Indeed, schooling may even be at odds with a culture's other ways of inducting the young into the requirements of communal living…what has become increasingly clear is that education is not just about conventional school matters like curriculum or standards of testing. What we resolve to do in school only makes sense when considered in the broader context of what the society intends to accomplish through its educational investment in the young. How one conceives of education, we have finally come to recognize, is a function of how one conceives of culture and its aims, professed and otherwise. (Bruner, 1996: pp. ix–x)

Bruner's work on the MACOS project involved young researchers such as the now famous Howard Gardner, who introduced the concept of multiple intelligences:

> In the heyday of psychometric and behaviorist eras, it was generally believed that intelligence was a single entity that was inherited; and that human beings — initially a blank slate — could be trained to learn anything, provided that it was presented in an appropriate way. Nowadays an increasing number of researchers believe precisely the opposite; that there exists a multitude of intelligences, quite independent of each other; that each intelligence has its own strengths and constraints; that the mind is far from unencumbered at birth; and that it is unexpectedly difficult to teach things that go against early naïve theories that challenge the natural lines of force within an intelligence and its matching domains. (Gardner, 1993: p. xxiii)

Freud's protégé, Carl Jung, took exception to his teacher's model, and instead conceptualized all psychological experience as inclusive of feminine and masculine/animus anima elements, along with the archetypal darker shadow self. His characterization of archetypal images and symbols emanating from a collective unconscious and manifesting in our subconscious opened up the field to entirely new conceptualizations of mind. Current conceptions of contemporary organizations return to this evocative paradigm, suggesting that organizational behavior also has unconscious elements that can be understood in terms of archetypes (e.g., Neville, 2007).

A second Freudian protégé, Adler, who also took his own path, saw power rather than pleasure as the ultimate reward, and developed a typology of personal development that culminated in self actualization through the divesting of individual power and the conferring of it upon others who were more needy, usually through philanthropic contributions to the greater good. This diffusion of power into the whole of social being provides insight into motivation with which many educators may identify.

Social cognition acknowledges the influence of cultural context and features social constructivism in the process of learning. These, and the concept of the zone of proximal development, are attributed to Lev Vygotsky whose work was not fully appreciated in the West until decades after it was written in Russian. At the time of his death at the early age of 38, Vygotsky was considering the role of emotions as the motivating sphere of consciousness in learning and the role of the teacher to provide the gift of confidence (Mahn & John-Steiner, 2002).

Motivation is considered a factor in learning involving a need, desire or want (Kleinginna & Kleinginna, 1981) that arouses, directs or causes persistence (Franken, 1994). Motivation is considered to be extrinsic when it is stimulated from outside the person and intrinsic when it is stimulated from inside the person. Teachers are said to be intrinsically motivated by the work itself, the satisfaction of making a difference in children's lives. Motivational needs are considered to range from behavior or external through social, biological, cognitive to affective. Basic or cognitive needs are associated with physiological and safety needs and the pursuit of attaining one's goals, and spiritual needs, to experiencing a sense of purpose in one's life. Behavioral explanations of motivation explain it in terms of stimulus and response conditionings. The resolution of cognitive dissonance is one example of a cognitive explanation for motivation. Inherent in cognitive theories of learning is the deliberate creation of disequilibrium as a condition of learning through which changes in behavior bring about new learning (Moon, 2004).

The concepts of equilibrium and disequilibrium in learning are relevant to preparation for leadership in that leading change involves the deliberate creation of disequilibrium. In terms of organizational learning and change, Neville (2007) challenges Lewin's view of transformation:

> For half a century organizational development theory has worked from the assumption that equilibrium is the natural state of an organization. This equilibrium may be disturbed from time to time by a period of turbulence, but the organization hopefully returns to equilibrium after this experience. Kurt Lewin's very influential unfreeze-reframe-refreeze model of organizational change is in tune with this 'natural' process. However, this particular truth about organizations is now challenged by another truth. In a machine-like, steady state universe it was appropriate to expect to find machine-like, steady state organizations. In a dynamic, alive, evolving universe, we expect to find dynamic, alive, evolving organizations. (Neville, 2007: p. 70)

Neville's conceptualization of a dynamic expanding view for organizations evokes images of spiraling and opening up in life affirming process of discovery, a very different view from the mechanistic imagery of the past century.

Attribution theory (Heider, 1958; Weiner, 1974) considers interpretations individuals make about experiences of success or failure as internal or external. Internal control is a desirable construct for the learner as it creates the held possibility of effort resulting in success. Expectancy theory (Vroom, 1964) posits the notion that three factors must all be present for motivation: belief in the likelihood that the desired outcome will occur; links between success and reward; and value of the goal. Franken (1994: p. 439) suggests that self concept is related to self-esteem in that "people who have good self esteem have a clearly differentiated self-concept... When people know themselves they can maximize outcomes because they know what they can and cannot do". Bandura's (1986, 1997, http://chiron.valdosta.edu/whuitt/col/motivation/motivate.html) explorations in self-efficacy position the importance of confidence that one can accomplish a desired task or goal. The relationship between self-efficacy and motivation is important for school leaders to appreciate, especially in their dealings with teachers (Leithwood & Beatty, 2008).

According to attachment theory (Bowlby, 1969), the secure base is also critical to curiosity; in other words, a foundation for learning. Just as children may become anxious when their reach exceeds their grasp as teachers encourage them to enter their zones of proximal development (Vygotsky, 1934/1987), adults can be threatened by professional imperatives for new learning. Without a secure base from which to explore new learning both children and adults may revert to unreceptive modes and exhibit attachment behaviors:

> ... attachment behavior is in no way confined to children. Although usually less readily aroused, we see it also in adolescents and adults of both sexes whenever they are anxious or under stress... . A feature of attachment behavior of the greatest importance clinically, and present irrespective of age ... is the intensity of the emotion that accompanies it, the kind of emotion aroused depending on how the relationship between the individual attached and the attachment figure is faring. If it goes well there is joy, and a sense of security. If it is threatened, there is jealousy, anxiety and anger. If broken there is grief and depression. (Bowlby, 1988: pp. 3, 4)

Teachers' need for a secure base is foundational to their ability to become curious about their own practices; this so that they may engage in bold self-critique in their efforts to optimize conditions for student learning. The appreciation of children's needs for a secure base and a sense of belonging and connectedness are aiding in our understanding of success in schools (Beatty & Brew, 2005). Comprehensive school based programs for developing social capital are grounded in these theoretical concepts. Children, who experience deprivation in family situations, need to be provided with a sense of safety, security and belonging, which have emerged as critical protective factors in reducing the risk of anti-social behaviors and crime (Dean, Beatty & Brew, 2007). Emerging clearly in research is the important role of leaders in fostering school cultures that create the necessary conditions for learning (Silins & Mulford, 2002).

Given the relationship between a sense of security and openness to new learning, the connection between attachment theory and the teacher student relationship presents a focus worthy of further study (e.g., see Riley, forthcoming). Correspondingly, given the extreme career vulnerability of teachers to their principals and the impact of leaders upon school climate and culture (Beatty, 2002, 2007a, 2007b) through the effect upon levels of trust in adults (Bryk & Schneider, 2002) and children (Beatty & Brew, 2004, 2005), attachment theory may provide some helpful insights for explaining the links among emotions, trust and learning at all levels in school communities.

Social learning theory is particularly influential in today's education practices of cooperative learning situations. Maxine Greene (1992: p. 250) captures a vision of learning in community:

> Passions, then, engagements, and imagining: I want to find a way of speaking of community, an expanding community, taking shape when diverse people, speaking as who and not what they are, come together in speech and action.

Learning about Self and Others

Tools from psychology abound for understanding self and others. For instance, learning style inventories such as Kolb's LSI; Myers Briggs personality type and its offshoot, True Colors; Salovey & Mayer's application of Reuven Bar-On's (1988) emotional intelligence and many others, are used to provide lenses for learning about our similarities and differences. However, when such tools are used superficially, they can exacerbate the very conditions they are designed to address, by fostering further categorizing and judging. In this case, issues of social separation and fragmentation arise. The managerial appeal of their apparent efficiency tempts users of these tools to apply them in reductionistic mechanistic ways, which can be counterproductive. That is, it is only by deeply understanding the theoretical underpinnings of such instruments and their protocols, and becoming intimately familiar with the continua and their interrelationships with each other and within each of us as individuals, that the ideas inherent within them can be integrated usefully for building connections rather than create further distances between people. Used skillfully, these tools do hold potential for developing appreciation for diversity. Learning reciprocity is the ideal: again, we encounter matters of emotion:

> In order to establish open learning reciprocity, one must be open to influence, to being emotionally "moved", to being vulnerable. All too often people move into illusions of self-sufficiency, control and power dynamics to manage the inevitable and often frightening experiences of vulnerability and movement into a power/control mode can lead to a relational pattern of entitlement, self pre-occupation, and failure of empathy in one persona and accommodation, compliance and silencing in the other. While giving the appearance of connection, inauthenticity and a deep sense of disconnection prevail. At its extreme, we see this pattern in many abusive relationships (Jordan, 1993: p. 1)

ADULT LEARNING REVISITED

In her excellent volume, *The New Update on Adult Learning,* Merriam (2001: p. 1) revisits the traditional themes of andragogy, self-directionality, and the later arriving transformational learning, characterizing these and other advances in the field as an "ever-changing mosaic". Since the establishment of Mezirow's (1991, 2000) transformational adult learning theory, the emphasis has shifted from what we know to how we know, and the importance of trusting relationships, feelings and context (Baumgartner, 2001).

The recognition of informal and incidental learning is considered by Marsick and Watkins (2001) who present a new model involving a progression of meaning making in practice that honors context and distinguishes among various incidental learning processes. Hayes (2001) challenges patterns within essentialist gendered treatments of learning by proposing it is the learning situation that is gendered. Theories of situated cognition echo the context dependence of learning especially with respect to tools, and the qualities of social interaction that define communities of practice (Hansman, 2001). As Kilgore (2001: p. 54) explains, both critical and postmodern perspectives on learning define knowledge as taking form "in the eyes of the knower, rather than being acquired from an existing reality that resides 'out there' " even though critical theorists focus on political perspectives regarding systemic subjugation while postmodern theorists see all knowledge as "tentative, fragmented, multi-faceted, and not necessarily rational". The positioning of emotions and the images 'behind' them as fruitful for moving "toward a deeper, more conscious connection with these aspects of ourselves" (Dirkx, 2001: p. 69), echoes the call for deeper learning defined through qualitatively different kinds of engagement with the dynamic interplay among context, content and self. Such learning is fostered by the appreciation of recent research on the brain (Hill, 2001), somatic learning and the role of imagination in narrative learning or storytelling (Clark, 2001).

THE LEADING EDGE

Theories of learning and instructional practices that feature individual and collective development, personal transformation, increased integrative creativity and enhancement of consciousness provide common ground and universal entry points no matter what one's beliefs, values, background or origins. The engagement of leaders with issues of self-development and awareness of learning patterns *in here*, is qualitatively different from learning about leadership as something that happens *out there*. Programmatic approaches to this terrain engage different emotions, among them the courage to move toward the danger (Maurer, 1996) and discomfort (Boler, 1999) of one's own fears.

For some time, images of self-awareness, self-discovery and personal transformation have been advocated for effective leaders in and out of the domain of education (e.g., Bennis, 1989; Covey, 1990; Kouzes & Posner, 1993; Bolman & Deal, 1995; Bender, 1997; Loader, 1997; Gronn, 1999). Whether the personal journey is characterized in explicitly or implicitly affective terms, this is emotional work of the toughest kind. It takes courage to lead others by leading oneself in learning (Palmer, 1998). The same challenge presents itself for teachers of leadership:

> Good talk about good teaching can take many forms and involve many conversation partners —
> and it can transform teaching and learning. But it will happen only if leaders expect it, invite it,
> and provide hospitable space for the conversation to occur. (Palmer, 1998: pp. 160–61)

The engagement with learning for personal transformation requires emotional honesty and self-acceptance (Brill, 2000). Leaders who know themselves, are far more likely to be able to get to know others in a non-defensive non-aggressive way. Having faced their own anxieties and being fully aware of the normal presence of fear, leaders can, with the support of trusted colleagues, learn to face others with calm and self-acceptance. Furthermore, the non-anxious leader can access her/his own courage more readily when not fighting unacknowledged anxiety, shame and/or fear of shame (Scheff & Retzinger, 2000). It is in the acknowledgement of inner emotional realities and actual vulnerabilities that strength in self-awareness can be found. Leadership that goes beyond obedience and followership, the kind that dares to be creative requires emotional awareness and connectedness with self and others (Bolman & Deal, 1995).

Authentic leadership is a matter of self-empowerment (Kouzes & Posner, 1993). Knowing oneself and engaging in deep connection with inner longings for healing, are critical to good leadership in any setting. According to Bolman and Deal (1995) this is leading with soul by facing one's fears and inner longings for connection and relationship with others. Loader's (1997) narrative and descriptive treatise of his experience in the principalship confirms the importance of emotional factors. He describes principal hopes and dreams, courage and paranoia and describes the awareness of his own emotional realities that made him better equipped to handle and more effective at encouraging educational change. He offers the following advice to his fellow principals:

> Be energized by the uncertainties, mysteries and doubts. In the midst of your leadership write of
> your experiences to help us weary but excited fellow travellers. Perhaps you may be able to fill in
> the gaps and write the unwritten stories about 'The humpty dumpty principal'; 'The proper principal'; 'the pre-emptory principal'; the humble principal'; or other principals....Most attempts
> at reform have come from the outside, people wishing to impose curriculum and benchmarks....
> schools can transform themselves. Better schools will eventuate when those in the schools, particularly the principal, become not only more aware of their community and its requirements

but also more aware of what is happening within themselves. A sensitive, thoughtful, proactive leadership might yet deliver the quality outcomes that the community desires from schooling. (Loader, 1997: pp. 150–51)

Starratt (1991) links effective leadership back to relationships and connectedness:

If schools are to teach the larger connection — connections to our ancestors, to the biosphere, to the cultural heroes of the past, to the agenda of the future — they must begin with the connections of everyday experience, the connections to our peers, to our extended families, to the cultural dynamic or our neighbourhoods. (Starratt, 1991: p. 77)

BEYOND EMPATHY

Little's (1982) exploration of the connection between success and adaptability features 'reciprocation' which she defines as a matter of effort and humility. In contrast to Beale's image of the principal as all power wielding, with teachers reduced to "yes men" (Beale, 1936: p. 602), Little's notion of 'equal humility' is evocative and speaks to a missing ingredient in teacher-leader relationship — mutuality. The exchange factor is there, a reciprocity of sorts, but the stakes are different for the teacher and the leader. A pursuant lack of equal humility may also help to explain this phenomenon. While teachers and leaders occupy different positions within their school organizational hierarchy which makes their achievement of mutuality even more challenging, they may be aided by acknowledging that asymmetric reciprocity is as good as it gets:

… we each must be open to learning about the other person's perspective, since we cannot take the other person's standpoint and imagine that perspective as our own. This implies that we have the moral humility to acknowledge that even though there may be much I do understand about the other person's perspective through her communication to me and through the constructions we have made common between us, there is also always a remainder, much that I do not understand about the other person's experience and perspective…. the only correction to such misrepresentations of the standpoint of others is their ability to tell me that I am wrong about them. (Young, 1997: pp. 53 & 45)

Without an expressivist discourse, a reigning 'culture of silence,' on inner experiences can similarly foster misrepresentations that confound connectedness and shared discovery with others. Learning about learning requires the valuing of internality.

Critical theory, that acknowledges inequities that otherwise may go unacknowledged and unchallenged can provide comfort for those who suffer the pain of systemic subjugation. As bell hooks proclaimed in *Teaching to Transgress*, "I came to theory, because I was hurting — the pain within me so intense that I could not go on living. I came to theory desperate, wanting to comprehend- to grasp what was happening around and within me. Most importantly, I wanted to make the hurt go away. I saw in theory then a location for healing" (cited in Brookfield, 2005: p. 4). By providing a conceptually 'bigger picture' of social and political patterns, within critical theory there are openings for adult learning that work through the lenses of social, economic and political identities. As Brookfield (2005: p. 5) notes, "theorizing is a form of meaning making, born of a desire to create explanations that impose conceptual order on reality, however artificial this order might later turn out to be." Brookfield links the power of critical theory in adult learning and teaching to Mezirow's (1991) theory of transformative learning as adults develop increasingly comprehensive and discriminating perspectives on how they see the world:

When a theoretical insight concerning hegemony (the process by which we embrace ideas and practices that keep us enslaved) helps us understand our practice in a new way, it often takes a great weight of potential guilt off our shoulders. There is no shame in admitting that we need theoretical insights to help us understand how the same destructive scenarios keep emerging in our lives, despite our efforts to prevent these. Without theoretical help, it is easy to see how many of our private troubles are produced by systemic constraints and contradictions. Brookfield (2005: p. 5)

Theoretical points of departure are often helpful in leadership preparation. For instance, the use of an emotional epistemologies theoretical framework within leadership preparation programs has proven similarly transformative (Beatty & Brew, 2004; Beatty, 2006). The framework has been used implicitly and explicitly to make apparent to learners, the systemic prohibitions upon the inner experiences of teaching and leading, to challenge the professional silence on emotion, and to explore ways of reculturing schools by changing the feeling rules. In this way assumptions about emotions are questioned, and alternative perspectives on emotion's place in the inner, inter and wider cultural space of learning and leading are explored. Ackerman and Maslin-Ostrowski's (2002, 2004) theory elucidates the systemic likelihood of school leaders being wounded by virtue of the fact that leadership is the act of disturbing the status quo. Based on over a decade of empirical work with principals, they present findings of a range of personal and professional impacts which help to make such events and their results, transparent and shared. By challenging the norm of silent suffering and permanent damage, and creating a safe space for returning to the scene of the wounding, aspirant and incumbent leaders can connect with their colleagues' stories, and retrieve their own painful places. In sharing their stories with each other, the healing can begin, and a transformative process occur as the personal professional and organizational self becomes reintegrated (Beatty, 2000c; 2006).

Emerging theories underpinning the power of story in learning are fascinating. A brain-based approach provides the following explanation: When listening to a story, in the conscious, Beta state the language processing domain listens to the words, while the spatial visual domain fills in the pictures and affective material in a simultaneous and harmonious activity that blends thinking, seeing and feeling. Stories with multi-sensory detail are most easily remembered as they activate the fullest range of the brain's memory storage bases. At the same time as the story is told, and after, the mind searches for relationships, patterns and deeper meaning.

The reconsideration of shifts in epistemological perspectives in cognitive and emotional knowledge authority can assist in the discussion of leading edge learning design elements that are fostering redefinitions of leadership itself as dynamic inquiry and collaborative reflection in the process of *learning with* others (Beatty, 2006). Given the additional evidence of the increasing use of action learning sets, school enquiry visits, networked learning groups and enquiry within on-line learning communities we can see that like leadership, leadership preparation and development is evolving. Exemplary approaches that prepare leaders for addressing certain ambiguities and negotiated futures in schools and schooling point to the value of experiencing first hand membership in professional learning communities as a way of learning how to create them. In leading edge programs, leaders unlearn old messages and learn new ways of seeing and being that enable them to foster school cultures that survive and thrive in genuine collaborative inquiry.

Leaders who are assisted in becoming emotionally prepared for developing dynamic learning communities that embrace diversity and the diffusion of leadership throughout them, are better able to respond to the needs of all learners, including themselves. As all members of learning communities build trust, resilience and discerning responsiveness to the needs for change they also become better able to address both foreseeable and unforeseeable complexities together. Further research is warranted if we are fully to appreciate the inner life of leadership and to track the impacts upon school leaders who have benefited from approaches to leader preparation and development that acknowledge and mine the riches within this 'place' where all learning actually occurs.

ACKNOWLEDGMENT

I am grateful to Professor Ken Leithwood and Professor Petros Pashiardis for their sage editorial advice.

REFERENCES

Ackerman, R., & Maslin-Ostrowski, P. (2002). *The wounded leader: How real leadership emerges in times of crisis.* San Francisco, CA: Jossey Bass.

Ackerman, R., & Maslin-Ostrowski- P. (2004). The Wounded Leader and Emotional Learning in the schoolhouse. *School Leadership and Management, 24*(3), 311–328.

Ainsworth, M. D. S., Blehar, M. C., Waters, E., & Wall, S. (1978). *Patterns of attachment.* Hillsdale, NJ: Erlbaum.

Argyris, C., & Schon, D.A. (1974). *Theory in practice: Increasing professional effectiveness.* San Francisco: Jossey-Bass.

Argyris, C., & Schon, D.A. (1978). *Organisational learning: A theory of action perspective.* Reading, MA: Addison-Wesley.

Argyris, C., & Schon, D. A. (1996). *Organizational learning II: Theory, method, and practice.* Reading, MA: Addison-Wesley.

Argyris, C., Putnam, R., & McLain-Smith, D. (1985). *Action science: Concepts, methods, and skills for research and intervention.* San Franciso, CA: Jossey-Bass.

Ball, S. (2000). Performativities and Fabrications in the Education Economy: Towards the performative society. *Australian Educational Researcher 27*(2), 1–25.

Bandura, A. (1965). *Research in behaviour modification: New developments and implications.* New York: Holt, Rinehart and Winston.

Bandura, A. (1986). *Social foundations of thought and action: A social-cognitive theory.* Upper Saddle River, NJ: Prentice-Hall.

Bandura, A. (1997). *Self-efficacy: The exercise of control.* New York: W. H. Freeman.

Bar-On, R. (1988). The Development of a Concept of Psychological Well-Being. Unpublished Ph.D. dissertation. Rhodes University, South Africa.

Baumgartner, L. (2001). An update on transformational learning. In Merriam, S. (Ed.), *The new update on adult learning theory* (pp. 15–24). San Francisco, CA: Jossey-Bass.

Baxter Magolda, M. (1992). *Knowing and reasoning in College. Gender-related patterns in students' intellectual development.* San Francisco: Jossey-Bass.

Beale, H. (1936). *Are American teachers free? An analysis of restraints upon the freedom of teaching in America schools.* New York: Scribner.

Beatty, B. (2000a). The emotions of educational leadership: Breaking the silence. *International Journal of Leadership in Education, 3*(4), 331–357.

Beatty, B. (2000b). The Paradox of Emotion and Educational Leadership. A keynote address presented to the British Educational Administration and Management Annual conference, Bristol, UK. September.

Beatty, B. (2000c). Teachers leading their own professional growth: Self-directed reflection and collaboration and changes in perception of self and work in secondary school teachers. *Journal of In-Service Education, 26*(1), 73–97.

Beatty, B. (2002). Emotion Matters in Educational Leadership: Examining the Unexamined. Unpublished Doctoral Dissertation, Ontario Institute for Studies in Education, University of Toronto, Toronto.

Beatty, B. (2004). Book Review of J. Blase & J. Blase, Breaking the Silence: principal mistreatment of principals; R. Ackerman & P. Maslin-Ostrowski, The wounded leader. *Educational Administration Quarterly, 40*(2), 296–312.

Beatty, B. (2005). Emotional leadership. In Brent Davies (Ed.), *The essentials of school leadership* (pp 122–144). Thousand Oaks, CA: Sage.

Beatty, B. (2006). Becoming emotionally prepared for leadership. *International Journal of Knowledge Culture and Change, 6*(5), 1–19. Melbourne, Victoria, Au: Common Ground Publishing. Online version www.Magagement-Journal.com.

Beatty, B. (2007a). Going through the emotions: Getting to the heart of school renewal. *Australian Journal Of Education.* Special Issue. November.

Beatty, B. (2007b). Feeling the future of school leadership: Learning to lead with the emotions in mind. *Leading and Managing, 13*(2), 44–65. Special Issue. Australian Council for Educational Leadership.

Beatty, B. R., & Brew, C. R. (2005). Measuring student sense of connectedness with school: The development of an instrument for use in secondary schools. *Leading and Managing, 11*(2), 103–118.

Beatty, B., & Brew, C. (2004). Trusting relationships and emotional epistemologies: A foundational leadership issue. *School Leadership and Management, 24*(3), 329–356.

Beatty, B., & Robertson, J. (2001, April). *Leaders online: Emotions and educational leadership in the context of online discussion groups.* Paper presented at the Annual Meeting of the American Educational Research Association, Seattle, Washington.

Belenky, M. F., Clinchy, B. M., Goldberger, N. R., & Tarule, J. M. (1986). *Women's ways of knowing: The development of self, voice and mind.* New York: Basic Books.

Belenky, M. F., Clinchy, B. M., Goldberger, N. R., & Tarule, J. M. (1997). *Women's ways of knowing: The development of self, voice and mind* (2nd ed.). New York: Basic Books.

Bem, S. L., Martyna, W., & Watson, C. (1976). Sex typing and androgyny: Further explorations of the expressive domain. *Journal of Personality and Social Psychology, 34*(5), 1016–1023.

Bender, P. (1997). *Leadership from within.* Toronto: Stoddart.

Bennis, W. (1989). *On becoming a leader.* Reading, MA.: Addison-Wesley.

Blackmore, J. (1996). Doing 'emotional labour' in the education market place: Stories from the field of women in management. *Discourse: Studies in the Cultural Politics of Education, 17*(3), 337–349.

Blackmore, J. (2004). The dissonance between performativity and 'real work' in corporate times: Leading and teaching as emotional management work. *School Leadership and Management, 24*(4), 439–459.

Blanshard, B., & Skinner, B. F. (1967).The problem of consciousness—A debate. *Philosophy and Phenomenological Research, 27*(3), 317–337.

Blase, J., & Blase, J. (2003). *Breaking the silence: Overcoming the problem of principal mistreatment of teachers.* Thousand Oaks, CA: Corwin Press.

Blum, D. (2002). *Love at Goon Park.* Cambridge MA: Perseus Book Group.

Boler, M. (1999). *Feeling power: Emotions in education.* New York: Routledge.

Bolman, L., & Deal, T. (1995). *Leading with soul.* San Francisco, CA: Jossey-Bass.

Bordo, S. (1987). *The flight to objectivity: Essays on Cartesianism and culture.* Albany: State University of New York Press.

Bowlby, J. (1969). *Attachment and loss, Vol. 1.* New York: Basic Books

Bowlby, J. (1988). *A secure base: Parent-child attachment and healthy human development.* London: Routledge.

Brew, C. R. (2001). Women, mathematics and epistemology: An integrated framework. *International Journal of Inclusive Education, 5*(1), 15–32.

Brill, R. (2000). *Emotional honesty and self-acceptance: Educational strategies for preventing violence.* Philadelphia: Xlibris.

Brookfield, S. (2005). *The power of critical theory: Liberating adult learning and teaching.* San Francisco: Jossey Bass

Bruner, J. S. (1957). On perceptual readiness. *Psychological Review, 64*(2), 123–152

Bruner, J. S. (1996). *The culture of education.* Cambridge. MA: Harvard University Press

Bryk, A., & Schneider, B. (2002). *Trust in schools: A core resource for improvement.* New York: Sage.

Caldwell, B. (1997). Prologue: The external principal. In D. Loader (Ed.), *The inner principal* (pp. vii–ix). London: Falmer Press.

Chomsky, N. (1959). A review of B. F. Skinner's verbal behavior. *Language, 35*(1), 26–58.

Clark, C. (2001). Off the beaten path: Some creative approaches. In S. Merriam (Ed.), *The new update on adult learning theory* (pp. 84–92). San Francisco, CA: Jossey-Bass.

Covey, S. (1990). *The seven habits of highly effective people.* New York: Simon & Schuster.

Crawford, M. (2001, April). King John's Christmas: Developing leadership communities on line. Paper presented at the Annual Meeting of the American Educational Research Association, Seattle, Washington State.

Damasio, A. (1997). *Descartes' error: Emotion, reason and the human brain* (2nd ed.). New York: Harper Collins.

Dean, S. (2001). *Hearts & minds: A public school miracle.* Toronto, Ontario: Penguin Press.

Dean, S., Beatty, B. & Brew, C. (2007). Creating safe and caring learning communities: Understanding school based development of social capital. *ACEL Yearbook, 2007.*

Dirkx, J. (2001). The power of feelings: Emotion, imagination, and the construction of meaning in adult learning. In S. Merriam (Ed.), *The new update on adult learning theory* (pp. 63–72). San Francisco, CA: Jossey-Bass.

Eisler, R. (1987). *The chalice and the blade: Our history, our future.* San Francisco: Harper.

Eisler, R. (2007). *The real wealth of nations: Creating a caring economics.* San Franciso, CA: Berrett-Koehler

Ellis, C., & Flaherty, M. (Eds.). (1992). *Investigating subjectivity.* Newbury Park, CA: Sage.

Evans, R. (1996). *The human side of school change.* San Francisco, CA: Jossey-Bass.

Franken, R. (1994). *Human motivation.* Boston, MA: Brooks/Cole.

Freud, S. (1935). The unconscious (C.M. Baines, Trans.). In *Essays in metapsychology*: London: Liveright. (Original work published 1915)

Friedman, E. H. (1985). *Generation to generation.* New York: Guilford.

Fullan, M. G. (1999). *Change forces: The sequel.* Bristol, PA: Falmer Press.

Fullan, M. G. (2001). *Leading in a culture of change.* San Francisco, CA: Jossey-Bass.

Gardner, H. (1993). *Frames of mind.* New York: Basic Books

Goleman, D. (1995). *Emotional intelligence.* New York: Bantam Books.

Greene, M. (1992). The Passions of pluralism: Multiculturalism and the expanding community. *The Journal of Negro Education, 61*(3), 250–261.

Grogan, M. (1996). *Voices of women aspiring to the superintendency.* Albany: State University of New York Press.

Gronn, P. (1996). From translations to transformations: A new world order in the study of leadership. *Educational Management and Administration, 24*(1), 7–30.

Gronn, P. (1999). *The making of educational leaders.* London: Cassell.

Hansman, C. (2001). Context-based Adult Learning. In S. Merriam (Ed.), *The new update on adult learning theory* (pp. 43–52). San Francisco, CA: Jossey-Bass.

Hargreaves, A. (1998). The emotional politics of teaching and teacher development: with implications for educational leadership. *International Journal of Leadership In Education, 1*(4), 315–336.

Harlow, H., & Harlow, M. (1965). The affectional systems. In A. Schrier, H. Harlow, & F. Stollnitz (Eds.), *Behavior of non-human primates* (pp. 287–334). New York: Academic Press.

Hayes, E. (2001). A new look at women's learning. In S. Merriam (Ed.), *The new update on adult learning* (pp. 35–42). San Francisco, CA: Jossey-Bass.

Heider, F. (1958). *The psychology of interpersonal relations.* New York: Wiley.

Hill, L. (2001). The brain and consciousness: Sources of information for understanding adult learning. In

S. Merriam (Ed.), *The new update on adult learning theory* (pp. 73–82). San Francisco, CA: Jossey-Bass.

Hochschild, A. R. (1983). *The managed heart: The commercialization of human feeling*. Berkeley: University of California Press.

Huberman, M. (1993). *The lives of teachers*. (2nd ed.). (J. Neufeld, Trans.). Teacher Development Series. London: Redwood.

Hurley, J. (2007). *Stories of wounding*. A Keynote Address to Human Leadership Developing People. Melbourne Australia, May, 2007.

Jordan, J. V. (1993). *Challenges to connection. Work in progress No. 60*. Wellesley, MA: Stone Center Working Paper Series.

Kilgore, D. (2001). Critical and postmodern perspectives on adult learning. In S. Merriam (Ed.), *The new update on adult learning theory* (pp. 53–62). San Francisco, CA: Jossey-Bass.

Kleinginna, P., & Kleinginna, A. (1981). A categorized list of emotions definitions, with suggestions for a consensual definition. *Motivation and Emotion, 5*(4), 345–379. Dordrecht, The Netherlands: Springer.

Knapp, M.S., Copland, M.A., & Talbert, J.E. (2003). Leading for learning: reflective tools for school and district leaders. Seattle: University of Washington, Centre for the study of teaching and policy, February 2003, 12.

Kouzes, J., & Posner, B. (1993). *Credibility: How leaders gain and lose it, why people demand it*. San Francisco, CA: Jossey-Bass.

Leithwood, K., & Beatty, B. (2008). *Leading with teacher emotion in mind*. Thousand Oaks, CA: Corwin Press.

Leithwood, K., Jantzi, D., & Steinbach, R. (1999). *Changing leadership for changing times*. Philadelphia: Open University Press.

Little, J. W. (1982). Norms of collegiality and experimentation: Workplace conditions of school success. *American Educational Research Journal, 19*(3), 325–40.

Loader, D. (1997). *The inner principal*. London: Falmer Press.

Macmurray, J. (1962). *Reason and emotion*. New York: Barnes and Noble.

Mahn, H., & John-Steiner, V. (2002). The gift of confidence: A Vygotskian view of emotions. In G. Wells & G. Claxton (Eds.) *Learning for life in the twenty-first century: sociocultural perspective on the future of education* (pp. 46–58). Oxford: Blackwell.

Margolis, D. R. (1998). *The fabric of self: A theory of ethics and emotions*. New Haven, CT: Yale University Press.

Marshall, C., & Greenfield, W. (1987). The dynamics in the enculturation and the work in the assistant principalship. *Urban Education, 22*(11), 36–52.

Marsick, V., & Watkins, K. (2001) Informal and Incidental Learning. In S. Merriam (Ed.), *The update on adult learning theory* (pp. 25–34). San Francisco, CA: Jossey-Bass

Maslow, A. (1954). *Motivation and personality*. New York: Harper.

Maurer, R. (1996). *Beyond the wall of resistance*. Austin, TX: Bard Books.

Merriam, S. (Ed.) (2001). *The new update on adult learning theory*. San Francisco, CA: Jossey-Bass.

Merriam, S. (Ed.) (2001). Editor's notes. In S. Merriam (Ed), *The new update on adult learning theory* (pp. 1–2). San Francisco, CA: Jossey-Bass.

Merriam, S. (Ed.) (2001). Andragogy and self-directed learning: Pillars of adult learning theory. In S. Merriam (Ed), *The new update on adult learning theory* (pp. 3–14). San Francisco, CA: Jossey-Bass.

Mezirow, J. (1991). *Transformative dimensions of adult learning*. San Francisco, CA: Jossey-Bass.

Mezirow, J. (2000*). Learning as transformation: Critical perspectives on a theory in progress*. San Francisco, CA.: Jossey-Bass.

Miller, A. (1991). *The untouched key*. New York: Anchor Books.

Moon, J. (2004). *A handbook of reflective and experiential learning: Theory and practice*. New York: Routledge Falmer.

Mulkeen, T. A., & Cooper, B. S. (1992). Implications of preparing school administrators for knowledge work organisations: A case study. *Journal of Educational Administration, 30*(1), 17–29.

Murphy, J., & Adams, J.E. (1998). Reforming America's schools 1980–2000. *Journal of Educational Administration, 36,* 426–444.

Neville, B. (2007) *Olympus Inc: Intervening for cultural change in organizations.* Greensborough, Victoria, AU: Flat Chat Press.

OECD (2005). *Improving School Leadership* project http://www.oecd.org/document/53/0,2340,en_2649_3 7455_38529205_1_1_1_37455,00.html

Osterman, K. (2000). Students' need for belonging in the school community. *Review of Educational Research, 70*(3), 323–367.

Palmer, P. (1998). *The courage to teach.* San Francisco: Jossey-Bass.

Perry, W. G. (1970). *Forms of intellectual and ethical development in the college years: A scheme.* New York: Holt, Rinehart & Winston.

Piaget, J. & Inhelder, B. (1958). *The growth of logical thinking from childhood to adolescence.* New York: Basic Books.

Riley, P. (2007). To stir with love: Attachment, teacher behaviour and classroom management. Unpublished Doctoral Dissertation, Latrobe University, Bundoora, Victoria, Australia.

Saulwick, I. (2004). The privilege and the price: A study of principal class workload and its impact on health and wellbeing. Victoria, Au: Department of Education and Training.

Scheff, T. J., & Retzinger, S. M. (2000). *Shame as the master emotion of everyday life.* Retrieved May 12, 2002, from *Journal of Mundane Behaviour* http://www.mundanebehavior.org/issues/v1n3/scheff-retzinger.htm

Sergiovanni, T. (1992). *Moral leadership.* San Francisco, CA: Jossey-Bass.

Shields, C. M. (2005) School leadership in the 21st century: Broadening the base. In C, Miskel & W. Hoy (Eds.), *Educational Leadership and Reform* (pp. 77–116). Greenwich, CT: Information Age.

Silins, H., & Mulford, W. (2002). Leadership and school results. In K. Leithwood & P. Hallinger (Eds.), *Second International Handbook of Educational Leadership and Administration* (pp. 561–612). Norwell, MA: Kluwer.

Spillane, J. P., Halverson, R., & Diamond, J B. (2001, April). Investigating school leadership practice: A distributive practice. *Educational Researcher, 30*(3), 23–28.

Starratt, R. J. (1991). Building an ethical school: A theory for practice in educational leadership. *Educational Administration Quarterly, 27*(2), 185–202.

Tolman, E. (1949). The psychology of social learning. *Social Issues. 40,* 2–18.

Understanding School Based Development of Social Capital. *ACEL Yearbook, 2006.*

Vroom, V. (1964). *Work and motivation.* New York: Wiley.

Vygotsky, L. S. (1934/1987). *The collected works of L. S. Vygotsky: Vol. 1. Problems of general psychology.* New York: Plenum.

Webber, C. F., & Robertson, J. (1998). Boundary breaking: An emergent model for leadership development [Electronic version]. *Educational Policy Analysis Archives, 6*(21). Retrieved from http://olam.ed.asu.edu/epaa/v6n21.html

Weiner, B. (1974). *Achievement motivation and attribution theory.* Morristown, NJ: General Learning Press.

Woodward, K. (1990). Introduction. (Special issue on Discourses of the Emotions). *Discourse: Journal for Theoretical Studies in Media and Culture, 13*(1), 3–11.

Young, I. M. (1997). Asymmetrical reciprocity: On moral respect, wonder, and enlarged thought. *Intersecting voices: Dilemmas of gender, political philosophy and policy.* Princeton, NJ: Princeton University Press.

II
THE PRACTICE OF
LEADERSHIP DEVELOPMENT

9

School Development and School Leader Development: New Learning Opportunities for School Leaders and Their Schools

Stephan Gerhard Huber

In view of the ever-increasing responsibilities of school leaders (the term 'school leader' in this chapter is used as synonymous with principal, head teacher, administrator or other term describing the person who is in charge of an individual school) for ensuring and enhancing the quality of schools, school leadership has recently become one of the central concerns of educational policy makers. At the beginning of the new century, there is broad international agreement about the need for school leaders to have the capacities required to improve teaching, learning, and pupils' development and achievement. Consequently, in many countries, the development of school leaders is high on the agenda of politicians of different political wings. A major focus of professional development programs in many countries is the establishment and modification of training and development opportunities.

The findings of an international study of school leadership development[1] (see Huber, 2004), which surveys the development models for school leaders in 15 countries across Europe, Asia, Australasia, and North America, underpin a number of international patterns or tendencies in school leadership development seen from a global perspective:

1. Central quality assurance and decentralized provision
   While quality assurance is often established by a central superordinate institution (through central guidelines, standards or suitable quality control measures such as accreditation, certification and licensing procedures) on one hand, numerous decentralized providers are then responsible for actually conducting the programs on the other hand.
2. New forms of cooperation and partnership
   New arrangements concerning partnerships in numerous countries, especially collaboration with the school boards and particular schools within the specific region, enable the implementation of innovative teaching and learning strategies for program participants. These partnerships have also contributed to the creation of a pool of highly qualified and accredited or certified trainers in some countries.

3. Dovetailing theory and practice

Partnerships like these have also contributed to the increasing combination of the theoretical and practical aspects of school leadership development, as theoretical knowledge and practical experiences are interdependent and therefore have to be developed together.

4. Preparatory qualification

Increasingly, a preparatory qualification is offered. Training undertaken before taking a position of school leadership is considered more useful than relying solely on in-service training once one has been appointed to a leadership position.

5. Extensive and comprehensive programs

There is a significant tendency towards more extensive and comprehensive training programs that are then able to explore many of the challenges connected to this new leadership role and its responsibilities.

6. Multi-phase designs and modularization

School leadership development is more and more regarded as a continuous, life-long process linked to the career cycle and to specific needs of the leader and his or her school. Hence, there is a trend towards multi-phase designs and modularization of the programs.

7. Personal development instead of training for a role

Often, training for a management position in terms of a fixed 'role' has been replaced by offering professional development opportunities concentrating on personal learning and one's needs in the areas of knowledge, dispositions, and performances that are useful in a more complex environment. It is the personality and the personal development of the (aspiring) school leader that become the focal point of the programs.

8. The communicative and cooperative shift

The overall focus of school leadership development programs is no longer on administrative and legal agendas as in earlier programs, but has shifted to agendas focused on communication and cooperation.

9. From administration and maintenance to leadership, change and continuous improvement

In the programs, an important paradigm shift has occurred: from a focus on managing schools with an emphasis on administration and maintenance, to a focus on leadership, change and continuous improvement.

10. Qualifying teams and developing the leadership capacity of schools

There is a trend towards qualifying teams and developing the leadership capacity of schools instead of attracting individual aspiring school leaders.

11. From knowledge acquisition to creation and development of knowledge

Instead of knowledge acquisition in terms of imparting a seemingly set knowledge base, the creation and development of knowledge through information management is increasingly the focus and the needs of adult learners are taken into account.

12. Experience and application orientation

In the programs studied, there is a clear tendency towards experience-oriented and application-oriented learning instead of mainly relying on course-based training.

13. New ways of learning: workshops and the workplace

New ways of learning are explored, using the workshops and increasingly located in the workplace itself (using methods like mentoring and internships).

14. Adjusting the program to explicit aims and objectives

Increasingly, the process of developing school leaders is becoming more professional. This includes explicitly stating the program's aims that aspiring leaders must achieve and adjusting the program to these explicit aims and objectives.[2]

15. New paradigms of leadership

    Preparation programs more and more reflect the new conceptions of leadership, such as organizational-educational leadership, instructional leadership, transformational leadership, post-transformational or 'integral leadership'.

16. Orientation towards the school's core purpose

    School leadership development programs are more strongly oriented towards the schools' core purpose, namely teaching and learning, and the specific aims of schools within society today and in the future.

Even from this brief overview, it can be seen that those responsible for school leader development programs are aware that school leaders are facing a huge shift in their core responsibilities: schools are no longer seen as static organizations that need to be 'run' or administered, but as learning organizations that should be continuously 'developed' or supported to develop themselves. School development is highest on the agenda in educational policy. This has strong implications for how to 'lead' schools.

It should be interesting and instructive to examine in more detail how this insight is reflected in innovative school leader development programs.

If this is taken seriously, it means that not only school leaders have to be prepared explicitly for their task as 'school developers', but also that their development itself should become a means of school development.

IMPACT ON THE AIMS OF THE PROGRAMS: NEW CONCEPTIONS OF LEADERSHIP AND OF SCHOOL

A good starting point for exploring the connection of school development and school leader development is indicated by the aims of the programs: is school development reflected in the aims and objectives of school leader development programs?

Internationally, two basically different approaches to the setting of aims can be observed. Some programs focus on the individual school leaders and aim at imparting to them the relevant competencies.

Other models, however, actually link school leader development closely to school development and place improving or restructuring the individual school at their centre. In these cases, the program is combined with the development of the participant's school. Its purpose will then be to enhance not only the leadership competences of an individual, but (also) to help build and enhance the leadership capacity of a whole school.

Both approaches have consequences for macro- and micro-didactic considerations. If school development measures are a relevant and essential part of the school leader qualification, this enhances the opportunity to learn from real situations and to use the reality of school not only as a starting point and target, but also as an intensive and extremely complex learning environment, embedding school leadership development in the concrete working environment of the individual school.

Due to changes in the context of schools, school leadership has to adopt a new role. Hence, in programs attempting to prepare and sometimes accredit individual leaders, it seems clear that this new role can hardly be filled by means of old leadership conceptions. Therefore, some programs focus upon rather specific leadership concepts. If it is no longer central to see school as a stable system in which the existing structures have to be managed, conceptions like transformational leadership are used. Transformational leaders not only manage structures and tasks, but also concentrate on the people and relationships in order to win their cooperation and commitment. They attempt to exert an active influence on the culture of the respective school so that more cooperation, more cohesion, more self-reliance, and independent learning and working takes place.

If the school is to become a learning organization, this implies the active empowerment and cooperative commitment of all stakeholders. The previous division between the positions of teachers on the one hand and that of learners on the other cannot be maintained; nor can the division between leaders and followers. Leadership is no longer statically linked to the hierarchical status of an individual person, but empowers as many staff members as possible as partners in the organization.

Integral leadership, as suggested by the Dutch program Meesters in Leidingsseven, emphasizes an integrated perspective, which aims to overcome the classic divide between management and leadership. Both functions serve the educational aims of school leadership. Through working with the mental maps of school leaders, such an integrated perspective is developed.

In some programs, decisive fundamental considerations are new conceptions of school. The old idea of school as an 'administered addition of lessons', as the 'lowest body' in the school system's hierarchy is outdated. Many changes in the school system have occurred in recent years, even in more centralized school systems. Therefore it is quite important, when designing a preparation program, to make the aims of school in society and the goals of schools of the future central themes.

Reflections on leadership activities, the school, its role and function are articulated in some countries. Increasingly, there is more conceptual elaboration of the aims of schools development. Questions are being raised in more and more countries, such as: what is the aim of education in schools? How can this aim be realized through teaching and through the communicative everyday practice in school and the culture of a school? What should the organization and administration of school look like in order to reach this aim? And what is the role of school leadership in this context? As a consequence, leadership activities like decision making, dealing with conflict, problem solving, interpretation of regulations and instructions, as well as the everyday routines at school have to align with these fundamental premises.

The principle that 'school has to be a model of what education aims at' (Rosenbusch, 1997) thus has consequences for school leader development. Training and development of school leaders must be based on a clear conception of the aims of education and teaching-learning processes at school and this idea has to shape the programs with regards to their contents, methods, and scheduling, and so forth.

Internationally, some programs provide a model that quite clearly relates to a new conception of school: a changeable and adaptable organization, developing as a learning community, and a learner-centered school. A leadership conception such as transformational leadership, too, implies an idea of school as a culturally independent organism. Efforts to combine a cognitive approach and a systemic approach are also founded on conceptualizing school as an independent organizational unit. Here, approaches in New South Wales, Washington, New Jersey, California, Denmark, and the Netherlands are illuminating.

IMPACT ON THE TARGET GROUP: INCREASED EMPHASIS ON TEAMS TO ENHANCE HORIZONTAL AND VERTICAL COLLABORATION

As discussed above, some programs no longer focus on the individual school leader and on equipping him or her with competences needed for school leadership tasks; rather their focus is on developing the leadership capacity of the whole school. This orientation has an impact on the macro- and micro-didactic realization of the respective program. First, it affects the target group, particularly in programs linking school leadership development closely to school development processes.

If school development is the goal, often whole school leadership teams (as in the Danish program Leadership in Development), or teams of staff members are included. Teams sometimes include parents or representatives of of the political community. Such teams, and particularly teams comprised of teachers, school leaders, parents etc. are the target group of the in-service program School Leadership Teams of the California Leadership Academy. However, only a few programs are designed exclusively for teams. Yet, even programs whose target group are individual school leaders place more and more emphasis on team aspects and on collegial learning and problem solving. Recognizing the relevance of cooperation, there are efforts to make cooperative methods a principal feature of the programs.

Growing from a notion of the school as a learning organization and viewing development and change in individual schools and in the school structure systemically, it follows that not only staff within the school are needed as change agents, but that there must be change agents at different hierarchical levels to initiate and to promote development processes. A distribution of leadership responsibility may result in an increase in the successful promotion of change. 'Building change capacity within the school' demands that more and more people recognize the potential of other team members, promote it, support it and thus give a stimulus for genuine 'grounded changes'. It would be logical then to develop personnel from different hierarchical levels together, including those external to the individual school. This might include the education authority or administration together with school leaders, deputy school leaders, persons from steering groups, and perhaps even 'identified' informal leaders within the staff. However, none of the programs identified in this chapter are this inclusive. This may be regretted, as the result might be a more profound mutual understanding among the differing groups. Possible reservations about each other's roles or even prejudices might be diminished. Hence, traditionally difficult relationships might be improved. Much more relevant, however, would be that such programs would create a shared knowledge about the concerns for school quality and school development. Sharing knowledge could also improve multi-level communication though a common language, and might enhance horizontal as well as vertical cooperation.

A considerable issue in many countries is that the school system has become decentralized, which has strengthened the self-responsibility of the school, but educators persist in thinking and acting on a hierarchical basis. This is the case in ministries, created to mandate regulations and to control, as well as among the teaching profession used to being passive and waiting for conditions to change. Chances for self-initiative and for realizing newly gained freedom for educational action remain unidentified and consequently unrealized. A comprehensive training and development approach that spreads across the various levels of the school system might be very useful here and would enhance professionalization.

Part of such an approach is that continuous professional development would no longer predominantly take place away from school at an external institute, but would rather take place at the individual school, and focus on the initiation, implementation, and institutionalization of school development processes.

IMPACT ON THE PATTERN: MULTI-PHASE DESIGNS AND MODULARIZATION

An international comparison shows that there is a tendency to move away from the idea that adequate preparation and development could be completed in a specific time frame using a standardized program. Instead, school leadership development is more and more regarded as a continuous, life-long process linked to the career cycle and to the specific needs of the leaders and those of their school.

This continuous process could be divided — ideally speaking — into the following phases:

1. A continuous development phase for teachers: to provide training and development for teachers in the fields of school effectiveness, school improvement, and school leadership.
2. An orientation phase: to provide the opportunity for teachers interested in leadership positions to reflect on the role of a school leader in respect to their own abilities and expectations.
3. A preparation phase: to prepare prior to taking over a school leadership position or even before applying for it.
4. An induction phase: to support the school leader in his or her new position after taking over a leadership position.
5. A continuous professional development phase: to provide various training and development opportunities for established school leaders, tailored to their individual needs and those of their schools.
6. A reflective phase: to provide the opportunity for experienced school leaders to continue to grow introspectively by being involved in development programs for others as coaches and to gain new experiences through learning by teaching, supplemental train-the-trainer-programs, and exchange with the younger colleagues who participate in the programs.

Although this ideal model may not yet have been fully realized, tendencies in this direction are emerging. Instead of a standardized program for all participants to 'teach' all the required competences at once, more and more countries provide professional development through multi-phase designs. These phases are, ideally, based on a coherent conceptual model.

It can also be observed internationally that programs are increasingly modularized. Modules tend to be organized according to one's individual needs as they become evident during different stages of the school leader's career, but also to the needs of the school she or he leads. There is no mandatory sequence for completion. Moreover, individual school leaders may well rely on modules for support during crucial phases of their careers. They may be 'collected' and archived in a kind of personal portfolio.

IMPACT ON CONTENTS: COMMUNICATION, COOPERATION, AND CHANGE PERSONAL DEVELOPMENT INSTEAD OF TRAINING FOR A ROLE

As the role of school leaders becomes increasingly complex, it is evident that it is no longer sufficient to train potential candidates or school leaders for a fixed role, whose concept may be quickly outdated. Instead, aspiring school leaders must develop a vision within the context of their school and adapt their role and responsibilities to that context. To achieve successful adaptive leadership, the programs of some countries include components such as personal vision, personal and professional development, development of fundamental values and of one's ability to reflect, time and self management, developing mental models of the organizational structure, and activities in the school that mirror good leadership activities. Moreover, 'shadowing' or internship experiences have become reflective activities that support re-conceptualization processes.

The emphasis has shifted from focusing on a specific role to a broader concept that concentrates on personal learning and one's needs in terms of knowledge, dispositions, and performance that would be useful in a more complex environment. Often, the approach of training for a management position has been replaced by that of offering professional development opportunities for one's leadership style. It is the personality of the (aspiring) school leader that becomes the focal point of any program.

THE COMMUNICATIVE AND COOPERATIVE SHIFT

In spite of the increasing stress on school leaders due to the complexity of the role — particularly in countries with more devolved systems — school leadership programs are not preoccupied with administrative topics. On the contrary, the overall focus of school leadership programs is no longer on administrative and legal issues as it was in earlier programs, but has shifted to a focus on communication and cooperation.

The image of school leaders as experts in administration has shifted to school leaders as experts in communication and cooperation. This trend has become another international paradigm shift. Topics such as communication, motivation, collaboration, collegiality, and cooperation are essential parts of all programs. Internationally, it is recognized that understanding and effectively making good use of communication and cooperation is essential for one to become a successful school leader.

Communication and cooperation as essential components in leadership development programs also play an important role in the methods applied. Realizing that learning processes that take place in groups provide participants with better opportunities for experiential learning, more programs are moving in the direction of small and large group interaction. The aim then becomes one of creating reflective practitioners and this will intensify the teaching-learning experiences. In addition to traditional seminars, 'collegial learning' — learning together with other colleagues — is being realized through a variety of strategies including peer-assisted learning, peer coaching, critical partnerships, acquiring knowledge from experienced peers by shadowing or through mentoring programs or collegial networks (that were created for example as a result of experiences by the cohorts that existed during other training programs). When one uses these strategies, learning evolves through mutual reflection and problem-solving processes; it is about learning with and from colleagues.

From Administration and Maintenance to Leadership, Change and Continuous Improvement

Throughout the countries involved in this study (Huber, 2004), an important paradigm shift has occurred: from a focus on managing schools with an emphasis on maintenance, to a focus on leading and improving schools. The aim is no longer to make the organization function within a static or fixed framework, but it is considered essential that programs adequately respond to the challenges created by social, cultural, and economic changes. Schools are no longer static organizations, but must be considered learning organizations, each with their own unique culture. Therefore, leading a school no longer means simply maintaining the status quo, but, above all, developing a learning organization. Consequently, what is worthwhile has to be sustained and, at the same time, necessary changes have to be made, and after being successfully implemented, they have to be institutionalized.

This paradigm shift can be identified in the lists of themes of the courses of many school leadership development programs. They take into account that school leaders must be educational leaders and that is about initiating, supporting, and sustaining substantive and lasting change as well as continuous improvement in schools for the benefit of pupils. The focus is then on a collaborative and collegial style of leadership.

IMPACT ON METHODS: EMPHASIS ON EXPERIENTIAL METHODS AND COLLEGIAL LEARNING

From Traditional Course-Based Designs to Experiential Methods

Changed aims and adapted contents demand adequately innovative methods. There are basically different but not mutually exclusive approaches, when thinking about the best possible way to link school leader development to school development and to make the training of the school leader supportive for the improvement of the whole school.

In many countries, development programs are moving from learning solely centered around courses, towards learning centered around experiential methods. Such experience — and participant-oriented methods include problem-based learning, projects at one's own or a different school, internships, shadowing, coaching and mentoring. The programs investigated, however, differ greatly in their reliance on these possibilities of learning-in-practice.

Project work and/or internships are included, for example, in the National Professional Qualification for Headship in England and Wales, in the Management en Organisatieopleidingen of the Nederlandse School voor Onderwijsmanagement, in the Master Programme in Educational Leadership at the William Paterson University of New Jersey, in the Principal's Qualification Program in Ontario, and particularly extensively in the central program in France, in the Diploma in Educational Administration in Singapore, and in the Danforth Educational Leadership Program at the University of Washington. However, countries which still favor an approach to leadership development that is more or less centered around courses, also indicate that certain modifications are under consideration.

In many countries, programs use workshops and confront participants with modeled situations of school leadership work and carefully constructed cases, and involve them in a cooperative problem-solving process, such as the case method or, the problem-based learning (PBL) approach, for example at the University of Washington.

Learning from and for Practice: Problem-based Learning

Problem-based learning (PBL) has been applied for many years in management training by companies or in training medical staff. In the educational sector, especially concerning the development of educational leaders from school boards and schools, PBL has been developed predominantly by Bridges and Hallinger in the United States (see Bridges, 1992; Bridges & Hallinger, 1995, 1997). The PBL-approach uses concrete and complex problems experienced in everyday practice by school leaders as a starting point in order to involve the learners in a cooperative problem-solving process and to find solutions interactively.

Here, learning is cooperative, interactive and participative. More consistently than the case studies and simulations often applied in qualification programs, the PBL approach starts with real-life experiences and then looks for supportive knowledge as a tool and takes it from various academic fields, from experiences of practitioners, from the political context of the respective school board and from the previous knowledge of the participants. The slogan here is: "First the problem, then the content" (Bridges & Hallinger, 1995, p. 8). Everyday life problems are here seen as stimuli for learning and as offering a learning situation as well as learning material, and not only as the future context in which to apply what has previously been learned.

Certainly, problem-based learning is an interesting attempt at achieving practice relevance by using concrete problems taken from real life and by involving the participants in a cooperative problem-solving process. Yet in PBL, despite its link to reality, the problem situation remains constructed and 'imagined'. This surely has advantages: however close to the complexity of school leadership reality the constructed problem may be, it always remains consciously designed and structured enough to enable exemplary learning experiences. Additionally, the team offers a certain shelter, in which it is possible to experiment.

Going one step further means using genuine cases that are taken from the real life of a school's cases on the agenda at the time the development program takes place. Thus, the cases are grounded more concretely and more authentically in a school situation. One precondition, however, is that the trainers have enough contact with school leaders who can 'deliver' these case examples from their own schools. The school leaders then can also function as mentors to the trainer team and, due to their experience, give feedback when the solutions to the problem are presented by the participants. Hence, the participants of the project group become external consultants for the school leaders. Through this interaction, both parties may gain something. This method can also be used in online mentoring schemes. For example, experienced school leaders present a problem taken from their work to the group for whom they are responsible at seven to ten day intervals. The participants then work on the problem by investigating it or interviewing their own school leaders. After that, the participants post their suggestions and comments on the Web. After ten days, the school leader who has brought the problem up for discussion reports about how she or he has acted and whether it has been successful.

Using the Authentic Workplace: Internships

All these PBL approaches, however, take place in a workshop situation. Some programs leave the workshop and use the authentic workplace as a clinical faculty. It is argued that only the authentic working context can assure adequate complexity and authenticity leading to the learning processes required. For the participants of pre-service school leader development, internships at one school or several schools are organized parallel to the training. In these internships, they can observe the school leader by shadowing; during a shadowing process, the participants take notes of their observations. They achieve an authentic insight into the complexity and variety of school leadership activities and in the leadership style of a particular individual. Any kind of artificial behavior shown by the school leader who is shadowed is likely to stop after some time, as well as any awkwardness at the beginning or any attempt to specifically 'control' situations by selection of interactions. Both sides profit from the shared reflection on the observations made. The intern can partially take over leadership tasks and can carry out projects independently. In this way the school leaders at the internship schools function as mentors or supervisors. Here, exemplary learning processes take place in the reality of school.

The internships, or school attachments, in one's own or another school, differ with regard to their duration and their emphasis. In some countries the participants spend many hours observing the school leader in their school in order to experience school leadership at work and to prepare to take over leadership and management tasks on their own. Other internships, however, aim at applying knowledge directly to the workplace by making the interns plan and carry out innovative projects. These projects, again, are meant to be useful to the internship school. In general, a good deal of effort is needed to create a balance of observation and active working on one's own project.

In the medical and legal professions, application orientation through internships has been practiced in training programs for quite some time. Internships were suggested for educators in the United States for the first time in 1947 at a session of the National Conference of Professors in Educational Administration.

In the following decades, the number of US universities that integrated internships in their training programs increased continuously and rose to about 87 per cent of the university programs by 1987 (see Milstein et al., 1991). A particular strength of internships lies in the balance they create between knowledge and skills, "between learning about and learning how, rooted in a solid foundation of learning why" (Milstein, 1990, p. 122).

Within the whole qualification program the internship is considered as an integrating factor, bringing about a synthesis of what has been learned. This makes a more holistic learning process possible, and motivates meta-cognitive processes enabling 'reflection on action' and helping to work out the meaning of experiences retrospectively: 'Making meaning out of experiences' (see Schön, 1983; Kolb, 1984; Greenfield, 1985). The aim is, in the end, to improve competence for handling future situations. In particular, the participants have the chance to develop technical skills, human skills, and conceptual skills, and to improve cooperative and communicative competences for managing group processes, dealing with conflict, decision making, and problem solving. In addition, participants have the opportunity the gain the ability to keep a balance between the big picture and detailed knowledge, and to develop an understanding of mutual links and inter-dependencies in complex situations.

An essential factor for the success of the concept is that the activities of the participants in the internship and those in the seminars are carefully coordinated so that both complement each other. The workplace environment offers opportunities to know and experience the everyday life components of school leadership. Writing a learning journal, in which experiences and reflections are continuously collected, is demanded in most programs. It serves as a basis for feedback sessions of the participants and their mentor, but also for discussions in the seminar. The technique of writing journals itself is a method to reflect on experiences and to anchor what has been learned. An important condition, however, are seminars linked closely to the internship to avoid the danger of pure on-the-job-training. In the seminar, the participants exchange their experiences, structure them, process them, and reflect on them and receive further information and incentive for reflection. Thus, theoretical content receives an immediate and direct relevance for practical action. The seminar group offers the chance of partnerships, for exchange and cooperation and for setting up a network lasting beyond the time of the program.

During projects, a critical problem may emerge. It is problematic when a school leader needs the particular school project to successfully fulfill the qualification requirements. In such circumstances, the staff may feel 'used' and may not be ready to identify with the project. It may be different, however, if not only the school leader, but a team from the school takes part in the development program, initiates and implements school improvement projects, as it is the case in California (above all in School Leadership Teams) or in New South Wales. Fundamentally, the school must not become a stage for the actions of an individual, and the projects must not become the production of a stage play.

Learning from Colleagues: Mentoring

Mentoring can be found in the training and development programs of several countries, for example, France, England, Singapore, and the United States. Mentoring on the one hand is an essential part of internships; on the other hand it is used as a professional support when taking over a leadership position. Compared with shadowing, the participant is active at the workplace rather than acting soley as an observer. Mentoring can be described as a complex interactive process between persons with different levels of experience and expertise, which stimulates interpersonal and psycho-social development. The relationship between mentor and protégé or mentee is dynamic and has different stages.

An advantage of mentoring as one part of the qualification of school leaders is the possibility for the mentor to learn at a different school. The group meetings with other mentors and protégés bring new perspectives with which the aspiring or newly appointed school leader would not normally be confronted. The mentor is an experienced colleague, whose credibility is appreciated and whose competence and role are accepted. Mentoring is not intended to lead to copying the behavior of another person, as may be the case with shadowing. In mentoring the participants are active and their own actions are the central theme.

This procedure, however, carries with it the risk that — in unfavorable situations — it may turn out to be not much more than a kind of a low-level apprenticeship and a mere passing on of recipes. In this case, traditional values and a kind of school leadership oriented towards maintaining the status quo may be passed on to a new generation of school leadership personnel. Thody, too, recognizes this danger: "It will result in principals cloning principals" (Thody, 1993, p. 74). In an unfavorable case, a readiness to question established traditions, to think critically, to favor change and development may not be sufficiently increased, and new ideas for academic excellence may be disregarded.

Nevertheless, a school leader's carefully supervised learning at the workplace — in internships or through mentoring processes — offers a genuine chance to successfully make the entire school profit from the individual's development.

CONCLUSION

The comparison of school leader development in 15 countries gives an impression of global approaches and shifts. What can be stated clearly about school leader development from an international perspective is that there have been many changes in nearly every country. Many of the countries that have enhanced their leadership development programs have increasingly focused on linking leadership development with school development. The leadership abilities of an individual are here seen as a component of building the leadership capacity of the whole school.

However, the conception of school leadership, even viewed internationally, is still a rather narrow one. Perhaps there does need to be 'one supreme head' in each school. Maybe school leadership development programs are about finding and equipping such individuals. But perhaps there are other alternatives — collective leadership, the development of whole teams of staff, the reconceptualization of the school leader's role as simply one member of a team, a team made up of leaders all of whom need support, training, and development opportunities. It is this last issue which seems to us to challenge most forcibly the orthodoxy underpinning current provision, and which offers the most interesting avenue for future exploration.

Given the fact that school leadership is becoming more and more complex and that the tasks are often too demanding for one person alone, forms of 'cooperative leadership' or 'distributed leadership' seem to be possible solutions discussed internationally in the academic community and, increasingly, in the profession itself.

Taking the role of school leader for school development seriously means orienting school leader development towards school development itself. This implies focusing on and aiming at a notion of leadership that is no longer strictly linked to hierarchical status, but comprises a broad distribution of leadership responsibilities. Concepts such as distributed leadership or cooperative leadership may reduce the classic divide between leaders and followers. To accomplish this, it is required that a communicative and cooperative style of behavior and an organizational structure be established to allow for the sharing of responsibilities and tasks by more people than ever before.

Over all, school leadership and leadership development have no purpose in their own right, but serve a specific function. This function requires an orientation to the schools' core purpose, and hence, where needed, an adjustment of aims. In order to improve teaching and learning in schools, and, ultimeately, the quality of education received by students, the central focus is on improving the conditions under which these processes will have the greatest possible impact. It would then make no sense if school leadership development did not focus on the specific role of school leaders in the school improvement process and did not try to equip the participants with the skills urgently needed.

Development programs for school leaders therefore require a multi-stage adjusting of aims. The first question would be: what are the essential aims of education? From these, the corresponding aims for schools and schooling in general can be derived: what is the purpose of school and what are the aims of the teaching and learning processes? Considering the perspective of the new field of 'organizational education', one should ask: how does the school organization need to be designed and developed in order to create the best conditions possible so that the entire school becomes a deliberately designed, educationally meaningful environment? This would enable teaching and learning to take place as well as multi-faceted and holistic educational processes that would lead to achieving the schools' goals.

This leads to the essential concern of school leadership: what are the aims of school leadership regarding the school's purpose and the individual context of each school? How do school leaders lead to reach those aims?

Therefore, the aims of school leader development programs should answer questions such as: what is school and schooling about, and what is leadership and management about? What is the core purpose, what should be the aims? What kind of training and development opportunities are therefore needed to prepare and support (aspiring) school leaders in adjusting their perspectives, conceptualizing their role and function, developing the necessary competences, and mastering the manifold tasks within the individual school in order to provide conditions and support staff so that effective and efficient teaching and learning takes place for the sake of the pupils?

This should be the essential or core goal for aligning and evaluating school leadership development programs.

Whether school leadership development programs are successful enough, particularly with the focus on school development, is not researched sufficiently. The efficacy and effectiveness of programs remains a research desideratum. Hence, research on the role of school leadership for school development, on the impact that school leaders have on school improvement and school development, and on what impact school leader development programs have, still has to be intensified. Additional research and funding would be in the interest of education policy worldwide.

NOTES

1. The methods used in the comparative research project comprised two surveys, extensive documentation analysis, and additional country-specific investigations.
2. For a full account see Huber, 2004.

REFERENCES

Bridges, E. (1992). *Problem-based learning for administrators*. Eugene, OR: ERIC Clearinghouse on Educational Management.

Bridges, E. & Hallinger, P. (1995). *Implementing problem-based learning in leadership development*. Eugene, OR: ERIC Clearinghouse on Educational Management.

Bridges, E. & Hallinger, P. (1997). Using problem-based learning to prepare educational leaders. *Peabody Journal of Education, 72*(2), 131–146.

Greenfield, W. (1985). The moral socialization of school administrators: Informal role learning outcomes. *Educational Administration Quarterly, 12*(4), 99–120.

Huber, S. G. (Ed.). (2004). *Preparing school leaders for the 21st century*. In the Series Context of Learning, J. Chrispeels, B. Creemers, D. Reynolds & S. Stringfield (Eds.). London: RoutledgeFalmer.

Kolb, D.A. (1984). *Experiential learning*. Englewood Cliffs, NJ: Prentice Hall.

Milstein, M. (1990). Rethinking the clinical aspects in administrative preparation: From theory to practice. In S. L. Jacobson & J. Conway (Eds.), *Educational leadership in an age of reform*. New York: Longman.

Milstein, M. M., Bobroff, B. M. & Restine, L. N. (Eds.). (1991). *Internship programs in educational administration: A guide to preparing educational leaders* (pp. 9–130). New York: Teachers' College Press.

Rosenbusch, H. S. (1997). Die qualifikation pädagogischen Führungspersonals. In E. Glumpler & H. S. Rosenbusch (Eds.), *Perspektiven der universitären Lehrerausbildung* (pp. 147–165). Bad Heilbrunn/ Obb.: Klinkhardt.

Schön, D. (1983). *The reflective practitioner*. New York: Basic Books.

Thody, A. (1993). Mentoring for school principals. In B. Caldwell & E. Carter (Eds.), *The return of the mentor. Strategies for workplace learning* (pp. 59–76). London: The Falmer Press.

10

The Recruitment and Selection of School Leaders

Stephan Gerhard Huber and Petros Pashiardis

The pivotal role of the school leader as a factor in effective schools has been corroborated by findings of school effectiveness research over the last two decades. School improvement researchers have also demonstrated increasing recognition of the importance of school leaders for all stages of the school improvement process. The school leader is most often cited as the key figure in the individual school's development, either blocking or promoting change, acting as the internal change agent, overseeing the processes of growth and renewal. The school leader's role has to be seen in relationship to the broad cultural and educational contexts in which the school is operating.

Since schools are embedded in their communities and in the particular national educational system, and these in turn are embedded in the particular society, schools and their leaders have to cope with, to support or otherwise react to the social, economic and cultural changes and developments taking place. Schools, and consequently the expectations on school leaders, also change as a result of more subtle and indirect forces in society — social, political and economic changes — that are gathering pace across the world. Moreover, direct changes in the educational system have a particularly strong impact on the school leader's role. In most countries, the tasks and structures of schools and of the education system are changing. These change processes strongly influence the leadership of schools.

For these reasons, it is essential to select (and develop) suitable individuals for school leadership positions. Furthermore, in many educational systems around the world it is a difficult (if not an impossible) process to dismiss an incompetent leader to correct problems stemming from mediocrity in management. Therefore, the issue of who is allowed into formal educational leadership positions is indeed of fundamental importance for educational systems around the globe.

There is broad international agreement about the need for school leaders to have the capacities needed to improve teaching, learning, and pupils' development and achievement. To establish and modify appropriate training and development opportunities has become a major focus of professional development programs in many countries, as shown by an international comparative research project (Huber, 2004) about school leadership development. But — different than questions of selecting leadership personnel in the economic sector — in the educational sector, insights into appropriate selection procedures and criteria for school leaders are still lacking to a great extent.

This chapter looks at the growing importance placed on activities to select and recruit school leaders that has led to the development of systematic selection procedures in many countries in recent years. The central question is: do we have policies and strategies that ensure that qualified individuals are recruited to be principals?

The chapter is organized into three main sections, as follows. The first section briefly outlines the changing context in which school leaders find themselves as more and more countries devolve significant management decisions to the school level. It focuses on the new expectations this brings to the school leader's role, and how these expectations have placed a new emphasis on the development of management and leadership skills. It reports contemporary thinking about how the leadership role can be most effectively exercised, and considers what combinations of knowledge, skills and attributes are stipulated for school leaders, and therefore, what requirements should be addressed in the recruitment and selection process of these school leaders.

The second section offers an overview of current practices to select and recruit school leaders. This overview is international in scope, drawn from experience and a synthesis of existing literature as well as from the first findings of a comparative research study that embraces some 20 countries worldwide (in this first exploratory phase, data from around ten countries were gathered; see Huber & Hiltmann, in press). For the purpose of illustration, we offer brief summaries from five countries, including examples from Europe, Asia, Australia, and North America. The countries selected are: England, Germany, Singapore, Australia, and the United States.

The respective Country Reports focus on providing answers to questions such as:

What is the overall approach?
Are the selection procedures conducted centrally or de-centrally?
Who is responsible for conducting the selection procedure?
Do the countries have standards for school leaders?
Do the countries have prerequisites for applicants for leadership positions?
What are the steps of the selection process?
What methods are applied?
What criteria are relevant for the decision on who is selected?

The final section examines similarities and differences in approach. It asks what can be learned more generally about the selection and recruitment of school leaders from these examples and looks for common solutions. Finally, it identifies emerging issues.

THE ROLE OF SCHOOL LEADERSHIP

School Leadership and School Effectiveness

Extensive empirical efforts of quantitatively oriented school effectiveness research — mostly in North America, Great Britain, Australia and New Zealand, but also in the Netherlands and in the Scandinavian countries — have shown that leadership is a central factor for the quality of a school (see, for example, in Great Britain: Reynolds, 1976; Rutter et al., 1979; Mortimore et al., 1988; Sammons et al., 1995; in the US: Brookover et al., 1979; Edmonds, 1979; Levine & Lezotte, 1990; Teddlie & Stringfield, 1993; in the Netherlands: Creemers, 1994; Scheerens & Bosker, 1997; in Cyprus: Pashiardis, 1998; Kythreotis & Pashiardis, 2006; Huber, 1999a, offers a critical overview).

The research results show that schools classified as successful possess a competent and sound school leadership (this correlates highly significantly). The central importance of educational leadership is therefore one of the clearest messages of school effectiveness research (Gray, 1990). In most of the lists of key factors (or correlates) that school effectiveness research has compiled, 'leadership' plays an important part, so much so that the line of argument starting with the message 'schools matter, schools do make a difference' may legitimately be continued: 'school leaders matter, they are educationally significant, school leaders do make a difference' (Huber, 1997).

'Professional school leadership' is described as firm and purposeful, sharing leadership responsibilities, involvement in and knowledge about what goes on in the classroom. That means that it is important to have decisive and goal-oriented participation of others in leadership tasks, that there is a real empowerment in terms of true delegation of leadership power (distributed leadership), and that there is a dedicated interest in and knowledge about what happens during lessons (effective and professional school leadership action focuses on teaching and learning and uses the school's goals as a benchmark).

School Leadership and School Improvement

Studies on school development and improvement also emphasize the importance of school leaders, especially in the view of the continuous improvement process targeted at an individual school (see van Velzen, 1979; van Velzen et al., 1985; Stegö et al., 1987; Dalin & Rolff, 1990; Joyce, 1991; Caldwell & Spinks, 1992; Huberman, 1992; Leithwood, 1992a; Bolam, 1993; Bolam et al., 1993; Fullan, 1991, 1992, 1993; Hopkins et al., 1994, 1996; Reynolds et al., 1996; Altrichter et al., 1998; Huber, 1999b, offers a critical overview).

In many countries, the efforts made to improve schools have illustrated that neither top-down measures alone nor the exclusive use of bottom-up approaches have the effects desired. Instead, a combination and systematic synchronization of both has proved most effective. Moreover, improvement is viewed as a continuous process with different phases, which follow their individual rules. Innovations also need to be institutionalized after their initiation and implementation at the individual school level so that they will become a permanent part of the school's culture; that is the structures, atmosphere, and daily routines. Hence, the goal is to develop problem-solving, creative, self-renewing schools that have sometimes been described as learning organizations. Therefore, the emphasis is placed on the priorities to be chosen by each school individually, since it is the school that is the center of the change process. Thereby, the core purpose of school, that is education and instruction, are at the center of attention, since the teaching and learning processes play a decisive role in the pupils' success. Hence, both the individual teacher and the school leadership provided are of great importance. They are the essential change agents who will have significant influence on whether a school will develop into a 'learning organization' or not.

For all phases of the school development process, school leadership is considered vital and is held responsible for keeping the school as a whole in mind, and for adequately coordinating the individual activities during the improvement processes (for the decisive role of school leadership for the development of the individual school see, for example, studies conducted as early as in the 1980s by Leithwood & Montgomery, 1986; Hall & Hord, 1987; Trider & Leithwood, 1988). Furthermore, it is required to create the internal conditions necessary for the continuous development and increasing professionalization of the teachers. It holds the responsibility for developing a cooperative school culture. Regarding this, Barth (1990) and Hargreaves (1994), among others, emphasize the 'modeling' function of the school leader.

A Complex Range of School Leadership Tasks

The managing and leading tasks of school leadership are both complex and interrelated, so that there is no clearly defined, specific 'role' of school leadership, but at best a colored patchwork of many different aspects. Some areas or role segments relate to working with and for people, others to managing resources like the budget. All are part of the complex range of tasks the school leader faces in the 21st century (see e.g. Huber, 1997, 1999c, 2004).

International school leadership research already features a number of different alternatives for classifying school leadership tasks. Various approaches allocate school leadership action within various ranges of duties and assign responsibilities and activities to these (see the analysis of Katz, 1974, as an important 'precursor' for classifications of management tasks, but also classifications of school leadership tasks, for example, by Morgan, Hall, & Mackay, 1983; Jones, 1987; Leithwood & Montgomery, 1986; Glatter, 1987; Caldwell & Spinks, 1992; Esp, 1993; Jirasinghe & Lyons, 1996).

Louis and Miles (1990) also distinguish between 'management', referring to activities in the administrative and organizational areas, and 'leadership', referring to educational goals and to inspiring and motivating others. For them, 'educational leadership' includes administrative tasks like, for example, managing and distributing resources or planning and coordinating activities as well as tasks concerning the quality of leadership, such as promoting a cooperative school culture in combination with a high degree of collegiality, developing perspectives and promoting a shared school vision, and stimulating creativity and initiatives from others.

Given the manifold tasks and responsibilities of school leadership, as well as the necessary competencies, school leaders might be propagated as a kind of 'multifunctional miracle beings' (Huber, 2004). But, nobody can safely assume that they are or will or should be the 'superheroes of school'. What may be deduced, however, is that their role can hardly be filled by persons with 'traditional' leadership concepts. The idea of the school leader as a 'monarchic', 'autocratic' or 'paternal' executive of school has increasingly been seen as inappropriate, but viewing a school leader as a mere 'manager' or 'administrative executive' is inadequate as well, despite the managerial pressures of the present situation.

Other concepts describing the role of school leadership are transactional, transformational, instructional leadership, and distributed leadership (see e.g. Burns, 1978; Leithwood, 1992b; Caldwell & Spinks, 1992; De Bevoise, 1984; Hallinger & Murphy, 1985; Gronn, 2002; Spillane, Halverson, & Diamond, 2001, 2004; Moos & Huber, 2006; Hallinger, 2005).

In the German-speaking context, the notion of 'organizational education' (see Rosenbusch, 1997b) refers to the mutual influence of the school as an organization on one hand and the educational processes on the other. The core question of organizational education raises a two-fold issue: which educational effects do the nature and conditions of school as an organization have on individuals or groups within the organization — and, vice versa, which effects do the conditions and the nature of individuals or groups within the school have on the school as an organization. Concretely speaking: how does the school need to be designed in order to guarantee favorable prerequisites for education and to support educational work? Hence, the influence of the organization on the teaching and learning process needs to be acknowledged. Administrative and organizational structures have to be brought in line with educational goals. This does not only concern the structure of the school system or the management of the individual school, but also the leadership style with aspects of the distribution of tasks and responsibilities among the staff. Hence, empowerment and accountability issues seem to be important and have to be considered seriously in the light of educational aims and goals. In the context of organizational education, school leadership action becomes educational-organizational action, and educational goals become super-ordinate premises of this action. This means that school leadership action itself must adhere to the four main principles of education in schools: that school leaders themselves assume or encourage maturity when dealing with pupils, teachers and parents, that they practice acceptance of themselves and of others, that they support autonomy, and that they realize cooperation. This adjustment of educational perspectives affects the school culture, the teachers' behavior, and the individual pupils, particularly through the teaching and learning process on classroom level. Administrative and structural conditions have to be modified accordingly, and be in compliance with educational principles. Thereby, the unbalanced relationship (which is historically conditioned in many countries) between education on the one hand and organization and administration on the other hand can be clarified.

The leadership concept of 'organizational-educational management' assumes a definition of 'educational' which not only incorporates teaching and education processes with pupils, but also the interaction with adults, as well as organizational learning. Organizational-educational management is committed to educational values, which are supposed to determine the interaction with pupils and the cooperation with staff as well.

SELECTION AND RECRUITMENT AROUND THE WORLD

For this section, we have chosen five countries to give some examples across the world. We include examples from Europe, Asia, Australia and North America. The countries selected are: England, Germany, Singapore, Australia, and the United States. In each report, we will provide information regarding the context, the overall approach and organization of the selection procedure, advertising and marketing, prerequisites and pre-selection, job profiles in use, selection methods and selection criteria applied, and whether there is any evaluation of the selection procedure available.

England

In England's decentrally organized education system, nationally, the responsibility for education policy lies principally with the Department for Education and Skills (DfES).[1] Regarding the selection of school leadership personnel, the Department has set standards for their education and development programs. At the district level, the Local Education Authorities (LEAs) remain responsible for the performance of publicly financed schools in their respective districts, and their tasks include ensuring that there are sufficient school places and school buildings suitable for the education of children living in the district. The regional differences which shape the school system in England can be accounted for by the freedom with which the LEAs can establish schools and design and implement individual school profiles. In the course of the 'Education Reform Act 1988', the LEAs' capacities to determine the distribution of funds to schools, to develop curriculum locally, to appoint teaching staff, and to inspect schools have all been eroded, as the national policy has moved towards a partnership built around a strong government and strong schools that has squeezed the LEAs' powers. The individual schools have obtained considerably increased powers, which extend to the selection of teaching staff, and, significantly, the appointment and suspension of the teachers and of the head teacher. Specific regulations regarding the appointment of a head teacher and deputies, other teachers and support staff are laid down in the "The Education (School Staffing) England Regulations 2003" made under sections 35 and 36 of the Education Act 2002.

The following information about the current school leader selection procedure is primarily based on a recent two year study by the National College for School Leadership (NCSL, 2006).

Organization of the Selection Procedure   The responsibility for the selection of teaching staff, the establishment of salary and promotion policies and, significantly, the appointment and suspension of the teachers and of the head teacher lies with the respective school governing body. Members of this committee (governors) include the school leader, elected representatives of the parents, representatives of the teaching and the non-teaching staff and of the LEA, and partly so-called 'co-opted members' (invited influential representatives of politics and economy). This board is in charge of selecting and appointing new head teachers, too. A specific panel of five to seven governors is appointed to conduct the selection process.

Altogether, the selection and appointment procedure of school leaders can be divided in the following seven phases (see NCSL, 2006): (1) Continuous Preparation, (2) Defining of Need, (3) Attraction, (4) Selection, (5) Appointment, (6) Induction and (7) Evaluation.

The proper selection procedure (following the preceding marketing and other preparatory measures, and without the design of job profiles) typically starts with long-listing. It results in a first pre-selection on the basis of all applications received, and it defines which applicants will be invited to interviews with the board members. Due to the results of the interviews, another and more restricted selection is made (short-listing). Sometimes, the applicants chosen take part in an assessment center as the next step. In those cases the selection procedure in the narrow sense is finalized with the decision making process after the assessment center.

Advertising and Marketing   The School Governing Body informs the LEA of the vacancy and advertises the vacancy. The most commonly used recruitment efforts comprise the Times Educational Supplement, advertising in online job boards, publishing advertisements in regional newspapers, relying on word-of-mouth recommendation, and using the LEA-networks. Since 1985 the "Annual Survey of Senior Staff Appointments in Schools in England and Wales" carried out by the Education Data Surveys (www.educationdatasurveys.org.uk) provides information on the number of advertisements and vacancies. The 2007 report indicates a high need of head teachers and problems in filling vacancies: many schools failed to appoint a new head teacher after their first advertisement (36 per cent in the primary sector, 29 per cent in the secondary sector and 48 per cent in the special needs school sector).

The process of personnel marketing includes all the advertising efforts, the provision of application packs, visiting schools, providing information on the school's website, and letters by the Governors. According to a survey of the NCSL, 2006, the advertising costs per school ranged from 500 to 1000 pounds sterling. In regions with particularly difficult recruiting conditions, additional 'incentives' such as 'Golden Hellos' or relocation packages are offered to attract potential candidates.

Prerequisites and Pre-Selection   Since 1997 teachers aspiring to headship take part in a training and development program, the National Professional Qualification for Headship (NPQH), in order to qualify for application. From April 1 2009 on, it will be mandatory to have completed NPQH prior to appointment to a first headship. The program consists of six modules, whose contents are aligned to the National Standards for Headship (a national catalogue of requirements relevant for the qualification and assessment of candidates aspiring to headship; see Starkebaum, 1998). Besides going through the NPQH, applicants have to meet further requirements (Eurydice Report, 1996; now known as Eurybase):

'Qualified Teacher' status (teachers of special needs schools must have an additional qualification, e.g. as a teacher for students with sight defects), adequate teaching experience, appropriate management knowledge and skills.

There are no explicit demands regarding the time span of being a teacher and the kind of functions held so far. However, often some experience as a deputy head teacher is expected.

Job Profiles   According to the survey by the NCSL, 37 per cent of the schools included have formulated specific demands for the head teacher role based on the 'National Standards for Headteachers' (edited by the DfES). In most cases, this national catalogue was only slightly adapted or modified to fit to the local conditions.

Selection Methods   After screening incoming applications, various methods are employed to screen the candidates: panel interviews by the committee (75.3%), presentations by the applicants (89.2%), and finalizing interviews (88.5%). Psychological tests (7.2%) and talks with representatives of the parents (5.4%) are applied more rarely. External assessment centers are seen to be useful even though not widely used (NCSL, 2006). They can be conducted with external support by 5.7per cent of the schools. Providers are e.g. the Secondary Heads' Association (SHA), the Association of School and College Leaders (ASCL), and the National College of School Leadership (NCSL).

Provision of Assessment Center in England   Linked to the increase of demands on school leaders in the course of the Education Reform Acts, the assessment center as a method to find suitable candidates was introduced in 1990. The National Educational Assessment Centre, NEAC (1995), was developed by SHA and Oxford Brookes University, in cooperation with industry and economy. According to Schneider (1997), the pilot scheme was widely supported by authorities during the 1990s. It is the objective of an assessment center to gain evidence for the actual capacity and competencies of a candidate with regard to the criteria described in the National Standards or additionally formulated by the schools. The assessment center developed by NEAC is underpinned by a development model with twelve competencies, which can be grouped to four areas:

Administrative Competencies: problem analysis, judgment competence, organizing competence, decision making competence
Interpersonal Competencies: leadership potential, empathy, stress resilience
Communicative Competencies: oral and written communication
Personal Versatility: a broad range of interests, motivation, educational value.

The candidates taking part in the AC go through four to six position-related exercises: discussing a case, to which consensus should be found within a given time span; working on ten in-tray tasks related to every-day or more rarely occurring situations; analysing individual position-specific problems and presentating the results; watching a video of a lesson and discussion of the professional development plan of the teacher; analysing a current study on education and instruction in schools. After all observations have been recorded and coded, the team of assessors goes into the final assessment process. The selection process itself is completed after the AC with the decision making process. If an assessment center is used, the selection process itself is completed after the AC with the decision making process.

TABLE 10.1

	Primary Schools	Secondary Schools
Expertise in teaching and learning	94%	88%
Leadership and management skills	87%	94%
NPQH qualification completed	49%	57%
Proficiency in budgeting and finances	32%	37%
Experience in collaboration with the community	34%	35%
Former school leadership experience	13%	23%

Selection Criteria   The last phase of the procedure comprises information and feedback to the candidates (if judged not suitable, the candidates are entitled to be given reasons for rejection and another chance to apply again in the following year), the reference checks, and the finalizing of the contract. According to the NCSL (2006), there is widespread agreement on the conduct of reference checks. Due to their rather low validity, they serve more as an additional confirmation of the decision already made rather than as an actual basis for the decision. The appointment is made by the LEA in charge on the basis of the respective school committees' recommendation (for community, voluntary-controlled, community special or maintained nursery schools). In the case of a foundation, voluntary-aided or foundation special school, the school itself makes the appointment.

The newly appointed head teachers get most often an unlimited contract but unlike tenure track as civil servants they can be made redundant. Moreover, salaries vary to a great extent.

Information about the criteria relevant to the decision making process is provided by the survey by the NCSL as well. The governors interviewed regard the following criteria as most relevant, as shown in Table 10.1.

The newly appointed head teachers get a contract equivalent to that of employment in the civil service. Hence, in most cases they get a permanent contract (Eurydice, 1996).

Evaluation of the Selection Procedure   The school governing body is strongly advised to carry out an evaluation of the recruiting process. However, evaluation takes place in an informal manner, if at all. The NCSL survey found that in just 47 per cent of the cases evaluation had taken place.

First general findings regarding the practice and effectiveness of the English scheme for the selection of school leaders are as follows (NCSL, 2006):

Errors may occur in any phase of the actual selection procedure, yet the interviews seem to be particularly prone to mistakes. To guarantee that the best possible candidate is appointed to their school, the Governors have to be capable of correctly 'translating' the demands and needs of their school into selection criteria that the successful candidate will have to meet. Apparently, however, sometimes the Governors prefer the 'safe route'. In these cases they seek for an individual as similar as possible to the previous school leader in post instead of focusing on the future needs of the school. Moreover, there are great differences concerning the quality and the amount of support (e.g. interview training) that Governors get from their LEAs.

TABLE 10.2

Aspect	Description
Overall Approach	distinctive decentralization (responsibility lies with the schools)
Selection Body	School Governing Body
Advertising & Marketing	– advertised throughout England and Wales: Times Educational Supplement, in regional newspapers, online job boards – provision of application packs, visiting schools, providing information on the school's website, and letters by the Governors – advertising costs per school ranged from 500 to 1000 pounds sterling
Job Profile	based on national standards, formulated in 37% of the schools
Prerequisites	– participation in The National Professional Qualification for Headship (NPQH); mandatory from April 1st 2009 – 'Qualified Teacher' status, adequate teaching experience, appropriate management knowledge and skills (e.g. from experience as a deputy head teacher)
Selection Methods	– presentations by the applicants (89.2%), finalizing interviews (88.5%), interviews by the committee (75.3%), psychological tests (7.2%), talks with representatives of the parents (5.4%), sometimes reference checks (percentages refer to secondary schools) – depending on number of applicants and funding: an assessment center
Selection Criteria	– leadership and management skills (94%), expertise in teaching and learning (88%), NPQH qualification finished (57%), an understanding of budgeting and finances (37%), experience in collaboration with the community (35%), former school leadership experience (23%) (important criteria to governors) – appointment made by the LEA in charge on the basis of the respective school committees' recommendation
Evaluation	– differences in experiences and preparation of Governors influences quality of interviews – analysis of the NEAC assessment centre

Regarding formal evaluations, an evaluation of the NEAC-model, the progress of the first hundred AC-participants was examined. According to Schneider (1997), the collecting of competence-related evidence has a much higher validity (0.40 to 0.60) than the formal interview with a validity of 0.30 with regard to the prognosis of future success in the job. Unfortunately, in Schneider's (1997) study, details of how the data were collected and of the kind of interview conducted remain unclear. To sum up, Table 10.2 provides an overview.

In summary, the NSCL expects "some basic changes to rationalise the processes of recruitment and appointment. Possibilities include: changes to resignation dates and notice periods; the provision of formal, regional or national assessment centers; the proliferation of fast-track schemes to accelerate candidates; technology-enabled advertising and matching of candidates to posts; formalised training and support to governing bodies; advertising and looking for candidates beyond the teaching profession; standardisation of procedures across different children's services; the formalisation of different career paths; the development of context-specific job descriptions and person specifications; increased emphasis on succession planning and talent management at the school and local level" (NCSL, 2006, p. 54).

Germany

The German school system is under federal control. At a national level, independence in matters of education and culture lies with each state due to the federal principle. This means that each of the 16 federal states (the German 'Länder') has an individual school system ensured by jurisdictional and administrative laws. Hence, the legal basis for the selection and appointment of school leaders is within the responsibility of the respective state as well as formulated in its respective laws. School leaders are employed by each state as civil servants and in general have non-terminable (lifelong) tenure. Hence, for promotion the career regulations for civil servants are valid. Legally, all appointments have to be in accordance with the goal laid down in the 'Grundgesetz' (constitution), article 33, postulating an equal access to any public position for every German, according to her or his aptitude, competence, and professional performance.

For the first time, Rosenbusch, Huber and Knorr investigated in an unpublished exploratory study the selection of school leadership personnel in Germany in 2002 (see Huber & Gniechwitz, 2006).

Organization of the Selection Procedure   The selection and appointment of a school leader lies within the responsibility of the ministry for education of the respective German federal state. Regulations of the school laws vary from one 'Land' to another regarding how detailed they are. Summing up, however, it is evident that all states (with the exception of Berlin, Bremen, Lower Saxony, and North Rhine-Westphalia) do not go beyond a general description of the selection procedure. In the states mentioned as exceptions, criteria are formulated a priori in the school law, and, more precisely, in the official regulations and stipulations.

One finding of the 2002 exploratory study is that the departments of the ministries for education and the education authorities not only are in charge of the selection and appointment procedure, but they are also involved in the development of the selection methods. In some states, the authorities are supported by state academies or state-run teacher training institutes or the personnel department.

The filling of a vacant position needs long-term personnel planning by the authority. In this context, in a publication of the German School Leader Association (ASD, 2005) the creation of a 'pool' of applicants by the state is regarded as a relevant condition for a successful selection and appointment procedure. In Bremen, Berlin, Hamburg, Hesse, Lower Saxony, Saxony, Schleswig-Holstein, and Thuringia, the creation of such a 'pool' on the basis of the candidates' taking part in development programs early in their careers is being considered and realized in some pilot schemes. Other federal states are following.

Advertising and Marketing   In all federal states, vacant school leader positions (or those expected to become vacant) are advertised in the official information publications of the ministry, in regional official newsletters, and partly on the Internet. Generally speaking, advertisements comprise the name of the school, the details of the school profile, the exact title of the position, the level of salary, and relevant information about the formal requirements and deadlines for the application procedure. States such as Brandenburg and Hesse additionally use regional and national newspapers, and so does North Rhine-Westphalia, where (like in Lower Saxony) optionally public advertising by the 'Schulträger' (institution or political community in charge of the maintenance of the school) is not unusual. Only in exceptions (e.g. in Bremen and Lower Saxony), the text of the advertisement is precisely adapted to the individual school's needs. According to the authorities in charge of selection and to the School Leader Associations of the individual federal states, on a national average there are 1.3 to 5.6 candidates per vacant position. In some 'Länder', such as Baden-Württemberg, Bavaria, Berlin, Bremen, Hesse, Lower Saxony,

North Rhine-Westphalia, Saxony and Saxony-Anhalt, interviews with potential school leader candidates are conducted. Marketing measures in a classic sense are not in use.

Prerequisites and Pre-Selection   In all federal states, a new school leader is required to have had teacher training for, and teaching experience in, the respective type of school. Moreover, additional qualifications are an advantage, like experiences as a deputy school leader, in leading teams, working as an instructor in charge of the induction phase of teacher training, etc. Mostly, however, the state examinations after teacher training are decisive as well as the regular official performance assessments by superiors. The candidates who are evaluated as most suitable are appointed school leaders for life (see Eurydice, 1996; Huber, 2004).

With the exception of Bavaria, where the regular official performance assessment by superiors is taken into account, in all states the teachers aspiring to school leadership are evaluated for this purpose. Consequently, the assessment of one's professional performance and achievements is not only a basis for promotion (see the section about selection criteria), but also the central precondition for the application. In some states, there is a systematic training before the application as a prerequisite for taking over school leadership, as is the case in some other European countries (Knorr, 2004).

Job Profiles   Job profiles or competence profiles have been set up in eleven (out of sixteen) federal states (Huber & Schneider, 2007a, 2007b). Others may have them now as well. However, they are not always explicitly formulated as job profiles. Besides, it is striking that most of the descriptions comprise tasks and demands on, competencies required for and goals of school leadership. Some states explicitly claim that the advertisements for vacant positions are to be based on the criteria formulated in the profiles, which should be adapted to the local conditions. In some states, these descriptions also function as a basis for the evaluation/assessment of school leaders.

Selection Methods   The choice of selection methods differs widely across the federal states so that there is no Germany-wide selection procedure (Rosenbusch et al., 2002). After the applications have been received and passed on to the authorities in charge, the first step is a general check if the candidate is suitable with regards to the results of the regular official assessments by his superiors.

In Bavaria and Hesse, the focus is only on these formal criteria indicating performance and abilities as stated in the regular official assessment. This selection method is the explanation for the fact that the complete selection procedure takes comparatively little time. Interviews play only a minor part in Bavaria and Hesse. They are only a fall back if the applicant's documents and evaluation results do not show a clear match to the criteria in terms of selecting the best.

In the federal states Baden-Württemberg, Brandenburg, North Rhine-Westphalia and Saxony-Anhalt, among the selection methods are classroom observations (and analyses), chairing of conferences (not in Baden-Württemberg), and interviews.

In Lower Saxony, Thuringia, Saxony, Hamburg, and Berlin, the emphasis is on the interviews, though the type and length of interviews differ. The impression of the applicant gained through the interview is most influential on the decision as to who is selected. In those states, the time span of the procedure is the longest.

In Schleswig-Holstein und Bremen, too, the personal presentation of the applicant plays a decisive part. In Schleswig-Holstein, the interviews are conducted in the selection committee; in Bremen, however, the applicants do not personally introduce themselves to the panel. There, the interviews with the pre-selected candidates are conducted by the respective board at the school itself. A further particularity of those two countries is that they establish a pool of candidates on the basis of professional development talks, potential analyses, and training and development programs, which can, in the case of new appointments, shorten the length of the procedure to approximately three months.

For some years, in Lower Saxony, Hesse, and Schleswig-Holstein an explicit restructuring of the school leader selection procedure has been planned with regards to selection methods (see Niermann, 1999; Hoffmann, 2003; Denecke, Simon, & Wiethaup, 2005; http://www.modelle. bildung.hessen.de). New conceptions particularly stand out due to a linking of personnel planning, staff development and selection, in which different potential analysis procedures and/or components of an assessment center are applied after the candidates have taken part in a development program.

Selection Criteria   According to an unpublished study by Rosenbusch, Huber and Knorr (2002), in all federal states there is consensus that the best candidate shall be selected for a school leadership position. The written criteria of Bavaria, Berlin, Bremen und Schleswig-Holstein state that above all the objectivity and lucidity of the procedure are the most relevant factors in the selection process. The applicants shall get the chance to fully understand the decision made. In all federal states, in a genuine selection procedure, the aptitude, capability, and professional performance of the applicant are assessed on the basis of his or her evaluation of achievements as a teacher.

The assessment of the professional abilities and performance of the future school leader is the central basis for promotion and appointment (see Eurydice, 1996). In quite a number of states, additional emphasis is put on performance in the personal interview. With the exception of countries that only focus on assessments of professional performance, the criteria for the

TABLE 10.3

Aspect	Description
Overall Approach	centralized selection process in most federal states
Selection Body	the departments of the Ministries of Education in the respective German federal state
Advertising & Marketing	– in the official information publications of the ministry, in regional official newsletters, and partly on the internet – general advertisements of open positions (no specifications about the individual school's needs) – no information about any marketing activities
Job Profile	job profiles or competence profiles in eleven federal states, however, not always explicitly formulated as such
Prerequisites	– teaching experience in the respective school type – good results in previous performance assessments – completion of a qualification program (is currently under discussion)
Selection Methods	– general check of the results of the regular official performance assessments by superiors – mostly focused on formal criteria indicating performance and abilities as stated in the regular official performance assessment – additional selection methods such as classroom observations and analyses, chairing of conferences and interviews are used in some federal states
Selection Criteria	– additional qualifications are usually an advantage – the weighing of single selection criteria differ widely across the federal states; the criteria for the final selection remain mostly unclear
Evaluation	no information on the reliability or validity of the selection procedures or methods

final selection remain unclear. In some federal states, the individual schools have a say in the procedure, in most cases, however, in terms of having a counseling voice. In Hamburg, Bremen, Schleswig-Holstein, and Lower Saxony, the individual school actively takes part in the process through a specific panel.

Evaluation of the Selection Procedure   When comparing the duration of the selection procedures of the German federal states, there are some striking differences. In Bavaria, Bremen, and Schleswig-Holstein the average time span is between two and three months. Those three states are below the German average of approximately four to six months. In Saxony and Thuringia, for example, the procedure takes one year on average and is clearly longer than the German average.

As far as we know, interviewing authorities and school leader associations in Germany did not bring about any insights into the reliability and validity of individual selection procedures and methods, as no state could provide any information about such results. This situation has not substantially changed in Germany. At present, studies focusing on the validation of selection methods cannot be found. To sum up, Table 10.3 provides an overview.

Singapore

From 1824 to 1945, Singapore was a British colony. During those 120 years, Singapore replicated England's education system. In that time, the management, supervision, evaluation, selection, and the training and development of staff were within the responsibility of the schools themselves. After independence from the British Empire in 1945, the government decided to manage the education sector centrally and to control it more strictly.

Singapore's present school system is determined by a meritocratic policy approach with a strong emphasis on achievement, efficiency and economic success. Most influential in the education sector is the Ministry of Education (MOE). The ministry formulates and implements education policies, and it is responsible for the design of the curriculum and allocates resources. Furthermore, it controls the development and administration of the government and government-aided schools and also supervises private schools. The school division of the MOE aims to ensure that schools are effectively managed and that the education provided is in accordance with national objectives.

Moreover, the ministry is in charge of the selection, training and development of school leaders. The school leaders and the whole school leadership team are supervised, guided, supported, and assessed regarding their effectiveness by superintendents. Hence, school inspection is allocated directly at the ministry level.

The responsibility for the individual school lies with the school leaders, yet most schools actually are directly administered by the ministry (with regard to selecting staff, admitting pupils, buying material needed, etc.). Thus, the tasks of school leaders are almost completely reduced to implementing the stipulations of the ministry, assessing whether the quality of instruction is good, and launching improvement efforts if necessary. Singapore's education system is extremely competitive, and there is much pressure on the schools, the teachers, and the pupils, as pupil achievement is evaluated through standardized tests and the results are published in ranking lists (league tables).

Since the end of the 1980s, there have been calls for a decentralization of educational governance. School leaders have demanded more responsibility at school level in order to be able to introduce initiatives and respond more flexibly to changes. Since the beginning of the 1990s, the demand for more autonomy has met with a positive result.

In 1997, the MOE introduced the 'Thinking Schools, Learning Nation' concept. The school principal obviously plays a key role in this transition from a very result-oriented approach to viewing schools to a more process- and learning-oriented one. The principal has to make sure that the school reacts to varying needs and challenges, and she or he supervises the development of school programs. The main emphasis will be on character building, motivation and innovation, creative and committed learning. This could mean even more pressure to succeed for the single principal, since there will still be ranking lists and competition among schools while the range of criteria for all that has changed and increased. It could thus be argued that school principals in Singapore have to cope with conflicting demands. On the one hand, they need to holistically drive forward the vision of a thinking school: developing into a more organizationally independent and self-reflecting entity, even as they are ranked. In fact, schools are supposed to develop contrary to what has shaped them for decades. The school principal, therefore, plays an important role in this politically propagated societal change.

Organization of the Selection Procedure   Possible further career steps for teachers within their school (e.g. to become a head of department or deputy school leader) are regulated by a formal Career Advancement Chart (CAC). It was developed to plot the training needs and career prospects of all teachers, and it functions as a formal guideline for promotions, positioning a teacher within a school according to his or her academic achievement and teaching experience as well as evaluation reports.

Advertising and Marketing   Unfortunately, we could not access any information about the means of recruiting suitable applicants and ways of advertising vacant positions.

Prerequisites and Pre-Selection   As a prerequisite for a school leader position, the preparatory program Diploma in Educational Administration (DEA) was a requirement. The program was developed and implemented in conjunction with the MOE and the National Institute of Education of the 'Nanyang Technological University'. Recently, a new program has replaced the DEA. This shorter qualification called Leaders in Education Program (LEP) is, at its core, an executive program conceiving of the principal's role as that of a Chief Executive Officer. It is shorter in duration than the previous DEA, adopts an innovative process-as-content model to place the emphasis on learning, problem solving and decision making, draws on the expertise available in industry, and provides opportunities for field trips abroad.

Job Profiles   There is no information available about job profiles.

Selection Methods   In the selection procedure in a narrow sense, teachers are invited to interviews upon the recommendation of the district superintendent. The main criteria for the selection of school leaders are their academic achievement, their teaching experience and their evaluation reports.

Selection Criteria   The school leaders should at least hold a Masters degree. If there is an exception, the degree can later be completed at the ministry or at a university of education. The final decision regarding the appointment is made by the Board of Education.

TABLE 10.4

Aspect	Description
Overall Approach	highly centralized
Selection Body	– the Ministry of Education (MOE)
	– basis: a formal Career Advancement Chart
Advertising & Marketing	no information available
Job Profile	no information available
Prerequisites	– mandatory prerequisite: participation in the 'Leaders in Education Program' (LEP)
	– a Master degree
Selection Methods	interview on the recommendation of the district superintendent
Selection Criteria	– academic achievement, teaching experience and performance according to assessment reports (career up to now).
	– final decision regarding the appointment by the so called 'Board of Education'.
Evaluation	no information available

Evaluation of the Selection Procedure   It seems that evaluation is not conducted, as there is no information available about evaluation of the school leader selection procedure. To sum up, Table 10.4 provides an overview.

Australia

New South Wales (NSW) is one of the six federal states of Australia. Australia's federal structure of government assigns most of the responsibility for schooling to the six state and two territory governments. The federal government, through the Department of Education, Science and Training and (DEST) provides national cohesion across the various school systems, a system of vocational training, funding for universities, which operate relatively autonomously, and a policy framework linking education to the economy, society and culture of the nation. Each state and territory has developed its own system of educational administration within this framework, New South Wales is the largest public school system, with 2,200 schools, 750,000 pupils and 46,000 teachers. In New South Wales, as in most other states of Australia, reforms in the field of educational policy took place in the course of the 1990s. Central administration was reduced and schools were given more self-management in terms of site-based management, by which local school committees and school leaders were delegated an increased level of responsibility. Since then, to some extent, individual schools and their leaders have become more accountable. In the course of these developments, a new conception of leadership has become operational, namely School Leaders in Learning Communities. It is based on seven principles (Dawson, 1999):

- leaders are responsible for learning,
- leaders model effective learning,
- leaders lead teams,
- leadership is a function of ability, not position in the hierarchy,
- leaders exist throughout the school learning community,

- leaders are creative,
- leaders are ethical.

On the basis of this new conception of school leadership, the NSW Department of Education and Training launched a comprehensive training and development program, the School Leadership Strategy (SLS), which was centrally developed and implemented, with support being provided through local Inter-District School Leadership Groups (ISLGs) and the principal associations. The School Leadership Strategy (SLS) is a multi-phase systematic program, based on an understanding of schools functioning as learning communities with leadership distributed widely within each school. It is underpinned by the NSW DET School Leadership Capability Framework and the NSW Institute of Teachers' Professional Teaching Standards. The programs address the needs of future school leaders, and the broader leadership group within each school. The School Executive Induction Program and the Principal Induction Program are designed to induct new appointees into these leadership functions. The Principal Development Program and the School Executive Development Program provide continuing professional development for established school leaders, and for faculty with other leadership roles.

Organization of the Selection Procedure   Regarding the filling of vacant school leadership positions, different contexts have an impact on the process. In the case where a member of the school leadership team has to be appointed for an interim period, the selection is made by a committee within the school. When school leadership personnel have to be appointed for a longer period, until recently, a distinction was made between the appointment for lifetime or 'merit-based' for a specific time period. In the meantime, however, only merit based selections for limited periods are made. A panel comprised of different members according to the respective federal state is usually in charge of the organization of this selection procedure. In NSW, the panel consists of one representative of the NSW Teachers Federation; one representative of the Director-General, and one administrative/clerical representative of the Education Department.

Advertising and Marketing   Vacant positions are advertised in the Commonwealth Government Gazette and additionally in the ACT Schools Bulletin (in most cases in March). The advertising period is about 6 to 12 months, which is quite long, due to the effort to advertise and fill all vacant positions for the coming term at the same time.

Linked to the various training and development programs, there are extensive marketing activities: Since the entire qualification program is mainly organized and implemented by the ISLGs, these groups are of major importance. There are 20 of these groups altogether. They have been formed by two or three individual school districts respectively. The main task of each ISLG is to disseminate information about the programs, to coordinate the implementation at the local level, and to facilitate mentoring opportunities and the development of local collegial networks. It may be assumed that networks can also be used for recruiting applicants for vacant positions.

Prerequisites and Pre-Selection   Applicants for a school leadership position are expected to have taken part in one of the development programs and to hold the 'Certificate of School Leadership'. However, this is not a mandatory requirement for appointment to school leadership positions. All teaching staff are free to apply.

Job Profiles   The NSW Department of Education and Training through the Training and Development Directorate formulated a conceptual basis for a notion of leadership that is expected to cope with the enlarged demands on school leaders. Hence, this may be called a comprehensive job profile. There is, however, no information about the extent of this job profile being taken into account in the selection procedure itself or whether it is supplemented by any further locally decided demands.

Selection Methods   Within the frame of merit based selection, classic methods are applied. First, the written applications are considered. References are checked. The support of external consultants is used. On the basis of this pre-screening, a more restricted selection is made (short-listing). Applicants on the short-list are invited to an interview by the panel. While Chapman (1984b) still reported that the "most senior eligible applicant must be offered the position" (p. 45), today a merit based selection is made.

Evaluation of the Selection Procedure   Some basic evaluation was undertaken in the 1980s (Chapman, 1984a, 19984b). A team of the Commonwealth Schools Commission was founded with the primary objective to identify ways of supporting and improving the professional development of principals. For this purpose, four studies were conducted, one of which aims at developing a descriptive profile of principals, and another at summarizing the procedures which are currently followed in selecting and appointing principals and to identify the assumptions underlying these processes. Due to the changes in the 1990s, it must be assumed that the modes of selection and the criteria for the decision were modified. There is no information about evaluation studies on school leader selection and appointment after those changes in the 1990s.

However, there are some hints at general problems in the Policy Statements of the Australian Secondary Principal Association (ASPA). The Policy Paper School Leaders: Shortage and Suitability in Australian Public Schools from November 1999, for example, indicates some improvements of the selection procedure.

TABLE 10.5

Aspect	Description
Overall Approach	– interim position: fully decentralized (appointment by schools) – long-term positions: relatively decentralized (selection panel)
Selection Body	mixed selection panels
Advertising & Marketing	– in the Commonwealth Government Gazette and the ACT Schools Bulletin – long advertising period of 6 to 12 months – extensive marketing activities linked to the development programs
Job Profile	no information about profiles; but conceptual basis for the new leadership in schools is formulated by NSW Department of Education and Training
Prerequisites	– all teaching staff are free to apply – 'Certificate of School Leadership' (expected)
Selection Methods	– screening of written applications, references checks, interviews by the panel – partly supported by external consultants
Selection Criteria	principle of a merit-based selection process highly emphasized.
Evaluation	– no information about evaluation studies on school leader selection and appointment after the changes in the 90s. – some critique is formulated by the ASPA

More importantly, ASPA notes that some jurisdictions are questioning the ability of the merit based selection processes to ensure that the best person is actually offered the job. ASPA strongly endorses the principle of selection by merit but notes there are some strongly held views that current processes by which merit is determined are not always working well. Issues surrounding existing selection processes are: self-promotion is rarely a reliable predictor of future performance. information about past performance is a more reliable indicator but is hard to obtain.

To sum up, Table 10.5 provides an overview.

The United States

In the United States, distinctive decentralization of decision making processes in the education sector — as well as open enrolment and the accountability of schools to the public — has had serious effects on the principals' functions and range of tasks. The states have established standards, and various state universities have founded bodies for collaboration in order to be able to create consensus across the states and to assure as high a level of quality as possible. Thus, when issues of personnel marketing and the selection of principals are discussed, this should be closely linked to the characteristic features of the US education system and the present 'market' for educational leadership qualification programs. Generally speaking, the responsibility for the training and development of teachers aspiring to a leadership position lies with the universities.

Organization of the Selection Procedure   Due to the special role of university-based training and development programs, the selection procedure basically is two-phased. In the first phase, the teachers must obtain an adequate university degree as a prerequisite. This is closely linked to getting a license, which is a precondition for consideration as a potential candidate for a vacant position. It is only on that basis that the selection procedure takes place. As mentioned above, the tradition of university-based training and development programs is highly relevant. Of similar importance are the states' responsibility for education policy, which leads to a very great differentiation between states, and the development of school site management (including the individual school's autonomy in matters of personnel), which further increases individualization and differentiation.

Hence, the responsibility for the design of the selection procedure ultimately lies with the schools. In most cases, the selection committee, established by the school, is responsible. Quite often, the committee delegates the (pre-) selection procedures to other agents or implements them with the support of personnel consultants or personnel recruitment agencies. Services of that kind exist (according to a survey of the School Boards Associations of 2001, quoted after Riede, 2003a) in more than 34 states. Among them are private companies as well as services of the School Board Associations (see Riede, 2003b).

Advertising and Marketing   Advertisements for vacancies can be found on the career boards of the various professional associations or on the board of the National Association of Secondary School Principals (NASSP, 1998, 2002, 2004), which can be accessed by members only. Some companies and districts also set up their own candidate pool, circulate emails and leaflets around schools, or publish advertisements in newspapers. The United States may be the country in which most marketing is practiced (in terms of leaflets for programs, etc.), as these programs are integrated in the university culture of the American higher education system with its typical marketing culture.

Prerequisites and Pre-Selection   In general, the prerequisite for the application of teachers for a leadership position as a principal is a Masters degree in Education, Educational Leadership, Educational Administration or similar. Additionally, applicants for principalship have to earn a certificate (valid in the respective state or district). To acquire that, they must have taken the respective courses, have professional experience, and often have passed a special test or an assessment center interview. For a detailed survey of the conditions for licensing in the different states see the information offered by the National Center for Education Information in Washington (2003). Korostoff and Orozco (2002) also provide detailed information about all state agencies and universities and various ways to get a license.

Job Profiles   Evidence for fulfilling the demands of the profile can be provided by candidates through their license. However, in the selection procedure, there are additional demands specific to the individual school, which are individually formulated by private personnel agencies and the school itself.

Selection Methods   Little is known about the selection methods applied in the procedure of filling the position. Essentially, there is supposed to be an analysis of the curriculum vitae and a sequence of interviews with the personnel agency and members of the hiring committee. Analysis of various advertisements suggests that the following documents are usually required: current résumé, current transcripts, cover letter outlining qualifications for the position, professional letters of reference, copy of principal certification, and quite often, additionally the response to questions regarding the school or the vision of the future development of the school.

In an effort to find out more about what factors are really important in predicting performance for future principals, the assessment center method came into play in the United States in the 1950s as a tool for personnel selection.

The 12 leadership indicators identified by the NASSP (1998, 2002, 2004) are supposed to constitute a good predictor for future levels of performance for newly hired administrators in education. The assessment center (AC), a growing trend currently used in various areas of the United States, has several characteristics: (1) The use of multiple contrived situations (e.g. business simulations) to observe behavior, (2) the presence of several trained assessors who pool their evaluations along a variety of specified dimensions (e.g. the assessee's leadership, risk-taking, and administrative abilities), (3) the evaluation of several candidates at one time, and (4) extensive feedback, written or verbal, to either the candidate or management, or both.

Selection Criteria   The decision very often lies directly with the school, i.e. with the hiring or selection committee of the particular school. The heterogeneous composition of those bodies on one hand has the advantage that various perspectives can be taken into account. On the other hand, the members of committees usually have not been trained in the selection of personnel at all, or given access to criteria which may differ from the search for the "best-suited individual". Riede (2003a), for example, reports on issues of very able candidates having not been accepted out of 'political reasons' and less able ones having been favored. Roza et al. (2003) state that human resources directors and superintendents draw on different criteria for selection, the former preferring professional experience — typically defined as years of teaching experience — and the latter focusing on leadership competences and often being dissatisfied with the individuals appointed to the position.

Evaluation of the Selection Procedure   The NASSP has had their assessment center procedures (in place since the early 1980s) evaluated continuously (see Schmitt, 1980; Schmitt,

TABLE 10.6

Aspect	Description
Overall Approach	distinctive decentralization (responsibility lies with the schools)
Selection Body	– hiring or selection committees, established by the school – sometimes supported by personnel consultants or personnel recruitment agencies or services of the School Board Associations
Advertising & Marketing	– in career boards, newspapers etc. – recruiting companies also send leaflets around
Job Profile	national standards serve as a general job profile, complemented by specific requirements of the respective school
Prerequisites	teaching licenses, adequate university Master degree, principal license
Selection Methods	great variation among: tests (for licensing); analysis of the curriculum vitae, answers to written questions, reference checks, interviews, and assessment centres
Selection Criteria	no data (probably a result of the very decentralized process)
Evaluation	– studies on the validity of the NASSP assessment centre – no research findings on further selection methods – heterogeneous composition of the selection committee is not always an advantage

Meritt, Fitzgerald & Noe, 1982; Schmitt & Cohen, 1990a, 1990b; Williams & Pantili, 1992; Pashiardis, 1993; Schmitt, 1994). The research findings confirmed sufficient prognostic validity of the assessment center for the future achievement of principals. Research in further selection methods applied during the process of filling positions (e.g. interviews, potential analyses, self-assessment through psychological tests) still is a desiderate. By comparison, the effectiveness and the quality of preparatory training and development programs, including specific methods such as principal internships, and the effectiveness of the standards, are regularly evaluated and broadly discussed. To sum up, Table 10.6 provides an overview.

CONCLUSION

This chapter has drawn heavily on a recent comparative international study (Huber, 2007b; Huber et al., 2007; Huber & Hiltmann, in press) which describes current practice from around the world and identifies commonalities and differences. As this project is only in an exploratory first phase, we are still restricted in drawing our conclusions. Interestingly, there seems to be little international work available on how school leaders are selected and recruited.

Given our first five case study countries, some central similarities and differences can be highlighted.

First, as would be expected, the overall approach of school leader selection ranges from a distinctive decentralized one (with responsibility lying with the schools as in England and the USA) to a centralized one (as in many German states and particularly in Singapore, where the ministry is in charge). Accordingly, the selecting body is either a committee established by the school, the community (or district) or the department of the ministry itself. These decentralized versus centralized approaches impact on the advertising and marketing activities undertaken to fill vacant school leader positions. They are either quite intense and widespread (in the countries with a decentralized approach) or restricted to official information publications.

Second, different kinds of job profiles seem to be in use in many countries. Some are based on standards, some are solely driven by school law and school regulations in which the role of school leaders is described. In countries where the selecting body is school or district based, there is a variety of different kinds of profiles. Some are context rich, taking the local situation into account; others are less detailed.

Third, a conditio sine qua non as a prerequisite for applying for a school leadership position in most countries is having a teaching license and some experience of teaching in the respective type of school. Further prerequisites, however, range from relying mostly on the previous performance of the candidates as teachers, as in Germany, or their participation in a preparatory training course, to completion of a more extensive development program concluding with a certificate or a license, as is the case in England and the United States.

Fourth, the selection methods applied differ widely. While in Germany the emphasis is put on formal criteria indicating abilities (albeit adding further selection methods if considered desirable), in Singapore they rely solely on interviews. Although a great variety of methods are used in the England and the United States, interviews, however, seem to be indispensable.

Fifth, the evaluation of the selection procedures, of selection methods, is a research desideratum: It is usually the case that no information about the reliability and validity is available. In England and the United States, however, some studies on selection methods are being undertaken.

It is clear from this brief review that there is further need to compare both common and distinct elements and to include more countries in the wider second phase of our study. It can rightly be assumed, however, that increasing efforts concerning the selection of school leaders will be made in the near future. This is due to the rising awareness of the central role of school leaders, corroborated by international research findings, as well as to the increasing importance of school leadership in the change process of many school systems from a centralized towards a more decentralized system of self-managing schools.

In general, it seems a rigorous and systematic approach is needed.

First, the approach should be based on what is expected from school leaders in general but also in a specific organizational context. What expectations by regulations, professional standards, or the voices of different stakeholders exist and must be taken into account? The approach should also be based on what we know from research about good or competent school leadership with regards to school quality and school improvement.

What is needed is not only to take the more general perspective into account but also the specific organizational context. Given the desired fit of a person's competences to the requirements of a specific organization, more is required than just backmapping individuals against a general compilation of generic competences; a contextual fit is required.

Second, selection processes should use a wide range of diagnostic means in a kind of mixed method approach, for example, test instruments for attributes and traits, but also for cognitive competences, simulation exercises and observations in real situations for present behavior (skills and abilities), biographical documents and references for past performance and achievements, interviews and letters of motivation to find out about the candidate's motivation and attitudes.

Besides the use of diagnostic instruments for selection and recruitment purposes, some of these methods can be applied to the external evaluation/assessment of established school leaders, and also for candidates' self-assessment for orientation before applying for a leadership position or for a needs-assessment to plan one's individual professional development. Moreover, some of the instruments may be used to select participants for training and development programs. According to the respective purpose in terms of whether it is more self-reflection-and-development-oriented or whether it is external evaluation/assessment-oriented, different strategies by the candidates may be needed. When a self-assessment or a needs-assessment is the focus, an atmosphere of trust can be assumed and the participant can be supposed to behave authentically and reply without anxiety concerning social acceptance. If assessment (e.g. for selection) is the purpose, the candidate will be alert and less ready to show her or his weaknesses. This bias has to be taken into account when using certain instruments and methods.

Moreover, when using selection instruments from the economic sector, it is important not only to adapt them linguistically to the education context but also to check their reliability and validity and use a standardization procedure which is relevant to the population. This adjustment to the specific context and the population seems very important, as does the evaluation of the instrument.

In this respect, Huber et al. (2007) developed an online inventory for self-assessment comprising around 30 test scales related to the competence profile to undertake school development and school management (with around 400 items) and a complex problem analysis tool (in form of an in tray exercise), which have been standardized with around 500 teachers (the Competency Profile School Management - CPSM).

Finally, a professional selection approach focuses on a prognostic perspective. It is about assuming the future performance of a candidate positioning a specific role/context. It is not about 'rewarding' experienced individuals as teachers for their merits. We do not have empirical evidence for the existing practice in some countries, which is based on the assumption that a good teacher automatically becomes a good school leader. There is a risk of losing a competent teacher whilst not necessarily gaining a competent school leader. Professional diagnostics aim at prediction on a prognostic base, not solely on a retrospective base. In this respect, an even less valuable criterion would be the mere age of the candidate in terms of the years of experience in the profession.

As to what is missing but needed, we see several emerging issues.

First, there is still some need for a clearer conception of the competencies required for school leadership. It is clear from the brief country reviews that there is a further requirement to compare both the common and the distinct elements that we find in different countries, and to recognize that, though a competency based approach may have some advantages, there is still less consensus about what the key competencies are than there might be. However, school leadership has to deal with a great amount of complexity and uncertainty but also with dilemmas and contradictions and with different expectations, given all the different stakeholders from the system context as well as the local context. Agreement on competencies may therefore be problematic.

Second, we have become increasingly conscious during our work in this field that the conception of school leadership, even taken internationally, is a rather narrow one. Perhaps there does need to be 'one supreme head' in each school. Maybe school leadership requires other conceptualizations like collective leadership and the re-conceptualization of the school leader's role as simply one part of a team. This would allow a move away from the school leadership concept as a position for one person, the 'multifunctional miracle being' (Huber, 2004), the one-man/one-woman at the top, and to conceptualize school leadership as a function that a team serves to fulfill. It is this last issue which seems to us to challenge most forcibly the orthodoxy underpinning current approaches to recruitment and selection, and which offers the most interesting avenue of exploration for the future.

Third, we need research on the instruments' reliability and validity in particular, and on the effectiveness of selection procedures in general. Reliability of instruments is especially important and therefore, internal consistency methods in order to calculate reliability are extremely useful.

Especially Rasch analysis, Kendalls' W, and Cronbach's alpha, become very useful in order to determine the reliability of each of the factors included in questionnaires which will be used for selection processes.

Fourth, in this context, there are further considerations of efficiency that have to be determined in terms of a cost-benefit analysis. It can be assumed that there is higher efficiency and effectiveness when individuals take over leadership who have been carefully selected and are suitable for the demands. Undeniably, however, there are the costs associated with the various selection methods. As stated above, the more different sources of information or the more different perspectives one includes in the selection procedure, the more objective and reliable, but also the more expensive the process. Consequently, the dilemma is higher expense in tension with greater reliability and validity of the selection process. Yet, it is also important to ask how much has to be spent if the wrong individuals are selected, let alone the educational damage that an incompetent principal can inflict. In essence, a cost-benefit analysis of the type described above would probably prove that it is far more beneficial to spend greater resources initially during the selection process as opposed to having the wrong person in the job for a number of years, particularly in countries where school leaders become appointed as civil servants and retain the position and the salary level for many years.

Finally, it is very interesting to look at potential links between diagnostic procedures, leadership experiences, and training and development opportunities. Among the diagnostic procedures are self- or needs-assessment and assessment in terms of selection or external evaluation. Leadership experiences may comprise a position in the middle management or the senior management team or elsewhere in the school, or as a previously established school leader. Training and development opportunities may have different phases: orientation, preparation, induction, and continuous professional development. The kind of triad of diagnostic procedures, leadership experiences, and training and development opportunities might serve to illuminate and to enhance practice in terms of quality assurance and quality development in leadership.

NOTE

1. Reconstituted in 2007 as the Department for Children, Family and Schools. Scotland and Northern Ireland have different far-reaching ranges of freedom of decision in education policy and therefore differ from what is described here for England.

REFERENCES

Altrichter, H., Schley, W. & Schratz, M. (1998). *Handbuch zur Schulentwicklung*. Innsbruck: Studien-Verlag.

ASD Allgemeiner Schulleitungsverband Deutschland e. V. (German School Leader Association) (2005). *Schulleitung in Deutschland 2005. Ein Berufsbild in Weiterentwicklung*. Raabe: Berlin.

Barth, R. S. (1990). *Improving schools from within: Teachers, parents and principals can make a difference*. San Francisco: Jossey-Bass Publishers.

Bolam, R. (1993). School-based management, school improvement and school effectiveness: Overview and implications. In C. Dimmock (Eds.), *School-based management and school effectiveness* (pp. 219–234). London: Routledge.

Bolam, R., McMahon, A., Pocklington, K. & Weindling, D. (1993). Effective management in schools: A report for the Department for Education via the School Management Task Force Professional Working Party. London: HMSO.

Brookover, W., Beady, C., Flood, P., Schweitzer, J. & Wisenbaker, J. (1979). *School social systems and student achievement: Schools can make a difference.* New York: Praeger.

Burns, J. M. (1978). *Leadership.* New York: Harper.

Caldwell, B. J. & Spinks, J.M. (1992). *Leading the self-managing school.* London: Falmer Press.

Chapman, J. D. (1984a). *The selection and appointment of Australian school principals.* Canberra: Commonwealth Schools Comm. 1984, VII.

Chapman, J. D. (1984b). *A descriptive profile of Australian school principals.* Canberra: Commonwealth Schools Comm. 1984, IX.

Creemers, B. (1994). The history, value and purpose of school effectiveness studies. In D. Reynolds, B. Creemers, P. Nesselrodt, E. Schaffer, S. Stringfield & C. Teddlie (Eds.), *Advances in school effectiveness research and practice* (pp. 9–23). Oxford: Pergamon.

DeBevoise, W. (1984). Synthesis of research on the principal as instructional leader. *Educational Leadership, 41*(5), 14–20.

Dalin, P. & Rolff, H.G. (1990). *Das Institutionelle Schulentwicklungsprogramm.* Soest: Soester Verlag-Kontor.

Dawson, G. (1999, January). School leaders for the 21st century. Paper presented at the Twelfth International Congress on School Effectiveness and Improvement, San Antonio, Texas.

Denecke, F., Simon, R. & Wiethaup, U. (2005). Führung in Schule und Wirtschaft. Qualifizierung von Schulleitungen in Kooperation mit der Wirtschaft. *Schul-Management, 36*(1), 22–25.

Edmonds, R. (1979). Effective schools for the urban poor. *Educational Leadership, 37*(1), 15–27.

Esp, D. (1993). *Competences for school managers.* London: Kogan Page.

Eurybase: The Information Database on Education Systems in Europe. Available online: http://www.eurydice.org/portal/page/portal/Eurydice/DB_Eurybase_Home

Fullan, M. (1991). *The new meaning of educational change.* London: Cassell.

Fullan, M. (1992). *Successful school improvement.* Buckingham: Open University Press.

Fullan, M. (1993). *Change forces. The school as a learning organisation.* London: Falmer Press.

Glatter, R. (1987). Tasks and capabilities. In N. E. Stegö, K. Gielen, R. Glatter & S. M. Hord (Eds.). *The role of school leaders in school improvement* (pp. 113–121). Leuven: ACCO.

Gray, J. (1990). The quality of schooling: Frameworks for judgements. *British Journal of Educational Studies, 38*(3), 204–233.

Gronn, P. (2002). Distributed Leadership. In K. Leithwood & P. Hallinger (Eds.), *Second international handbook of educational leadership and sdministration* (pp. 653–696). Dordrecht: Kluwer

Hall, G. E. & Hord, S. (1987). *Change in schools: Facilitating the process.* Albany: State University of New York Press.

Hallinger, P. (2005). Instructional leadership and the school principal: A passing fancy that refuses to fade away. *Leadership and Policy in Schools, 4*(3), 221–240.

Hallinger, P. & Murphy, J. (1985). Assessing the instructional management behaviour of principals. *Elementary School Journal, 86*(2), 217–247.

Hargreaves, D. H. (1994). The new professionalism: The synthesis of professional and institutional development. *Teaching and Teacher Education, 10*(4), 423–438.

Hoffmann, E. (2003). Schulleiterin oder Schulleiter als Beruf Teil II: Auswahl und Qualifizierung. Ergebnisse des niedersächsischen Projekts "Arbeitsplatz Schulleitung". Schulverwaltung. *Ausgabe Niedersachsen und Schleswig-Holstein, 13*(2), 53–55.

Hopkins, D., Ainscow, M. & West, M. (1994). *School improvement in an era of change.* London: Cassell.

Hopkins, D., West, M. & Ainscow, M. (1996). *Improving the quality of education for all: Progress and challenge.* London: David Fulton Publishers.

Huber, S. G. (1997). *Headteachers' views on headship and training: A comparison with the NPQH.* Cambridge: School of Education, University of Cambridge.

Huber, S. G. (1999a). School effectiveness: Was macht Schule wirksam? Internationale Schulentwicklungsforschung (I). *Schul-Management, 2,* 10–17.

Huber, S. G. (1999b). School improvement: Wie kann Schule verbessert werden? Internationale Schulentwicklungsforschung (II). *Schul-Management, 3,* 7–18.

Huber, S. G. (1999c). *Schulleitung international. Studienbrief im Studium "Vorbereitung auf Leitungsauf-gaben in Schulen".* Hagen: Fernuniversität Hagen.

Huber, S. G. (2004). *Preparing school leaders for the 21st century: An international comparison of development programmes in 15 countries.* London: RoutledgeFalmer.

Huber, S. G. & Gniechwitz, S. (2006). *Auswahl von Schulleiterinnen und Schulleitern in den deutschen Bundesländer. Eine Synopse.* Interner Bericht. Erfurt.

Huber, S. G. (2007a). Anforderungen an Schulleitung: Was wird in den Ländern von den pädagogischen Führungskräften in der Schule erwartet? In A. Bartz, J. Fabian, S. G. Huber, Carmen Kloft, H. Rosenbusch, &. H. Sassenscheidt (Eds.), *PraxisWissen Schulleitung* (pp. 10–24). München: Wolters Kluwer.

Huber, S. G. (2007b). *Auswahl von Schulleiterinnen und Schulleitern. Ein international-vergleichendes Forschungsprojekt: Forschungsfrage und Projektdesign.* Interner Bericht, Zug.

Huber, S. G., Hiltmann, M., Hader-Popp, S. (2007). *Auswahl von Schulleiterinnen und Schulleitern. Ergebnisse einer internationalen Sondierungsuntersuchung.* Interner Bericht, Zug.

Huber, S. G. & Hiltmann, M. (in press). The recruitment and selection of school leaders – first findings of an international comparison. In S. G. Huber, (Ed.), *School leadership — international perspectives.* New York: Peter Lang.

Huber, S. G. & Schneider, N. (2007a). Anforderungen an Schulleitung: Funktion, Aufgaben, erforderliche Kompetenzen und Leitbilder in den deutschen Bundesländer. Eine Synopse der Beschreibungen in den deutschen Bundesländer. Interner Bericht. Zug.

Huber, S. G. & Schneider, N. (2007b). Anforderungen an Schulleitung: Was wird von den pädagogischen Führungskräften in der Schule erwartet? Beschreibungen aus den Ministerien der deutschen Bundesländer. In A. Bartz, J. Fabian, S.G. Huber, Carmen Kloft, H. Rosenbusch, H. Sassenscheidt (Eds.), *PraxisWissen Schulleitung* (pp. 11–35). München: Wolters Kluwer.

Huberman, M. (1992). Critical introduction. In M. Fullan (Ed.), *Successful school improvement* (pp. 1–20). Milton Keynes: Open University Press.

Jirasinghe, D. & Lyons, G. (1996). *The competent head: A job analysis of heads' tasks and personality factors.* London: The Falmer Press.

Jones, A. (1987). *Leadership for tomorrow's schools.* Oxford: Basil Blackwell.

Joyce, B. (1991). The doors to school improvement. *Educational Leadership, 48*(8), 59–62.

Katz, R. L. (1974). The skills of an effective administrator. *Harvard Business Review, 52,* 90–102.

Knorr, A. (2004). Personalauswahl. Unterschiedliche Verfahren in den Bundesländern. Schul-Management, 35(1), 30–32.

Korostoff, M. & Orozco, L. (2002). Who Will Educate Our Candidates? The Politicalization of Educational Leadership Preparation Programs. Paper presented at the 2002 American Educational Research Association Annual Conference, New Orleans, LA, April 2, 2002. Available: http://hdcs.fullerton.edu/faculty/orozco/aera2002.html

Kythreotis, A. & Pashiardis, P. (2006). The influences of school leadership styles and culture on students' achievement in Cyprus primary schools. Paper presented at the 87th Annual Meeting of the American Educational Research Association. San Francisco.

Leithwood, K. A. (1992a). The principal's role in teacher development. In M. Fullan & A. Hargreaves (Eds.) *Teacher development and educational change* (pp. 86–103). London: The Falmer Press.

Leithwood, K. A. (1992b). The move toward transformational leadership. *Educational Leadership, 49*(5), 8–12.

Leithwood, K. A. & Montgomery, D. J. (1986). *Improving principal effectiveness: The principal profile.* Toronto: OISE Press.

Levine, D. U. & Lezotte, L. W. (1990). *Unusually effective schools: A review and analysis of research and practice.* Madison: National Centre for Effective School Research.

Louis, K. S. & Miles, M. B. (1990). *Improving the urban high school, what works and why.* New York: Teachers College Press.

Moos, L. & Huber, S. G. (2006). School leadership, school effectiveness and improvement: Democratic and integrative leadership. In T. Townsend (Ed.). *International handbook of school effectiveness and school improvement* (pp. 579–596). New York: Springer.

Morgan, C., Hall, V. & Mackay, H. (1983). *The selection of secondary school head-teachers.* Open University Press: Milton Keynes.

Mortimore, P., Sammons, P., Stoll, L., Lewis, D. & Ecob, R. (1988). *School matters: The junior years.* Wells: Open Books.

National Association of Secondary School Principals (NASSP). (1998). *Developmental Assessment Center – frequently asked questions.* Reston, VA: NASSP.

National Association of Secondary School Principals (NASSP). (2002). *Selecting and developing the 21st century principal – frequently asked questions.* Reston, VA: NASSP.

National Association of Secondary School Principals (NASSP). (2004). *Promoting excellence in school leadership. Reston,* VA: NASSP.

National College for School Leadership (NCSL). (2005). *Leading Appointments A study into and guidance on headteacher recruitment. Interim-report.* Nottingham, UK.

National College for School Leadership (NCSL). (2006). *Recruiting headteachers and senior leaders. Overview of research findings.* Nottingham, UK.

National Educational Assessment Centre (NEAC). (1995). *The Competencies.* Oxford Brooks University: NEAC.

Niermann, W. (1999). Qualifizierung und Auswahl von Schulleiterinnen und Schulleitern. *Pädagogische Führung, 10*(4), 175–179.

Pashiardis, P. (1993). Selection methods for educational administrators in the U.S.A. *International Journal of Educational Management, 7*(1), 27–35.

Pashiardis, P. (1998). Researching the characteristics of effective primary school principals in Cyprus: A Qualitative Approach. *Educational Management and Administration, 26*(2), 117–130.

Reynolds, D. (1976). The delinquent school. In P. Woods (Ed.), *The process of schooling.* London: Routledge & Kegan.

Reynolds, D., Bollen, R., Creemers, B., Hopkins, D., Stoll, L. & Lagerweij, N. (Eds.). (1996). *Making good schools: Linking school effectiveness and school improvement.* London: Routledge.

Riede, P. (2003a). The Hard Business of Searching. For search firms, filling a superintendency can be as demanding as the job itself. The School Administrator Web Edition, June 2003. Available: http://www.aasa.org/publications/saarticledetail.cfm?ItemNumber=1714

Riede, P. (2003b). Power Brokers Revisited. A directory of firms that conduct national or regional superintendent searches. The School Administrator Web Edition, June 2003. Available: http://www.aasa.org/publications/saarticledetail.cfm?ItemNumber=1968

Rosenbusch, H. S. (1997a). Die Qualifikation pädagogischen Führungspersonals. In E. Glumpler & H. S. Rosenbusch (Eds.), *Perspektiven der universitären Lehrerausbildung* (pp. 147–165). Bad Heilbrunn/Obb.: Klinkhardt.

Rosenbusch, H. S. (1997b). Organisationspädagogische Perspektiven einer Reform der Schulorganisation. *SchulVerwaltung, 10,* 329–334.

Rosenbusch, H. S., Huber, S. G. & Knorr, A. (2002). *Personalauswahl. Unterschiedliche Verfahren in den Bundesländern.* Interner Bericht, Bamberg.

Roza, M., Celio, M. B., Harvey, J. & Wishon, S. (2003). *A matter of defintion: Is there truly a shortage of school principals?* (2nd ed.). A Report to The Wallace Foundation, Center on Reinventing Public Education, University of Washington.

Rutter, M., Maughan, B., Mortimore, P. & Ouston, J. (1979). *Fifteen thousand hours.* London: Open Books.

Sammons, P., Hillman, J. & Mortimore, P. (1995). *Key characteristics of effective schools: A review of school effectiveness research.* London: OFSTED.

Scheerens, J. & Bosker, R. (1997). *The foundations of educational effectiveness.* Oxford: Pergamon.

Schmitt, N. (1980). Validation of the NASSP Assessment Center: An overview and Ssme preliminary findings. *NASSP Bulletin, 64*(438), 107–117.

Schmitt, N. (1994). Equivalence of NASSP Standard Assessment Center and an Abbreviated Center. Report submitted to National Association of Secondary School Principals. Reston, VA.

Schmitt, N., Meritt, R., Fitzgerald, M. P., & Noe, R. A. (1982). The NASSP assessment center: A validity report. *National Association of Secondary School Principals Bulletin, 66,* 134–142.

Schmitt, N. & Cohen, S. A. (1990a). *Criterion-Related Validity of the NASSP Assessment Center. Report submitted to the National Association of Secondary School Principals*. Reston, VA.

Schmitt, N. & Cohen, S. A. (1990b). Criterion-related validity of the assessment center for selection of school administrators. *Journal of Personnel Evaluation in Education, 3*, 203–212.

Schneider, Franz J. (1997). Assessment Centre. Zur Auswahl von Schulleitern und stellvertretenden Schulleitern in England. *Schul-Management, 28*(1), 32–35.

Spillane, J. P. Halverson, R. & Diamond, J. B. (2001). Investigating school leadership practice: A distributed perspective. *Educational Researcher, 30*(3), 23–28.

Spillane, J., Halverson, R., Diamond, J. (2004). Towards a theory of school leadership practice: Implications of a distributed perspective. *Journal of Curriculum Studies, 36*(1), 3–34.

Starkebaum, K. (1998) Schulleiterausbildung in England und Wales. Blickpunkt Schulleitung, *Magazin des Schulleitungsverbandes, 62*(3/98), 8–11.

Stegö, N. E., Gielen, K., Glatter, R. & Hord, S. M. (Eds.). (1987). *The role of school leaders in school improvement*. Leuven: ACCO.

Teddlie, C. & Stringfield, S. C. (1993). *Schools make a difference: Lessons learned from a 10-year study of school effects*. New York: Teachers' College Press.

Trider, D. & Leithwood, K. A. (1988). Influences on principal's practices. *Curriculum Inquiry, 18*(3), 289–311.

Van Velzen, W. G. (1979). *Autonomy of the school*. S'Hertogenkosch: PKC.

Van Velzen, W. G., Miles, M. B., Ekholm, M., Hameyer, U. & Robin, D. (Eds.). (1985). *Making school improvement work: A conceptual guide to practice*. Leuven: ACCO.

Williams, J. & Pantili, L. (1992). A meta-analytic model of principal assessment. *Journal of School Leadership, 2*(3), 256–279.

11

Curriculum and Pedagogy

Edith A. Rusch

Constructing an international perspective of the curricula that form worldwide educational leadership programs is somewhat like trying to develop a worldwide picture of women's lives. I have a vivid memory of the first time I realized that my understandings of professional women's issues were based on a singular Westernized view and that my carefully crafted knowledge base was most incomplete and almost useless once I moved beyond the United States. In that moment, in the Russian state of Tartarstan, I became a more humble learner.

This task was somewhat simpler because I approached it with the perspective that the only commonality I might find around the world was an agreement on the meaning of curriculum, which is a "system of teaching somebody something by some process" (Taba, 1967, p. 4). Each program, in each country I examined, has a system of learning experiences intended to increase the knowledge and skill base of aspiring and practicing educational leaders. The most common system is one of 10–15 separately designed courses, sporadically interrelated or connected, offered to adult learners in structured and timed setting, using a variety of pedagogical techniques, ranging from knowledge acquisition to active and problem-based knowledge use. Often, courses from a wide variety of locations have somewhat similar titles and very common content. In some cases, the series of courses that comprise an educational leadership program appear to be a highly developed and well-thought-out system, with learning experiences designed to scaffold toward sophisticated outcomes. Additionally, the processes that engage students in the program of study have a fair amount of similarity, suggesting that educators around the world ascribe to some common theories about adult learning. But that is where the similarities end. What constitutes a course (time and credit) has wide variance. The number of courses that comprise a program and when, or if, an individual should engage in a course of study, have even wider variance. Throughout the world, cultural or political ideology is also a formidable factor, for both curriculum and pedagogy. In some cases, like that of the United States, political ideology has fostered a stream of privately sponsored and highly touted programs which are challenging the longest-standing tradition — that school leaders are educated in university settings. In other cases, like China, current political ideology is reversing the cultural and political traditions that formerly guided the training and appointment of school leaders. And yet in other cases, like the United Kingdom and many nations in Africa, the systems to create the systems are under construction.

DISCLAIMERS AND LIMITATIONS

The review that follows was enhanced by the extraordinary connections available through the Internet. This source is more useful than the traditional academic references in journals and books because program descriptions rarely are published in peer refereed sources. However, some journal articles and books provided wonderful baseline information that led to searches of university, agency, and individual websites. The work of Ray Bolam (1991, 2003, 2004), Tony Bush and David Jackson (2002), Phillip Hallinger, (2003), Stephan Huber and Mel West (2002), Joseph Murphy (1991, 1999), Allan Walker and Clive Dimmock (2006) and many others provided in-depth accounts, both current and historical, about program development around the world. I drew heavily from the work of these colleagues and attempted to add as much currency as possible. Fortunately, many university and agency websites around the world offer comprehensive and easily accessible information about programs, individual courses, and pedagogy.

I began by accumulating information about and examples of programs worldwide, hoping to represent every continent. That approach quickly eliminated some major continents and regions like South and Central America and Russia, because information is not readily available or educational leadership is an underdeveloped field of study. In other cases, like the United States and the United Kingdom, information and examples were so readily available that the selection process was a challenge. Criteria that guided my final selections included:

- Available Information about national/governmental standards or directions that supported a fuller understanding or critique of the university program(s);
- Program descriptions that included mission statements and some description of course content (beyond titles);
- A balance of longstanding programs (US) with emergent programs (South Africa);
- A sampling of emerging entrepreneurial and non-traditional leadership programs.

The data acquired through this process, although thick and rich, may not be as current or as accurate as one might like. The sections that follow should be read with the knowledge that they represent a broad brushstroke of information, synthesized in arbitrary ways. Furthermore, evaluations of the curriculum and pedagogy of different programs are rarely systematically conducted or presented in the extant literature. Thus, the purpose of this chapter is to provide descriptions of illustrative samples of programs and to present an analysis of curriculum and pedagogy of leadership development and preparation from an international perspective. The chapter begins with descriptions of the curriculum of some illustrative formal university-based preparation programs and then moves to descriptions of more entrepreneurial leadership preparation programs. Following an examination of the curriculum of leadership preparation and development, the chapter focuses briefly on examples of pedagogical practices. Finally, the chapter presents an analytical discussion of commonalities and differences in educational leadership curriculum and pedagogy and ideas for further research.

FORMAL UNIVERSITY-BASED PROGRAMS

Centralized and/or Standards Driven

Curricular structures described in this section are often guided by national or government-driven standards set by Ministries or Departments of Education. In cases like South Africa, Hong Kong and the United Kingdom, centralized standards are recent and programs may or may not connect to the standard requirements. In cases like Singapore and the United States, national or state standards have long been a factor in the development of formal programs.

An effective curriculum that qualifies as a "system of teaching and learning" (Taba, 1967, p. 4) has tightly interrelated objectives, content, learning activities, teaching strategies, and evaluative measures. A curriculum in an educational leadership program, whether based in a university or offered by a private provider typically frames the program objectives as a mission, vision, purpose, or belief set that guides the selection and design of content, which become separate and specific courses. One challenge advanced educational programs face is that individual courses are constructed and taught by individual faculty with specialized knowledge and expertise, who may or may not connect their content, learning activities, or teaching strategies with the larger framework of the program. The programs chosen, to varying degrees, represent that coherence and are not intended to be inclusive of all type programs but rather to illustrate some themes and practices across international contexts. In order to develop a more global perspective on the directions educational leadership curriculums are taking, I examined program mission, vision, purpose and belief statements for commonalities and anomalies and then compared those goals and objectives to the course offerings (content) in an attempt to determine the degree to which a system of teaching and learning was possible.

Africa *Nigeria The University of Lagos* This university provides one example of Nigerian advanced degree programs that are attempting to meet the standards of the National Universities Commission. The program aims to develop "skills, abilities, and competencies that enable [graduates] to cope" with the many challenges facing the Nigerian educational system. The mission goes on to note that a graduate will emerge with the "the spirit and culture of both entrepreneurship and intrepreneurship (University of Lagos website). The goals of the M.Ed Educational Administration program include developing "highly motivated, conscientious and efficient educational managers" with the intellectual and professional knowledge and skill base to make them adaptable to any changing situation, not only in the life of their country but also in the wider world" (University of Lagos website). An additional goal of the program is to prepare educational managers who can advance Nigeria's educational objectives.

The language in the mission and objectives suggest a curriculum filled with change, innovation, and comparative studies of educational reform. However, the program still mimics the traditional management programs in the United States, with a mix of courses in educational administration fundamentals, policy, politics, law, finance, and research. Although internship experiences are required, the learning activity leads to a thesis. There is no indication that coursework is available to develop entrepreneurs or intrapreneurs.

South Africa In 1995, David Johnson examined the changing landscape of formal management education in South Africa and noted a changing program emphasis from administration or top-down management to "more value-added principal centered leadership" (p. 228). Numerous higher education institutions, particularly the White Afrikaans speaking institutions, had offered formal degree programs for educational administration for many years (Johnson, 1995). However, as the political and social landscape changed, White, English-speaking universities and historically disadvantaged universities began to collaborate in order to increase opportunities for potential school leaders. After reviewing the current state of educational management training opportunities, Johnson (1995) concluded that most efforts in South Africa were still piecemeal and not driven by any central focus that recognized the unique needs of educators in a nation with "changing realities" (p. 235).

Johnson's call for more coherency appears to have been heeded. More recently, a National Task Team on Educational Management Development (NTTEMD) reviewed existing and emerging programs across the country and granted full accreditation to seven programs, provisional or conditional accreditation to eight programs, and withdrew or did not grant accreditation to three programs. Four programs are voluntarily ending and are listed as "teaching out the program."

Nelson Mandela Metropolitan University   This fully accredited program offers a vision:

> to be a centre of excellence contributing to sustainable development in education. Our mission is to develop education who can act as leaders and mentors in a transforming environment. This we will achieve by offering relevant, researched and advanced study programmes that address the current changing needs of our country. (Nelson Mandela Metropolitan University website)

References to "sustainable development" and "current changing needs" highlight the unique challenges of leader work in African nations where "even the most advanced country in this continent has thousands of schools without power, water, sanitation, or telecommunications" (Bush & Oduro, 2006, p. 360).

The module-based curriculum (Table 11.1) that supports the mission includes many standard titles found in longer standing programs across the world, with each module including a methodology course and a 25,000–30,000 word treatise on an approved topic, an assignment typical of doctoral programs in the UK. One course that looks at eco-systemic perspectives is more reflective of the developmental needs of this nation.

University of Johannesburg   A program that visibly attends to content related to teaching and learning is at the University of Johannesburg. Labeled as an Advanced Certificate in Educational Management and Leadership, the two-year program is taught in nine modules and addresses four themes: Teaching and Learning, Leadership, Policy and Governance, and Finance and Resources. The program begins with Instruction in South African Leadership followed by courses related to the four themes that are taught each year, suggesting a clear scaffolding of content with attention to deep knowledge in these selected areas. Students also have an elective choice in Mentoring or Gender Issues. Unlike the other two programs described above, Johannesburg students develop a Portfolio of Evidence related to practical application of their learning, as opposed to required research projects.

East Asia Singapore   Some of the liveliest educational leadership program development is taking place in this world region. Led by Singapore, which began formal preparation in the

TABLE 11.1
Course Modules

Educational Management	Special Needs Education	Curriculum Policy, Development and Management
Research Methodology Treatise (Undertaken on an approved topic: 25 000 – 30 000 words)	Policy Frameworks: Special Education the Inclusive classroom: Theory and Practice	Curriculum Policy Curriculum Planning Curriculum Implementation
Educational Leadership	Educational Needs: An Eco-systemic Perspective	Curriculum Evaluation
Educational Change		
Management of the Curriculum Management of Human Resources	Professional Help to Address Needs of Children	

late 1980s, programs are highly centralized and developed by the National Institute of Education in cooperation with the Ministry of Education. Today, according to Walker, Hallinger, and Qian (2007), programs that were designed around executive management skills are now focused on concepts of learning organizations, complexity theory, innovation, and creating new knowledge. The intent is to develop school leaders who can navigate complex and unpredictable problems and issues, who regard schools as learning communities where they establish management teams, and draw colleagues into leadership roles (Huber & West, 2002).

Nanyang Technological Academy   This ministry-approved program promotes Singapore as "the hub of educational achievement in South East Asia" and a leader in educational advancement on the world stage (Nanyang Technological Academy website). The mission of the program is "to provide the sorts of leaders who will continue to keep Singapore at the cutting edge of knowledge and who will lead their institutions to sustainable success" (Nanyang website).

The Leaders in Education Programme (previously known as Diploma in Educational Administration Programme) is a full-time six-month preparation program for aspiring school leaders. Using the "authentic workplace of the school and international locations", program content addresses designing and managing learning school organizations that can sustain a competitive advantage in a fast-changing and turbulent environment; strategic choice and marketing; innovative communication and information technology; designing an integrative and innovative curriculum in order to achieve excellence in teaching and learning; and building human and intellectual capital" (Nanyang Technological Academy website).

Using the concept of "networks of influence" (Choy, Stott, & Tin, 2003), Singapore is investing in formal leadership preparation for department chairs and teacher mentors. Viewing department chairs as key curricular and instructional leaders in a school, these educators complete a 17-week, full time program that includes content in management of teams, delegation skills, teamwork, conflict management, instructional leadership, curriculum evaluation, staff development, teacher appraisal, and resource/budget management. Students spend time visiting a variety of schools to expand their understanding of management strategies and school improvement issues.

Educators who have attained a school leadership position complete a Master of Arts in Educational Management program. Program goals include gaining current knowledge about critical issues in educational management, attaining skills for applying intellectual approaches to principal work, and gaining coping skills to deal positively and effectively with management challenges. Students can choose to take a ten-course program or complete an eight-course program and a dissertation. Topics covered include: organizational learning and development, human development and learning, assessment quality and standards, supervisory leadership and curriculum design, management of educational technology applications, finance and resource management, quantitative and qualitative research methods, comparative issues in education, contemporary issues in school marketing, mentoring for professional development and leadership succession, school and organizational effectiveness, globalization, educational change and pedagogical reform.

Taiwan   The Ministry of Education, which controls the structures, politics and processes of the Taiwanese educational system, is currently more focused on upgrading pre-service teacher education. Examination of ministry documents show a dedication to school reforms guided by learning organization concepts, with attention to increased community involvement, a promotion of innovation and creativity, and interest in international approaches. Yet, coursework currently available at institutions that offer degrees in educational administration do not appear to have much connection to the vision of the Ministry of Education. For example, National Taiwan Normal University, National Chung Cheng University, and Taipei Municipal Teachers College all offer masters' programs focused on "promoting professional knowledge" (Ming-Dih, 2003). Required coursework in the 36 credit hour programs appear to focus primarily on preparing students to engage in research. Most programs identify required core courses such as Studies in Educational Administration, Studies in Educational Policy and at least two courses related to research methods. The programs also offer lengthy lists of elective or selective courses ranging from law to marketing to conflict and risk management and conclude with a capstone project of a thesis or dissertation. According to Ming-Dih (2003), both formal and informal coursework in the Taiwanese system is "on-the-job" training that leads to an advanced graduate degree (p. 196).

Mainland China   Required pre-service training for school leaders has only been in effect since 1995 (Su, Adams, & Mininberg, 2000) and in order to retain a position, a principal or school headmaster must complete additional training every five years (Peoples Daily, 2000).

Walker, Hallinger, and Quin (2007) documented the changing landscape in Chinese leadership preparation, noting that newly appointed and currently practicing principals are now required to have preparation in areas beyond the historically required training in political ideology. In addition to coursework in political theories, administrators now have learning experiences in modern educational theories and practices, management theories, ethical and moral thinking, and the social sciences. But compared to formal pre-service training programs in other parts of the world, administrators have only a few months of preparation and training, comprised of short term courses that are focused primarily on theory. In a comparative study of Mainland Chinese and California-based US principals, Su and his colleagues reported that pre-service preparation included Computer Applications, English as a Foreign Language, and a thesis. Practicing principals also indicated that they had no preparation in curriculum development, supervision of personnel or instruction, school-community relations, field experiences or guided internships (Su et al, 2000).

Hong Kong   A comparison of program missions, curricular structures and instructional processes led me to conclude that Hong Kong, in contrast to Taiwan and Mainland China, have some of the most advanced and sophisticated programs in this region. In 1999, the Hong Kong Education Department's Task Group on the Training and Development of School Leaders brought forward a new framework for principal development. By 2002, after numerous revisions, institutions interested in preparing school leaders were required to follow "a dictated [but] coherent framework for educating both aspiring and practicing administrators (Walker, Hallinger, & Qian, 2007).

Chinese University of Hong Kong   The MA program in School Improvement and Leadership at the Chinese University of Hong Kong is a two year course focused on improving schools and student learning. The program has five core modules, one guided project and three elective modules. The core modules include the following courses:

Issues and Advances in School Improvement
Leadership for Student Learning
Evaluation for School Improvement
Field Experience
Action Research in Education
Guided Improvement Project

TABLE 11.2
Cross-Department Offerings

Department of Educational Administration and Policy	Department of Curriculum and Instruction	Research Methods Modules
Effective School Leadership Managing Change in School Building Learning Communities	Curriculum: Perspectives and Design Curriculum Evaluation: Theory and Practice Curriculum Change and Implementation	Quantitative Methods in Educational Research Qualitative Methods in Educational Research

Then students select one course from a set of modules taught by various departments across the College of Education (see Table 11.2).

Australasia   Central requirements do not drive leadership preparation in this part of the world, however aspirants and practicing administrators do not lack opportunities to enhance their administrative skills. Universities in New Zealand and Australia have invested in formal university-based graduate programs for many years, focused primarily on research more than practice. Like many other nations, the press for accountability and increased achievement has led to the development of non-university-based programs that frequently are viewed to address the current educational needs of school leaders.

New Zealand   University of Waikato   The degree program at the University of Waikato aims to develop "the ability to reflect, interpersonal competence and basic values" (University of Waikaido website). This educational management program joins hands with the Waikato Management School and the Law School to offer coursework. Required content includes Resource Management, Issues in Ed Administration, Educational Leadership, Organizational Development, and Educational Research Methods. This program also attends to the needs of the indigenous Maori population by offering an option to focus on Kaupapa Maori Research. Electives offered are Assessment, School Leadership & the Community, Leadership for Social Justice, Developing Educational Leadership, and Professional Educational Leadership (University of Waikato website).

Australia   Aspiring principals in this nation do not need specialized training or advanced graduate programs to attain a principalship. Consequently, throughout many states, universities have counted on the urge for lifelong learning to attract students to degree programs in educational management or leadership. Consequently, most formal programs have focused on the development of scholarship more than the learning of practice. But like many nations around the world, tough accountability standards and an increased focus on achievement has fueled new approaches to principal preparation.

University of Wollongong   Increased flexibility is the primary impetus behind a major program revision at this New South Wales university. In addition to a full range of educational courses that address current issues, students also have the opportunity to link their studies with the Master of Business Administration to gain expertise in Finance and Strategic Planning. Students choose 24 credit hours from course offerings in Educational Leadership that include, Foundations of Educational Leadership, Introduction to Educational Management, Policy Studies: Global Change and Educational Leadership, Leadership of Effective Change, Leadership of Curriculum and Instruction, Information Systems and Educational Leadership, Quality Learning and Teaching,

Mentoring Beginning Teachers, Developing and Managing People, Law for Educational Leaders. This program also has a research requirement that culminates in a thesis.

The program uses modern technologies and a powerful on-line learning system to deliver coursework focused on "cross-cultural perspectives and change factors" (University of Wollongong website). In order to build community among students participating in this on-line program, students are required to attend a campus-based Professional Learning Conference every semester while completing the program.

Recently, the New South Wales Department of Education and Training, in collaboration with the NSW Secondary Principals' Council and the NSW Primary Principals' Association, developed a set of standards for preparation, the School Leadership Capability Framework (SLCF) (NSW Department of Education and Training website). A review of university programs in the area suggests that the preparation and training this state agency is offering is influencing revisions in graduate degree programs.

Europe France "Notoriously centralized" (Derry, Brundett, Slavikova, Karabec, Murden, & Nicolaidou, 2006, p. 6) is the term used to describe France's approach to training school leaders. *Formation au Premier Emploi* directed by the French Ministry of National Education requires administrative aspirants to complete long-term coursework and seminars on the topics of Administration, School Law, Management Techniques, Budgeting, Teachers Evaluation, Interpersonal Skills, and Leading Conferences and Staff Groups (Huber & West, 2002). Although the content tends to match traditional management courses, students complete extensive internship experiences, in school sites, private companies, and with local educational authorities (Huber & West, 2002).

Specialized programs that lead to a DESS diploma, the equivalent to a masters degree, are now offered at several French universities, but these programs must comply with the goals set at the national level by the Ministry of Education. Coursework tends to focus primarily on management techniques with offerings like Context and Strategic Management, Organization Management, Models of Educational Organizations, Collective Bargaining, Productivity and Quality Care; Facility Management, Instructional Leadership, and Curriculum and Instruction (Huber & West, 2002). These programs also include a required four-semester internship.

Netherlands Currently, this nation relies on local authorities to determine expectations for school leaders. Without a central framework for schooling or any specific requirements for holding an administrative position, leadership preparation is a market driven enterprise. Aspiring and practicing administrators, who perceive a need for administrative training, choose from a wide variety of available programs. Despite the absence of central standards and requirements, Huber and West (2002) observed that Dutch educators can choose some of the most innovative leadership programs in the world.

Meesters in Leidingsseven One example noted by the authors was the *Meesters in Leidingsseven*, a program that engages participants' peer-assisted learning to work on local school problems. Partners begin by developing a "cognitive map" of a school, which they then use for "school development planning" (Huber & West, 2002, p. 1077). Essentially, students learn and engage in a process that focuses on the needs of an individual school each is familiar with, but use a skill and process that transfers to any other school community.

Nederlandse School voor Onderwiqsmanagement A stark contrast to the program described above, is the *Nederlandse School voor Onderwiqsmanagement*, run by a consortium of five universities. This program, which leads to a Masters degree in Educational Management, focuses primarily on the development of competencies for leading schools and other institutions in the educational sector" and "improving the chances of the participants to get employed" (Huber & West, 2002, p. 1078). Enrolled students begin this program by completing a needs assessment that then guides the development of an action plan of course work, leading to competencies in three areas: pedagogical and educational, counseling, and controlling organizations. Students spend four-semesters choosing courses from a list of decidedly management-centered offerings, such as Organizational Management and Operational Management. Students work on a school project throughout the program, thus completing 140 hours of internship experiences each semester. A final assessment includes a "rigid battery of exercises" related to the core purpose of the headship (Shuttleworth, 2003, p. 132).

United Kingdom In 1991, Bolam reported that applicants for "headships and deputy headships are not required to have completed an accredited course in school management and administration"; additionally, he noted that "accredited courses, as such, do not exist" (Bolam, 1991, p. 81). When examining the evolution of leadership preparation in the UK today, one finds a unique dynamic between a government-supported preparation institute and UK universities. Universities had long given attention to educational management, with masters and doctoral degrees becoming "an increasingly important part" of a comprehensive university program (Brundett, 2001, p. 235). Typically focused on theory, knowledge acquisition, and thesis writing, these programs matched the models found in the United States. As institutions responded to a growing cry for more practice-oriented coursework, a hodgepodge of certificates and diplomas emerged with the intent of integrating theory with practice. According to Bolam (2004), the difference between management training and management education in the UK was the degree to which the learning experiences were practical and useful.

As political discourse led to stringent accountability measures and school management devolved to the local level, both practicing and aspiring head teachers found themselves in need of new knowledge and skills. Short courses (1-20 days) abounded throughout the country, focused on content that matched emerging government educational policy. These courses, which did not lead to any kind of advanced degree, focused on educational issues like teacher appraisal, team building, and staff development, while others addressed the emerging market approach to schooling. Practicing administrators now learned how to market their schools, handle institutional evaluations, and work with governors. Although practitioners found the short courses useful, criticisms related to the depth of preparation of school heads continued.

National College for School Leadership Government intervention, in the form of competitive grants, fostered the development of the National College for School Leadership (NCSL). With the ambitious goal to "be a driving force for world-class leadership … and to stimulate national and international debate on leadership issues (Bolam, 2004, p. 254), NCSL set out to change the landscape of leadership preparation in the UK. According to Dean (2007), "NCSL has done so well with its charge that it has eclipsed the country's postsecondary education system and local education authorities (LEAs) as the primary means of preparing school leaders" (p. 1). In fact, certification from NCSL is now a requirement for educators who aspire to the headship. Headquartered at, but separate from, the University of Nottingham, the National College of School Leadership is organized around three key principles: (1) effective leadership starts with knowing and managing oneself; (2) learning is an extraordinarily diverse endeavor; and (3) leaders must develop others in order to grow the next generation of leaders.

With those goals, the program offers multiple tracks for aspiring and practicing leaders with content specifically focused on the three principles, noted above. Currently the program is offered throughout the UK in NCSL-approved centers, some of which are affiliated with universities. Any approved program must be based on pedagogical approaches that mix independent study with team learning, e-learning with face-to-face learning, experiential learning, and intervisitation (the practice of visiting a variety of schools and businesses to see leadership in other contexts). After interviewing NCLS framers, Dean (2007) reported that the pedagogical requirements:

> reject the shallow, which focuses on memorization, information, replication, extrinsic rewards, compliance, dependence ... and embrace deep and profound learning, which focuses on dialogue, reflection, linkages between theory and practice, the use of expert professionals, and the like. In our programmes we emphasize skills, like listening, dialogue, engagement ... not debate, winning arguments. We teach school leaders how to come to a point of shared meaning with their staff. (p. 23)

London Centre for Leadership in Learning   One example of this program in action is found at The London Centre for Leadership in Learning, which operates out of the Institute of Education at the University of London. Their program, Head for the Future, provides the NCSL mandated courses and curriculum that leads to certification for the headship. The program design includes the following modules:

> Orientation: 360 degree assessment of professional qualities, leadership style, and climate. Feedback leads to an action plan for the "journey as a leader" and the nomination of a sponsor.
>
> Focusing on Change: This residential module explores "models of outstanding leadership and the comparative data from your colleagues with a focus on the connection between these and school outcomes, the current and future educational landscape and a preferred future for your school" (Institute of Education brochure). At this point, students form small teams that work together for the remainder of the program.
>
> Committing to Change: This action-oriented module takes place in students' home school. It includes active analysis of the culture and climate in the setting, garnering support from peers inside and outside the school community, self-paced activities, and use of online learning support tools. The online tools are information-rich resources that include recent research, school cameos, discussion and reflection pieces. Participants keep a learning log as they respond to the on-line units. Peer teams formed during Phase II meet during this time period.
>
> Leading the Change: Over a period of nine months, students enact an agenda for change in their local school, with online, facilitator, and sponsor support. The school improvement project supports the development of students' leadership skills in practice.
>
> Heading for the Future: The culmination of the program is a 1-day workshop for celebration and sharing. Content during this session includes succession planning and a recap of "lessons learned" from the activities of all the participating students (Institute Brochure).

Perhaps one of the most interesting and challenging outcomes of the NCLS movement is that longstanding masters degree programs are now operating in tandem with NCLS preparation programs. In some cases, universities chose to concentrate their efforts on research-oriented doctoral programs. In other cases, it appears that some institutions have revamped their curriculum in an effort to attract a specific market. Two examples follow.

Institute for Education, University of London   Parallel to the London Centre Head for the Future program, this institute offers an MA in Applied Leadership and Management, an MBA in Leadership (International) and an MBA in School Business Leadership (International). Each of these programs is designed to attract practicing administrators, most often educators who have achieved senior leadership positions.

The MA Applied Educational Leadership and Management is a distance learning program with a mission to:

> Increase your understanding of educational management and leadership, apply theory and research to your own working environment, foster your continuing professional development through reflection on practice, allow you to consider issues related to the policy context of education, and give you the chance to contribute towards improvement of educational systems and institutions and to reflect on the quality of learning and teaching. (Institute of Education website)

Students can choose one of four program directions: Educational Leadership and Management, Urban Educational Leadership, Learning-Centred Leadership, or System Leadership

The MBA in School Leadership, designated as International, is "designed explicitly to meet the needs of senior leaders in schools ... recognize and critically explore important debates in and around school leadership" Program goals include:

- Develop scholarship and academic skills to support reflective practice
- Enable critical reflection on key areas of theory
- Conduct empirical research and values underpinning school management and leadership
- Analyze how the policy context impacts on school leadership and management
- Support the creation of personal and professional knowledge through research and enquiry.
- Support your development and role as strategic thinkers, leaders of learning and
- School improvement, and managers of resources. (Institute of Education website)

The international focus of the program takes place during the module Leading in Diverse Cultures and Communities when students engage in a comparative study of leadership by traveling to an international setting.

This institution also offers an internationally focused degree in School Business Leadership. The program responds to the specific needs of bursars and school business managers in self-managing schools in both the state and independent sectors.

North America *Canada*   Advanced degrees in education are preferable for attaining a principalship in most Canadian provinces, but unlike its neighbor, the United States, there are no licensure requirements that centralize a preparatory curriculum. Many Canadian principals have little formal pre-service training, other than an incidental course or a local school-based leadership development program (Aitken, Bedard, & Darroch, 2003). However, the lack of centralized requirements has not precluded the development of university-based comprehensive masters programs in educational leadership. Examination of university-based programs across several provinces revealed great variation in purpose and design of curriculums and delivery systems across Canada.

University of Lethbridge (Alberta)   Following the lead of sister institutions in Alberta, this university also revised the content and organization of their master's curriculum in leadership. Instead of organizing the curriculum around traditional disciplines and administrative role functions, this faculty-developed learning experiences around three themes: Leader as Educator, Leadership as Moral Steward, and Leader as Community Builder. Students engage in problem-based learning that intentionally integrates the three themes in all courses. The 10-course program culminates either in a thesis or an internship and leadership portfolio. Course descriptions suggest a postmodern focus. For example, the Foundations of Modern Educational Theory and Practice includes study of "Post Modernity and Critical Theory and the Impact On Educational Leadership" and "Gender Equity and Leadership" (Aitken, Bedard, & Darroch, 2003, p. 42). A majority of courses focus on the development of instructional leadership. One example is found in the content of course in School Culture and the Instructional Program, which includes:

- Nature of Instructional Leadership-Curriculum/ Instruction/Supervision/ and the Learning Environment
- Best Practices for Student Learning
- Measurement, Evaluation, and Assessment Strategies
- Developing Learning Community and School Culture.
- Adult Learning Theory and Professional Growth Plans (Aitken, et.al. 2003, p. 43)

The intentional integration of the three themes is also visible in the course titled Governance, Collaboration, and Community Engagement. That content includes:

- Community Relationships
- Site-based Decision Models
- Shared Decision Making
- School Councils
- Ethics, Values, and Moral Leadership
- Consensus Building and Negotiation Skills (Aitken, et.al., 2003, p. 43)

University of Manitoba (Manitoba)   The designated theme of this program is "to provide an in-depth and theoretical understanding of educational administration as a moral and technical endeavor" (University of Manitoba website) and the primary purpose of the program is to design and implement research projects that lead to a thesis. One curricular route culminates in a thesis and requires courses in Educational Administration as a Field of Study and Practice, Theoretical Perspectives of Educational Administration, and six hours of Research. A course-based route adds Philosophy of Education to the requirements. Students also have a choice of six hours (two courses) of electives. Their choices include: Personnel Issues of Administration; Politics, Finance; Organizational Planning and Development; Analysis of Organizations; and Curriculum. Neither curricular pathway includes an internship or field experience.

Ontario Institute for Studies in Education (Ontario)   The province of Ontario appears to provide more centralized control over the pre-service preparation of principals with a professional organization, the Ontario College of Teachers, controlling the licensing of degrees (Huber & West, 2002) In his review of ten Ontario university programs, Huber observed that "some convergences of curriculum content is emerging-at least in relation to two crucial areas ... teaching and learning issues and the personal and interpersonal skills of leadership" (p. 1097). Although content may be similar, there is variation in pedagogical approaches.

For example, the Ontario Institute for Studies in Education (OISE) engages small teams of students in problems of practice from each other's schools (Huber & West, 2002). Supporting coursework includes studies of Leadership, Communication Strategies, Human Resources, Interpersonal skills, School Programs, Students with Exceptionalities, and Resource Management. In addition, during a 10-12 week required internship in an organization (not always schools), students must administer tasks that have some element of risk. This activity culminates with a full evaluation report.

McGill University (Ontario)   The Educational Leadership program at McGill University has a mission to:

> foster the ongoing development of reflective practitioners who have a sense of educational action, the capacity to anticipate needs, the ability to exercise professional judgment within the realities of policy frameworks, and the ability to both lead and support institutional and organizational change at all levels. (McGill University website)

Their curriculum focuses on "institutional improvement in schools and other centers of formal or informal learning" (McGill website) and required course are Educational Studies, Leadership in Action, Leadership Theory, and Research. Students can choose six hours of electives from Resource Management, Policy Issues, Workplace Learning, Managing Change; Curriculum, Planning and Evaluation, Law, Organizational Theory, School Improvement, Literacy, Media Literacy, and Communications.

United States

Voice of the Profession: Practitioner and Academic   For decades, academics have conducted a search for an appropriate knowledge base in response to critics who experienced preparation as less-than-helpful for the job of leading schools. Decades of critiques were fully documented by Murphy and Forsythe (1999), who concluded that most preparation programs "had very little to do with education" (p. 20). Starting in the late 1980s, a series of activities nurtured by the University Council for Educational Administration (UCEA) led to the creation of the National Policy Board of Educational Administration (NPBEA). The NPBEA brought together ten professional groups with vested interests in strengthening the fundamental education of school leaders. The formation of the NPBEA provided professional administrative organizations the opportunity to voice concerns about how preparation connected to daily practice. Since 1990, educational leadership programs nationwide have seen a flurry of white papers, commission reports, notebooks of Knowledge Domains, handbooks, and foundation or federally funded demonstration projects.

Rise of Standards Movement   UCEA, an organization dominated by faculty at research-intensive institutions, must be given credit for pushing forward and sustaining the work on improving pre-service leadership programs. In 1992, this organization put forward a set of knowledge domains to guide program review and development. The UCEA domains include:

- Societal and cultural influences on schooling
- Teaching and Learning processes
- Leadership and Management processes
- Policy and Political Studies
- Legal and Ethical Dimensions of Schooling
- Economic and Financial Dimensions of Schooling

UCEA's persistent engagement in the NPBEA professional conversation also opened the door to a proposed set of model standards for the preparation and evaluation of school leaders. Supported by the Council of Chief State School Officers (state superintendents) and NPBEA, the Interstate School Leaders Licensure Standards (ISLLC) were performance-based criteria designed to link preparation and practice standards across 50 very diverse states. However, one major challenge stood in the way; all 50 states retain the right to establish and govern standards for education. Although ISLLC standards represented a noble effort to bring national coherence to educational leadership curriculums, actual implementation required masterful political work.

Critics of the standards movement object to the lack of attention to social justice, the loss of attention to foundational knowledge in programs, and the fact that rigid standards can be barriers to diverse ideas, diverse individuals, and innovative programs (English, 2006). As this chapter neared completion, the proposed revisions to the ISLLC standards were released to UCEA members for preliminary review. The most prominent changes included a reduction in the number of elements that comprise each of the six standards and a marked change in emphasis on social justice issues. The effects of the current standards movement on the actual practices of school leaders still remains to be discovered and comprehensive empirical work that examines the value-added or value-lost, sadly, is not in evidence.

Voice of the Politician: State Licensure   Individuals from outside the United States who have examined US program designs (Huber & West, 2002, Bush & Jackson, 2002, Brundett, 2001) describe the system as centralized because of licensure standards and the existence of the Interstate School Leaders Licensure Consortium (ISLLC) standards. From its inception in 1992, ISLLC is probably the most effective attempt to bring consistent standards to the preparation and licensing of school leaders throughout all 50 states. However, any student of centralized preparation standards must take into account that education is always a state's right, a US political concept that allows any state to ignore a national effort. In many cases, state political agencies have requirements that do not match or support the ISLLC standards or if they do, those requirements may not link to the Educational Leadership Consortium Council (ELCC) standards that drive national accreditation for some university programs. Finally, centralized standards are also thwarted by the fact that National Council for the Accreditation of Teacher Education (NCATE) or ELCC accreditation is not required, and in some states, private universities do not adhere to state requirements either. In their recent study on exemplary programs, Darling-Hammond and her colleagues noted, "although many states have adopted standards to guide leadership development, they have differed in how they use and enforce these standards and how they encourage programs to improve" (Darling-Hammond, LaPointe, Myerson, Orr, & Cohen, 2007, p. 127).

Educational leadership preparation programs in universities pay attention to standard movements for several reasons. First, state licensure standards determine who gets credentialed so they can apply for and accept jobs. Second, the ISLLC standards were developed and continue to be examined and modified by a consortium of practitioner professional associations. Maintaining the support of those professional associations is the lifeblood of university programs. Finally, standards often are a legitimizing notion, and adherence to something like ISLLC or ELLC/NCATE becomes a normative exercise for an emergent program that wants to gain legitimacy in the eyes of students and the controlling state agencies.

Voice of State-directed Reform Movements   Another individual element that can influence state-specific university-based leadership preparation programs is a state's focus on school reform. Although the No Child Left Behind (NCLB) Act has certainly contributed a singular national focus to expected student achievement, the actual processes and practices of implementation vary widely from state to state. Some states have invested heavily in aligned and coherent professional reforms for classrooms, curriculum, instruction, and preparation programs for teachers and administrators. For example, in states like Kentucky, principals must be prepared to participate in all aspects of the Kentucky Educational Reform Act (KERA) and thus, preparation programs were modified to incorporate each and every element of the state's emerging standards. Another example can be found in the state of Oregon; the states' Standards and Practices Commission determined several years ago that licensed educators needed to demonstrate cultural competence due to the changing demographics of the state's population. In turn, preparation programs were modified in response to this new standard.

Perhaps the lesson in this tangled description of US program structures is that the longer a country has engaged in formal education of school leaders, the more one will find stepped-up efforts to control, centralize, and standardize those programs. In turn, one may also find persistent efforts to avoid or resist centralized notions.

Comparing Curricula

Providing a detailed comparison of US preservice curriculums is as challenging a task as developing a portrait of worldwide trends. In some ways, the US is comprised of 50 'countries' that happen to belong to the United States. In order to give an international readership a sense of the complexity of preparatory curriculums, particularly in a ISLLC and NCLB dominated era, I arbitrarily chose states in various regions of the country, selected one public and one prive institution from that state, and charted the preparation program using the broad curricular themes promoted by UCEA, plus clinical, practicum, or field-based experiences. Hopefully, Tables 11.3–11.6 will provide readers with a sense of how state context can control program curriculum, despite national efforts to forge common standards.

Texas   Texas Administrative Code requires that candidates for principal certificates be assessed on eight content and skill areas (see Table 11.3 for example). The code specifically states that this set of knowledge and skill standards must be used to develop curricula and courses in any approved leadership preparation program. The content and skill themes include the following:

- Learner-Centered Values and Ethics of Leadership
- Learner-Centered Leadership and Campus Culture
- Learner-Centered Human Resources Leadership and Management
- Learner-Centered Communications and Community Relations
- Learner-Centered Organizational Leadership and Management
- Learner-Centered Curriculum Planning and Development
- Learner-Centered Instructional Leadership and Management.

Each theme has extensive and very specific detail, suggesting that the content of university-based preparation courses has been designed at the state level and is encoded in state regulations.

For example, the Communications and Community Relations theme requires that prospective principles know how to:

1. Demonstrate effective communication through oral, written, auditory, and nonverbal expression.

TABLE 11.3
Texas

Trinity University (Private) 36 credit hours   Program Intent: The program prepares men and women who will bring to the principalship a deep commitment to leadership, a sound background in teaching and learning, strong management skills, political acumen, knowledge of the change process, a commitment to lifelong learning and a vision of excellence (See Trinity University website)

Societal and Cultural Influences	Teaching and Learning	Leadership and Management	Policy and Politics	Legal and Ethical Dimensions	Economic & Financial Dimensions	Clinical Exp Practicum	Other
	Curriculum Development (3)	Educational Administration & Organization (3) The School Management Functions (3) Administration of the Elementary & Secondary School (3) Problems in Administration (3) Advanced Problems in Administration (3)			School Law & Finance	Supervised Practicum (3) Internship (3)	Research Methods I (3) Independent Study: Problems in Practice

University of Texas, Austin (Public) 42 credit hours   Program Intent: To foster a deep commitment to social justice and equitable schooling for all students and an emphasis on the role of school principals as instructional leaders who are highly involved in organizing and developing schools focused on effective teaching and learning. (See University of Texas, Austin website)

Societal and Cultural Influences	Teaching and Learning	Leadership and Management	Policy and Politics	Legal and Ethical Dimensions	Economic & Financial Dimensions	Clinical Exp Practicum	Other
	Systems for Observation & Analysis (3)	Public School Administration (3) Decision-Making (3) Principalship (3) School Improvement (3)		School Law (3)	School Business Management (3)	Internship 12 credit hours	Special Education Procedures & Processes (3)

2. Utilize effective conflict management and group consensus building skills.
3. Implement effective strategies to systematically gather input from all campus stakeholders.
4. Develop and implement strategies for effective internal and external communications.
5. Develop and implement a comprehensive program of community relations which utilizes strategies that will effectively involve and inform multiple constituencies, including the media.
6. Provide varied and meaningful opportunities for parents to be engaged in the education of their children.
7. Establish partnerships with parents, businesses, and other groups in the community to strengthen programs and support campus goals.
8. Respond to pertinent political, social, and economic issues that exist in the internal and external environment. (Texas Administrative Code website)

Ohio   The state of Ohio requires prospective school leaders to complete a master's degree plus 15 additional credit hours for licensure. Curricula in a typical Ohio leadership preparation program begins with a standard 36 credit hour masters program built from the courses described in Table 11.4 and then students take 15 additional credit hours to qualify for state certification. In order to be certified, a prospective school leader must complete a program that includes a concentration in one of the following: educational research, personnel administration, curriculum, instruction and professional development, pupil services administration, school-community relations, and administration of career and technical education. State regulatory code requires that licensed individuals must demonstrate competency in five areas specific to the Ohio Standards for Principals. The competencies include:

- Creating a shared vision and clear goals for a school and ensuring continuous progress toward achieving the goals
- The implementation of high-quality standards-based instruction that result in higher achievement for all students
- Allocation of resources and management of operations that ensures a safe and productive learning environment
- Sustaining collaborative learning and shared leadership to promote achievement for all students
- Engagement of parents and community members in the educational process so that community resources support achievement of all students. (Adapted from Ohio Standards for Principals website)

Like Texas, the Ohio standards have specific elements for each standard, but this state has added an elaborate rubric with Proficient, Accomplished, or Distinguished performance indicators for each element of each standard. Leader preparation programs that wish to remain viable in the state of Ohio will no doubt pay careful attention to these performance indicators as they select course content and learning experiences so their graduates have the capacity to demonstrate skills and knowledge beyond basic proficiency. One example of how the rubric might influence a leadership curriculum is found in Standard 4 that focuses on Collaboration. Table 11.5 illustrates one of the three elements detailed for this standard.

TABLE 11.4
Ohio

Ashland University (Private institution) Ohio 45 credit hours Program Intent: To prepare ethical and competent educational leaders who are able to work with diverse groups; to integrate critical thinking skills, communication skills and technical skills; and to exercise reflection, judgment, and wisdom in decision-making. (See Ashland University website)

Societal and Cultural Influences	Teaching and Learning	Leadership and Management	Policy and Politics	Legal and Ethical Dimensions	Economic & Financial Dimensions	Clinical Exp Practicum	Other
Contemporary Education: Issues & Practices (3)	Principles & Procedures of Curriculum Development (3 Leadership Skills in Supervison-Administration (3 Improving Classroom Instruction (3)	Intro to School Administration (3) Human Behavior in Administration (3) Professional Development for Administrators	Educational Politics, Policies & School-Community Relations (3)	School Law & Ethics (3)	Resource Management in Administration	Ed Adm I (3) Building Principal Internship (3)	Qualitative Research (3) Educational Statistics (3)

Miami of Ohio (Public) (48 hours) Program Intent: To provide a rigorous and innovative academic environment that incorporates problem solving in school settings. (See Miami University of Ohio website)

Societal and Cultural Influences	Teaching and Learning	Leadership and Management	Policy and Politics	Legal and Ethical Dimensions	Economic & Financial Dimensions	Clinical Exp Practicum	Other
Foundations of Multicultural Education (3 Collaboration & Support for Child/Youth/ Family (3)	Curriculum Theory & Program Development (3) Supervision of Instruction (3) Curriculum Development for Instruction (3) Learning Theories Applied to Education (3)	Educational Leadership Theory (3) Organizational Change (3) Topics in Educational Leadership (3) The Principal & Change (3) School Personnel Administration (3)	Politics of Education (3)	School Finance (3)	School Law (3)	Internship (3)	

TABLE 11.5
Principals Advance the Leadership Capacity of all Educators

Proficient	Accomplished	Distinguished
a) Principals serve as role model for the leadership behaviors they seek to instill in others b) Principals participate in leadership development activities with staff c) Principals identify strengths and interest of the building staff in order to identify potential leaders	d) Principals mentor and coach staff and student leaders e) Principals build on staff's skills and interests to advance the leadership capacity of all	f) Principals create leadership growth opportunities for staff, students, parents, and community members g) Principals encourage other educators to assume leadership roles outside of the school building

The Ohio code also points out that preparatory programs should be based on "occupation-relevant knowledge" that has been informed by business, education, and communities (Ohio Standards website) on collaborative leadership.

Oregon   The Oregon Teachers Standards and Practices Commission has sole authority in this state to approve university-based preparation programs (see Table 11.6). Although they do not publish a specific set of course requirements, a candidate for a beginning administrator's license must complete an approved master's program that includes knowledge of Oregon school finance and law. In addition, applicant for licensure must be able to demonstrate cultural competence.

Observations: Curricula for Leadership Preparation in the US

It should be clear from the information on the above charts that the United States does not ascribe to a national curriculum for preparing school leaders. Although there are many similarities across the 50 states, there are many more discrepancies and anomalies due to a particular state's investment in education and the preparation of its leaders. Just as professional educators from countries in Europe or Asia gather and exchange ideas and influence each others' curricular directions, professional educators from states in the US gather and engage in similar exchanges. The ISLLC/ELCC standards have profoundly influenced a national conversation about the content, skills, and disposition found in courses in preparation programs; however that conversation is always tightly tied to an individual state's regulations and codes for administrative licensure. In addition, the impetus to modify leadership preparation curricula is often swayed by the degree of school reform underway in particular states and there is minimal consistency in those efforts.

ENTREPRENEURIAL LEADERSHIP PREPARATION PROGRAMS

This examination of worldwide programs turned up examples of emergent curricular design that fall outside the purview of university-based or government-approved programs. Two of the examples (Australia and the US) exemplify these types of programs. In Australia, the New School Leadership Capability Framework was developed by a collaborative group of professionals in

TABLE 11.6
Oregon

Lewis & Clark College (Private) 38 credit hours Program Intent: Innovative curriculum and personal attention give both aspiring and experienced administrators a useful and reflective educational experience. The program is particularly committed to involving more women and minorities in educational leadership and focusing on collaborative leadership. (Lewis and Clark College website)

Societal and Cultural Influences	Teaching and Learning	Leadership and Management	Policy and Politics	Legal and Ethical Dimensions	Economic & Financial Dimensions	Clinical Exp Practicum	Other
Engaging the Community for Effective Schools (2.5)	Teaching & Learning in El/Middle/ Sec School (3) Instructional Leadership (3)	Leading & Managing for Teaching & Learning (3) Constructive Classroom Assessment (2)		Ethics, Policy & the Law (1.5)	Budgeting for School Equity (1)	Practicum (4) Project Seminar (2)	Educational Research (2) Using Data for School Improvement (3)

* Students select 9 hours of subject area electives and complete 2 credit hours of Core courses

Portland State University (Public) Program Intent. To prepare educational leaders to respond positively, creatively, and proactively to the diversity within our communities. It offers prospective school leaders an experience that reflects the faculty's commitment to teaching, research, and service along with the department's mission to provide and develop responsive leadership. Underlying the work of our faculty is the assumption that at every level, traditional approaches to education and schooling should be challenge (Portland State University website).

Societal and Cultural Influences	Teaching and Learning	Leadership and Management	Policy and Politics	Legal and Ethical Dimensions	Economic & Financial Dimensions	Clinical Exp Practicum	Other
Human Relations & Educational Foundations (4)	Teaching, Learning & Curriculum (4)	Introduction to Educational Administration (4) Human Resource Development & Org. Change (4)				Educational Leadership Project I (1) Practicum: IAL (3) Educational Leadership Project II (1) Practicum: IAL (3) Educational Leadership Project III (1) Practicum: IAL (3)	Principles of Educational Research (4)

response to the lack of required administrator preparation. In the United States, The New Leaders for New Schools program was designed to meet the specific needs of low-achieving urban schools but also was a response to the criticisms of traditional university-based programs. The third example, The Matthew Goniwe School of Leadership, in Guatang, South Africa, emerged in 1996 under the leadership of the first national Minister of Education in Guatang, who recognized that leadership preparation was critical to advancing the development of Guatang and South Africa. The descriptions provide insights into the types of program formats and curricula that comprise these entrepreneurial programs, but in no way represent a full-scale compilation of the entrepreneurial programs that may be available.

The School Leadership Capability Framework (New South Wales, Australia)

This preparation program was developed by the New South Wales (Australia) Department of Education and Training in collaboration with the NSW Secondary Principals' Council and the NSW Primary Principals' Association. It is based on the research on effective principals, conducted by Professor Geoff Scott in 2002. The School Leadership Capability Framework (SLCF) is based on five interrelated domains and three higher order leadership skills. The offerings connected with this program serve both practicing and aspiring principals and are established in such a way that participants have the opportunity to engage in ongoing learning experiences that are not linked to a degree structure or university curriculum.

Principal aspirants begin with a self analysis of leadership capabilities and then, using action research, online learning, and qualified mentors explore the issues and concepts in the educational, personal, strategic, organizational, and interpersonal domains. The framework of emotional intelligence guides personal and interpersonal development and the action research work incorporates the use of diagnostic maps and the development of "ways of thinking." The diagnostic maps are developed by careful reflection and examination of previous situations in order to develop new insights and skills into handling new situations. Participants are also linked online to a Conflict Resolution Network committed to creating a "conflict-resolving community in a culture of peace and social justice. Conflict Resolution builds stronger and more cohesive organizations and more rewarding relationships. So we make Conflict Resolution skills, strategies and attitudes more readily and universally accessible" (New South Wales Department of Education & Training website). The initial preparation experiences carry over and continue as newly hired principals stay connected with experienced mentors and continue to build skills in the five domains. By using Australia's extensive Internet technology, school leaders are constantly linked to sources and each other.

New Leaders for New Schools (NLNS)

United States This program, based primarily in large US urban centers like New York, Chicago, and Boston, came about as political figures (mayors) took over failing city school systems. In their search for school leaders who could develop and sustain reform, these mayors turned to private foundations to sponsor an intensive, fast-paced, and hands-on leadership training program. Candidates begin the NLNS program with a five week "boot camp" that focuses on instructional leadership, a culture of high student achievement, and day-to-day management operations. Next, students are assigned to a local school to work directly with a "strong" principal who coaches them as they work with a teaching team to raise student achievement. Throughout the year, candidates participate in a Foundations course that represents the academic core of the NLNS's curriculum. The curriculum is organized around three strands that align to NLNS's Principal Leadership Competencies, which came from research on 90-90-90 schools (schools where at least 90 per cent of students are students of color, 90 per cent are on free or reduced lunch and at least 90 per cent are achieving at or above proficiency). Themes that inform each strand include family involvement, diversity, education policy, and reform. The three strands are:

School Leadership addresses the key skills and behaviors demonstrated by successful principals who promote high academic achievement for all children, including: high-quality teaching and learning, the alignment of curriculum, standards, and assessment, the effective use of data to drive student achievement, high-functioning teacher teams, effective leadership and management, positive school culture, and strong relationships with families and the broader community.

Personal Leadership addresses the essence of leadership — the skills, insights, perspectives, personal voice and authority, and change management strategies necessary to lead a school that has high expectations for every child.

Technical Leadership addresses the critical building and organizational management topics needed to support high student achievement and a positive school culture, including any local knowledge, networks, and skills a successful principal needs to support a high-quality school in their particular district, city, and state (http://www.nlns.org/NLWeb/Index.jsp).

The programs in Australia and the United States have some common features. Both are organized for maximum flexibility and hands-on engagement. Participants spend far less time studying 'about' educational leadership and far more time practicing the actual work of leading school. Therefore each program devotes considerable time to reflecting on actual practice, problem solving and problem-finding based on actual practice, and both make extensive use of mentors who coach aspiring and newly assigned principals to improve their practice. Though neither is formally affiliated with a university program, each notes that academics are part of the instructional group. However, each program draws on a much more diverse instructional team to instruct courses or workshops. Each of these programs also devotes considerable effort to growing a network of lifetime professional relationships, in the belief that this approach to leadership education will eventually improve the effectiveness of schools.

One major difference between the Australian and US programs is found in the required course products. US participants are required to complete journals, projects, comprehensive school plans, and a portfolio of evidence in order to demonstrate Principal Leadership Competencies. These requirements are no doubt necessary in order for graduates of this program to qualify for licensure in the state. In some locales, the New Leaders for New Schools program has partnered with local universities in order to satisfy state credentialing requirements. For example, in Boston, the program has partnered with Northeastern University where students enroll for 24 credit hours of coursework and then develop an individualized learning plan that reflects their work with Boston's program, The Principal Residency Network. Once again, this points out the high level of influence that state regulations have on leadership education in the United States. (See Littkey & Schen, 2003, for further description.)

Matthew Goniwe School of Leadership (Guatang, South Africa)

The Matthew Goniwe program represents a *start-up* program in the truest sense of the phase. When South Africa, and many other nations on the African continent, began to move to be part of the developed world, framers of new governments realized the lack of leadership capacity at all levels. In some cases, international agencies, like the US-based Aspen Institute have provided initial training for emergent leaders. But in the case of Guatang, South Africa, a new minister of education decided more was needed if his province was to move forward. The Matthew Goniwe School of Leadership was established as a non-profit company, funded primarily by the Guatang Department of Education. The mission states:

> The Matthew Goniwe School of Leadership and Governance exists to expand and enhance the vision and quality of leadership that guides education and learning in the schools of Guatang Province and beyond. It is dedicated to bringing to educators at all levels leading-edge research, thinking, frameworks, strategies, and professional growth experiences that elevate their understanding of learners, learning, and learning systems and translate those understandings into constructive action. (Matthew Goniwe School of Leadership website)

In an area that requires no formal training to be a school principal, the Goniwe School is attempting to provide support for all newly appointed principals. The program consists of seminars that can eventually lead to an Advanced Certificate in Education. The Goniwe School program is an example of curricular structures that emerge without university involvement or centralized government standards. In their efforts to build capacity, seminar organizers draw from the wisdom of Roland Barth (US) and the research of Tony Bush (UK). All seminars focus on problems of the moment, with content such as the following:

- Entering a school that has no functional system
- Schools without facilities or poor infrastructure
- Schools in extreme poverty-stricken areas
- Impact of HIV/AIDS
- Issues of race, ethnicity, and diversity
- Crime and domestic violence
- Issues of gender
- Issues of age
- Poor parental support
- Complying with demands of parents e.g. prioritizing rugby results above all else. Matthew Goniwe School of Leadership website)

A BRIEF LOOK AT PEDAGOGY

My own student experience with leadership preparation several decades ago was filled with course lectures, class discussions, occasional guest speakers, extensive note taking, course exams based on recall, and a steady stream of research papers. Today's leadership classrooms, worldwide, are very different spaces, reflecting, in my opinion, more sophisticated knowledge about adult learning, and recognition that the complex work of school leadership requires not only hands-on practice, but extensive critique of and reflection on that practice. What follows is a representative sample of the pedagogical practices found in program or course descriptions from a variety of leadership preparation programs around the globe.

Chinese University of Hong Kong

Learning takes place using a combination of case studies, journal writing, problem-based cases, experiential activities and self-guided learning in which students apply leadership knowledge to their own personal and school contexts (see Chinese University of Hong Kong website).

France

Pedagogical approaches include lectures, speeches, seminars, training sessions, consultations, role play and simulations, peer counseling, case study, readings, writing a study journal, reflective writing, school projects and a 4 semester, 140-hour internship (Huber, 2002, p. 1078).

National College for School Leadership

The processes used in the NCSL program are similar to those practiced by the New School Leadership program (Australia). After completing a self-assessment, learning experiences include taught sessions, seminars, workshops, case studies, simulations, group reviews and presentations, research findings and videos. Participants also work online, in teams, on problems of practice, working on school-based projects under the tutelage of mentor. Additionally, all participants in the NCSL have the opportunity to use a sophisticated electronic network of support services to continue their collaborative efforts at improving schools (Huber & West, 2002).

University of Nanking, Singapore

Course include journals, international visits, industrial attachments, focused discussion meetings, seminars with overseas educators, formal reading and theoretical 'future school assignments.'

University of Waikato, New Zealand

Learning experiences included lectures, seminars, workshops, email exchange, and international study tours.

University of Calgary Alberta, Canada

A unique pedagogical aspect of this program is an online partnership with the University of Waikato in New Zealand. Students engage in an online cross-cultural project related to the development of school culture.

Portland State University, United States

IAL incorporates an integrated curricular approach that focuses on actual problems of practice rather than on traditionally discrete academic disciplines/courses. The IAL experience results in artifact-creation — a collection of materials that attest to a participant's administrative beliefs, accomplishments, and experiences. This portfolio could be invaluable in seeking administrative employment (Portland State University website).

The brief descriptions provided above clearly show a rich array of active learning experiences. One prominent feature in many programs around the world is attention to working on real problems of practice, in a supportive environment. Not only does that support include mentors and coaches, students also learn and practice using diagnostic tools like Cognitive Maps (Netherlands) and Diagnostic Maps (Australia). Many school leaders understand the importance of developing learning communities and fostering high achievement, but even if they know what to do, a lack of guided and supported practice with the *doing* inhibits them from engaging in the work.

A CIRCULAR RESPONSE: EDUCATIONAL LEADERSHIP CURRICULUM AND PEDAGOGY

When I began this *round-the-world journey* to the curricular and pedagogical structures of educational leadership programs, I posited that the information would reveal patterns of influence between longstanding and emergent programs. Following Bush and Jackson's (2002) observation, that we have "an international curriculum for school leadership preparation (p. 420), I expected to find constant patterns across the world. I also assumed that a deep history of leadership preparation must lead to highly evolved programs, thinking that highly evolved programs never fell into the category of *emergent*. Truthfully, all my assumptions were quite flawed.

Certainly some of the historical influence does appear, particularly if one traces the visiting scholars who have traveled to new regions of the world, either to engage in research and guest instruction, or to actually relocate to develop a particular country's program. But as I examined the convergent and divergent patterns of learning leadership across the world, I was reminded far more of the Theory of Circular Response, advanced almost a century ago by Mary Parker Follett (1869–1933), a US-based Progressive-era scholar-activist. Follett devised her theory after working with newly arrived immigrants to the Boston area, where she organized instruction and support services so these new residents could become vital contributing citizens of a new country. The Theory of Circular Response, according to Follett, was based on the notion that individuals and environments were constantly creating and recreating each other. She argued cause and effect were limited descriptions of moments in time, suggesting that the relationship and interaction among various elements, over time, was a much more powerful method for understanding human behavior. Follett proposed three principles. First, the response to a situation must be based on a belief that an environment is always changing; she advised people not to be rigid. Second, in her view, the response must be governed by a belief that you are now interacting with the environment, and third, that interaction changes the environment you are observing.

Merely examining my own circular response to this journey, I have learned that programs outside my own country seem to include or focus on international perspectives far more than US-based programs. Aspiring school leaders who examine international perspectives on reform or globalization issues would seem to be more aware of or prepared for the flatter world described by Thomas Friedman (2005).

Programs that are just emerging, such as those in the African continent, include focused attention on key societal issues, like HIV/AIDS, sustainable development, and gender issues in leadership. Although formal leadership training emerged during a highly developmental period of US history, early programs rarely addressed any social issues, despite their prominence in American daily life. At the same time, 'emergent' is a circular term. Just a cursory examination of US-based curriculums brings insights into the issues confronting various sections of the country.

The influence of centralized standards or guidelines, although prominent in both longstanding and emerging programs is less connected to innovative curriculum than one might expect. Walker and Dimmock (2006) cited Huber's study of programs, which found that the most effective programs had centralized guidelines, yet the guidelines for developing learning organizations promoted in some Eastern Asian countries are a vivid contrast to the guidelines focused on accountability that are prevalent in the US and the UK. Additionally, centralized guidelines are not necessarily leading to new curricular designs in Taiwan or traditional South African institutions. If there is any centralized standard that influences leadership preparation around the world, it is that social and intellectual concerns for increasing the educational attainment of children are foremost in program design.

Traditions and replication of classic curricular designs abound in longstanding and emergent programs. Many nations maintain models of advanced graduate work based on the traditions of European universities, requiring students to demonstrate mastery of leadership knowledge by completing a lengthy thesis or multiple research papers. What is more interesting to observe, are the number of programs that have replaced the research requirement with internships in multiple types of settings or organizations. The notion of active practice of leadership practice appears to have gained acceptance as a scholarly activity across the world.

One additional commonality appeared as I examined the emerging or entrepreneurial programs, such as the first-time ever programs on Mainland China and Guatang, South Africa, or the non-university programs emerging in New South Wales, Australia and the urban centers of the United States. Each of these programs has a very different perspective on the amount of time an aspiring school leader needs to spend in a formal classroom setting. It remains to be seen if and how the entrepreneurs will influence longstanding university-based degree programs.

The reward, or souvenir, of this journey is understanding the great potential of the Theory of Circular Response-the opportunities we have today to create and recreate each other. Advanced technology allowed me to *visit* universities, agencies, courses, and faculty around the world. Every interested educator with access to the Internet can replicate my journey. Brundett ((2001) observed that, "educational leadership programs tend to reflect the central intellectual and social concerns in the wider society" (p. 241). Today that wider society is truly global and I would hope that my professional colleagues would let go of national or parochial rigidities, maximize their interactions with this emerging global environment, and attend carefully to the new leadership preparation environment we are creating.

REFERENCES

Aitken, A., Bedard, G., & Darroch, A. (2003). *Designing a master program in educational leadership: Trends, reflections, and conclusions* (ERIC Document: ED 475 008). Alberta, Canada: University of Lethbridge.

Bolam, R. (1991). Management and the quality of schooling: Some implications of research and experience in England and Wales. In P. Ribbins, R. Glatter, T. Simkins, L. Watson (Eds.), *Developing Educational Leaders: International Intervisitation Programme 1990*. Essex, England: Longman.

Bolam, R. (2003). Models of leadership development: Learning from international experience and research. In R. Bolun (Ed.), *Leadership in Education* (pp. 74-89). London: Sage.

Bolam, R. (2004). Reflections on the NCSL from a historical perspective. *Educational Management Administration and Leadership, 32*(3), 251-267.

Brundett, M. (2001). The development of school leadership preparation programs in England and the USA. *Educational Management and Administration, 29*(2), 229-245.

Bush, T., & Jackson, D. (2002). A preparation for school leadership. *Educational Management and Administration, 30*(4), 417-429.

Bush, T., & Oduro, G. (2006). New principals in Africa: Preparation, induction, and practice. *Journal of Educational Administration, 44*(4), 359-375.

Choy, C. K., Stott, K., & Tin, L. (2003). Developing Singapore school leaders for a learning nation. In P. Hallinger (Ed.), *Reshaping the Landscape of Leadership Preparation* (pp. 163-174). Lisse, The Netherlands: Swets Zeitlinger.

Darling-Hammond, L., LaPointe, M., Myerson, D., Orr, M. T., & Cohen, C. (2007). *Preparing school leaders for a changing world: Lessons from exemplary leadership development programs.* Palo Alto CA: Stanford University West Ed.

Dean, D. (2007). The National College of School Leadership: A case study in distributed leadership development. *Journal of Research on Leadership Education 2*(1) Retrieved from http://www.ucea.org on 6/20/07.

Derry, A., Brundett, M., Slavikova, L., Karabec, S., Murden, B., & Nicolaidou, M. (2006). Unpublished manuscript.

English, F. (2006). The unintended consequences of a standardized knowledge base in advancing educational leadership preparation. *Educational Administration Quarterly, 42*(3), 461-472.

Friedman, T. (2005) *The world is flat: A brief history of the twenty-first century.* New York: Farrar, Strauss & Giroux.

Hallinger, P. (Ed.). (2003). *Reshaping the landscape of leadership.* Lisse, The Netherlands: Swets & Zeitlinger.

Huber, S., & West, M. (2002). Developing school leaders: A crtcial reveiw of current proactice, approaches, and isues, and some direciton for the future. In K. Leithwood & P. Hallinger (Ed.), *Second International Handbook of Educational Leadership and Administration* (pp. 1071-1102). Dordrecht: Kluwer.

Johnson, D. (1995). Developing an approach to educational management in South Africa. *Comparative Education, 31*(2), 223-241.

Littkey, D., & Schen, M. (2003). Developing school leaders: One principal at a time. In P. Hallinger (Ed.), *Reshaping the landscape of leadership preparation* (pp. 87-100). Lisse, The Netherlands: Swets & Zeitlinger.

Ming-Dih, l. (2003). Professional development for principals in Taiwan: The status quo and future needs. In P. Hallinger (Ed.), *Reshaping the landscape of leadership preparation* (pp. 191-204). Lisse, The Netherlands: Swets & Zeitlinger.

Murphy, J. (1991). The effects of the educational reform movement on departments of educational leadership. *Educational Evaluation and Policy Analysis, 13*(1), 49-65.

Murphy, J (1999). The reform of the profession: A self portrait. In J. Murphy & P. Forsythe (Eds.), *Educational administration: A decade of reform* (pp. 39-68). Thousand Oaks, CA: Corwin Press.

Murphy, J. & Forsythe, P. (1999). *Educational administration: A decade of reform.* Thousand Oaks, CA: Corwin Press.

Peoples Daily. (2000). Retrieved on 8/17/2007 from http://english.people.com.cn/english/200003/23/eng20000323U102. html.

Shuttleworth, D. (2003). *School management in transition: Schooling on the edge.* London: Routledge-Falmer.

Su, Z., Adams, J. & Mininberg, E. (2000). Profiles and preparation of urban school principals: A comparative study in the United States and China. *Education and Urban Society, 32*(4) 455-480.

Taba, H. (1967). *Teacher's handbook for elementary social studies.* Palo Alto, CA: Addison Wesley.

Walker, A., & Dimmock, C. (2006). Preparing leaders, preparing learners: The Hong Kong experiencee. *School Leadership and Management, 26*(2), 125–147

Walker, A., Hallinger, P., & Qian, H. (2007). Leadership development for school effectiveness and improvement in East Asia. Unpublished manuscript.

UNIVERSITY WEBSITES

Ashland University Ohio, USA Retrieved on 9/06/07 from http://www3.ashland.edu/academics/education/edadmin/

Chinese University of Hong Kong, China Retrieved on 8/13/07 from http://www.fed.cuhk.edu.hk/EAP_MA_DegreeProgram.htm/

Hong Kong Institute of Education, China Retrieved on 6/03/07 from http://www.ied.edu.hk/acadprog/postgrad/prog/med/edu_mgt.htm

Institute of Education, University of London, United Kingdom. Retrieved on 6/20/97 from http://ioewebserver.ioe.ac.uk/ioe/index.html

Lewis and Clark College Oregon, USA Retrieved on 9/06/07 from http://graduate.lclark.edu/dept/eda/

London Centre for Leadership in Learning, United Kingdom Retrieved on 6/20/07 from http://ioewebserver.ioe.ac.uk/ioe/cms/get.asp?cid=9087

McGill University, Toronto Canada Retrieved on 2/28/07 from http://www.mcgill.ca/edu-integrated/cel/

Nanyang Technological Academy Singapore Retrieved on 6/14/07 from http://www.nie.edu.sg/nieweb/programs/loading.do?id=Graduate&cid=10453001&ppid=10485788

Nelson Mandela Metropolitan University South Africa Retrieved on 6/20/07 from http://www.nmmu.ac.za/default.asp?id=3603&sid=&bhcp=1

Rowan University New Jersey, USA Retrieved on 9/06/07 from http:// www.rowan.edu/colleges/education/departments/education_leadership

Seton Hall New Jersey, USA Retrieved on 9/06/07 from http:// education.shu.edu/elmp/index.htm

Simon Fraser University Retrieved on 2/28/07 from http://www.educ.sfu.ca/gradprogs/masters/education_leadership/index.html

Trinity University, Texas, USA Retrieved on 9/24/07 from http://www.trinity.edu/departments/Education/Degree_Programs/sch

University of Hong Kong Retrieved on 6/03/07 from http://www.hku.hk/educel/

University of Johannesburg, South Africa Retrieved on 6/17/07 from http://www.nmmu.ac.za/default.asp?id=3603&sid=&bhcp=1

University of Kentucky Kentucky, USA Retrieved on 8/16/07 from http://www.uky.edu/Education/EDL/edelma.html

University of Lagos Nigeria, Africa Retrieved on 6/17/07 from http:// www.unilag.edu/index.php?page=about_departmentdetail&sno=6

University of Leicester Retrieved on 6/20/07 from http://www.le.ac.uk/education/research/arg/edleadershipmanagement/edleadership.html

University of Louisville Kentucky, USA Retrieved on 9/06/07 from http://louisville.edu/education/departments/elfh/ed-leadership

University of Manitoba Canada Retrieved on 2/28/07 from http://www.umanitoba.ca/education

University of Miami Ohio, Ohio USA Retrieved on 3/09/07 from http://www.units.muohiio.edu/eap/EDL/programs/Grad/slp

University of Newcastle New South Wales, Australia Retrieved on 6/20/07 from http://www.newcastle.edu.au/faculty-old/education-arts/programscourses/10975.html

University of Texas Austin Texas, USA Retrieved on 9/06/07 from http://edadmin.edb.utexas.edu/prospective/pselp/principalship/index.php

University of Waikato, New Zealand Retrieved on 8/08/07 from http://edlinked.soe.waikato.ac.nz/programmes/index.php?prog_id=28

University of Wollongong, New South Wales, Australia Retrieved on 6/20/07 from http://www.uow.edu.au/educ/postgrad/edlead/index.html

Non-University Programs

Matthew Goniwe School of Leadership Guatang, South Africa Retrieved on 2/28/07 from http://www.mgslg.co.za/

School Leadership Capability Framework Program, New South Wales, Australia Retrieved on 8/08/07 from https://www.det.nsw.edu.au/proflearn/areas/sld/devstage/ap.htm

New Leaders for New Schools USA Retrieved on 2/28/07 from http:// www.nlns.org/NLWeb/Index.jsp

Standards and Administrative Regulations

Educational Leadership Constituent Council (ELCC) Retrieved on 2/28/07 from http://www.npbea.org/ELCC/index.html

Interstate School Leaders Licensure Consortium Retrieved on 2/28/07 from http://www.ccsso.org/projects/Interstate_Consortium_on_School_Leadership/ISLLC_Standards/

Ohio Standards for Principals Retrieved on 9/28/07 from http://www.ode.state.oh.us/GD/Templates/Pages/ODE/ODEDetail.aspx?page=3&TopicRelationID=312&ContentID=8561&Content=37548

Texas Administrative Code Retrieved on 10/01/07 from http://info.sos.state.tx.us/pls/pub/readtac$ext.ViewTAC

12

Mentoring and Coaching Programs for the Professional Development of School Leaders

Bruce G. Barnett and Gary R. O'Mahony

The induction and transition of principals into the profession is of great concern, especially if there are particular events or circumstances that either encourage or discourage capable educators from seeking the position. Duke (1987) argues:

> School leaders do not emerge from training programs fully prepared and completely effective. Their development is a more involved and incremental process, beginning as early as their own schooling and extending through their first years on the job as leaders. Becoming a school leader is an ongoing process of socialization. (p. 261)

Therefore, there is an increasing need to implement effective administrator professional development programs that reflect the needs and practices of what actually occurs in schools (e.g., Barth, 2003; Daresh & La Plant, 1985). While the importance of developing effective school leadership practices has remained a key element for developing effective schools (Austin, 1979; Lipham, 1981), recent system-wide responses tend to focus on identifying a set of standards and management competencies to be performed, bearing little resemblance to what principals actually do in leading and changing schools. These "designer leadership development programs" (Gronn, 2003), based almost entirely on achieving certain competencies and standards, will not create the types of leaders necessary for this new regime as "the wide variation between [institutions] may give rise for differentiated strategies" (Lupton, 2004, p. 31). Although some policy makers still lean towards "informed prescription" of leadership development curriculum (Barber, 2002), there is more emphasis on the profession providing foundations for sharing craft knowledge.

International trends in leadership development exemplify the growing recognition to provide support for aspiring and practicing school leaders. For example, the United Kingdom has taken a strong lead in recent years in developing policies focusing on learning-centered leadership and personalized development (Southworth, 2002). Furthermore, Huber's (2003) study of 15 countries indicates that many mandatory or quasi-mandatory programs have mushroomed throughout Europe, Asia, Australasia, and North America. Finally, Weindling's (2004) investigation of 43 principal induction programs from 14 nations reveals that despite local differences, most programs tend to address issues related to instructional leadership, school improvement, change management and skill development. These trends indicate there is enormous interest in administrator preparation and development (Hallinger, 2005).

THE CASE FOR MENTORING AND COACHING

There have been major paradigm shifts in leadership development moving from developmental supervision models to more professional learning network models (Hallinger, 2005; Murphy, 2001). No doubt the pressures faced by today's school leaders take a toll on their physical and emotional wellbeing. Despite the growing recognition of school leaders' emotional intelligence (e.g., Goleman, 1995, 1998), there still exists a lingering suspicion and mistrust of the word "emotions" in leadership development. Therefore, as school systems and professional developers have sought effective means for supporting the development of school leaders' skills, cognitive abilities, and emotional intelligence, mentoring and peer coaching programs have flourished (Crow & Matthews, 2003). There is an abundance of literature heralding the value of mentoring and coaching in business (Clutterbuck 1998; Hall 1976; Kram, 1985; Zeus & Skiffington, 2000), teacher education (Jonson, 2002; Portner, 1998), and graduate education (Brause, 2002; Erkut & Mokros, 1981). Daresh (2004) concludes that while these and other similar studies provide valuable evidence regarding mentoring in different organizational settings, the focus needs to be limited to school leaders, specifically beginning school principals. Barnett and O'Mahony (2002) justify the growing popularity of mentoring and coaching for educational leaders:

- These programs provide a flexible way for two people to devote time for interacting and reflecting on important school leadership issues.
- They are an off-line activity and usually occur outside the normal operational activities and therefore have an element of social interaction and personalized support.
- Coaching and mentoring are related to the essence of the work of leadership.
- They focus on the individual by engaging hearts and minds.
- Personalized feedback greatly enhances learning and development of leadership skill and attitudes.
- These approaches co-exist with other learning strategies that link learning to the workplace.

Given the growing trend to provide mentoring and coaching opportunities for aspiring, beginning, and experienced principals, this chapter provides an overview of these forms of professional development for school leaders. The first part of the chapter describes important conceptualizations of leadership development that underlie the relevance of mentoring and coaching. The remainder of the chapter examines how mentoring and coaching programs have taken shape around the world, the possible outcomes these programs have on participants and their schools, and implications for future research on mentoring and coaching programs for school leaders.

DEVELOPMENTAL CONCEPTUALIZATIONS OF MENTORING AND COACHING

Mentoring and coaching are an important peer-support process for assisting administrators to learn new skills, better understand their school environments, and clarify their career orientations and aspirations. Because school administration has become so complex, principals need constant development throughout their careers (Crow & Matthews, 2003; Weindling, 2000). Clearly, mentoring and coaching focus on personal and professional development. If so, what developmental concepts and principles drive mentoring and coaching processes? This question is directly addressed in this section. We begin by describing the developmental aspects of leaders' career orientations and then discuss the power of reflection and knowledge construction as cornerstones to leaders' development.

DEVELOPMENTAL GROWTH PROCESSES

At their core, mentoring and coaching are aimed at facilitating principals' growth. Often the term *development* is used to describe this growth process. Daresh (2004), for instance, identifies various developmental concepts underlying mentoring: professional development, cognitive development, career development, and adult development. For our purposes, two important developmental issues will be addressed: (1) the phases principals experience throughout their careers and (2) the relationships that emerge during the mentoring and coaching processes.

Phases of Career Development

Researchers have sought to understand the developmental phases newcomers experience as they transition into the role as well as throughout the remainder of their careers. A synthesis of studies of the organizational socialization of principals reveals three major stages define principals' careers: (1) encounter, (2) adjustment, and (3) stabilization (Hart, 1993). Other examples of these broad stages of development can be seen in the work of researchers studying beginning and experienced principals. For instance, Parkay and Hall (1992) describe a five-stage developmental model to explain the career transitions of principals: (1) survival, (2) control, (3) stability, (4) educational leadership, and (5) professional actualization. Another conceptualization by Day and Bakioglu (1996) indicates principals experience four developmental phases: (1) initiation, (2) development, (3) autonomy, and (4) disenchantment. The biggest difference in these two models is that principals either reach a pinnacle in their careers where they feel extremely competent and self-fulfilled (Parkay and Hall's *professional actualization* phase) or they become burned out, losing their self-confidence and motivation to perform the role (Day and Bakioglu's *disenchantment* phase).

Some stage models of principal development account for significant learning experiences that occur *before* becoming a principal. These conceptualizations acknowledge novices have been shaped by earlier personal, social, and professional experiences, which influence their expectations and perceived capabilities to do the job. Examples of these pre-entry phases include: *idealization* (O'Mahony, 2003; O'Mahony & Matthews, 2003), *warm up* (Reeves, Moos, & Forrest, 1998), and *preparation prior to headship* (Weindling, 2000). Perhaps the most attention given to the factors affecting new principals' initial conceptualizations and expectations is Ribbins' (1998) four-stage model of principal socialization. The first two stages — *formation* and *accession* — occur prior to becoming a principal. Formation is how future principals' personalities are influenced by their formative experiences with family, friends, and schooling. Accession refers to the professional career experiences that influence future principals' knowledge, skills, and attitudes, such as their formal leadership preparation program and jobs performed within and outside education.

Mentoring and coaching have been touted as important support mechanisms for school administrators at various stages of their careers (Mertz, 2004; Reyes, 2003). Crow and Matthews

(2003), for example, indicate that mentors can be useful for: (1) principal interns and aspirants, (2) new assistant principals, (3) new principals, and (4) mid-career principals. Most often, however, attending to the developmental needs of aspiring and beginning principals is the focus of mentoring and coaching. These supportive relationships are intended to socialize novices as they are inducted into the profession. Professional socialization refers to the "processes of becoming a member of a profession and developing an identity with that profession" (Vallani, 2006, p. 18), and mentoring is an important mechanism for assisting teachers to transition to this new role (Daresh, 2004).

Stages of Relationship Development

For mentoring and coaching processes to succeed, solid relationships based on trust, confidentiality, and mutual respect must be developed between partners. These types of relationships do not develop immediately; therefore, many authors acknowledge the mentoring and coaching relationship will evolve through a series of stages. Some of the earliest conceptual models arise from studies of mentoring in business settings. Phillips (1977) identified six stages: initiation, sparkle, development, disillusionment, parting, and transformation. Kram (1985) contends there are four stages of progression: initiation, cultivation, separation, and redefinition. One of the first conceptualizations of relationship development for educators was Gray and Gray's (1985) five-level model of the Mentor/Protégé Helping Relationship. Calabrese and Tucker-Ladd (1991) elaborate on these general phases, indicating a successful mentoring relationship is a social contract that develops over time based on trust, collaboration, inclusiveness, modeling, and reciprocation. Despite using different terms, the literature indicates that "healthy mentor/protégé relationships involve a progression from relative protégé dependence at the beginning of the relationship to autonomy and self-reliance as the protégé grows into a colleague and peer" (Head, Reiman, & Thies-Sprinthall, 1992, p. 12).

Far less has been written about coaching for principals; however, a few prominent examples illustrate the developmental nature of the relationship. Robertson (2005) describes three general phases of a successful coaching relationship: (1) *initiation* is the time when trust and confidence develop, (2) *implementation* emerges as they discuss deeper educational issues, conduct observations, and provide constructive feedback to one another, and (3) *institutionalization* emerges when the person being coached becomes more autonomous and takes more direction of the relationship. Similarly, O'Mahony and Barnett (2006) conceptualize the coaching process for principals occurs over four stages: (1) establishing the relationship and understanding the context, (2) building and understanding direction, (3) progressing and reviewing the program, and (4) consolidating and continuing the learning.

In the early stages of the coaching relationship, establishing a foundation of trust is essential for moving the process forward. Following through on agreements, such as scheduling specific time to meet, preparing an agenda, and sharing different perspectives, are important first steps in solidifying the relationship (Bloom, Castagna, Moir, & Warren, 2005; Rich & Jackson, 2005). Conducting a context interview early in the relationship allows coaches to obtain important background information about the leader's school, which helps them establish specific goals and outcomes (Robertson, 2005). Also, as coaches prepare to work with another person, they contemplate their own and the other person's motives for entering into a coaching relationship by considering such questions as "What am I hoping for myself?" "What approach do I think is best?" "What does the coachee actually want?" and "What expectations does the coachee have of me?" (deHann, 2005, pp. 21–22). The relationship is intended to mature and change as coaches demonstrate their commitment to the coachee's learning, provide emotional support, and assist the coachee to attain agreed upon goals (Bloom et al., 2005). As the relationship develops, coaches and coachees may find themselves involved in a variety of different relationships, as described by deHann (2005):

- The guild master/freeman relationship: coachee presents issues and coach responds;
- The doctor/patient relationship: coachee reveals uncertainties and emotions to which the coach provide possible solutions;
- The midwife/mother relationship: coach anticipates the coachee's problems and provides assurance they can be resolved;
- The peer review relationship: both parties mutually review coachee's practices to take a critical view of the coachee's approach;
- The old boys' relationship: coachee uses coach as a sounding board to try out new ideas.

REFLECTION AND CONSTRUCTING KNOWLEDGE

One of the most often mentioned concepts associated with mentoring and coaching is how reflection can stimulate individuals' thinking and action (e.g., Brown, 2005; Conyers, 2004; Hibert, 2000; Zellner, Ward, McNamara, Gideon, Camacho, & Edgewood, 2002). As Barnett (1995) notes, "the image of a successful mentor is that of someone who...encourages a protégé to become a more reflective, inquiring professional" (p. 54). Daudelin (1996) describes the relationship between reflection and learning as follows:

> *Reflection* is the process of stepping back from an experience to ponder, carefully and persistently, its meaning to the self through the development of inferences; *learning* is the creation of meaning from past or current events that serves as a guide for future behavior. (p. 39, emphasis added)

Although it is beyond the scope of this chapter to describe all the ways to encourage reflection, some of the more promising types of activities mentors and coaches use to foster reflective thinking will be briefly examined. Robertson (2005) outlines three types of activities coaches can use to facilitate reflection: (1) complete self-assessment tools at the beginning of the relationship, (2) establish goals and action plans based on the self-assessment results, and (3) observe and describe the leadership practices of others, including the coach. Another fruitful exercise to stimulate reflection is journal writing, which can assist aspirants and novices to identify the types of leadership activities they are practicing and assess their personal and professional goal attainment (Zellner et al., 2002).

Perhaps the most important reflective tool, however, is the ability to pose reflective questions to stimulate mentees' and coachees' thinking and action (Barnett & O'Mahony, 2006a). Reflective questioning techniques are particularly useful for mentors and coaches since this approach "encourages the respondent to explore his or her *own* thinking; it is not intended to direct the respondent to a conclusion pre-determined by the questioner" (Lee & Barnett, 1994, p. 17, emphasis in original). Effective mentors and coaches not only pose questions that encourage mentees' and coachees' thinking about events, their meanings, and implications for future actions (e.g., Barnett, O'Mahony, & Matthews, 2004; Lee & Barnett, 1994; Robertson, 2005), but they also stimulate thoughtful reflection through active listening and posing questions in non-threatening ways (Calabrese & Tucker-Ladd, 1991; Rich & Jackson, 2005; Robertson, 2005)

Clearly, reflecting and learning to construct knowledge are interwoven concepts. To better understand these concepts and their applicability to mentoring and coaching, we describe the connections between cognitive development and reflection and then highlight a non-Western approach to reflection.

Constructing Knowledge

What knowledge do school leaders who are being mentored and coached need? One answer to this question is revealed by asking administrators what they need to know as they experience the role for the first time. They tend to identify specific tasks associated with their roles, such as setting goals, improving curriculum and instruction, and managing the budget (Elsberry & Bishop, 1996). Another way to answer the question is to turn to research studies of effective school leaders to see how they think and act. A recent summary of research on effective leadership conducted by Leithwood, Day, Sammons, Harris, and Hopkins (2006) indicates successful leaders build vision and direction, understand and develop people, redesign the organization, and manage teaching and learning; they also understand that student learning is influenced by staff commitment and motivation as well as workplace conditions.

A second question also is relevant: How do school leaders who are being coached and mentored learn this knowledge? At a conceptual level, Lieberman and Miller (1992) distinguish three types of knowledge: (1) knowledge *for* practice, which is gained by reading existing research, (2) knowledge *in* practice, which occurs through reflecting on exemplary practice of others, and (3) knowledge *of* practice, which happens as leaders engage in and reflect on their own leadership. Mentoring and coaching tend to address the last two types of knowledge. There is ample literature and research indicating that mentors and coaches influence the reflective and cognitive abilities of the individuals they are mentoring or coaching (e.g., Hobson, 2003). Daresh (2004), in summarizing the literature on mentoring, contends that the role of mentors is to assist novices to form ideas and understand their patterns of thinking. As mentor relationships develop, successful mentors match the type of support provided to novices' cognitive development stage (Gray & Gray, 1985; Head, Reiman, & Thies-Sprinthall, 1992; Thies-Sprinthall & Sprinthall, 1987). Cognitive coaching, a process to assist newcomers' mental processing, aims to develop the mental capacities of the mentor and coach in order to allow the novice to become an autonomous, self-dependent learner (Costa & Garmston, 1994). Finally, there is mounting evidence that when individuals develop their cognitive abilities, their reflective and problem-solving abilities improve (Allen, 1995; Leithwood & Steinbach, 1992; Short & Rinehart, 1993).

Reflection from a Non-Traditional Perspective

Most discussions and explanations of reflection and knowledge construction tend to use a rational-linear approach by breaking the reflective process down into discrete steps, phases, and/or elements. One of the earliest proponents of this rational-linear thinking was John Dewey (1910), who advocated a five-step reflective model. Since then, a host of other models have been developed to capture the essence of reflection (e.g., Barnett, O'Mahony, & Matthews, 2004).

Reflection can be conceptualized from a non-Western perspective; however, this perspective has not found its way into the mainstream literature on reflection, professional development, or mentoring and coaching. Tremmel (1993) suggests that non-Western philosophies, such as Zen Buddhism, are another way to view reflective practice since it is "best understood in-action and in the midst of everyday practice" (p. 442). As human beings become more mindful of what is occurring in their everyday lives and pay attention to their surroundings and inner emotions, they begin to experience the Zen way of life (Tremmel, 1993). When reflection is viewed from this vantage point, it is a holistic, free-flowing process, where individuals are keenly aware of their actions and feelings as they are in the midst of their actions (a process that is somewhat similar to Donald Schön's (1983) notion of "reflection-in action"). Tremmel (1993) suggests that mindfulness and paying attention as reflective processes can be encouraged as individuals: (1) engage in "freewriting" exercises where all conscious thoughts are written down as they occur, (2) are reminded to pay attention to their thoughts and feelings as they are occurring, and (3) write "slices of life" vignettes of an event in their life in great detail and then examine their thoughts and feelings associated with the event. Regardless of the perspective of reflection that is taken, effective mentors and coaches are able to assist other people to examine a situation from various viewpoints, consider options for resolving dilemmas, and determine the most beneficial course of action to take. With these conceptualizations in mind, we now turn our attention to the key ingredients to effective mentoring and coaching programs for school administrators.

MENTORING PROGRAMS FOR SCHOOL ADMINISTRATORS

What is Mentoring and Why Use It?

The increased popularity of the term *mentoring* has led to it becoming one of the prominent fads to sweep the education scene. While mentoring has been used in business since the 1970s, its more recent application in education has seen it used as a way of describing various supportive relationships and as a panacea for many problems that beset educators (Weindling, 2000). Confusion surrounding the term is unfortunate since the promise of mentoring should be seen in its primary role of helping others rather than as an end in itself. By itself, mentoring should not be seen as a school improvement strategy or, as a way of directly improving student learning, but as a facilitating process to support the professional growth of individuals. Healy (1997) points to the difficulty in defining mentoring and deriving its potential benefits:

> The seeds of empirical study have been cast too broadly to yield a harvest of cumulative knowledge given the inconsistent, idiosyncratic definitions of mentoringÖemployed Ö The absence of a definitional consensus is stymieing efforts to synthesize empirical findings into a coherent body of knowledge and to identify important unanswered questions. (pp. 9–10)

Despite a lack of consensus on a common definition, we concur with Danielson and McGreal (2000) that a mentor is someone "with experience, expertise, wisdom and/or power who teaches, counsels and helps less experienced or less knowledgeable persons to develop professionally and personally" (p. 251). The terms *coaching*, *counseling*, and *mentoring* are sometimes used interchangeably. However, they are quite different activities even though there is some overlap between them, varying on the length and focus of the relationship. *Coaching* in the workplace context usually takes place over a relatively short time span. For example, a principal or a colleague would provide "just in time" coaching assistance to someone who is having difficulty getting a power point presentation completed. Short cuts and well-timed assistance over a few hours or days will help the person to learn the task satisfactorily. *Counseling* also usually occurs over a short time frame, however, the focus is on attitudinal, motivational, or behavioral issues that interfere with someone's job performance. This situation can occur when a colleague whom the person respects, provides some advice that assists the person to fit in better into the workplace. *Mentoring*, however, is usually carried out over a longer time frame and is intended to encourage formal and informal career development, reciprocal learning between mentors and mentees, reflection for personal and professional growth, and trust between mentors and mentees (Crow & Matthews, 2003). These three approaches may occur simultaneously in informal and formal ways as peers and significant others encourage their colleagues' growth and development.

Features of Mentoring Programs

Daresh (2004) points out that within the past 10 years in the United States that 32 states have enacted laws and policies that call for mandated support programs to assist beginning school administrators. As mentoring for school administrators has become more popular, programs have been developed by a variety of organizations, including professional associations, states, districts, universities, and collaboratives among various agencies (Vallani, 2006). Not only have these mentoring programs been used for beginning school administrators, but they also are becoming quite popular at the preservice level in university educational leadership preparation programs (Capasso & Daresh, 2001; Daresh, 2004). Although no two mentoring programs are identical, the most effective U.S. programs contain these elements:

- Organizational support from the superintendent and other key decision makers in the organization
- Clearly defined outcomes that provide information on the knowledge and skills to be attained
- A clear process for screening, selecting, and matching mentors and protégés to ensure qualified administrators are identified to work with novices
- Training for mentors and protégés regarding their roles, skills, and strategies for working together
- A learner-centered focus which addresses the needs of the protégé (Riggins-Newby & Zarlengo, 2003)

Two of the most important elements — mentor selection and matching and mentor training — are examined in more detail.

Mentor Selection and Matching

The effectiveness of mentoring programs depends greatly on the nature of selection and matching of mentoring pairs (Hobson, 2003). Studies in the United Kingdom and the United States on the mentoring of head teachers and principals emphasized their importance to the success of the mentoring process (Bolam, McMahon, Pocklington, & Weindling, 1993; Bush & Coleman, 1995; Daresh & Male, 2000; Draper & Michael, 2000; Monsour, 1998). While providing a universal set of assumptions and methods for mentor selection and matching is problematic, Hopkins-Thompson (2000) indicates mentors should be role-models and Bolam et al. (1993) go further in suggesting mentor programs need to establish selection and matching protocols. Newton (2001) strongly argues for mentors to be selected from a national register based on a clear and understood criteria, and nationally-determined protocols be established to guide mentoring activities. This is echoed by Hopkins-Thompson (2000) in the U.S. context by suggesting that mentors must be highly skilled in communication, listening, analysing, providing feedback, and negotiating. They also have to be respected administrators, who are committed to the process as well as trustworthy individuals capable of establishing the level of candour needed for such work. She establishes that these components must be clearly defined in a list of criteria for selection, suggesting that great principals do not necessarily make ideal mentors. She further suggests that protégés need to be screened and identified regarding their level of commitment to the profession, personal development, and motivation.

Hopkins-Thompson (2000) suggests that mentor-protégé pairings can be done through self-selection, but also may involve the use of assessment information, such as the Myers-Briggs or Kolb's learning styles to identify preferences. Other programs use interest inventories to create pairs according to identified indicators. Walker and Stott (1994) suggest that selection is the vital issue in mentoring programs in Singapore. Selection and matching decisions are made by the government ministry of education, and although the criteria used are not specifically defined, the decision makers clearly take into account administrators' and their schools' perceived performance. Walker and Stott (1994) recommend the matching process is best approached collaboratively, with mentor, protégé, and the organizing body all having some input.

Some disagreement, however, exists in relation to mentor selection and matching. Some argue that pairs should be geographically close together, allowing frequent contact and sharing of local and system perspectives (Blandford & Squire, 2000; Draper & Michael, 2000). However, some researchers have noted that local rivalries, such as those resulting from local mentoring pairs in competition for the same students, can hinder the development of support systems and cooperative working relationships between pairs in the same locality (Daresh & Male, 2000; Draper & Michael, 2000). Because some mentoring partnerships may not be successful, the need to include provisions for protégés to be paired with different mentors is always a necessary consideration (Monsour, 1998). Clearly, some degree of compatibility between mentors and individuals with whom they are working is essential for a successful relationship to develop.

Mentor Training

Capasso and Daresh (2001) and Hopkins-Thompson (2000) argue that the training of mentors and protégés should be based on program needs and skills. For example, the National Association of Secondary School Principals (NASSP) mentoring and coaching module provides an excellent example of skill-based comprehensive program for training and mentoring. For mentors, skills include communication, needs analysis, and feedback; training should focus on how to use developmental analysis strategies, develop growth plans, and encourage reflective practice. Observation, communication, listening, and feedback skills also should be highlighted and programs needs to address organizational norms, values, and expectations in order to provide mentors with a common language and understanding about the process of mentoring (Daresh & Capasso, 2002). Daresh and Playko (1991), in developing a comprehensive mentor training programs, indicate the following topics should be covered: (1) orientation to the mentoring role, (2) instructional leadership skills, (3) human relations skills, and (4) mentor process skills.

Benefits and Limitations of Mentoring

Benefits to Mentees   Research indicates mentoring is seen as an effective mechanism in assisting new principals' transition to the job (Hansford, Tennent, & Ehrich, 2003). Numerous studies cite the benefits for beginning principals, including reduced feelings of isolation (Bolam et al., 1993; Grover 1994), reduced stress and frustration (Grover, 1994), the opportunity to reflect on the new role (Pocklington & Weindling, 1996; Southworth, 1995), accelerated rates of learning (Hopkins-Thompson, 2000), professional growth (Grover, 1994), and improved technical expertise and problem analysis (Bush & Coleman, 1995; Grover, 1994). Daresh (2003b) discovered that individuals immersed in formal mentoring programs have identified these major benefits:

- Feeling more confident about their professional competence
- Understanding the connections between their daily actions and educational theories
- Improving their communication skills
- Learning tricks of the trade in leading and managing their schools
- Feeling they belong in the school and profession

Benefits to Mentors Mentors also report advantages from their mentoring experiences, especially increased opportunities for collegiality, networking, and professional development (Hansford, Tennent, & Ehrich, 2003). Daresh (2004) suggests being a mentor can be a stimulating personal experience for experienced principals, especially those who are seeking a professional challenge. The rewards for mentors often lie in their sense of job satisfaction and an investment in the altruistic development of others (Clutterbuck, 1998). They also report a sense of achievement in seeing the values and culture of a school system incorporated into the practices of a newcomer (Daresh, 2004) and in receiving recognition from their peers (Daresh & Playko, 1993). As they share information and ideas (Daresh, 2004; Monsour, 1998) and discuss professional issues with an equal partner (Bush & Coleman, 1995), they report improvements in their performance and problem analysis (Bush & Coleman, 1995; Hopkins-Thompson, 2000), gain insights into current practice (Bush & Coleman, 1995), become aware of different styles of leadership (Ganser, Marchione & Fleischmann, 1999), improve their reflective tendencies (Hopkins-Thompson, 2000), and increase their self-esteem (Hopkins-Thompson, 2000). Daresh and Playko (1993) have argued that mentoring can play a role in energizing school leaders and facilitating the development of communities of learning. Crow and Matthews (2003) have found no empirical research that demonstrates a direct relationship between mentoring and student achievement; however, there are suggestions that mentoring can contribute to a school culture that emphasizes collegiality, cooperation and collaboration-features that are found in on effective schools (Fullan, 1999; Little, 1982).

Limitations While mentoring has been proclaimed as the savior of leadership development, it is only one form of professional learning and should not be promoted as the single answer. Pitfalls can occur in the mentoring relationship. In the worst case scenario, mentors perpetuate the status quo by discouraging innovation (Hart, 1993; Crow and Matthews, 2003), lack the commitment to assist new principals (Mertz, 2004), attempt to clone themselves (Hay, 1995), promote their own personal agendas at the expense of protégés (Muse, Wasden, & Thomas, 1998), and seek personal gains for themselves (Daresh & Playko, 1993). Based on their review of 40 empirical studies of mentoring, Hansford, Tennent, and Ehrich (2003) found the most commonly-cited problem for mentors and their protégés is the lack of time to devote to the relationship.

Besides problems associated with how mentors conduct themselves, organizational factors may limit the extent and success of the mentoring process. Some organizational pitfalls include:

- Lack of planning and financial resources. Inadequate training and support for mentors can erode the ongoing focus and continuity for new school leaders (Anderson, 1990). As the financing and support of the professional development for school leaders waxes and wanes, mentoring programs can become under-resourced professional mandates. Daresh (2004) argues that while the cost of mentoring programs may not be extremely high, there may be a resistance to resource a program for a small group of educators, namely beginning principals.

- Lack of understanding of the value of mentoring process. When mentoring is not respected as a legitimate approach to learning, it will not be successful or effective. For instance, if mentoring is seen as a deficit model to overcome weaknesses or to provide tangential support to newcomers in their socialization, these programs may not assist beginning principals (Daresh, 2004). In addition, when school systems reinforce the notion that mentoring is an extra, unnecessary burden for administrators, the process can be sabotaged.
- Selection of inappropriate individuals as mentors. Daresh (2004) suggests that if mentoring is a critical component in organizational and professional socialization, then mentors must be expected to be able to adjust their roles from confidant to guide to meet the needs of protégés as they move from novices to more competent leaders. Not all effective principals make good mentors. When school systems use mentoring as a reward for certain individuals, they may not have the beginning principals' interests in mind.
- Lack of political support. Most mentoring relationships operate outside the line management structure of the organization and therefore can by-pass the normal power structure, which may be resented by other powerful members of the organization. Because most new principals have little political clout, without advocates within the system, mentoring programs run the risk of being marginalized or eliminated (Barth, 1991).

Examples of Mentoring Programs

To provide a better sense of the types of leadership mentoring programs operating in different countries, we will describe: (1) SAGE Mentoring Programme in Australia, (2) First-Time Principals' Mentoring Programme at the University of Auckland, and (3) mentoring programs operating in Singapore and the United Kingdom. (For a description of additional international mentoring programs for principal induction, see Dick Weindling's (2004) report published by the National College of School Leadership in England.)

SAGE Mentoring Programme (Victoria, Australia)   The SAGE Mentoring Programme was developed to support new principals across nine regions in the state of Victoria. Since its inception in 1999, the SAGE two-day training program has been delivered to approximately 1000 school leaders. SAGE was conceived to: (1) build a cadre of trained mentors for succession planning, induction, leading teacher accreditation, and deputy principal programs, (2) assist new principals in developing the capability to create an educational vision, lead school improvement efforts, deliver programs through people, and build commitment, and (3) nurture, develop, and facilitate the growth of principals, deputy principals, and leading teachers through the provision of an accredited mentoring program.

Throughout the two-day SAGE training program, participants engage in numerous hand-on, reflective learning activities:

- Completing a learning style instrument, revealing the mentor's and the protégé's preferred styles
- Using a written inventory to examine mentors' tendencies for interacting with others, controlling situations, and developing trusting relationships

- Creating a jointly-developed Memorandum of Understanding, which specifies the mentor's and protégé's working agreements, timelines, and expected outcomes
- Practicing how to ask reflective questions and provide meaningful feedback
- Anticipating how to accommodate the changing nature of the mentoring relationship

SAGE participants have indicated high degrees of satisfaction with the program content and delivery. Revisions have been made based on participants' feedback and regional reviews. For instance, all the activities and materials have been aligned with five essential elements of effective mentoring and a Training of Trainers version was implemented to assist regional teams in learning how to adapt the program to meet their regional needs.

First-Time Principals' Mentoring Programme (New Zealand)   The New Zealand First-Time Principals Programme (NZFTPP) was initiated by the Ministry of Education and is delivered by a project team from the Faculty of Education at The University of Auckland. Since its inception in 2002, over one third of New Zealand's school principals have completed the program, with 87 mentors having been appointed and trained. During the first two years of the program, mentoring occurred over one year and was comprised of two half-day school-based visits, telephone and email contact. More recently (2005-2007), the program incorporated a shadowing experience; first-time principals shadow their mentors, who then shadow the first-time principal. Comprehensive guidelines, rubrics, and templates for all of the mentoring activities have been developed over time for both the mentors and the first-time principals.

Feedback from first-time principals and mentors reflect the following trends:

- High levels of participant satisfaction with the quality of mentoring and the overall mentoring program
- High levels of mentor satisfaction with the quality of the training they receive
- High levels of awareness about the predominant issues that the first-time principals are experiencing
- Increased awareness by first-time principals of the leadership practices and attributes that are desirable for effective educational leadership

Mentor Programs in Singapore   Beginning in the mid-1980s, the Singapore Ministry of Education, universities, and local districts began collaborating to implement mentoring programs for practicing assistant principals to help prepare them for the principalship (Coleman, Low, Bush, & Chew, 1996; Walker & Stott, 1994). Mentors attend seminars and workshops to hone their communication and feedback skills and participate in sessions with other mentors to discuss ways to address common problems they are experiencing. Vice-principals selected for the program enroll in academic coursework and work full time at their mentors' schools for two four-week blocks during the year. Mentors provide vice-principals with opportunities to engage in typical tasks; near the end of the eight-week practicum, vice-principals take over the lead administrative role on the campus (Coleman et al., 1996).

As the program has evolved, program organizers have learned a number of lessons about mentoring in the Singapore educational context. Mentors report being satisfied knowing they have helped influence their colleagues' careers, improving their own analytical skills, and clarifying their own practices. Furthermore, program organizers have discovered mentoring works best when: (1) trust is established in a non-threatening, informal atmosphere, (2) mentors' clearly communicate their expectations with vice-principals, (3) mentors are prepared for their role by trained facilitators, (4) mentoring is not overly prescriptive, but can be flexible based on the developing relationship, and (5) other staff members are informed of the purpose of having the vice-principals on their campuses (Walker & Stott, 1994).

Mentor Programs in the United Kingdom   Few formal induction programs for new head teachers in the United Kingdom existed before the early 1990s. Prior to that time, Local Education Authorities (LEAs) provided some induction preparation for new principals; however, many of these programs lasted one day (Male, 2006; Weindling & Earley, 1987). Beginning in 1992, a series of formal mentoring programs have been established, including the Headteacher Mentoring Scheme in 1992, Headteachers' Leadership and Management Programme (HEADLAMP) in 1995, New Visions Programme for Early Headship in 2001, and Headteacher Induction Programme (HIP) in 2003 (Hobson, 2003; Male, 2006). HEADLAMP is the most well-subscribed induction program with approximately 5000 head teachers having participated. HEADLAMP participants received funding for their first two years as head teachers to attend leadership and training programs to facilitate their growth and development. During this time, many LEAs offered mentorship programs for new head teachers, who used their HEADLAMP funds to pay for this learning experience. Although many head teachers took advantage of the funds offered through HEADLAMP, little monitoring of how the funds were spent and evidence documenting the impact of these development experiences exist (Male, 2006). One study concluded that the quality of induction programs varied greatly across the country (Office for Standards in Education, 2002).

Comparing Mentoring in Singapore and the United Kingdom   Very little research comparing mentoring programs in different countries appears in the literature. An exception is a cross-cultural study conducted by Coleman and his colleagues (1996) of school administrators who served as mentors to vice-principals in the Singapore system with those in the UK system (particularly mentors working with new head teachers during the HEADLAMP era). Similarities in mentors' perceptions in the two countries indicated: (1) the mentor relationship must be based on trust, (2) mentors gain great satisfaction when supporting a new colleague, (3) new principals have established professional networks, (4) new principals are eager and excited to learn about school leadership, and (5) new principals appreciate the opportunities assess their own practice through reflection with their mentors. Various differences in the perceptions between mentors in the two countries also were discovered:

- UK mentors stressed the need to listen while Singapore mentors emphasized the importance of personality traits (openness, sincerity, patience).
- Singapore mentors were much more likely to notice improvements in their protégés' management skills than UK respondents.
- Singapore mentors indicated protégés gained a sense of the realities of the principalship whereas UK mentors sensed headteachers' personal development resulted from the experience.
- For UK mentors, protégés benefited by discussing situations in a safe, non-judgmental, and confidential environment while Singapore mentors felt protégés learned new skills and knowledge about management.
- UK mentors found it difficult not to solve problems for their protégés and Singapore mentors were uncomfortable providing summative assessments of their protégés (Coleman et al., 1996).

COACHING PROGRAMS FOR SCHOOL ADMINISTRATORS

As noted earlier, there is an abundance of mentoring programs for individuals who aspire to the principalship as well as those who are beginning the role for the first time. Coaching programs for aspirants and practicing principals are far less common; however, there are several programs that have surfaced in recent years. Therefore, this section addresses the same issues discussed earlier about mentoring, focusing on coaching for school leadership development. We begin by describing how coaching has been conceptualized and comparing this type of supportive role with mentoring. Descriptions of the elements and guiding principles of coaching are examined as well as its benefits and limitations. The section concludes with descriptions of several coaching programs for beginning and experienced principals operating around the world.

What Is Coaching and Why Use It?

Peer coaching has a long history in teacher development (e.g., Garmston, 1987); however, far less emphasis has been placed on the value of coaching for leadership development. deHann (2005) suggests that managers can benefit from coaching by reflecting on their strengths and identifying obstacles to their growth and development. Topics of interest include coachees' workplace relationships, how they deal with difficult situations, and their decision-making tendencies. Several recent publications address how coaching can be an effective means for developing school leaders' talents. Robertson (2005), for instance, indicates that coaching involves two people setting and achieving professional goals, being open to new learning, and engaging in dialogue for the purpose of improving leadership practice. Bloom et al. (2005) provide a clear vision of the successful coach:

> A coach... provides continuing support that is safe and confidential and has as its goal the nurturing of significant personal, professional, and institutional growth through a process that unfolds over time. A coach brings an outside perspective and has no stake in the status quo in an organization. (p. 10)

As mentioned earlier, despite attempts to clearly define mentoring, the term has been confused with coaching and counseling (Mertz, 2004). Various authors have sought to identify the overlap between coaching and mentoring. For instance, Hobson (2003) contends that mentoring is more encompassing since "coaching tends to be seen as a form of mentoring, or as one aspect of mentoring, but having a more narrow focus, notably relating to an individual's job-specific tasks, skills or capacities" (p. 1). Male (2006) views mentoring as a generic term, which is intended to provide non-evaluative, non-prescriptive support for novices' personal and organizational socialization to the principalship. Others maintain that successful mentors must possess certain types of expertise to pass along to novices whereas coaches facilitate learning and do not need to be experts in various aspects of leadership. As Grant (2001) suggests, "[m]any mentors may have good coaching skills and many mentoring relationships undoubtedly involve high levels of nurturance, but mentoring per se does not require coaching skills" (pp. 6–7).

Although most leadership coaching programs described in the literature are from Western cultures (e.g., see the programs described later in the section from the United States and Australia), Stober and Grant (2006) indicate that cultural expectations can influence the coaching process. For example, when coaches are aware of the existing norms regarding power relationships between managers and employees in the Malaysian culture, they can take this information into account when working with coachees. In addition, the study reported earlier by Coleman et al. (1996) revealed that mentors in Singapore tended to see their roles more as coaching for skill development than for providing peer support. Coaching for skill development and learning is more likely to be viewed as an appropriate strategy for aspirants in Singapore while peer support is more appropriate for novices who are actually in the principalship role (Coleman et al., 1996; Hobson, 2003; Strong, Barrett, & Bloom, 2003).

Features of Coaching Programs

Earlier, we identified a variety of underlying developmental constructs (professional development, cognitive development, career development, and adult development) that serve as a conceptual foundation for mentoring and coaching. Coaching as a developmental process also has been viewed from other conceptual vantage points, including the humanistic, behavioral, cognitive, psychological, and systemic perspectives (Stober & Grant, 2006). Our intent in this section is not to describe the elements and features of these perspectives, but to summarize two important considerations when establishing coaching programs for school leaders: (1) the principles of successful coaching programs and (2) how coaches develop effective relationships with their coachees.

Guiding Principles of Coaching Programs

Because the expectation of leadership coaching is for coaches to assist coachees in reflecting on their practices without evaluating or judging their performances (Calabrese & Tucker-Ladd, 1991; Robertson, 2005), their relationship is viewed as being a reciprocal and dynamic learning process between two people who have held similar leadership roles (O'Mahony & Barnett, 2006). One of the more comprehensive explanations of the underlying principles guiding effective leadership coaching programs has been provided by Robertson (2005):

1. The process is dynamic, meeting the changing needs of and resulting in new learning for each person. In this way, it is also reciprocal.
2. The coach is a facilitator of the learning process, not the "teacher" of how something should or should not be done, unless invited.
3. The coached person takes responsibility for his or her own learning, and sets the agenda and goals for coaching sessions.
4. The partners have a good understanding of each other's roles and the social and political context within which they both work.
5. The coaching relationship takes time to develop effectively and sustain, with educational change, innovation and improvement occurring over time.
6. The coaching partners require the interpersonal, communication, and coaching skills to work together in different ways. (p. 29)

Given this intent, what are the guiding structures and elements that comprise effective coaching programs for school leaders? Hopkins-Thompson (2000) mentions five interrelated components of successful coaching programs: (1) organizational support, (2) clearly defined outcomes, (3) screening, selecting, and training coaches, (4) focus on learner.needs, and (5) continual monitoring and evaluation. In providing more specificity of what coaching programs need to attend to, Bloom and his colleagues (2005) provide specific guidelines for selecting and preparing coaches as well as assessing the quality of their relationships. For instance, they suggest leadership coaches must have at least five years of successful educational leadership experience; have demonstrated the ability to informally mentor new principals; must complete a formal application and training program prior to their selection; and participate in ongoing professional development activities, including job shadowing and periodic meetings with other coaches.

Coaching Relationships

Clearly, for coaching to succeed, a strong relationship must develop between the two partners. Strong relationships emerge as partners begin to trust one another, share different perspectives, see problems as learning opportunities, provide emotional support, and strive to attain agreed goals (Bloom et al., 2005). deHann (2005) describes the importance of first impressions in getting the coaching relationship off on the right foot, such as whether partners arrive on time, how they greet one another, and what their body language communicates. Astute coaches also begin their relationships by considering why the coachee has decided to engage in this relationship, understanding the situational factors that have led the coachee to use a coach, and reflecting on their own motivations for entering the relationship (deHann, 2005). Coaches can demonstrate their commitment to making the relationship work by scheduling specific times to meet, preparing an agenda, carefully observing and listening, and keeping a journal (Rich & Jackson, 2005).

Literature confirms that three of the most important ingredients to establishing a successful coaching relationship are: (1) developing trust, (2) questioning and observing, and (3) providing feedback (e.g., Bloom et al., 2005; Rich & Jackson, 2005). Trust between coaching partners emerges over time and is based on one another's sincerity (do they mean what they say and say what they mean), reliability (do they do what they say they will do), and competence (do they possess the necessary knowledge and skills) (Bloom et al., 2005). As Larson & LaFasto (1989) remind us, trust is quite fragile and can be eroded when any of these factors are violated. One powerful way coaches can demonstrate their listening and questioning skills is to help coachees become aware of their statements that are *assertions* (facts that can be verified by other sources) or *assessments* (personal judgments or opinions) (Bloom et al., 2005). Coaches can help coachees examine assessment statements by asking them to consider the standards being used to make judgments and what facts may support their assessments. As mentioned earlier, reflective questioning is a powerful way to pose non-judgmental questions that encourage coachees' thinking about events, their meanings, and implications for future actions (Barnett, O'Mahony, & Matthews, 2004; Lee & Barnett, 1994; Robertson, 2005). Finally, when providing effective feedback coaches need to keep the coachee's and school's needs in mind, provide data-based information, link outcomes to actions, acknowledge the coachee's areas of strength, and present sensitive feedback at the appropriate time (Bloom et al., 2005).

Benefits and Limitations of Coaching

The advantages and pitfalls of mentoring have been captured in the popular and research literature. Although far less has been written about the pros and cons of coaching, we briefly describe what has been reported about leadership coaching.

Benefits   In his extensive review of research on mentoring and coaching for new leaders, Hobson (2003) notes the lack of empirical studies revealing the effects of coaching. Despite the lack of research findings, suggestions have been offered as to the merit of coaching. deHann (2005), for example, outlines the possible contributions of coaches:

- Person-focused — coach contributes understanding and validation of person
- Insight-focused — coach provides deeper understanding and objectivity
- Problem-focused — coach stimulates new ideas and recommendations
- Solution-focused — coach provides feedback and direction for future actions

In addition, suggestions in the popular literature suggest coaching can reduce isolation, increase leaders' self-awareness, improve their skills, consider the broader school context when making decisions, and become more reflective (Rich & Jackson, 2005).

A recent empirical study of a peer coaching program for new principals in California reveals the effects on new principals' skills, satisfaction, and retention (Strong, Barrett, & Bloom, 2003). (This program is described in more detail below.) Because of their coaches' interactions and support, most new principals reported being able to focus on instructional leadership issues, including developing their personal vision, clarifying long-term school goals, and making more sound instructional decisions. They also were highly satisfied with the program and many felt the coaching program was responsible for their motivation to remain in the job.

Limitations   Once again, limited evidence exists regarding the problems associated with coaching; however, some authors suggest disadvantages surface when comparing mentoring and coaching. On one hand, Hobson (2003) found mentors in the UK "felt that the term 'coaching' was not appropriate in describing the mentoring of new headteachers" (p. 22). On the other hand, coaching may overcome some of the inherent problems of mentoring. For instance, mentors: (1) employed in the same district as protégés may be reluctant to share confidential information with one another, (2) who work full time in another school may lack the time to work with their protégés, and (3) may be successful practitioners, but lack the tools and skills to provide individual support (Bloom, Castagna, & Warren, 2003). Other factors have surfaced that can influence the quality of a coaching program include the lack of adequate time to devote to the relationship (Bloom, Castagna, & Warren, 2003; Hobson, 2003; Robertson, 2005), flaws in matching coachees and coachees (Hobson, 2003), inadequate training for coaches (Hobson, 2003), the great sense of loss when the coaching relationship ends (Robertson, 2005), and the difficulty of maintaining the habit of using reflective questioning strategies (Robertson, 2005).

Examples of Coaching Programs

To provide a sense of some of the prominent administrative coaching programs operating around the world, we will summarize: (1) Effective Leaders Improve Schools in the Chicago Public Schools, (2) New Administrator Program at the University of Santa Cruz, and (3) Coaching for Experienced Principals in Australia.

Effective Leaders Improve Schools (Chicago Public Schools)   In 2005, the Chicago Public Schools (CPS) received a three-year U.S. Department of Education grant to implement the Effective Leaders Improve Schools (ELIS) project. The overarching goal of ELIS is to improve the recruitment, selection, training, and support for aspiring and new principals (Daresh & Cunat, 2006). A major component of ELIS is to select and prepare experienced principals as coaches to work with novices during their first year on the job. During the first two years of ELIS, practicing or recently retired CPS principals, particularly ones who had a reputation for leading schools where student achievement has improved, were hired part time to serve as *internship coaches* for aspiring principals and *induction coaches* for new principals. Ongoing support and development of coaching is provided throughout the program, including ongoing data collection to determine coaches' impact, coaching institutes during the year, and periodic study sessions between coaches and their assigned aspirants or novices (Daresh, 2006a; Daresh & Cunat, 2006).

To determine how coaching is working and adjustments that may need to be made, the Center for Research in Educational Policy (CREP) at the University of Memphis is conducting a formal evaluation of the program (Wright & Ross, 2006). ELIS participants report the value of forming meaningful relationships and becoming more reflective about their practice (Daresh, 2006a). Additional reactions were reported:

- Internship coaches indicated aspiring principals practice skills needed to be an effective school leader, provide feedback to teachers to improve their practice, and work effectively with students.
- Induction coaches were comfortable providing feedback, gain professional satisfaction from the experience, are pleased with the willingness of new principals to contact them, and see novices establishing safe and supportive learning environments in their schools.
- Aspiring principals' responses suggested they have a clear understanding of the internship program, their experiences are helping them grow as leaders, their change projects address important school improvement initiatives, and they are progressing towards becoming effective urban school leaders.
- New principals were satisfied with how their coaches are assisting them to address new challenges and obstacles, focusing their attention on observing classrooms and assessing quality instruction, and providing constructive feedback (Daresh, 2006a; Wright & Ross, 2006).

Based on feedback from ELIS participants, several changes have been made. To provide more time for personalized contact, full-time coaches are being hired to work with aspirants and beginning principals. More attention is being devoted to collecting data about the impact of the coaching experience on aspirants and new principals and data collection instruments have been simplified to reduce confusion and excessive record keeping.

New Administrator Program (Santa Cruz, California)   Beginning in the late 1990s, the University of Santa Cruz (California) instituted the New Administrator Program (NAP), a coaching program for first- and second-year school administrators (Strong, Barrett, & Bloom, 2003). The overall purpose of NAP is to support beginning principals to become instructional leaders by addressing daily management issues and instructional and educational activities dealing with school improvement and reform (Strong, Barrett, & Bloom, 2003).

Coaches are retired principals who worked in a different district than the new principals they are coaching (Strong, Barrett, & Bloom, 2003). Three to six hours of coaching are provided per month during one-on-one sessions every two weeks for first-year principals and every three weeks for second-year principals. NAP places a strong emphasis on developing the instructional leadership skills of beginning principals; coaches observe beginning principals conducting classroom visits, teacher evaluation sessions, and staff meetings. Novice principals also attend the New Site Administrators Institute, a series of nine seminars during the year. Beginning principals and coaches engage in a variety of professional development activities to prepare and support their growth and development, analyzing case studies, watching videos of new principals describing their challenges and coaching sessions, and completing a 360 degree feedback instrument (Bloom et al., 2003).

Several informal, small-scale studies have been conducted of NAP principals and coaches. Strong, Barrett, and Bloom (2003) found the most common issues shaping coaching conversations were: (1) staff issues (uncooperative teachers, retaining teachers), (2) district constraints (excessive paperwork, unrealistic deadlines), (3) multiple demands on their time, (4) analyses of student data, (5) acceptance by parents and community members, and (6) the legacies of previous administrators. Perhaps the most significant finding from this investigation revealed that over 50 per cent of respondents indicated the coaching support they received was responsible for them remaining in the job. Coaches gained satisfaction by helping novices to identify their decision-making tendencies, clarify their career aspirations, reduce their stress, see the big picture, explore standards-based instruction, and allocate personal time for their families; they also became better at practicing active listening, asking reflective questions, and understanding school administrators' expectations (Bloom, Danilovich, & Fogel, 2005).

Coaching for Experienced Principals (Victoria, Australia)   The Victorian Department of Education and Training (2005) recently emphasized their commitment to supporting professional development programs intended to build school leaders' leadership capacity. In response to this initiative, the Australian Principals Centre (APC) instituted the Coaching for Enhancing the Capabilities of Experienced Principals Program (CEP). The program is unique in that it is intended to support experienced principals, rather than novices, using an executive coaching model (Zeus & Skiffington, 2000).

During the first year of the program (2004–2005), 62 coaches (retired principals, state department, employees, practicing principals, and corporate consultants) and 97 experienced primary and secondary principals participated. Subsequent cohorts had similar numbers of coaches and principals participating (Barnett & O'Mahony, 2007). Once coaches are selected, they attend a two-day training program to clarify expectations about their roles, examine how to develop experienced principals' transformational leadership skills, and explore effective coaching skills (O'Mahony & Barnett, 2006; Barnett & O'Mahony, 2006b). Coaches and their partners use the results from the 360 degree Educational Leadership Feedback Instrument (ELFI) to ensure the coaching relationship focuses on transformational leadership (Leithwood & Jantzi, 2005). Coaches are expected to spend at least 10 hours with their partners over the year; however, most coaches exceed this minimal requirement. Throughout the year, regional staff and APC staff monitor coaching relationships through telephone calls, email messages, and site visits.

Principals reported instituting a wide array of transformational leadership projects and being very satisfied with the program, particularly how it was advertised, delivered, and supported. They developed a greater sense of self-confidence and awareness of their preferred leadership styles, were better able to delegate responsibilities to other staff members, and became more strategic in implementing school improvement (O'Mahony & Barnett, 2006). Despite the short duration of the program, many principals wanted to extend the experience to be able to receive additional support from program organizers and their coaches. Coaches also appreciated the training they received, especially in how to utilize the ELFI results as a starting point in working with their partners.

EFFECTS OF MENTORING AND COACHING

An abundance of popular and research literature cites the benefits school leaders, mentors, and coaches obtain when engaging in this professional development experience; however, Daresh (1995) warns that definitive claims about the impact of mentoring still remain elusive:

Despite repeated and persistent suggestions that mentoring programs might serve as a central part of initial pre-service leadership preparation programs, induction schemes, and ongoing in-service and professional development activities, however, there has been a remarkable lack of systematic analysis of this issue in the research literature. (p. 7)

Earlier we mentioned there are very few studies documenting the effects of leadership coaching programs (e.g., Hobson, 2003; Strong et al., 2003), especially when compared to the impact mentors have on aspiring and practicing school leaders. Although definitive research on the value of mentoring and coaching does not exist, an extremely useful way for examining the effects of these types of professional development programs has been developed by Guskey (2000), who suggests five increasingly deeper levels of impact can be assessed:

- Level 1 — Participants' reactions. The perceptions of participants regarding the content and delivery of the program.
- Level 2 — Participants' learning. The types of learning reported by participants.
- Level 3 — Organization support and change. How the school's policies and practices affect the successful implementation of the program.
- Level 4 — Participants' use of new knowledge and skills. How knowledge and skills are being applied by participants.
- Level 5 — Student learning outcomes. How student performance has been affected in schools where participants are working.

Using this five-level framework, research studies on mentoring and coaching for each of these five levels will be summarized below.

Participants' Reactions (Level 1)

Mentoring Studies The perspectives of those participating in mentoring programs can be obtained immediately following a professional development session or experience using questionnaires, focus groups, interviews, and journals (Guskey, 2000). In general, beginning principals involved in mentoring programs are quite satisfied, as indicated in the case studies from Australia (O'Mahony, 2003), New Zealand (Robertson, 2005), and the United States (Daresh, 2006a; Wright & Ross, 2006). Similarly, studies from the United Kingdom indicate benefits of mentoring for new headteachers centered on helping them resolve problems and issues of concern, reflecting on what it means to be a headteacher, obtaining another perspective, and receiving emotional support (Pocklington & Weindling, 1996). Finally, mentors report high degrees of satisfaction in investing in the learning of inexperienced colleagues, being recognized by peers, and seeing new principals affecting their schools' values and cultures (Clutterbuck, 1998; Daresh, 2004; Daresh & Playko, 1993).

Coaching Studies In general, school leaders react favorably to having a peer coach, reporting high degrees of satisfaction (e.g., Robertson, 2005; Strachan & Robertson, 1992; Strong et al., 2003). For example, 27 new principals rated their coaches as a 9.6 on a 10-point scale (Strong et al., 2003) and a survey of 42 experienced principals indicated over 90 per cent felt their experience was successful or very successful (O'Mahony & Barnett, 2006). Despite the short duration of many coaching programs, many school leaders desire additional contact with their coaches following the formal operation of the program (O'Mahony & Barnett, 2006; Strong et al., 2003). Coaching relationships tend to fail when there are mismatches between coaches and school leaders or when coaches do not establish credibility. Finally, coaches indicate being renewed by the opportunity to assist other school leaders (Strong et al., 2003) and appreciate the preparation they receive in learning how to become more effective coaches (Barnett & O'Mahony, 2006b; O'Mahony & Barnett, 2006).

Participants' Learning (Level 2)

Mentoring Studies   Perceptions of what participants have learned from their mentoring experiences can be gathered through portfolios, case studies, and oral and written exercises (Guskey, 2000). Mentors appear to support newcomers to "learn the ropes" (Duke, 1987; Hart, & Bredeson, 1996), such that beginning principals are affected in many ways. New principals report the experience greatly assists in their job transition, reducing feelings of isolation, stress, and frustration (Bolam et al., 1993; Daresh, 2003b; Grover 1994). Being able to reflect on their initial job experiences also has been reported to affect novices' technical expertise, problem analysis, and communication skills (Barnett, Miller & O'Mahony, 2003; Bush & Coleman, 1995; Daresh, 2003b; Grover, 1994; O'Mahony, 2003). The examples of mentoring used in the ELIS and SAGE programs described above provide additional confirmation of how aspiring and new principals' understanding of school improvement and the challenges of urban school leadership are heightened by mentors' involvement (Daresh, 2006a; Wright & Ross, 2006). Mentors also report advantages based on their experiences, claiming the experience affects their problem analysis strategies (Hopkins-Thompson, 2000; Bush & Coleman, 1995), awareness of varying leadership styles (Ganser, Marchione & Fleischmann, 1999), ability to reflect (Hopkins-Thompson, 2000), and self-esteem (Hopkins-Thompson, 2000). Daresh and Playko (1993) have argued that mentoring can play a role in energizing school leaders and facilitating the development of communities of learning.

Coaching Studies   Perceived learning outcomes have been obtained from aspiring, new, and experienced principals involved in coaching. A study of aspiring principals in Singapore suggests mentors performed more like coaches, noting improvements in their protégés' knowledge and skills about management as well as the chance for protégés to gain a sense of the realities of the principalship prior to taking on the role (Coleman et al., 1996; Walker & Stott, 1994). Learning outcomes for new principals have been reported. For instance, novices find it useful to work with coaches on issues dealing with staff discontent, time restrictions, district demands, acceptance by parents and community members, and the legacy of previous administrators (Strong et al., 2003). In addition, conventional wisdom suggests novices tend to spend the majority of time on managing the school, rather than being instructional leaders; however, mounting evidence suggests that when coaches purposely attend to instructional matters (e.g., classroom visits, teacher evaluation, student data analysis), novices are capable of spending time and reflecting on their instructional leadership responsibilities (Bloom et al., 2003; Daresh, 2006b; Strong et al., 2003). Finally, coaching may have effects on principal retention since first-year principals report they might have left the job if they had not had a coach working with them (Strong et al., 2003).

While most coaching programs are intended to assist novices, experienced principals benefit from having leadership coaches since they can provide an external perspective and are not immersed in the internal school's politics. Veteran principals perceive they gain a more strategic, or "big picture," view of their schools (Robertson, 2005) and are better more adept at practicing transformational leadership in affecting school improvement (Barnett & O'Mahony, 2007; O'Mahony & Barnett, 2006). Reports from principals and coaches indicate they gain self-confidence, become more aware of their leadership styles, and are better able to delegate tasks to teachers and leadership team members (Barnett & O'Mahony, 2006b; O'Mahony & Barnett, 2006).

Organization Support and Change (Level 3)

Mentoring Studies   Examining school policies and gathering input from participants about the organizational structures affecting their mentoring experiences can reveal factors that facilitate or impede the practices being advocated in the professional development program (Guskey, 2000). Empirical studies examining how organizational structures affect mentoring are sparse; however, a host of suggested factors that can influence the quality of the mentoring program have been espoused. Examples of organizational structures that can affect mentoring include inadequate support from upper level administrators, no or poor training and support for mentors, selection of unqualified mentors, and lack of political support (Anderson, 1990; Barth, 1991; Daresh, 2004; Riggins-Newby & Zarlengo, 2003). As demonstrated in the ELIS Project in the Chicago Public Schools, district leaders can demonstrate their support and commitment to mentoring by expecting mentors' interactions to focus on agreed-upon performance standards, establishing mentor advisory committees, and implementing ongoing workshops for mentors and mentees (Daresh, 2006a; Daresh & Cunat, 2006).

Coaching Studies   Based on the experiences of program developers who have implemented coaching programs for school administrators, various structural elements have been reported to affect program quality. Hopkins-Thompson (2000), for instance, mentions five necessary components of successful coaching programs: (1) organizational support, (2) clearly defined outcomes, (3) rigorous screening, selection, and training of coaches, (4) focus on learner needs, and (5) continual monitoring and evaluation. In addition, there appears to be some evidence that coaching relationships can be compromised if not enough time is devoted to the relationship (Bloom et al., 2003; Hobson, 2003; Robertson, 2005), coaches and coachees are not well matched (Hobson, 2003), and coaches are not trained (Hobson, 2003). Finally, based on their experiences delivering a variety of peer coaching programs in New Zealand and Australia, Strachan and Robertson (1992) and O'Mahony and Barnett (2006) discovered that:

- Coaches need preparation to learn new skills.
- One year is not long enough for coaching partnership to fully develop.
- Successful coaching relationships are based on mutual respect, honesty, and trust.
- Coaching partners need to maintain regular and sustained contact.
- Lack of time and distance between coaching partners are major inhibiting factors.
- Partnerships are likely to be successful when between people with leadership experiences in similar types of schools are matched.
- Many coaching partnerships continue beyond the formal operation of the program.

Participants' Use of New Knowledge and Skills (Level 4)

Mentoring Studies   Because studies dealing with mentoring effects are self-reports from participants and their mentors, the types of learning reported at Level 2 is difficult to substantiate in participants' workplace actions. To fill this gap, mentored principals can document their experiences using portfolios and be observed in practice to determine how their actions change over time when working with a mentor (Guskey, 2000). In addition, perceptions of others in the school (e.g., teachers, staff members, parents) regarding the principals' actions can be obtained to ascertain if they notice changes in their behaviors.

Coaching Studies   To determine if coaching relationships are making a difference in the actions of school administrators, they can be observed in practice, interviewed, and provide documentation using portfolios (Guskey, 2000). Once again, studies dealing with coaching effects tend to be self-reports from participants and their coaches, so no corroborating evidence exists to demonstrate whether school leaders' are actually putting new ideas into practice.

Student Learning Outcomes (Level 5)

Mentoring Studies   Collecting student work and gathering input from students, teachers, and community members are viable ways to determine this level of impact (Guskey, 2000). Leithwood and his colleagues (2006) maintain that next to the classroom teacher, the principal is the most important person in influencing the lives of students in their classrooms. While myriad problems exist in attempting to trace how principals' professional development experiences ultimately affect student learning outcomes in their schools, few studies noting these relationships have been conducted. A notable exception is the work of Leithwood, Riedlinger, Bauer, and Jantzi (2003) who examined student achievement gains in schools where principals attended a two-year professional development program. Speculation exists that mentors can influence student learning (Daresh, 2006b); however, no tangible evidence supports this assertion.

Coaching Studies   Perhaps the most important level of impact is whether students directly benefit from the actions of principals who have been coached. Unfortunately, as is the case with mentor research, coaching programs hint that principals will become more effective and affect student learning (Robertson, 2005), but no studies were located to substantiate this claim.

As our analysis suggests, few empirical studies provide clear evidence of the impact or effectiveness of mentoring programs for school leadership development. Virtually all studies rely on the perceptions of participants, rather than making a coherent link between structures, processes, and subsequent student learning outcomes. Clearly, more empirical research is needed to obtain a comprehensive view of the impact of mentoring and coaching. To address these shortcomings, we now direct our attention to future research in the final section of the chapter.

IMPLICATIONS FOR FUTURE RESEARCH ON MENTORING AND COACHING PROGRAMS

Methodological Critique

As we have mentioned repeatedly, most reports of mentoring and coaching programs are based on personal opinions and/or descriptions of individual programs. Daresh (1995) suggests that there have been many claims of the utility of mentoring programs for aspiring administrators, beginning principals, and experienced principals, yet the literature provides little systematic analysis of the merits of these interventions. Similarly, Hobson's (2003) extensive review of literature on mentoring and coaching programs for new leaders confirms West and Milan's (2001) finding that there is little empirical evidence revealing the effects of coaching on school leaders. As Hobson (2003) found:

[t]he effectiveness of mentoring and coaching tends to be partial and inconclusive and becomes increasingly so as one narrows the focus from (1) the effectiveness of mentoring/coaching *in general*, through (2) the effectiveness of mentoring/coaching *for leaders* and (3) the effectiveness of mentoring/coaching for *new leaders*, to (4) the effectiveness of mentoring/coaching for *new headteachers*. (p. 4, emphasis in original)

Hobson (2003) continues his methodological critique, indicating there are significant gaps in the research designs since most studies: (1) are based on mentors' and protégés' perceptions and (2) ignore whether principals' performance is affected by their mentoring experiences. Furthermore, most studies reveal positive impressions from these respondents; however, because of the significant investment of time and resources, they might be reluctant to reveal underlying problems, difficulties, and concerns with the mentoring process and its effects. By relying almost exclusively on mentor's and protégés' perceptions, other important data sources have been ignored, such as teachers' viewpoints as well as students' impressions and performance. Perhaps more importantly, without observing mentored principals or obtaining others' reactions to their interactions, we have little confidence that mentoring has made any difference in principals' actions (Bolam, McMahon, Pocklington, & Weindling, 1993; Southworth, 1995). As mentioned earlier, this gap is even more pronounced when applying Guskey's (2000) framework. Not only is there little evidence that school adminstrators' workplace actions have changed (Level 4), but there also is a dearth of information regarding the organization support structures that facilitate or impede mentored or coached principals' actions (Level 3) and whether student learning is influenced in schools where principals have been mentored or coached (Level 5).

Future Research Agenda

To counteract these types of methodological and substantive omissions, a variety of suggestions are offered to shape future research on mentoring and coaching. What types of research designs would be appropriate? As we have noted, most research is piecemeal and based on perceptions of participants in individual mentoring or coaching programs. Therefore, the advice of West and Milan (2001) is particularly relevant to expand our current research designs. They recommend future studies should:

- Increase the number of respondents sampled within and across programs. Examples of research that has attempted this approach is the study of two cohorts of Australian coaches and experienced principals (Barnett & O'Mahony, 2007) and the comparative study between mentoring programs in Singapore and the United Kingdom (Coleman et al., 1996; Walker & Stott, 1994).
- Obtain information from other stakeholders (e.g., district officials, teachers) to reduce the subjectivity of only capturing mentors', coaches', and their partners' impressions. An excellent illustration of this strategy was utilized by Leithwood, Jantzi, Coffin, and Wilson (1996) who obtained teachers' perceptions of the leadership skills of beginning principals who attended specific leadership preparation programs.
- Incorporate control groups of school administrators who have not been mentored or coached. These types of quasi-experimental designs are rare; however, Strong, Barrett, and Bloom's (2003) study of coaching for first- and second-year principals and Leithwood, Reidlinger, Bauer, and Jantzi's (2003) investigation of principals' involvement in a professional development program both incorporated control groups for comparative purposes.

What topics or issues should be addressed in these expanded studies? A host of recommendations for future areas of research on mentoring and coaching have been raised in the literature.

First, Daresh (2001) suggests evaluating a large sample of mentoring programs on a set of common dimensions, including whether: (1) financial expenditures were within the proposed budget, (2) participants' and the districts' needs were met, (3) input from participants was utilized in program revisions, and (4) weaknesses were addressed by program designers.

Second, to compare and contrast mentors' and coaches' perceptions across many programs, they could use a common set of criteria to evaluate aspirants' or beginning principals' capabilities. Capasso and Daresh (2001) advocate using the standards of the National Association of Secondary School Principals (NASSP) for such a data collection effort. Besides asking about their partners' skills (e.g., organizational ability, written and oral communication, decisiveness, stress tolerance) they could also determine how well aspirants or novices demonstrate vision, motivate and inspire others, are sensitive to others' needs, and allocate resources (Capasso & Daresh, 2001).

Third, while some literature exists on the implications of gender and race when matching mentors and coaches with novices (e.g., Davidson & Foster-Johnson, 2001; Enomoto, Gardiner, & Grogan, 2002; Wilcox, 2002), additional studies with larger samples sizes in a variety of contexts would be extremely beneficial. Fourth, the developing relationships between mentors, coaches, and their partners might be examined. One method to assess this evolving relationship is to collect data throughout their relationship (similar to the study reported earlier by Barnett & O'Mahony, 2007). Another way is to focus on the motivational aspects of the relationship. A promising area for research in this area has been suggested by Mertz (2004). She advocates determining participants' *intent* (e.g., the reasons why they have decided to participate in the mentoring or coaching relationship) and their *investment* (e.g., the amount of time and effort they are willing to devote to the relationship). Examining these issues at the beginning, during, and near the conclusion of mentoring and coaching relationships would provide useful longitudinal information on how partners' psychological intent and investment evolves over time and what contributes to these changes.

Finally, as mentioned earlier, an almost non-existent area of research is the impact of mentoring and coaching on participants' skills and on students' learning. One way of determining participants' skill development would be to apply the aforementioned NASSP standards, using a pre- and post-test design. For instance, self-reports as well as assessments from mentors, coaches, and individuals in the workplace could be collected prior to and at the conclusions of the mentoring/coaching experience. (This type of 360 degree feedback regarding experienced principals' skills is obtained with the ELFI at the beginning of the Australian CEP program.) Another way to assess skill development would be to incorporate Guskey's (2000) recommendations about using portfolios, direct observation, video and audiotapes, and individual and focus group interviews with participants and others in the school. Determining how student performance has been affected by school leaders who have been mentored or coached is far more complicated because of the lack of control groups, contextual differences between schools, and measurement errors resulting from using different tests (Leithwood et al., 2003). Despite these challenges, studies incorporating standardized test results; questionnaires; interviews with students, teachers, and parents; and student portfolios could begin to address this long-neglected area of research (Guskey, 2000).

One reason the research on mentoring and coaching effects is piecemeal is that most studies are conducted by individual university researchers or research centers. To achieve the research agenda we are recommending requires funding and inter-institutional collaboration. Perhaps the most promising inter-institutional collaboratives could be supported by research and development (R&D) centers and university systems. For instance, the Southern Regional Education Board serves a 16-state region in the United States and has a rich history of conducting multi-state studies dealing with leadership preparation, effective high schools, and middle school education. In addition, the National Foundation of Educational Research in the England has sponsored research within and outside the UK and Europe on such topics as literacy, health education, and research-engaged schools. Finally, large state-wide university systems, such as those operating in California, Texas, and New York could sponsor cross-institutional research studies designed to collect comparable data in different regions of the state. Without the involvement of these types of research organizations, the types of comprehensive research initiatives suggested have little chance of being conducted and we run the risk of not advancing our knowledge base in order to utilize mentoring and coaching processes for school leaders more effectively.

REFERENCES

Allen, J. D. (1995). The use of case studies to teach educational psychology: A comparison with traditional instruction. Paper presented at the annual meeting of the American Educational Research Association, San Francisco, CA.

Anderson, M. (1990). *Principals: How to train, recruit, select, induct and evaluate leaders for America's schools.* Eugene, OR: ERIC Clearinghouse on Educational management, University of Oregon.

Austin, G. R. (1979). Exemplary schools and the search for effectiveness. *Educational Leadership, 37*(1), 10–11.

Barber, M. (2002). From good to great: Large-scale reform in England. Paper presented at the Futures of Education Conference, Zurich, Switzerland.

Barnett, B. G. (1995). Developing reflection and expertise: Can mentors make the difference? *Journal of Educational Administration, 33*(5), 45–59.

Barnett, B. G., & O'Mahony, G. (2002). One for the to-do list: Slow down and think. *Journal of Staff Development, 23*(3), 54–58.

Barnett, B. G., & O'Mahony, G. R. (2006a). Developing a culture of reflection: Implications for school improvement. *Reflective Practice, 7*(4), 499–523.

Barnett, B. G., & O'Mahony, G. R. (2006b). Peer coaching for experienced principals: Building their capacity as transformational leaders. Paper presented at the annual convention of the University Council for Educational Administration, San Antonio, TX.

Barnett, B. G., & O'Mahony, G. R. (2007). Developing productive relationships between coaches and principals: The Australia experience. Paper presented at the annual meeting of the American Educational Research Association, Chicago, IL.

Barnett, B., O'Mahony, G. R., & Matthews, R. J. (2004). *Reflective practice: The cornerstone for school improvement.* Moorabbin, Victoria: Hawker Brownlow Education, Australia.

Barth, R. (1991). *Improving schools from within: Teachers, parents and principals make the difference.* San Francisco: Jossey-Bass.

Barth, R. (2003). *Lessons learned: Shaping relationships and the culture of the workplace* (2nd ed.) San Francisco, CA: Jossey- Bass.

Blandford, S., & Squire, L. (2000). An evaluation of the Teacher Training Agency Headteachers' Leadership and Management Programme (HEADLAMP). *Educational Management and Administration, 28*(1), 21–32.

Bloom, G., Castagna, C., Moir, E., & Warren, B. (2005). *Blended coaching: Skills and strategies to support principal development.* Thousand Oaks, CA: Corwin Press.

Bloom, G., Castagna, C., & Warren, B. (2003, May/June). More than mentors: Principal coaching. *Leader.* Association of California School Administrators.

Bloom, G., Danilovich, D. L., & Fogel, J. (2005). *Leadership* (September/October), 30–33.

Bolam, R., McMahon, A., Pocklington, K., & Weindling, D. (1993). *National evaluation of the headteacher mentoring pilot schemes.* London: DFE.

Brause, R. (2002). Doctoral dissertations: Dilemma for doctoral students, doctoral courses, and doctoral faculty. Paper presented at the annual meeting of American Educational Research Association, New Orleans: LA.

Brown, F. (2005). Leveling the playing field for new principals. *Principal, 84*(5), 22–24.

Bush, T., & Coleman, M. (1995). Professional development of heads: The role of mentoring. *Journal of Educational Administration, 33*(5), 60–73.

Calabrese, R. L., & Tucker-Ladd, P. R. (1991). The principal and assistant principal: A mentoring relationship. *NASSP Bulletin, 75*(533), 67–74.

Capasso, R. L., & Daresh, J. C. (2001). *The school administrator internship handbook: Leading, mentoring and participating in the internship program.* Thousand Oaks, CA: Corwin Press.

Clutterbuck, D. (1998). *Learning alliances: Tapping into talent.* London: Chartered Institute of Personnel Development.

Coleman, M., Low, G. T., Bush, T., & Chew, O.A. J. (1996). Re-thinking training for principals: The role of mentoring. Paper presented at the annual meeting of the American Educational Research Association, New York, NY.

Conyers, J. G. (2004). Thinking outside to support newcomers. *School Administrator, 61*(6), 18–21.

Costa, A. L., & Garmston, R. F. (1994). *Cognitive coaching: A foundation for renaissance schools.* Norwood, MA: Christopher-Gordon Publishers.

Crow, G. M., & Matthews, L. J. (2003). *Finding one's way.* Newbury Park, CA: Corwin Press.

Danielson, C., & McGreal, T. L. (2000). *Teacher evaluation to enhance professional practice.* Princeton, NJ: Educational Testing Service.

Daresh, J. C. (1995). Research base on mentoring for educational leaders: What do we know? *Journal of Educational Administration, 33*(5), 7–16.

Daresh, J. C. (2001). *Leaders helping leaders: A practical guide to administrative mentoring* (2nd ed.). Thousand Oaks, CA: Corwin Press.

Daresh, J. C. (2003b) *Teachers mentoring teachers.* Thousand Oaks, CA: Corwin Press.

Daresh, J. (2004). Mentoring school leaders: Professional promise or predictable problems? *Educational Administration Quarterly, 40*(4), 495–517.

Daresh, J. C. (2006a). Mentoring for aspiring and beginning principals in the Chicago Public Schools ELIS Project. Paper presented at the annual convention of the University Council for Educational Administration, San Antonio, TX.

Daresh, J. C. (2006b). Mentors for principals: Guardians of the past or change agents? Paper presented at the annual meeting of the MidWestern Educational Research Association, Columbus, OH.

Daresh, J. C., & Capasso, R. L. (2002). Where are the future school principals? Explaining a lack of interest. Paper presented at the annual meeting of the American Educational Research Association, New Orleans. LA.

Daresh, J. & Cunat, M. B. (2006). Chicago's "Effective Leaders Improve Schools" (ELIS) Project: First year overview. Paper presented at the annual meeting of the MidWestern Educational Research Association, Columbus, OH.

Daresh, J. C., & La Plant, J. (1985). Developing a research agenda for administrator in-service. *Journal of Research and Development in Education, 18*(2), 39–43.

Daresh, J. C., & Male, T. (2000). Crossing the border into leadership: Experiences of newly appointed British headteachers and American principals. *Educational Management & Administration 28*(1), 89–101.

Daresh, J. C., & Playko, M. A. (1991). Preparing mentors for school leaders. *Journal of Staff Development, 12*(4), 24–27.

Daresh, J. C., & Playko, M. A. (1993). *Leaders helping leaders: A practical guide to administrative mentoring.* New York: Scholastic

Daudelin, M. W. (1996). Learning from experience through reflection. *Organizational Dynamics, 24*(3), 36–48.

Davidson, M. N., & Foster-Johnson, L. (2001). Mentoring in the preparation of graduate researchers of color. *Review of Educational Research, 71*(4), 549–574.

Day, C., & Bakioglu, A. (1996). Development and disenchantment in the professional lives of headteachers. In I. Goodison & A. Hargreaves (Eds.), *Teachers professional lives*. London: Falmer Press.

deHaan, E. (2005). A new vintage: Old wine maturing in new bottles. *Training Journal*, November, 20–24.

Dewey, J. (1910). *How we think*. New York: D. C. Heath.

Draper, J., & Michael, P. (2000). Contextualising the headship. *School Leadership & Management, 20*(4), 459–473.

Duke, D. (1987). *School leadership and instructional improvement*. New York: Random House

Elsberry, C. C., & Bishop, H. L. (1996). A new deal for new principals. *Principal, 75*(3), 32–35.

Enomoto, E., Gardiner, M. E., & Grogan, M. (2002). Mentoring women in educational leadership. In F. K. Kochan (Ed.), *The organizational and human dimensions of successful mentoring programs and relationships* (pp. 207–220). Greenwich, CT: Information Age Publishing.

Erkut, S., & Mokros, J. (1981). *Professor as models for college students*. Wellesley, MA: Center for Research on Women.

Fullan, M. (1999). *Change forces: The sequel*. Philadelphia: Falmer Press.

Ganser, T., Marchione, M. J., & Fleischmann, A. K. (1999). Baltimore takes mentoring to the next level. In M. Scherer (Ed.), *A better beginning: Supporting and mentoring new teachers* (pp. 69–76). Alexandria, VA: Association for Supervision and Curriculum Development.

Garmston, R. (1987). How administrators support peer coaching. *Educational Leadership, 44*, 18–26.

Goleman, D. (1995). *Emotional intelligence: Why it can matter more than IQ*. New York: Bantam Books.

Goleman, D. (1998). *Working with emotional intelligence*. New York: Bantam Books.

Grant, A. M. (2001). Towards a psychology of coaching. Retrieved March 22, 2007 from: www/psych.usyd.edu.au/psychcoach/Coaching_review_AMG2001.pdf

Gray, W. A, & Gray, M. M. (1985). Synthesis of research on mentoring beginning teachers. *Educational Leadership, 43*(3), 37–43.

Gronn, P. (2003). *The new work of educational leaders*. London: Sage.

Grover, K. L. (1994). A study of first elementary principals and their mentors in the New York City Public Schools. Paper presented at the annual meeting of the American Educational Research Association, New Orleans. LA.

Guskey, T. R. (2000). *Evaluating professional development*. Thousand Oaks, CA: Corwin Press.

Hall, D. (1976). *Careers and organizations*. Pacific Palisades, CA: Goodyear.

Hallinger, P., (2005) Instructional leadership: How has the model evolved and what have we learned? Paper presented at the annual meeting of the American Educational Research Association, Montreal, Canada.

Hansford, B. C., Tennent, L., & Ehrich, L. C. (2003). Educational mentoring: Is it worth the effort? *Education Research and Perspectives, 39*(1), 42–75.

Hart, A. W. (1993). *Principal succession: Establishing leadership in schools*. New York: State University of New York Press.

Hart, A. W., & Bredeson, P. V. (1996). *The principalship. A theory of professional learning and practice*. San Francisco, CA: McGraw- Hill.

Hay, J. (1995). *Transformational mentoring: Creating developmental alliances for changing organizational cultures*. London: McGraw-Hill.

Head, F. A., Reiman, A. J., & Thies-Sprinthall, L. (1992). The reality of mentoring: Complexity in its process and function. In T. M. Bey & C. T. Holmes, (Eds.), *Mentoring: Contemporary principles and issues* (pp. 5–24). Reston, VA: Association of Teacher Educators.

Healy, C. C. (1997). An operational definition of mentoring. In H. T. Frierson (Ed), *Diversity in higher education* (pp. 9–22). Greenwich, CT: JAL.

Hibert, K. M. (2000). Mentoring leadership. *Phi Delta Kappan, 82*(1), 16–18.

Hobson, A. (2003). *Mentoring and coaching for new leaders*. Nottingham, England: National College for School Leadership.

Hopkins-Thompson, P. A. (2000). Colleagues helping colleagues: Mentoring and coaching. *NASSP Bulletin, 84*, 29–36.

Huber, S. (Ed.) (2003). *Preparing school leaders for the 21st century: An international comparison of development programmes in 15 countries*. London: Taylor & Francis.

Jonson, K. F. (2002). *Being an effective mentor: How to help beginning teachers succeed.* Thousand Oaks, CA: Corwin Press.

Kram, K. (1985). *Mentoring at work: Developmental relationships in organizational life.* Glenview, IL: Scott, Foresman and Company.

Larson, C. E., & LaFasto, F. M. J. (1989). *Teamwork: What must go right/what can go wrong.* Newbury Park, CA: Sage.

Lee, G. V., & Barnett, B. G. (1994). Using reflective questioning to promote collaborative dialogue. *Journal of Staff Development, 15*(1), 16–21.

Leithwood, K., Day, C., Sammons, P., Harris, A., & Hopkins, D. (2006). *Seven strong claims about successful school leadership.* Nottingham, England: National College for School Leadership.

Leithwood, K., & Jantzi, D. (2005). A review of transformational school leadership research 1996 to 2005. Paper presented at the annual meeting of the American Educational Research Association, Montreal, Canada.

Leithwood, K., Jantzi, D., Coffin, G., & Wilson, P. (1996). Preparing school leaders: What works. *Journal of School Leadership, 6*(3), 316–342.

Leithwood, K., Riedlinger, B., Bauer, S., & Jantzi. D. (2003). Leadership program effects on student learning: The case of the Greater New Orleans School Leadership Center. *Journal of School Leadership, 13*(6), 707–738.

Leithwood, K., & Steinbach, R. (1992). Improving the problem-solving expertise of school adminstrators: Theory and practice. *Education and Urban Society, 24*(3), 317–342.

Lieberman, A., & Miller, L. (1992). Revisiting the social realities of teaching. In A. Lieberman & L. Miller (Eds.), *Staff development: New demands, new realities, new perspectives.* New York: Teachers College Press.

Lipham, J. M. (1981). *Effective principal, effective school.* Reston, VA: National Association of Secondary School Principals.

Little, J. W. (1982). Norms of collegiality and experimentation: Workplace conditions of success. *American Educational Research Journal, 19*, 325–340.

Lupton, R. (2004). *Schools in disadvantaged areas: Recognising context and raising quality.* London: Economic and Social Research Council.

Male, T. (2006). *Being an effective headteacher.* London: Paul Chapman Publishing.

Matthews, L. J., & Crow, G. M., (2003). *Being and becoming a principal: Role conceptions for contemporary principals and assistant principals.* Boston: Allyn & Bacon.

Mertz, N. T. (2004). What's a mentor, anyway? *Educational Administration Quarterly, 40*(4), 541–560.

Monsour, F. (1998). Twenty recommendations for an administrative mentoring program. *NASSP Bulletin, 82*(594), 96–100.

Murphy, J. (2001). The changing face of leadership preparation. *The School Administrator, 58*(10), 14–18.

Muse, I. D., Wasden, F. D., & Thomas, G. J. (1998). *The mentor principal: A handbook.* Provo, UT: Brigham Young University.

Newton, P. (2001). The Headteachers' Leadership and Management Programme (HEADLAMP) review. Nottingham: National College of School Leadership.

Office for Standards in Education (2002). *Leadership and management training for headteachers* (HMI Report 457). London: Author.

O'Mahony, G. R. (2003). *Learning the role: Through the eyes of beginning principals.* Unpublished PhD dissertation. Melbourne, Victoria: Deakin University.

O'Mahony, G. R., & Barnett, B. G. (2006). Advancing school improvement in Australia: The influence of peer coaching on experienced principals. Paper presented at the annual meeting of the American Educational Research Association, San Francisco, CA.

O'Mahony, G., & Matthews, R. J. (2003). Learning the role: Through the eyes of beginning principals. Paper presented at the annual meeting of the American Educational Research Association, Chicago, IL.

Parkay. F. W., & Hall, G. E. (Eds.) (1992). *Becoming a principal.* Boston, MA: Allyn and Bacon.

Phillips, L. L. (1977). Mentors and protégés: A study of the career development of women managers and executives in business and industry. Unpublished doctoral dissertation. Los Angeles: University of California.

Pocklington, K., & Weindling, D. (1996). Promoting reflection of headship through the mentoring mirror. *Educational Management & Administration, 24*(2), 175–191.

Portner, H. (1998). *Mentoring new teachers.* Thousand Oaks, CA: Corwin Press.

Reeves, J., Moos, L, & Forrest, J. (1998). The school leader's view. In Macbeth, J. (Ed.), *Effective school leadership.* London: Paul Chapman/Sage.

Reyes, A. (2003). The relationship of mentoring to job placement in school administration. *NASSP Bulletin, 87*(635), 45–64.

Ribbins, P. (1998). On ladders and greasy poles: Developing school leaders' careers. Paper presented at the third ESRC Seminar, Milton Keynes, England.

Rich, R. A., & Jackson, S. H. (2005). Peer coaching: Principals learning from principals. Pairing novice and experienced principals provides both with opportunities to promote reflective thinking in their decision-making. *Principal, 84*(5), 30–33.

Riggins-Newby, C. G., & Zarlengo, P. (2003). *Making the case for principal mentoring.* Providence, RI: Brown University.

Robertson, J. (2005). *Coaching leadership.* Wellington, New Zealand: NSCER Press.

Schön, D. A. (1983). *The reflective practitioner.* New York: Basic Books.

Short, P. M., & Rinehart, J. S. (1993). Reflection as the means of developing expertise. *Educational Administration Quarterly, 29*(4), 501–521.

Southworth, G. (1995). Reflections on mentoring new school leaders. *Journal of Educational Administration, 33*(5), 17–28.

Southworth, G. (2002). Instructional leadership in schools: Reflections and empirical evidence. *School Leadership and Management, 22*(1), 73–91.

Southworth, G. (1995). Reflections on mentoring for new school leaders. *Journal of Educational Administration, 33*(5), 17–28.

Stober, D. R., & Grant, A. M. (Eds.) (2006). *Evidence based coaching handbook: Putting best practices to work for your clients.* Hoboken, NJ: John Wiley & Sons.

Strachan, J. M. B., & Robertson, J. M. (1992). Principals' professional development. *New Zealand Journal of Educational Administration, 7,* 45–51.

Strong, M., Barrett, A., & Bloom, G. (2003). Supporting the new principal: Managerial and instructional leadership in a principal induction program. Paper presented at the annual meeting of the American Educational Research Association, Chicago, IL.

Thies-Sprinthall, L., & Sprinthall, N. A. (1987). Experienced teachers: Agents for revitalization and renewal as mentors and teacher educators. *Journal of Education, 169*(1), 65–79.

Tremmel, R. (1993). Zen and the art of reflective practice in teacher education. *Harvard Educational Review, 63*(4), 434–458.

Victorian Department of Education and Training (2005). Annual report 2004–05. Retrieved February 2, 2006 from: http://www.det.vic.gov.au/edulibrary/public/govrel/reports/05DET-rpt.pdf

Vallani, S. (2006). *Mentoring and induction programs that support new principals.* Thousand Oaks, CA: Corwin Press.

Walker, A., & Stott, K. (1994). Mentoring programs for aspiring principals: Getting a solid start. *NASSP Bulletin, 78*(558), 72–77.

Weindling, D. (2004). *Innovation in headteacher induction.* Retrieved February 4, 2005 from: http://www.ncsl.org.uk/index.cfm?pageID=randd-research-publications

Weindling, D. (2000). Stages of headship: A longitudinal study of the principalship. Paper presented at the American Educational Research Association, New Orleans, LA.

Weindling, D., & Earley, P. (1987). *Secondary headship: The first years.* Windsor, England: NFER-Nelson.

West, L., & Milan, M. (2001). *The reflecting glass: Professional coaching for leadership development.* Basingstoke, England: Palgrave.

Wilcox, K. (2002). Matching mentors and protégés: Dynamics of race, ethnicity, gender, and job location.

In F. K. Kochan (Ed.), *The organizational and human dimensions of successful mentoring programs and relationships* (pp. 243–268). Greenwich, CT: Information Age Publishing.

Wright, P. M., & Ross, St. M. (2006). Chicago Public Schools Effective Leaders Improve Schools. Program evaluation: Year 1 summary. Paper presented at the annual convention of the University Council for Educational Administration, San Antonio, TX.

Zellner, L., Ward, S. M., McNamara, P, Gideon, B., Camacho, S., & Edgewood, S. D. (2002). The loneliest job in town: Sculpting the recruitment and retention of the principal. Paper presented at the annual meeting of the Southwest Educational Research Association, Austin, TX.

Zeus, P., & Skiffington, S. (2000). *The complete guide to coaching at work*. Sydney, Australia: McGraw-Hill.

13

Evaluation of School Principals

Petros Pashiardis and Stefan Brauckmann

Evaluation can be defined as the process through which information and data are collected in order to reach decisions concerning the improvement of staff or the identification of the most effective personnel. It is important to realize that from the day we are born till the end of our lives we go through a series of evaluations and judgments both at the personal and at the professional levels. Evaluations sometimes aim at improving us and at other times aim at ranking or providing us with professional rewards. Evaluations can also be used to impose sanctions. Stemming from the above, it is important to provide some answers to the basic question of why it is necessary to carry out evaluation.

When discussing the evaluation of principals in this chapter there will be necessarily a strong emphasis on what is objective, measurable, and controllable in practice as far as is feasible. Even within this inevitably reduced frame of reference there are many different perspectives and we acknowledge the fact that even the most "objective" data can (and will) be subjectively interpreted. Therefore, when using sophisticated evaluation schemes, all we can hope for is to reduce the inevitable subjectivity that follows. The purpose and practice of the evaluation of principals is likely to be viewed differently by national policy makers, school governors and managers, teachers, students, the parents of students and, of course, researchers, although there is likely to be a common core of interest in educational outcomes that is relevant for all.

Ginsberg and Thompson (1993, as cited in Lashway, 2003) maintain that principal evaluation is difficult because of the complexity and ambiguity of their work (Lashway, 2003). Moreover, the nature of their role is highly context sensitive and thus standard procedures could not work reliably in all situations. In a study in northern California interviews were obtained from 14 principals and 6 superintendents on the politics of principal evaluation (Davis & Hensley, 2000). Both principals and superintendents admitted that "most feedback was qualitative and subjective in nature" (p. 391). Furthermore, it is often argued that evaluation is not utilized in a productive and meaningful way (Reeves, 2004). For example, principal evaluation on the one hand might be wholly positive or lack any constructive feedback for improvement. On the other hand, there may be overly negative results which might cause resentment in those addressed.

In order to be able to respond to the contemporary demands of evaluation, we will address the following topics:

1. Why should school principals be evaluated? In essence, in this section we are trying to explore the culture of educational evaluation (e.g. system monitoring, school inspection) as well as the core purpose of the evaluation of school principals.

2. How are school principals evaluated? What are the means through which evaluation is conducted and by whom? What are the major evaluation methods utilized?
3. Critical review of evaluation practices. What do we know about what works and what does not in the case of principal evaluation?
4. Challenges for Evaluation Practices and Future Research on Evaluation. How does evaluation relate to principals' career stages? We conclude with some propositions for future research.

WHY SHOULD SCHOOL PRINCIPALS BE EVALUATED?

At the beginning of the 21st century, we are experiencing a rapidly changing environment, characterized by complexity and uncertainty. The only stable factor is continuous change. We have witnessed numerous changes in every domain of the human enterprise, from technology to biogenetics as well as huge demographic shifts, state interdependence and globalization, increased competition pressures, knowledge expansion. These societal changes have transformed the school environment into a more dynamic and complex one than in the past (Crow, 2006).

These changes, inevitably, have had a significant impact on education. Increased demands for effectiveness and improved quality have resulted in increased monitoring of the education system at various levels. Evaluation is necessary so that the proper improvements may be made at various levels of the system. For example, the Program for International Student Assessment (PISA), the Third International Mathematics and Science Study (TIMSS) and other ongoing assessments focus on the school level (e.g. school inspection) and on the individual level (teacher evaluation, student achievement). As part of the self-evaluation process, a profile of the school and the whole education system is created by assessing the strengths and weaknesses of each school. Evaluation also provides answers for students and parents in relation to problems facing the individual school and the school system. In addition, evaluation creates reports about the educational system and through these reports holds the school accountable to the community from which it gains support. Finally, evaluation satisfies statutory, normative or other regulations and, as a consequence, improves the whole learning experience of the children at school.

The widespread evaluation culture (seen on almost every governance level) therefore impacts the role of principals and their place in the school environment. Governments and local stakeholders exert ever greater pressures upon school leaders to perform. Communities question school programs, policies and procedures. Parents demand greater participation in school programs and in the day to day running of the schools. Legislators demand more widespread results and higher student achievement and performance standards. However, tensions result in circumstances where it is difficult to provide an effective response to societal expectations (Stevenson, 2006). Tensions can be understood as the result of the conflict between self-image and the expected social role. The factors contributing to these tensions include accountability demands, lack of sufficient resources, and the instability induced by an uncertain and complex environment.

In view of this complex, accountability-led school environment, where various pressures and tensions are evident, it is essential to be able to effectively evaluate the principal's performance. As Heck and Marcoulides (1996) report, there is a growing interest in accountability and principal evaluation. For example, in the United States, the No Child Left Behind (NCLB) legislation has raised the expectations for school units and principals and "has led to their greater public scrutiny" (Crow, 2006, p. 310).

Emphasis on school administrator accountability has changed the ways and processes through which districts evaluate their principals (White, Crooks & Melton, 2002). Moreover, accountability systems require evaluation to be aligned with the standards-based educational environment in order to accurately evaluate principals' effectiveness (Davis & Garner, 2003).

In general, one could argue that the purpose of evaluation is also reflected in the dichotomy of formative/summative evaluation. Formative evaluation is related to the principal's improvement and self-growth while summative evaluation relates primarily to purposes of retention, tenure or merit pay (Marcoulides, Larsen & Heck, 1995). Formative evaluation focuses on process as well as outcomes while summative evaluation is primarily outcomes-based (White, Crooks & Melton, 2002). Formative evaluation serves as a tool for further development while summative evaluation is mainly a tool for accountability (Davis & Garner, 2003). In short, formative evaluation of principals has the person as the main focus whereas summative evaluation has the system as the main focus. Therefore, the purpose of evaluations is twofold: to help a school leader improve (through the provision of constructive feedback) and to help the system make summative decisions about vacancies or rewards that ought to be given for exceptional performance.

In a study carried out in Alberta, Canada, Thomas, Holdaway and Ward (2000) investigated the policies and practice of evaluating principals, including the purpose for their evaluation. Data collection included documents, questionnaires and structured interviews. In phase one of the study, 67 superintendents were asked to provide relevant documents while in phase 2 all superintendents and 100 principals were asked to complete a questionnaire. However, only 63 (out of the 67) superintendents and 62 principals (out of the 100 selected) returned the questionnaire. In phase three of the study, interviews with 10 superintendents and 10 principals were conducted. The results indicated that the most common purpose found in the documents was to "promote professional growth and improvement" (84 per cent). Superintendents also rated the above statement in the questionnaire (mean 2.83 on a 3-point scale) as the most important purpose while the principals considered most important the statement "assess the extent to which expectations are being met" (mean 2.34). However, it must be noted that principals ranked "promote professional growth and improvement" (mean 2.18) as fourth in importance.

The study of Davis and Hensley (2000), investigating the politics of principal evaluation, revealed that most principals perceived the formal evaluation process as more summative in nature than formative. Having this in mind, they did not find the evaluation process useful in shaping their professional development and generally distrusted the evaluators' intentions. On the other hand, superintendents found that the evaluation process provided useful information about principal performance.

The main conclusion which can be drawn from these studies is that there is a gap between official or stated and perceived purposes of evaluation. While superintendents declare a focus primarily on formative purposes of evaluation in line with official documents, principals perceive evaluation more as summative or as a way to respond to external accountability demands. Ongoing consultation with principals regarding evaluation policy and practice and frequent monitoring of how far the process is in line with prestated and agreed upon processes may increase the effectiveness of evaluation.

In closing, it should be remembered that principals' evaluation practices can be used for different purposes. Firstly, they can serve during the selection process of qualified candidates for the principal's position. However, this issue is treated in detail in another chapter of this handbook. Secondly, principals can be evaluated while on the job in the form of a qualifications evaluation both in a summative and formative way.

HOW ARE SCHOOL PRINCIPALS EVALUATED?

Methods of Evaluation

What are the means through which evaluation is conducted and by whom? Different methods of evaluation have been utilized internationally for the evaluation of principals. Some of the most important ones will be presented in this section.

External evaluation at the systemic level can be exercised through:

1. Principal evaluation as part of the whole school evaluation,
2. Standards-based evaluation

External evaluation at the individual level can be exercised through:

1. Direct observation
2. Peer evaluation
3. Observation of simulated activities

Internal evaluation at the individual level can be exercised through:

1. Self-evaluation
2. Portfolio evaluation

Principal Evaluation as Part of the Whole School Evaluation

Evaluation can be focused on the whole school. Such evaluation is usually concerned more with academic results, ignoring other critical aspects of a school's life. Evaluation information will be used by policy-makers to make decisions about the allocation of resources to schools and whether to impose sanctions on low performing schools. In this case, the leader's performance is assessed alongside that of the school. Pashiardis and Orphanou (1999) suggest that evaluating schools and holding them accountable in relation to standardized scores might motivate principals and result in more enthusiastic and positive attitude towards educational outcomes. This was the main finding of a quantitative study on the perceptions of 115 elementary school teachers in Cyprus regarding their principals and their leadership styles. Cyprus as well as other countries do not have standardized exams and, therefore, principals do not really know if they are doing a good job, based on this criterion. It is interesting to note that in a qualitative study carried out by Pashiardis (1998), successful primary school principals indicated that they want to have standardized exams and to be compared with other schools.

Standards-Based Evaluation

It is important to note that accountability systems require evaluation to be aligned with the standards-based educational environment (if there are standards) in order to accurately evaluate principals' effectiveness (Davis & Garner, 2003). As Philips (2003) further reports, standards-based qualification systems are becoming increasingly popular in an effort to raise the skills of current and future employees. The Interstate Leaders' Licensure Consortium (ISLLC) Indicators (Council of Chief State School Officers, 1996) and the National Standards for Headteachers

(Department for Education and Skills, 2004) are quite popular in the US and the UK respectively. In the United States, a district or state may use a set of standards such as the ISLLC and decide upon levels of performance (Lashway, 2003). For instance, an evaluation academy design was developed by the Region VII Education Service Center in Kilgore, Texas, designed to provide standards-based evaluation profiles to participants (White, Crooks & Melton, 2002). The academy focused on making principals examine and clearly understand the school leadership standards in order to be able to effectively analyze their own performance.

Direct Observation

Marcoulides, Larsen and Heck (1995) maintain that different means of evaluation, including direct observation can be used to evaluate the leaders' progress. Direct observation involves the evaluation of leadership behavior in real school settings. In the state of Kentucky, principals are evaluated annually through observation of their on-the-job-performance and review of progress in achieving their professional growth targets (Browne-Ferrigno & Fusarelli, 2005). More specifically, in a study conducted by Thomas, Holdaway and Ward (2000) already mentioned, direct observation was regarded as important by five superintendents (of ten) and four principals (of ten). However, one superintendent remarked that this source of information is not useful in the case of paying a limited number of visits per year to each school.

Peer Evaluation

Peer evaluation constitutes a useful way of evaluating a principal's progress. This form of evaluation rests on the assumption that the effectiveness of a leader depends mainly on how others see him/her (Pashiardis, 2001). Principals acquire knowledge from many different sources (Sackney & Walker, 2006). Teachers, other school principals and their superintendents can take the role of a peer or a friend, evaluate the principal's progress and provide him/her with critical feedback. This was reported by Sackney and Walker (2006) in an examination of a number of Canadian studies showing how beginning principals learn to build capacity in learning communities. Discussing plans, problems and actions with critical friends, the principal can gain constructive support in becoming a reflective thinker and improving his/her performance (Quong, 2006). Critical friends bring an external perspective highlighting what may not be apparent to insiders (Earl & Katz, 2002). They facilitate reflection on school issues, remind the leaders of what they have achieved and to what extent, and help them move towards the next goals.

Evidence so far indicates that principals are quite favorably disposed towards the use of the peer evaluation method. They appreciate its value and contribution towards their professional development and progress. However, as Smith (2002) points out, successful principals take advantage of a critical friend if they are convinced that he or she is there to support and not to undermine the leader.

Observation of Simulated Activities

Evaluation can also take the form of observing a leader's simulated practice. Simulated practice can be identified in problem-based evaluation such as responding to case studies (Wong, 2004). Wong (2004), referring to this practice in schools in Hong Kong, points out that this is an important way of appraising principals' knowledge and skills. Porter et al. (2005) recommend the use of vignettes, a case-based evaluation in which principals are required to respond to a problem or dilemma of a scenario or short case. Rubrics are developed so as to evaluate leadership dimensions based on the principals' responses. This is an opportunity to evaluate the leader's ability in applying knowledge and strategies to specific problems. However, evaluation through simulated practice may not relate directly to actual everyday performance. Yet, when used in combination with other evaluation methods validity can be greatly enhanced.

Self-Evaluation

Supervision of the principal's development can be self-monitored by the principals in order to judge their effectiveness in various roles such as personnel management and evaluation, conflict resolution, and public relations (Marcoulides, Larsen & Heck, 1995; Johnson & Rose, 1997). Vaughan (2003) proposes self-evaluation as a way to improve performance. The principal may be seen as a continuous learner who focuses not only on the tasks but also on the processes underlying the tasks. The principal becomes a "skilled self-organized" individual who engages in a "learning to learn dialogue" (Vaughan, 2003, p. 379). At the same time, it is important to highlight that the process of self-evaluation takes time, effort and patience (Johnson & Rose, 1997).

White, Crooks and Melton (2002) conducted a field study in a leadership assessment academy in Texas which focused on providing formative, self- assessment profiles to participants. Data were collected during ten three-day sessions over a period of four years through participant observation, document analysis, questionnaires and interviews as well as through case simulations. Five authentic assessment methods were used:

- *Business interviews*: The participant conducts an interview of a community businessperson so as to assess the principals' skills in applying professional knowledge to the business sector.
- *Case Simulation*: This is a technology-integrated simulation approach which examines complex leadership issues. The assessment provides information about participants' reflective thinking and decision-making skills.
- *Basic Leadership Inventory*: This method provides important information determined by the school faculty on the participants' leadership ability in areas which include leadership behavior, communication skills and organizational management.
- *In-basket writing*: This method focuses on assessing the participant in solving specific problems faced by the school leader. The participants review an in-basket case study and write a letter responding to the case.
- *Student-performance skills:* This object is used to assess the participants' skills in analyzing student achievement data sets and generating development plans for school academic success.

Commenting on the design dynamics of the academy, White, Crooks and Melton (2002) point out that the process of self-assessment increases responsibility for one's own performance and establishes a collaborative relationship between assessors and assessees. Also, the multiplicity of assessment methods and reflective lenses provides participants with multiple perspectives in analyzing their strengths and weaknesses and informing their professional development plans. On the whole, the academy gives special emphasis to assisting principals to cultivate reflective thinking and mental processes associated with effective school leadership.

In the context of self-evaluation practices, Robbins and Alvy (2003) further stress the importance of keeping a self-reflection journal and using it as a tool for evaluating one's own job and bringing greater insight to the experiences and problems faced at school. In the long-term, this can take the form of a portfolio.

Portfolio

A portfolio is a "conceptual container" in which principals place artifacts to document their accomplishments (Lashway, 2003). According to Johnson and Rose (1997), a professional portfolio could be used by administrators to demonstrate their leadership capabilities, to reflect on their learning and to set future goals. The principal identifies a goal and gathers evidence to show that there has been progress towards the desired outcome. Evidence might include journal entries, parent newsletters, staff meeting notes, photographs of classroom activities, records of dropout rates, test scores, handbooks and whatever else the principal considers important data (Lashway, 2003; Robbins & Alvy, 2003). The development of a portfolio is a valuable tool for reflecting on one's professional growth during a particular school year or over one's career (Robbins & Alvy, 2003).

Johnston and Thomas (2005) conducted qualitative research on the usefulness of a four-year portfolio evaluation system for beginning principals which was field tested in the state of Ohio. The Portfolio Assessment for School Leaders was designed by the Interstate School Leaders Licensure Consortium and the Educational Testing Service (ETS). It is important to note that the portfolio components were aligned with the ISLLC standards. The participants were 26 principals who completed the portfolio between September 1999 and January 2002. Data were collected through focus group interviews, phone interviews, surveys, the principals' completed portfolios, annual regional evaluation reports and regional meeting minutes. Almost half of the principals (12 of 26) mentioned that they benefited from the portfolio process. They reflected on problems and developed new initiatives guided by their work. On the whole, the principals reported the existence of a "reciprocal process" between their portfolio work and their development as leaders. On the other hand, there were those principals (7 of 26) who did not find the portfolio meaningful to their practice and saw it only as extra work. In the middle, were the remainder of the principals (7 of 26) who valued the portfolio only at the end of the process. The research also revealed that those who valued the portfolio process most were part of a "supportive social network of professional development" (p. 383). This indicates that if portfolio evaluation is used as a means to professional development then it has the potential to be a learning tool and not just a tool for complying with policy demands. In other words, its real value lies in serving the formative purposes of evaluation.

Based on the above, one may conclude that different means or methods can be used to evaluate a principal's performance. Each one is characterized by its own advantages or drawbacks. However, no single method seems to outweigh the others. In fact, a combination of methods responding to a specific purpose seems to be the ideal process.

Composition of the Evaluation Team

As far as the composition of the evaluation team is concerned, it is widely accepted that there should be multiple sources of information (Heck & Marcoulides, 1996; Johnson & Rose, 1997; Lashway, 2003). Teachers, students, parents and members of the general public depend on the principal for leadership and direction. Therefore, they should be given an equal opportunity to evaluate the principal's performance. According to a study by the NAESP (Doud & Keller, cited in Lashway, 2003), there is an increasing tendency to involve parents, teachers and principals themselves in evaluation procedures (Lashway, 2003). A "360 degree" model is proposed by Porter, Murphy, Goldring, Elliott & Linn (2005) in which leaders, teachers and other stakeholders rate specific behaviors in terms of their frequency or importance. In a study conducted by Thomas, Holdaway and Ward (2000) in Alberta, Canada superintendents and principals stressed the need for more stakeholder involvement in evaluation processes.

It should be borne in mind that role makes a difference in perceptions about performance (Heck & Marcoulides, 1996). This was one of the findings of a multilevel analysis evaluating the principal's performance. Principals and teachers of a sample of 56 schools responded to a questionnaire comprising 34 administrative actions. The results showed that principals rated themselves higher than teachers did, suggesting that school role makes a difference in evaluating leadership. However, if the views of the principal do not match the views of the staff then it seems that there may be problems and dysfunctionalities in the day-to-day operations of the school (Pashiardis, Savvides & Tsiakkiros, 2005). The degree of congruence of the principal-teacher perceptions could be derived by analyzing the results from leadership effectiveness questionnaires, semi-structured interviews and shadowing. In the case that other stakeholders' views are investigated, the methodology used may need to be sensitive to the role of the person providing the evaluation. For example, the state of Kentucky has established School-Based Decision Making Councils (Browne-Ferrigno & Fusarelli, 2005). These Councils are entitled to select principals from a number of candidates recommended by superintendents. Also, in Hong Kong the School Management Committee (SMC) is responsible for hiring people to the post of principal. The government only sets minimum academic and professional qualifications. The selection criteria, procedures and panel membership are determined by the SMC. However, a close relationship with the sponsoring body which appoints the SMC will be likely to affect the success in securing a principalship position (Wong & Ng, 2003).

CRITICAL REVIEW OF EVALUATION PRACTICES

What do we know about what works and what doesn't in the case of principal evaluation? In this section we provide a critical review of the different evaluation methods as presented in the previous section. The evidence concerning what works and what doesn't is indeed scarce and inconsistent. Moreover, it is always contextual. In any case, we offer some of the major criticisms which can be found in the literature on principal evaluation. The criticisms mainly revolve around two major areas:

- Content/Process/Output aspects of evaluation
- Methodological aspects of evaluation

First we proceed with a more in-depth examination of the content, procedural and instrumental aspects of evaluation.

Content/Process/Output Aspects of Evaluation

Firstly, standards-based systems offer a number of benefits for evaluating principals. Such specific systems can hold principals accountable through the use of indicators of school leadership (Kimball, 2006). Performance evaluation includes specific leadership indicators or different levels of performance as well as guidance on how to evaluate principals in relation to standards

(Heck & Marcoulides, 1996). As a result, the evaluation data may become more accurate and more reliable.

On the other hand, there are those who strongly criticize the use of standards-based evaluation systems or indicate their inadequacies. More specifically, Reeves (2004) highlights that standards in many evaluation instruments are unclear, incoherent or unrealistic. He criticizes standards that do not explicitly state expectations and stresses that only scarce data exist on the effectiveness of standards as tools for improving leadership evaluation procedures. Standards are also criticized for not being responsive to the context of the particular school in which a principal is placed. A sound evaluation system would be underpinned by social systems theory, which suggests that there is a close relationship of interdependence between the environment and the system. Consequently, standards should take into account the local and wider context, in short, all those factors which might influence the principal's functioning. This stance is taken by Heck and Marcoulides (1996) who maintain that performance evaluation should be based upon the local school setting. For example, both school level data and student achievement affect the way principals are perceived to be leading. Therefore, if comparisons are to be made about principal performance across schools, a weighting system may be needed to accommodate the influence of contextual factors.

Gronn and Ribbins (2003) suggest that the potential inexperience and unfamiliarity of school councils with selection criteria and evaluation processes might create a gap between national standards and local choices. Davis and Garner (2003) agree that "one size fits all" may not be appropriate for all cases and therefore may render evaluation a counterproductive process. As an alternative, each organization may establish its own leadership domains according to its own culture and needs (Reeves, 2004).

A criticism aimed specifically at the ISLLC standards in the United States is that they underemphasize certain aspects of effective leadership practices. These include the leaders' participation in curriculum development, the promotion of effective instructional and student evaluation practices, the recognition of individual and school achievements, and the leaders' response to the context-specific needs of teachers, students, and other stakeholders (Waters, Marzano & McNulty, 2003; Davis, Darling-Hammond, LaPointe & Meyerson, 2005). However, Murphy (2005) responds by claiming that leadership practice is complex and context-dependent and thus it is impossible to provide a full, definitive list of competencies. The standards were developed "to direct not determine action". Success criteria can be contextualized in accordance with school level data, existing school performance, and the principal's career stage (Murphy, 2005).

Leithwood, Aitken and Jantzi (2001) point out that process measures can detect unsatisfactory features of a school's functioning, allowing one to change these features for school improvement. These processes can be used to demonstrate a school's accountability. Educators have control over these processes in contrast to the standards against which outcomes are compared. Outcomes are influenced by many variables such as an individual's background and the wider community. In a study conducted in Alberta, Canada, 32 out of the 63 principals noted that school and community characteristics influenced principal evaluation, for instance "the nature of the school, the type of the students, the spiritual atmosphere in the school, and the size, culture, language, and unique needs of the community" (Thomas, Holdaway & Ward, 2000, p. 231). It is therefore important to acknowledge the particular context or situation in relation to leadership behavior.

Student achievement is also used to evaluate the principal's performance (Scheerens & Witziers, 2005; Reeves, 2004). Nevertheless, one-dimensional evaluations based only on test scores are usually flawed. More specifically, it is argued that leadership is a necessary but not sufficient condition for high academic achievement (Marcoulides, Larsen & Heck, 1995). Evaluation based upon student achievement may place too much emphasis on test scores when the principals may not have direct control over all the elements which contribute to these (Heck & Marcoulides, 1996; Kythreotis & Pashiardis, 2006; Usdan, McCloud & Podmostko, 2000).

Standardized tests cannot give a complete picture of learning (Johnson & Rose, 1997). Smith (2002) argues that standardized tests cannot be regarded as authentic evaluation since they cannot represent the complex, real world of school. Hoy and Miskel (2005) also contend that evaluating organizational effectiveness only in terms of student achievement underestimates the importance of the social systems theory, which advocates that school organizations represent open systems with inputs, processes and outputs. School performance should therefore be evaluated in the whole context of a school's operation and not just student achievement (Kellaghan & Greany, 2001; Reeves, 2004). Similarly, Vaughan (2003) and Smith (2002) indicate that performance evaluation needs to address processes as well as outcomes.

Methodological Aspects of Evaluation

It can be observed that the summative purposes of evaluation attract more attention than the formative ones (White, Crooks & Melton, 2002; Usdan, McCloud & Podmostko, 2000) and therefore more criticism. According to White, Crooks and Melton (2002) principal evaluation is characterized by top-down processes for the purposes of reward or punishment rather than for professional development. The same stance is taken by Usdan, McCloud and Podmostko (2000) who maintain that principal evaluation rarely provides opportunities for reflection and professional growth. Nevertheless, effective evaluation also needs to address the professional growth of the administrator (Davis & Garner, 2003). In this context, both the evaluator and the evaluatee have a responsibility for reflection, analysis and improvement (Reeves, 2004). As Vaughan (2003) indicates, the principal may be seen as a continuous learner who focuses not only on the tasks but also on the processes underlying the tasks. The conditions and processes could more effectively be improved through the use of formative methods of evaluation. Thomas, Holdaway and Ward (2000) also report that the majority of principals and superintendents who responded to their questionnaire desire to move towards formative evaluation.

Reliability and validity of principal effectiveness measures are also critical (Heck & Marcoulides, 1996; Marcoulides, Larsen & Heck, 1995; Davis & Garner, 2003). Any evaluation model should be able to yield valid and reliable data about the principal's performance. Validity refers to the extent that the model measures what it is designed to measure. Reliability refers to the consistency of the results when performance is repeatedly measured. According to Reeves (2004), if five different superintendents evaluate a principal in five different ways, then such a process is not consistent and therefore unreliable. Reliability is suggested to be the key to fairness and therefore candidates must be treated in the same way.

Also contested is the degree to which the evaluation of leadership has been undermined by the paucity of valid tools for measuring leadership performance (Porter et al., 2005). Expert panels have sometimes been employed in order to review the specific instruments to be used for evaluation. Porter et al. (2005) propose a Leadership Evaluation System (LAS) utilizing a multicomponent system of evaluating leadership behaviors. These components include a set of behavior-rating scales, scoring rubrics, vignettes, logs, and collections of evidence. This combination of a number of evaluation methods may enhance the quality of information and the validity of evaluating the principal's performance. Validity increases by using multiple data sources and by examining the multilevel nature of organizations (Heck & Marcoulides, 1996). As far as reliability is concerned, it may be increased by carrying out repeated measurements over time and taking into account local school data.

Finally, an evaluation instrument requires field-testing (Reeves, 2004) against a wide range of leaders, beginning principals and veterans. During the field testing period, the use of at least two evaluators conducting independent evaluations of a particular leader allows comparison. If they come to different conclusions, the instrument appears to exhibit ambiguity and signifies that leadership domains and performance descriptions are not specific enough. During the field testing period, the leaders may also evaluate themselves and their results should be compared to those of the evaluators. When there is agreement about a performance level, then the leadership domains and performance specifications can be judged reliable. The field test will provide feedback about the leadership evaluation process before it is implemented at the school level. In this way evaluation results will be more accurate, fairer and more useful to the evaluation team and the principal him/herself.

After having reviewed some of the major criticisms of principal evaluation, at this point, it is important to gain a deeper understanding of the career trajectories of teachers as they potentially move towards, into and through the principalship. This is important, as school leaders may need a differentiated approach to their evaluation, depending on their career position.

CHALLENGES FOR EVALUATION PRACTICES AND FUTURE RESEARCH ON EVALUATION

The main aim of this section is to explore what we should know and what we should do, depending on career point. We conclude with some propositions for future research.

Challenges for Evaluation Practices

The previous review of the literature indicated that the role of the principal has become complex and demanding. This is the result of: (a) external, societal, and economic changes, (b) the growing accountability movement, and (c) pressures for raising school performance. In this changing context of leadership practice, a shortage of qualified candidates for the principal's position is observed in numerous parts of the world (Stevenson, 2006; Davis et al., 2005; Usdan, McCloud & Podmostko, 2000). Thus, it is necessary to provide support both for the aspiring as well as for serving principals in order to attract them to the profession and help them to achieve increased effectiveness.

Leadership evaluation is a significant aspect of a principal's development and a currently evolving field of research (Porter et al., 2005). The improvement of the principal's performance is a central issue concerning educators and policy makers. One aspect of the issue which attracts much attention is the debate about the nature of the motivation related to a specific career stage. Motivation is defined as "an internal state that stimulates, directs and maintains behaviour" (Hoy & Miskel, 2005, p. 157). According to Vaughan (2003), performance-related pay has become increasingly popular. This means that high performance is rewarded with increased pay or extra money to spend for school purposes (Rasch, 2004; Heck & Marcoulides, 1996; Hoy & Miskel, 2005). For example, in Cincinnati, Ohio, the administrators' pay raises partly depend on whether they achieve high student performance. However, when evaluation is used to determine pay-for-performance, fear and competition emerge. It is arguable that this kind of reward system suppresses the employee's internal motives and morale (Vaughan, 2003). According to Earl and Katz (2002), extrinsic motivation results only in short-term, superficial outcomes. Alternatively, intrinsic motivation could more effectively motivate principals to improve their performance (Rasch, 2004; Earl & Katz, 2002). This is partly because sanctions or praises are not effective; it is in fact the activity itself which rewards the principal's performance to a great extent. Of course, depending on the career stage, pay-for-performance or other motivation techniques could affect him/her to a different extent; this will vary amongst individuals and amongst different cultures.

This is why, in part, principal evaluation schemes need to be closely aligned with the socialization phases or the various career stages of a principal from preparation prior to the principalship, to entry, development, achieving autonomy, and finally the moment of exit. Identification of career stages produces profiles for principal's trajectory (Weindling & Dimmock, 2006). When an individual principal's behavior is compared to these collective profiles, the degree of deviation can be traced and interpreted accordingly. The knowledge of the stages through which principals move can significantly inform the practices of evaluation. Nevertheless, the achievement of the desired objectives for school improvement requires that realistic career frames are created for school leaders. Too many ambitious expectations may lead to the leaders' physical and professional burn out.

Learning to be a principal is a continuous developmental process of socialization (Weindling & Dimmock, 2006). According to Merton's (1963) socialization theory, it is constituted by two overlapping phases (Weindling & Dimmock, 2006, p. 334):

- Professional Socialization refers to learning what it means to be a principal, from personal experience and formal training prior to taking up the post.
- Organizational Socialization refers to the knowledge, values and behaviors which are required to perform a particular role within the organization.

Hart distinguishes three categories of socialization (Cheung & Walker, 2006, p. 392):

- Encounter, adjustment, stabilization.
- Anticipation, accommodation, role management.
- Confrontation, clarity, location.

Weindling (1999) adapted the categories to describe a three-stage model of socialization (Cheung & Walker, 2006). The first stage includes the processes of encounter, anticipation or confrontation. In this stage, a new principal learns to make sense of the new environment. The second stage consists of adjustment, accommodation and clarity. In this stage, the principal tries to "fit in", creates interpersonal relations with school stakeholders and learns to manage ambiguous situations. The third stage consists of stabilization of the principal in the new position.

In addition, the National Foundation for Educational Research (NFER) Secondary Heads Project conducted by Weindling and Earley (1987, cited in Weindling & Dimmock, 2006, pp. 335–337) indicated that no matter how good the preparation of the principals is, they will have to go through a transition phase during which there is an attempt to make sense of the particular organizational situation (Weindling & Dimmock, 2006). Weindling (1999) used the results of the NFER study and other authors in order to create a model of stages of transition through the principalship (headship) (Weindling & Dimmock, 2006, pp. 335–337):

- Stage 0   Preparation prior to headship.
- Stage 1   Entry and encounter (first months). This is the beginning of organizational socialization at which the new head attempts to make sense of the new situation.
- Stage 2   Taking hold (three to 12 months). The new head attempts to challenge the status quo and decide on the new priorities.
- Stage 3   Reshaping (second year). This is the period of implementing major changes in the school.
- Stage 4   Refinement (years three to four). Previous changes are refined.
- Stage 5   Consolidation (years five to seven). Consolidation of previous changes.
- Stage 6   Plateau (years eight and onwards). After a seven years period the heads have initiated most of the changes they wanted and they have reached a plateau.

The NFER data show that principals were less likely to reach a plateau if they had moved to a second headship (Weindling & Dimmock, 2006). The latter would move to Stage one and then move at different rates through the rest of the stages. The NFER data suggest that primary principals can move through the stages more quickly due to the smaller size of primary schools and their less hierarchical structures.

As principals move through the various stages of their career, their evaluation needs change considerably. Therefore, evaluation should be differentiated in such a way as to respond to the needs and career profiles of the specific phase the principal is experiencing. Evaluation should distinguish between the pre-principalship stage, the initial stage, the seasoned stage, and the exiting principalship stage. Pre-principalship evaluation should take into account the Professional Socialization stage as described by Merton (1963) , which is similar to Stage 0 of Weindling (1999). Initial Principalship evaluation should address the challenges faced by beginning principals including the Organizational Socialization stage as described by Merton and Stages 2 and 3 described by Weindling as well as the latter's adapted model of encounter, anticipation or confrontation. Seasoned principalship evaluation should be informed by Weindling's Stages 4 and 5 as well as the model of adjustment, accommodation and clarity. The exiting principalship evaluation should take into account Stage 6 as well as Weindling's recommendation on the stabilization, role management and location model.

Recommendations for Future Research

As Lashway (2003) points out, research on principal evaluation is still inadequate. Effective leadership evaluation has been notably absent. Most leadership evaluations may be "infrequent, late, unhelpful, and largely a source of administrative bother" (Reeves, 2004, p. x). Taking into account these observations as well as the findings from the literature review, we offer a number of recommendations relating to future research on principal evaluation. The use of a differentiated form of evaluation should, in every case, help principals cope with tensions between personal perceptions and outside demands (Cheung & Walker, 2006). Hence, principals can become more successful in building adaptive confidence in themselves and other members of the learning community as they enter uncertain situations, learn from their mistakes and adapt as they move through their career (Sackney & Walker, 2006).

As far as leadership competencies are concerned, there are specific trends traced while examining the standards adopted by a number of countries. These involve creating a vision, distributing leadership, acting in an ethical manner, using information technologies, and collaborating with the wider community. According to Hage and Powers (cited in Crow, 2006), the evaluation criteria for principals in the post-industrial era should emphasize creativity and innovation in contrast to the criteria of efficiency and quantity of work which characterized the rationality of the industrial society (Crow, 2006). In the new knowledge society the principals have to create school environments which respond to the demands of life-long learning (Crow, 2006). They have to respond to the expanding technology needs of teachers and students and support an inclusive learning environment. Nevertheless, the success criteria should be contextualized in accordance with influencing factors such as the school level, the existing school performance, and the principal's career stage (Murphy, 2005). Thus, it becomes an indispensable need for policymakers and public education officials to collect information regarding the supply, effectiveness and changing roles, as well as career needs, of principals (Usdan, McCloud & Podmostko, 2000). Therefore, more research is needed in the area of career progression of principals and their needs as they evolve.

It is also important to include dispositions as well as behavioral standards for evaluation (Hill, 2005; Cheng, 2002; Murphy, 2005). This is a necessary provision since leadership practice and evaluation is influenced by values and beliefs. More comparative research is needed in this area in order to establish the universal and the contextual.

Reliability and validity of principal effectiveness measures are also central. As a result, evaluation should examine the appropriate skills for the principal's role, be flexible enough to allow for variations in how the role is perceived, and include multiple data sources (Heck & Marcoulides, 1996). Multilevel data analysis can be effectively used. However, as Heck and Marcoulides (1996, p. 12) highlight, "any evaluation model that tries to capture all of the subtleties of the role and operationalize all of the day-to-day activities of the principal is doomed to failure". Browne-Ferrigno and Fusarelli (2005) believe that research needs to address the issue of whether high-stakes accountability has made the job too demanding. Longitudinal and cross-case inquires are needed on the implementation of standards for the evaluation of principals as well as their influence on student achievement.

In summary, evaluation is not just the design of a plan or process; it involves the creation of a new culture. It is, in fact, "the result of gradual steps that serve to build trust in the process and confidence in the ability to succeed in it" (Hill, 2005, p. 29). It is therefore crucial to try to build such a culture of evaluation for the sake of the educational system as a whole. As Usdan, McCloud and Podmostko (2000) indicate, state and local school systems, higher education, businesses and principals themselves will need to work together to find ways to support the profession and to ensure enhanced quality and improved results.

In conclusion, we would like to stress once more that there is an urgent need for education systems worldwide to revisit the issue of principal evaluation. This position is based on research evidence showing that the principal's role is indeed crucial for students' improved academic achievement. Therefore, there is a need for new evaluation systems which are based on meritocracy. Such an evaluation needs to be systematic and must examine who produces excellent results and why. These new systems need to provide us with the ability to differentiate between excellent and mediocre principals and therefore reward those who perform best and, at the same time, provide the necessary professional growth activities for those who do not perform as well. We need a variety of arguably revolutionary principal evaluation systems to help transform educational systems into modern and open ones able to react effectively to the challenges posed to education around the globe. These new evaluation schemes need to provide answers to crucial questions, such as: how do we reward and differentiate better principals from not so good ones? And how do we connect these rewards with enhanced student learning?

Finally, there is a need to review and refine the existing systems of evaluation. The issue of the quality, functionality and effectiveness of any evaluation system should be the concern of all stakeholders, especially when important decisions are made regarding the professional future of principals. Consequently, evaluation itself should become the object of evaluation. This concept of meta-evaluation, first introduced by Scriven (1995), involves the attempt to control and understand the way it functions, with the objective of identifying the problems which might occur and taking corrective action for their early treatment. According to Pashiardis, Savvides and Tsiakkiros (2005), the implementation of meta-evaluation procedures is necessary in order to secure that:

- the wider objectives and the more specific goals of the evaluation are achieved;
- the proposed evaluation procedures are correctly implemented;
- the evaluation is valid and reliable.

Through such meta-evaluation it is hoped that those who undertake the implementation of principal evaluation will realize that they are expected to exhibit enhanced responsibility knowing that their work itself will be evaluated.

REFERENCES

Browne-Ferrigno, T. & Fusarelli, B. C. J. (2005). The Kentucky Principalship: Model of School Leadership Reconfigured by ISLLC Standards and Reform Policy Implementation. *Leadership and Policy in Schools, 4*, 127–156.

Cheng, Y. C. (2002). *The Changing Context of School Leadership: Implications for Paradigm Shift*. In K. Leithwood & P. Hallinger (Eds.). *Second International Handbook of Educational Leadership and Administration* (pp. 485–518). Dordrecht: Kluwer Academic.

Cheung, R. B. & Walker, A. (2006). Inner Worlds and Outer Limits: The Formation of Beginning School Principals in Hong-Kong. *Journal of Educational Administration, 44*(4), 389–407.

Council of Chief State School Officers (1996). *Interstate School leaders Licensure Consortium: Standards for School Leaders*. Washington, DC: Council of Chief State School Officers.

Crow, G. M. (2006). Complexity and the Beginning Principal in the United States: Perspectives on Socialization. *Journal of Educational Administration, 44*(4) 310–325.

Davis, E. E. & Garner, E. (2003). *Current Practices of Evaluating Superintendents and Principals in a Standards-Based Environment*. Technical Report 2002–2005. Pocatello, ID: ICEE.

Davis, S., Darling-Hammond, L., LaPointe, M. & Meyerson, D. (2005). *School Leadership Study - Developing Successful Principals. Review of Research*. Stanford, CA: SELI.

Davis, S. H. & Hensley, P. H. (2000). The Politics of Principal Evaluation. *Journal of Personnel Evaluation in Education, 13*(4), 383–403.

Department for Education and Skills (2004). *National Standards for Headteachers*. Nottingham: DfES.

Earl, L. & Katz, S. (2002). Leading Schools in a Data-Rich World. In K. Leithwood & P. Hallinger (Eds.). *Second International Handbook of Educational Leadership and Administration* (pp. 485–518). Dordrecht: Kluwer Academic.

Gronn, P. & Ribbins, P. (2003). Evolving Formations: The Making of Secondary School Principals on Selected Small Islands. In P. Pashiardis & P. Ribbins (Eds.). *International Studies in Educational Administration. Special Issue on the Making of Secondary School Principals on Selected Small Islands, 31*(2), 76–94.

Heck, R. H. & Marcoulides, G. A. (1996). The Assessment of Principal Performance: A. Multilevel Evaluation Approach. *Journal of Personnel Evaluation in Education, 10*, 11–28.

Hill, J. S. (2005). Developing a Culture of Assessment: Insights from Theory and Experience. *Journal of Political Science Education, 1*, 29–37.

Hoy, K. & Miskel, I. (2005). *Educational Administration. Theory, Research and Practice*. New York: McGraw Hill.

Johnson, N. J. & Rose, L. M. (1997). *Portfolios. Clarifying, Constructing and Enhancing.* Lancaster, PA: Technomic Publishing Company.

Johnston, M. & Thomas, M. (2005). Riding the wave of administrator accountability: a portfolio approach. *Journal of Educational Administration, 43*(4), 368–386.

Kellaghan, T. & Greany, V. (2001). *Using assessment to improve the quality of education.* Paris: International Institute for Educational Planning (UNESCO).

Kimball, S. M. (2006). *Case Study of the Initiation of Standards-Based Principal Performance Evaluation in Washoe County School District.* Consortium for Policy research in Education, Wisconsin Center for Education Research, University of Wisconsin-Madison.

Kythreotis, A. & Pashiardis, P. (2006). Exploring Leadership Role in School Effectiveness and the Validation of Models of Principals' Effects on Students' Achievement. CCEAM Conference "Recreating Linkages between Theory and Praxis in Educational Leadership". Nicosia, Cyprus, 12–17 October, 2006.

Lashway, L. (2003). Improving Principal Evaluation. Clearinghouse on Educational Policy Management. *Eric Digest* 172.

Leithwood, K., Aitken, R. & Jantzi, D. (2001). *Making Schools Smarter. A System for Monitoring School and District Progress.* Thousand Oaks, CA: Corwin Press.

Marcoulides, G. A., Larsen, T. J. & Heck, R. H. (1995). Examining the Generalizability of a Leadership Model: Issues for Assessing Administrator Performance. *International Journal of Educational Management, 9*(6), 4–9.

Merton, R. (1963). *Social Theory and Social Structure.* New York: The Free Press.

Murphy, J. (2005). Unpacking the Foundations of ISLLC Standards and Addressing Concerns in the Academic Community. *Educational Administration Quarterly, 41*(1), 154–191.

Pashiardis, P. (1998). Researching the Characteristics of Effective Primary School Principals in Cyprus. A Qualitative Approach. *Educational Management and Administration, 26*(2), 117–130.

Pashiardis, P. (2001). Secondary Principals in Cyprus: The Views of the Principal Versus the Views of the Teachers- A Case Study. *International Studies in Educational Administration, 29*(3), 11–23.

Pashiardis, P. & Orphanou, S. (1999). An Insight Into Elementary Principalship in Cyprus: The Teachers' Perspective. *International Journal of Educational Management, 13*(5), 241–251.

Pashiardis, P., Savvides I. & Tsiakkiros, A. (2005). Meta-Evaluation of the Proposed Systems. In P. Pashiardis, I. Savvides & A. Tsiakkiros (Ed.). *The Evaluation of Teachers' Work: from Theory to Praxis* (pp. 343–349). Athens: Ellin Publishing House (in Greek).

Philips, D. (2003). Lessons from New Zealand's National Qualifications Framework. *Journal of Education and Work, 16*(3), 289–304.

Porter, A., Murphy, J., Goldring, E., Elliott, S. & Linn, R. L. (2005). A Proposal to Develop and Test an Education Leadership Performance Assessment. Report Submitted to the Wallace Foundation by Vanderbilt University.

Quong, T. (2006). Asking the Hard Questions: Being a Beginning Principal in Australia. *Journal of Educational Administration, 44*(4), 376–388.

Rasch, L. (2004). Employee Performance Appraisal and the 95/5 Rule. *Community College Journal of Research and Practice, 28*, 407–414.

Reeves, D. B. (2004). *Assessing Educational Leaders. Evaluating Performance for Improved Individual and Organizational Results.* Thousand Oaks, CA: Corwin Press.

Robbins, P. & Alvy, H.B. (2003). *The Principal's Companion.* Thousand Oaks, CA: Corwin Press.

Sackney, L. & Walker, K. (2006). Canadian Perspectives on Beginning Principals: Their Role in Building Capacity for Learning Communities. *Journal of Educational Administration, 44*(4), 341–358.

Scheerens J. & Witziers, B. (2005). *Educational Leadership and Student Performance.* University of Twente: Department of Educational Organisation and Management.

Scriven, M. (1995). A unified theory approach to teacher evaluation. *Studies in Educational Evaluation, 21*, 111–129.

Smith, W.J. (2002). *School Leadership and Self-Assessment: Guiding the Agenda for Change.* In K. Leithwood & P. Hallinger (Ed.). *Second International Handbook of Educational Leadership and Administration* (pp. 485–518). Dordrecht: Kluwer Academic.

Stevenson, H. (2006). Moving Towards, Into and Through Principalship: Developing a Framework for Researching the Career Trajectories of School Leaders. *Journal of Educational Administration, 44*(4), 408–420.

Thomas, D. W., Holdaway, E. A. & Ward, K. L. (2000). Policies and Practices Involved in the Evaluation of School Principals. *Journal of Personnel Evaluation in Education, 14*(3), 215–240.

Usdan, M., McCloud, B. & Podmostko, M. (2000). *Leadership for Student Learning: Reinventing the Principalship. School Leadership for the 21st Century Initiative. A Report of the Task Force on the Principalship.* Washington, DC: Institute for Educational Leadership.

Vaughan, S. (2003). Performance: Self as the Principal Evaluator. *Human Resource Development International, 6*(3), 371–385.

Weindling, D. (1999). Stages of Leadership. In T. Bush, L. Bell, R. Bolam, R. Glatter & P. Ribbins (Eds.), *Educational Management: Redefining Theory, Policy and Practice* (pp. 90–101). London: Paul Chapman.

Weindling, D. & Dimmock, C. (2006). Sitting in the "Hot Seat". New Headteachers in the UK. *Journal of Educational Administration, 44*(4), 326–340.

White, D. R., Crooks, S. M. & Melton, J. K. (2002). Design Dynamics of a Leadership Assessment Academy: Principal Self-Assessment Using Research and Technology. *Journal of Personnel Evaluation in Education, 16*(1), 45–61.

Wong, P. (2004). The Professional Development of School Principals: Insights from Evaluating a Programme in Hong-Kong. *School leadership and Management, 24*(2), 139–162.

Wong, K. & Ng, H. (2003). On Hong Kong: The Making of Secondary School Principals. In P. Pashiardis & P. Ribbins (Ed.). *International Studies in Educational Administration, Special Issue on the Making of Secondary School Principals on Selected Small, 31*(2), 35–53.

Waters, T. Marzano, R. J. & McNulty, B. (2003). *Balanced Leadership: What 30 Years of Research Tells Us About the Effect of Leadership on Student Achievement.* Denver, CO: Mid-continent Research for Education and Learning.

14

Understanding and Assessing
the Impact of Leadership Development

Kenneth Leithwood and Ben Levin

This chapter grapples with some of the thornier challenges that have arisen from the relatively recent expectation that leadership development initiatives justify themselves by explicitly demonstrating their contributions to student learning. While this view would not necessarily be accepted by all those working in leadership development, it represents, in our view, a policy orientation that is strong around the world so forms the dominant orientation of this chapter. Arising from the ubiquitous and almost universal press for greater public accountability, the overriding challenge facing assessors is to determine the nature of the connection between efforts to improve leadership, actual changes in such leadership, and the effects of those changes on both organizational characteristics and (most importantly) students. The argument underlying the demand to justify leadership development is that if leadership does not affect what students learn, then leadership development does not matter. Equally, if planned leadership development initiatives do not improve leadership practice, then they do not merit the resources spent on them no matter how much leadership itself matters. We return at the end of the chapter to the question of how this approach might be mediated by diverse national or local contexts and cultures.

The expectations underlying this logic have arisen out of a newly-minted conviction about the importance of leadership to the future of our schools. Policy makers aiming to improve schools on a large scale assume, almost without exception, that the success of their efforts depends significantly on the nature and quality of leadership, especially leadership at the school level (Brown, Anfara, Hartman, Mahar & Mills, 2002; Fullan, 2007). They are likely correct. A compelling body of empirical evidence now demonstrates the significant effects of leadership on school conditions and student learning. This evidence comes from multiple and quite different sources, although as we discuss later this evidence comes almost entirely from the 'developed' world and very largely from a small number of countries. As well, the vast majority of the research addresses leadership at the school; we know much less about leadership at larger (district, regional, national) levels.

One source of evidence is large-scale quantitative studies of overall leadership effects on both student test scores (Hallinger & Heck, 1996a; 1996b; 1998; Leithwood & Riehl, 2005) and student engagement with school (Leithwood & Jantzi, 2006). Reviews of this evidence indicate small but significant effects on student participation in and identification with school as well as on student achievement primarily in literacy and mathematics. Waters, Marzano and McNulty (2003) also point in their recent meta-analytic review to substantial evidence of the significant effects of quite specific leadership "responsibilities".

Case-study and other qualitative evidence, collected in schools serving disadvantaged children using "outlier designs", add to this growing evidence about important leadership effects. These studies usually report very large leadership effects not only on student learning but on an array of school conditions, as well (e.g., Mortimore, 1993; Scheurich, 1998; Harris, 2006). Finally, research on leader succession provides arguably the most compelling source of evidence about leadership effects. This evidence demonstrates that few school improvement initiatives survive a change in principal leadership and that important attitudes toward leadership are significantly and negatively influenced by frequent changes in such leadership. Similarly, leader succession research in non-school organizations points to very large leader effects, especially the effects of leaders at the apex of the organization (Day & Lord, 1988; Thomas, 1988).

As the value of good leadership has assumed the status of an undisputed "fact" in the international policy community, the need to develop good leadership has taken on considerable urgency. Although the research on leadership is centred in only a few countries, the interest in improving education leadership is worldwide. Foundations, governments, international agencies and professional associations have turned their attention to the quality of formal leadership development, and have raised central questions about the impact of existing efforts including the question of how one would assess this impact. But the empirical basis for answering these questions remains quite small — certainly much more limited than the evidence for the impacts of leadership itself. Like the general literature on leadership, research is restricted to a small number of countries, primarily English speaking or industrialized. To illustrate, McCarthy's (1999) analysis of leadership preparation programs across the United States concluded that we do not actually know whether, or the extent to which, such programs actually achieve the goal of "producing effective leaders who create school environments that enhance student learning" (p. 133). Broader efforts to assess the impact of training (Hesketh, 1997) or of management development (Collins, 2002) on organizational outcomes also have not been very successful. The vast majority of evaluations of leadership development efforts are, in fact, limited to assessing participants' satisfaction with their program experiences and sometimes their perception of how such programs have contributed to their work in schools (McCarthy, 2002). While participant satisfaction and skill development may be valuable in their own right, they do not address the questions about impact on school outcomes that are considered important in today's policy environment and are the main reason for increasing investment in leadership development. Moreover, given the variety of program models in place, embodying many different ideas about how to produce changed leadership practice, it would be challenging to demonstrate effects even if the links from leadership to student outcomes were clearer and stronger.

This current state of relative ignorance is not a function of slothful behavior on the part of those who should know better. Arriving at a credible estimate of leadership development impacts, especially impact on students, is a very complex task. It is a cauldron of conceptual and methodological challenges. We unpack some of these challenges and offer some responses we think might improve on much past practice. We begin with a discussion of the impact of leadership itself, as this is essential background to a discussion of the impact of leadership development efforts.

CONCEPTUAL CHALLENGES IN ASSESSING THE EFFECTS OF LEADERSHIP DEVELOPMENT INITIATIVES

1. Understanding How Leaders' Influence "Seeps Through" to Students

Most efforts to conceptualize the relationships among leadership programs, leaders' practices and student learning assume that the effects of leaders on student learning are largely indirect, a view that is implicit in the evidence cited earlier. For these sources of leadership to effect student learning they must exercise some form of positive influence on the work of other colleagues such as teachers, as well as the status of key conditions or characteristics of the organization (school culture, for example) that have a direct influence on students. Leaders can have a direct relationship or influence on these variables and these variables, in turn, have a direct influence on student learning. One of the primary challenges in assessing the effects of leadership development efforts is, therefore, to determine the most defensible set of variables mediating and moderating leadership effects. A second significant challenge is to uncover the nature of the relationships among these variables. Figure 14.1 is the general framework guiding our understanding how leadership "seeps through" to, or is "linked" to student outcomes. This figure and its elements are described more fully in Leithwood and Levin (2005); here we provide only a brief overview.

In regard to outcomes — the dependent variables in Figure 14.1 — we discuss later in the chapter our concerns with the narrow focus on short-term student outcomes as the main — and often only — dependent variable in much of the leadership effects research but we also assume that student learning in some form is a main outcome of schooling and therefore likely to be a key consideration in most studies of leadership and leadership development effects.

Antecedents are internal or external factors that shape the way leaders construct their experience and actions. The two kinds of antecedents are interdependent in that the extent and nature of influence of an external antecedent depends on what sense is made of it internally and the importance the leader attaches to it as a stimulus for their own behavior. The influence of external antecedents, in other words, is "constructed" from the internal cognitive and emotional resources of the individual leader. Put simply, what leaders do depends on what they think and how they feel.

The dotted line joining antecedent and moderating variables in Figure 14.1 acknowledges that one study's antecedents may be another study's moderators; these may be theoretically

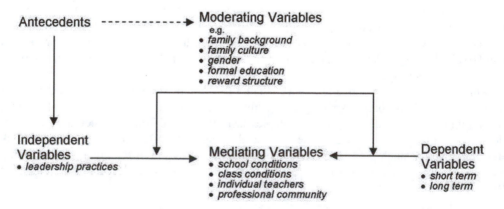

FIGURE 14.1 A general framework for guiding leadership effects research.

defensible differences. "Policy context" is an example of a variable that might be either an antecedent or a moderator. If the research question is: What is the impact of accountable policy contexts on the frequency with which principals display transformational leadership behaviors, then policy context is an antecedent. But if the question is: To what extent do accountable policy contexts enhance or depress the impact of transformational leadership behaviors on the development of collaborative school cultures, then policy context is a moderator.

The theory-driven nature of how variables are classified is a point worth a bit more attention. The same variable actually might be assigned antecedent, moderator, mediator or dependent variable status depending entirely on the theory or framework used to guide a leadership effects study. Employee trust is an example of a moderating variable included in research about the effects of leadership on teachers' efficacy, for example. However, trust is viewed as a dependent measure in leadership studies when researchers are curious about the forms of leader behaviors which promote its development (e.g., Kouzes & Posner, 1995). Trust is also conceived of as a mediating variable in studies, for example, concerned with the effects of leader behaviors on employees' acceptance of decisions (Tyler & Degoey, 1996). For purposes of this discussion, leadership development is an antecedent variable, as described more fully below.

Figure 14.1 indicates that leadership effects operate through mediating and moderating variables. Thompson (2006) describes moderating variables as describing when or for whom a relationship between variables holds, and mediating variables as describing how the relationship works. In more technical language, Baron and Kenny explain that mediating variables:

> represent the generative mechanisms through which the focal independent variable[e.g., leadership] is able to influence the dependent variable of interest [e.g., student learning]. (1986, p. 1173)

A wide range of mediating variables can be found in the leadership research. However, often very similar ideas are expressed in slightly different terms by different researchers, so we believe that the four categories in the figure represent most of the variables identified in the existing research.

Figure 14.1 also includes a set of "moderating variables". These are features of the organizational or wider context in which leaders work that interact with the dependent and/or mediating variables. These interactions can change the strength or nature of relationships between, for example, the independent and mediating variables or the mediating and dependent variables. As Baron & Kenny explain, moderating variables:

> partition a focal independent variable into subgroups that establish its domains of maximal effectiveness in regard to a given dependent variable.[…]Moderator variables are typically introduced into a study when … a relation holds in one setting but not another, or for one subpopulation but not another. (1986, p. 1173)

For example, if previous evidence suggested that male and female teachers respond differently to the same set of leadership behaviors, then teachers' gender would be a promising moderating variable to include in a study of leadership effects.

Since moderating variables help explain how or why certain effects will hold, the careful selection of moderating variables is a key step in designing assessments of leadership and leadership development efforts and one that has been neglected in much educational leadership research to date. Indeed, inadequate attention to moderating variables is one of the more plausible explanations for contradictory research findings and the general skepticism about the potential of research to provide clear guidance for policy and practice. This charge, it should be noted, is not unique to large-scale quantitative research, which at least has a tradition of worrying about such matters. Case study or other qualitative, research is especially well suited to the task of surfacing promising moderators for subsequent consideration.

2. Adding Leadership Development to the Conception

Assessing leadership development efforts is more complicated than the already challenging task of "just" assessing leadership impacts because there is an extra link in the chain — not just from leadership to results, but from leadership development through actual leadership practices to results. This assessment challenge is also less well developed both conceptually and empirically.

Building from Figure 14.1, and concerned specifically with leadership development programs, Figure 14.2 captures a range of ways to frame the evaluation of leadership development program effects. In this figure there are six discrete models for such evaluation, along with many additional hybrids. Each of these models is distinguished by its choice of dependent variable and the number of additional variables mediating the effects of leadership programs and leadership practices on that dependent variable. This framework is consistent with Guskey's (2000) general model for evaluating professional development programs. Guskey's model consists of five "levels" of data to be collected: participants' reactions; participants' learning; organization support and change; participants use of new knowledge and skills and student learning outcomes.

Models 1, 2 and 3 are direct effects models. They propose no mediating variables between a leadership program and either participants' satisfaction (model 1) or participants' internal processes (knowledge, skill, dispositions — model 3); in the case of model 2, the qualities and features of the program are assessed against a set of ideal features drawn from previous research and/or professional judgment. Model 1 is the simplest, least valuable, but most commonly used of the six alternatives.

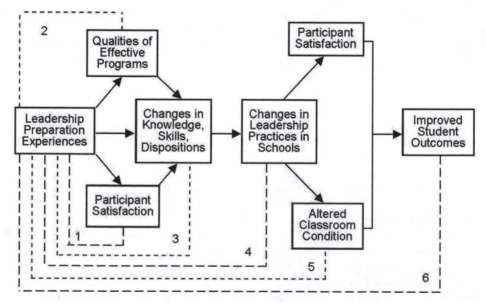

FIGURE 14.2 Alternative frameworks to guide the evaluation of leadership programs.

Model 2, a relatively recent alternative, has emerged with accumulations of evidence about the characteristics of effective programs; both the University Council for Educational Administration (Peterson, 2001) and the Texas Principal Preparation Network (Eddins, 2002). Reflecting UCEA's perspective, for example, Peterson (2001) argues that programs must have; a clear mission and purpose linking leadership to school improvement; a coherent curriculum that provides linkage to state certification schemes; and an emphasis on the use of information technologies. He also suggests that programs should be continuous or long-term rather than one-shot, and that a variety of instructional methods should be used rather than relying on one or a small set of delivery mechanisms.

Evaluations guided by models 3 and 4 are, in many respects, highly defensible responses to the outcomes usually demanded of education programs in most fields. That is, programs change the capacities and/or actual practices of participants. Indeed, it is reasonable to argue that, given the methodological difficulties associated with models 5 and 6, that this ought to be viewed as the near-term standard for evaluating leadership preparation programs. Very few examples of such evaluation can be found at present. One such example is Leithwood et al.'s (1996) summative evaluation of 11 university-based programs sponsored by the Danforth Foundation. With Wallace Foundation support, Darling-Hammond and her colleagues (2007) are just now beginning a second such example.

The simpler models may also make up parts of more complex models 4 through 6; model 6 potentially subsumes all the others. In case of model 4, the criterion variable for judging leadership program effects is change in program participants' actual practices in their organizations. Model 5 requires, in addition, evidence that such leadership practices lead to desirable changes in school and classroom conditions. Finally, model 6 expects everything — the criterion for judging a leadership program successful is that the students in the participants' schools learn more.

By mixing and matching, other hybrid models are possible, although we do not have much to say about them in this chapter. For example, one could easily create a direct effects model in which only leadership programs and/or leadership practices and student outcomes were linked. But the likelihood of such a model detecting changes in students learning due to either experience in a leadership program or only changes in leaders' practices is remote (Hallinger & Heck, 1996a).

Three recent studies with which we are associated provide more specific illustration of the range of alternatives within model 6. Figure 14.3 summarizes the framework used to guide a recently completed, five-year evaluation of an annual series of development initiatives provided for a selected set of practicing school principals in the greater New Orleans, Louisiana, region

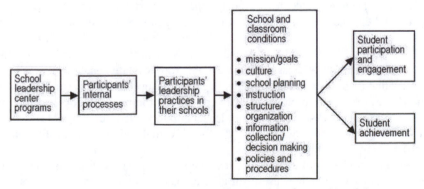

FIGURE 14.3 Framework guiding the evaluation of the Greater New Orleans.

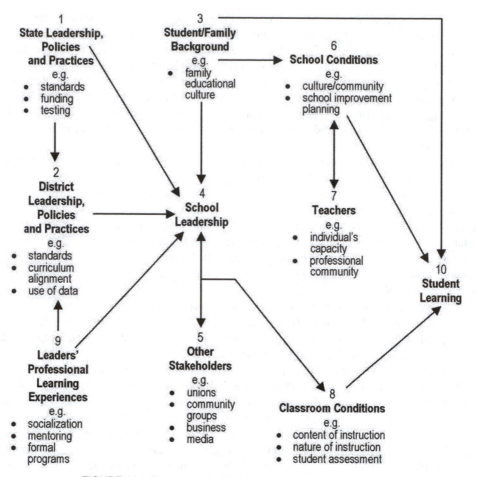

FIGURE 14.4 Framework for Wallace-supported leadership study.

of the United States (Leithwood et al., 2003). In this case, internal processes were primarily cognitive in nature and a transformational model (after Leithwood, Jantzi & Steinbach, 1999) was used to conceptualize leadership practices. Variables in the school and classroom, influenced by organizational design theory, were derived from evidence reported in Leithwood and Aitken (1995). Two sets of student outcomes served as dependent variables in this evaluation — student participation and engagement in class and school, and achievement as measured by the state's annual tests.

A second illustration is a study supported by the Wallace Foundation, now in the third of its five-year duration (Leithwood, Seashore Louis, Wahlstrom & Anderson, 2003). This is a research rather than evaluation project and the framework guiding data collection is summarized in Figure 14.4. This framework is based on an extensive review by the principal investigators of policy-oriented literature linking district and school leadership to student learning. The study inquires, among other things, about the contribution of leaders' formal and informal professional learning experiences to their leadership practices.

In this study, both school and district leadership are conceptualized as a combination of (potentially distributed) practices useful in all contexts, as well as additional practices espe-

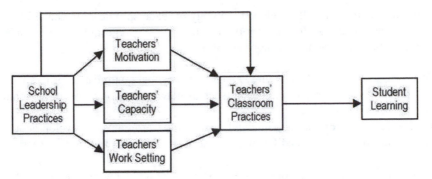

FIGURE 14.5 Framework guiding UK external evaluation.

cially helpful in the contexts of outcomes-oriented school accountability policies and highly diverse school communities (Riehl, 2002). This framework explicitly accounts for student and family background variables, as well as the influence of "other stakeholders" on school leaders' practices. Mediating school leader effects on student learning are a series of classroom and school conditions not unlike those found in the New Orleans study. However, teachers (their capacities, communities, etc.) are distinguished as a separate set of variables in this study. State and district tests will be among the measures of student achievement, the dependent variable in this study.

A third illustration is embedded within the recently completed external evaluation of England's literacy and numeracy strategies (Earl, Watson, Levin, Leithwood & Fullan, 2003). One part of this evaluation was a study of school leadership effects on changes in classroom practices and student learning (Leithwood & Jantzi, in press); Figure 14.5 summarizes the framework for this study. As in the two previous examples, a transformational model was used to conceptualize leadership practices which might be distributed across several sources within the school. Mediating leadership effects on classroom practices and learning were a set of teacher-related variables — motivation, capacity, work setting — based on a model of workplace performance from industrial psychology (Rowan, 1996) but adapted and extended for use in this study (Leithwood, Jantzi & Mascall, 2002). This study was not intended to address issues of leadership preparation but the framework could easily be extended for that purpose, illustrating yet another model 6 possibility.

3. Conceptualizing the Critical Characteristics of Leadership Development Initiatives

Many efforts are now underway aimed at improving leadership in education. These efforts are quite varied from, for example, one-shot workshops and conferences to university graduate programs, to in-house development programs offered by school districts or states or provinces. These programs may or may not have a clear theory of leadership and leadership development guiding their approach. Any look at the range of offerings suggests that they embody quite different assumptions about how leadership is developed. Yet assessing these varied leadership development efforts requires a clear definition of what those efforts are, preferably in a form that permits comparison of costs and effects across different types. In particular, in jurisdictions where resources are scarce, including most developing countries, the question of the merits of investment in leadership development has to be weighed against other priorities such as basic preparation of teachers or provision of textbooks.

We are not aware of a well-developed typology of leadership development efforts, so offer an initial formulation here as the basis for our discussion. We suggest classifying leadership development efforts along seven dimensions as follows:

- Structure — from highly structured (such as a principal qualification program or a graduate degree) to non-formal or informal (such as networks, book clubs, or personal mentoring arrangements).
- Career stage — from pre-appointment qualification programs to development while in a leadership role (such as qualification programs) to programs for highly experienced leaders.
- Duration — from one-time or short-term (such as individual workshops or conferences) to longer-term or multi-part (such as graduate degrees or formal qualification programs).
- Nature of tasks — from formal and didactic to attempts at real-world simulation.
- Specialization — from generic (such as an MBA or leadership seminar directed to many sectors) to those specifically about leadership in education.
- Credential — from no credential (such as attending a conference) to a local credential (such as a qualification issued by a particular district or jurisdiction) to a broadly recognized credential (such as a university graduate degree).
- Location — from programs provided in the workplace to those provided off site.
- Provider — from programs provided by the employer to those provided by education groups (such as a principals' organization) to those provided by external third parties (such as universities or for-profit organizations).

These differences are not of equal importance, but they do illustrate the wide range of potential modes of delivery, and it is immediately obvious that different models or combinations are likely to have quite different effects.

4. Clarifying the Meaning and Scope of "Student Outcomes"

Most studies that have attempted to link leadership or leadership development to student outcomes have relied on short-term measures of academic achievement, most typically test scores. This is an instance of the common tendency in social science research to use the data that are available rather than the data that would actually be most meaningful. In our view — and, we believe, in the view of much of the public — short-term measures of academic achievement should be seen as only one measure of student outcomes. We agree that leadership in education matters only if it contributes to better educational outcomes for students. But we use the phrase 'student outcomes' in reference not just to the shorter-term measures of academic achievement that tend to dominate research in this area, but to the entire range of outcomes of schooling that are of concern to students and the public. Because education is largely appreciated for its instrumental value, most people actually care far more about longer-term indicators of education success, such as high school graduation, repetition in grade or course failure, suspension and expulsion, and student engagement.

Indeed, there is a strong case to be made that the important outcomes of education are even broader and longer-term measures such as participation in further or higher education, employment, health, social participation and life satisfaction (Picot, Saunders & Sweetman, 2007). While all of these are linked to academic skills assessed in schools, it is also the case that short-term school success is a quite imperfect predictor of these larger outcomes. For example, literacy as assessed by non-school measures clearly has an independent impact on many life outcomes (Riddell, 2007).

5. Detecting the Unique Effects of Leader Development Initiatives

Significant resources are being devoted at local and national levels to the development of leaders in education and more generally. This is the case in countries with dramatically varying levels of wealth and basic education infrastructure. Increasingly, assessments of leadership development efforts in education search for effects on student learning. But formal development experiences are just one of many influences on leaders' actual behaviors and they are less powerful than others such as leaders' internal states, existing skills, beliefs, values and dispositions. Internal states constitute the perceptual filters and meaning-making "tools" through which all other potential influences must pass if they are to change leaders' behaviors. In order to change leaders' behaviors, other types of influences must actually change some aspect of a leader's internal states.

The next most powerful set of influences on leadership development is likely the social, cultural and historical contexts of leaders' work (e.g., Vadeboncoeur, 2007). As in most areas of education, the bulk of the published empirical evidence on education leadership comes from relatively few countries. We believe that many dynamics of human behavior and organization are common across settings. For example, in all settings questions of power, respect, hierarchy, and acceptance of diversity are part of organizational life and require ongoing management. Yet these dynamics may be played out in very different ways in different settings as illustrated in Wong's (1998) description of the differences in approaches to leadership in western and Chinese settings.

These differences are not only matters of national culture, either. Within a given jurisdiction there can be important regional differences or differences resulting from the socio-economic context. For example in high poverty or high conflict settings expectations for educational outcomes and leadership may be quite different than they are in more affluent or more peaceful settings (Thrupp, 1999). Contexts dominate leaders' organizational socialization and exert an irresistible and direct influence on leaders' internal states. They reshape and add to a leader's stock of "tacit" knowledge (Polanyi, 1962), in particular, a form of knowledge which guides the largest proportion of human behavior while, at the same time (and by definition), being unavailable for conscious reflection and evaluation. As Mertz (2007) has recently demonstrated, much of the tacit knowledge that leaders acquire through organizational socialization reinforces existing norms, values and practices even when something quite different might be more productive.

Social, cultural and historical contexts also exert a powerful influence on a range of important emotions or dispositions including, for example, leaders' sense of efficacy, openness to the ideas of others and optimism in the face of significant challenges in the workplace (Zaccaro, Kemp & Bader, 2004). These dispositions and emotions strongly influence leaders' goals and motivations and so determine how and when leaders' exercise their repertoires of knowledge and skill.

This brief glimpse at the sources of leadership development, other than formal training or professional development, should remind us that judgments about the impacts of formal professional development must somehow "partial out" these other sources if they are to detect the unique effects of such formal experiences. Hence, issues of evaluation design are critical matters in deliberations about how to assess leadership development programs.

METHODOLOGICAL CHALLENGES IN ASSESSING THE EFFECTS OF LEADERSHIP DEVELOPMENT INITIATIVES

Evaluators of leadership programs, and researchers inquiring about leadership effects, face additional thorny methodological challenges in their efforts to demonstrate program and leader effects, especially in regard to student outcomes. We discuss five such challenges in this section of the paper. Several are illustrated using the experience of Leithwood and colleagues (2003) during the evaluation of a leadership development program in New Orleans that used U.S. state (Louisiana) achievement data as the measure of program and leadership effects.

1. Measuring Leadership Practices

Some education sector leadership models have been specified in detail and tested with instruments which are quite well developed. This is the case, for example, with Hallinger's instructional leadership model (see Hallinger & Murphy, 1985), Leithwood's transformational school leadership model (Leithwood & Jantzi, 2000) and Marks and Printy's (2003) synthesis of both of these forms of leadership. Several versions of Bass' (1985) Multifactor Leadership Questionnaire have been used extensively to study transformational leadership effects primarily in non-school organizations, but in schools and districts, as well (e.g., Nguni, 2005). Many other instruments are available for measuring leadership, especially in organizations outside the education sector (Clark & Clark, 1990).

Without diminishing their many contributions, one limitation of some of the most widely cited reviews of leadership effects on student learning is that they confound estimates of such effects by failing to distinguish among alternative approaches to, or models of, leadership (e.g., Hallinger & Heck, 1996b); this is an important issue to grapple with in both the assessment of leadership and leadership development programs. If leadership matters, then the particular approach should be factored into the research. Other reviews seem to infer comprehensive assessments of leadership effects while actually limiting themselves to the behaviors associated with a particular model of leadership (e.g., Witzier, Bosker & Kruger, 2003). Furthermore, some original studies of leadership effects use secondary data sources originally created for other purposes, typically estimating the effects of potentially incoherent or incomplete models of leadership. These problems are difficult to avoid in the development of the field, but as knowledge deepens researchers will need to be more careful in the way they conceptualize their work and in the data analyses they perform.

Virtually all large-scale quantitative leadership effect studies in education restrict their attention to some features of what leaders do. Such studies are usually guided by a leadership model which is intentionally reductionist in nature. The aim of this work is to assess the explanatory power of a particular set of leadership behaviors associated with the chosen model. Real leaders, of course, do much more in their schools than provide, for example, instructional or transformational leadership. Almost all leaders will demonstrate the use of practices associated with strategic leadership, moral leadership and the like at least on occasion. Such outside-the-model practices are often captured in the much wider net of qualitative case study research and this is one of the reasons for the discrepancy between the size of leadership effects reported in qualitative and quantitative studies.

A review of research (Bell, Bolam & Cubillo, 2003 — available at www.eppi.org.uk) prepared for the British Evidence-based Policy and Practice Centre (EPPI) started with more than 4000 references to leadership studies but found only eight that met the criteria of a well-specified leadership model and empirical evidence on student outcomes. In addition, many leadership program evaluations neither specify nor measure the leadership practices they aim to improve, electing instead for more global measures of participant satisfaction with the contribution of the program to participants' personal and implicit leadership efforts or espoused leadership theories.

These shortcomings in the actual measurement of leadership point to the importance of clearly specifying those leadership practices that are hypothesized to effect student outcomes. Failure to do this arises from both practical and conceptual sources. Practically, available resources will often press researchers and evaluators to rely on existing evidence, even where it is an imperfect match for their purposes. Conceptually, a major source of the problem is lack of agreement about the definition of leadership, as discussed earlier.

These challenges notwithstanding, improvements in our understanding of leadership and leadership development effects on students depends on the use of reliable leadership measures explicitly based on clearly defined and conceptually coherent images of desirable leadership practices.

2. Measuring Student Achievement

This section moves our earlier discussion about student outcomes from conceptual to methodological concerns. As that earlier discussion made clear, the current preoccupation with student test scores as the main if not only dependent measure in inquiries about leadership effects is open to serious challenge. That said, given the overall public and political climate around education, the preference for assessing leadership effects on student test scores is not likely to go away anytime soon. In fact, Hallinger and Heck (1996a) decried the extent of use of such measures in studies of leadership a decade ago but the press to use them has grown rather than diminished in the interim.

While purpose-built achievement measures could be used by researchers and evaluators (although they would have their own limitations), in practice, most research studies and program evaluations end up using existing measures partly because they are available and partly because that is what research funders ask for. These measures are typically part of national or local testing programs that have three well-known limitations as estimates of leadership effects: a narrow focus, questionable or unknown reliability, and the questionable accuracy with which they are able to estimate change over time. We have encountered a handful of less pervasive, practical limitations in some of our own recent work which we also identify in this section.

Narrow Focus   Most large-scale testing programs confine their focus to mathematics and language achievement with occasional forays into science. Only in relatively rare cases have efforts been made to test students in most areas of the curriculum not to mention cross-curricular areas such as problem-solving or teamwork. Technical measurement challenges, lack of resources and concerns about the amount of time for testing explain the narrow focus of most large-scale testing programs. But this means that evidence of leaders' effects on student achievement using these sources is really evidence of effects on students' literacy and numeracy.

Because improving literacy and numeracy are such pervasive priorities in so many schools at the moment, this is a limitation that will not concern many researchers and evaluators. There is evidence, however, that leadership effects are of a different magnitude for even these two areas of achievement. For example, literacy is more substantially shaped than is numeracy by pre-school and home experience and so may be less susceptible to improvement through good instruction

The lesson for researchers and program evaluators is that the size and significance of leadership effects on other areas of achievement cannot be assumed or extrapolated, and should be investigated directly. It is plausible to think, though we have no evidence on the point, that leadership could have its strongest effects in areas such as student engagement, commitment, and interest in ongoing learning.

Reliability   Lack of reliability at the school level is a second limitation of many large-scale testing programs. Most of these programs are designed to provide reliable results only for large groups of students. But as the number of students diminishes, as in the case of a single school or even a small district or region, few testing systems claim even to know how reliable are their results (e.g., Wolfe, Childs & Elgie, 2004). The likelihood, however, is that they are not very reliable, thereby challenging the accuracy of judgments about leadership effects. A very large proportion of schools would have grade cohorts of fewer than 30 students, so having 2 or 3 particularly strong or particularly challenging students in a grade can make a very large difference in a school's scores. Researchers and program evaluators would do well to limit analysis of achievement to data aggregated above the level of the individual school or leader. As more than a small aside, this suggestion is in direct conflict with the systems of school reporting in many places, which report school by school results without regard to population size and measurement error.

Estimating Change   Conceptually, monitoring the extent to which a school improves the achievement of its students over time is a much better reflection of a school's (and leader's) effectiveness than are its annual mean achievement scores. Technically, however, arriving at a defensible estimate of such change is difficult. Simply attributing the difference between the mean achievement scores of this year's and last year's students on the test to changes in a school's (and/or leader's) effectiveness overlooks a host of other possible explanations:

- Cohort differences: This year's students may be significantly more or less advanced in their capacities when they entered the cohort. Such cohort differences are quite common, as any teacher will attest;
- Test differences: While most large-scale assessment programs take pains to ensure equivalency of test difficulty from year to year, this is an imperfect process and there are often subtle and not-so subtle adjustments in the tests that can amount to unanticipated but significant differences in scores;
- Test conditions differences: Teachers are almost always in charge of administering the tests and their class's results on last year's tests may well influence the nature of how they administer this year's test (more or less leniently) even within the guidelines offered by the testing agency;
- External environment differences: Perhaps the weather this winter was more severe than last winter and students ended up with six more snow days - six fewer days of instruction, or a teacher left half way through the year, or was sick for a significant time;
- Regression to the mean: this is a term used by statisticians to capture the highly predictable tendency for extreme scores on one test administration to change in the direction of the mean performance on a second administration. So schools scoring either very low or very high one year can be expected to score less extremely the second year, quite aside from anything else that might be different.

Linn (2003) has demonstrated that these challenges to change scores become less severe as change is traced over three or four years. It is the conclusions drawn from comparing scores over a single year that are especially open to misinterpretation, but it is just these single year comparisons that are most commonly made. The lesson for researchers and program evaluators is to use as their dependent variable changes in student achievement over longer periods of time (three or more years).

3. Policy and Structural Challenges

We became particularly sensitive to the three methodological challenges raised here during the Leithwood et al. (2003) program evaluation in Louisiana. Although we use that context to illustrate the challenges, these are challenges likely to be encountered in many other program evaluation contexts.

Policy Changes Over Time   The Leithwood et al. (2003) study was a five year longitudinal evaluation that was complicated by changes in the state's achievement measures. Given the frequency of policy shifts in student assessment practices in many jurisdictions, it may become impossible to maintain a consistent set of data over several years. Not only can the tests change, but scoring rubrics and cut-offs may also be modified.

Cell Sizes   Considerable variation in the organization of program participants' schools meant that there were very small numbers of students available for analysis within any one type of organization. Few schools had identical sets of data. Across participants' schools, at least eleven different grade configurations could be found. None of these configurations included enough schools to carry out detailed analyses by configuration using the same measures. For example, a school mean for the Iowa achievement test was calculated to develop a gain score from 2000 to 2002. The number of grades contributing to the school mean varied across schools from one to five. This raised questions about the comparability of, for example, a mean score for grades 3 and 5, a mean score for a single grade 3, or a mean score for a grade 6 and 7 combination. But limiting comparisons only to identical grades would have virtually ruled out most analyses, particularly for schools within the same participants' cohort.

Missing Data   Missing or incorrect data may also be a problem for researchers and evaluators. Indeed, school records of achievement data, should they be used, are quite likely to be inadequate for research purposes. In the Louisiana study achievement data for a few schools were available for one year but not subsequent years, even though the grades to which the tests were administered were included in the schools. Data may be missing, or coded incorrectly, or simply misplaced over the years. This reduced the number of schools available for comparison across years. A few schools changed the grade levels tested further complicating the comparability issue by the lack of data for the same grade(s) each year.

4. Research Design

Statistical models used in quantitative research on leader effects — typically some path analytic technique — are capable of measuring both leaders' direct effects on student learning, as well as their indirect effects through influence on school and classroom conditions which, in turn, also influence student learning. Statistical models of this type are extremely useful in the evaluation of leadership programs, beyond models 1 to 3, in those vast majority of evaluations in which only data related to participants, their schools and students can be collected.

A challenging issue in leadership development research is the extent to which it is possible to use experimental or quasi-experimental designs. Participation in leadership development can hardly assumed to be random; participants are likely to differ in important ways from non-participants. However random assignment would not necessarily correct this problem in that the background attributes of leaders — the same attributes, to a considerable extent, that shape their desire to participate in development activities — would also influence the learning they derive from participation. Hence it is difficult to implement classic control group evaluation designs. As well, such models involve tradeoffs: for example, tradeoffs between the theoretical complexity (and explanatory power) of a mediated effects model and the difficulties of either random assignments in real world conditions or locating comparison groups sufficiently similar to the leadership preparation group to rule out competing hypotheses to the program experience as explanation for any observed differences in dependent measure.

Most survey-based research on the nature of school leadership uses data collected from teachers about their perceptions of the leadership provided by administrative leaders (e.g., Day & Harris, 2002; Leithwood, Jantzi & Steinbach, 1999). Such evidence is a considerable improvement on leader self-report data and is consistent with the theoretical claim that leadership is an attribution.

A further issue in research design relates to the situational nature of leadership. If we want to assess the impact of leadership in situ, then presumably we need a definition of leadership that is precise enough so that we can recognize it. Yet, as discussed earlier, many factors shape school outcomes and may also affect the nature of leadership. For example, presumably one important task of school leaders is to recruit and retain good teachers, but that task may be much more difficult in settings that also face other constraints to good outcomes, such as geographical isolation, high poverty or high ethnic diversity. Other aspects of leader activity, such as strategies for involving parents, relations with students and approaches to curriculum may also vary considerably within schools. If this is so, how is it possible to assess leadership impact across settings?

Two strategies are possible. The most commonly used strategy is simply to rely on an average impact score. While this doesn't tell us much about the areas of low and high impact in a school, it does tell us the overall level of impact which may be sufficient for some evaluation purposes; indeed, most of the quantitative evidence we now have of leadership impact is based on this strategy.

A second strategy used quite extensively in leadership research is to start with schools judged to be exemplary on the basis of student outcomes and then determine what leaders in those schools do. Even better is a design that compares outliers — exceptionally high versus low scoring schools. While these designs have some value as research strategies (but for a critique of outlier research see Levin, 2006), they are of no value for program evaluation purposes. One cannot pick leaders and schools for evaluation; the program picks them for you.

5. Unit of Analysis

The New Orleans evaluation used the school as the unit of analysis. But determining what the unit of analysis should be is a fundamental challenge for any social science research, one that is often not thought through adequately in study design. In one sense, leadership development experiences are expected to have an impact on individual leaders who in turn have an impact on other individuals and on entire organizations.

Impact on individual leaders is relatively easy to assess. Usually this is done through attitude or opinion measures administered to leaders themselves, a largely unsatisfactory form of evidence. But this evidence tells us little or nothing about their practices or their impact since we know that people's self-reports of behavior may be quite different from the way their behavior is perceived by others. Alternatively, it is certainly possible to assess leaders' acquisition of knowledge and skill in variety of quite direct ways using tests, case problems, simulations and the like (e.g., Leithwood & Steinbach, 1995).

Whatever the form of evidence about changes in leader practices, however, such change, as Figure 14.2 makes clear, is only part of the chain of variables measured through more sophisticated evaluation designs. As well, if one embraces a distributed model of leadership, then a focus on individuals may hide important contributions to development in the school made by others. Some analysts argue that we focus too much on people in positions of authority and fail to see the way in which key leadership functions in schools may be exercised by many different people. Certainly adopting a model of shared or distribute leadership would mean thinking differently about the assessment of leadership impact.

There are also problems with using entire schools as the unit of analysis for leadership impact. A school model assumes that leadership impacts are direct and evenly distributed, but as our earlier discussion shows, neither of these assumptions is necessarily correct. Take the issue of staff mobility. One reasonable expectation for good leadership is that staff stability should be high, since many changes in staff are likely to make it more difficult to improve learning and teaching. However changes in leadership are associated with increased turnover of staff as leaders recruit new staff who are more aligned with the leader's values.

THINKING INTERNATIONALLY ABOUT LEADERSHIP DEVELOPMENT

As already noted in this chapter, the research on leadership development is heavily concentrated in relatively few countries. Our view is that the increasing emphasis on leadership, its development, and its impact on student achievement is a broadly international phenomenon that is taking place in most if not all countries. However given our position on the importance of antecedents in shaping leaders' understanding and behavior, including their response to leadership development efforts, we recognize that leadership development efforts will vary in design and impact from one country or culture to another. Cultural beliefs around the importance of individuals versus groups or teams, or the expression of personal opinions, or deference to hierarchy, or commitment to tradition will all affect the ways in which leadership development should be designed and responses from participants to any given development program. The models in this paper are, we emphasize, a particular orientation drawn from a relatively small number of societies. While we believe they have a broad and generic applicability, this is an empirical question still to be tested.

CONCLUSIONS AND RECOMMENDATIONS

This chapter has described both the promise and the challenges associated with conceptualizing the relationship between leadership programs, changes in leader practices and the effects of such changed practices on schools and students. We also grappled with some of the methodological challenges facing evaluators and researchers with an interest in program and leader effects, offering suggestions about how these challenges might be addressed.

We began by describing the current state of knowledge on the impact of leadership and of leadership development activities. The former has a more extensive and powerful empirical base than the latter. We discussed the problem of how best to frame the relationship between leadership programs, leadership practices and student outcome. We offer a relatively generic response to this question, suggesting that any comprehensive framework would include independent, dependent, antecedent, moderating and mediating categories of variables. Frameworks guiding a handful of current and recently completed studies illustrate variations on the generic framework. We define and illustrate the state of knowledge about these variables through reviewing leadership research. We also discussed some of the main difficulties in conducting both program and leadership effects research, such as the narrow and unreliable nature of commonly used student assessment instruments.

Our conclusions and recommendations bear on selected aspects of these points. Because the impact of development programs rests on actual leadership practices, it is necessary to consider future research and evaluation on both leadership itself and leadership program effects. Given the importance of leadership in the current education policy environment around the world, better knowledge about effective leadership and its development should be a high priority.

Future leadership effects research should, in our view:

- Measure a more comprehensive set of leadership practices than has been included in most research to date: these measures should be explicitly based on coherent images of desirable leadership practices. Such research is likely to produce larger estimates of leadership effects on student outcomes than has been provided to date;
- Measure an expanded set of dependent (outcome) variables: these are variables beyond short-term student learning including longer term effects such as student success in tertiary education, employment and commitment to learning over the life span.
- Describe systematically how leaders successfully influence the conditions mediating their effects on students so that development programs can pay attention to these practices. We now have considerable evidence about the most powerful variables mediating school leader effects but we know much less about how leaders influence these mediators;
- Attend more systematically to variables moderating (enhancing, reducing) leadership effects: lack of attention to this category of variables seems likely to be a major source of conflicting findings in the leadership research literature. Furthermore, when studies do attend to moderators, their choice has often been atheoretical and difficult to justify.
- Reflect substantial methodological variety: this will be essential if a robust body of context — relevant knowledge is to be developed.
- Future research on the effects of leadership development programs should:
- Be guided by conceptual frameworks similar to those we have recommended for leadership effects research. Our review suggests that the few efforts to evaluate leadership program effects, in most parts of the world, have generated the type and quality of evidence required to answer with confidence questions about their organizational or student effects. This problem could be addressed by considering leadership programs as one category of antecedent variables stimulating changes in leadership practices as described in our models.
- Be more explicit about the assumptions or theory, both about leadership and about its development, that guide any particular leadership development program. The multiplicity of approaches to development require more explicit comparison in terms of their effects
- Provide comparative information about a range of program effects. Formal programs vary greatly on many dimensions and in any case are just one of many influences on leaders' practices. To appreciate fully the value of such programs, their effects need to be com-

pared to the effects of such other antecedents as on-the-job learning, leaders' traits and early family experiences. Such information would inform not only program improvement efforts but also leadership selection processes, and would also assist with cost-effectiveness judgments in planning for leadership development.

- Be organized and funded at levels consistent with the expectations for what is to be accomplished: few documented program evaluations provide the type of comprehensive data we call for here. Although this is partly a matter of research practice, funding is also a reason. If future leadership program evaluations are to assess the direct and indirect effects of such programs on student learning as well as leaders' practices, then a different level of research effort, and consequently of funding will be required than has been typical to date.

Implementing these recommendations will require considerable attention to a significant number of conceptual and technical issues at the core of designing and conducting high quality, high impact research and evaluation. Just doing more research of the type that is typically being done now — at least as it is reflected in the published literature — seems unlikely to advance our understandings about how leadership programs and leaders most productively improve student learning. While the impetus for this improvement in research strategies must come from governments and large professional organizations, researchers could also contribute through:

- better connections among researchers working in this field;
- more cumulative and replicative research using previous tools and concepts rather than constant invention of new frameworks and measurement instruments;
- pooling of data across studies to allow larger samples with greater statistical power (which would, in turn, require more consistency in measures as noted).

This volume will, we hope, be an important step in moving that discussion forward so that we can improve leadership development in the service of better outcomes — broadly considered — for students.

REFERENCES

Baron, R. M., & Kenny, D. A. (1986). The moderator-mediator variable distinction in social psychological research: Conceptual, strategic and statistical considerations. *Journal of Personality and Social Psychology, 51*(6), 1173–1182.

Bass, B. M. (1985). *Leadership and performance beyond expectations.* New York: The Free Press.

Bell, L., Bolam, R., & Cubillo, L. (2003). A systematic review of the impact of school headteachers and principals on student outcomes. Retrieved March 20, 2004, from http://eppi.ioe.ac.uk/EPPIWebContent/reel/review_groups/leadership/lea_rv1/lea_rv1.pdf

Brown, K. M., Anfara, V. A., Hartman, K. J., Mahar, R. J., & Mills, R. (2002). Professional development of middle level principals: Pushing the reform forward. *Leadership and Policy in Schools, 1*(2), 107–143.

Clark, K. E., & Clark, M. B. (Eds.). (1990). *Measures of leadership.* West Orange, NJ: Leadership Library of America, Inc.

Collins, D. (2002). Performance-level evaluation methods used in management development studies from 1986 to 2000. *Human Resource Development Review, 1*(1), 910–1110.

Darling-Hammond, L., LaPointe, M., Meyerson, D., & Orr, M. (2007). *Preparing school leaders for a changing world: Executive summary.* Stanford, CA: Stanford University, Stanford Educational Leadership Institute.

Day, C., & Harris, A. (2002). Teacher leadership, reflective practice and school improvement. In K. Leithwood & P. Hallinger (Eds.), *Second international handbook of educational leadership and administration* (pp. 957–978). Dordrecht: Kluwer Academic Publishers.

Day, D. V., & Lord, R. G. (1988). Executive leadership and organizational performance: Suggestions for a new theory and methodology. *Journal of Management, 14*, 453–464.

Earl, L., Watson, N., Levin, B., Leithwood, K., & Fullan, M. (2003). *Watching and Learning 3: Final report of the external evaluation of England's National Literacy and Numeracy Strategy.* Toronto: OISE/ University of Toronto.

Fullan, M. (2007). *The new meaning of educational change* (4th edition). New York: Teachers College Press.

Guskey, T. R. (2000). Evaluating professional development. Thousand Oaks, CA: Corwin Press.

Hallinger, P., & Heck, R. (1996a). The principal's role in school effectiveness: An assessment of methodological progress, 1980–1995. In K. Leithwood & P. Hallinger (Eds.), *International handbook of educational leadership and administration* (pp. 723–783). Dordrecht: Kluwer Academic Publishers.

Hallinger, P., & Heck, R. (1996b). Reassessing the principal's role in school effectiveness: A review of empirical research, 1980–1995. *Educational Administration Quarterly, 32*(1), 5–44.

Hallinger, P., & Heck, R. (1998). Exploring the principal's contribution to school effectiveness: 1980–1995. *School Effectiveness and School Improvement,* (9), 157–191.

Hallinger, P., & Murphy, J. (1985). Assessing the instructional management behavior of principals. *Elementary School Journal, 86*(2), 217–247.

Harris, A. (2006). Leading change in schools in difficulty. *Journal of Educational Change, 7*(1), 9–18

Hesketh, B. (1997). Dilemmas in training for transfer and retention. *Applied Psychology: An International Review, 46*(4), 339–361.

Kouzes, J. M., & Posner, B. Z. (1995). *The leadership challenge: How to keep getting extraordinary things done in organizations* (Revised ed.). San Francisco, CA: Jossey-Bass.

Leithwood, K., & Aitken, R. (1995). *Making schools smarter: A system for monitoring school and district progress.* Thousand Oaks, CA: Corwin Press.

Leithwood, K., & Jantzi, D. (2000). *The Transformational School Leadership Survey.* Toronto, ON: OISE/ University of Toronto.

Leithwood, K., & Jantzi, D. (2006). Transformational school leadership for large-scale reform: Effects on students, teachers, and their classroom practices. *School Effectiveness and School Improvement, 17*(2), 201–227.

Leithwood, K., & Jantzi, D. (in press). Linking leadership to student learning: The role of leader efficacy. *Educational Administration Quarterly.*

Leithwood, K., & Levin, B. (2005). *Assessing school leader and leadership programme effects on pupil learning.* London, UK: Department for Education and Skills (DfES) RR662.

Leithwood, K., & Riehl, C. (2005). What we know about successful school leadership. In W. Firestone & C. Riehl (Eds.), *A new agenda: Directions for research on educational leadership* (pp. 22–47). New York: Teachers College Press.

Leithwood, K., & Steinbach, R. (1995). *Expert problem solving processes: Evidence from principals and superintendents.* Albany, NY: SUNY Press.

Leithwood, K., Jantzi, D., & Mascall, B. (2002). A framework for research on large-scale reform. *Journal of Educational Change,* (3), 7–33.

Leithwood, K., Jantzi, D., & Steinbach, R. (1999). *Changing leadership for changing times.* Buckingham, UK: Open University Press.

Leithwood, K., Jantzi, D., Coffin, G., & Wilson, P. (1996). Preparing school leaders: What works? *Journal of School Leadership, 6*(3), 316–342.

Leithwood, K., Riedlinger, B., Bauer, S., & Jantzi, D. (2003). Leadership program effects on student learning: The case of the Greater New Orleans School Leadership Center. *Journal of School Leadership and Management, 13*(6), 707–738.

Leithwood, K., Seashore Louis, K., Anderson, S., & Wahlstrom, K. (2004). *How leadership influences student learning: A review of research for the Learning from Leadership Project.* New York: The Wallace Foundation.

Levin, B. (2006). Schools in challenging circumstances: A reflection on what we know and what we need to know. *School Effectiveness and School Improvement, 17*(4), 399–407.

Linn, R. (2003). Accountability: responsibility and reasonable expectations. *Educational Researcher, 32*(7), 3–13.

Marks, H., & Printy, S. (2003). Principal leadership and school performance: An integration of transformational and instructional leadership. *Educational Leadership Quarterly, 34*(3), 370–397.

McCarthy, M. M. (1999). The evolution of educational leadership preparation programs. In J. Murphy & K. S. Louis (Eds.), *Handbook of research on educational administration* (2nd ed., pp. 119–140). San Francisco, CA: Jossey-Bass

McCarthy, M. M. (2002). Educational leadership preparation programs: a glance at the past with an eye toward the future. *Leadership and Policy in Schools, 1*(3), 201–221.

Mertz, N. (2007). The organizational socialization of assistant principals. *Journal of School Leadership, 16*(6), 644–675.

Mortimore, P. (1993). School effectiveness and the management of effective learning and teaching. *School Effectiveness and School Improvement, 4*(4), 290–310.

Nguni, S. (2005). Transformational leadership in Tanzanian education: a study of the effects of transformational leadership on teachers' job satisfaction, organizational commitment and organizational citizenship behaviour in Tanzanian primary and secondary schools. Radboud University, Nijmegen, The Netherlands.

Peterson, K. D. (2001). The professional development of principals: Innovations and opportunities. Paper presented at the first meeting of the National Commission for the Advancement of Educational Leadership Preparation, Rancine, WI.

Picot, G., Saunders, R., & Sweetman, A. (2007). (Eds.). *Fulfilling potential, creating success: Perspectives on human capital development.* Montreal, QC and Kingston, ON: McGill-Queen's University Press.

Polanyi, M. (1962). *Personal knowledge.* Chicago, IL: University of Chicago Press.

Riddell, C. (2007). The impact of education on economic and social outcomes: An overview of recent advances in economics. In G Picot, R. Saunders & A. Sweetman (Eds.) *Fulfilling potential, creating success: Perspectives on human capital development* (pp. 55–100). Montreal, QC and Kingston, ON: McGill-Queen's University Press.

Riehl, C. (2002). The principal's role in creating inclusive schools for diverse students: A review of normative, empirical and critical literature on the practice of educational administration. *Review of Educational Research, 40*(1), 55–81.

Rowan, B. (1996). Standards as incentives for instructional reform. In S. H. Fuhrman & J. J. O'Day (Eds.), *Rewards and reform: Creating educational incentives that work.* San Francisco, CA: Jossey-Bass.

Scheurich, J. J. (1998). Highly successful and loving, public elementary schools populated mainly by low-SES children of color: Core beliefs and cultural characteristics. *Urban Education, 33*(4), 451–491.

Thomas, A. B. (1988). Does leadership make a difference to organizational performance? *Administrative Science Quarterly, 33,* 388–400.

Thompson, B. (2006). *Foundations of behavioral statistics: An insight-based approach.* New York: Guilford.

Thrupp, M. (1999). *Schools making a difference: Let's be realistic.* Buckingham, UK: Open University Press.

Tyler, T. R., & Degoey, P. (1996). Trust in organizational authorities: The influence of motive attributes on willingness to accept decisions. In R. M. Kramer & T. R. Tyler (Eds.), *Trust in organizations: Frontiers of theory and research* (pp. 331–356). Thousand Oaks, CA: Sage.

Vadeboncoeur, J. (2007). Engaging young people: Learning in informal contexts. In J. Green & A. Luke (Eds.), *Rethinking learning: What counts as learning and learning what counts* (pp. 239–278). Washington, DC: American Educational Research Association.

Waters, T., Marzano, R. J., & McNulty, B. (2003). Balanced leadership: What 30 years of research tells us about the effect of leadership on pupil achievement. A working paper. Aurora, CO: Mid-continent Research for Education and Learning.

Witzier, B., Bosker, R., & Kruger, M. (2003). Educational leadership and pupil achievement: The elusive search for an association. *Educational Administration Quarterly, 34*(3), 398–425.

Wolfe, R., Childs, R., & Elgie, S. (2004). *Final report of the external evaluation of the EQAO's assessment process.* Toronto: OISE/University of Toronto.

Wong, K. C. (1998). Culture and moral leadership in education. *Peabody Journal of Education, 73*(2), 106–125.

Zaccaro, S. J., Kemp, C., & Bader, P. (2004). Leader traits and attributes. In J. Antonakis, A. T. Cianciolo & R. J. Sternberg (Eds.), *The nature of leadership* (pp. 101–124). Thousand Oaks, CA: Sage.

III

INTERNATIONAL REFLECTIONS

15

Leadership Preparation and Development in North America

Michelle D. Young and Margaret Grogan

Canada, Mexico and the United States are increasingly tied together in a complex and evolving trinational relationship. The spillover effect of economic integration after NAFTA (the North American Free Trade Agreement which came into effect on 1 January 1994, the trade bloc in North America created by the Agreement and both the North American Agreement on Environmental Cooperation (NAAEC) and The North American Agreement on Labor Cooperation (NAALC), whose members are Canada, Mexico, and the United States) has focused attention on shared transnational concerns, such as immigration, labor, education, social welfare and the environment (NAMI, 2007). And while increased integration of these three nations seems inevitable, they currently have quite distinct traditions, politics, economies and education systems. In this chapter we review one aspect of North American education systems, the development of educational leaders.

According to Kandel (1970), to truly understand and appreciate the educational workings of a nation, it is essential to know something of its history and traditions, and of the political and economic conditions that determine its development. Education systems, he goes on to explain, inevitably tend to reflect the aims, aspirations, traditions and characteristics of the nations they serve. We begin the chapter with a general overview of North America and then focus in turn on Canada, Mexico and the United States. For each of these North American countries, we attempt to provide helpful contextual information that will assist the reader in situating leadership development practices.

Regardless of our efforts, however, there are at least three serious limitations to this chapter. First, to understand, appreciate, and evaluate the reality of preparation in North American countries it is essential to know something about the countries' histories and traditions, the forces governing social traditions, and the political and economic traditions. While we do give limited attention to these issues, we do not attempt to provide the type of comprehensive treatment that deep understanding would require. Second, despite the volume of literature and interest in comparative and international education, the study of leadership education has not become established as an important area of research. Thus, we encountered a few too many dead-ends in our attempt to review scholarship on the preparation of educational leaders in North America (e.g., a few too many published resources).[1] Third, North America is home to 23 different nations and we have limited our chapter only three of those nations: Canada, Mexico and the United States.

THE NORTH AMERICAN CONTINENT

North America is a racially and ethnically diverse continent of 23 different countries. Officially, the countries of (and territories often associated with) North America include Canada, United States, Mexico, Guatemala, Honduras, El Salvador, Nicaragua, Costa Rica, Panama, Tobago, Grenada, Trinidad, St. Martin, Anguilla, Antigua and Barbuda, Aruba, Bahamas, Barbados, Belize, Bermuda, British Virgin Islands, Cayman Islands, Cuba, Dominica, Dominican Republic, Greenland, Guadeloupe, Haiti, Jamaica, Martinique, Montserrat, Navassa Island, Netherlands Antilles, Puerto Rico, Saint Barthelemy, Saint Kitts and Nevis, Saint Lucia, Saint Martin, Saint-Pierre and Milquelon, Saint Vincent and the Grenadines, Turks and Caicos Islands, and the US Virgin Islands.

The continent covers an area of about 24,490,000 square kilometers (i.e., 9,450,000 square miles), which is approximately 16.4 per cent of the planet's land masses (Applied History Research Group, 2001). As of October 2006, its population was estimated at over 514,600,000. The largest of the North American cities are located in Mexico, the United States and Canada; they include Mexico City, New York City, Los Angeles, Chicago, Toronto, Houston, and Montreal. These are followed closely by San José, Costa Rica, Panama City, Panama and La Havana, Cuba.

The economy of North America comprises more than 514 million people with a gross domestic product of over $15.560 trillion (US dollars). Canada and the United States are the wealthiest and most developed nations in the continent; the countries of Central America and the Caribbean are much less developed, while Mexico — a newly industrialized country — lies somewhere in between these two extremes. Canada, the United States and Mexico developed the North American Free Trade Agreement in 1994 to facilitate trade and protect intellectual property rights and investments across borders (Wikipedia, 2007).

Socially and culturally, North America presents several well-defined areas. For example, Canada and the United States have a similar culture and similar traditions, primarily as a result of both countries being former British colonies. Similarly, Spanish-speaking North America also shares a common past as former Spanish colonies. In the majority of Central American countries and Mexico where civilizations like the Maya developed, indigenous people continue to preserve traditions across modern boundaries (Applied History Research Group, 2001). Finally, Central American and Spanish-speaking Caribbean nations have historically had more in common due to geographical proximity and the fact that, after winning independence from Spain, Mexico never took part in an effort to build a Central American Union.

The primary languages spoken in North America include English, Spanish, and French, though many other languages are used throughout the continent. English is spoken primarily in the United States and Canada (where French is also a co-official language) and Spanish is the most common language spoken in Mexico and Central America.

Similarities in language and culture are not all that Canada and the United States share. The education systems of these two countries, while certainly not identical, share a number of similarities as well. Moreover, the influence of the two systems on one another (particularly of the United States practices on Canadian practices) has been important in leadership development programs. Given these conditions, we will begin our discussion of leadership development with these two countries in turn, followed by a discussion of Mexico's work in leadership development. No attempt has been made in the present chapter to compare the statistics of education except in a most superficial way. Over time it may be possible to make more direct comparisons as methods and standards of measurement evolve.

LEADERSHIP DEVELOPMENT IN THE UNITED STATES

As in many countries, the positions of school leaders were originally bestowed upon head teachers. Over time, as school systems in the United States have become more complex and definitions of educational leadership have evolved, the requirements for taking a leadership position have increased. In many states, in order to lead a school or school district one must hold a special license or certification that warrants an individual's expertise to hold an educational leadership position. Typically, though it is not the case in all states, certification is tied to the completion of graduate level educational leadership courses and/or programs.

The preparation of educational leaders in the United States can trace its origins to the early part of the twentieth century, though it came strongly into its own in the 1950s. Since that time, leadership development in the United States has consisted of both pre-service and in-service preparation. For the most part, in-service preparation is provided by professional organizations or through collaborative efforts between universities and school districts following initial preparation. The graduate field of leadership preparation, on the other hand, is the primary means of providing pre-service preparation for principals and superintendents in the United States. An estimated 450–500 programs in schools and colleges of education offer leadership preparation through masters (472 institutions), specialist (162 institutions) and doctoral (199 institutions) degrees (Baker, Orr, & Young, 2005).

Over time, the content and character of leadership preparation has changed, shifting in the 1980s from a more conventional emphasis on school management to an emphasis on leadership that reflects emerging work in decentralized systems characterized by shared governance, participatory decision making, and school-based councils and again in the late 1990s to learning focused leadership. Embedded within the concept "leadership for learning" is the expectation that school and district leaders will have a working knowledge of learning, teaching, curriculum construction and alignment (Björk, 1993; Cambron-McCabe, 1993; Murphy, 1993). These shifts have resulted in a similar change in the focus and content of leadership preparation professional development.

Critique and Reform in Leadership Preparation

Between 1986 and 2007, both the preparation and professional development of educational leaders have been the focus of much criticism and reform (Young, Petersen, & Short, 2002). Several national commissions, task forces, and individual scholars have examined the nature of leadership and university-based leadership preparation programs. They were instrumental in shedding light on how demands for reform were altering the nature and direction of preparation programs. The first major effort to address criticisms of the field was undertaken in the mid-1980s when the National Commission on Excellence in Educational Administration (NCEEA) was developed. In 1987, the NCEEA issued a set of eight recommendations:

> calling for the redefinition of educational leadership; the establishment of a national board to shape policy related to school administration; the modeling of administrator preparation programs after other professional schools; a reduction in the number of preparation programs; the increased recruitment, preparation, and placement of ethnic minorities and women; the establishment of partnerships with the public schools in the preparation of school administrators; increased emphasis on professional development or practicing administrators; increased emphasis on professional development for practicing administrators; and reform of licensure and certification. (Forsyth, 1999, p. 75; see also Griffiths, Stout, & Forsyth, 1988; NCEEA, 1987)

These recommendations influenced thinking about school leadership and were widely endorsed in the United States. Following the release of this report, much emphasis was placed on leadership preparation. For example, the Danforth Foundation launched a major initiative to support preparation reform and innovation, the National Policy Board in Educational Administration (NPBEA) was established, and, across the United States, states engaged in efforts to strengthen standards designed to ensure the quality of administrator training (Young, Petersen, & Short, 2002).

Since the mid-1980s, several efforts have also been undertaken to define the knowledge base in educational leadership and to create standards for use in leadership preparation programs (Donmoyer, 1999; Donmoyer, Imber, & Scheurich, 1995). Efforts to define standards have been undertaken chiefly by organizations involved in the National Policy Board for Educational Administration (NPBEA) (Domnoyer, Imber, & Scheurich, 1995; Leithwood & Duke, 1997; NPBEA, 2002) with university faculty and practitioners playing a limited role. In the mid-1990s, the University Council for Educational Administration (UCEA) engaged scholars from across the country in defining the knowledge base in educational administration. Considered a controversial project by some, the UCEA Knowledge Base project resulted in the development of a document warehouse of essential readings on educational administration. The document warehouse, titled *Primis* and published for UCEA by McGraw Hill, enabled faculty to develop course readers from the identified knowledge base; the project also produced much generative discussion.

Soon thereafter, the NPBEA initiated the development of the Interstate School Leaders Licensure Consortium (ISLLC) standards for the professional practice of school leaders. The purpose of the ISLLC standards, according to consortium's sponsoring organization — the Council of Chief State School Officers (CCSSO) — was to provide a clear, organized set of curriculum content and performance standards that could be used to drive the preparation, professional development, and licensure of principals. By 2001, 35 states had adopted or adapted the standards for use in guiding the practice, preparation and professional development of educational leaders (CCSSO, 2001). Complimenting this effort, the Education Testing Service (ETS) used the ISLLC standards to develop a performance-based assessment, the School Leaders Licensure Assessment (SLLA), to assess proficiency in those same standards and thus the effectiveness of leadership preparation and professional development.

The ISSLC standards have substantially influenced preparation and professional development in the United States. In 2000, the NPBEA established a working group with representatives from AACTE, ASCD, AASA, NASSP, NCPEA, NAESP, NASB, and UCEA to design program accreditation standards for the National Council for the Accreditation of Teacher Education's (NCATE) review of educational leadership programs. These standards, which were adopted by NCATE in the spring of 2002, are currently under revision. The new version, which is predicted to be more research-based than the original set, should be in place for state level adoption and use by accrediting associations in early 2008.

In addition to these national efforts, attempts have been made to develop a base of empirical data upon which to guide preparation program reform efforts. Both individual researchers and organizations have participated in these efforts. For example, in 1999 UCEA conducted a study of principals and superintendents, their jobs, preparation and the problems they faced. In 2005, following the recommendations of the National Commission on the Advancement of Educational Leadership Preparation (NCAELP), UCEA published a meta-analysis of research on leadership preparation conducted by Joe Murphy that provided an overview of the state of research on preparation (M. Young, 2002a). Then, in 2005 UCEA worked with the National Council for Professors of Educational Administration (NCPEA), the Teaching in Educational Administration (TEA) special interest group and Division A of the American Educational Research Association

(AERA) to develop a research taskforce focused on leadership preparation. The research base developed from these efforts and the increasing emphasis on evaluation in accreditation reviews have encouraged a more data-based program improvement in the field.

A current national effort focused on program evaluation, jointly supported by UCEA and the Evaluation Research Taskforce, involves a Collaborative Evaluation Process in which programs document their practices and engage in shared evaluation research of programs' impact on leadership practices, using common follow up surveys of their graduates (Orr, 2005). Another promising approach that is becoming increasingly used to support program improvement is the Critical Friends process in which programs prepare documentation and evidence on their content, design and delivery based on a set of questions which reflect the principles of effective leadership preparation, to be reviewed by a team of leadership preparation experts. These experts serve as critical friends for feedback and suggestions for program improvement.

These efforts have had an important impact on preparation programs in the United States. For example, in response to criticisms concerning the fragmented nature of conventional preparation programs, many institutions have used core beliefs about the purpose of educational leadership and schools as a foundation for redesigning their programs. Some have used core beliefs to essentially reinvent their programs from recruitment and selection to curriculum and pedagogy.

Contemporary Leadership Preparation in the United States

So what exactly have these reforms produced? What does preparation entail in the United States? In this section, we review the most common aspects of leadership preparation programs in the United States. In doing so, we use a number of programs which have been identified by experts in the field as exceptional or innovative (Darling-Hammond, et al., 2007; Jackson & Kelley, 2002; Orr, 2006). These common program components include: *Student selection, curriculum, pedagogy, field-based experiences, and partnerships.*

Student Selection In the typical program, program applicants are identified, selected, and screened to reflect leadership potential. A key feature of these programs is the degree to which applicants are screened and selected for the programs. In some cases, applicants submit an essay and a set of recommendations from individuals who they feel can speak to their leadership potential. Based on this information and, in most programs, the applicant's score on the graduate record exam, program faculty select candidates who they believe will gain from and contribute to the program in meaningful ways. According to Orr (2006) student selection practices, in many programs, reflect the program's purpose and assumptions about leadership and its development. For example, the process used by the University of Texas at Austin assumes that principals must be able to transform schools into educational environments that work for each and every child, and, as a result, program faculty select candidates who are excellent teachers and who can provide evidence of teacher leadership (UCEA Review, 2007). In addition to evaluating each application portfolio, a team of observers visits each applicant's classroom to assess teaching quality and to personally interview the applicant and his or her principal.

In many programs applicants are selected as a cohort. Again program assumptions about leadership and adult learning may come in to play in that some programs attempt to identify a mix of students that will support one another's learning and development. For example, Brigham Young University uses cohorts with the intention of developing professional learning communities. At BYU, then, cohorts are used to facilitate student learning. Similarly, Wichita State University intentionally organizes student cohorts into learning families for the duration of their two-year program, meeting weekly for courses that are linked to practicum assignments for each semester in their concurrent field work and to work in student and faculty teams to complete field-based projects. More typically, cohort structures are used as a means of simplifying program delivery.

Curriculum   In effective programs, there is a clear, well-defined curriculum that reflects agreement on the relevant knowledge and skills needed for educational leaders in their first year, or first few years in the profession (Jackson & Kelley, 2002). As such, contemporary leadership preparation curriculum reflects the heightened emphasis on school improvement (e.g., courses focused on change, transformational leadership, applied research and data analysis), social justice (e.g., courses focused on issues of diversity and leadership for special needs students), and democracy (e.g., courses on ethics, collaboration, and distributed leadership; Orr, 2006).

Although programs ultimately determine course content, national leadership standards — the ISLLC standards — frame preparation program focus and alignment in many states. To date, almost 40 states have adopted or adapted the ISLLC standards as platforms for programs and licensure, with many requiring university alignment, and use the standards for program review and accreditation (Anthes, 2004). In 2002, these standards were integrated into NCATE and EL-CC's standards for leadership preparation programs for accreditation and recognition. By 2005, one-third of all institutions (representing 34 per cent of all institutions with leadership programs nationwide) had received national recognition by NCATE for one or more leadership preparation programs, many based on the new standards (Fede, 2005, personal communication). Thus, state licensure policy and the ISLLC standards have had a major hand in shaping and defining the knowledge base of leadership preparation programs.

Pedagogy   Problem-based and case-based teaching methods are increasingly the primary mode of teaching in educational leadership preparation programs. These pedagogical tools offer situated learning and an opportunity to experiment with multiple perspectives within a traditional classroom setting. A number of preparation programs have incorporated problem-based learning, an approach adapted for educational leadership by Bridges (1992), as a means of grounding aspiring leaders in the problems of their field, expanding their problem-framing and problem-solving capabilities, and working on problems collaboratively with others.

Building on some of the work in adult learning, UCEA has focused on the possibility of developing a signature pedagogy in the development of school leaders, one that would include problem-focused learning, action research and other transformative learning experiences (Brown, 2005, Mezirow, 1991; Murtadha, 2006). Drawing from new developments in adult learning theory and principles, such as Mezirow (1991) and Kolb (1984), faculty are incorporating experiential learning, reflective practice, structured dialogue, problem-based learning and learning communities into their courses. Kolb's work, which emphasizes the importance of experiential learning through experience, reflection, conceptualization, and experimentation, is commonly used in the contemporary programs.

Reflective practice is increasingly structured into and throughout programs as a means of provoking and challenging students presuppositions, helping them to surface theories-in-use that shape behavior, and enabling them to try on other frames for leadership development (Osterman, 1995). According to Mezirow (1991), learning becomes transformational when facilitated through guided reflection, particularly when it challenges the validity of presumptions rooted in prior learning. Reflection work is an integral part of many programs with formal reflections frequently incorporated into final portfolios.

Field-Based Experiences   In recent years, internships, practica and other field-based experiences have become more central to leadership preparation. Many internships involve over 600 contact hours and span at least two semesters. In some programs, the internship extends through a program's two-year duration. In a handful of programs, like that of Brigham Young University, the internship is full-time; however in most programs the internship is a part time experiences. In the latter situation, field-based experiences are typically integrated into course work. In these programs, the curriculum is sequenced and mapped against the annual cycle of regular work responsibilities and the random, non-routine responsibilities of the principal, or against a vision of the knowledge, skills and abilities needed to be an effective school leader. Moreover, adult learning strategies on active learning, reflection, portfolio development, and transformative learning have been incorporated into internships to make encourage theory to practice connections and generally make them more meaningful learning experiences.

Partnerships   Less than 20 years ago, district-university collaborations were small-scale initiatives involving districts and regional colleges and universities. Today, however, district and university collaborations in leadership preparation programs are increasingly common and involve colleges and universities of many sizes. Moreover, the nature of the collaborations tend to be much more substantive and reciprocal, reflecting leadership needs for local contexts (e.g., student achievement or teacher turnover). District leaders are no longer satisfied to participate on advisory boards; rather they participate as partners in program design and delivery in their schools and district. Program delivery is in university-district partnership programs are often located in the districts themselves using the schools and district problems and data resources as learning contexts. In a growing number of such partnerships, districts provide paid opportunities for selected candidates to participate. For example, in the multi-district partnership developed at BYU, districts grant participants a one-year paid sabbatical.

Professional Development in the United States

In the United States, a variety of forms of leadership professional development are provided by multiple associations, organizations, and groups. These include programs from: national associations such as NASSP, ASCD, NSDC, and NAESP, state administrator associations, university institutes, comprehensive school reform programs, state departments of public instruction, major national and state programs, regional laboratories, district leadership academies, independent consultants, and, more recently, for-profit firms. These groups offer a variety of workshops, academies, and professional development opportunities of various lengths. According to Peterson (2002), many such programs have carefully designed curricula, quality instruction, and a clear mission; however, there is such a wide array to choose from that administrators may find it difficult to choose a program that best fits their needs.

For the most part professional development takes place outside the university, with one exception, superintendent training. The preparation of district superintendents, perhaps because it is a form of pre-service education, tends to still take place within university preparation programs. However, Grogan and Andrews (2002) argue that very few universities have developed programs specifically for the superintendency, even though many states require licensure for individuals who wish to be superintendents. On the other hand, much attention has been given to defining what school system leaders need to know and be able to do. One example is the AASA standards: performance-based standards and indicators were explicated in, *Skills for Successful School Leaders* (Hoyle, English, & Steffy, 1985). The eight standards included: 1) designing, implementing, and evaluating school climate; 2) building support for schools; 3) developing school curriculum; 4) conveying instructional management; 5) evaluating staff; 6) developing staff; 7) allocating resources and, 8) engaging in research, evaluation and planning.

According to Grogan and Andrews (2002), the task of preparing district administrators is complicated by the fact that there are typically a variety of academic paths to the superintendency. In various states, these include coursework and field experiences leading to the superintendent's license, an Ed.D. or a Ph.D. degree. Interestingly, the educational leadership doctorate is often viewed as synonymous with superintendent preparation. This may eventually change, however, as the conflation of doctoral degrees, regardless of their content focus, with expertise for professional educational leadership positions has caused alarm in some circles. A growing number of education schools and colleges have joined a Carnegie Foundation taskforce focusing on redesigning the education doctorate.

Women in Educational Administration in the United States

There is a fairly robust literature on women in educational leadership in the United States, spanning the last three decades. Research has focused on the differences between men and women leaders, the working conditions of women leaders, mentoring, and so forth. Of most interest has been trying to understand why there are so few women in educational leadership. While, the representation of women in administrative positions in K–12 and higher education institutions is increasing, they are still not present in proportion to their number in teaching. To illustrate, while women make up 75 per cent of all teachers in the United States, they make up only 44 per cent of principals and 18 per cent of all superintendents, nationwide.

Over the last decade and a half, research on gender and school administration has provided insight into this situation. For example, Ortiz and Marshall (1988) found that women do not have the same opportunities as men in administration. They attributed this problem primarily to stereotypes attached to both women and leadership. According to Charters and Jovick (1981), society conditions both men and women to believe that women are not as capable of holding leadership positions as men (see also Bell & Chase, 1993; Blackmore & Kenway, 1997; Marshall, 1993; Marshall & Kasten, 1994; Shakeshaft, 1987; Skrla, 2000). Furthermore, Shepard (1999) asserted that external barriers (e.g., recruitment, selection, evaluation, and reward systems), as well as norms and expectations of most schools and school districts, ensure that women are less likely than men to serve in leadership positions. Similarly, Walby (1990) argued that the criteria used to recruit and hire administrators favor men over women.

Less attention has been given to women's experiences with pre- and in-service education. However, we do know that women are no longer under-represented in preparation or doctoral programs. On the contrary, in a state by state analysis conducted by Young and Fuller (2007), it was found that women make up on average between 52–64 per cent of the candidates enrolled in educational leadership preparation programs. Whether or not these programs meet the needs of women students is debatable. Young and McLeod (2001) warn that "traditional leadership literature [including leadership theories] essentially legitimizes traditionally male behavior and perspectives and delegitimizes the behavior and perspectives of women" (p. 491). Moreover, Young and McLeod found that "exposure to nontraditional leadership styles is a key element in facilitating women's paths into administration" (p. 491). If women observe variations in leadership styles and expectations, they are more likely to believe that leadership is not only something they can do, but also something they might want to do.

Continuing Issues Concerning Leadership Development in the United States

Although, much of the recent attention focused on leadership preparation and professional development in the United States has been the result the standards and accountability movement, the focus on quality content and delivery and useful assessment has been growing within the academy. Preparation and professional development remain, for the most part, as independent, or at best loosely linked, endeavors with separate providers, content and purposes. Thus far, little attention has been given in the United States to coordinating career-long learning experiences for leaders, which might provide leaders with more cumulative, higher quality and deeper learning experiences (Peterson, 2002). Similarly, limited attention has been given within the field to learning from the experiences of other countries. While there has been a quiet tradition of faculty exchange and comparative and international scholarship on educational leadership in the United States, the content of few leadership programs are impacted by international scholarship and few programs have more than cursory treatment of global education issues. This is not the case in Canada, where a more global perspective is taken in K–12 and higher education.

EDUCATIONAL LEADERSHIP PREPARATION IN CANADA

Similar to the United States, educational Administration has been a field of study in some Canadian universities since at least the 1950s. In his book on doctoral research in educational administration at the University of Alberta, Erwin Miklos (1992) analyzed the dissertation research topics, methods and methodologies used from 1958 to 1991. The study provided a comprehensive view of what students of educational administration were exposed to and what captured their attention during those years. In total, 329 Ph.D. dissertations and one Ed.D. dissertation were reviewed. About half of the studies investigated areas related to organizational studies or policy analysis and the other half to change, the context of educational administration, decision making and the administrator. Miklos argued that the characteristics of the studies "serve as indicators of the nature and state of research conducted within educational administration in general" (p. 173). He noted the influence of the social science movement and the struggle to understand every-day practice — a theme that appears to recur in discussions about what is taught in Canadian educational administration programs (see also Deblois, 1992).

In the early days, as was the case in the United States, administrator preparation programs offered students a theoretical foundation from the social sciences or humanities and from the business literature. "[S]tudents of educational administration came into direct contact with social scientists either through taking courses in the disciplines or in having professors from these areas participate in interdisciplinary seminars" (Miklos, 1992, p. 6). The expected outcome was an increased capacity to be able to analyze administrative and educational problems. This enthusiasm for direct contact with professors of social science subsequently waned, but the orientation towards the social sciences continues to persist. Most of these university degree programs served both those who were preparing to become researchers in the field and those who aspired to be practicing administrators. The qualifications for individuals to gain positions as school administrators across Canada differ by province, but it was not until the mid 1980s that Ontario started to require certification. Teaching experience at different divisional levels was the most important preparation early on and remains essential today.

Influenced heavily by the field of educational administration in the United States, Canadian professors of the educational administration have long been engaged in the task of defining for themselves and their students what constitutes the Canadian context of educational administration. Some of the writers "suggest that there is something of a love-hate relationship between Canada and the U.S.; some Canadians admire many aspects of American culture, but fear its excesses" (Hickcox, 1981, p. vii). During the education boom of the 1960s and 70s, many "Yankee" professors were hired in Canadian universities bringing with them ideas and theories of educational administration popular in the United States to the students farther north. Some question the assumptions that undergird U.S. approaches to the field. Greenfield (1981) argued that "the theory of educational administration and the belief in a general science of organization are an American invention of the twentieth century" (p. 15).

Characteristics of Educational Administration Unique to Canada

Education in Canada is controlled by the provincial governments. About 95 per cent of the population is educated in publicly funded schools and the rest in private or federally or First Nations-controlled schools (Levin & Young, 1994). Provinces provide the legislation that allows for the creation of school boards to govern school districts, but "the final authority over most areas of educational decision making remains at the provincial level, with a minister of education" (Levin & Young, p. 27). Worthy of note is that Protestant and Catholic parents in Canada have the right to establish their own schools and to receive public funding for them. These separate schools and school boards differ from province to province but, in general, the province retains the power to control curriculum and teachers. Levin and Young remark that schools play an important role in the creation of a Canadian identity amongst a very religiously and culturally diverse population. This has lead to increased standardization of curricula and schools nationwide although much attention is paid to linguistic diversity and, in particular, to the rights of the English-speaking and French-speaking populations in each province.

Canadian schools are organized into district units governed by school boards that employ superintendents and principals to supervise the operation of schools. The role of the school administrator is to ensure that organizational goals are met and that policies and procedures are followed. By the late 1980s and 90s, there was a growing public dissatisfaction with the way schools were performing (Deblois, 1992). Linking poor student performance to the absence of leadership in schools, university preparation programs came under fire. Some of the criticisms included the irrelevance of administrative theory to the day-to-day work of the principal and too much emphasis on the control aspect of administration in contrast to too little emphasis on the values aspect. The call for a values component echoes a chord found in the work of a number of Canadian scholars of educational administration and might be seen as one of Canada's major contributions to the educational administration literature. Though they were not the only educational administration scholars to write and research about values, several Canadian scholars have attended to values issues in their work.

Some of the most prominent include Paul Begley, Elizabeth Campbell, Christopher Hodgkinson, Lyse Langlois, and Kenneth Leithwood. Their work has influenced leadership preparation not only in Canada, but in other English and non-English-speaking countries around the world. In the late 1990s, the University Council for Educational Administration established The UCEA Center for the Study of Educational Leadership and Ethics, a partnership between the Ontario Institute for Studies in Education and the University of Virginia (in the United States). The center was established to conduct research on the relationships and intersections between educational leadership and ethics and values with the understanding that future generations of school and district leaders would be prepared to be moral and ethical leaders. Hodgkinson's

(1978) values typology sparked much of the early interest in this research, and Begley (1999) developed a line of inquiry applying values typology to the work of Canadian school leaders dealing particularly with the value-conflicts and diversity they were confronted with in the 1990s and the 2000s.

Leithwood (1999) articulates two challenges for those preparing leaders in this vein. He highlights first the need to sensitize leaders to the crucial professional values "on which the design of high-reliability learning communities are dependent" (p. 45). His second argument is that leaders need to be prepared to prioritize their values depending on the needs of the organization. Campbell (2003) points out that principal leadership programs fail to focus enough (and in some cases, not at all) on moral and ethical principles, but focus rather on technical and instrumental models of decision-making. Based on her research with school administrators and teachers, Campbell asserts that ethics training is essential because a principal's behavior, attitudes, decisions and leadership practices can contribute to or detract from an overall ethical school environment.

Such work attends to Greenfield's (1981) criticism that the pervasive influence of United States scholarship on educational administration "… prevents us from seeing our schools and seeing their cultural and social context" (p. 16). Although scholarship from the United States has been influential in Canadian leadership research and development programs, Canadian scholars have been skeptical that the research on social problems and issues of diversity in United States schools can inform practice in Canada. Langlois and Lapointe (2007) contribute important contextual understanding of the leadership issues in linguistic-minority school settings in Canada. Their study of principals of French-language minority schools in seven Canadian provinces found that principals were guided by an ethic of critique that helped to protect the French-language identity as well as providing for linguistic and cultural survival.

Urban issues and challenges of race integration in the United States that thread the texts and other materials used for principal preparation are seen as less than helpful (Hickcox, 1981, 2002). Citing fundamental differences in constitutional provisions, Greenfield makes the point that "The Canadian constitution promises 'peace, order and good government' thus implying institutional control of the individual, while the American constitution offers its citizens 'life, liberty and the pursuit of happiness,' and thereby implies that citizens should be free of restraint by unnecessary or unwanted institutions" (p. 21). Canadian views of schools and government involvement in schooling differ sharply from those found in the United States.

Certification/Qualifications

Some provinces require school principals and vice-principals to be certified, but many others do not. Ontario, New Brunswick, and the Northwest Territories, are among those that do (Hickcox, 2002; Normore, 2004). In Ontario, for instance, certification is obtained by gaining teaching experience and taking postgraduate coursework. Sometimes coursework is embedded in a master's degree, in intense summer experiences or threaded throughout the program (Normore, 2004; Rees 1991). Universities are primarily responsible for delivering such coursework though previously teachers' federations and the ministry were involved. Administrator preparation programs in Quebec reflected major transitions from a professional religious leadership to lay administrators. Principals there are exposed to inservice opportunities and usually move into the position from the vice-principalship (Deblois, 1992).

Within the context of a provincial discussion about introducing certification in British Columbia, a recent study of educational leadership programs there found little consensus on what leadership means and how best to develop it. Programs followed a competency approach to leadership development and assessment and advocated the integration of theory and practice (Stack, Coulter, Grosjean, Mazawi, & Smith, 2006). Because of so little conceptual agreement amongst designers of these programs, the authors did not endorse current efforts to standardize leadership training in the province. Content in the courses, which led mainly to master's degrees, drew primarily on social science, learning, leadership, administration and research. Most of these programs were delivered via the cohort model and on-campus instruction was often complemented by flexible or distance delivery modes of instruction. The authors identified some general concerns associated with the programs including the nonexistence of aboriginal leadership as a focus of study, the absence of faculty trained in the area, the relative absence of aboriginal students and the lack of indigenous content taught within the leadership curricula. Foster and Goddard (2003) noted similar findings in their study of aboriginal schools in the northern part of the province. They urge researchers, policy makers and practitioners "to consider ways in which traditional indigenous beliefs and values might inform models of leadership that contribute to the rebalancing of economic and political power in northern communities and their schools" (p. 11).

A similar concern for the development of a conceptual model of leadership was expressed in another scholarly report on designing a master's program in educational leadership at the University of Lethbridge in Alberta (Aitken, Bedard, & Darroch, 2003). Alberta does not require certification for the principalship, but many school boards expect candidates to have a master's degree. The authors argue that the new models of school leadership need to reflect Alberta's restructured, decentralized approach to education. The evolution of shared decision making and site-based decision-making requires school leaders to be skilled collaborators and to use inclusive strategies. Expectations include working with school councils, responding to parent concerns and collaborating and dialoguing with teachers. New core and concentration courses in the program draw upon a knowledge base for developing leaders "that stresses self-understanding, using inquiry, shaping school communities, and understanding and interpreting people and contextual differences" (p. 28). This represents a move towards a more holistic and integrated preparation of leaders away from the traditional disciplinary, role-oriented approach.

Women in Educational Administration in Canada

There was little concern expressed over the absence of women from school and district leadership positions in Canada until the mid 1980s (M. Young, 1994). Rees' (1991) research found that, in Ontario, after the education ministry adopted an affirmative action/employment equity policy in 1986, preparation opportunities for women improved. However, most helpful to women were the changes in application procedures and residency requirements for the summer intensive courses that provided certification. By the late 1980s, women comprised about half those who were successfully certified as administrators in Ontario. Their placement in positions did not follow as quickly though. The majority of superintendents and principals in Canada traditionally have been, and continue to be, men (Levin & B. Young, 1994; B. Young, 2002b). Barriers to women include stereotypical notions of who is best suited to lead schools. "If we think that to be a successful high-school principal a person must be large and have a powerful voice, then we automatically exclude most women (and many men) from consideration" (Levin & B. Young, 1994, p. 199). Beth Young (1994) found that women became more visible and more vocal in Canadian departments of educational administration from the mid 1980s. By the early 1990s, women made up about 20 per cent of the professors in English-speaking regions. However, there has been little research on women's issues as practicing principals and superintendents in Canada. "Feminist thought is only beginning to affect Canadian educational administration" (B. Young, 1994, p. 364).

Moreover, statistical information revealing the numbers of women in administrative posts in Canada is very hard to come by. Beth Young (2002) argues that little responsibility has been taken at the provincial and federal level for collecting and reporting such data, but a 1999 survey of Alberta's school districts conducted by the Alberta Teachers' Association (ATA) discovered that no women held superintendencies in that province (B. Young, 2002). Women fare a little better at other levels it seems. According to the Canadian Teachers' Federation, women hold one out of five secondary school principalships and three out of ten vice-principalships (B. Young, 2002). Reynolds (2002) offers a historical perspective of women's increasing presence in the principalship from the 1940s through the 1970s. She was not sure, though, that her findings boded well for the future. She leaves open the question of whether organizational structures and available discourses have changed enough to guarantee equitable access to leadership positions for the next generation of women. The extent to which preparation and selection of leaders for schools are gendered processes is unclear. Although researchers like Rees, Reynolds and Beth Young raise the questions, few studies have investigated the current Canadian context.

Canada as Part of a Global World

In comparison to the United States, Canadian reflections on education and the leadership of Canadian schools and districts are situated in a larger, global context. While both countries view themselves as nations of immigrants, Canada takes this aspect of its identity to heart. For example, in Canada cultural and linguistic diversity is considered one of the most important issues facing school leaders, whereas in the United States this is not the case.

Whereas schools in both countries are at the forefront of dealing with enormous demographic changes over the past century, the United States continues to encourage assimilation and while tensions exist in Canada between the traditional assimilationist approaches and the more sensitive approach to preserve cultural integrity at some level. "[C]lassrooms are increasingly heterogeneous in their ethnic make-up. Teachers may have substantial numbers of students whose first language is not English, and whose culture, or whose parents' culture, is quite different from the dominant culture in Canada" (Levin & M. Young, 1994, p. 296). As Ungerleider (2005) argues, "Canada depends to a greater extent [than other nations] on its public schools to communicate the values that define and distinguish Canadians from others and Canada from other nations" (p. 12).

School leaders are increasingly being called upon to handle these challenges in productive ways that build community out of fragmented groups of stakeholders (Ryan, 2003; Shields, 2002). Studies drawing on the experiences of leading in contemporary Canadian schools have helped to develop an expanded notion of community to include communities of difference. Shields describes it as a form of cultural democracy in which prejudice is critically scrutinized and race and ethnicity matter. Mahwinney (2005) clarifies the different approaches in the two countries:

> Canadians refer to multiculturalism as a public policy holding two dimensions: recognition of cultural diversity and social equality for members of minorities. In contrast, in the U.S. multiculturalism acknowledges the role of minorities in the nation's history and culture. It is therefore, mainly a statement about identity.... Education policy in the U.S. largely focused on creating [a] societal culture, has also been designed to minimize and negate cultural identities of ethnic and minority groups. (p. 15)

The preparation of school leaders in Canada reflects such Canadian policy frameworks — although not exclusively. The value of scholarship and preparation practices from the United States, the United Kingdom and other countries cannot be underestimated for their breadth and scope.

Educational Leadership Preparation in Mexico

In comparison to the scholarship on leadership development in the United States and Canada, little has been written in English about the preparation of school leaders in Mexico. Additionally, only a few articles address the roles and responsibilities of principals in elementary or secondary schools. From such articles and from other scholarship addressing broader educational topics, we have gained a somewhat fragmented picture of leaders in schools and how they get there.

Much of the decision-making power in schools resides with the Educational Worker's Union (SNTE) described as Latin America's largest trade union (*Economist,* 2006). School principals along with classroom teachers belong to this union that hires and occasionally fires teachers. Teachers are not evaluated by anyone outside the union and many teachers are not formally trained. School principals are primarily responsible for the routine management of school operations (Ornelas, 2004). Levinson (2004) describes principals as being similar to "governors" or "presidents" who behave as if their positions are threatened by new curricular reforms to introduce civic and ethics to students in secondary schools. Waite and Allen (2003) argue that the pyramidal hierarchies in education, like all bureaucracies in Mexico, invite corruption and abuse of power. According to the authors, appointments to become head of schools are based as much on patronage and nepotism as upon leadership skills. Ornelas (2004) makes a similar point that educational supervisors are usually political appointees. "'[D]emocratic education' involves a different, more collegial role for school administration, yet current administrators are resistant..." (Levinson, 2004, p. 278).

MEXICAN CONTEXT

Since the 1990s much energy has gone into education reform in Mexico. Guided by the Federal Secretariat of Public Education (SEP), reforms in the early 90s were aimed at improving the quality of education and at achieving a more equitable education system (Ornelas, 2004). The goals of educational reform were essentially the same during the terms of presidents Salinas de Cortari, 1988–1994, Ernesto Zedillo, 1994–2000, and Vicente Fox, 2000–20006. However, Mr. Fox added the improvement of school management as an important new priority (Ornelas, 2004). A shift toward decentralization placed the responsibility for basic education with local governments instead of at the federal level. Local governments now oversee their system of education, the calendar, and personnel issues. However, the main educational functions of curricular design, evaluation of teachers, and the distribution of resources remains under the control of the national department of education (SEP). Yet, the reforms are the most far reaching Mexico has seen in modern times. According to Martin and Guzman (2005), the reforms include major decentralized administrative innovation, changes in teaching practice and performance expectations, new compensatory programs in neglected areas, and the development of more accountable student evaluation systems.

Under President Fox's goal of quality in education, which continues to guide reform under the new administration, the focus is on the teachers as the most important actors in the education reform. At the same time, school principals and supervisors are expected to lead the change effort through new and more effective management skills (Ornelas, 2004). Parents and other community organizations have a limited role to play in the development of their local schools, but they are not allowed any input into teaching methods or content. As part of the move towards decentralization, under the Zedillo administration, two projects were designed to change administrative approaches to the improvement of education. One was a pilot project (PE) that adopted school-based management and the other was the Quality Schools Program (PEC). Both programs were critical of the lack of principal decision-making powers and the lack of principal involvement in instructional issues (Ornelas, 2004). The projects (PE and PEC) both advocate the participation in decision-making of a school community. Teachers, administrators, students and parents would work together to identify local issues and seek local remedies. Ornelas (2004) cites positive evaluations of the projects in helping to improve the leadership of school principals though he does not explain how or in what sense.

While the reforms appear to have opened up new possibilities for notions of leadership in schools as opposed to school management, there appear to be few studies reported in English of school leaders on the job and none that discuss how leadership preparation and development needs to change to meet these new goals (see Cisneros-Cohernour & Bastarrachea, 2005; Cortina, 1989; Cuellar, 1989; Iturbe & Talan, 2006; Slater et al., 2000, 2003). Similarly, only four studies reported in English look at school leadership preparation (see Slater et al., 2001, 2002, 2003, 2006).

Principals in Mexico Compared to Principals in the United States

Each of the Slater et al. studies noted above takes a comparative approach to leadership preparation and training by gathering data from Mexican students enrolled in a master's degree at the Instituto Politecnico Nacional in Mexico City and from students in a master's program at Southwest Texas State University. The studies are designed and collaboratively conducted by professors from both the Mexican institution and from the United States institution. The main theoretical framework used in all is Hofstede's work on cultural difference. The earliest of those studies (Slater et al., 2001, 2003) identified some clearly different approaches to leadership preparation in the two countries. Using focus groups and written comments from about 25 students in both programs, the researchers analyzed the data and found some recurring themes across both groups to allow for a comparison. A particular difference that helps illuminate the preparation of leaders in Mexico is the mention of the importance of a global, collective approach to solving problems in Mexican schools in contrast to the more individualistic approach found in the United States students' comments. There was a greater sense of commitment to take on the problems in the Mexican students' comments. The authors attribute these fundamental differences to the different programmatic emphases — in Mexico, there is more focus on the study of history and the social conditions of education and there is a requirement for students to conduct a research-based thesis.

In the Slater et al. 2002 study, Kouzes and Posner's (1995) Leadership Practices Inventory (LPI) was administered to a cross cultural sample of 56 university students preparing for educational leadership at the same two universities mentioned above. There were 28 students in each setting. The United States program of studies was narrowly focused on preparation of teachers for the principalship and superintendency, but the Mexican program educated individuals for administrative positions in a range of organizations including elementary and secondary schools and higher education (Slater et al., 2002). Findings were that for each of the leadership categories, the United States subjects scored higher than their Mexican counterparts according to the mean rank scores. There was also a difference in the order of the rankings for each group — the Mexican students ranked encouraging the heart at the top of the list while the United States students ranked enabling others first. Interestingly, each group's top ranking was ranked last by the other group.

Relevant to the preceding discussion, the authors found that in contrast to the United States, Mexican aspiring leaders did not score highly on the leadership practice of challenging the process. By way of possible explanation, Slater et al. (2002), suggest that Mexican educational leaders value uncertainty avoidance. They also point out that to challenge the process would involve challenging authority, which would be inconsistent with Mexican traditional cultural processes. In addition, since the Mexican culture is polychronic, there is not the same sense of urgency to change as there is in a monochronic culture like the United States. In a follow-up study, Slater, Boone, Fillion et al., (2003) examined attitudes about the same leadership practices through leadership essays written by 26 United States university students and 26 Mexican students. As in the first study, the Mexican group wrote more about encouraging the heart and the United States group focused more on challenging the process. Since the Mexican students did not score highly on any of the leadership practices espoused by Kouzes and Posner in either study, Slater et al., raise the issue of whether United States leadership theories are particularly useful to understand leadership in Mexican schools.

Prompted by findings in these earlier studies of leadership aspirants in both countries, Slater, Boone, et al., (2006), used a qualitative approach to investigate how school administrators view ideal images of educational leadership in Mexico City and South Texas. This cross-cultural study aimed first to clarify how the different groups conceived of ideal leadership and, then, to inform leadership preparation in both countries. Again, the United States university preparation program was more focused on school and district leadership than the Mexican university, which offered a master's degree in leadership for various organizational settings. The participants in the study were asked to reflect on leadership and to relate their best leadership experiences — as a formal, graded assignment in the United States case, but as an in-class essay in the Mexican case. In addition, many of the United States students already had leadership roles in schools in contrast to the Mexican students who apparently did not. The distinct differences between the backgrounds and experiences of the participants and the differing circumstances under which they completed the assignment does call into question the comparability of the essays produced.

Nevertheless, consistent with previous studies, the authors of this study also found distinct differences of opinion about the valued qualities of leadership between the two groups. The Mexican students identified teamwork, trust, enovation,[2] humility and honesty as important characteristics of leadership while the United States participants emphasized involvement, technical communication, innovation and learning. The authors found there were some shared images of leadership across the two groups such as risk taking and charisma, but cultural mores shaped the ways those characteristics were demonstrated. In the essays from Mexico City, leadership was portrayed as rotating from person to person depending on the task. "There was less position authority and more persuasion" (p. 167). In addition, these essays expressed little confidence in the process of leadership and more faith in the integrity of the person. There is a much greater sense of the place of history in the Mexican system — leaders are expected to help others gain a sense of pride in past accomplishments and hope for future success. Slater et al. (2006) conclude that these ideas communicate a different philosophy of education in each country and, in each case, the students seem to have been well prepared to operate as educational leaders in the two distinct cultures. However, the authors raise the important question of whether, in this global world today, some overarching international perspectives should guide educational leadership preparation.

Women in Educational Leadership in Mexico

Finally, two studies available in English looked at the issues of women in educational leadership in Mexico (Cortina, 1989; Iturbe & Talan, 2006). Though these studies focus on women, they contribute to our understanding of leadership preparation in general. Women *are* found in administrative positions in the schools — especially at the elementary level, but they form a small minority in the powerful national ministry of education (SEP) and the union (SNTE). "As a result, women exercise little influence on policy-making and the daily management of the schools in which they work" (Cortina, p. 358). Because the Mexican hierarchical bureaucracy concentrates educational authority outside the schools, little autonomy or decision-making power is devolved to the buildings themselves. One important point regarding preparation for leadership seems to be that women traditionally had access only to the normal schools rather than the universities (Cortina). In the past, women and less privileged men could enter the normal schools and get a teaching certificate instead of trying to get into the elite high schools, which ultimately prepared students for higher education and especially the professions. Iturbe and Talan (2006) make the point that the presence of significant numbers of women in elementary leadership positions is also a result of men having more choices to gain university degrees that lead to better paying positions. Few male or female teachers have the kind of university degree that is required for upper level leadership such as in SEP.

According to Cortina, (1989), the rise to power in SNTE depends on seniority and contacts within the union itself. Some move into the SNTE leadership after a career in public school administration. However, most important, SNTE plays a key role in advancing or curtailing an individual's career in administration. Cortina argues that "The informal networks of friendship and social relations that constitute the daily life of teachers act as a barrier in the promotion of women" (p. 365). Active involvement in union activities and politics is necessary for promotion to the superintendency and the principalship in Mexico. "Women's lives continue to be restricted by cultural patterns and power relationships between men and women at home, the workplace and their communities" (Iturbe & Talan, p. 1). Therefore, it seems that preparation for educational leadership in Mexico is much less dependent on formal qualifications such as degrees than it is on key opportunities to interact with powerful elites in the educational establishment who can foster an individual's career. One other important factor in career advancement appears to lie, historically at least, in the desirability of training as a teacher in a public normal school as opposed to a private one. This is because the union and the authorities from SEP protect those who graduate from public institutions (Cortina, 1989). Whether that remains true today is not clear. In any case, the approach to educational leadership as well as the approach to leadership preparation in Mexico contrasts strongly with the approaches to both in the other North American countries.

CONCLUSION AND DISCUSSION

Direct comparisons of educational leadership development in North America are difficult to accomplish. Each of the three countries we examined in this chapter has a very different history, culture, economy and political structure that has and continues to influence the politics that govern educational leadership development. Although the Canadian and United States systems have some important beliefs and practices in common, they are not exactly the same. The purpose of this chapter, or course, was not to develop a design for a North American leadership development tradition. That practices, devices, methods, organization, all the detailed aspects which go to make up an educational system cannot be transferred intact from one environment to another, has been amply proved in both practice and research. This fact, however, illustrates only the "wrong use of comparative education and emphasizes the importance of adaptation as over against assimilation in education. Comparative education has an entirely different function, particularly at the present time when so many of the problems of education are almost universally identical" (Kandel, 1970, p. xviii). According to Kandel, comparative work, such as that contained in this volume as well as more serious empirical research, enables a study of the problems of education systems, "an analysis of the causes which have produced them, in a comparison of the differences between the various systems and the reasons underlying them, and, finally, in a study of the solutions attempted" (Kandel, 1970, p. xix).

Thus, while this chapter serves as a description of three distinct systems of leadership development in North America, it may also serve as a window to identifying common educational problems that through analysis can assist scholars in North America and elsewhere in developing an understanding of and/or push thinking about such problems.

On the other hand, an argument could also be made for seeing Canada, the United States and Mexico as a North American Region. Mahwinney (2005) advocates the writing of education policies in a reinvented vernacular of the United States and Canada (and we would add Mexico) that acknowledges "history of the First Nations, their territorial defeats and victories, the similar subsequent victories of Spanish, French and English colonists, and the waves of immigrants that have woven their identities into the territorial fabric of North America" (p. 16) If we consider the value of the idea of transnational citizenship, this regional concept can provide a powerful organizing force for new notions of school leadership.

We are left, then, with the intriguing challenge of how best to prepare school leaders to embrace and enact leadership that envisions a much greater connectivity between peoples of the region and world. To be sure, as professors in the field, our first task must be to dialogue with each other about our separate national contexts of educational leadership. Trans-cultural/national research studies should follow in an attempt to understand the much richer, more multi-faceted social, political and economic environments our students already operate within. New theoretical underpinnings of leadership will no doubt emerge and new knowledge of global leadership practices will surface.

NOTES

1. Our own language limitations also served to undermine our efforts to review research on leadership preparation that was not published in English.
2. Enovation means change that emerges within the organization according to Slater et al. (2006).

REFERENCES

Aitken, A., Bedard, G., & Darroch, A. (2003). *Designing a master program in educational leadership: Trends, reflections and conclusions.* ERIC Full text ED475008.

Anthes, K (2004). Administrator license requirements, portability, waivers, and alternative certification. ECS State Notes Leadership /Licensure. Denver CO: Education Commission of the States.

Applied History Research Group. (2001). *Peopling North America: Migration movements & migration.* Applied History Research Group, Calgary University. Retrieved September 12, 2007 from: http://www.ucalgary.ca/applied_history/tutor/migrations/

Baker, B., Orr, M. T. & Young, M. D. (2005). Academic Drift, Institutional Production and Professional

Distribution of Graduate Degrees in Educational Administration. Paper presented at the annual meeting of the American Educational Research Association, San Francisco, CA.

Begley, P. T. (1999). Value preferences, ethics and conflicts. In P. T. Begley (Ed.), *Values and educational leadership* (pp. 237–254). Albany, NY: SUNY Press.

Bell, C., & Chase, S. (1993). The under representation of women in school leadership. In C. Marshall (Ed.), The new politics of race and gender (pp. 141–154). London: The Falmer Press.

Björk, L. (1993). Effective schools-effective superintendents: the emerging instructional leadership role. *Journal of School Leadership, 3*, 246–259.

Blackmore, J., & Kenway, J. (1997). *Gender matters in educational administration and policy: A feminist introduction*. London: The Falmer Press.

Bridges, E. (1992). *Problem-based Learning for Administrators*. ERIC Clearinghouse on Educational Management, University of Oregon.

Cambron-McCabe, N. (1993). Leadership for democratic authority. In J. Murphy (Ed.). *Preparing tomorrow's leaders: Alternative designs* (pp. 157–176). University Park, PA: University Council for Educational Administration.

Campbell, E. (2003). *The ethical teacher.* Philadelphia: Open University Press

Charters, W., & Jovick, T. (1981). The gender of principals and principal/teacher relations in elementary schools. In. P. Schmuck, W. Charters, & R. Carlson (Eds.), *Educational policy and management: Sex differentials* (pp. 307–331). New York: Academic Press.

Cisneros-Cohernour, E. & Bastarrachea, W. (2005, April). *Examining the impact of culture on leadership in Mexico*. Paper presented at the Annual Meeting of the American Educational Research Association, Montreal, Canada, April 11–15.

Cortina, R. (1989). Women as leaders in Mexican education. *Comparative Education Review, 33*(3), 357–376.

Cuellar, A. (1989). *School principals in Mexico: A research agenda*. ERIC document #ED318113.

Darling-Hammond, L., LaPointe, M., Meyerson, D., & Orr, M. T. (2007). *Preparing school leaders for a changing world. Lessons from exemplary leadership development programs*. New York. Wallace Foundation.

Deblois, C. (1992). School administrator preparation programs in Quebec during a reform era. In E. Miklos, & E. Ratsoy (Eds.). *Educational leadership: Challenge and change.* (pp. 355–368). Edmonton: Department of Educational Administration, University of Alberta.

Donmoyer, R. (1999). The continuing quest for a knowledgebase: 1976–1998. In J. Murphy & K. Seashore Louis (Eds.), *Handbook of research on educational administration: A project of the American Educational Research Association* (2nd ed., pp. 25–44). San Francisco: Jossey-Bass.

Donmoyer, R., Imber, M., & Scheurich, J. J. (1995). *The knowledge base in educational administration: Multiple perspectives*. Albany, NY: State University of New York Press.

Economist (2006, November). Mexico's mezzorgiorno, *381*(8504) 7–9.

Forsyth, P. B. (1999). Redesigning the preparation of school administrators: Toward consensus. In S. D. Thompson (Ed.), *School leadership: A blueprint for change* (pp. 23–33). Newbury Park, CA: Corwin Press Inc.

Foster, R. & Goddard, T. (2003). Leadership and culture in schools in northern British Columbia: Bridge building and/or re-balancing act? *Canadian Journal of Educational Administration and Policy, 27* [Online]. Retrieved June 5, 2007, from http://www.umanitoba.ca/publications/cjeap/articles/miscellaneousArticles/fostrverd.html

Fullan, M. G. & Newton, E. E (1988). School principals and change process in the secondary school. *Canadian Journal of Education, 13*(3), 404–422.

Greenfield, T. B. (1981). Who's asking the question depends on what answer you get. In R. Townsend. & S. Lawton (Eds.), *What's so Canadian about Canadian educational administration?* (pp. 13–28). Toronto: Ontario Institute for Studies in Education.

Greenfield, T. B. (1981). Who's asking the question depends on what answer you get. In R. Townsend. & S. Lawton (Eds.), *What's so Canadian about Canadian educational administration?* (pp. 13–28). Toronto: Ontario Institute for Studies in Education.

Griffiths, D. E., Stout, R. T., & Forsyth, P. B. (Eds.). (1988). *Leaders for America's schools*. Berkeley, CA: McCutchan Publishing.

Grogan, M & Andrews, R.(2002). Defining Preparation and Professional Development for the Future. *Educational Administration Quarterly 38*(2), 233–256.

Hickcox, E. (1981). O say can you see our home and native land. In R. Townsend. & S. Lawton (Eds.), *What's so Canadian about Canadian educational administration?* (pp. 1–8). Toronto: Ontario Institute for Studies in Education.

Hickcox, E. (2002). *Shaping the principalship in Manitoba*. Paper commissioned by the Manitoba Council for Leadership in Education.

Hodgkinson, C. (1978). *Towards a philosophy of administration*. Oxford: Basil Blackwell.

Iturbe, E. & Talan, R. (2006, October). *Women leadership in Mexico*. Paper presented at the Commonwealth Council for Educational Administration and Management, Nicosia, Cyprus, October 12–16.

Jackson, B. L. & Kelley, C. (2002). Exceptional and innovative programs in educational leadership. *Educational Administration Quarterly, 38*(20), 1992–212

Kandel, I.L. (1970). *Comparative education*. Westport, CT: Greenwood Press.

Kouzes, J. M., & Posner, B. Z. (1995). *The leadership challenge: How to keep getting extraordinary things done in organizations*. San Francisco: Jossey-Bass.

Langlois, L. & Lapointe, C. (2007). Ethical leadership in Canadian school organizations. *Educational Management, Administration & Leadership, 35*(2), 249–262.

Leithwood, K. (1999). An organizational perspective on values for leaders of future schools. In P. T. Begley (Ed.), *Values and educational leadership* (pp. 25–50). Albany, NY: SUNY Press.

Levin, B., & Young, J. (1994). *Understanding Canadian schools*. Toronto: Harcourt Brace & Company, Canada.

Levinson, B., A., U. (2004). Hopes and challenges for the new civic education in Mexico: Toward a democratic citizen without adjectives. *International Journal of Educational Development, 24*, 269–282.

Mahwinney, H. B. (2005, Winter). Scaling up education policy futures to inform a new vernacular for North American geopolitical socioeconomics. *UCEA Review, XLV*(1), 15–17.

Marshall, C. (1993). (Ed.). *The new politics of race and gender*. London: The Falmer Press.

Marshall, C., & Kasten, K. (1994). *The administrative career: A casebook on entry, equity, and endurance*. Thousand Oaks, CA: Sage.

Martin, C. & Guzman, E., (2005). Performance evaluation or standardized testing of aptitudes? Innovations at the margins of Mexico's school system. *International Journal of Educational Development, 25*(2), 145–155

Mezirow, J. (1991). *Fostering critical reflection in adulthood: A guide to transformative and emancipatory learning*. San Francisco: Jossey-Bass.

Miklos, E. (1992). *Doctoral research in educational administration at the University of Alberta, 1958–1991*. Edmonton: Department of Educational Administration.

Murphy, J. (Ed.). (1993). *Preparing tomorrow's school leaders: Alternative designs*. University Park: PA: UCEA.

Murtadha, K. (2006). A signature pedagogy. *Journal of Research on Leadership Education, 1* (1), 5–15.

National Commission on Excellence in Educational Administration (NCEEA). (1987). *Leaders for America's schools*. Tempe, AZ: University Council for Educational Administration.

National Policy Board for Educational Administration (NPBEA). (1989). *Improving the preparation of school administrators: An agenda for reform*. Charlottesville, VA: Author.

Normore, A. (2004). Recruitment and selection: Meeting the leadership shortage in one large Canadian school district. *Canadian Journal of Educational Administration and Policy, 30* [Online]. Retrieved June 5, 2007 from http://www.umanitoba.ca/publications/cjeap/articles/miscellaneousArticles/fostrverd.html

Ornelas, C. (2004). The politics of privatization, decentralization and education reform in Mexico. *International Review of Education, 50*, 397–418.

Orr, M. T. (2005, November). *From pipeline to practice: A comparative evaluation of leadership preparation*. Annual convention of the University Council for Educational Administration. Nashville, TN.

Orr, M. T. (2006, April). Research on Leadership Education as a Reform Strategy. *Journal of research on leadership education, 1*(1).

Ortiz, F., & Marshall, C. (1988). Women in educational administration. In N. Boyan (Ed.), *Handbook of research on educational administration* (pp. 123–142). New York: Longman.

Osterman, K. (1990). Reflective practice: A new agenda for education. *Education and Urban Society, 22*(2), 133–152.

Peterson, K. (2002). Professional Development. *Educational Administration Quarterly. 38* (20, 1992–212

Rees, R. (1991). The Ontario principals' qualifications course: Towards employment equity. *Journal of Educational Administration and Finance, 5/6*, 37–52.

Reynolds, C. (2002). Changing gender scripts and moral dilemmas for women and men in education, (1940–1970). In C. Reynolds (Ed.), *Women and school leadership* (pp. 29–48). Albany, NY: SUNY Press

Ryan, J. (2003). *Leading diverse schools*. Boston: Kluwer Academic Publishers.

Shakeshaft, C. (1987). *Women in educational administration*. Newbury Park, CA: Sage.

Shakeshaft, C., Brown, G., Irby, G., Grogan, M., & Ballenger, J. (2007). Increasing gender equity in educational leadership, In S. Klein, B. Richardson, D. A. Grayson, L. H. Fox, C. Kramarae, D. Pollard, & C. A. Dwyer. (Eds.). *Handbook for achieving gender equity through education* (2nd ed., pp. 103–129). Florence, KY: Erlbaum.

Sheilds, C.M. (2002). Learning from educators: Insights into building communities of difference. In G. Furman (Ed.), *School as community* (pp. 143–164). Albany, NY: SUNY Press.

Shepard, I. S. (1999, February). Persistence of graduate student sin educational administration in seeking and securing positions: A gender difference exists. Paper presented at the AASA National Conference on Education, New Orleans, LA.

Shields, C.M. (2002). Learning from educators: Insights into building communities of difference. In G. Furman (Ed.), *School as community* (pp. 143–164). Albany, NY: SUNY Press.

Skrla, L. (2000). *The social construction of gender in the superintendency*. Manuscript submitted for publication.

Slater C. L., et al. (2002). A cross-cultural investigation of leadership in the United States and Mexico. *School Leadership & Management, 22*(2), 197–202.

Slater, C. & Arisa, M. (2000). Educational leadership in the United States and Mexico. *Journal of Interdisciplinary Education, 3*(2), 137–150.

Slater, C. L., Boone, M., Fillion, S., Galloway, H., Alvarez, I., & Topete, C. (2003). The stories of educational leaders in the United States and Mexico. *World Studies, 4*(1–2), 85–87

Slater, C. L., Boone, M., Price, L., Martinez, I., Alvarez, I., Topete, C., & Olea, E. (2002). A cross-cultural investigation of leadership in the United States and Mexico. *School Leadership & Management, 22*(2), 197–202.

Slater, C. L. Boone, M., Alvarez, I., Topete, C., Iturbe, E., Base, M., Fillion, S., Galloway, H., Korth, L., & Munoz, L. (2006). Ideal images of educational leadership in Mexico City and South Texas. *The Educational Forum, 70*(2), 154–170.

Slater, C. L. et al. (2006). Ideal images of educational leadership in Mexico City and South Texas. *The Educational Forum, 70*(2), 154–170.

Slater, C. L., McGhee, M., Capt, R., Alvarez, I., Topete, C., & Iturbe, E. (2001). A comparison of the views of educational administration students in the United States and Mexico. Paper presented at the Annual Meeting of the American Educational Research Association, Seattle, WA, April 10–14.

Stack, M., Coulter, D., Grosjean, G., Mazawi, A., & Smith, G. (2006). *Fostering tomorrow's educational leaders*. [Online]. Retrieved June 10, 2007, from http://slc.educ.ubc.ca/Downloads/Educational LeadershipNetworks.pdf

Ungerleider, C. (2005,Winter). Education policy trends from a Western Canadian perspective. *UCEA Review, XLV*(1), 11–13.

Waite, D., & Allen, D. (2003). Corruption and abuse of power in educational administration. *Urban Review 35*(4), 281–296

Walby, S. (1990). *Theorizing patriarchy*. Cambridge, MA: Basil Blackwell.

Wikipedia. (2007). North American Free Trade Agreement. Retrieved September 12, 2007, from http://en.wikipedia.org/wiki/NAFTA.

Young, B. (2002a). The "Alberta advantage": "DeKleining" career prospects for women educators. In C. Reynolds (Ed.), *Women and school leadership* (pp. 75–92). Albany, NY: SUNY Press

Young, M. (2002b). *National Commission for the Advancement of Educational Leadership Preparation: Ensuring the University's Capacity to Ensure Learning Focused Leadership.* Columbia, MO: UCEA.

Young, M. D., & Fuller, E. (2007). Principal Career Paths. Paper presented at the Annual Meeting of the American Educational Research Association, Chicago, Illinois.

Young, M. D., Petersen, G. J., & Short, P. M. (2002). The complexity of substantive reform: A call for interdependence among key stakeholders. *Educational Administration Quarterly, 38,* 137–175.

Young, M. D., & McLeod, S. (2001, October). Flukes, opportunities, and planned interventions: Factors affecting women's decisions to become school administrators. *Educational Administration Quarterly. 37*(4), 462–502.

16

Leadership Development in Latin America

Alexandre Ventura, Jorge Adelino Costa
and Terezinha Monteiro dos Santos

It is very difficult to present an overview of educational leadership in Latin America given the diversity of policy and practice. Therefore the authors have chosen to focus on three of the most important countries in the region: Argentina, Brazil and Chile. The variety of contexts and the limited space of a single chapter have constrained the authors so that they have had to be selective. This does not imply an underestimation of the importance or interest of the other countries in the region. Throughout the chapter, there will be consideration of the similarities and contrasts in Latin America focusing on school leaders, that is, head teachers and their direct assistants (for example, vice-presidents or assistant head teachers).

It has been difficult to find relevant research, not only in respect to a regional overview, but also for each country. Although there are many books and articles on the subject of the preparation and development of school leaders, most reflect a theoretical approach and do not relate to the realities of the actual situation on the ground. Most writing employs a normative "should be" approach and does not describe or engage with what is going on in schools. The authors of these writings, inspired by international literature on the subject, restrict themselves to presenting desirable scenarios and practice. On the one hand, this presents a difficulty for the chapter, but on the other, it strengthens the need for a contribution focused on Latin America. We will begin with a brief description of the historical, geographical, political, and social context of Latin America.

Latin America has a population of about 529,333,000. In this region of the world, Portuguese and Spanish are the primary languages and Roman Catholicism is the dominant religion.

Argentina, with a population of 40,403,000, is divided into 23 provinces, and one autonomous city, Buenos Aires, which is the capital of the country. Traditionally, Argentina is seen as having one of the best standards of living in Latin America. However, due to the prolonged economic, political and social crisis that has assailed the country in recent times, the once middle class of Argentina has suffered a remarkable deterioration. The poor are increasing in number.

Brazil is the largest and most populous country in Latin America, and fifth largest in the world in both area and population (183,983,000 inhabitants in 2007). Brazil's population is very diverse, including European, Amerindian, African and Asian elements.

Politically, Brazil is a federal, presidential, representative, democratic republic. In terms of economy, it possesses large and well-developed agricultural, mining, manufacturing, and service sectors and therefore has the strongest economy in Latin America. It is the only Portuguese-speaking country in the region.

Chile occupies a long and narrow coastal strip wedged between the Andes Mountains and the Pacific Ocean. The capital of Chile is Santiago and the official language is Spanish. As of 2007, its population, with 70 per cent Catholic, was estimated at 16,285,000.

EDUCATIONAL LEADERSHIP CONTEXTS

We now present some of the main characteristics that contextualize educational leadership preparation and development in this part of the world.

A Centralized Tradition

A document concerned with the challenges in education (IIPE, 2000, pp. 19–20), which was published by the UNESCO International Institute for Educational Planning in Buenos Aires, suggests that the educational systems of Latin American countries were, in general, built as centralized state apparatuses. They have a pyramidal structure with the Ministry of Education at the vertex and successive hierarchical levels — provincial authorities, supervisors, directors, teachers. Decision-making processes are concentrated at a central level and exchange and communication systems are designed to operate in a vertical direction. The preferred method of operating is by prescription and control. The authority establishes what should be done and bodies of civil servants verify that what has been stipulated is carried out (IIPE, 2000, pp. 19–20). This centralized and hierarchical system was clearly inspired by the traditions brought to Latin America by European colonizers.

The UNESCO document further adds that this organizational structure worked adequately while the educational systems had a limited size and while they dealt with a relatively small body of teachers, who enjoyed a guaranteed homogenous training and a superior social status to most of their fellow citizens (IIPE, 2000, pp. 19–20).

Recent Educational Reforms Common in most Latin American Countries

In Latin America, once a certain level of expansion of the educational system was reached, by means of models of centralized administration and services based on proposals with a high degree of homogeneity, the various countries started defining new educational policies (IIPE, 1998, p. 16). Burki and Perry (1998, p. 91) point out that the:

> Latin American school has been a remarkably stable system. Not only have the key actors remained unchanged for centuries, but the shared values, expected behaviors, and rules of the game — the institutional framework — also have been remarkably stable. Only recently has a first generation of education reforms attempted change. A major challenge to implementation of these school reforms, in fact, has been the strength of the system and its resistance to change.

The recent measures adopted by Latin American countries are characterized by the implementation of decentralization processes and the transfer of educational services to lower level jurisdictions (provinces, departments, municipalities) with the aim of optimizing the quality of the education provided, based on the assumption that bringing the administration closer to the schools would improve the search for more appropriate responses and correct the bureaucracy-related difficulties that occurred as a result of the previous educational model (IIPE, 1998, p. 16).

As Machado (2001, p. 4) indicates, in Latin America, where great geographic, cultural, ethnic and socio-economic diversity exists, adopting a decentralization processes that facilitate the autonomy of the school as a place of change is an essential condition for progress. This diversity, however, as the same author points out, makes it harder to make a decision that will serve an infinity of realities, situations and contexts (Machado, 2001, p. 4).

The new functions adopted by the governments of Latin America were defined around certain axes of priority intervention, to be developed through programs planned by central entities, with frequent participation of provincial or municipal administrative agents in their implementation. These axes of involvement are:

1. The creation of national systems for improvement of the quality of education. The aim is to develop national systems of external evaluation to be applied to pupils at all levels, establishing, in this way, criteria to evaluate the quality of the results obtained;
2. The conception of compensating strategies to address situations of inequality. Governments finance and accomplish actions, through specific programs, directed at schools in unfavorable situations. The criterion of intervention is the focus of actions and resources, the participation of the community, the revalorization of the work of teachers, the attention to pedagogical priorities and the articulation of actions with provincial authorities to articulate efforts and results;
3. Update and adjustment of the curriculum content. The definition of new content is used as a strategic tool to underpin the organization of an articulated, coherent and equitable educational system;
4. Establishment of mechanisms for teacher training in schools, with the aim of capacitating them in the content and competences related to the reform;
5. Global restructuring of the teacher initial training system, including structural and curricular change in the training institutions, the opening of new career pathways, and the regrouping of institutions;
6. Equipping schools with pedagogical and technological resources. This equipment includes, for example, books and audiovisual resources to libraries in schools located in poor areas; computers to be used by pupils and teachers, which allow, for example, the participation of the school in a network; grants and materials for the development of teaching and learning projects (IIPE, 1998, pp. 17–18).

Having mentioned the general trends in Latin American countries, a closer look will now be taken at the main trends in the three specific countries under examination.

Decentralization — School Autonomy

From the 1980s onwards, the discussion around the democratization of school management and school autonomy has been linked to educational reform concerned with decentralization and autonomy measures. Since the 1980s, educational policy is characterized by the search for efficiency and quality, and by a concern for the training of human resources to allow for an increase of international competitiveness of each national economy and to answer the challenges raised by globalization, the knowledge society and multiculturalism (Ball, 1998; Castro & Carnoy, 1997; Whitty, Power & Halpin, 1998, cited by Gorostiaga, 2006, p. 4).

The changes that were implemented because of reform processes in general, and decentralization in particular, brought new challenges to schools (for example, related to staff training and management). Decentralization requires personnel with different training, both at the level of the school and at that of the educational system. There is, similarly, a change in the role of school principals, as the school becomes the "owner of its own destiny" (Machado, 2001, p. 5). As Machado points out, decentralization brings, in fact, an increase in the amount of work that has to be done in schools: more internal meetings so as to allow for collective planning and to share experiences. New responsibilities arise, connected to budget management, human resources management, accountability, and the interaction with the community (Machado, 2001, pp. 10–11).

Such changes have created certain sociological trends, of which one is the notion of a crisis in education, with an emphasis on the deterioration of the public school. In Argentina this crisis in the public school system is seen as a result of "bad management" by state administration.

The education reform process of the 1990s put schools at the centre of the processes of change — schools were seen as "transformation units". This notion placed schools as the object of direct and indirect intervention, justified by arguments connected with school autonomy and various mechanisms, such as administrative and structural reform, the training of directors and teachers and the financing of projects, among others (Sverdlick, 2006, p. 69).

During the reform processes in the 1990s in some Argentinean provinces, local educational policies were virtually reduced to putting in place devices designed by the central government (Sverdlick, 2006, p. 70). Simultaneously during those years, the policy of school autonomy increasingly placed an emphasis on school management. Within the framework of these reforms, an autonomous school was one that possessed more liberty of action, organization and management. The state ceased to be responsible for school management and the responsibility of school leaders to improve the efficiency of the school increased. Such autonomy was defined by the absence of the government. Therefore, if the expected results were not produced, one had to look for problems in the "efficiency" of school management. In this way, there was a move towards a concealed privatization, thereby decreasing the responsibility of the state for what is public (Sverdlick, 2006, p. 71).

When one looks to Brazil, since the 1980s, the issue of school democratization has constituted a recurrent theme in debates on education. As a result of the struggles fought by educators and progressive politicians, the principle of "democratic management of the public educational system", consecrated in the Federal Constitution and reaffirmed in the Fundamental Law of National Education of 1996, has influenced the policies of school management in recent years (Teixeira, 2000). Villela (2007) indicates that according to this Fundamental Law, the different municipal and state educational administrations must define their specific priorities, as well as the participation of education professionals in the development of the pedagogical project of each school and the participation of the community in school activities.

Accompanying the Federal Constitution, the Constitutions of several states and the Organic Law of many municipalities have also adopted the principles of democratic management in public schools (Colares, 2000, pp. 39–40). At this time, actions aiming at the development of collective participation were intensified (Colares, 2000, p. 40). Moreover, the democratic management of school implies a new profile for the school principal; the principal must be capable of putting into practice the basic principles of administration — planning, organizing, leading and supervising — and have the ability to coordinate (Teixeira, 2000).

The policy of giving autonomy to schools was promoted from the mid-1980s in the context of wider political processes that aimed at decentralization and were put in place to encourage greater participation by citizens. The instruments more commonly used by the states to give autonomy to schools are: collegiate management structures with the authority to manage funds, the election of principals and a school development plan (Espínola, 2000, p. 11).

When turning to Chile, we can observe that the last three decades have presented a strong move towards privatization. The "voucher" system, introduced in Chile in 1980, granted schools an important form of autonomy; by transferring resources directly to schools, the schools receive a fixed amount per pupil enrolled (Espínola, 2000, p. 11). This system aimed to improve the quality of education by providing parents with the opportunity to choose a school according to the quality of education it offered (Espínola, 2000, p. 19). The state financed private schools at the same level it did public/municipal schools. Finally, in the 1980s the transfer of basic and secondary education institutions and their personnel from the Ministry of Education to the municipalities was also regulated using as a justification the need for improvement in the efficiency and quality of educational services (Aceituno, 2004, p. 5).

Challenges for the Decentralization Process

One issue arising from the decentralization process throughout Latin America is the limited experience that the personnel of the provincial administrations possess in order to fulfill the extended and more complex functions required of them. Lack of experience generated administrative and pedagogical problems that increased inefficiency and led to deterioration in the quality of services (IIPE, 1998, p. 19). Furthermore, regional or local administrations do not always possess the administrative technologies they need for their management tasks at a time of increased responsibility. The administration exhibits weak planning teams, a lack of planning systems and insufficient coordination between the processes of educational planning, budgetary planning and effective allocation of resources (IIPE, 1998, p. 20). Moreover, the development of decentralization generated a new demand for training civil servants to work in administrative positions at the school level (Tiramonti, 1998, p. 45).

In fact, the process of decentralization has raised new challenges connected to educational management and policies in all of Latin America. For example, there is the issue of the increase and the diversification of civil servants and other individuals involved with the management of education (Braslavsky, 2001, p. 11). Historically, in many Latin American countries, education was managed by civil servants of the national administration in which all power of decision making was concentrated (Braslavsky, 2001, p. 11). Today, national, provincial and municipal civil servants, school principals, employees of non-governmental organizations and of for-profit companies participate in the management of education (Braslavsky, 2001, p. 11).

Moreover, in some countries, the decentralization of the educational system meant not only the transfer of parts of the system from central to regional governments, but also the transfer of aspects of school management responsibilities to the schools themselves, which are intended to work in collaboration with the local community (Krawczyk & Vieira, 2003, p. 83).

However, decentralization and empowerment of local players are policies and not outcomes. The impact of strategies related to management on the quality of teaching and learning is not guaranteed to be positive. As Oliveira (2002, p. 77) points out, the autonomy given to schools under decentralization brought with it some paradoxes. On the one hand, there is discussion about the democratic management of schools, and about the creation of collegial bodies comprised of representatives from all segments of the population that attend the school. On the other hand, schools face legal constraints legitimized by (alleged) concerns about the quality of teaching, the management of school budgets, conception of the curriculum and the pedagogical organization of classes.

The policies of decentralization and autonomy have been intensely debated at an international level, either from a perspective of being seen as a way of assisting schools in responding to the interests and demands of the communities in which they are situated, or in relation to the impact they have (or not) on the efficiency and quality of educational systems.

Focusing on our three countries once more, in Argentina, during the 1990s, the majority of the provinces promoted greater autonomy in schools, namely through the "educational project of the institution" (*Proyecto Educativo Institucional – PEI*). A policy that was implemented with the aim of improving the quality of schools (through specific improvement projects) and to achieve democratization in schools through the development of participation of the citizenry (Gorostiaga, 2006, p. 7). As with all processes of change, the implementation of "educational projects of the institution" was met with some resistance from school inspectors, school principals and teachers. The resistance was mainly associated with the lack of an institutional culture of collaboration, the lack of financial support and, in secondary schools, the phenomenon of "taxi" teachers who work in several schools without assuming a strong commitment to any. At the same time, the educational projects at the institutional level do not seem to have generated increased participation or processes of critical questioning about the reality and change possibilities for schools, as is shown by studies that included interviews of employees and school directors (cf. Señoriño & Vilanova, 2001).

Analyzing the educational policies adopted by Brazil, it can be inferred that the country has a similar policy of decentralization and deconcentration to that of other countries (Mattos, 1999, p. 44).

Finally, in Chile, decentralization takes on more complex traits, due to the transfer of the management of some public schools to private entities, to the opening of private schools, to the guarantee that demand is met and to the funding of private schools. This process involves the establishment of partnerships between the central and municipal governments and private entities and parents (Krawczyk & Vieira, 2003, p. 85) and it has posed problems.

THE MAIN ISSUES OF EDUCATIONAL LEADERSHIP

As a response to a perceived centralized, bureaucratic, inefficient and ineffective public educational administration, several educational reforms have been implemented in Argentina, Brazil and Chile. In this way, from the 1980s onwards new educational policies have been developed mostly under guidelines provided by international organizations (such as the World Bank, the Inter-American Development Bank, and the International Monetary Fund), which are based on notions such as: municipalization, privatization, decentralization, democratic management, school autonomy, among others.

In the countries on which we are focusing, school management assumes at present a central role in the process of school improvement, as the development of school autonomy brings with it new functions and responsibilities for those working in schools, and in particular to those in charge of their management. To Braslavsky (2001), Braslavsky and Acosta (2001) and Villela (2007) the new concept of school principal comes hand in hand with the policy of school autonomy and with the development of pedagogical and other school projects. It is associated, moreover, with the necessity of creating opportunities for the permanent training of school principals and with all involved in the teaching/learning process.

With regard to how the position of school principal is filled, what training the individual should possess and what his roles should be, gains increasingly more attention. This has brought into focus the necessity of improving training to adequately prepare the school principal to master the challenges the position entails (Mitrulis, 2007, p. 2).

Ontological and Epistemological Foundations

For many years, schools in Latin America were considered simply groups of classrooms, or as smaller units of a centralized educational system. Principals acted as medium-level administrators and were limited to transmitting orders and regulations. As schools continue to acquire more independence to improve their academic results, it is necessary for principals to assume a new role. If decisions are made at a school or community level, principals are enabled to head efforts to improve the teaching-learning process in their schools (Borden, 2002). As Burki and Perry (1998, p. 92) point out:

> *Directors (note: school principals)* of the traditional public school are selected from the teaching faculty and sometimes return to the faculty after serving this administrative duty. Usually, directors retain membership in the teachers association. The responsibilities and authority of directors are severely constrained, especially regarding the recruitment and evaluation of teachers. Their principal duty is the administrative enforcement of basic employment rules. They usually are not expected to initiate change, evaluate staff, or provide support to teachers with performance problems, and they have very few ways to reward good performance or address the specific needs of individual teachers. Besides, directors typically receive no specialized training in school management that would equip them to carry out these responsibilities, so they seldom know the arcane and complex requirements for removing or disciplining teachers, even in cases of extreme cause. Like teachers, directors have divided allegiances. They are agents of the education ministry, but their day-to-day work cannot be carried out without the cooperation of the teaching faculty, whom they may one day rejoin. (authors' emphasis)

School Principal and Leadership Issues in Latin America

In Latin America, the requisites that are perceived to constitute the essence of being a school principal at present are: strategic management; leadership; communication, negotiation, and problem-solving skills and the ability to delegate competences. Furthermore, it is expected that he/she is able to anticipate scenarios, to promote team work and also to act with rigor and professional ethics (cf., Braslavsky & Acosta, 2001; Scotuzzi & Silva, 2007). However, even with the implementation of reforms to decentralize education, principals in Latin America continue to carry out only the administrative dimension of school management (Borden, 2002).

This may be because principals are not seen as leaders, that they are not sufficiently trained, that they do not know or understand the importance of their position, or that they have not received sufficient support to allow them to spearhead the change process in their schools.

School principals have little power to manage resources. However, the problem is still more serious. "Teachers and directors, who have the best information about the school, have little authority to act on that knowledge. They cannot change the curriculum, select different textbooks, or in other ways change production relationships within the school" (Burki & Perry, 1998, p. 96).

Therefore, "these problems translate into a lack of incentives for school principals to set organizational goals and monitor the school educational outcomes. School principals do not possess the resources to motivate teachers and give them incentives to improve their teaching skills and innovate their classroom practices" (Burki & Perry, 1998, p. 96). Sociologically, one can say that school heads in Latin America lack power, authority, training and resources. At the same time, the role now expected of the school director requires the abandonment of characteristics common to authoritative management, sometimes internalized, as the tendency to impose the individual's way of thinking, being authoritarian, not considering diverging opinions, not admitting criticism, using their power in an abusive way, being insecure, oppressive and controlling, not believing in the other's abilities, seeing the other as a menace, not being open to dialogue, and centralizing power (Westrupp, 2003, p. 75).

Impact of International Institutions on the Understanding of School Leadership

Several international institutions have played a significant role in the morphology and performance of education systems in Latin America. According to Kempner & Jurema (2002, pp. 332–333):

> in the 1960s and 1970s educational policies emanating from international agencies were based on the theory of human capital. In the 1980s and 1990s policies focused more on globalization and the knowledge society, under the guidance of theories of modernization and total quality assessment.

Furthermore, the perception is that many international agencies announce loans and educational reforms with a neoliberal perspective as a salvation for developing countries. Bueno (2004, p. 448) indicates that the 1970s, in particular, were prolific in the import and "transplant" of planning, evaluation, administration and supervision models. Although it was emphasized that such models should be "open" and flexible, they were generally adopted as strict guidelines, and the secret to their success seemed to rest in the rigor of following the steps that were proposed. In this way, despite what was officially stated, the idea of the model was associated with a "closed" package, with defined limits, whose parameters served to classify, frame and measure the quality and adequacy of the actions undertaken (Bueno, 2004, p. 448).

Kempner and Jurema (2002, p. 333) believe that "as international policies have embraced globalization theory, educational policy has operated further and further from the school ground and more toward the managerial and organizational levels in what is seen as an educational enterprise".

On the issue school leadership and the policy of school autonomy, the following questions are being asked: What is leadership? How do we obtain schools principals/leaders? In this context, OREALC/UNESCO decided to create, in 1998, a research and development program, which, by order of the Meeting of Ministers of Latin America and the Caribbean, took place in 2002, and originated the School Leadership Network (*Red de Liderazgo Escolar*), with the aim of developing leadership competences in the countries of this region. Between 1998 and 2005, more than a thousand school principals were trained by OREALC/UNESCO or by other associated institutions.

UNESCO was also instrumental in the creation of the Latin American Encounter on Educational Leadership and Training (*I'Encuentro Latinoamericano de Liderazgo en Educación y Capacitación*). The meeting, entitled *"Leadership of Directors for Inclusive and Quality Education"* (*"Liderazgo Directivo para una Educación Inclusiva y de Calidad"*), which took place in September 2006, and was organized by the Regional Bureau for Education in Latin America and the Caribbean (OREALC/UNESCO), the Chilean Ministry of Education and the Hineni Foundation. During that meeting, the institutions responsible for the event shared their experiences with representatives of Education Ministries of the participating countries, with teachers, academics, education researchers, and in particular school principals. The issue of training in school leadership was also discussed.

Gradually, it became evident that the increased competitiveness introduced to the management of schools required principals with a different profile. According to the World Bank, there was a need for differentiated training for the school principal, which can lead to the separation of the career of the principal from that of the teacher (Lopes, 2002, p. 42). Brazil is a typical example of the influence of the World Bank in Latin America. In 2002, this agency financed educational projects totaling over a billion dollars in the states of São Paulo, Paraná, Minas Gerais, Espírito Santo and in nine states of Northeast Brazil (Kempner & Jurema, 2002, p. 342). However, because Brazil is such a diverse and complex society, World Bank initiatives have not been equally accepted across all states.

School Leaders' Training and Development

During the Forum, "The training of human resources for educational management in Latin America", which took place in 1998, the experiences of human resources training in Argentina, Brazil, Chile and Uruguay were presented. The following characteristics of a human resources training "predominant model" in Latin America were delineated (IIPE, 1998, p. 20):

- Centrally planned and managed;
- Centered in technical knowledge and theory;
- Conceived more from a supply than from a demand standpoint;
- With an emphasis on the arrival point (the profile of an ideal civil servant) without recognizing the departure point (the body of knowledge, beliefs and attitudes possessed by the individuals to be trained);
- With a reduced conception of "modernization", which is perceived as the introduction of technologies rather than as the updating of a vision for education.

Tiramonti (1998, p. 45) indicates that the centrality that the school has acquired as a sphere where policies become concrete and where efforts to improve the services provided must converge, has led school principals to become protagonists in a change process, converting them to potential demanders of specific training in school management. The supply of this kind of training in Latin America does not satisfy this potential demand.

Initial Training

The state of training in educational management in countries like Argentina, Brazil and Chile is extremely complex. This complexity is associated with the existence of a very heterogeneous assortment of training providers (higher education institutions, teacher training institutes, national or provincial/state programs, teachers unions training institutions, and foundations) in educational management and policies (Braslavsky, 2001, p. 16).

Most of the degrees and postgraduate programs in Argentina that deal with educational management and policies can be classified as generalist. This means that, although they include curricular spaces dedicated to training in educational management and policies, they do not assume the aim of offering specialized training in those fields of action (Braslavsky & Acosta, 2001, p. 43). In general terms, both at the level of initial and of postgraduate training, several tensions can be observed: on the one hand, there is a tension between focusing the training offered on the intervention or on the analysis of educational policy and management; and on the other, the tension between offering a training directed at a macropolitical level (municipalities, provincial and central governments) or at a micropolitical level (schools) (Braslavsky & Acosta, 2001, p. 51).

According to Martelli (1999, p. 25) educational administration studies in Brazil first started in 1932, as a course of the Pedagogy degree of the Institute of Education of Rio de Janeiro. The School Administration course was included in the curriculum of the School Administrators Specialization degree of the Institute of São Paulo in the following year (Martelli, 1999, p. 25). In 1946, the Organic Law of Formal Education stimulated the creation of degrees of administration of primary education in other states of the country.

As Castro (2007, pp. 1–2) indicates, the training of school principals began with the advent of the School Administration Degrees. Among the first schools to offer such a degree was the Minas Gerais School of Training. This school had as its main goal the improvement of technical and scientific teacher training, thus preparing teaching staff of the regular schools and the managers of the basic schools. This training is seldom a forum for discussion of knowledge and for sharing management experiences and/or practices. Very often, this training is mandatory, being seen as another certification (Ribeiro, 2007). Recent analyses have shown that these training programs have a low impact on the transformation of reality. This can be explained by a number of characteristics of the training itself: short duration courses which attend to topical and immediate needs; subjects based on generalizations with low articulation between theory and practice; content out of context; individual training instead of teamwork; methodology based on the transmission of knowledge rather than on solving daily school management issues (Mitrulis, 2007, p. 2).

Besides the initial and specific training in school administration, the preparation for the performance of the school principal is, very often, made on the job, introducing them to the context of the practices and institutional projects of their schools, as well as to central level educational policies.

Furthermore, in Brazil, amidst the current public policies of school principals' training, the Progestão program is being adopted by many Brazilian states. This program consists of an in-service training course, with both in-room classes and web-based classes. The program is the result of an initiative of the CONSED (National Council of the Secretaries for Education) in partnership with a group of Educational Secretariats, with the Spanish National University of Distance Education (UNED) and with the Roberto Marinho Foundation (Scotuzzi & Silva, 2007).

This course of 270 hours is taught in modules which are organized as problem-solving situations that are identified in the daily running of the schools and whose analysis require the articulation between theory and the practical experience of the professionals. In the State of São Paulo, for instance, there is a further introductory module on school diagnostic evaluation (Scotuzzi & Silva, 2007). This module has as its main targets school teams with principals, vice-principals, pedagogical coordinators, supervisors and teachers, technical staff and central and regional level managers of the educational system.

We should further note that, as a support for this program of principals' in-service training, the CONSED has organized, in collaboration with UNESCO and other agencies, the National Prize of School Management Reference. The aim here is the dissemination of the culture of self-evaluation of the management process, and to highlight and guide management practices that can help improve schools' performance and the level of academic success (Mitrulis, 2007, p. 4).

Finally, with regards to Brazil, it should be stressed that the Fundamental Law of National Education of 1996 establishes that to be a school administrator one has to possess a Degree or a Graduate Degree in Pedagogy (Art. 64). The basic four-year curriculum of the degree in Pedagogy is organized in subjects connected to the general training of the teacher (sociology of education, philosophy of education, history of education, psychology and didactics), subjects connected with methodology and teaching practice, and subjects concerned with the political-administrative structure and dynamics of education systems (school administration, education policies, education management, structure and functioning of the education system, etc).

Many higher education institutions with degrees in Pedagogy also offer some specialization options to students, the most common being educational administration, educational supervision, or psycho-pedagogy. The tendency nowadays is to transfer the specific specialized training in these areas to graduate studies, to university specialization courses and to courses of on the job training (Draibe, Souza, & Borba, 2001, p. 86).

In the curricula of some institutions that provide degrees in pedagogy and pre-school education in Chile, a subject dealing with school administration was introduced, but its only intention is to acquaint students with the concepts pertaining to this area. It does not prepare them to fulfill the role of school managers (Undurraga & Araya, 2001, p. 128).

Some regions of the country do not have any training program in the area of educational management and policies. Most of these study programs are concentrated in the Santiago region (Undurraga & Araya, 2001, p. 132). In order to deal with this geographic issue, some higher education institutions have created and developed distance learning programs, which rely on the autonomous learning abilities of the student (Undurraga & Araya, 2001, p. 132).

Selection Processes for School Leaders

In general, the school leaders of Brazilian schools reach their position through a legal process. The selection process of the school principal, however, varies in different regions of the country, and the way in which the principal is chosen has an impact on the relations that are established inside the school (Scotuzzi & Silva, 2007). The data collected by Mendonça (2001, p. 88) allowed him to identify four ways of filling the position of principal. The first one is by political indication, in which a government authority freely nominates an individual of its choice, even when the name of the individual is the result of political-partisan pressures. The second one is a public tender offer, which is a selective process that entails a presentation of the candidate's academic qualifications and also written and oral examinations. The third one is election in which a candidate is chosen as a result of a voting process in the school community. The fourth one is selection and election whereby an election is held amongst the candidates previously selected by means of written examinations. Dourado (2006, p. 62) adds to these mechanisms two others: the career principal and the principal who is indicated by triple or sextuple lists or mixed processes.

However, in many regions of the country, school leaders are still appointed by a recommendation made by political authorities, especially at the municipal level (Draibe, Souza & Borba, 2001, p. 85). This practice eliminates any individual that opposes the policies of the Mayor or Governor (Dourado, 2006, p. 62). It allows for the school to become a space where authoritarian practices take place, and indicates a strong interference of the government in school management (Dourado, 2006, p. 62). To the politician, having the school principal as a political ally is to have the potential to indirectly influence the control of a public institution that relates to a significant segment of the population (Mendonça, 2001, pp. 88–89). Exclusion from the position follows, in this sense, the same logic (Mendonça, 2001, p. 89). If the individual given the position loses the political confidence of the politician who has granted it, exclusion comes as a natural consequence — the stripping away of a privilege (Mendonça, 2001, p. 89).

The practice of choosing school principals via election can be said to be new in Brazilian schools and, in many states, it is a practice not yet adopted (Martelli, 1999, p. 42). The election of principals is the process that has embodied the fight against clientelism and authoritarianism in school administration. Teixeira (2000) considers that the main virtues of the election of the school principal reside in the possibilities for debate and, consequently, for participation and commitment of the several actors involved. Moreover, the election of the principal has been pointed out as an effective channel for the democratization of school relations (Dourado, 2006, p. 64). The process of increasing democratization of the selection of principals has contributed to the rethinking of school management and the role of the principal.

Description of School Leaders' Work

In Latin American countries, as in others, when measures to achieve and develop school autonomy have been put in place, the functions of school principals have been questioned and the competences they need in order to fulfill their position have been discussed. For school principals to be able to perform the new roles that are expected of them, they need to have access to specific training in the area of school management and regularly to refresh their knowledge of education, striving to improve the functioning of the school, what is learned there and also the work of teachers. As Lück, Freitas, Girling, and Keith (2001, p. 25) mention, the actions of the school principal are directly associated with effective schools.

According to Machado (2001, pp. 8–9), one of the main roles of school leaders is to communicate with the central government, to receive directives on central educational policies, and to share their knowledge and experience with other school principals.

In the context of the process of educational decentralization and school autonomy in Argentina, the Federal Law of Education is the legal document that establishes the competencies and the functions of those responsible for the management of schools at a local level. Therefore, it is up to each province to plan, organize and administer the educational system of its jurisdiction; to organize and lead the educational services under the management of the state, to authorize and supervise private schools pertaining to its jurisdiction; to apply the decisions made centrally, with their respective adjustments; to promote the participation of organizations to support technical-pedagogical contributions from professionals to improve educational practices (Candia, 2004, p. 190).

It is up to the principal of each school, and all those involved with it, to use their greater autonomy to establish the priorities of the school in curricular issues and teaching methods, subjects/courses offered and activities that take place inside and outside the classroom. It is, in fact, as we are told by Gorostiaga, Acedo, and Xifra (2003), in this context that each school begins developing its own institutional educational project (*Proyecto Educativo Institucional*). In this process, the ideal is for all teachers and school principals to define, collectively, the administrative structure of the institution, in order that this document will respect, on the one hand, the specific context of the school, and on the other, the guidelines set at the central level. Nevertheless, to our mind, and in the words of Experton (1999), cited by Gorostiaga, Acedo, and Xifra (2003), the decentralization that occurred in the provinces by means of the intrajurisdictional deconcentration of functions connected with curricular design seems to have been essentially rhetorical.

The process of the municipalization of education in Chile, by bringing new responsibilities/duties to municipal governments, has altered the functions held by the central government. The roles and competences of the Ministry of Education were, from the implementation of this process onwards, limited to the following: proposing and evaluating educational and cultural policies, studying and proposing general educational norms, assigning the necessary resources for the development of educational and cultural activities, and granting official recognition to educational institutions (Candia, 2004, p. 195). Furthermore, in Chile, the functions of school principals are decreed in the Complete School Day Law (*Ley Jornada Escolar Completa* – JEC, N° 19.532), that sets their pedagogical, administrative and financial roles. As pointed out by a document of the Chilean Ministry of Education (Ministerio de Educación, 2005, p. 4), related to their pedagogical duties, the school principal must formulate, support and evaluate school goals and objectives, plans and programs and the strategies for their implementation. They must also organize, guide and observe the technical-pedagogical work and professional development of the teachers of the school, and establish communication channels between the school and the community (Ministerio de Educación, 2005, p. 4). In administrative terms, the school principal must organize and supervise the work of the personnel (teaching and non teaching staff) employed at the school, and propose the hiring and replacement of personnel (teaching and non-teaching staff) (Ministerio de Educación, 2005, p. 4). In financial matters, the school principal must assign, manage and control all the resources that are consigned to the school (Ministerio de Educación, 2005, p. 5).

DILEMMAS FACING EDUCATIONAL LEADERSHIP AND FUTURE TRENDS

The development of school autonomy and the increase of the number of training opportunities for school principals all over Latin America have brought some difficulties:

- the difficulty in articulating educational policies made centrally with strategic decisions made in a particular context;
- the difficulty in managing schools because of the intervention of a very heterogeneous group of actors;
- the difficulty in managing a less hierarchical/rigid management structure, in which actors from different decision-making levels interact and in which those in charge of school management must act, on the one hand, in accordance with central educational policies and, on the other, with respect to local necessities;
- the mismatch between educational policies and the initial training provided by higher education institutions for those who will become school principals (e.g. Brazil and Argentina);
- the difficulty in operationalizing educational policies and management in specific contexts with new challenges (e.g. the respect for ethnic, cultural, religious and linguistic diversity; the struggle to achieve equality, transparency, democratic values, efficiency and effectiveness) (Braslavsky, 2001, pp. 12–14).

Moreover, Sverdlick (2006, pp. 75–78) points out some problems and difficulties that, in her view, are faced by school management specifically in Argentina: firstly, an important problem in the relationship between the administration and the system is mutual distrust (on the one hand, certain signs of distrust can be perceived on the part of those in charge of educational management related to the effective implementation of change by teachers; on the other, teachers feel that these individuals do not truly understand how life in school works).

Secondly, the process of delegitimizing and of stripping teachers of their authority has been mentioned repeatedly by those who attribute a responsibility (professional and individual) to teachers and that identify gaps/problems in the teaching profession (what teachers do not know, what they cannot do, the notion that they do not keep abreast of the changes that occur). To this process can be added the legacy of the 1990s governments, which, because of their paternalistic attitude, have led teachers to wait and not act until they know what the administration sees as the right solution to the different problems and also to wait for the redefinition of what is expected of schools and of teachers. Nowadays many teachers feel unsure when questioned on the knowledge they possess and confused in respect of what is expected of them. Furthermore, schools and teachers continue to ask for instructions and "recipes", but at the same time protest against them.

Thirdly, the procedures/guidelines that are prescribed by the central administration normally have a universal sense/feel, which leads schools to view those directives as not particularly responding to their specific problems (conflict/tension between educational management at a local and at the central level).

Fourthly, several school devices connected with management should be questioned and reformulated. An example, which has widespread use, is the "educational project of the institution" (*Proyecto Educativo Institucional – PEI*). The PEI, considered an instrument of reform, was designed to be used as a tool to assist for school principals with the individual work of each school. Nevertheless, several investigations conducted by the authors have indicated that, at best, this project only exists in schools because it is required by the government. Mechanisms oriented towards improving school management have displaced the centrality of pedagogical issues in the school principal's tasks. The tasks of planning lessons, evaluating, doing follow-up, have lost their pedagogical character in favor of criteria connected with evaluation and supervision. There is, consequently, some difficulty in regaining the pedagogical sense of some of the strategies.

Fifthly, there are some tensions between political time versus school time. The questions are: How to respond to an urgent issue without undermining medium and long term plans? How to respect the rhythms of change and of production of knowledge that take place inside schools in the limited time that a government mandate lasts? In reference to Argentina, Sverdlick (2006, p. 78) indicates that the distance that exists between the universe of central government and schools, and the day-to-day life of the schools is a necessary reality. The awareness of this reality should stimulate an analysis of the points of articulation and complementarity that make possible a convergence, so as to act on problems and produce change (Sverdlick, 2006, p. 78).

In lieu of a conclusion, as this chapter clearly indicates, there is a strong need for further research on the topic of leadership preparation and development in Latin America. The investment of time on behalf of researchers has been mainly in what we can call a "recipes-import" approach. Most of the literature published in this part of the world uses a "should be" normative approach inspired by American and European models. Future research should focus on the description of the actual situation in the region and on specific countries, and produce indigenous perspectives on leadership preparation and development.

REFERENCES

Aceituno, R. C. (2004). *Fundamentos de la Calidad de la Educación en Chile: de lo Macro a lo Micro*, Facultad de Ciencias Económicas y Administrativas, Universidad de Chile, Seminario para optar al t'tulo de ingeniero comercial.

Borden, A. (2002). *Directores de escuela en América Latina: ¿L'deres del cambio ó sujetos a cambio? Documento de Trabajo para el Diálogo Regional de Pol'tica*, Washington: Banco Interamericano de Desarrollo (BID).

Braslavsky, C. (2001). Necesidades y respuestas en la formación para la gestión y la pol'tica educativa en América latina: tendencias y construcción de estrategias compartidas. In C. Braslavsky & F. Acosta (Eds.), *El estado de la enseñanza de formación en gestión y pol'tica educativa en América Latina* (pp. 7–25). Buenos Aires: UNESCO: Instituto Internacional de Planeamiento de la Educación.

Braslavsky, C., & Acosta, F. (2001). El estado de la enseñanza de la formación en gestión y pol'tica educativa en Argentina. In C. Braslavsky & F. Acosta (Eds.), *El estado de la enseñanza de formación en gestión y pol'tica educativa en América Latina* (pp. 27–75). Buenos Aires: UNESCO: Instituto Internacional de Planeamiento de la Educación.

Bueno, M. S. S. (2004). O Banco Mundial e modelos de gestão educativa para a América Latina. *Cadernos de Pesquisa*, 34(122), 445–466.

Burki, S. J., & Perry, G. E. (1998). *Beyond the Washington consensus: institutions matter.* Washington: The International Bank for Reconstruction and Development/The World Bank.

Candia, A. N. (2004). Razones y Estrateg'as de la Descentralización Educativa: Un Análisis Comparado de Argentina y Chile. *Revista Iberoamericana de Educación*, Número 34, Enero - Abril 2004, 179–200.

Castro, M. d. (2007). A formação do gestor de ensino fundamental no Brasil: das origens às atuais diretrizes curriculares de pedagogia, *IV Congresso Luso-Brasileiro de Pol'tica e Administração da Educação.* Faculdade de Psicologia e de Educação da Universidade de Lisboa, 12, 13 e 14 de Abril de 2007, working paper.

Colares, M. L. I. S. (2000). Concepções de gestão educacional: estudo com diretores de escola pública do ensino fundamental formados em pedagogia e habilitados em administração escolar pela Universidade Federal do Pará, Universidade Estadual de Campinas, Mestrado em Educação.

Dourado, L. F. (2006). *Gestão da educação escolar.* Curso técnico de formação para os funcionários da educação - Profuncionário, Bras'lia: Universidade de Bras'lia, Centro de Educação a Distância.

Draibe, S. M., Souza, A. N. d., & Borba, M. O. G. (2001). El estado de la enseñanza de la formación en gestión y pol'tica educativa en Brasil. In C. Braslavsky & F. Acosta (Eds.), *El estado de la enseñanza de formación en gestión y pol'tica educativa en América Latina* (pp. 77–113). Buenos Aires: UNESCO: Instituto Internacional de Planeamiento de la Educación.

Esp'nola, V. (2000). Autonom'a escolar: factores que contribuyen a una escuela más efectiva: Banco Interamericano de Desarrollo.

Gorostiaga, J. M. (2006). La democratización de la gestión escolar en la Argentina: una comparación de pol'ticas provinciales. *Archivos Anal'ticos de Pol'ticas Educativas*, 15(2), 1–23.

Gorostiaga, J. M., Acedo, C., & Xifra, S. E. (2003). Secondary Education in Argentina during the 1990s: The Limits of a Comprehensive Reform Effort. *Education Policy Analysis Archives*, 11(17).

IIPE (1998). La formación de recursos humanos para la gestión educativa en América Latina. Instituto Internacional de Planeamiento de la Educación - Buenos Aires, Argentina, 11 y 12 de noviembre 1998.

IIPE (2000). Competencias para la profesionalización de la gestión educativa - Módulo 1 Desaf'os de la Educación. Buenos Aires: UNESCO/Instituto Internacional de Planeamiento de la Educación IIPE/ Ministerio de Educación Argentina.

Kempner, K., & Jurema, A. L. (2002). The global politics of education: Brazil and the World Bank. *Higher Education*, 43, 331–354.

Krawczyk, N. R., & Vieira, V. L. (2003). A reforma educacional no México e no Chile: apontamentos sobre as rupturas e continuidades. *Educar, Curitiba*, 22, 77–98.

Lopes, N. F. M. (2002). *A função do diretor do ensino fundamental e médio: uma visão histórica e atual*, Universidade Estadual de Campinas, Mestrado em Educação.

Lück, H., Freitas, K. S. d., Girling, R., & Keith, S. (2001). *A escola participativa: o trabalho do gestor escolar.* Rio de Janeiro: DP&A.

Machado, A. L. (2001). *El rol de los gestores educativos en el contexto de la descentralización de la escuela.* Santiago: UNESCO/Comité Regional Intergubernamental del Proyecto Principal de Educación en América Latina y el Caribe.

Martelli, A. C. (1999). Gestão escolar: mudança de paradigma ou uma nova nomenclatura para um velho modelo?, Universidade Estadual de Campinas, Mestrado em Educação.

Mattos, M. J. V. M. d. (1999). *A reforma educacional de Minas Gerais: a implementação da autonomia escolar*, Universidade Estadual de Campinas, Mestrado em Educação.

Mendonça, E. F. (2001). Estado Patrimonial e Gestão Democrática do Ensino Público no Brasil. *Educação e Sociedade*, 22(75), 84–108.

Ministerio de Educación (2005). Marco para la buena dirección. Estándares para el desarrollo profesional y evaluación del desempeño.

Mitrulis, E. (2007). Repercussões de um programa de um programa de formação de gestores em exerc'cio, *IV Congresso Luso-Brasileiro de Pol'tica e Administração da Educação.* Faculdade de Psicologia e de Educação da Universidade de Lisboa, 12, 13 e 14 de Abril de 2007, working paper.

Oliveira, C. (2002). Gestão da educação: união, estado/distrito federal, munic'pio e escola. In L. M. Machado & N. S. C. Ferreira (Eds.), *Pol'tica e gestão da educação — dois olhares*. Rio de Janeiro: DP&A.

Ribeiro, D. S. (2007). Formação de gestores escolares: perspectivas conceituais, *IV Congresso Luso-Brasileiro de Pol'tica e Administração da Educação*. Faculdade de Psicologia e de Educação da Universidade de Lisboa, 12, 13 e 14 de Abril de 2007, working paper.

Scotuzzi, C. A. S., & Silva, J. M. A. d. P. e. (2007). Pol'ticas Públicas de Capacitação de Gestores Escolares: uma análise da situação no Estado de São Paulo - Brasil, *IV Congresso Luso-Brasileiro de Pol'tica e Administração da Educação*. Faculdade de Psicologia e de Educação da Universidade de Lisboa, 12, 13 e 14 de Abril de 2007 (working paper).

Señoriño, O., & Vilanova, S. (2001). Construcción del proyecto educativo institucional: concepción de los directivos. *Revista Iberoamericana de Educación*, 22-7-01.

Sverdlick, I. (2006). Apuntes para Debatir sobre la Gestión Escolar en Clave Pol'tica. Una Mirada por la Situación en Argentina. *REICE - Revista Electrónica Iberoamericana sobre Calidad, Eficacia y Cambio en Educación*, 4(4), 65–84.

Teixeira, L. H. G. (2000). Seleção de diretores de escola: avanços, pausas e recuos de um processo, *23a Reunião Anual da Associação Nacional de Pós Graduação e Pesquisa em Educação*. Caxambu, Anuário GT Estado e Pol'tica Educacional, Goiania, v. 1.

Tiramonti, G. (1998). Orientaciones para la formación de funcionarios públicos en el área de educación. In I. I. d. P. d. l. Educación (Ed.), *La formación de recursos humanos para la gestión educativa en América Latina*. IIPE-Buenos Aires, Argentina, 11 y 12 de noviembre 1998: Instituto Internacional de Planeamiento de la Educación.

Undurraga, C., & Araya, C. (2001). El estado de la enseñanza de la formación en gestión y pol'tica educativa en Chile. In C. Braslavsky & F. Acosta (Eds.), *El estado de la enseñanza de formación en gestión y pol'tica educativa en América Latina* (pp. 115–142). Buenos Aires: UNESCO: Instituto Internacional de Planeamiento de la Educación.

Villela, D. d. P. (2007). Gestão Educacional e Formação dos Gestores Escolares, *IV Congresso Luso-Brasileiro de Pol'tica e Administração da Educação*. Faculdade de Psicologia e de Educação da Universidade de Lisboa, 12, 13 e 14 de Abril de 2007, working paper.

Westrupp, M. F. (2003). *Gestão escolar participativa - Novos cenários de competência administrativa*, Universidade do Estado de Santa Catarina, Mestrado em Educação e Cultura. Retrieved October 10, 2006 from: http://enciclopedia.us.es /http://www.unicef.cl/indicadores/educa.htm

17

Leadership Development in Europe

Jorunn Møller and Michael Schratz

In this chapter we show how leadership training and development is framed by the different historical and socio-cultural contexts. We first trace the images of school leadership by analyzing both their historical distinctions and the emerging forces for consensus caused by the spread of political expectations and the impact of transnationalism. Against this background, we explain how, in recent years, the role of schools, the position of school leaders[1] and the approach to leadership training have changed radically across countries. We discuss approaches to leadership development in relation to the particular context and in relation to what seems to have become more dominant discourses of leadership development at policy level. Preferences in perspectives on leadership development are by and large closely connected to countries' approaches to educational governance and accountability, of which we provide an overview. We conclude by showing how political control and professional content may influence future approaches to leadership development in Europe.

Since it is impossible to cover all European countries in this chapter, we have selected four cases by which we discuss the similarities, contrasts and conditions with regards to leadership development more in-depth across different regions. The selected cases include England, Scandinavia (Denmark, Norway and Sweden), German-speaking countries (Germany, Austria and Switzerland) and Eastern Europe represented by the Czech Republic and Hungary. Cross-national comparisons remind us that theory and practice in educational leadership and management are socially constructed and more contextually bound than some are prepared to admit. The difference is even greater when the countries compared do not share a common cultural heritage and a common language (Johnson et al., in press). In leadership research, in projects initiated by the Organization for Economic and Cultural Development (OECD) and the European Union, and in networking amongst national agencies, English has become the dominant language. Consequently, the English-speaking world will probably to a large degree influence the global discourse about leadership development. The dominating perspectives on educational leadership have discursive power and set an agenda for the educational discussion. This is one of the reasons for choosing England as one of our main cases, even though much has already been written about England's approach to leadership development. However, it is an empirical question to what degree England influences the global discourse about leadership development in Europe.

IMAGES OF SCHOOL LEADERSHIP: HISTORICAL DISTINCTIONS

The socio-cultural context influences what is defined as effective school leadership and how it can be best developed and supported. In the following, we will provide brief descriptions of the historically determined "models" that leadership training and development in the selected countries will most likely be seeking.

England: The Headmaster Tradition

In England, it is possible to trace a heroic model with a strong moral purpose underpinning the approach to leadership training and development, which has its origin in a "headmaster tradition" going back to the 19th and early 20th centuries. According to this model, the notion of school leadership as moral leadership was a dominant construct, and the moral order of all schools was seen to be closely related to the moral order and the social order of the wider society, which deeply resides in the basic class structure (cf. Bernstein, 1977). The most important function of schools at each social class level was to provide appropriate moral socialization relevant to the class destinations of its students. The "headmaster tradition" of school leadership developed over time in the contexts of upper-class education in England, and this tradition placed a premium upon leaders with a strong and assertive personality. There was, however, a difference between being a headmaster in the "public schools"[2] compared to the "state schools". School leadership in the public schools was exercised in conditions of greater autonomy compared to elementary state schools where it was enacted under class-cultural inspection (Baron, 1970; Grace, 1995).

During the period from the 1940s to the 1970s, the political culture became more democratic and participative, membership of the governing body became socially more heterogeneous, and the explicit class-cultural control in English state schooling was removed. This period was characterized by a transformation towards greater autonomy for all schools and particularly for those in the working-class, elementary tradition. As a general tendency, the ideology of the "headmaster tradition" was extended to and recontextualized in state schools (first to the grammar schools, later to the comprehensive schools), and for many years this "headmaster tradition" empowered head teachers vis-à-vis the formal authority of the governing body. It was a period of growth in status and influence of professionalism and expertness, although the head teachers did not have power in matters of finance, resources and in recruitment of personnel (Grace, 1995).

The Education Reform Act 1988 significantly altered the education system in England. A combination of neo-liberal market reforms and neo-conservative government regulation reformed schooling during the late 1980s and 1990s. The autonomous teachers were held responsible for a decline in educational standards, and the politicians shared a belief that the power of Local Education Authority (LEA), universities and teacher unions needed to be broken in favor of more robust forms of managerial accountability. The Office for Standards in Education (OFSTED) was established, and a new framework for inspection was devised. The second mechanism for accountability was national Standard Attainment Tests (SATs) for all students aged 7, 11 and 14 years, and a third mechanism was the introduction of merit pay.

The Reform Act introduced such concepts as a national curriculum, local management of schools and stronger accountability of state schooling to parents who may choose where to place their children. School governing bodies were empowered, so that almost all schools are now highly decentralized in terms of their budgets and management but highly centralized in terms of the curriculum and its assessment. Heads have become more managerially autonomous, but they are less educationally autonomous compared to the 1970s.

Although new models of school leadership have been developed during the last two decades, the "headmaster tradition" still resides in the English school system. In many ways the headmaster tradition has been recontextualized within modern management culture rather than being abolished (Grace, 1995). For example, there is growing empirical evidence that despite the pressures some head teachers have found 'room to maneuver' (Helsby, 1999). Also, presently, there is debate around the potential of "shared leadership" or "distributed leadership", yet these new images focus on developing personal styles and courage relative to the perceived and actual pressures (Day, 2007). Even the emerging model of system leadership paradoxically has a strong individual and heroic focus.

Scandinavia: The Welfare State

The welfare state, which is a distinguishing feature of the Scandinavian region (i.e. Norway, Denmark and Sweden), was intended to create equitable life conditions for all social groups, regardless of social background, gender, ethnicity and geographical location. School access for children from all socio-economic groups is considered very important, and Education Acts in all three countries stipulate that all activity should be carried out in accordance with fundamental democratic values, and that everyone working in the school should encourage respect for the intrinsic values of each person as well as for the environment shared by all.

Scandinavia has a strong ideological tradition of viewing schools as an expression of democratic political ideals and as a mechanism for preparing children to play constructive roles in a democratic society and a strong commitment to comprehensive education and social justice. Democratic leadership in the schools is grounded in the societal view that education should promote democracy as a fundamental social value and an ethical guide to citizenship (Johansson, 2004; Moos, Møller & Johansson, 2004; Møller, 2006).

Individual autonomy is part of the tradition in schools and related to the history of teaching in Scandinavia. Trust in teachers' work has for long been a tacit dimension in principals' approach to leadership, establishing accepted zones of influence (Berg, 2000). This implies the idea of a school leader as "primus inter pares" (first among equals), and it points to the flat organizational structure of a school. This feature was mirrored in the title of the leadership positions in schools. For instance, up to the late 1960s the title "overlærer" (*primus inter pares*) was used in Norway for the person in charge of leading compulsory schools. The titles have changed since then, but the person in charge at each primary and lower secondary/high school was still, particularly by teachers, considered "first among equals". Neither has there been a strong emphasis on leadership as an academic discipline.

However, during the 1990s established zones of control were challenged, as some parents and people outside schools questioned the individual autonomy each teacher had in his or her classroom. The focus shifted the power relationship between the adults in the school system, and the recent development has focused more on the planning, efficiency and control of the educational process. This shift essentially moved the head teacher from being "the first among equals" to a manager, at least in the dominant discourses and in national policy documents.

There is evidence that the tradition of striving for equity through centralized welfare state governance is changing throughout Scandinavia towards a school policy based on choice, deregulation, evaluation and managerialism.[3] In addition, the historical development of the Scandinavian nations has viewed democracy as central to the workplace. It has been and continues to be important for everyone to have a sense of control over their working conditions, and to some degree there has been a similarity of lifestyle between managers and workers. Resilient unions have contributed to robust elements of negotiations in the workplace and a form of institutionalized trust relations. A strong welfare state has simultaneously played a powerful role in shaping job security. Such conditions may have probably set up barriers against implementing a strong, hierarchical and powerful leadership model within a Scandinavian context (Sejersted, 1997). As such, it is possible to distinguish a Nordic model of society which is based on cooperation and compromise, with a special balance between the state, the market and civil society. It emerges as a composite of two large European models; the Continental model's emphasis on a large public sector, social welfare and security, and the Anglo-Saxon model's emphasis on economic liberalism and competition (Telhaug, Mediås & Aasen, 2006, pp. 278–279).

German-Speaking Countries (Germany, Austria, Switzerland): Balancing Centre and Periphery

The three countries are united by one language, but their social fabrics are historically based on different developments. Whereas Austria and Germany have their roots in formerly influential monarchies, Switzerland is rooted in a strong direct democracy where citizens should have full influence on the state.[4]

Each of the three countries has a framework of a federal parliamentary democratic republic, but the different historical developments have led to different specifications of how federal democracy is executed. The Swiss Federal Constitution limits federal influence in the formulation of domestic policy and emphasizes the roles of private enterprise and cantonal government. Germany is a parliamentary federal republic consisting of sixteen states (*Bundesländer*), after it had been divided into the Federal Republic of Germany and the German Democratic Republic from 1949 until 1990. After the fall of the Austro-Hungarian Empire (1918), the Austrian Republic had to undergo several political phases until it became what is now known as the Second Austrian Republic (1955–present) and has changed from a strongly multi-ethnic empire to a small country trying to construct a new identity considering the manifold past.

As far as schooling is concerned, the three countries have different ways of distributing power according to their socio-cultural traditions. In Switzerland, by tradition, the local community has a strong influence on what happens in schools, whereas the confederate level has no or little say. The individual citizens (represented by a lay body) take responsibility for staffing schools and monitoring success. It was not common for primary schools to appoint a school leader until recently. In Germany, the legislative power is divided between the federation and the state level. The federate level has only power to legislate "if and to the extent that the establishment of equal living conditions throughout the federal territory or the maintenance of legal or economic unity renders federal regulation necessary in the national interest" (Art. 72 Basic Law). Accordingly, responsibility for educational matters in Germany lies primarily with the states, whereas the federal government only plays a minor role. As is the case with government administration in general, responsibilities for legislation and implementation in school education in Austria are divided between the Federation and the *Länder*. Commentators on Austrian society point to the strong emphasis placed on social cohesion, trust, and stability in organizational structures. In the school system, there are many consultative processes with groups and organizations involved in decision-making, a condition which often makes it difficult to reach the necessary majority for significant changes.

All three German-speaking countries have been compelled to align their systems nationally because it became more and more difficult and expensive to have parallel structures on the national and federal state or cantonal levels in the context of the political developments described above. In order to avoid criticism or resistance to centralization, non-government institutions or agencies have been created to take over overall responsibility. At the Humboldt University Berlin, the IQB (Institute for Educational Progress) was founded by the KMK (Standing Conference of the Ministers of Education and Cultural Affairs) of the federal states in Germany. The IQB supports all 16 federal states in Germany in their endeavor to ensure that the quality of educational processes is monitored and continually improved. Similar developments in centralizing and standardizing the education systems are taking place in Austria and Switzerland.

Schools in German-speaking countries are presently experiencing transforming changes from an administrative style of management towards a leadership oriented way of facing contemporary challenges, since they have been confronted with pressures from all sides. This change of conditions in schools of German-speaking countries has led not only to a re-definition of the tasks demanded of heads and an increased power of control (Schratz 1996a), but also to the introduction of a revised definition of the function of school inspection (cf. Rosenbusch, 1995; Schratz, 1996b; Rolff & Schmidt, 2002). Thus, decision-making structures concerning the development of schools and teaching have been shifted to the schools themselves, and completely new tasks are demanded of all others in the system. Self-evaluation is becoming a necessary task providing evidence for improvement and external evaluators have more and more become the "guardians" monitoring success or failure (Schratz, 2006).

For quite some time the relationship between "leaders" and "followers" could not be dealt with productively because of the negative connotations of the German word "Führung". Researchers still argue if the concept of leadership was a meaningful way out of the underlying dilemma in the ongoing debate. In German-speaking countries, the organizational structure of schools is marked by a very flat hierarchy which leads to a "myth of equality" among the teaching staff. The inner hierarchy is thus concealed and the distribution of organizational tasks is complicated. Additionally, heads of school are often regarded as being "primus inter pares", which leads to additional problems in orchestrating the dimensions of "sollen" and "wollen" (duty and desire) among the teaching staff (Schratz, 2003).

Former Eastern Europe (Hungary and the Czech Republic): Decentralizing to Western Models

In most Eastern European countries, we notice a recurring tendency: They look at "old" European countries as role models for leadership training to align their own education systems with what they call "international trends" and European dimensions and standards (Slavikova, 2007). We will look at two countries which have only recently joined the European Union: the Czech Republic and Hungary. Their political systems underwent dramatic changes in the past two decades and they serve as an example of what has happened in other former Eastern countries. Since 1989, with liberation from the Soviet hegemony, they have changed at different speeds, and are still changing, and so are the expectations about schools and school leadership. The large-scale social and economic changes of the 1990s were partly preceded and partly accompanied by those political processes which led to the evolution of parliamentary democracy. The single party regime and the planned economy were replaced by a multi-party democracy and a market economy, which both had a significant influence on the education sector.

The new era also brought a significant change in public administration: The central and local authorities now share the responsibility for public education, and the structure of decision-making has shifted from a centralized pattern to a more decentralized one. After the political changes in 1990, fundamental changes took place in the social and economic field. In the economic sector, the transition to market economy has influenced the employment structure dramatically and led to an economic crisis with an adverse effect on public services. Public expenditure was reduced largely, labor market demand changed significantly. Health care, public administration and education came in for significant structural reforms.

In 1985, in Hungary, even before the change of the political system, a public education law was passed by Parliament which gave professional autonomy to the schools. After 1989, this process was speeded up. Educational administration moved from a strictly centralized position to a strongly decentralized form (Baráth & Cseh, 2002, & Baráth, 2006). In the past decade, the internal conditions of schools were greatly influenced by social changes that took place simultaneously with the transition of the economy. In the 1990s, the gap between different groups of society widened, and the number of underprivileged people increased. With the appearance of unemployment after the regime change and with pay rising for more highly educated people, the population's demand for education has grown. The educational expansion of the 1990s has contributed to an increase of educational demands from younger people.

With different speeds — most rapidly in the Czech Republic and Hungary — schools have started to become places of varying degrees of autonomy. In some Eastern countries, the movement towards school autonomy happened even faster than in Western or Central Europe, due to the radical changes in the overall system after the fall of the Iron Curtain. Schools were supposed to be able to absorb the metamorphoses of the external circumstances. Though school heads were considered able to manage the new situation, the development of their personal capacity was rather neglected. A predominant role under the new constellation was given to head teachers, who were granted considerable power. However, their readiness to cope with the new situation was lacking, and so was the external support to schools.

"Borrowing" concepts and frameworks from other countries and implementing them seems to work even more successfully in these countries. A lot of new vocabulary from quality assurance concepts has been introduced and accepted very quickly. After the breakdown of the communist system, educational management, both as theory and practice, began to depart from its past and search for an identity of its own in the theoretical fundamentals of management and the cultural models of school management popular in the United States and Western Europe. As a result of the changes, society witnessed a reform in school management. The problems of school autonomy and the role of school heads as professional managers are widely debated. Discussion of ideas related to participative, strategic, innovative and situational management, and the application of managerial principles to the sphere of education started at different phases in the respective countries. As educational systems are moving toward decentralization and varying degrees of autonomy, educational management has become a very specific and complex task, which seems likely to become even more difficult and demanding in the future. This means that specific training for educational leaders is needed on a large scale.

The need for a scientific background of educational leadership and management requires improved institutional capacity for research in the field of management and leadership and its consolidation as professional activity. This would encourage the recognition of school leaders as professional managers and the training of managers for the needs of the educational system. For understandable reasons, the immediate need for training was perceived first as "managing" the school, whereas leadership has followed later as a distinctive issue.

IMAGES FOR SCHOOL LEADERSHIP: FORCES FOR CONSENSUS

Today there is a tension between those who argue for top-down conceptions of "strong" leadership and those who argue that strong leadership can only be achieved through a participative approach. According to Grace (1995, p. 186), the 'major trend could be called the *masculine-strong leadership* and it can be seen to have re-contextualized earlier masculine cultures of leadership in contemporary forms which seem relevant to market conditions in schooling'. His analysis is based on the UK, but 'grand man' theory seems, currently, to be a dominant trend amongst politicians in many European countries.

This section of the chapter looks at possible reasons for an emergent consensus which are the impact of trans-nationalism and the spread of political expectations.

Europeanization: The Impact of Trans-Nationalism

The changing social environment in Europe has been accompanied by major legislation which has led to new governance structures across most European countries. These governance structures provide the context for educational reforms affecting the roles and responsibilities of school leaders, and consequently the approach to leadership development.

In this process, the European Union (EU) and Organization for Economic Co-operation and Development (OECD) seem to play powerful roles in driving and attenuating policy. For instance, the EU has instigated numerous efforts for an integration of what is coined a European dimension in education, particularly since the ratification of the Maastricht Treaty on European Union in 1992. The aspiration is to create a feeling of belonging within the European Community and a European identity. However, in a diverse Europe with great differences in relation to language, ethnic background, culture and history, this is a massive challenge (Karlsen, 2002). EU activities and programs are expected to enhance mobility through exchanges of students and teachers, school partnerships and foreign language learning, as well as transnational research projects.

At the same time, through the International Association of the Evaluation of Educational Achievement (IEA), the OECD has implemented large scale international comparisons like TIMSS (Third International Mathematics and Science Study) and PISA (Program for International Student Assessment). Teachers and school principals are subject to pressure from governments to improve national ranking in the different subjects, and these studies have a global effect and influence the way all countries define quality (Brown, 1998). What is often termed neo-liberal concepts are currently used in arguing for reforms to education, and they are guided by a vision of a weak state and strong marketization.

In 2006, the Organization for Economic Co-operation and Development initiated the "Improving School Leadership" project (ISL) in which eighteen European countries[5] participated. It aims at providing policy makers with information and analysis to assist them in formulating and implementing school leadership policies leading to improved teaching and learning. A major assumption behind the project is that successful school leadership is viewed as key to large-scale education reform and to improved educational outcomes. To a large degree this assumption is based on the school effectiveness literature (cf. Reynolds & Teddlie, 2000). Such an international project as ISL may lead to more standardization in each country's approach to leadership development and influence the way all countries define more innovative practices. Already, in many countries there is a trend towards developing standards as a central plank of educational reform, borrowing frameworks and ideas particularly from England and the United States. There seem to be numerous examples of policy copying, following site visitations, study tours, electronic networking amongst national agencies and authorities.

Glocalization: The Spread of Political Expectations

Even though there are many examples of policy borrowing and there is a growing homogenization of approaches to governance due to global forces, local traditions ensure that they are played out differently in national contexts, a phenomenon which Beck (2000) has termed "glocalization". Across our selected European countries various strategies for school governance can be identified. In the following a short overview will be provided to set the political context for leadership development in these countries. The approaches contain a quasi-market approach which involves high-stake-testing, New Public Management (NPM), Old Public Administration (OPA), professional control and self evaluation (cf. Leithwood, 2001; Mulford, 2003; Olsen, 2002).

A *quasi-market approach* is characterized by competition among schools, school choice, and publicly ranking schools based on aggregated student achievement scores (Leithwood, 2001). *New Public Management* (NPM) is inspired by a model of private corporations operating in competitive markets, and is primarily an instrument for efficient service production, governed by a performance-oriented culture with a focus on results, entrepreneurship and efficiency (Olsen, 2002). NPM has traits like decentralization, privatization, contracting out, competition, and emphasis on economic rewards and sanction (Mulford, 2003). As such, there are many similarities between a quasi-market approach and NPM. Both have elements of managerial approaches to public administration. *Old Public Management* assumes administrators socialized into an ethos of rule following and public service or a structure characterized by a bureaucratic model.

Professional approaches to accountability encompass both the implementation of professional control of site-based management and the professional standards movement as it applies to the practices of teachers and school leaders and control of entry to the profession by government. The power of teachers increases, but at the same time the teachers are held accountable for the school's effects on students. There is also an expectation that school leaders monitor the progress of staff towards the achievement of professional standards. *Self evaluation* is mainly characterized by a focus on improvement and claims for strengthening professional accountability. Goals, planning and continuous evaluation provide the key to improvement, and the benefits are seen as primarily for teachers and students. But it is possible to discern two other competing logics connected to self evaluation. They embrace, first, the accountability logic which holds that schools are financially and morally obliged to monitor and report on their own performance. Second, the economic logic which derives from recognizing that external quality assurance is expensive and does not offer value for money. Hence, self evaluation offers a cost-free alternative (MacBeath, 2006).

In comparing these separate approaches it is possible to distinguish tensions between top-down and bottom-up change strategies; and the external accountability of league tables versus self-evaluation for institutional learning. Such strategies influence the role of school leaders in different ways, and they set the context for approaches to leadership development.

In Table 17.1, we have summarized our criteria for the different approaches to governance in some European countries to illustrate both similarities and contrasts within Europe. A distinction between different elements within each approach is made to demonstrate possible overlaps between the different approaches, and to indicate whether or not each criterion applies to each of the different countries.

TABLE 17.1

Different Approaches to School Governance in Some European Countries

	Denmark	Norway	Sweden	England	Switzerland[1]	Germany	Austria	Czech	Hungary
Quasi-market									
Competition among schools	Partial	No2	Partial	Yes	No	Partial	Partial	Partial	Yes[3]
School choice	Partial	No	Yes	Yes	No	Partial	Partial	Partial	Yes[4]
Public ranking	No	No	No	Yes	No	No	No	No	Partial[5]
New Public Management									
Decentralization	Yes	Yes	Yes	Yes	Partial	Partial	Partial	Yes	Yes
Privatization	Partial	No	Partial	Yes	No	No	No	No	Yes[6]
Contracting out	No	No	No	Partial	Partial	No	No	Partial	Partial[7]
Output governance	Yes	Yes	Yes	Yes	Partial	Partial	Partial	Partial	Partial
Economic rewards / Sanctions	No	No	No	Yes	No	No	No	No	No
Old Public Management									
In-put regulated	No	No	No	No	Yes	Yes	Yes	Yes	No
Hierarchical system	Yes	Yes	Yes	Yes[8]	Yes	Yes	Yes	Yes	No
An ethos of rule following	Partial	Partial	Partial	Partial	Yes	Partial	Partial	Partial	Partial[9]
Professional Control									
Site based management	Partial	Partial	Yes	Yes	Yes	Partial	Partial	Partial	Partial[10]
Professional standards	In process[11]	No	No	Yes	Yes	In process	No	No	No
Professional monitoring & accountability	Partial	Partial	Partial	Yes	In process	Partial	In process	In process	Partial
Control of entry to the profession by government	Partial	Partial[12]	Yes	Yes	Yes	Yes	Yes	Yes	Partial[13]
Self evaluation									
Improvement logic	Yes	Yes	Yes	Yes	Partial	Yes	Yes	Yes	Yes
Accountability logic	Yes	Yes	Yes	Yes	Yes	Yes	Yes	Yes	Yes
Economic logic	No	No	No	Yes	No	No	No	No	No

(Continued)

TABLE 17.1
Continued

[1] Answers for compulsory schools. More competition, choice and NPM in upper secondary level.

[2] Some counties have established competition at upper secondary level.

[3] Schools fight for students because of the demography tendencies (decreasing seriously). Schools advertise themselves. There are big differences among their possibilities.

[4] Parents can freely choose school for their children, however the educational government plans to limit it on primary school level (ISCED 1 and 2).

[5] There are different rankings about the performance of the secondary schools, like ration of students get language exam, get into university, etc. Measurement of the students' performances is under development.

[6] Yes means: the Public Educational Law allows to found and launch schools. Most of the private schools belong to the church on primary level (5.0 percent), the schools owned by foundations 2.1 percent.

[7] The profit organizations are strongly on the market of the evaluation of schools (ordered by the maintainers), in-service training of teachers.

[8] Even though decentralization has been a key word in educational reforms, new constructs in which principals are seen as managing directors are growing in prominence and power. Seen from the teachers' perspective, there is still a hierarchical system in place. There is a tendency to exert more control over teachers' work and time.

[9] The administration system has completely changed: it was centralized and became strongly decentralized. In spite of this many actors of the system could keep style of OPA.

[10] Behind the educational law, the national curriculum and the requirements of the final exam most of the decision is taken by schools and/or their maintainers. However the level of accountability is law.

[11] A codex for successful school leadership has recently been introduced in Denmark, but so far it has not been implemented as part of an evaluation system.

[12] The Danish and Norwegian governments control the entry to the teaching profession, but there is no such requirement for the entry to the leadership profession.

[13] Working as teacher requires teacher certificate. After 2015 only those who have certificate in school management can be nominated as school director before his/her appointment.

As demonstrated in Table 17.1, it is not easy to apply only one category to each of the countries. New Public Management overlaps to some extent the quasi-market approach, and professional control may include self evaluation. It is, nevertheless, possible to spot some distinctive approaches to school governance across countries. For instance, standards and benchmarking have become a central metaphor of educational reform, particularly in England. Failure to improve in England can lead to rigorous inspection, state take-over or dissolution. Simultaneously, there has been a contested history of publishing test scores in England, and the teacher unions' press for a more school-based approach has recently gained positive results (MacBeath, 2006).

Benchmarking, league tables and professional standards are more recent phenomena in other European countries. For instance, Denmark has in 2006 devised a codex for leadership, which later can be developed into a standards framework for school principals' work. But compared to England, the Scandinavian schools are under less threat of sanction if the test and exams scores are low, or if the school is not well thought of in the community.

Austria is characterized by a strongly input-regulated, hierarchical system, which is interwoven with federal elements, causing parallel structures on the national and federal state level. According to the bureaucratic model, school leaders only have autonomy within limited boundaries. They are not able to appoint new teachers according to the needs of their schools as personnel selection is conducted by the regional education authorities or the Ministry. Also, school leaders have limited autonomy within the boundaries of the curriculum and budgetary decision-making is restricted.

PREPARING FOR AND DEVELOPING SCHOOL LEADERSHIP

Europe is in many ways an example of an area of great heterogeneity, and the availability and the quality of professional development of school leaders across European countries is mixed. However, there seems to be a trend toward formal requirements to qualify for leadership positions in most countries which implies a stronger professionalization of school leaders.

The Professionalization of Principals

The professionalization of school leaders can be viewed as a sociological project, relating to the authority and status of the school leadership profession. As such, it can be measured in terms of symbolic strength, requirements for formal qualification, and its possible exclusiveness. Professional unions may play an important role in protecting this status. For instance, unlike the case of the United States and Canada (cf. Bredeson, 1996), the formal education of candidates for school leadership in university-based preparation programs has not been a significant component of the professional socialization processes for school leaders in Europe. In addition, it is quite common for teachers and school leaders to be members of the same trade union (OECD, 2007). As demonstrated by Table 17.2, which compares information from European countries participating in the OECD's Improving School Leadership project, including our selected cases, most countries have established professional associations/unions in which both school leaders and teachers participate, but in addition they also have associations for school leaders (Hegtun, 2007).

Only England and Scotland require pre-service training, and only Norway and the Netherlands do not require teacher education or any other formal credentials, at this point, for school leadership positions.

TABLE 17.2
Professionalization of School Leaders across Countries

Countries	Unions and professional associations for school leaders and teachers		Major requirements to qualify for school leadership positions/ Regulatory framework and legislation that applies to school leadership preparation (pre-service) programs			
	Teachers and school leaders	Only school leaders	Formal pre-service-training of school leaders	Teacher education and experience	Teacher education, experience and formal preparation as leaders after being appointed	No formal requirements
Denmark	x			x		
Norway	x	x				x
Sweden	x	x			x	
Austria	x				x	
Germany	x	x		x	(x)	
Switzerland	x	x		x	x	
Czech Republic	x			x	x	
Hungary	x			x	(x)	
England	x	x	x		x	
Scotland	x	x	x		x	
Finland	x				x	
Flemish Belgium	x	x		x		
France	x	x			x	
Ireland	x	x		x		
Netherlands	x	x				x
Slovenia	x				x	
Spain	x				x	

A requirement for formal training and compulsory pre-service education for school leaders has only recently emerged on the agenda of some European countries, for which England, with the establishment of the National College of School Leadership, seems to take a lead role. Professional standards for principals are being developed and these standards represent expectations of what is considered preferred practice among school leaders. In practice standards increasingly lead to new forms of regulation of preparation programs and accreditation. For instance, in the Czech Republic levels of formal preparation of school heads have been established nationally about two years ago, and providers have to follow national standards.

In the following section we present the different approaches to leadership training and development in the selected country cases.

England: Centralizing Decentralization

Three major phases in the approach to leadership development in England can be distinguished (Bolam, 2004). The first one includes ad hoc provision in the late 1960s and early 1970s. During this period, the Local Educational Authorities (LEA) and Her Majesty's Inspectorate ran many practical courses in order to support school leaders in their job, and several universities ran Diploma and Masters courses in educational management.

The second phase represents a move towards more coherence and coordination. One example was the establishment of the National Development Centre for School Management Training. The Education Reform Act in 1988 gave even stronger emphasis to the management role and education of school leaders, and many university programs on leadership and management expanded in the next few years. It recognized how vitally important leadership was to the success of schools, and this became the rationale for many new initiatives during the 1990s. A major development was the establishment of the Teacher Training Agency (TTA), which set up the first national qualification for aspiring heads, the National Professional Qualification for Headship, (NPQH) in 1997. When this program was established, the government made a decision not to link it with university programs. In addition, HEADLAMP (Head teachers' Leadership and Management Programme) provided new head teachers with a grant of money to be spent on their development needs. During this period, the two main head teachers' unions became increasingly active in promoting and delivering both training and development programs for school leaders, and British Educational Leadership, Management and Administration Society) (BELMAS) promoted networking and research and the dissemination of information (Bolam, 2004).

The next major step was taken when the National College of School Leadership (NCSL) was established in November 2000, and finally launched by Prime Minister Tony Blair in 2002. The College is wholly funded by central government, has an annual budget of £100 million, and makes extensive use of modern technologies and e-learning. The NCSL's very ambitious aims include providing a national focus for school leadership development and research; to be a driving force for world class leadership in the schools and the wider education service, a provider and promoter of excellence, a major resource for schools, a catalyst for innovation, and a focus for national and international debate on leadership issues. The goals include developing excellent school leadership to transform children's achievements and well-being, to develop leadership within and beyond the school, and to identify and grow tomorrow's leaders. It puts an emphasis on practice and learning through reflection on leaders' experiences. As such, their programs have been informed by the notion of "best practice", and recently they have changed this notion to "next practice" in order to look forward and promote innovation in schools. In order to distribute evidence-based research the College collaborates with researchers to highlight key findings in summary and with a focus on practice.

The college distinguishes between programs for emergent leaders, established leaders, newly appointed leaders, experienced heads looking to refresh and update their skills, and consultant leaders which include those who have proved effective and are willing to help heads in other schools and therefore are ready to further their training, mentoring and coaching skills. They have also appointed 68 national leaders of education who will work in weaker schools to help school improvement.

The college's reach is impressive. It covers 47 per cent of all school leaders, and it is also a major sponsor of school leadership research. However, there are some pitfalls of this national strategy for leadership education in England. Some will claim there is an "unhealthy domination" of leadership development in England by the NCSL, not least because of the "monopoly" of NPQH. In addition, some question if scale is chosen at the expense of quality and depth, practitioners seem to have limited engagement with research and theory, and fewer people are taking Masters degrees in educational leadership and management (Bush, 2004).

The description above is largely based on articles in a special issue of the journal, *Educational Management, Administration and Leadership*, which was published in 2004. In these articles there is a general tendency to view the NCSL as a largely beneficial development. However, critical perspectives are gaining more ground. For instance, Gronn (2003) has argued that in some ways NCSL is promoting a process of what he has coined as "designer leadership" to underscore how managerial, national standards for school leaders have become a defining theme for leadership in the appearance of regimes of assessment. These involve much more control over what kind of school leader it is possible to be. As such, it is possible for the government to regulate education from a distance. So even though decentralization acts as delegation of responsibilities, schools are tied to greater central monitoring. This can be called "decentralized centralism" (Karlsen, 2000). NCSL has also been critiqued for framing school leadership to disseminate managerialist education policy into schools (Thrupp, 2005). According to Thrupp (2005), critical perspectives which do not fit with government policy are largely ignored in the NCSL's publications and the College falls clearly into line with the DfES 5 Year Strategy. Also, in a situation with budgetary crisis facing education as a whole in UK, the College with a budget of £100 million sterling may be vulnerable to discussion about how cost effective it is (Bolam, 2004).

Scandinavia: Loose Coupling

Until the early 1990s, no formal education for school leaders was offered by Norwegian university colleges and universities. However, national and regional authorities have instigated in-service training. In the period from 1980 to 2000, such efforts were guided by broad national in-service programs for school leadership. Simultaneously, the dominant teacher unions strongly contested the need for formal, university-based preparation programs for school leaders. According to their view, earlier experience as a teacher was a sufficient and substantial qualification for a position as principal. Also, the unions argued for keeping this option as a career path for teachers. Neither did the teachers welcome a leadership profession which could influence their control over classroom activities (Tjeldvoll, Wales, & Welle-Strand, 2005).

In 1998 a network of universities and colleges which provided in-service training and Masters programs in educational leadership, was established and funded by the Ministry of Education and Research. The focus of the network, which allowed for breadth and diversity, was to develop and share experiences about providing leadership programs and tailor-made courses, to promote more extensive and better use of ICT-based programs, and to develop a stronger research agenda for school leadership in Norway. Although now several universities and colleges offer Masters programs in educational leadership, it cannot be considered a strong national strategy for leadership development, mainly because the school owners, i.e. municipalities and county authorities, are responsible for ensuring that school leaders have the necessary competence, and also for evaluating, developing and implementing leadership programs and courses. This political course has resulted in growing competition between the higher education institutions which compete in bidding for the provision of programs for local and regional authorities across the country, alongside private consultancy companies. Also, institutions have to overcome the geographical challenges of attracting students from a wider area in order to survive. As such, the ties within the network are rather weak (Wales & Welle-Strand, 2005).

Accordingly, preparation and development for school leaders vary across municipalities and counties. Currently Norway has no mandatory requirement for any leadership qualification. With the exception of a recently established agency, which deals with accreditation of college-based programs for school leaders, there is no national monitoring of the content and structure of the courses which are offered. Whether formal education in the form of a Master's degree is a requirement for employment is currently for the municipalities as employers to decide.

Similarly, Denmark has neither had national guidelines nor requirements for formal preparation for school leadership. Only recently have the teacher unions developed a codex for school leadership which later can be developed into a framework of standards for school principals' work, similar to that in England. There is no certified education or any comprehensive government supported in-service programs for school leaders. There seemed to be a consensus for many years that leadership didn't require any education exceeding the teachers training and some years of teaching and schooling practice. As in Norway, programs are offered by the municipalities, and they exist alongside with those made available from the universities, and those developed by independent and private providers. The State does not provide a national direction, and the responsibility for leadership development is located at municipal level. Newly appointed principals are offered courses in management, and sometimes a mentor-program is available. Recently, a Master's program in educational leadership has been developed at The Danish University of Education in collaboration with Copenhagen Business School. The government is planning a diploma course in leadership that is going to be compulsory for school leaders.

In Sweden, state involvement in the training of school leaders has occurred since the late 1960s (Johansson, 2004) with the provision of short-term courses in a number of educational and administrative areas. Since 1986 a national training program for principals has been offered by The National Agency for Education, but since 1992 courses have been delivered at various universities, while the Agency has retained the responsibility for these programs. Tuition is funded by the State, while the municipalities and other employers bear the costs of travel and subsistence allowances, stand-in teachers and reading material.

For the present programs, which started in 2002, the National Agency for Education defines the goals, content and coverage of the training and distributes State funding allocated for this purpose to eight universities that carry out the program. The Agency is also responsible for the follow-up and evaluation of the training on a regular basis, and the principals have at least 10 per cent reduction in their work load while they are participating. The municipalities can decide if they will enroll their school leaders into this program, and most of them do. During the first three years of appointment as a school leader, the majority of Swedish principals join this three year program covering thirty course-days. The Swedish strategy can be characterized as a combination of centralization and decentralization; it is a balance between political and professional power over leadership training, but compared to Norway and Denmark, the State seems to have a stronger position.

During the spring of 2006, the new National Agency for School Improvement proposed a national program with a mandatory course in management. The National Agency for Education expected to be responsible for this program, indicating that the State intended to weaken the ties with the universities which offered the national training program. After the general election in 2006, the new government presented a revised proposal for leadership training which will be mandatory for all principals appointed after 2007. It requires a certificate of 30 credits (ECT) within the first four years of appointment. The program will be governed by the National Agency for Education and cover 15 credits in management and 15 credits in school leadership, and the universities will be the providers of the program in school leadership. This proposal represents continuity with what has been in place, and it will also strengthen the ties with universities by requiring courses at advanced level.

German-Speaking Countries: Struggling for Ownership

Leadership development programs vary in the different German-speaking countries and reflect the federal or cantonal structures of their school systems. According to the federal system, in *Germany* the Bundesländer provide their own qualification programs for school leaders (some in cooperation) through their in-service training institutions. The programs differ according to structure, time span and contents (cf. Huber, 2004, p. 172). In states where there have been particular school reform initiatives, the necessity for a qualification for school heads has become a priority, e.g. because of its decentralization initiative Lower Saxony has started a certified trainer training program to assure quality in their state-wide leadership qualification.

Despite the activities of the University of Bamberg offering symposia for school leadership as early as 1988, it has not been possible to introduce university programs for educational leadership in Germany (cf. Rosenbusch, 1995). However, two universities (Hagen and Kaiserslautern) offer distance courses for school management. In North Rhine-Westphalia the *Dortmunder Akademie für Pädagogische Führungskräfte*, an institution offering courses in educational management, was recently opened as an initiative by the local university. The federal states with their hierarchical school structure organize their own development programs in order to influence on the content and structure as well as the recruitment of lecturers/trainers.

Since Switzerland allows little federal influence on educational programs, there have been several initiatives offering pre- and in-service management courses for school heads by different providers. The earlier ones started at the University of St. Gall with a strong business faculty offering courses to the school sector. The Academy for Adult Education in Lucerne has a long tradition offering country-wide courses in cooperation with the umbrella organization of the Swiss Teachers Association. Also individual cantons or joint ventures between several (for reasons of size and resources) have started offering courses serving their school leaders. For financial reasons the situation in Switzerland has a more open market culture in management courses. The participants themselves or the communities or the canton of their schools have to pay the costs, whereas in Germany and Austria the courses offered as in-service training are usually financed by the federal states. Towards the end of the last century the first attempts to harmonize the different training programs all over Switzerland started. Meanwhile, most cantons have turned their previously non-academic teacher education seminars into institutions of higher learning (*Päda-*

gogische Hochschulen), which have taken over the role of organizing pre- and in-service courses for school leaders.

Since the 1990s, Austria has had a compulsory systematic initial training program for newly appointed school heads consisting of a six week school management course, organized in a part-time arrangement so that the novice heads can start working as school leaders in their new position. The program consists of collective work in residential meetings (24 days) and individual self-study covering three or four terms (cf. Fischer & Schratz, 1999). Most of the training programs are offered by the regional in-service training institutions which in autumn 2007 will become part of the *Pädagogische Hochschulen* (similar to the Swiss situation).

In 2004, the Austrian Ministry of Education started the *Leadership Academy* (LEA)[6] as an innovative approach to enhance leadership development within the German-speaking countries. It aims at educating all 6500 school leaders and other executives in leadership positions in the Austrian school system (cf. Schley & Schratz, 2006). As a virtual organization, the LEA functions as a project organization and is not built as a physical environment (in contrast to the English NCSL). A project management team, a scientific research team, an organizational support team linked with the Universities of Innsbruck and Zurich and the Ministry of Education cooperate in making it work. Network coordinators in all Austrian provinces function as the regional support system assuring regional networking. The website www.leadershipacademy. at is the central communication platform which offers participants of the LEA immediate and project focused support in the members sections. Each cohort meets four times for three full days each before its members graduate. In-between they meet regularly at provincial, group and partner levels. Each cohort consists of 250 to 300 participants from the educational system. They come from all provinces and school types as well as the Ministry and regional education authorities (e.g. inspectorate). This ensures right from the beginning that the "whole system" is involved in a joint learning process in order to make a system-wide impact on change and transformation possible.

The LEA is composed as a network building its foundation on the smallest organizational entity, the learning partnership. This learning partnership is the home base for two participants each of whom align in a trustful, reciprocal, coaching partnership. They support each other through exploratory questions, help to define project milestones and guide each other through their individual learning processes. Three learning partnerships respectively merge in collegial team coachings (CTCs) forming learning groups of six, who consult and coach each other collegially. The approach is solution-oriented, through which working in a "problem space" is transferred towards a "solution space" in the realm of "next practice". This goal oriented, creative and inventive work is the foundation and philosophy of the CTC. The heterogeneous coaching groups of six are combined together at regional level. These regional groups are coordinated by their respective network coordinators who organize all LEA Generations in the *Bundesländer*.

Eastern Europe: Breaking New Ground

After the break with the previous political system, most Eastern European countries began to break with their past and search for an identity of their own. However, they asked for or received support for implementing "Western" models of education from ex-patriots coming "back home" or international organizations offering ready-made programs for system-wide change. Policy advisers gave a high priority to changing the school system to initiate a process of re-education. The transition toward radical social and economic change in society poses new requirements to management and to the introduction of a professional approach in management and leadership. Educational leaders were seen as an important target group to become the change agents in the new development dynamics (cf. Schratz, 1994). Many former countries of the Eastern part of Europe started a transformation process with the aim of aligning their education systems with international trends, particularly the US and European models. What was understood by that depended very much on the partners (consultants, international organizations, governmental and non-governmental organizations).

When the educational administration moved from a strictly centralized position to a strongly decentralized form, the development of their capacity was rather neglected. The development in the Czech Republic in the early 1990s is a good example. A predominant role under the new regime was given to head teachers. They were granted a lot of power, but their readiness to cope with the new situation was omitted, and so was the need of external support to schools. As a consequence, some schools turned out to be led and developed by strong and creative, or even visionary, personalities, able to face up to the new requirements from the outside and proactively lead the school in a certain direction. Ideally, they did so in coordination with teachers, in view of a jointly agreed idea of the future, accepted by the wider environment of the school. But during the first half of the 1990s, a number of principals communicated poorly with the school's environment and tried as best as they could to survive, despite the challenging conditions under which they had to work. The practice of many heads and teachers oscillated between these two extremes (Pol, 1997).

The need for large-scale professional training was a challenge for most systems because after 1989 about 90 per cent of the previous school heads were dismissed for political and ideological reasons. The new generation of school leaders mainly had to be recruited from the teaching force, who themselves had experienced a different type of school system. Whereas school heads were previously mainly executors of orders in a centralized system, they suddenly had to become the gate openers for a new era of self-managing schools. They became part of a radical reform in school management. Quickly the education systems started moving toward decentralization and varying degrees of autonomy, which resulted in a particular need for (post) modern management and leadership. Problems of school autonomy and the role of principals as professional leaders were actively discussed and there were debates on the application of managerial principles from the world of economy into the sphere of education (cf. Pol & Rabuőicová, 1999).

The changes in legislation had a great impact on school leaders. Whereas in some countries they were granted employers' rights so that they could select, hire and dismiss school staff, financial autonomy was improved and school budgets were introduced etc., in other countries there has been a combination of rising levels of responsibility with only a minimal increase in power and authority for heads. The new rights, obligations and duties delegated to schools and their heads required new forms of professionalization in management and leadership. Professional school leaders should be capable of working independently in a situation of autonomy, indeterminacy and dynamically changing social environment. Experiences had shown that newly appointed heads without education or training in school management had a hard time coping with their newly delegated rights and responsibilities. Such lack of professional training slowed down change processes, impeded innovation and affected the moral and psychic environment in the respective schools. This pressure led to different ways of setting up training programs for future or practicing school heads.

There are various providers for the development of school heads according to the respective governance system introduced in each country. In contrast to the state monopoly, a stronger market-orientation can be found in many Western European countries. This is especially valid for Hungary in the fields of school evaluation, consultancy, and in-service training of teachers. One-sided interventions from the outside in the pioneer phase have been replaced by partnerships in cooperative projects which have lead to mutual exchange (cf. Fischer & Schratz, 1996; Schratz & Steiner-Löffler, 1997). Membership with the European Union as accession countries has enhanced the exchange in leadership through participation in various EU funded education projects like Socrates and Comenius.

The institutionalization of professional development of school leaders has also been enhanced by university partnerships, such as the collaboration with the Netherlands School of Educational Management (NSO) at the University of Amsterdam. In Hungary from 1992–1998, such a partnership has lead to the foundation of the Hungarian-Netherlands School of Educational Management (HUNSEM) at the University of Szeged. The program includes skill development training and field work. HUNSEM not only offers degree courses in educational management, but also focuses on research in the field of educational leadership.[7]

In the Czech Republic any provider can offer training programs for school leaders, but they have to match national standards for qualification training programs for school leaders. Heads are now expected to start formal preparation as leaders within two years of appointments. Also, current heads are expected to enroll in the program. Introducing the new paradigm in teaching educational management (based on case studies and student experience) to the systems of higher education has been a difficult process, since new concepts collide with the old paradigm which was based on lecturing on managerial theory and evaluating student performance through exams.

CONCLUSIONS: REFORMING TRAINING FOR SCHOOL LEADERSHIP

We started this chapter by tracing historical and cultural patterns of social development in different European regions and went on to explain how, in recent years, the role of schools, the position of school leaders and the approach to leadership training have changed radically across countries. Traditional working attitudes and privileges are under threat in the present period which is characterized by managerial accountability in many countries, and principals are exposed to a number of contradictory pressures. There seems to be a growing convergence of policy, focused on recreating leaders as public servants under greater central control because of the increasing dominance of managerial accountability (Ranson, 2003). In the concluding section, we will incorporate a discussion of political control and the professional content of leadership programs.

Political Control

Decentralization of the educational system, irrespective of motives, puts in focus the balance between political and professional power over education (Lundgren, 1990). In most countries, a movement from centralized to decentralized governance is taking place, which influences this power relationship. Figure 17.1 provides a cognitive map which includes these dimensions and creates four quadrants between the extreme poles (cf. Maritzen, 2000, p. 38). In the grid, the horizontal axis refers to the tension between political versus professional power over education, while the vertical axis refers to central versus local governance of leadership education and training. The first quadrant (A) shows a system of central governing where the politicians are in command. The second quadrant (B) shows a centralized system where the educational experts in the governing boards or agencies have the power. The third quadrant shows a model for local

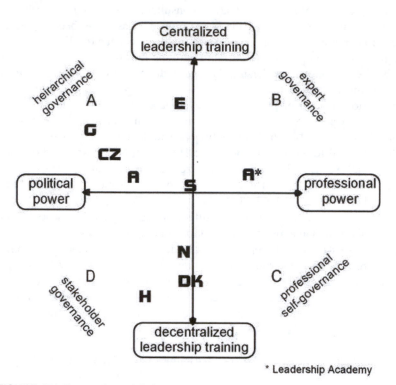

FIGURE 17.1 Four main models for governing leadership training and development.

governance where the professionals set the agenda (C), and in the fourth quadrant the local politicians and other stakeholders hold the power (D). It is also possible to trace the direction of ongoing changes.

Figure 17.1 enables a rough sorting of how leadership training and development in different countries are positioned according to centralization vs. decentralization, and according to political vs. professional power over training programs. One dimension of the comparison of models of leadership education is who are the providers? Who is responsible for the program, who has developed it, who sets the standards, and who carries it out? Across European countries there is a wide variety of how leadership training and development are organized. In some countries the ministry or an agency is the main provider, in other countries different kinds of partnerships between universities and regional providers have been established; some countries allow for a high degree of local choice, others are more centralized.

If centralization is enhanced with political power, we experience hierarchical governance, which can be found in hierarchical educational systems. If the central power is exercised by the profession, expert governance takes place (e.g. in PISA, where global test items are developed centrally by experts in the area of testing). If the central power is passed down the line, it can be exercised by communities, school boards and similar, and we can talk about stakeholder governance. If the power is exercised by the professionals in the field, it will be professional governance.

Such categorization illuminates similarities and differences, but will certainly also raise debate. For instance, we have chosen to locate Sweden just in the middle. Their approach can be described as decentralized centralism. The State is setting standards and is making the programs mandatory, but the universities are in charge of carrying out the programs and interpreting the standards. There is also a balance between political and professional power.

We have located the Czech Republic in the first quadrant, because the Ministry has announced mandatory standards for the highest qualification preparation course for school leaders. This is a strong centralized initiative. In addition there are a number of other preparation courses for school leaders in the country, and these are highly decentralized and demonstrate great variety. However, they only have minor significance for formal preparation of heads. In contrast, Hungary at present can be located in the fourth quadrant, but there might be a move toward the first quadrant. They have passed a law with regards to requirements years ago, but it has not been implemented in practice, and there is great competition among the providers of leadership courses. Also, the education system is highly decentralized.

In moving from central governance towards more local governance, the question of holds has the responsibility is sharpened (Lundgren, 1990). The diffuse borderline between political and professional responsibility seems to represent a major problem. As shown in Figure 17.1, the positioning of the leadership training programs of most countries are in the quadrant of hierarchical governance, which means that the central government has a strong influence on the provision of leadership training. In some cases like Norway and Denmark, we find more decentralized training provisions which are governed by the local or regional stakeholders in collaboration with professional organizations. However, in these two countries the loosely coupled initiatives across different municipalities have created too much variety in quality. Therefore, there is likely to be a change to a more centralized direction within the next few years, similar to the development which is happening in Sweden. Simultaneously, there will probably be a lengthy debate about the balance between political and professional power.

The ministries have the power to make leadership programs mandatory. As such, they will usually be strongly influenced by the political agenda. In this perspective, the Austrian Leadership Academy provides a different scenario. It can be seen as a paradox that in Austria, which we have characterized as being influenced by Old Public Administration, has chosen an approach to leadership development by granting power to experts or the professionals themselves whereas initial training is rather dominated by political stakeholders. Also, the Leadership Academy has been chosen as an innovative case study by OECD. Within the next few years we will know if this fact is driving and attenuating Austrian policy on leadership training.

Professional Content

In the literature on professional learning and leadership development, there is an increasing tendency to apply the term "learning trajectories" (Wenger, 1999; Engeström, 1999). A main argument for introducing this term is that professionals, for instance school leaders, are members of a range of different institutions simultaneously, and these may work together to provide very distinct learning opportunities. To be competent is to be competent in particular settings, and occupational competence develops in the workplace as individuals make sense of lived experience by engaging in dialogue and reflecting on practice. Pre-service, initial and in-service-training and development for school leaders across different European countries have increasingly given priority to learning from practice and more tacit forms of knowledge.

For instance, in German-speaking countries qualification programs for school heads were for a long time determined, more or less, by behavioral-theoretical concepts which were used to assess the most effective 'instruction'. This was strongly related, hierarchically, to the (central) education system. In implementing the content of the qualification program, however, it became apparent that a typical course of procedure in a school as an organization could not be standardized. Thus one often hears views reflected in these statements:

> One sets out alone, accompanied only by training courses in which — generally — knowledge which has its roots in other irrelevant contexts is passed on. We take note of the concepts, which science has at its disposal. Problems which would be worthy of closer scrutiny, however, have already been pre-formulated. Everyday practice obviously presents quite different problems, according to the given situations and we are constantly challenged by new questions which need to be answered. We are really and truly 'searchers'. We act and react as such. (Watschinger, 1999, p. 37) [authors' translation]

Since such behavioral-theoretical concepts have proven to be ineffective, in many places there is a search for more open-minded concepts for in-service training in which the aim is to achieve an opening-up of the developmental potential of the individual participant and to promote more participative methods of learning.

Another tendency to counteract theoretical approaches in German-speaking countries has been the hiring of experienced professionals (school heads, inspectors or people from educational administration) who pass on their own experience to novices. In other words, an apprenticeship model is promoted. This approach also includes what can be called "train-the-trainer-programs". In such arrangements the practical theories of senior professionals are often seen and taken for granted as best practice, whereas research-based theory is devalued.

In former Eastern European countries, leadership training programs were often developed in partnership with countries from the former West. In such cooperative arrangements it was soon realized that an apprenticeship model combined with 'best practice' approach did not work because of the cultural historical differences in the respective countries. Therefore a one-to-one transfer was not possible. Especially in the initial phase a learning trajectory which emphasized building a community of practice was foregrounded because embedded knowledge had to be shared. In addition, collective sense-making of the past, present and future in the new socio-political situation was necessary between the different cultures. However, the more the cooperatively developed leadership programs reached the status of the new provision, the more they tended to move towards the model of the course-based and apprenticeship trajectory. They soon become the "official" leadership training programs in which new school heads have to enroll, or providers have to align to performance standards to achieve the desired training outcome.

In Scandinavia there is a distinction between the leadership training programs, of which the municipalities are in charge and the programs provided by universities and university colleges. The development in Norway can be used as an example. So far, the Norwegian Association of Local and Regional Authorities (KS) has argued against a mandatory leadership program. According to this association, the school owner, i.e. the municipalities, should keep the responsibility for leadership education since they can best evaluate the need in co-operation with their school leaders. Municipalities and counties do not wish for intervention by the State in the form of mandatory requirements. They encourage the formation of a local network where schools and school leaders can learn from each other. "Best practice" is held as a basic principle, and it is the schools' or the schools owner's perspective, not a centrally hatched model by experts and researchers which is preferred. Reflection on experience or sharing of knowledge is their accepted mode of leadership training.

The universities are, on the other hand, promoting programs which imply a higher education degree and therefore will include a professional knowledge base. They argue that trajectories of lifelong learning and community learning tend to neglect knowledge issues which are important to school leaders' professional learning. As such, there are tensions and contradictions in the way school leadership is being conceptualized (Møller, 2007), and in judgments on what would be the most promising leadership development. Even though learning from practice has shown great potential, it may both preserve and mask the preservation of the status quo. Alternatively, it encourages a reserved embrace of the latest trends without equipping professionals to analyze the models more critically. Action research and participative research with school leaders and teachers have demonstrated that knowledge of theoretical concepts is crucial for participants' understanding. Observation is more than merely "seeing what is" because it includes the theoretical framework in which school leaders interpret what they see (Møller, 1996).

Future Approaches to Leadership Development

Our analysis of leadership development programs in different European countries shows similarities in the way both policy and professional levels struggle in setting up programs which aim at balancing supply and demand, and our analysis indicates a move towards more centralization. However, the analysis also reveals cultural differences with regard to how the power is distributed between political and professional power.

It is reasonable to assume that the less preparation head teachers have, the more likely they are to fall back on their lay theories of leadership that are often premised on a very narrow experiential base of prior experience as a teacher. Also, due to rapid changes in society, lay theories are likely to maintain outdated concepts of heroic leadership rather than a concept of sustainable leadership. Therefore, in addition to formal leadership training support for inter-generational learning should be provided. Leadership programs have the potential to influence the principals' learning trajectories, their emerging leadership identities, depending on which form of leadership is considered appropriate within the life cycle of the particular school (Sugrue, 2005).

The importance of theoretical concepts as a tool for analyzing what happens in every-day practice should not be underestimated. Theoretical knowledge helps to enlighten leadership practice and reflect it within a broader contextual framework. De-contextualized knowledge of scholarship should receive equal recognition with contextualized knowledge. This implies formal, university-based preparation programs for school leaders alongside collective sense-making, reflection on action and socialization into communities of practice. Theoretical education has the potential to promote critical thinking if it includes an understanding of the type of control that state and society exercise on the school, a historical perspective on educational leadership within a national and local context, and an understanding of the micro-politics in schools. Although theoretical knowledge can never prescribe exactly what to do in a specific situation, personal constructs cannot be discriminated from the concepts which are in use. Subjective theories are expanded in dialogue with research-based theories in a knowledge building process. Establishment of a partnership between college/university and educational authorities, which also includes internship, could represent a promising approach.

ACKNOWLEDGEMENT

We thank the following colleagues for their support in getting valuable information on their countries: Dr. Tibor Baráth, University of Szeged (Hungary), Ivan Ivanov Hristov, University "St. Kliment Ohridski", Sofia (Bulgaria), Prof. Olof Johansson (Sweden), Dr. Norbert Maritzen, Hamburg (Germany), Associate Prof. Lejf Moos, (Denmark), Prof. Milan Pol, Masaryk

University, Brno (Czech Republic), Prof. Manfred Prenzel, University of Kiel (Germany), Dr. Anton Strittmatter, Biel (Switzerland). We are also indebted to the reviewer for his/her valuable comments on our first version of this chapter.

NOTES

1. We use the terms *school leader, head teacher* and *principal* as synonymous in this chapter.
2. In England "public school" is used as a label for private and independent schools. In other European countries a public school means a state school.
3. The same tendency can be identified in Finland and Iceland (Johannesson, Lindblad, & Simola 2002).
4. We will only refer to the German-speaking language group in Switzerland.
5. In addition to the European countries, New Zealand, Australia, Israel and Korea are participating.
6. The Academy has been chosen by the OECD as an innovative case study for the project *Improving School Leadership*.
7. A similar project took place in Bulgaria, where several universities have joined to offer a school management education program: From 2002 to 2004 an international team of scholars and consultants from the Netherlands School of Educational Management (NSO) under Amsterdam University, and five Bulgarian state universities, had been working on the implementation of the "Transformation of educational management in Bulgaria" project (with financial support from the Dutch Ministry of Foreign Affairs).

REFERENCES

Baráth, T. (2006). Az iskolavezetés jellemzői és az intézmény eredményessége, hatékonysága. In *Új Pedag—giai Szemle*. 2006/7-8. 56–72. (Features of school management, school efficiency and effectiveness. In *New Pedagogical Review* 7-8, 56–72.

Baráth, T. & Cseh, G. (2002). Az intézményi auton—mia feltételrendszere – Szervezeti és jogi jellemzők. Kézirat. (The condition system of institutional autonomy – Organizational and legislation characteristics. Unpublished manuscript.)

Baron, G. (1970). Some aspects of the headmaster tradition. In P.W. Musgrave (Ed.) *Sociology, history and education*. London: Methuen.

Beck, U. (2000). *What is globalization?* Cambridge: Polity Press.

Berg, G. (2000). Steering in and steering of the school. In C. Day, A. Fernandez, T.E. Hauge & J. Møller (Eds.), *The life and work of teachers. International perspectives in changing times* (pp.195–210). London: Falmer Press.

Bernstein, B. (1977). *Class, codes and control: Vol. 3. Towards a theory of educational transmissions* (2nd ed.), London: Routledge.

Bolam, R. (2004). Reflections on the NCSL from a historical perspective. *Educational Management Administration & Leadership*, 32(3) 251–267.

Bredeson, P. (1996). New directions in the preparation of educational leaders. In Leithwood, K., Chapman, J., Corson, D., Hallinger, P. & Hart, A. (1996). *International handbook of educational leadership and administration* (pp. 251–278). Dordrecht: Kluwer Academic Publishers

Bush, T. (2004). Editorial: The National College for School Leadership: Purpose, Power and Prospects. *Educational Management Administration & Leadership*, 32(3) 243–249.

Brown, M. (1998). The tyranny of the international horse race. In R. Slee and G. Weiner with S. Tomlinson (Eds.), *School effectiveness for whom? Challenges to the school effectiveness and school improvement movements* (pp. 33–47). London: Falmer Press.

Day, C. (2007). Sustaining success in challenging contexts. Leadership in English schools. In C. Day & K. Leithwood (Eds.), Successful principal leadership in times of change. An international perspective (pp. 59–709). Dordrecht: Springer,

Engeström, Y. (1999). Situated learning at the threshold of the new millennium. In Bliss, J., Säljö, R. & Light, P. (Eds.), *Learning sites. Social and technological resources for learning* (pp. 249–258). Amsterdam: Pergamon

Fischer, W. & Schratz, M. (1996). *Veden' a rozvoj skoly. Do budoucnosti s novou kulturou r'zen'*. Brno: Nakladatelstv'.

Fischer, W. & Schratz, M. (1999) Schule leiten und gestalten. Mit einer neuen Führungskultur in die Zukunft. Innsbruck: Studienverlag.

Grace. G. (1995). *School leadership. Beyond education management. An essay in policy scholarship*. London: Falmer Press.

Gronn, P. (2003). *The new work of educational leaders. Changing leadership practice in an era of school reform*. Thousand Oaks: Paul Chapman Publishing.

Hegtun, A. (2007). "Improving School Leadership". Professional skoleledelse – noe alle vil – trenger vi OECD for å få det til? (Professional school leadership – do we need OECD to accomplish the goal?). Unpublished Master thesis in Educational Leadership, Faculty of Education, University of Oslo.

Helsby, G. (1999). *Changing teachers' work*. Buckingham: Open University Press.

Huber, S. (2004). *Preparing school leaders for the 21st century. An international comparison of development programs in 15 countries*. London: RoutledgeFalmer.

Johannesson, I.A., Lindblad, S. & Simola, H. (2002). An inevitable progress? Educational restructuring in Finland, Iceland and Sweden at the turn of the millenium. *Scandinavian Journal of Educational Research,* 46(3), 325–340.

Johansson, O. (2004). A democratic, learning and communicative leadership? *Journal of Educational Administration,* 42(6), 697–708.

Johnson, L., Møller, J., Jacobson, S. & Wong, K.C. (in press). Cross-national comparison in the International Successful School Principalship Project (ISSPP): The United States, Norway and China. Scandinavian *Journal of Educational Research*, 52(5).

Karlsen, G. (2000). Decentralized centralism: framework for a better understanding of governance in the field of education. *Journal of Education Policy*, 15(5), 525–538.

Karlsen, G. (2002). Educational policy and educational programmes in the European Union: a tool for political integration and economic competition? In J. A. Ibàñez-Martin & J. Gonzalo (Eds.), *Education in Europe policies and politics* (pp. 23–49). Dordrecht: Kluwer Academic Publishers.

Leithwood, K. (2001). School leadership in the context of accountability policies. *International Journal of Leadership in Education*, 4(3), 217–235.

Lundgren, U. (1990). Educational policy-making, decentralisation and evaluation. In Granheim, M., Kogan, M. & Lundgren, U. (Eds.), *Evaluation as policymaking. Introducing evaluation into a national decentralised educational system* (pp. 23–42). London: Jessica Kingsley Publishers.

MacBeath, J. (2006). Evaluation in European schools: A story of change. Keynote address to the European Commission, Frascati, April 14.

Maritzen, N. (2000). Funktionen des Schulprogramms im Rahmen eines Steuerungskonzeptes. *Pädagogik* 4, 36–40.

Moos, L., Møller, J. & Johansson, O. (2004). A Scandinavian perspective on educational leadership. *The Educational Forum*, 68(3), 200–211.

Mulford, B. (2003). School leaders: Changing roles and impact on teacher and school effectiveness, paper commissioned by OECD Education and Training Policy Division.

Møller, J. (1996). Rethinking educational leadership. *EERA Bulletin*, 2(3), 13–24.

Møller, J. (2006). Democratic Schooling in Norway: Implications for Leadership in Practice. *Leadership and Policy in Schools*, Special issue on "International Perspectives on Leadership for Social Justice", 5(1), 53–69.

Møller, J. (2007). Educational leadership and the new language of learning. *International Journal of Leadership in Education*, 10(1), 31–48.

OECD (2007). Improving school leadership. Participating country background reports. Retrieved May 12,

2007, from http://www.oecd.org/document/53/0,2340,en_2649_34859095_38529205_1_1_1_1,00. html

Olsen, J. P. (2002). Towards a European administrative space. ARENA, Working Paper, No 26, August.

Pol, M. (1997). Management of Czech schools: with or without teachers´ participation? Budapest, RSS CEU. Final report.

Pol, M. & Rabuöicová, M. (1999). Governance and participation in Czech schools. In R. Bolan, F. v. Wieringen (Eds.), *Research on educational management in Europe* (pp. 110–122). Münster: Waxmann.

Ranson, S. (2003). Public accountability in the age of neo-liberal governance. *Journal of Educational Policy*, 18(5), 459–480.

Reynolds, D. & Teddlie, C.; with Creemers, B., Scheerens, J, and Townsend, T. (2000). An introduction to school effectiveness research. In C. Teddlie & D. Reynolds (Eds.), *The international handbook of school effectiveness research* (pp. 3–26). London: Falmer Press.

Rolff, H.-G. & Schmidt, H. J. (2002). *Schulleitung und Schulaufsicht*. Neuwied: Luchterhand.

Rosenbusch, H. S. (1995). *Lehrer und Schulräte. Ein strukturell gestörtes Verhältnis*. Bad Heilbrunn: Klinkhardt.

Schley, W. & Schratz, M. (2006). Leadership Academy – Professionalisierung von Führungspersonen. *Schulmanagement*, 2, 28–30.

Schratz, M. (1996a). Die neue Qualität von Schulleitung - Schule als lernende Organisation. In W. Specht & J. Thonhauser. (Eds.), *Schulqualität: Entwicklungen, Befunde, Perspektiven* (pp. 173–222). Innsbruck: Studienverlag.

Schratz, M. (1996b). *Die Rolle der Schulaufsicht in der autonomen Schulentwicklung*. Innsbruck: Studienverlag.

Schratz, M. (2003). From administering to leading a school: Challenges in German-speaking counties. *Cambridge Journal of Education*, 33(3), 395–416.

Schratz, M. (2006). Schulinspektion und die Folgen für Schulentwicklung und Schulprogramm. *Lernende Schule*, 9, 14–17.

Schratz, M. & Steiner-Löffler, U. (1997). Rady Skol v Rakousku. In M. Pol & M. Rabusicova (Eds.), *Správa a Rizen' Skol* (pp. 82–95). Brno: Paido.

Sejersted, F. (1997). Lederskap og demokratisk kapitalisme (Leadership and democratic capitalism). In H. Byrkjeflot (Ed.), *Fra styring til ledelse (From management to leadership)* (pp. 33–53). Bergen: Fagbokforlaget.

Slavikova, L. (2007). School leadership for an integrated Europe. Paper presented at the International Conference "New Policies for School Leadership", 10–12 May, 2007, in Vilnius.

Sugrue, C. (2005). Principalship. Beyond pleasure, pain and passion. In Sugrue, C. (Ed.), *Passionate principalship: Learning from life histories of school leaders* (pp. 161–184). London: RoutledgeFalmer.

Telhaug, A.O., Mediås, O.A. & Aasen, P. (2006). The Nordic model in education: Education as part of the political system in the last 50 years. *Scandinavian Journal of Educational Research*, 50(3), 245–283.

Thrupp, M. (2005). The National College for School Leadership: A Critique. Retrieved May 9, 2007, from http://www.soc-for-ed-studies.org.uk/pdfs/thrupp.pdf

Tjeldvoll, A., Wales, C. and Welle-Strand, A. (2005). School leadership training under globalisation: Comparisons of the UK, the US and Norway. *Managing Global Transitions*, 3(1): 23–49.

Wales, C., & Welle-Strand, A. (2005). School Management Training. HEAD Country Report: Norway. Studies in Education Management Research, No. 16, Centre for Education Management Research (CEM), Norwegian School of Management (BI).

Watschinger, J. (1999). Peer-Gruppe entsteht. In P. Höllrigl & E. M. Lanthaler (Eds.), *Mit kritischen Freunden unterwegs. Zu einer neuen Qualität von Schulführung* (pp. 35–41). Bozen: Pädagogisches Institut der deutschen Sprachgruppe.

Wenger, E. (1999). *Communities of practice. Learning, meaning and identity*. Cambridge: Cambridge University Press.

18

School Leadership Development in Africa

Ruth Otunga, David K. Serem and Jonah Nyaga Kindiki

African countries share similar geographical, historical, social, cultural and economic contexts. School leadership development in Africa is influenced by these factors. Historically, African countries South of Sahara were mainly colonized by Britain and France. The Germans' influence was not sustained during wars for the scramble for Africa. For this reason, Africa is mainly divided into English-speaking (*Anglophone*), French-speaking (*Francophone*) and Portuguese-speaking (*Lucophone*) countries. Other languages spoken in Africa include Arabic, Italian and Afrikaans, a multitude of other African languages in the various countries. In Kenya for example, there are over 40 African languages spoken with Kiswahili as the main language of communication (Mbaabu, 1996). Consequently, Africa has variations in forms of formal education, depending on the specific foreign influence.

The structures of education systems especially regarding teacher education for primary (elementary), secondary (high school) and tertiary institutions in Anglophone and Francophone African countries are similar to those found in Britain or France (UNESCO, 1999). These similarities depend on colonization history. Africa is not homogeneous; it has peculiarities. It is, therefore, not possible to cover in detail all the preparation and development issues of school leaders in Africa.

This chapter will adopt a pan-African focus: setting the African context, approaches to school leadership preparation and development in selected countries, characteristics, roles and contexts of school leaders, current research underpinning school leadership preparation and development, dilemmas of school leadership, research needs, future issues and international links for African school leaders.

SETTING THE AFRICAN CONTEXT

It is not easy to understand fully school leadership development in Africa without a clear understanding of how education in the continent has evolved over the years. Eshiwani (1993) and Mugambi (1989) emphasize that traditionally before the coming of the Europeans, especially the missionaries who introduced formal education, an African child received as much education as was necessary in an informal manner from parents, relatives and opinion leaders in the community. The child learnt through Traditional African Education (TAE) arrangements. The principal objective of TAE was to equip the child with knowledge, skills and behavior to enable him or her to live in society (Kindiki, 1999).

On one hand, Islamic influence was dominant in Northern Africa as well as along the East and West coast of Africa due to the presence of traders from Arabic countries. Thus Islamic education (*Madrasa* system) existed in East Africa and other areas where Arabs had settled before the coming of the Europeans. Muslim immigrants from Arabia introduced Islamic education to the coast of East Africa (Eiseman & Wasil, 1987). Islamic education was formal and its principal objective was to teach Islamic law and '*suna*', that is, practices or traditions of Islam as established by Prophet Mohamed. Islamic education was designed for teaching sons and daughters of Moslem and African converts the Islamic beliefs and rituals. Their teacher was '*maalim*'. The first group of the '*madrasas*' was of primary type as it concentrated on the teaching of the 3Rs (Reading, Writing, and simple Arithmetic) taught in the Arabic language (Kindiki, 2007).

On the other hand, Europeans came to Africa to explore, colonize and spread Christianity. Initially, colonial governments had little interest in education of the Africans. In fact, the management of education during this period was left to the missionaries such as the work of Ludwing Krapf and J. Erhardt in 1884 (Ssekamwa & Lugumba, 2001). Schools were started at the mission centers where they offered education in conjunction with religious teachings. They wanted to bring social change to Africans, sometimes forcing them to change their beliefs, attitudes and practices such as worship, dressing and circumcision practices. At early stages, children of the loyalists and converts were enrolled in those schools and learnt the 3Rs. Education offered by missionaries was aimed at training interpreters, builders, office messengers, orderlies and domestic servants. In later stages, missionaries reformed education and mainly offered religious education, simple technical education, agricultural training and basic numeracy, reading and writing. With time, more African children were attracted by this type of education. During this period, the missionaries established missions and schools without the help of colonial governments. But persistent demands for education forced colonial governments to take some steps towards management and control of education (Kindiki, 2007).

Clearly, colonial governments contributed much to the development of education in Africa. A lot of educational reforms in Africa have also taken place in the post independence era. African governments have constantly formed various commissions or task forces to examine ways of reforming education including looking into leadership preparation and development. A good example is in Kenya where many education commissions have been set up including Ominde (1964), Ndegwa (1970/71), Bessey (1972), Gachathi (1976), Waruhiu (1979/80), Mackay (1981), Kamunge (1988), Koech (1999) and Kamunge (2005). These have gathered views on required adjustments to the education system as well as the necessary school leadership preparation and development to put in place effective functioning of the various phases of the school system.

APPROACHES TO SCHOOL LEADERSHIP PREPARATION AND DEVELOPMENT

The discussion on school leadership preparation and development in this section is perceived in terms of Anglophone and Francophone Africa. Typical representative countries from Anglophone Africa used in the discussion include Kenya, Nigeria and South Africa. These are economies representative of regional locations. Additionally, they are unique in their own way; thus, Nigeria is the most densely populated country in Africa and largest producer of oil in Sub-Saharan Africa. South Africa, an economic giant in Africa, gained its political independence later than other African countries. Kenya is a representative of the Eastern Africa regions with a fairly strong economy.

Francophone Africa is represented by the Democratic Republic of Congo (DRC), Senegal and Rwanda. DRC is a mineral-rich country which has been adversely affected by civil wars; Senegal had adverse French influence on the West Coast in the form of the Goree slave market, while Rwanda in Eastern Africa is one of the smallest countries and has had the largest genocide in the recent years.

School leadership preparation and development in African countries vary depending on the historical background. In Kenya, formal education is currently based on the 8-4-4 system of education, established in the late 1980s, which means eight years of primary education, four years of secondary school and four years minimum of university education. The introduction of 8-4-4 education system has led to tremendous changes in the secondary school curriculum. This is in line with the need for a broad-based curriculum that prepares students for self-reliance, vocational training and further education (UNESCO, 1999).

In reference to teacher education and training of primary or basic school teachers in Kenya, students are admitted to teacher training colleges and must hold the Kenya Certificate of Secondary Education after completing four years of secondary education. This teacher training course lasts two years, and graduates are awarded a Primary 1 (p. 1) certificate, depending on their success in centrally set and administered examinations. Training of secondary school teachers is carried out at two levels. In universities, graduate teachers take four years for the Bachelor of Education Degree (B.Ed). However, graduates holding B.A, B.Sc or B.Com take a one-year postgraduate diploma course in education to become professional teachers. Teachers are also trained at diploma level colleges. The three-year diploma course leads to an ordinary Diploma in Education

The diploma holder teachers teach either at primary or secondary schools depending on the need. Some even teach at tertiary institutions, especially those in technical disciplines. Public universities are the major secondary school teacher training institutions. There is no formal training for higher education teachers who wish to teach in universities. Candidates must have a first class or upper second Honors Degree, followed by a Masters Degree as minimum qualification (UNESCO, 1999).

Although Kitavi & Van Der Westhuizen (1997) assert that pre-service training of school head teachers or principals in Kenya is not required, serious thought has always been invested in school leadership preparation and development. This is evidenced by the May, 1968 conference on teacher education which resulted in the formation of a steering committee which made a recommendation that 'principals should have not only excellent academic qualifications, but also appropriate experience and outstanding qualities of leadership and imagination' (Ssekamwa and Lugumba, 2001, p. 145).

The decades from 1980 have witnessed considerable efforts by the Ministry of Education to provide in-service management training for principals of schools. It has been recognized in Kenya, as elsewhere, that changes within society and within the educational system itself require continuous in-servicing of staff to enable them acquire appropriate knowledge, skills and attitudes for their roles (Lodiaga & Olembo, 1990).

In 1988, the government of Kenya established the Kenya Educational Staff Institute (KESI) to offer in-service training for the heads of educational institutions including school principals. Further, the KESI mandate was to be diversified to develop both serving and potential school leaders. However, although it has been in existence for almost two decades, the institute provides in-service training largely to serving principals and rarely to other school leaders such as deputy principals, heads of departments, school committees and Boards of Governors (BOG).

The current Kenyan government development strategy is for Constituency Development Fund (CDF), free education in primary schools and the waiving of tuition fees in all public secondary schools both of which place additional responsibilities on school leaders. There is, therefore, a need for education leaders to be adequately trained and continuously in-serviced to keep abreast of the developments in school leadership.

There are also other initiatives targeting school leaders in Kenya. The Kenya Institute of Education (KIE) provides in-service training for leaders at primary schools, secondary schools and tertiary institutions, except universities, in matters of curriculum implementation (Kamunge, 1988). There is also the Kenya Institute of Administration (KIA) which provides leadership development skills to education leaders mainly from the Ministry of Education.

There is the Kenya National Union of Teachers (KNUT) formed in 1957, an umbrella body for all primary teachers in Kenya, which handles welfare issues of teachers regarding their profession. The KNUT mandate has expanded over time beyond welfare and currently provides workshops and in-service education on school leadership issues. This organization is very active and has well equipped offices in every district with permanent staff chosen democratically from among the teachers themselves. Indeed, as Ssekamwa and Lugumba (2001) put it, "Kenya has one of the best organized and strongest teachers unions in Africa" (p. 37).

There is also the Kenya Secondary Schools Principals Association (KSSPA) which holds annual conferences in different parts of the country during which Ministry of Education officials and high ranking and experienced educators are invited to discuss leadership issues in schools. During these conferences, principals share experiences while the Ministry officials and experienced educators discuss and disseminate current up-to-date information on school leadership.

Unlike Kenya, secondary education in Nigeria is divided into junior and senior secondary and technical and vocational education. The Junior School Certificate is awarded after three years of junior school. The Senior School Certificate is awarded after three years of senior secondary education. It replaced the West African GCE "O" level in 1989. Pupils who complete junior secondary are streamed into senior secondary school, technical college, an out of school vocational training centre or an apprenticeship. Technical secondary education is available in secondary commercial schools which offer six-year courses including academic subjects and specialization. At the end of the course, students may take the examinations for the Senior School Certificate. Vocational education produces low level personnel and is offered in technical colleges or business and engineering skills training centers. Technical colleges are the only alternative to senior secondary schools as a route to further formal education and training after junior secondary education (UNESCO, 1999).

Teacher education in Nigeria, at primary or basic school takes four years post primary study at a grade 2 teacher training college which leads to a Grade 2 Certificate or Higher Elementary Teachers' Certificate. Holders of the former Grade 3 Certificate may take an upgrading course to become grade 2 teachers. As from 1998, the Nigerian Certificate in Education conferred by colleges of education was required for teaching in primary schools. Holders of the Nigerian Certificate of Education may teach in junior secondary schools and technical colleges. Senior secondary school teachers are trained at the universities. They must hold a B.Ed. or Bachelor's plus a postgraduate diploma in education. Most students study for three years at an advanced teachers' college for a Nigerian Certificate of Education, which also gives access to university. As from 1998, no teacher with a qualification below this level was able to teach in any school (UNESCO, 1999).

Nigeria, like any other African country, has no formalized procedures for preparing and developing school leaders. The primary school principals are held accountable in many areas of school functions. However, there is no formal leadership training, but all are expected to gain knowledge through experience (http://www.jstor.org/view, p. 2). At secondary school level, the principal's skills are developed through planned in-service education by the ministry responsible for Education by organizing seminars and workshops. However, principals largely learn through their own experiences in schools and interactions with other principals.

South Africa's National Qualifications Framework (NQF) recognizes "three broad bands of education: General Education and Training, Further Education and Training and Higher Education and Training" (http://www.southafrica.info/SA, 8/28/2007, pp. 1–2). Under the South African schools act of 1996, education is compulsory for all South Africans from age seven (grade 1) to age 15 or the completion of grade 9. General Education and Training also includes Adult Basic Education and Training. Further Education and Training takes place from grades 10 to 12, and also includes career-oriented education and training in other further education and training institutions — technical colleges, community colleges and private colleges. Diplomas and certificates are qualifications recognized at this level. On the other hand, Higher Education and Training, or tertiary education, includes education for undergraduate and postgraduate degrees, certificates and diplomas, up to the level of the doctoral degree.

The South African secondary education system comprises five years of schooling, although the first year of the junior secondary phase is the primary school. At the end of senior secondary phase — lasting three years, pupils sit for the Senior Certificate Examination. The 1996 Constitution confirms the right to basic education and additionally that Government must progressively make available and accessible through reasonable measures further education, that is, the senior secondary phase preceding higher education. In the senior cycle, students may study subjects either at Higher Grade, Standard Grade or Lower Grade. N-courses are also on offer for some technical school and college candidates. A Senior Certificate is awarded after passing externally moderated examinations by the time of completion of senior secondary school. Technical secondary education is provided by technical centers and secondary and vocational schools. Provision is also made for further education colleges in terms of the Draft Bill (Further Education and Training Bill, 1998). Technical high schools may *inter alia* offer courses leading to Senior Certificates with matriculation endorsements, which statutorily constitute the minimum general admission requirements for access to universities. *Technikons* require Senior Certificates but not necessarily with matriculation endorsements.

Teacher education in South Africa involves training of primary, secondary and higher education teachers. Training of primary or basic school teachers by 1999 required training colleges that previously reported to the provinces to transfer to the national Department of Education and certain universities run three-or four-year diploma courses qualifying holders to teach in primary schools. This also applies to some universities and *technikons*. The general admission requirement for diploma studies at any of these colleges is a Senior Certificate with a pass mark in one of the two college languages of instruction that is English and Afrikaans. Degree-level courses for training secondary school teachers are required and are run by all universities and *technikons*. A Senior Certificate with matriculation endorsement or a certificate of complete or conditional exemption is required for university study, whilst *technikons* have different requirements, usually senior certificates and further requirements as stipulated in their joint stature. Forty per cent of academic staff in higher education obtained their highest qualification at the University in which they are employed, 30 per cent at another South African University and 30 per cent at a foreign university (UNESCO, 1999).

In the face of radical global changes, South African schools have become sites for radical change and principals are working under the most difficult conditions. School principals have a multifaceted and enormous task of establishing an environment that could lead to effective schooling. However, many of the principals are either not coping with the numerous changes or they do not have the necessary skills, knowledge and attitudes to manage their schools effectively and efficiently. It is, therefore, essential for the authorities or educationists to develop training programs for principals of schools so that they can manage their schools as necessary (http://www.educationpublishing.com/isea, 8/31/2007).

Successful schools require leaders who are able to perform at optimum levels, have the knowledge, skills and disposition to meet the complex challenges of schools today and in the future. Every principal, assistant principal and school teacher must share responsibility for his or her own professional development (http://www.principals.org/s_nassp/sec, 8/28/2007). The National Association of Secondary school principals (NASSP) helps to train successful school leaders by providing tried and proven assessment and development programs designed to meet complex school challenges. Internal experienced staff and carefully selected facilitators are used to do program planning, development and implementation services. Facilitators trained by NASSP are carefully selected, exceptionally experienced educators who are committed to empowering current and aspiring school leaders (http://www.principals.org/s_nassp/sec, 8/28/2007).

In Francophone countries, for instance Senegal, secondary schooling lasts seven years, divided into four-year lower secondary and three-year upper secondary education. The lower cycle (called *"moyen"*) is offered by CEGs and CEMs (lower secondary only) or *lycees* and ends with the *Brever de Fin d'Etudes moyennes* (BFEM). The three-year upper cycle ends with the *Baccalaureat*, which may be taken in five series depending on the specialization taken in the last two years. In technical tracks, *centres de formation* professionally train non-BFEM holders in three years leading to a CAP (*Certificat a' Aptitude*) and BFEM holders in two years leading to a BEP. One further year leads to the BP. In *lycees techniques*, three-years upper secondary lead to a *Baccalaureat technique*. The Bac gives access to higher education. Various *Brevets de technicians*, of *Bac* level, are offered in three years, but do not give access to university.

In Senegal, primary school teachers (*Instituteurs*) take a four-year course at one of the *Ecoles normales regionales* leading to a *Certificat d'Aptitude pedagogique* (CAP). Assistant teachers holding a *Brevet de Fin d'Etudes moyennes* (BFEM) and having professional experience may take a one-year course at the *Centre de* formation *pedagogique* also leading to the CAP.

Secondary school teachers are trained at *Ecoles normales superieres* which were partly integrated into the University of Dakar in 1971. *Licence* holders take a one-year course leading to a *Certificat d'Aptitude a l'Enseignment moyen* (CAEM); *Baccalaureat* holders take a two-year course leading to a *Certificat d'Aptitude a l'Enseignement des Colleges d'Enseignement moyen* (CAECEM). Upper secondary teachers who hold a *Maitrice* take a two-year course leading to a *Certificat d'Aptitude a l'Enseignement secondaire* (CAES). Vocational trainers pass their own *Certificats d'Aptitude* four or five years after the Bac (CAEMTP and CAESTP) or two years after a *Licence*.

Training of higher education teachers, *Assistants* and *Maitres* assistants must hold a *Doctorat de 3eme Cycle*. The latter must also be listed on a *"liste d'aptitude"* maintained by the *Conseil Africain et Malgache pour l'Enseignement superieur* (CAMES). Maitres de Conference and Professors must hold a *Doctorat d'Etat* and be listed on a "listed on a *"liste d'aptitude"* (delivered by the CAMES).

Senegal is in the *Sahel* region (Sahara Desert) of Africa and is not economically well endowed. There are no serious initiatives towards school leadership development programs. However, there are a few foreign aid initiatives directed towards school leadership development. For example, in 2006, the USAID spent "$14.7 million to build rural middle schools, train school principals and teachers and empower community management of these schools" (http://Senegal.usaid.gov, 8/28/2007).

Congo (Democratic Republic of Congo) secondary education comprises several types of schools: schools of arts and crafts where studies last three years; teacher training schools where studies last between four and six years; professional schools where studies last for five years; schools of humanities and technical studies where courses last for six years. Pupils must have obtained the *Certificat d'Etudes primaries*. Studies in the long cycle (six years) lead to the *Diplome d'Etudes secondaires du Cycle Long*. Students holding this diploma are eligible to enter higher education. Vocational schools prepare pupils for a profession without the possibility of entering a university.

DRC teacher education, particularly training of primary or basic school teachers, involves training in short cycle courses (four years after primary education) or in long cycle (six years primary education).

Training of secondary school teachers includes those who hold degrees in other subjects then pedagogy must follow the *Cours d'Agregation a I'Enseignment*. The higher institutes train pedagogy specialists in various fields. They may teach in the first cycle of secondary education, whereas *Licencies en Pedagogie appliquee* and *Agreges* teach in the second cycle. There are also five ranks of teachers in higher education: assistant, project head, associate professor, professor and full professor. An assistant must hold a *Licence* or its equivalent and is nominated for a two-year period, twice renewable. A project head needs four years as an assistant and two publications in a scientific journal. An associate professor must hold a first-level doctorate. Promotion requires four years from the previous level together with several publications. There is a service de *pedagogie universitaire* which organizes training sessions for higher education teachers.

Democratic Republic of Congo has been adversely affected by civil wars and schools are to a large extent struggling to survive. There are no clearly known and identifiable national programs for school leadership development. School leaders more or less depend on on-the job experiences enhanced by infrequent in-service programs and seminars organized and run by the Ministry of Education.

In Rwanda, secondary education is divided into two three-year cycles. The first cycle is common to all pupils. The second cycle covers Modern or Classical Humanities. On successful completion of the second cycle, pupils are awarded the *Diplome des Humanities completes*. There is a variety of two-year technical secondary courses for pupils who have completed two to three years of academic secondary education, although pupils could also enter directly from primary school. There are also four-year courses.

Primary school teachers in Rwanda are trained in secondary school teacher training institutions (*Ecoles normales inferieures*) in a five-year post-primary course (the first three years cover the same curriculum as the first cycle of general secondary education and are followed by two years' pedagogical training). Secondary school teachers are trained at the *Ecole normale superieure* in conjunction with the National University. Students who successfully complete the three-year course leading to the *Agregation de I'Enseignment secondaire inferieur*, may teach in the lower secondary cycle, and those who successfully complete the five-year course leading to the *Agregation* de *I'Enseignment secondaire superieur*, may teach in the upper secondary cycle. Higher education teachers are trained at the *Universite nationale du Rwanda* and often go abroad to complete their training.

Rwanda is among Africa's poorest countries. It has been plagued by civil wars which culminated in the 1994 genocide and thus political instability (http://www.spiegel.de/international/ spiegel, 8/28/2007). This situation has heavily and negatively impacted on school leadership development initiatives. The Ministry of Education makes efforts to provide school leadership short courses in an effort to empower school principals to do their work. There is also heavy reliance on imported expertise especially from the East African region particularly Kenya and Uganda. This expertise is used to offer in-service and to induct school leaders particularly through consultancy services.

Besides the internal African countries' school leadership development initiatives, there is the International Confederation of Principals (ICP) based in UK, whose membership is open to any organization of school principals whose aims are consistent with those of ICP (including the English National College for School Leadership). One of the objectives of the ICP is to develop relationships between school leaders in Africa, which began at the inaugural African convention of principals held in August 2000 at Saint Stithians College, and to broaden these connections to include international members of the ICP (http://www.globalgateway.org.uk. 8/28/2007). The National Association of Secondary School Principals (NASSP) of South Africa and Kenya Secondary School Principals Association (KSSPA) benefit from ICP.

CHARACTERISTICS, ROLES AND CONTEXTS OF SCHOOL LEADERS

Discussion on school leadership in Africa involves consideration of the characteristics, roles and contexts of school leaders. Indeed, one of the features that distinguish effective schools in Africa, as elsewhere, is the caliber of the principals' leadership qualities. It is generally acknowledged that the principal is the linchpin in any school. A bad principal can ruin a good school and, by the same token, a great principal can sometimes overcome even the worst obstacles. Success in school leadership depends upon professional training, ability, professional opportunities and career planning (Kimbrough & Nunnery, 1983). Literature is emphatic that leadership has to be distinguished from management. Managers are concerned with "doing things right" and leaders are more concerned with "doing the right thing". The distinguishing characteristics of an effective leader of a school include: a sense of vision, which is communicated to all staff and students, a sense of responsibility, concern for task completion, energy, persistence, risk-taking, originality, self-confidence, capacity to handle stress, capacity to influence, capacity to co-ordinate the efforts of others in the achievement of purpose (Stogdill, 1974 in Harris et al., 1996 in Kindiki, 2004).

A school principal in Africa should first and foremost be a professionally trained teacher who has experience in classroom instruction. As a trained teacher, the principal must also be aware of the teachers' code of conduct in the specific country. These qualities place them in a position of instructional leaders, who should provide counsel and even suggest innovative developments in matters of the teaching profession (Ssekamwa, 2001).

In the countries described, there are a range of normative expectations. The school principal is expected to be a public relations person in and outside the institution. Within the school, the principal works with the teachers, sub-ordinate staff and students. Outside the school, principals works with the parents, the surrounding community, the education officers and other government agents, the politicians and other interest groups such as church organizations. The way he/she relates to all these determine the atmosphere within the school and the extent of success.

Principals are expected to always look out for opportunities for their teachers and other workers to better their prospects both materially and professionally. They should obtain useful information on promotion and advancement prospects and make such information available to the right people, so those interested may take action; they may also be in a position to support in terms of recommendation. They should recognize contribution, empathize when necessary and celebrate victories. Furthermore, the principal should search for opportunities that will result in academic excellence for the school.

A principal in Africa needs to be aware of the various tribes' (or clans'), religions, political ideologies, gender and social classes that are likely to influence the school functioning but should not allow any of these to be the determining factor in his/her decision making process; rather they will be guided by careful identification and utilization of talent among those with whom they work (Ssekamwa, 2001).

Principals should take the initiative where it is necessary and feasible to expand the school infrastructure, to improve the existing facilities and carry out required renovations. They may also be a change agent who should be aware of the current trends in education, for example, during the implementation of the 8-4-4 system of Education in Kenya, the principals were recognized and utilized as the main engines for change.

A school principal in Africa should be a resource mobilizer and a collaborator for the progress of the school. A good example is in Ndiareme B. Primary School in the outskirts of Dakar, Senegal. The school principal, Maguette Mbow, mobilizes the parents and the local community to support the school. She even wrote "a letter to U.N. Secretary General, Kofi Annan, to remind him of his promise five years ago to support her school" (http://www.ungei.org/gapproject/Senegal, 8/28/2007, p. 6). According to her, "we have to work in synergy if we want to succeed" (p. 3).

Furthermore, Serem (1985) identified the following responsibilities concerning the role of the principal: making frequent and formal classroom visitations, making the school a safe and secure place in which to work and centralized instructional leadership; ensuring that classroom atmosphere is conducive to learning for all students; establishing high, but attainable learning standards in all academic areas as an important goal of the school. Others include holding conferences with Parents Teachers Association (PTA) and other lay groups, planning and coordinating public relations programs; helping the Board of Education in determining the educational needs of the community among others.

A number of criticisms can be made regarding this list; first, the imprecision of the language; second, some successful school leaders do not exhibit such characteristics; third, schools are slowly beginning to democratize their management, placing greater emphasis on management teams rather than individual leaders. It has become more common to establish to what extent the senior management team possesses the appropriate combination of qualities (Belbin, 1981, cited in Harris et al., 1996).

But the most important quality of an effective school leader is having a clear vision for the school which must be translated into meaningful goals. Thus:

> Outstanding leaders have a vision for their schools-mental picture of a preferred future-which is shared with all in the school community and which shapes the programs for learning and teaching as well as policies, priorities, plans and procedures pervading the day-to-day life of the school. (Caldwell & Millikan, 1993, cited in Harris et al., 1996, p. 34)

Kitavi and Van Der Westhuizen (1997, p. 251) quoting Weldy (1979) conclude about the importance of principals that:

> In many ways the school principal is the most important and influential individual in any school. it is his/her leadership that sets the tone of the school, the climate for the learning, the level of professionalism and morale of the teachers and degree of concern for what students may or may not become. If a school is a vibrant innovative, child-centered place, it has a reputation for excellence. If students are performing to the best of their ability, one can always point to the principal's leadership as the key to that success.

None of the above studies has taken an inclusive approach to discussing the importance of school leaders other than the principal. However, the roles of school leaders rest on the principal as the leading professional. It is the principal who initiates a participative approach as a motivator and guide, involving teachers in decision-making and seeing them as agents of change within the school (Mortimore, 1997). The school principal also works cooperatively with other leaders; deputy principals, heads of departments, committees for primary schools, Board of Governors in case of secondary schools and Ministry of Education officials to realize the goals set.

In Africa, however, most school systems are centralized and school principals are expected to operate within the specified boundaries of the nationally set goals of education. They may only make small variations that should not alter the national vision envisaged. Such alterations may be made with the blessing of the PTA, the BOG, school teaching staff and in consultation with the relevant Ministry of Education officials.

CURRENT RESEARCH UNDERPINNING SCHOOL LEADERSHIP PREPARATION AND DEVELOPMENT

Current research underpinning school leadership preparation and development in Africa is scanty (Kitavi & Van Der Westhuizen, 1997). A good deal of research exists on the characteristics, roles, contextual problems faced by principals in improving schools. The growing body of empirical research from some developed countries such as the United States (Anderson, 1991; Parkay & Rhodes, 1992), Australia (Beeson & Matthews, 1992) and the UK (Harber & Dadey, 1993; Harber & Davies, 1997) are too broad and relate to research on and the reality of the job of the principal in developing countries in general. Such studies do not take an inclusive pan-African focus. Interestingly, many lines of inquiry identify principals as the key ingredient for successful schools, and that there are obstacles that they face. In fact, studies axiomatically affirm that school principals face problems which hinder them from being effective educational managers. However, rarely do such studies mention the key role-played by other school leaders like deputy principals, heads of departments, school committees or Board of Governors and the Ministries of Education officials in school leadership functions.

Schools in Africa operate in different philosophical contexts. The main argument here is that the African context is different from that of most schools in developed countries. Inevitably, the need to generalize about 'African school leaders preparation' means that there is a risk that contrasts between individual African countries and the existence of similarities with developed countries are not sufficiently highlighted in what is a broad continuum rather than an absolute divide. However, what is certainly the case is that most of the literature on educational leadership has been written in developed, industrialized countries and describes educational conditions and realities as they exist in those countries. It would be inaccurate to assume automatically that these conditions prevail in Africa.

There is, nevertheless, a danger that in stressing the problematic context of education in Africa, too negative a picture may be painted. It is, therefore, important to bear in mind that considerable progress has been made in Africa in a whole range of fields of school leadership development over the past two or three decades. For example, the UNDP report on human development for developing countries, shows that there is significant progress in the life expectancy, access to safe water, primary school enrolment, per capita food production, agricultural and food production, a decline in fertility rates, increased female access to education, decreased infant mortality and the extension of democracy particularly in African countries (Harber & Davies, 1997). These have implications for school leadership preparation and development.

DILEMMAS TO SCHOOL LEADERSHIP

There are school leadership dilemmas in Africa. Education in many Anglophone and Francophone African countries is a precious commodity widely given and sought after. African governments for instance spend more than half their annual budget on education. However, in spite of the high budgetary allotment to education, little is known about the problems faced by school leaders.

Despite the growing awareness of the problems faced by principals, very little is known in general about problems faced by other school leaders. Researchers are becoming aware of the unique problems faced by principals. Robust inclusive research on educational leadership in Africa is indispensable. Such research is necessary because school principals and other school leaders face problems which markedly differ from problems faced by their counterparts in developed countries.

These studies have failed to conceptualize the history and issues that impact the development of school leaders in Africa. Similarly, they have not investigated the problems facing school leaders in Africa and the skills leaders require in order to be effective and efficient. Such research also fails to consider the characteristics, contexts and role played by school leaders in African countries as distinct from other developing countries. The most serious problems faced by African school leaders are many and varied. But we confine our discussion to a selected few which include demographics, economics, resources, violence, health and cultural issues.

Demographic consideration is one glaring dilemma that affects school leaders in both Anglophone and Francophone Africa in terms of their effectiveness in getting children educated in the light of rapidly expanding school-age populations. Whereas in developed countries primary and secondary education is universally available, only about 75 per cent of eligible children on average attend primary schools in Africa (Harber & Davies, 1997). This situation is exacerbated by high drop out rates as well as over-age students such as is the case in Mozambique, Lesotho, Rwanda and Mali (Colclough and Lewin, 1993 in Harber & Davies, 1997; Hough, 1989 in Harber & Davies, 1997).

Exacerbating these demographic trends is rural-urban migration which leads to overcrowded schools, high repetition and drop-out rates, together with deterioration in the quality of teaching in the urban areas and at the same time declining enrolment in rural areas (UNESCO, 1994, pp. 29–30, Harber & Davies, 1997, pp. 11–12). This scenario poses leadership challenges to school principals who are forced to mentally adjust to accommodate these difficulties and at the same time counsel the classroom teachers to do likewise.

The economic difficulties are significant for school leadership in Africa. The Structural Adjustment Programmes (SAPs) initiated by the World Bank and International Monetary Fund (IMF) in 1979–80 have had serious implications for the education sector in developing countries, especially in Africa. The actual funds available for expenditure on education meant that school leaders are constrained in terms of infrastructure development, educational materials provision and human resource engagement and development for educational institutions.

The decrease in money available for public expenditure has affected spending on education in many Anglophone and Francophone African countries. To get loans from the IMF and the World Bank to help them revive the economy and pay debt, many countries like Kenya have had to agree to SAPs which deliberately cut down on state funding of health, welfare and educational provision. In countries with SAPs, expenditure on education declines more than those without. Private households are less able to make up the shortfall by contributing to education because of sharply increased austerity created by the negative multiplier effects of SAPs; hence there is a drop in pupils' enrolment rates in such countries. Samoff (1994) lists the effects of structural adjustment on education in developing countries.

In Kenya, for example, the implementation of SAPs policies has forced the government to cut down expenditure on education and other important services, yet teachers' salaries are poor and their purchasing power has fallen dramatically along with those of other public service workers. Teachers in many Anglophone and Francophone African countries are paid irregularly or have to wait for months for their pay package (Colclough and Lewin, 1993; Graham-Brown, 1991). Many teachers have to take an extra job or even two in order to survive, and this has affected their teaching morale. Consequently, the principals' role as a leading professional in curriculum implementation and supervision is seriously affected.

Likewise, Ilon (1994) illustrates that governments are under pressure from poorer segments of society to provide access to quality education that leads to high paying jobs. Satisfying this demand becomes increasingly difficult given pressures to decrease public spending, so the realities of shrinking education investment bring compounding conflict with poorer groups who complicate the school leaders' role.

Resource is another dilemma faced by school leaders in Africa. Teachers work under very deplorable conditions, overworked, underpaid and, as previously stated, sometimes not paid at all for months. Harber and Davies (1997, quoting Lulat, 1988) add that schools in developing countries sometimes use textbooks in classrooms that are long out of date, and that the number of textbooks available is often not enough to go round. Furthermore, it is not uncommon in rural African schools to see a single textbook for a given subject shared by a whole class and a lack of qualified teachers to handle the various subjects. These obviously impact on the rating of the school leaders' performance. In response, the principals find innovative ways of survival, for example, introduction of a cost sharing strategy where parents buy textual materials or pay some fees to the schools or even collaborate with neighboring resource endowed schools to share the available resources.

The teachers work in overcrowded and under furnished classrooms coupled with poor means of communication. This situation affects teaching negatively both in motivation and morale which translates into high absenteeism which, in turn, has negative implications for productivity (Kitavi & Van Der Westhuizen, 1997).

Since schools in Africa operate in different and difficult resource contexts, school leaders need to be innovative, applying practical strategies in circumstances of economic stringency. The most obvious focus of these practical strategies would tend to be internal management of schools themselves and the context in which they operate. School management styles themselves are not always universal. Schools have points of difference as well as similarities, driven by the management of scarce resources for school improvement in contexts of economic stringency. These constraints limit the range of possible outcomes and force schools into providing courses and deploying resources in ways which are cost-effective (Bullock & Martin, 1999). This limited resource base has a serious influence on the way school leaders organize and run institutions.

Inaccessibility of parents is another dilemma. Because of poverty, most parents in Africa are busy most of the time either looking for the next meal of the day or looking for the next term's school fees. Others are ignorant of the importance of parental involvement in their children's education. This implies that school leaders, particularly principals, will at times be confronted with the dilemma of making some decisions on certain students, which may create conflicts with the inaccessible parent (Kitavi & Van Der Westhuizen, 1997).

Violence disrupts the smooth running of schools in Africa, and this, too, has an impact on the effectiveness of school leaders. Harber and Davies (1997) argue that in the past years many developing countries, particularly African countries, have been plagued by war and violent unrest.

Examples of countries that have suffered from this include Burundi, Chad, Ethiopia, Eritrea, Guinea-Bissau, Kenya, Liberia, Mali, Namibia, Nigeria, Rwanda, Sierra Leone, Somalia, South Africa, Sudan, Uganda, Zaire (DRC), Zimbabwe, Angola and Mozambique. In some African countries, military dictatorships have carried out violent acts against their own people. The statement below summarizes the violence dilemma that has also plagued African countries:

> …And in many parts of the world, children have been tortured and forced to watch or participate in atrocities. Hundreds and thousands have been crippled by landmines. Many more have been recruited into armies, given drugs and weapons and desensitized to others' pain. Uncounted millions of these young people are suffering from post-traumatic stress disorders, a new and chilling term in the international lexicon. (UNICEF 1994b, p. 4, in Harber & Davies, 1997)

Long-term violence in a society can create a culture of violence, which is difficult to eradicate. School leaders in some African countries have had to confront this problem in the line of their duties and indeed some have lost their lives. Such violence and conflicts result in political instability, which has serious implications for school leadership. Innovative school leaders work in collaboration with the curriculum development agencies in their countries to incorporate aspects of trauma and stress management in the various school subjects to initiate the healing process for the learners.

Health concerns for school children should be considered by school leaders. Specifically, HIV/AIDS is a serious social and a health concern for school leaders in Africa today (Coombs, 1995; Harber & Davies, 1997; Bartlett et al., 1999). The devastating effects of HIV/AIDS coupled with the poverty rates in African countries put most school-going children in a vulnerable position, unable to conceptualize the need for and value of education. With such children in schools, the school principals may have a difficult task trying to do their work and are sometimes forced to deal with issues beyond their mandate. In such cases, school principals have to link up with relevant NGOs, concerned government agencies and local community initiatives in support of the affected learners. HIV/AIDS education is also progressively gaining currency in school curricula in many African countries in an effort to manage its negative effects.

Cultural diversities influence school leadership. The location of institutions and the dominant cultural underpinnings influence the leadership style and performance of the school principal. For example, in some communities, girls' education is seen as being of no value since their role is to be confined to the kitchen, while in others boys become adults after circumcision at the age 13 to 14 years and are considered ready to be out of school. In predominantly Muslim communities such as is the case in Somalia, West African countries and parts of East African countries, girl's education is in jeopardy. Consequently, the principals' role in achieving the millennium development goal to "eliminate gender disparity in primary and secondary education, preferably by 2005 and all levels of education no later than 2015" is an up hill task (UNDP, 2003, p.1). The school principals have to work closely with the local communities to discover effective strategies that would keep learners in school.

Lack of deliberately planned programs for leadership preparation and development for school leaders in most African countries, worsened by lack of financial resources makes the situation desperate. Most principals have no empowering knowledge and skills beyond what was acquired in pre-service teacher education programs which renders most of them in a precarious position. In most cases, school principals have to make deliberate efforts to up-date themselves through individual initiative and experiences on-the-job.

RESEARCH NEEDS, FUTURE ISSUES AND INTERNATIONAL LINKS FOR AFRICAN SCHOOL LEADERS

From the foregoing, further research is required in Africa to support school leadership preparation and development. The means by which most principals in Africa are trained, selected, and inducted, indicate potential for improvement. School leaders are not only limited to principals, but also deputy principals, heads of department, school committees, Board of Governors and Ministries of Education officials (Kitavi & Van Der Westhuizen, 1997).

Given the importance of school leaders and particularly the principal, there is a need to focus leadership training and research on specific needs, concerns, challenges and problems faced by school leaders in Africa. With better understanding of the problems affecting school leaders, educational systems in Africa may consider adjusting and re-focusing their current practices of selecting, preparing, and inducting principals and other school leaders.

Teacher colleges, universities and other educational institutes involved in the professional development of principals could consider redesigning programs that will assist individual students undertaking teacher education training programs after they assume their position as principal to provide leadership training as far as school management is concerned. Universities could champion preparation and organization of materials to be used in seminars, conferences and refresher courses for school leaders, in a planned and scheduled manner. Such programs could not only include principals, but also deputy principals, heads of department, school committees, Board of Governors and Ministry of Education officials themselves who make policy decisions that considerably affect the running of schools.

Specific African countries need to initiate research agendas into their countries to be able to address country-specific issues in school leadership and development. Such issues may include pre-service teacher education programs *vis-á-vis* the principal's role in school, the role of school leaders, the training needs of school leaders and the support programs for school leaders.

There should be a deliberate move to link the various facets of the school system to strengthen school leadership activities in African countries. These should be linkages among the ministries of education, teacher education programs and school leadership programs. Such linkages are likely to compel African countries to take planned, deliberate steps towards improving school leadership development efforts that are currently scanty. It is also suggested that universities in the various African countries be encouraged to research and also play a leading role in delivering school leadership preparation and development activities.

It should also be remembered that school leadership preparation and development issues are universal to some extent and, therefore, African countries in tackling these issues should look beyond African borders for support. They could establish links and be willing to share the experiences of relevant international organizations such as the International Confederation of Principals (ICP). These linkages are likely to benefit the African countries' efforts to move in the right direction.

REFERENCES

Anderson, M.E. (1991). *Principals: How to Train, Recruit, Select, Induct and Evaluate Leaders for America's Schools*. University of Oregon, College of Education. Eric Clearing House.

Bartlett, S., Hart, R., Satterthwaite, D., Barra, X. and Missair, A. (1999). *Cities for Children: Children's Rights, Poverty and Urban Management*. London: UNICEF. Earthscan Publications Ltd.

Beeson, G.W. and Matthews, R.J. (1992). 'Becoming a Principal in Australia'. In F. W. Parkay, and Hall, G. E. (eds.), *Becoming a Principal: The Challenges of Beginning Leadership*. Boston: Allyn & Bacon, pp. 308–328.

Bullock, A. and Martin, J. (Eds.) (1999). *Distance Education in Research Methodology: Ways of Doing Research. Unit 4: Researching the Institution.* The University of Birmingham. School of Education and School of Continuing Studies.

Colclough, C. and Lewin, K. (1993). *Educate All the Children.* Oxford: Clerendon press.

Coombs, P.H. (1995). *The World Crisis in Education: The View from the Eighties.* New York: Oxford University Press.

Eiseman, T.O. and Wasil, A. (1987). Koranic Schooling and its Transformation in Coastal Kenya. *International Journal of Educational Development.* Vol. 7, No. 2, pp. 89–97.

Eshiwani, G.S. (1993). *Education in Kenya Since Independence*. Nairobi: East Africa Educational Publishers.

Graham-Brown, S. (1991). *Educational in the Developing World. Conflict and Crisis.* London: Longman.

Harber, C. (2000). *Lecture Handouts*. The University of Birmingham.

Harber, C. and Dadey, A. (1993). The Job of Headteacher in Africa: Research and Reality. *International Journal of Educational Development.* Vol. 13, No. 2, pp. 147–160.

Harber, C. and Davies, L. (1997). School Management and Effectiveness in Developing Countries. London: Cassell.

http://www.jstor.org/view. *A Journal of Opinion*: Vol. 23, No.2, p. 18. (8/28/2007).

http://www.southafrica.infor/sa_glance/education/education.htm (8/28/2007).

http://www.principals.org/s_nassp/sec.asp (8/28/2007).

http://www.educationpublishing.com/isea Vol.32, No.3, 2004 (8/31/2007).

http://www.ungei.org/gapproject/senegal_333.htm (8/28/2007).

http://www.spiegel.de/international/spiegel (8/28/2007).

Ilon, L. (1994). Structural Adjustment and Education: Adapting to a Growing Global Market. *International Journal of Educational Development.* Vol. 14, No .2, pp. 95–108.

Kimbrough, R. B. and Nunnery, M. Y. (1983). *Educational Administration: An Introduction* (3rd ed.). New York: MacMillan.

Kindiki, J.N. (1999). 'Community Participation in Education in Primary and Secondary Schools in Kenya'. Unpublished M.Ed Dissertation. School of Education. The University of Birmingham. Birmingham, England, United Kingdom.

Kindiki, J.N. (2004). 'Investigating School Effectiveness in Slum Contexts: The Case of Nairobi, Kenya'. Unpublished PhD Thesis. School of Education. The University of Birmingham. Birmingham, England, United Kingdom.

Kindiki, J.N. (2007). Management and Policy in Education: Rhetoric and Practice. Unpublished Teaching Manual. Moi University, Eldoret, Kenya.

Kitavi, M. and Van Der Westhuizen, P. (1997) Problems Facing Beginning Principals in Developing Countries: A study of Beginning Principals in Kenya. *International Journal of Educational Development.* Vol. 17, No.3, pp. 251-263.

Lodiaga, J. and Olembo, J. (1990). 'Headteacher Training in Kenya'. In B. McNie, R. White, and J. Wright (eds.). *Headteacher Management Training and the Development of Support Materials: A Planning Overview.* London: Commonwealth Secretariat, pp. 41–49.

Mbaabu, I. (1996). *Language Policy in East Africa.* Nairobi: Educational Research and Publication.

Mortimore, P. (1997). "Can Effective Schools Compensate for Society". In A.H. Halsey, H. Lauder, P. Brown, & A.S. Wells, (eds.). *Education, Culture, Economy, Society.* New York: Oxford University Press, pp. 376–487.

Mugambi, J.N.K. (1989). *Christian Mission and Social Transformation. A Kenyan Perspective.* Nairobi: Nairobi Council of Churches of Kenya.

Parkay, F.W. and Rhodes, J.W. (1992). 'Stress and Beginning Principals". In F.W. Parkay and G.E. Hall (eds.). *Becoming a Principal: The Challenges of Beginnng Leadership.* Boston: Allyn & Bacon, pp. 103–122.

Republic of Kenya (1964). *Kenya Education Commission Report (Ominde Report)*.Nairobi: Government Printer.

Republic of Kenya (1976). *Report of the National Committee on Educational Objectives and Policies (Gachathi Report)*.Nairobi: Government Printer.

Republic of Kenya (1981).*Presidential Working Party on the Establishment of the Second University in Kenya (Mackay Report)*. Nairobi: Government Printer.

Republic of Kenya (1988). *Report of the Presidential Working Party on Education and Manpower Development for the Next Decade and Beyond* (Kamunge Report). Nairobi: Government Printer.

Republic of Kenya (1999). *Totally Integrated Quality Education and Training (Koech Report)*. Nairobi: Government Printer.

Republic of Kenya (2005).*The Background Report of Kenya (Kamunge Report)*. Nairobi:Ministry of Education, Science and Technology.

Samoff, J. (1994). *Cooperation,But Limited Control and Little Ownership: Observations on Education Sector Studies in Africa, 1990–1994*. Paris: UNESCO.

Ssekamwa, J.C. & Lugumba, S. M. E. (2001). *A History of Education in East Africa* (2nd ed.). Kampala: Fountain Publishers.

Ssekamwa, J. C. (2001*). Professional Ethics for Teachers*. Kampala: Nets Africana Ltd.

Serem, D. K. (1985). A Comparative Study of the High School Principalship Role in Traditional and Outcome-Based Environments in Wyoming Central Association High Schools. Unpublished PhD Dissertation.

UNDP (2003). *Human Development Report 2003: Millenium Development Goals: A Compact Among Nations to End Human Poverty*. New York: Oxford University Press, Inc.

UNESCO (1999). *Guide to Higher Education in Africa: Association of African Universities*. London. MacMillan Reference Ltd.

Weldy, G.R. (1979). *Principals: What They Do and Who They Are*. Reston, VA: National Association of Secondary School Principals.

19

Preparing and Developing School Leaders in the Middle East: Towards Mediating Westernization with Indigenous and Evidence-Based Practice and Theories of Educative Leadership

Reynold Macpherson and Omid Tofighian

The purpose of this chapter is to review the preparation and development of the leaders of primary and secondary schools in the Middle East. The chapter has an introduction, three major sections and a brief summary of preliminary recommendations. Given the unevenness of international understandings of this region, the first major section demonstrates that school leadership in each location in the Middle East occurs in a unique and complex patchwork of cultures. Each patchwork reflects the vagaries of a general political history of conquest and decolonization, peace and *jihardism*, oil wealth and modernization, and, reconciliation and development. The second major section introduces a common heritage of traditional Islamic schooling and then provides a snapshot of each country's developing education system and its approach to preparing and developing its school leaders. It shows that the ideological context of leadership is in transition from traditional to modernized forms of Islamism, in most cases being overlaid by self-managed Westernization. The third section begins with a general Islamic perspective on leadership and summarizes the options regarding the preparation and development of school leaders from English, American and European perspectives. The concluding reflections suggest that the ontological, historical, cultural and epistemological challenges faced by each Middle Eastern country might best be addressed by mediating Westernization with indigenous and evidence-based concepts of best practice and theory about educative leadership. By educative leadership we mean leadership services that achieve intended learning outcomes in educators, educational institutions and education systems (Duignan & Macpherson, 1993).

CONTEXT

Definitions

The terms "Middle East", "Arab" and "Muslim", and the nature of being or identity associated with each of these terms, are all contested. The definition of the Middle East used by the International Air Transport Association (IATA, 2005) includes the nations of Bahrain, Egypt, Iran, Iraq, Israel, Jordan, Kuwait, Lebanon, Palestinian Territories, Oman, Qatar, Saudi Arabia, Sudan, Syria, United Arab Emirates, and Yemen. The Arab League, the "United Nations" of the Arab World, has a different list. Powerful outsiders have also proposed alternatives, a not uncommon practice throughout the ages, as we will show. We will use the most common and least controversial list from the IATA.

The media in the West frequently bundle the terms Middle East, Arab and Muslim. The Middle East is commonly defined as a predominantly Islamic Pan-Arabic community wracked by frequent internal wars (Clements, 2001). This definition is riddled with problems and, as it will be shown, tends to blame the traumatized victims of serial conquest and colonization. The concept of ethnic nationality is technically inappropriate; most of the nation states in the Middle East are multi-ethnic, variously including Africans, Arabs, Assyrians, Armenians, Azeris, Berbers, Chaldeans, Druze, Greeks, Jews, Kurds, Maronites, Persians and Turks, not counting large numbers of expatriates. Most of the nation states in the region cannot speak plausibly with one voice; the main language groups heard include Arabic, Armenian, Assyrian (also known as Aramaic or Syriac), Azeri, English, Hebrew, Kurdish, Farsi (Persian), and Turkish. Many members of these states do not have a unitary sense of being a nation in political, religious or military terms; most nations have substantial minorities whose affiliations cross borders. The region has also seen the birth of The Bahá' Faith, Christianity, Islam, Judaism, and Zoroastrianism, as well as many other smaller religions and many sects of each. This pluralism, in terms of ethnicity, language and religious conviction, could be one reason why the region has experienced extended periods of relative peace and tolerance through the ages, despite the more salient examples of violence and militancy.

The concept of Pan-Arabism, or being part of the "Arab nation" irrespective of state, is also problematic. It probably started as a 19th century European and somewhat romanticized concept of a nation (Lewis, 2004). It assumes that the human race divides naturally into nations, each with discernible characteristics and political attributes, purposes and rights. Any nation, it follows, unable to express its nationhood in statehood is being denied its rights, and conversely, that any state not based on a nation is illegitimate. Most European and Arabic-speaking peoples over the last 2,000 years have not defined themselves primarily in terms of a nation state, but as members of a religious community, as subjects of an empire, and as members of a tribe. A safer generalization is that Pan-Arabic political identity and loyalty has three basic dimensions, with huge variations (Lewis, 2004). First is membership in the Islamic community, where the fundamental purpose of life is to prepare for the next. Second is allegiance to a specific polity or dynasty. The third level of identity is ethnic or tribal in nature, such as Bedouin. Each identity is weighted and counts differently in combination with the others in different circumstances.

The Impact of Empires

The complexity of identity also traces to the vicarious impact of civilizations in the region. The earliest were in Mesopotamia (approximately Iraq today), namely the Sumerian, Babylonian and Assyrian empires, and the Pharaonic Empires of Ancient Egypt. From about 500BC the Achaemenids foundered the Persian Empire, Alexander the Great briefly established the Macedonian Empire, followed by the Ptolemaic Empire in Egypt and the Seleucid Empire in Syria. The Roman Empire then enveloped the Middle East, North Africa and Europe from the 1st to the 5th century AD, and latterly, spread Christianity. When power was transferred from Rome to Constantinople in the 4th century, the Greek-speaking Christian Byzantine Empire ruled from the Balkans to the Euphrates, alongside the Persian Empire (as revived by the Parthians and Sassanids). Each region in the Middle East had a unique experience of these empires with plural legacies.

The rise of Islam on the Arabian Peninsula from 634AD then created a region in the Middle East with a new and relatively common cultural identity that overlaid without eradicating the earlier plural identities. It did not include Anatolia (Turkey today) which remained Christian until the arrival of the Turks some 400 years later. The Arabic Empire's dominance of the Middle East ended in the 11th century when the Seljuk Turks sought to impose their culture for 200 years until their empire gradually devolved into sultanates. Pope Urban II mobilized the nasty, expensive and ultimately futile Crusader campaigns from 1099 (Holt, 1986). Saladin retook Jerusalem in 1187 and the last of the Crusader fiefdoms disintegrated in 1291. The Arab *Ayyubid sultans* then regained control of Egypt and Syria from the Turks in the early 13th century, until the *Mongols* of the *Golden Horde* swept through as far west as the Egyptian border, before leaving again by the 14th century. The Turkish *Mameluk* sultans of Egypt regained control of Palestine and Syria, and other Turkish sultans took charge of Iraq and Anatolia. Then, for 400 years from the early 15th century, the Ottoman Empire was in ascendancy, maintaining a border between the Christian World and their Muslim world north of the Danube.

Two residual effects of these empires related to education are still explicit today, in addition to traces of anti-Christian hatred dating from the Crusades. First is the unique cultural patchwork that comprises each Middle Eastern nation, each with its own bewildering array of local and regional cultures. These multi-layered profiles are in sharp contrast to the countries on the Arabian Peninsula where the Arabs continued to run their own affairs; the resultant cultural homogeneity there helped underpin the development of the Gulf Cooperation Council (GCC; comprised of Bahrain, Kuwait, Oman, Qatar, Saudi Arabia and United Arab Emirates; Ministry of Information and Culture, 1998). Notably, the GCC sustained a 25-year campaign from 1981 to position the GCC as a leading force for regional security, industrialization, economic integration and liberalization, mediation, unity, and increasingly, educational reforms in the Arab world (Government of the United Arab Emirates, 2004). Recent evidence suggests that the GCC interfaces more effectively with Europe and the United States than any other alliance in the Arabic World (Woodward, 2006). The key point here is that non-GCC Middle Eastern countries had unique experiences of empires, especially during the disintegration of the Ottoman Empire, an issue we now examine.

The Post-Ottoman Period

The Ottoman Empire gradually succumbed to Western Europe's growing economic power, which in turn can be attributed to capturing the resources of the New World, the development of capitalism, the technology of the industrial revolution and, most notably, by the emergence and political accommodation of pluralism (Yapp, 1987). Pluralism flowered in Europe and Britain once the Protestant reformation had broken the theological monopoly of the Catholic Church and legitimated individualism and entrepreneurialism. Hence, from 1700 to 1918, as the Ottoman Empire retreated steadily from Europe, the "Modern Near East" took shape but fell further and further behind Europe economically and politically, and remained broadly antagonistic to international relations, trade with the West and pluralism. By the 19th century the Ottoman Empire was regarded patronizingly in Europe as "the sick man of Europe," which legitimated financial exploitation and another wave of colonization. This descriptor was reputedly initiated by Czar Nicholas I of Russia in conversation with the British Ambassador, Sir Hamilton Seymour, in January 1853 (Lewis, 2004).

The desperate Ottomans turned to Germany for protection in return for even greater financial and military dependence. They were not alone in adopting this strategy, with long-term consequences. Many Middle Eastern rulers sought help from European powers in the late 19th and early 20th centuries in order to modernize and compete more effectively. Egyptian and Persian rulers, for example, imported Western models of constitutional government, civil law, secular education and industrial development. They rapidly developed railway and communication systems, schools and universities, and created a new professional class of army officers, lawyers, teachers and administrators. The approaches used to prepare and develop school leaders today in different Middle Eastern countries often date from these times.

There were other common strategies used by Middle Eastern nations, again to common effect (Ovendale, 1998). The modernization of education eroded the traditional leadership provided by Islamic scholars. Defaults on international loans deepened dependencies on European powers, discredited internal reformers and triggered radical conservatism. Professional armies sometimes seized power for themselves, imposed reforms and then refused to give up their power, and so prevented the development of political democracies. And when the Ottoman Empire finally collapsed in 1918, the many peoples of the Middle East discovered that they had been twice betrayed, partially explaining their distrust of the West ever since.

Britain had secretly signed the Sykes-Picot Agreement with France to partition the Middle East between them. Britain had also secretly signed the Balfour Agreement with the international Zionist movement to help establish a Jewish homeland in Palestine, once the site of the ancient Kingdom of Israel where a largely Arab population had since been living. The Middle East was then re-colonized using the fig leaf of protectorates. The French took Syria and split off the Christian areas to create Lebanon. The British installed Sherif Hussein's son Faisal as king of their protectorate, Iraq. They split Palestine with the eastern section becoming another protectorate, Transjordan (later Jordan), where they installed another of Sherif Hussein's son as king, Abdullah. They administered the rest of Palestine themselves and allowed the already substantial Jewish population to increase. Most of the Arabian Peninsula fell to another British ally, Ibn Saud, who established the Kingdom of Saudi Arabia in 1922. These changes concluded the post-Ottoman period and were followed by a realignment of the world order.

The Impact of Geopolitics

The world's largest easily accessible oil and gas reserves were discovered in the Middle East in the mid-20th century. That discovery placed the region central to global energy politics and provided a unique opportunity for the newly rich countries to diversify and become early members of the emergent world knowledge economy. It also made the monarchs of oil states very wealthy, extremely powerful at home, and increasingly dependent on Western military power and professional expertise. In some of the more conservative Islamic states, oil wealth also served to retard the adoption of political, economic and social reforms, education in particular (Ahmed, 1998). And when the costs of World War Two forced the reluctant departure of the British and French colonial powers, a series of national independence movements flowered, with schools commonly expected to give expression to nationhood.

In Palestine, however, the competing forces of Arab nationalism and Jewish colonization could not be reconciled, especially when intensified by growing Arab resistance to accelerating Jewish immigration onto their land, and the bitter determination of the Jewish people traumatized by the Holocaust to establish a defendable home. In 1947 the United Nations proposed to partition Palestine into a Jewish state and a Palestinian state. The Palestinians rejected the plan, the Jewish settlers declared the State of Israel, and the Arab states attacked and were defeated. About 800,000 Palestinians then became refugees in neighboring countries and, two generations later, continue to live in appalling conditions (Schulze, 1999).

Hence, for the period between 1954 and 1969 the republican revolutions in Egypt, Syria, Iraq and Libya retained popular support by regularly promising to destroy Israel, defeat the United State of America and its Western allies, and bring prosperity to Arabs (Ovendale, 1999). Many of these regimes developed alliances with the Soviet Union, but when these relationships failed to deliver the promised prosperity, resistance mounted, and many regimes became despotic. Education typically languished in such conditions. During the same period, the United States reinforced its support to its allies in the region, principally the feudal monarchies of Iran, Jordan, the Gulf Emirates and Saudi Arabia, despite their uneven commitment to the principles of human rights and good government. Iran was a key US ally, and the Shah's regime was dislodged in 1979 by a broad front of popular resistance groups who were then displaced by an anti-Western theocracy. Saudi Arabia remained a close US ally, despite its continued commitment to the destruction of Israel. However, the defeats of the Arab armies by Israel in 1948, 1967 and 1973, and Egypt's independent peace treaty with Israel in 1979, undermined the possibility of a united Pan-Arabic front (Laqueur, 1974). The growing Jewish population, strong backing from the United States, and Israel's development of nuclear weapons increasingly convinced exiled Palestinians and other Arabs that military means would probably never prove successful. The geo-political stalemate meant that the rights of the Palestinians were left unresolved, with education remaining significantly under developed, as evident in Table 19.1.

The next shock, the collapse of the Soviet Union as a super power, impacted on Middle Eastern education in many ways. It resulted in even larger numbers of Jews settling in Israel, ended an easy source of credit, armaments and diplomatic support for anti-Western regimes, enabled the flow of cheaper oil and gas onto world markets, and thus reduced Western dependency on Middle Eastern energy sources. Resources for schooling typically dwindled further. Authoritarian state socialism evaporated as a plausible model for national development. Rulers left economically and politically stranded by the collapse of the Soviet Union turned to Arab nationalism as a substitute for state socialism, and in the case of Iraq, exaggerated it to the point where it led to a lengthy war with Iran in the 1980s, and the invasion of Kuwait in 1990. The US-led coalition that evicted Iraq from Kuwait included Egypt and Syria, although the permanent military presence of the United States in the Persian Gulf, especially in Saudi Arabia — the guardian of the two most holy sites in Islam — caused deep offence to many Muslims and triggered militant *jihardism*,[1] the growth of the Al-Qaeda[2] network, and the revitalization of traditional Islamic schooling in *madrasahs* — an issue we come back to (Burke, 2004).

This helps explain why the global trend in the 1990s in the West towards political democracy, market economies and educational reforms had relatively little impact in the Middle East, except in Israel, Turkey and the Lebanon which do not have Islamic majorities. Most legislative bodies in the Middle East remained comparatively powerless. The majority of the populations in the Gulf States remained "guest workers," not citizens. The development of market economies was held back by political restrictions, corruption and cronyism, overspending on arms and prestige projects, and overdependence on oil revenues. The most successful economies, such as in Bahrain, Qatar and the United Arab Emirates, were those that combined oil wealth with benevolent and modernization-minded leadership, persuaded their nationals to become minorities in their own countries, attracted large expatriate professional communities, offered effective internal security and made cautious moves towards economic, social and political liberalization (Al-Fahim, 1995; Government of the UAE, 2005). Despite these examples to the contrary, the Middle East fell further behind Europe and the rapidly developing market economies of India and China (in terms of educational outcomes, production, trade, communications, and most other indicators of social and economic progress). Two common assertions heard in the West were that, oil apart, the Arab world exports less than Finland, and that the Arabs are trapped in a cycle of backwardness. These echoes of the "sick man of Europe" myth led sophisticated investigative journalists to suggest that it was intended to legitimate a creeping conquest of the Middle East as a great war for civilization (Fisk, 2005). Arabs, especially Palestinians, seethed with resentment at these self-serving myths, and some groups transformed their "history of hatred" for the West into militant *jihardism*, with *madrasahs* continuing to play a key formative role (Lewis, 2004).

The General Political Context of Public Education

The events of the early 21st century are recent enough not to require summary or to offer premature interpretation. Instead, the point drawn here is that any form of development in the Middle East is contingent on the residual and ongoing effects of an unfolding political history, with the development of public education and its school leaders being no exception. As the next section will further reinforce, school leadership in the diverse cultural settings of the Middle East has long been expected to serve the ideological interests of fluid alliances of interest groups, national governments and colonial powers, each determined to achieve the ends they favor through a range of political means; from degrees of militancy to economic reforms. Indeed, four broad dimensions of the context described above can be identified;

1. a politics of decolonization — evident in how polities have responded to the impact and departure of empires over centuries, especially in more recent times as republican independence movements, anti-Western authoritarian state socialism, Pan-Arabism, and radical Arabic nationalism
2. a politics of *jihardism* — seen in how polities have responded to the perceived defilement of Muslim holy lands and sites, the plight of the Palestinians, the existence of Israel, Islamic sectarianism, and to the presence of Western occupation forces in Saudi Arabia and in Iraq
3. a politics of oil wealth and modernization — evident in how polities have tried to reconcile Muslim philosophies and theocracies with monarchies, authoritarian socialism and nationalism, professionalism, political democracy, cultural secularization, capitalism, and global energy politics, and
4. a politics of reconciliation and development — seen in the persistent capacity of polities to sustain periods of peace and growing prosperity, multiculturalism, industrialization, economic reforms, social and political liberalization, and real progress towards providing universal human rights, modern education and good government.

With this general political history as a backdrop, we now move to the history, nature, outcomes and purposes of education in Middle Eastern countries and indicate the approach they are each using to train and develop school leaders. We acknowledge that the stated intentions of governments can be very different to the experience of local realities, and that the validity of data used to summarize intentions inevitably contains degrees of error. It proved very difficult to gain access to the details of preparatory and developmental programs and very little recent research has been reported. The automatic translation of Arabic policies at web sites cannot do justice to the richness of the original texts. Hence, the following analysis must be regarded as provisional until more sophisticated local research is reported.

EDUCATION AND EDUCATIONAL LEADERSHIP IN THE MIDDLE EAST

The purpose of this second major section is to summarize the nature of public schooling in each of the countries of the Middle East, and the nature of their approach to preparing and developing school leaders. The third and following section will clarify a general notion of Islamic leadership, relate the approaches being used to prepare and develop practitioners in the Middle East to international approaches, and then suggest how knowledge production of best practice and theory about educative forms of leadership might be better managed.

Traditional Islamic schooling occurs in Arabic in a local *madrasah* (the Arabic term مدرسة actually means *any* form of school, except universities) (Berkey, 1992; Lapidus, 1984; Rahman, 2006). The nature of current *madrahsahs* in different countries today is contested. The first of two traditional Islamic curricula, the *hifz*, aims to help a student to memorize the Quran, and when demonstrably successful, to graduate as a *hafiz*. The alternative and approximately 12-year *alim* curriculum typically includes *Tafsir* (interpretation of the Quran), *Shariah* (Islamic law), *Hadith* (the recorded sayings and deeds of Prophet Muhammad), *Mantiq* (logic) and Muslim History. Some *madrasahs* offer more advanced courses in Arabic literature, English and other foreign languages, as well as science and world history. The successful completion of an *alim* course leads to recognition as an Islamic scholar. It may lead on to service as an *imam* (prayer leader), or when complimented by service to *hifz* and *alim* courses, may result in being nominated to lead a *madrasah*. Since some *madrasahs* also serve as community and residential colleges, and may offer evening classes and education and training to adults, women, orphans and other disadvantaged people, educational leaders are expected to learn the additional organizational skills required on the job.

With these two forms of traditional Islamic schooling in mind, Table 19.1 offers a summary of the history, nature, outcomes, and developmental policies of education in each of the countries of the Middle East, as well as what can be deduced about their current approach to the preparation and development of school leaders.

The first theme evident in this overview is the extent to which each of the countries of the Middle East is using public schooling to address the challenges of decolonization, militant *jihardism*, modernization, and reconciliation and development. The second is that, with exceptions related to the ideology of the Government, most expect their aspirant school principals to learn on the job, to participate in Ministry leadership skills training courses and then to participate in higher learning. A third theme, with the exception of Israel and Lebanon, is that school leaders are expected to either reproduce a traditional Islamic society, as interpreted locally, or to help establish an open Islamic knowledge economy or society (Herrera, 2004). In the light of these three

TABLE 19.1

Overview of the Public Education Systems of Middle East Countries and Their Approach to Preparing and Developing School Leaders

Key: ICT = Information and communication technology, MOE = Ministry of Education, Training = pre-service preparation, PG HE = postgraduate higher education, PD = in-service professional development

Country	History	Nature of Schools Today	Adult Literacy	Key Educational Policies	Preparation and Development of School Leaders
Bahrain	Traditional Kuttab schools with modernization starting after WW1[1]	Traditional and modern schools, standardized public curricula[2] and examinations for promotion.[3]	75% in 1985 80% by 2000 86% by 2002–2004[4]	Membership of the global information economy	Computer training, ICT education, leadership skills training
Egypt	Muslim and Christian clergy provided religious, literacy and arithmetic skills until secularization. Recent reforms downscaling the role of government.[5]	Standardized public curricula[6] and examinations for promotion[7] administered by the MOE.[8] The President's Musa Vision[9] stresses democratic and economic reforms, greater Egyptian expertise, and skilled labor for the private sector.[10]	43% by 1985 53% by 1997 57% by 2002 71% by 2002–2004[11]	MOE vision[12] requires pioneer leaders for a decentralized system to prepare citizens for a knowledge society in a new social contract based on democracy, justice and sustainability.	Skills training, PG HE and PD to develop effective schools, distinguished teachers, high quality and relevant curricula, educational technology, community participation, and educational administration.
Iran	Modern schools developing first in cities and then in rural areas. Steady improvement of social and economic infrastructure over the past two decades.	Blend of traditional and modern schools in a large education system.[13] Curricula reformed several times in the last two decades to respond to changes in society, the economy and in youth.	63% in 1990 77% in 2002–2004[14]	MOE[15] modernizing schools through ICT and through in-service training for teachers in cooperative and student-based learning methods.	Training, PG HE and PD to decentralize management, improve community participation, devolve authority to provinces and schools, localize curricula.
Iraq	Modernization from WW1. By the late 1980s, the centralized K-12 education system[16] was serving about six million students with limited accountability.	School attendance decreased after the invasion of Kuwait.[17] UN-imposed sanctions cut resources. 80% of Iraq's 15,000 schools required rehabilitation, toilets, libraries and laboratories by 2004s.[18]	55% for males and 23% for females in the 1980s 36% overall by 1990 71% by 2002–2004[19]	Recent policy[20] to remove Baathists, increase salaries, retrain teachers, rehabilitate schools, create Iraqi-led reform of curriculum.	Training, PG HE and PD intended to achieve equity in access; quality and relevance; national unity; planning, evaluation, decentralization and cut corruption.[21]

Israel	Comprehensive pre-primary,[22] primary and middle,[23] and secondary school[24] systems, with post-secondary education integrated with military service. Israel cut spending from 2004 due to recession and security.[25]	School self-management started 1992, despite opposition, accelerated from 2004 with strong centralization and regionalization; to encourage Ultra-Orthodox and Arab sectors to improve the effectiveness of their schools and reduce inequalities.[26]	91% 1990 97% by 2002-2004.[27]	Include universal values; the values of Israel's society and heritage; remembrance of the Holocaust and heroism; develop child's personality, abilities and creativity; various disciplines; physical activity; and culture and recreation.[28]	Training, PG HE and PD available to prepare and develop principals to self-manage school development in a pluralist society in a contested context.
Jordan	Transjordan created in 1921 had about 25 religious schools providing Arabic literacy and Islamic studies. By 1997 Jordan had 4,442 schools, with more than 63,000 teachers and an enrolment of 1.3 million students.	Free and compulsory for all children aged 6-15.[29] High participation in post-compulsory education. Nearly one-third of the total population of 4.2 million engaged in forms of education.[30]	80% for males and 50% for females by 1979 90% and 79% by 1994 95% and 84% by 2002–2004[31]	MOE developing the human capital of its citizens[32] with access to basic education to meet national development plans.[33]	Training, PG HE and PD to create human resources that remain competitive, by providing life-long learning to the work force so it can contribute to sustainable economic development."[34]
Kuwait	Madrasahs with little change after the discovery of oil in 1939,[35] The August 1990 invasion by Iraq and 7-month occupation destroyed many schools and a belief in Arabic and Islamic solidarity.[36]	Traditional schools being reconstructed with strong private sector.[37] The role of public school principals is of minor significance, unrelated to teaching, plagued by poor staff morale and staff and resource shortages, and has a conservative focus on routine.[38]	55% by 1975 79% by 1995 93% by 2002-2004[39]	MOE[40] regulates all schools and seeks to modernize teaching, maximize access by all citizens[41] and prepare students for the world's knowledge economy.[42]	Training and PD are focusing on school reconstruction, student counseling, planning, curriculum development, evaluation and supervision..[43]
Lebanon	The 'classroom of the Middle East' until civil war started in the 1970's with a gradual deterioration in educational infrastructure since.[44] French Baccalaureate system with French, Arabic and English.	Primary schools stress basic literacy and numeracy. Secondary schools prepare students for university studies, technical or vocational training, or the workforce.[45] Teachers licensed by the MOE.	76% in 1985 84% in 2000[46] No figures since due to civil war.	Prepare students for a global knowledge society, promote national unity through a mandatory public school curriculum.[47]	Training, PG HE and PD in school management and leadership. Feedback from unscheduled, irregular and rigorous inspections by Ministry officials.[48]

(continued)

TABLE 19.1
Continued

Country	History	Nature of Schools Today	Adult Literacy	Key Educational Policies	Preparation and Development of School Leaders
Oman	Major development of education from 1970 when Sultan Qaboos acceded to the throne.[49] % of GNP spent on education rose from 4.5% in 1998 to 26% by 2006.[50]	School system modeled on the British system[51] with an extensive adult literacy programs.[52]	54% in 1990 81% by 2002–2004[53]	National education plans are to enable modernization, achieve self-satisfaction for citizens, diversify the economy and advance technical development.	Training, PG HE and PD in a school management, evaluation, instructional leadership, etc., with specialist bachelor and masters degrees.[54]
Palestinian Territories	MOE established in 1994 focused on re-building schools, setting standards, curriculum development, teacher training, and establishing the Ministry. The Israeli invasions (triggering the1987–1992 intifada[55] and the Al Aqsa intifada[56]) disrupted education.[57]	70% of 2,267 schools in 2005 were being operated by the MOE, 24% by the United Nations Relief and Works Agency for Palestine Refugees in the Near East, and 6% private.[58] One third of the 3.15m population are students at all levels of education. Shortages of teachers and poor facilities persist.	92% in 2002–2004[59]	Reconstruction remains the primary aim. The MOE has trialed the devolution[60] of administrative, financial and technical authority and monitoring to District level.	Very little pre- or in-service training for school leaders. Proposed focus on school-based management, community capacity building, local governance, plus external support and supervision.[61]
Qatar	Home tuition and religious instruction in mosques until the discovery of oil in the 1960s.[62] Rapid modernization in recent years through the encouragement of private education at all levels.	Primary schooling in basic literacy and numeracy. Secondary schooling for university, technical or vocational training. Male secondary students may specialize in religious, commercial or technical studies. Females may choose primary teacher training.	74% in 1985 77% by 2000 89% by 2002–2004[63]	The Government of Qatar expects education to enable all citizens and the country to be successful in the global knowledge economy.	The MOE encourages school leaders to attend the training courses they provide and to advance their qualifications given the influx of Western higher education institutions.
Saudi Arabia	Traditional religious instruction. No access for nomads until oil revenues were used to create modern infrastructure, including primary schools.	Education is free, not compulsory and widely available throughout the country. Most Saudi children attend public schools with early curriculum weighted in religious instruction.	15% for adult men and 2% for adult women by 1970 71.5% and 50% by 1995[64] 87% for adult men and 69% for adult women by 2002–2004[65]	Building society, achieving personal ambitions and capacities, scientific research in an Islamic world, school development, special and gifted education.[66]	Training, PG HE and PD approved by the MOE and related to salary increases, promotions and appointments, specializations and the needs of schools and the system.[67]

Sudan	Traditional schools in the northern and rural areas,[68] with British schools in cities.[69] Civil war from 1983 destroyed many schools in the South. The 1969 and 1991[70] Governments intensified the Islamization of education.	Traditional Islamic education. Little schooling for girls or rural education.[71] Many scholars and aid agencies have left,[72] access by nomads has worsened,[73] with many more refugees now seeking basic education.[74]	22.9% in 1956 30% in 1990 61% by 2002–2004[75]	The MOE expects the education system to serve national social and economic development objectives according to a traditional Islamic ideology.	Training and PD is intended to implement the state's Islamic ideology.
Syria	Modernization through national education system that responded to political changes with reforms to curricula and improved access.[76]	Baath Party promoted education as a foundation of economic development. English and French are compulsory in elementary schools. Computer literacy is mandatory in high schools.	58% in 1981 80% by 2002–2004[77]	The main objectives of MOE policy are to raise literacy, meet the country's manpower needs, and modernize the economy.[78]	Training, PG HE and PD focus on school management, educational leadership, literacy and ICT.
United Arab Emirates	Rapid development since UAE established in 1971. Deficits found in 2005; obsolete curricula, poorly maintained school buildings and low salaries.[79]	One third of national students attend private schools.[80] AED 46bn over 10 years[81] to achieve international standards,[82] salaries and conditions,[83] and modernize Islamic curricula.[84]	53.5% in 1989 79% by 2000 86% by 2002–2004[85]	Diversified economy, success in the ICT revolution, an open Arabic and Islamic knowledge society.[86]	Training, PG HE and PD in English and computing, instructional leadership, ISLLC licensed,[87] and US benchmarked degrees.[88]
Yemen	Arabic literacy and Islamic studies in South Yemen until secularization after WW2. North Yemen modernized schooling after the 1962 revolution. Unification in 1990 after oil found and Soviet support to South Yemen cut.[89]	Economic reforms from 1995 included school modernization, adult literacy and life-long learning. Many families continue to send their children overseas for their university education.[90] Internal security remains a challenge for the Yemeni Government.[91]	66% in the urban centers and near 20% in rural areas, with a large disparity between the rates for males and females, although recent data are not available.[92]	Eradicate illiteracy, promote vocational and technical education.[93] Priorities include school licensing, teaching materials, syllabi, books, home-school relationships, access for girls, guidance, and PD for teachers	Training and PD is targeting administrative skills for school and system leaders, including planning, evaluation, community engagement, instructional leadership and supervision.

(continued)

TABLE 19.1
Continued

1 See http://www.education.gov.bh/english/index/index.aspx

2 See http://univ.cc/search.php?dom=bh&key=&start=1

3 http://www.me-schools.com/countries/bahrein.htm

4 http://www.uis.unesco.org/profiles/EN/EDU/countryProfile_en.aspx?code=480

5 General Authority for Educational Buildings, Egypt (2006). "Schools pilot launched," Middle East Economic Digest, 50(50), p. 23.

6 See http://univ.cc/search.php?dom=bh&key=&start=1

7 http://www.me-schools.com/countries/bahrein.htm

8 http:// www.emoe.org/english.htm

9 http://translate.google.com/translate?hl=en&sl=ar&u=http://www.emoe.org/&sa=X&oi=translate&resnum=1&ct=result&prev=/search%3Fq%3DMinistry%2Bof%2BEducation%2BEgypt%26hl%3Den%26lr%3D

10 http://www.me-schools.com/countries/egypt.htm

11 http://www.uis.unesco.org/profiles/EN/EDU/countryProfile_en.aspx?code=2200

12 Loc cit.

13 http://www.iranchamber.com/education/articles/educational_system.php

14 http://www.uis.unesco.org/profiles/EN/EDU/countryProfile_en.aspx?code=3640

15 http://213.176.19.4/medu/index.aspx

16 http://www.me-schools.com/countries/iraq.htm

17 http://www2.unesco.org/wef/countryreports/iraq/rapport_1.html

18 Iraqi Ministry of Education (2004). School Survey 2003-2004 in Iraq, Baghdad: MOE and UNICEF.

19 http://www.uis.unesco.org/profiles/EN/EDU/countryProfile_en.aspx?code=3680

20 http://www.cpa-iraq.org/pressreleases/20040403_ed_PR.html

21 http://www.cpa-iraq.org/ES/ed.html

22 http://cms.education.gov.il/EducationCMS/Units/Owl/English/Organization/pre-primary/

23 http://cms.education.gov.il/EducationCMS/Units/Owl/English/Organization/Primary/ORGANIZING+THE+SCHOOL+SCHEDULE.htm

24 http://cms.education.gov.il/EducationCMS/Units/Owl/English/Organization/Secondary/

25 http://cms.education.gov.il/NR/rdonlyres/0D4A1917-8256-42D4-A55A-AFAD4D2A3A3B/7138/DirectorGenerals.pdf

26 Volansky, A. (2006). "Education leadership in pluralistic societies: The case of Israel," International Studies in Educational Administration, 34(1), 106-117.

27 http://www.uis.unesco.org/profiles/EN/EDU/countryProfile_en.aspx?code=3760

28 http://cms.education.gov.il/EducationCMS/Units/Owl/English/Legislation/Principal/STATE+EDUCATION+LAW.htm

29 http://www.me-schools.com/countries/jordan.htm

30 http://www.jordanembassyus.org/new/jib/factsheets/education.shtml

31 http://www.uis.unesco.org/profiles/EN/EDU/countryProfile_en.aspx?code=4000

32 http://www.moe.gov.jo

33 http://www.kinghussein.gov.jo/resources3.html

34 http://translate.google.com/translate?hl=en&sl=ar&u=http://www.moe.gov.jo/&sa=X&oi=translate&resnum=3&ct=result&prev=/search%3Fq%3Deducation%2Bin%2Bjordan%26hl%3Den%26lr%3D

35 http://www.kuwait-info.com/sidepages/edu_over.asp

36 Al-Jaber, Z. (1996). School management in Kuwait after the Iraqi aggression: Problems for principals', Educational Management and Administration, 24(4), 411-24.

37 http://www.me-schools.com/countries/kuwait.htm

(continued)

38 Al-Jaber, loc cit.

39 http://www.uis.unesco.org/profiles/EN/EDU/countryProfile_en.aspx?code=4140

40 http://www.moe.edu.kw

41 http://www.kuwait-info.com/sidepages/edu_minedu.asp

42 See http://translate.google.com/translate?hl=en&sl=ar&u=http://www.moe.edu.kw/&sa=X&oi=translate&resnum=3&ct=result&prev=/search%3Fq%3DKUWAIT%2BEDUCATION%2BMINISTRY%26hl%3Den%26lr%3D

43 Al-Jaber, Z. (1996). The leadership requirements of secondary school principals in Kuwait: A post-invasion analysis, *Journal of Educational Administration, 34*(4), 24–38.

44 http://www.uis.unesco.org/profiles/EN/EDU/countryProfile_en.aspx?code=4220

45 See http://csrd.lau.edu.lb/Publications/StudentReports/Education%20in%20Lebanon.htm

46 http://www.me-schools.com/countries/lebanon.htm

47 http://www.lebweb.com/site/lebanon-schoolnet-edu-lb-35030

48 Al-Morad, T. (2006). Personal communication, 1 November.

49 http://www.me-schools.com/countries/oman.htm

50 http://www.uis.unesco.org/profiles/EN/EDU/countryProfile_en.aspx?code=5800

51 http://www.moe.gov.om/moe_2006/en/index.php

52 http://www.moe.gov.om/moe_2006/en/viewpage.php?pg=innerpages/basiceducation.htm&show=1

53 http://www.uis.unesco.org/profiles/EN/EDU/countryProfile_en.aspx?code=5800

54 Ahmed Bin Khamis Al Jamri, (2006). Personal communication. Consultant, Embassy of the Sultanate of Oman to the United Arab Emirates, Abu Dhabi, 25 December.

55 See http://www.unesco.org/education/news_en/131101_palestine.shtml

56 See http://www.forcedmigration.org/psychosocial/inventory/pwg007/pwg007-sect1-2.htm

57 See http://www.grassrootsonline.org/Palestine%20Now/pal_0923/education.html

58 See http://www.mohe.gov.ps/

59 http://www.uis.unesco.org/profiles/EN/EDU/countryProfile_en.aspx?code=5880

60 http://siteresources.worldbank.org/INTWESTBANKGAZA/Resources/EducationSectorAnalysisSept06.pdf

61 Ibid, pp. 31-6, 36.

62 http://www.me-schools.com/countries/qatar.htm

63 http://www.uis.unesco.org/profiles/EN/EDU/countryProfile_en.aspx?code=6340

64 http://www.me-schools.com/countries/ksa.htm

65 http://www.uis.unesco.org/profiles/EN/EDU/countryProfile_en.aspx?code=6820

66 http://www.moe.gov.sa/openshare/EnglishCon/About-Saud/Education.htm_cvt.htm

67 HE Abdullah Bin Moamar (2007). Personal communication. Ambassador of the Royal Embassy of Saudi Arabia to the United Arab Emirates, Abu Dhabi, 30 January.

68 http://www.sudan-embassy.co.uk/infobook/educate.php

69 http://www.sudanupdate.org/REPORTS/education/ED-ART.HTM

70 http://www.sudanupdate.org/REPORTS/education/ED-ART.HTM

71 http://countrystudies.us/sudan/51.htm

72 http://allafrica.com/stories/200611100021.html

73 http://www.oxfam.org.uk/what_we_do/issues/gender/links/1003sudan.htm

74 http://portal.unesco.org/education/en/ev.php-URL_ID=39631&URL_DO=DO_TOPIC&URL_SECTION=201.html

75 http://www.uis.unesco.org/profiles/EN/EDU/countryProfile_en.aspx?code=7360

76 http://www.me-schools.com/countries/syria.htm

TABLE 19.1
Continued

[77] http://www.uis.unesco.org/profiles/EN/EDU/countryProfile_en.aspx?code=7600

[78] http://www.syrianeducation.org.sy/

[79] Problems Face Education: Unsuitability of Curricula, Collapsing School Buildings, and Low Salaries, Al Ittihad, (translated from Arabic), 19 November 2005, pp. 8-9.

[80] http://www.me-schools.com/countries/uae.htm

[81] 46 billion dirhams will be spent developing the education system in the next ten years, Al Ittihad, (translated from Arabic), 20 November 2005, p. 8.

[82] Spending on education is 60% less than international standards, Al Ittihad, (translated from Arabic), 21 November 2005, p. 9.

[83] New salary scales and long-term contract system, Al Ittihad, (translated from Arabic), 22 November 2005, p. 9.

[84] The full development and modernization of Islamic curricula, Al Ittihad, (translated from Arabic), 23 November 2005, p. 9.

[85] http://www.uis.unesco.org/profiles/EN/EDU/countryProfile_en.aspx?code=8120

[86] http://www.education.gov.ae

[87] Council of Chief School State Officers (1996). Interstate School Leaders Licensure Consortium, Washington, DC. pp. 21.

[88] Macpherson, R.J.S., Kackelhoffer, P. and El Nemr, N. (2007). "The Radical Modernization of School and Education System Leadership in the United Arab Emirates: Towards Indigenized and Educative Leadership," International Studies in Educational Administration, 35(1), 60-77.

[89] http://www.britannica.com/eb/article-45275/Yemen

[90] http://www.britannica.com/eb/article-45267/Yemen

[91] http://www.britannica.com/eb/article-45275/Yemen, p.23

[92] http://www.uis.unesco.org/profiles/EN/EDU/countryProfile_en.aspx?code=8850

[93] http://www2.unesco.org/wef/countryreports/yemen/rapport_1.html

themes, the next and final major section will begin by reviewing Islamic leadership concepts. It will then suggest, to system and school leaders and professors in the Middle East, that they mediate any use of Western preparatory and developmental programs with indigenous perspectives and evidence-based practice gathered by research.

LEARNING ALONE, FROM OTHERS, OR THROUGH SCIENCE?

A General Perspective of Islamic Leadership

The key issue of this section is how a Middle Eastern country might manage knowledge production and applications regarding effective school leadership. To this end, we begin with a general concept of leadership in Islamic societies that is neither exclusively traditional nor modern. Instead, our portrayal encompasses the essential features that have made, and still make, individuals or groups of people characteristically Islamic. This element of our argument is important for two reasons.

First, until Thom Greenfield's intervention in the West, the study of the development of educational leadership placed far more emphasis on the structures and functions of institutions than on the role of leaders' characters (Greenfield & Ribbins, 1993). We will show that this is an all-important issue in Islamic societies. We will therefore present a general account of leadership in the Islamic World to clarify the cosmology, values and culture that supports an Islamic idealization of a leader's character and leadership services. A similar approach was taken by Schraw and Olafson (2002), who analyzed the dynamics between teachers and practices and the epistemological influences that helped form the beliefs pertaining to knowledge held by teachers. Consequently, they argue, classroom practices were significantly affected by cultural influences and school criteria.

Second, as noted above, the Middle East is actually made up of numerous ethnic and religious groups, many loosely coupled as an Islamic community. A comprehensive model of leadership in the Middle East must eventually recognize the existence of alternative examples of leadership in specific localities, and spell out the consequences regarding our general notion of Islamic leadership. Indigenized variations to a general model are therefore inevitable, and we argue, to be welcomed locally out of respect for the local patchwork of cultures, and then tested. However, to include the different perspectives and nuances existing amongst the variety of minority groups in the region at the outset is well beyond the scope of this paper. Hence, although our approach can not be comprehensive, it is offered as a beginning because of the pervasiveness of Islamic concepts throughout most Middle Eastern institutions and peoples.

We begin by exploring the dynamic relationship between leadership, "followership" and the Islamic environment in which they occur, as portrayed by modern Middle-Eastern empirical research. We then look behind this portrayal to the Islamic cosmology that gives leadership and followership their meanings and uncover the epistemology used to test knowledge claims about educational leadership. This method of evaluating the method used to justify knowledge claims is normally not a feature of Middle-Eastern research nor of evaluating Western constructivist approaches to education (Phillips, 1997). We begin with systematic studies.

Research Findings

Tamadonfar (1989) found that a pragmatic leadership style was a far more accurate generalization of effective Islamic leadership, than the sometimes more salient examples of fundamentalism or sectarianism seen in Islamic polities. Leaders in Islamic settings were found to possess a particular character, and exhibit values, knowledge, skills and dispositions; that together facilitate their rise into leadership roles (Beekun & Badawi, 1999). Related evidence showed that such leaders simultaneously develop, and become dependent on, the allegiance of followers (Tamadonfar, 1989, pp. 48–53). The developmental dynamic between character formation and the growth of allegiance requires a particular socio-economic and organizational structure and a cultural milieu, if character, allegiance and cultural context are to become fully integrated and evident as significant positional authority (Beekun & Badawi, 1999; Tamadonfar, 1989). Regarding character, Beekun and Badawi found that an Islamic leader's moral character, personality, motives, and goals correlate highly with perceptions of their competency. It was shown to be imperative that a leader exhibit honesty, competence, prudence, inspirational appeal, strength of character, patience, humility, magnanimity, self-understanding, consultative skill, an egalitarian outlook, modesty, willingness to follow as well as lead, and a keen sense of responsibility (Beekun & Badawi, 1999).

The allegiance of followers, according to Beekun and Badawi's research, is a result of *constantly becoming* a leader in an Islamic institution or community by creating and recreating networks of followers that are based on reciprocal obligations. Obedience is required of followers in an Islamic environment if and when the leader has the character and ability to consolidate networks based on reciprocity. The ongoing enactment of leadership and followership is therefore based on interaction; blind subservience is considered inappropriate and constructive and confidential criticism is expected, although whatever their views, followers must then behave in a way that sustains the unity of the organization or community. Public dissent by a follower is unacceptable. Conversely, a key determinant of a leader's success is the capacity to understand and accommodate the diversity of followers' characters when recreating networks. Beekun and Badawi also found that the environment encompassing a leader and followers in an Islamic culture sometimes alters the perception of a leader and causes the person to adjust their leadership style and technique, but not strategy. Typical examples of modifications of style and technique occurs when the organizational climate is made difficult by the competency of some members, the complexity of the task being addressed, the stage of development of a workgroup, the policy orientation of the organization or institution, and the maturity level of different members. Tamadonfar (1989) and Beekun and Badawi (1999) provide compelling evidence that the most effective style of leadership in Islamic cultural settings is primarily pragmatic in nature, rather than ideological or sectarian, and achieved through networks of followers that are sustained by interaction and reciprocity.

Interpretation

Interestingly, Tamadonfar (1989) uses two Western frameworks to advance interpretation of effective leadership in Islamic societies; elite theory and a theory of charismatic authority. First, he argues, Islamic societies can be interpreted as fundamentally elitist. The term "elite" has a particular meaning in this context that differs from the Western understanding of an elite society, which holds that an elite is established according to a social, economic or ethnic hierarchy. In Islamic societies, positions of privilege should, ideally, be granted to those who achieve and sustain moral excellence and are steadfast in the locally prevalent Islamic ideology. As a result, "the Prophet, the caliphs or imams and their companions; and currently the leader (the imam or *vali-i faqih*) and the clerical establishment — are primarily distinguished from non-elites by their knowledge of Islam, their commitment to the Islamic principles and possession of superior moral values" (Tamadonfar, 1989). Again, reciprocity is essential for this arrangement to function. The elite — leader or leaders — are obliged to provide and sustain social cohesion and moral standards. Reciprocity in process and outcomes is therefore one key basis of legitimacy in Islamic polities, and defines what governs who rules, how they rule and what their rule entails for leaders and followers. The Arabic term for this capacity to influence processes and outcomes informally, behind the scenes, on a reciprocal basis, is *wasta*.

In the public domain, however, Tamadonfar (1989) argues, charisma plays a central role in an Islamic approach to leadership and followership. His evidence indicates that the charisma of leaders in Islamic cultures tends to shade into perceptions of their legitimacy. There can be such a close relationship between moral virtue, religious piety and charisma that they can become synonyms. It is not uncommon for individuals who are in positions of authority to depend on perceptions of their characters to distinguish themselves from the rest of their communities. The ability to integrate personal charm with virtue, and thus give expression to God's divine order, reinforces the longevity of leadership and ensures the devotion of followers. The next section shows that this combination of moral elitism, reciprocity and charisma traces directly from a classical theory of Islamic cosmology and is the basis of determining the legitimacy of leadership.

Islamic Cosmology

Space precludes an overview of Islamic philosophy, other than to note that following the life of Muhammed (570–632), the profession of faith was confronted by Iraqi gnosticism, Christian Hellenism, Persian dualism and Greek syllogistic logic. This triggered a period of vigorous philosophical activity involving such as Al-Kindi (died after 866), Al-Farabi (870–950), Al-Ash'ari, (873/4–935/6), Ibn Sina or Avicenna (980–1037), Al-Ghazali (1058–1111) and Ibn Rushd or Averoes (1126–1198). This vigor was then followed by about 500 years of "ever increasing rigidity of Islamic theology and law, epitomized … in the legal phrase, 'the closing of the door of *ifthād* (independent reasoning)' (Flew, 1979, p. 182). Hence, from this extraordinary group of philosophers, and their works, we selected the influential critique of leadership developed by the 10th century Islamic philosopher and scientist, Abu Nasr Al-Farabi, whose fame spread to the medieval West where he was known as Abunaser or Alfarabius.

According to Al-Farabi, the cosmos is ordered by a hierarchy. First in rank is God, understood in philosophical terms as the First Principle or Cause. Each subsequent rank is regarded as another "emanation" from God. In the second emanation are abstract and pure concepts. These immaterial existents, also referred to as the Active Intellect, are closer than any other emanations to the First Principle or Cause of the Universe. Under them, in the third emanation, are the heavenly bodies (stars, planets, etc.), and finally, in the forth, are the material bodies. All of the entities in each emanation conform to the nature and law of the First Principle, Al-Farabi argued, and attempt to follow it, take it as their guide and seek to imitate it. However, the entities in each level of emanation are only capable of copying the First Principle according to their capacity, and capacity to copy is limited by the position that the entity holds in the cosmic hierarchy. Only the entities of the second emanation can directly imitate the entity of the first, God. Otherwise, an entity can only seek to copy an entity of inferior rank and quality. Hence, for Al-Farabi, God's Universe is made up of multiple imitations of the First Principle, and is segregated into different levels of excellence, which range from superior to inferior replicas; with some entities being closer to God while others are far more removed.

Following the Platonic tradition, Al-Farabi argued that the ideal leader is a *philosopher ruler* of pragmatic bent. In his *Al-Madinah al-Fadilah,* he actually referred to this ruler as a philosopher-king-prophet, implying that the ruler receives direct revelation or knowledge from the First Principle (Al-Farabi, Abu-Nasr Muhammad, trans. R. Walzer, 1985). On pragmatic matters, for example, for a leader to cause something to exist or occur, such as an initiative, a group or an institution, the leader must know the essence of the purposes of the project, prior to attempting to make it a reality. Al-Farabi therefore advised that a leader must be able to understand the *quality* of practical knowledge, the *nature* of available resources, and to use *deductive reasoning* in order to link the essential nature of a planned entity and project to the unifying abstract concepts underlying it (Lameer, 1994). Essential to this leadership by a philosopher ruler, Al-Farabi argued, were twelve personal attributes; physically impressive, action oriented and able to accomplish objectives, able to understand and accommodate other's expectations and intentions, able to remember facts learned and things seen and heard with a lively intelligence, able to speak clearly, loves learning and knowledge, truthful and dispels untruths, an aversion to base and worldly pleasures, self-respect directed towards improving the spirit and personal honor and never towards the acquisition of material goods, just and supportive of those who believe in justice, supportive of all that is beautiful and noble, and strong willed and brave.

Applications

Given the rarity of such philosopher-rulers, Al-Farabi developed a pragmatic alternative. The First Principle or Cause remained equivalent to God. The ideal ruler was recast as a plausible archetype; a supreme philosopher king who seeks to replicate God's active intellect by searching for the source or essence of things. The second tier of archetypes were defined as "rulers of excellence" to different degrees, in specific circumstances, each possessing the information and intellectual capacity needed for practical reasoning, and thus able to elaborate the foundations set by the philosopher ruler, yet without necessarily contributing new insights (Mahdi, 2001). The third tier of archetypes did not need to be philosophers, according to Al-Farabi, since they were not required to reason but to apply the codified wisdom of precedents, and thus were able to function in the absence of the two higher ruling archetypes (Galston, 1990).

Al-Farabi also approved two substitutes; dual leadership to combine talents, and a form of oligarchy where members had, together, acquired the necessary competencies of a philosopher ruler and rulers of excellence to be able to rule in harmony. These two substitutes were consistent with his metaphysical cosmology wherein degrees of leadership emanate from the concept of the ideal ruler and are ranked in a hierarchy in which the bottom entity or ruler imitates or refers to the position above themselves for guidance and insight. In effect, Al-Farabi's cosmology and hierarchy of ruling archetypes became operational when they became a "just state" with sociopolitical structures that enveloped all rulers, citizens and peasants. It is notable that Al-Farabi stressed that the ranks were egalitarian, due to their interdependence, and so tried to prevent a society declining into an exploitative or despotic state. He disliked the idea of an ethnically or economically based stratification or segregation in a society.

Finally, Al-Farabi spoke indirectly to the issue of preparing and developing school leaders. The process of emanations from the First Principle down through rulers of excellence and then to non-philosophical operational managers requires that aspirants search for understandings, skills and dispositions by seeking guidance from, studying and imitating their leaders (Davidson, 1992). This means aspirants being modest in the knowledge that their best efforts will only ever achieve a third order and approximate replica of their philosopher-ruler-prophet's leadership service, yet being rewarded in knowing that this is part of God's divine process of forming an excellent community, organization or institution fashioned on First Principles.

We must stress at this point that our intention was not to represent a general Islamic view of leadership as irrational, feudal or driven by religious dogma but as rational within the terms of its own cosmology, and as readily adaptable to Western structures. Clearly, Al-Farabi's theory of leadership appropriates neo-Platonic and Aristotelian ideas to construct an Islamic cosmology and metaphysical theory based on logical principles. It is, we again stress, a rational system wherein religious law must be interpreted using a logical system of thought. Our proposal for a strategic approach to leadership training later in the text is not at odds with incorporating Al-Farabi's leadership quality traits, while noting that trait theory has been found by Western scholarship to suffer from some serious limitations. We now turn to the issue of selecting a national school leadership development strategy.

Alternative School Leadership Development Strategies

The preliminary evidence in the second major section above suggests that most Middle Eastern countries no longer follow a theocratic approach to school leadership preparation and development, the notable exceptions being the Sudan and rural parts of the Yemen. Instead, most countries are adopting and adapting knowledge, skills and dispositions regarding school leadership from North America and Europe through local universities and branches of Western universities where learning is often offered by Western-educated personnel. This process constitutes gradual to accelerated forms of Westernization (Herrera, 2004). As there is felt need and means to further develop these provisions, the increasing secular Governments of the Middle East have a number of strategies to choose from.

The first strategy is where a government takes control of the "professionalization" of school leadership, as in the UK. The second strategy is where the profession of Educational Administration itself takes control of the licensure of school leaders, as in the United States. A third potential strategy is to have the "great and good blend the best" from diverse European and other approaches. A fourth potential strategy is to "grow your own" theory of best practice using a bottom up and largely qualitative research processes, as proposed by historically critical researchers. Once these four approaches have been described, we highlight two issues that all strategies will continue to encounter in the Middle East. First is the privileged role accorded in an Islamic epistemology to revelation whereby the making of meaning and the gaining of wisdom is held to indicate the movement of the soul towards God's truth. Second is that Westernization will inevitably give carriage to the values of the Western Enlightenment, values that will challenge the cosmology and political cultures of Islamic societies, just as they have and continue to do so in Western societies that guarantee public and Greek-style dialectical critique. We note in passing that this Greek style of critique is very close to what Islamic philosophers following Al-Farabi's tradition have used over centuries and use today (Aziz, 1986; Butterworth, 2001).

The Government-sponsored professionalization of school leadership is a strategy most highly developed in England where the Government established a National College for School Leadership (NCSL). The aim of the NCSL is to ensure that school leaders "manage their own schools and work collaboratively with others" (NCSL, 2007a) at each of five different stages in their career; emergent aspirant, leaders not seeking headships, entry to headship, advanced leadership, and consultant leadership. The milestones within the Leadership Development Framework comprise the now mandatory qualification for headship (National Professional Qualification Headship, NPQH), prior to local selection by school governors, as well as continuing access to three other optional national programs (NCSL, 2007b). A key feature of the NPQH is that it requires participants to demonstrate leadership skills or competencies in a number of areas of activity. This is appropriately modest since a skills training program can not be expected to help people learn how to think on their feet and to make sound judgments; the gaining of wisdom tends to come with experience and to be enabled by higher education designed to advance analytical, strategic, critical and epistemological capacities. A review of the approach concluded that "Questions remain how far governmentally inspired leadership programs have moved beyond the more reductivist elements of a competence paradigm towards educational programs that develop the kind of reflective knowing and higher order cognitive abilities that will undoubtedly be required by leaders in the increasingly complex world of educational leadership in the 21st century" (Brundrett, Fitzgerald & Sommefeldt, 2006).

An alternative to a professionalization strategy controlled by a government is a licensing strategy controlled by the profession. This is the approach adopted by most states in the United States. By 2005, 46 states had adopted the Interstate School Leaders Licensure Consortium (ISLLC) leadership standards for administrator certification and preparation programs (Sanders & Simpson, 2005). The ISLLC standards provide a common language of leadership expectations, despite some differences in state policies, and constitute a national Gold Standard on competencies that are claimed to be "grounded in the knowledge and understanding of teaching and learning" (Interstate School Leaders Licensure Consortium, 2007). The Consortium was actually created by the National Policy Board for Educational Administration (NPBEA), a national professional association of administrators in education. The standards were written by representatives from states and professional associations during 1994–95 and first published in 1996. In more recent times the states have asked for the standards to be revised to reflect "a decade of policy experience and significant political and social changes" (Council of Chief School State Officers, 1996). A feature of the ISLLC Standards is that they require those seeking licensure to demonstrate leadership skills or competencies in six areas not dissimilar to those require by the English NPQH. Notably, they do not expect a demonstration of wisdom or the higher order scientific and critical capacities offered by masters and doctoral programs. If adopted uncritically, however, they could promote an offensively nationalist, pluralist, secular and culturally transformative view of schooling, over anticipating national reforms in Middle Eastern settings, and be an ineffective preparation for the leadership of Islamic or private schools, depending on local policies and priorities. In countries with relatively few checks and balances regarding good government, a solely ISLLC-based approach could train a professional class of leaders in education in managerial technique without giving them the socially-critical and epistemologically-critical capacities needed to advance the development of a theory of practice suitable for a knowledge society.

A third potential strategy is to learn from diversity elsewhere by commissioning a group of the great and good to blend the best. European countries have taken many different approaches to the preparation and development of school leaders, to the point where their national systems are, at the very least as diverse as those described above in the Middle East. This reminds us of Europe's similarly complex and appallingly conflicted social and political history. Four particularly insightful case studies of reforms in the national education systems of Cyprus, England, Greece and Sweden illustrate the point (Pashiardis, Thody, Papanaoum & Johansson, 2003). Given the greater differences than similarities demonstrated between these four European cases, relatively few generalizations can be derived concerning the wisest approach to developing a national system of leadership preparation and development, other than identifying a large number of variables that may need to be taken into account. On the other hand, the US, English and Swedish experiences suggest distinct advantages over the current situation in Greece, Cyprus and in many of the nations of the Middle East, where most school leaders are selected on the basis of their performance in the classroom, the length of their service and standing in the school community, and then be expected to learn on the job through interaction with other school and system leaders, and by being encouraged to advance their understandings through higher education. The result in such circumstances inevitably means that educational leadership, as a body of knowledge, skills and attitudes, evolves as a rich, idiosyncratic, vicarious and scientifically untested form of folk art. Our point here is that having the great and good blend of the best in each national system design preparatory and development programs could run the danger of compounding well-intentioned ignorance, unless the knowledge production process is mediated by science, in the broad sense, which implies the need for an epistemologically-critical basis.

This brings us to the advice of social scientists and the fourth strategic option. Ribbins, a leading British researcher long concerned with the quality of knowledge, skills and attitudes in the field of Educational Administration, has suggested the wider use of historiography (Ribbins, 2006). This method entails describing, understanding and explaining the production of knowledge about educational leadership over time and in a specific national context, in order to improve the quality of knowledge production, and thus the quality of the learning to be offered to neophytes and experienced practitioners. Reflecting on knowledge production in the field in a specific nation, he argues, will mean being intellectually modest and culturally critical about what we know, how we know it, when we know it, who knows it, and why, prior to making strategic decisions about improving the preparation and development of school leaders.

We find this fourth approach more congenial than the other three, although elements may be blended, providing that a number of pre-conditions are satisfied. First, those designing preparatory and developmental learning systems for school leaders will need to be critically aware of the *epistemological relativity* of the intended learning outcomes, the delivery systems, the learning activities, and the scope and sequence of the content of the leadership programs that they are proposing (Schraw & Olafson, 2002). Second, each Middle Eastern nation will have to determine its position regarding the balance of the ideological, vocational and aesthetic purposes of schooling, and determine where they are and where they want to go on a continuum between the reproduction and the transformation of Islamic curriculum. This condition, not incidentally, rules out accepting *a priori* that transformational leadership is the most appropriate model of practice and theory. Ribbin's scintillating review of the scholarship used to create knowledge of transformational leadership, and to secure its dominance in the West, found that knowledge production jumped straight to identifying and measuring four key variables in behaviors and skills: idealized influence; individualized consideration; intellectual stimulation, and inspirational motivation. Missing from these knowledge production process were qualitative knowledge claims derived from stories told by practitioners, presumably essential to establishing relevance and coherence with the realities of experience. Similarly missing, after the achievement of its dominance, was any systematic enquiry into how practitioners have engaged with this model. The model is, ironically, a flight of faith.

Of greatest concern to those of Muslim faith, committed as they are to living by God's rules within the terms of an Islamic cosmology, is that there is no justification of the essential "rightness" of the model and therefore no promise that learning will potentially guarantee that their souls *will* move closer to God's truth (Hodgkinson, 1978). The upshot, as Ribbins (2006) pungently observed, is that "the knowledge claims [about transformational leadership] are limited and disrespectful of other ways of knowing."

This is not an insignificant matter, given the nature of popular Islamic epistemology in some circles, as exemplified by a South Asian Muslim scholar, Al-Attas (with original emphases);

In contrast to the position of modern science and philosophy with regard to the sources and methods of knowledge, we maintain that knowledge comes from God and is acquired through the channels of the sound senses, true report based on authority, sound reason, and intuition … [and] … that just as there are levels of reason and experience, so are there levels of authority and intuition. Apart from the authority of men of science and learning generally, the highest level of authority in our view is the Holy Qur'an and the Tradition including the sacred person of the Holy Prophet. They represent authority not only in the sense that *communicate* the truth, but in the sense that they *constitute* the truth. They represent authority that is established upon the higher levels of intellectual and spiritual cognition and transcendental experience that cannot simply be reduced to the normal level of reason and experience … knowledge consists of units of meaning which are coherently related to other units thereby forming notions, ideas, concepts, conceptions and judgments. Thought (*al-fikir*) is the soul's movement towards meaning, and this needs imagination (*al-khayal*). Intuition, that is, either in the sense of sagacity (*al-hads*), or in the sense of illuminative experience, (*al-wijdan*), is the arrival of the soul at meaning, or the arrival in the soul of meaning, either by acquisition of proof as in the former case, or it comes by itself as in the latter case. (Al-Attas, 1989, pp. 9, 13, 16)

This could be too easily dismissed as a variant of the Ancient Neoplatonism of Plotinus that found its way into medieval European thought via St. Augustine, until displaced by the rise of modern science and the scientific method (Flew, 1979). While this is a technically accurate evaluation, it remains a troubling fact to us that there are about 1.3 billion Muslims in the world, about 20–30 million in Europe and 6–7 million in the United States, that, to varying degrees, may hold to or would intuitively accept this general view of the growth of knowledge. It is also our concern that this popular Muslim world view would bring with it its own approach to historiography. For example, it may seek to describe, understand and explain the production of knowledge over time in terms of the "*recognition and acknowledgement, progressively instilled in man, of the proper place of things in the order of creation, such that it leads to the recognition and acknowledgement of the proper place of God in the order of being and existence*" (Al-Attas, 1991, original emphasis). This takes us back to the critical role of epistemology in knowledge production (Lumby, 2006).

Becoming Epistemologically Critical

Our view is that, apart from Attas' use of spiritual symbolism, his position is at odds with philosophical traditions that require a basis not in faith but in evidence and reason. The position is inconsistent with the position taken by Al-Farabi and at least two other great Islamic philosophers, Avicenna and Averoes, who both required that the rightness of a model be demonstrated using evidence and logic. A faith-driven view of education and leadership that is not open to empirical reality tests or critique is difficult to accept at face value, to reconcile with prior knowledge, or to use in the many real worlds of practice (Kezar, 2000).

One of the promises of becoming epistemologically critical is that it may help a person to better understand the extent to which their webs of belief are likely to be right. This takes us to the role of *adab* in Islamic epistemology; the form of knowledge that preserves man from errors of judgment. *Adab* has been defined as a "recognition and acknowledgement of the reality that knowledge and being are ordered hierarchically according to their various grades and degrees of rank, and one's proper place in relation to that reality and to one's physical, intellectual and spiritual capacities and potentials" (Kezar, 2000, p. 27). *Adab* has long required leaders to ensure that people are accorded their human rights guaranteed under Islam, especially concerning equality, freedom, security, wealth, honor and lineage (Wafi, 1998). Abdek-Hady, a modern Arabic scholar, takes the view that *adab* also requires Islamic leaders to relate the foundations of Islam to contemporary issues, specifically, to the nature being human, the place of women, globalization, terrorism, the environment, and Islamophobia (Abdek-Hady, 2006).

Adab also provides manners and protocols (*adab al-Islam*) for all situations, including an ontology and axiology suitable for effective school leadership. A relatively standard list requires considerable personal discipline; being deliberative with a primary concern for consequences, being kind and gentle to others, being clean and pure in body and mind, being elegant and orderly, being courteous and never impudent, being humble and never arrogant, avoiding harm to self and others, preferring silence to unneeded talk, treating others as you wish to be treated, never expecting of others that you do not expect of yourself, favoring the right hand, achieving self-sufficiency without extravagance, being generous without meanness and avarice, being grateful and patient, being faithful, being moderate in everything, never copying other cultures and religions, avoiding any contradiction with Islamic values, maintaining gender identity, maintaining a disciplined balance in harmony with the community, and remaining flexible and tolerant (Al-Kaysi, 1986). Further, the notion of aspiring to a position of responsibility or seeking a place offering power and influence, are both repugnant to Islam. Given an example relayed by Abu Musa, a Companion of the Prophet, it has been argued that one must be called to an office on the basis of one's known worth, upright character and merit, and in the interim, a person should strive to become what the Qur'an styles as a *Salehin* leader; an upright person who balances service to self-interests with service to the interests of others (Latif, 1961). And how is such knowledge refined?

WHENCE TRUSTWORTHY KNOWLEDGE, SKILLS AND ATTITUDES?

In this necessarily brief concluding section we provide some provisional advice concerning the development of trustworthy knowledge, skills and attitudes as the basis for the preparation and development of school leadership. We offer four recommendations that that might be considered with caution.

First, the diverse pathways taken in pluralistic Western societies, as they move from an idiosyncratic folk art to more standardized practices in school leadership, have all been paved with the best of intentions and with assumptions that are highly specific to context, and reflect idealized notions of appropriate schooling and effective leadership. Despite the values of the Western Enlightenment, the most appropriate balance of ideological, vocational and aesthetic purposes in education remains a contested issue in the West, as it should be, according to those values.

A key implication is that good government at all levels in Islamic society may have to encourage clarifying the rightness of education policy settlements and determining the most appropriate combination of strategies, and to keep facilitating such contestation through increasingly democratic processes. The Western "enlightenment concept of democracy rests on four bases: accountability, representativeness, respect for the rule of law and the capacity; through free speech, for debate, exchange and deliberation" (Hutton, 2007, p. 305). It is important to understand and anticipate the longer-term consequences, since Westernization will inevitably give carriage to the full set of Enlightenment values.

The second caution relates to the urge in the Middle East to modernize and diversify in haste using oil and gas revenues. The sense of urgency is understandable in the light of comparative prosperity, the West's creative race to control carbon emissions and to find alternatives to hydrocarbon energy sources, and the West's dominant capacity to provide the human capital required to build knowledge societies. An uncritical transfer of school leadership competencies from

Western sources may prove very helpful in a technical managerial sense, in the short term. On the other hand, such a transfer may also bring intercultural and ideological challenges to deeply embedded aspects of Islamic cosmology, epistemology and culture. These challenges will signal the need for school and system capacity building in systematic analysis, interactive critique, action research *in situ* and inclusive policy making, in order to achieve sustainable improvements to schools and systems.

This problem solving infrastructure, will, in turn, require a wider context of good government that actively encourages pluralism, international trade, effective public institutions and the sharing of technology, if Europe's example is to serve as a guide:

> These four key elements — the pluralism developed by near-continual war and state competition; profitable long-distance trade and the companies it created; a robust institutional infrastructure; and the universalization of technology — kindled Europe's miracle ... and uniting, underpinning and embodying all four elements was the Enlightenment and the public institutions it underwrote. (Hutton, 2007, p. 305)

The third caution is that the normal patterns of Western knowledge production regarding educational leadership have a limited proven technical capacity to accommodate diversity as a norm in pluralistic societies. Perceptive research in England has shown that its favored methodologies tend to impose cultural homogeneity as an assumption during theory building. One unacceptable consequence noted is that practitioners may be encouraged to manage diversity by side stepping discrimination and exclusion, and focus on differences that are less likely to provoke discrimination (Lumby, 2006). A more strategic alternative would be to help leaders of schools with Muslim students in a Western context learn how to understand and alter the dynamics of creating out-group and in-group identity constructions, "impose inclusion" and deliver on the students" "right to equality as British citizens with multiple identities" (Shah, 2006, p. 230).

The fourth caution is that the Middle East could inherit long-standing problems from the West if it adopts and adapts its dominant methods of creating theories of best practice uncritically. The process of knowledge production in the West concerning school leadership is suffering from retarded development. Research regarding school leadership typically and skillfully uses contextual analysis (to map the policy and values context of practice), ethnographic studies (to map theories-in-use and to propose links between agency and outcomes), and empirical surveys and meta-analyses to develop and arbitrate causal networks (Ribbins & Gronn, 2006).

Our view is that these research outcomes are impressive but do not achieve scientific closure or provide adequate justification. Researchers are yet to use randomized control trials (RCTs) to link leadership actions to learning outcomes with precision. As a co-developer of educative leadership practice, theory and research in Australasia, the lead author submits a plea of *mea culpa*. Our field's sister discipline of nursing has developed equally contextualized, grounded and complex causal stories, but has then used RCTs in recent decades to move forward, both scientifically and as a profession, to more fully developed evidence-based practice and theory. Researchers in Educational Administration in the Middle East may wish to take this short cut to international fame. Alternatively, they may like to note and respond to the absence of political philosophy in the field; practitioners are central to the use of power but we do not question the justifications for current political arrangements.

In sum, the provisional evidence assembled in this chapter suggests that Middle Eastern countries intending to improve the preparation and development of school leaders would be well advised to learn from other countries and intellectual traditions with a great deal of caution. Program designers are advised to mediate the adoption and blending of Western models with the systematic and scientific creation of indigenous and evidence-based practice and theory of educative leadership, and if conditions permit, develop a defensible political philosophy of educative leadership.

NOTES

1. The term 'jihard' traditionally refers to the daily struggle that an Islamic person makes to resist evil temptations.
2. The term itself means a foundational ideology and cosmology, as well as a methodology for militant Islamism.

REFERENCES

Abdek-Hady, A. M. (2006). *Islamic Thought and Culture,* United Arab Emirates: Al-Falah Books.

Ahmed, A. (1998). *Discovering Islam: Making sense of Muslim history and society*, London: Routledge.

Al-Attas, S. M. N. (1989). *Islam and the philosophy of science*, Kuala Lumpur, Malaysaia: International Institute of Islamic Thought and Civilization.

Al-Attas, S. M. N. (1991). *The Concept of Education in Islam*, Kuala Lumpur, Malaysia: International Institute of Islamic Thought and Civilization.

Al-Fahim, M. (1995). *From Rags to Riches: A Story of Abu Dhabi,* London: London Centre of Arab Studies.

Al-Farabi, Abu-Nasr Muhammad, trans. R. Walzer, (1985). *Al-Farabi on the Perfect State, Abu Nasr al-Farabis – Mabiadi ara'ahl al-madina al-fadila*, Oxford: Clarendon.

Al-Jaber, Z. (1996). The Leadership Requirements of Secondary School Principals in Kuwait: A post-invasion analysis, *Journal of Educational Administration, 34*(4), 24–38.

Al-Kaysi, M. I. (1986). *Morals and Manners in Islam: A Guide to Islamic Adab,* Leicester, UK.: The Islamic Foundation.

Aziz, A. A. (1986). *Arabic Thought and Islamic Societies*, Kent: Croom Helm.

Beekun, R. I. and Badawi, J. (1999) *Leadership – an Islamic perspective*, Brentwood, MD: Amana.

Berkey, J. (1992). *The Transmission of Knowledge in Medieval Cairo*, Princeton, NJ: Princeton University Press.

Brundrett, M., Fitzgerald, T. and Sommefeldt, D. (2006). The Creation of National Programmes of School Leadership Development in England and New Zealand, *International Studies in Educational Administration, 34*(1), 89–105.

Burke, J. (2004). *Al-Qaeda: The True Story of Radical Islam*, London: Penguin.

Butterworth, C. (2001). *Alfarabi – ThePpolitical Writings*, *Selected Aphorisms and Other Texts*, Ithaca, NY: Cornell University Press.

Clements, F. A. (2001). *Historical Dictionary of Arab and Islamic organizations,* Lanham, MD: Scarecrow Press.

Council of Chief School State Officers (1996). *Interstate School Leaders Licensure Consortium*, Washington, DC. pp. 21. http://www.ccsso.org/projects/Interstate_Consortium_on_School_Leadership/ ISLLC_Standards/ Accessed online 9.10.07

Davidson, H. A. (1992). *Alfarabi, Avicenna, and Averroes, on Intellect: Their Cosmologies, Theories, of the Active Intellect, and Theories of Human intellect*, New York: Oxford University Press.

Duignan, P. A. and Macpherson, R. J. S. (1993). Educative Leadership: A Practical Theory, *Educational Administration Quarterly*, *29*(1), 8–33.

Fisk, R. (2005). *The Great War for Civilization: The Conquest of the Middle East,* London: Fourth Estate.

Flew, A. (1979). *A Dictionary of Philosophy,* London: Pan Books.

Galston, M. (1990). *Politics and Excellence – The Political Philosophy of Alfarabi*, Princeton, NJ: Princeton University Press.

General Authority for Educational Buildings, Egypt (2006). Schools Pilot Launched, *Middle East Economic Digest, 50*(50), 23.

Government of the United Arab Emirates. (2004). *Statements issued by HH Sheikh Khalifa Bin Zayed Al Nahyan to the media since the first GCC Summit in Abu Dhabi on May 25, 1981.* UAE: Office of the Deputy Prime Minister for Information Affairs.

Government of the UAE. (2005). *Sheikha Fatima and Humanitarian Works,* United Arab Emirates: Office of Deputy Prime Minister.

Greenfield, T. and Ribbins, P. (Eds.) (1993). *Greenfield on Educational Administration: Towards a Humane Science,* London: Routledge.

Herrera, L. (2004). Education, Islam, and Modernity: Beyond Westernization and Centralization, *Comparative Education Review*, *48*(3), 318–26.

Hodgkinson, C. (1978). *Towards a Philosophy of Administration,* Oxford: Basil Blackwell.

Holt, P. M. (1986). *The Age of the Crusades: The Near East from the Eleventh Century to 1517.* London: Longman.

Hutton, W. (2007).*The Writing on the Wall: China and the West in the 21st Century*, London: Little, Brown.

Interstate School Leaders Licensure Consortium (2007) *About ISLLC* http://www.umsl.edu/~mpea/Pages/AboutISLLC/AboutISLLC.html Accessed online 9.10 07

International Air Transport Association. (2005). "IATA - Middle East and Northern Africa." http://www.iata.org/worldwide/middle_east/ Accessed 9.10.07.

Iraqi Ministry of Education (2004). *School Survey 2003–2004 in Iraq*, Baghdad: MOE and UNICEF.

Kezar, A. (2000). The Importance of Pilot Studies: Beginning the Hermeneutic Circle, *Research in Higher Education*, *41*(3), 385–400.

Lameer, J. (1994. *Al-Farabi and Aristotelian Syllogistics: Greek Theory and Islamic Practice*, Leiden: E.J. Brill.

Lapidus, I. (1984). *Muslim Cities in the Later Middle Ages,* Cambridge: Cambridge University Press.

Laqueur, W. (1974). *Confrontation: The Middle East War and World Politics.* London: Abacus.

Latif, S. A. (1961). *Principles of Islamic culture,* University of Madres: Goodwood Books.

Lewis, B. (2004). *From Babel to Dragoman: Interpreting the Middle East,* London: Phoenix.

Lumby, J. (2006), International Perspectives on Leadership and Management, *Management in Education*, *3*(2), 235.

Lumby, J. (2006). Conceptualizing diversity and leadership: Evidence from 10 Cases, *Educational Management, Administration and Leadership, 34*(2), 151–66.

Mahdi, M. S. (2001). *Alfarabi and the Foundations of Islamic Political Philosophy*, Chicago: University of Chicago Press.

Ministry of Information and Culture, UAE. (1998). *Arab Gulf Cooperation Council (GCC),* London: Trident Press.

NCSL (2007a) *Welcome to the National College for School Leadership*, Nottingham, NCSL. http://www.ncsl.org.uk/ Accessed 9.10.07

NCSL (2007b) *Leadership Development Framework,* Nottingham, NCSL. http://www.ncsl.org.uk/publications/ldf/index.cfm Accessed 9.10.07

Ovendale, R. (1998). *The Longman Companion to – The Middle East since 1914.* (Second Edition). London: Longman.

Ovendale, R. (1999). *The Origins of the Arab-Israeli Wars* (3rd ed.), London: Longman.

Pashiardis, P., Thody, A., Papanaoum, Z. and Johansson, O. (2003). *European Educational Leadership: A Search for Consensus in Diversity,* CD-ROM, European Union: Socrates Program.

Phillips, D. C. (1997). How, Why, What, When, and Where: Perspectives on Constructivism in Psychology and Education, *Issues in Education*, *3*(2), 151–68.

Rahman, T. (2006). *Denizens of Alien Worlds,* Karachi: Oxford University Press.

Ribbins, P. (2006). Knowledge and knowing in the study of leadership in education: A place for history? Unpublished paper.

Ribbins, P. and Gronn, P. (2006). Researching principals: Context and culture in the study of leadership in schools. Unpublished paper.

Sanders, N. M. and Simpson, J. (2005). *State Policy Framework to Develop Highly Qualified Administrators*, Washington, D.C.: Council of Chief State School Officers.

Schraw, G. and Olafson, L. (2002). Teachers' Epistemological World Views and Educational Practices, *Issues in Education*, 8(2), 99.

Schulze, K. E. (1999). *The Arab-Israeli Conflict*. Essex, UK.: Pearson Educational.

Shah, S. (2006). Leading multi-ethnic schools: A new understanding of Muslim youth identity, *Educational Management Administration and Leadership*, 34(2), 215–37.

Tamadonfar, M. (1989). *The Islamic Polity and Political Leadership: Fundamentalism, Sectarianism, and Pragmatism*, Boulder, CO: Westview.

Wafi, A. A-W. (1998). *Human rights in Islam*, Riyadh: Naif Arab Academy for Security Science.

Woodward, B. (2006). *State of Denial*, London: Simon and Schuster.

Yapp, M. E. (1987). *The Making of the Modern Near East 1792–1923*. London: Longman.

20

Leader Development Across Three Chinese Societies

Allan Walker, Shuanye Chen and Haiyan Qian

This chapter outlines and analyses the current state of leader development across three rapidly reforming Chinese societies — People's Republic of China (China), Taiwan and Hong Kong Special Administrative Region (HKSAR). Our descriptive and analytic frame is founded on the assumption that Leader Development Programs (LDPs) do not operate in isolation but within a broader international, societal and local context. This context has many faces, including cultural, economic, political, religious, and social aspects. In terms of education, these influences help shape to a greater or lesser degree the purpose, extent and content of education policy. Although not necessarily in a linear or formal fashion, education reform policy influences interest and action in leader development. Given the influence of context, any understanding of leader development must begin with at least a basic understanding of different levels of education trends as well as what is involved in policy and programs.

Whereas an understanding of current education reform and leader development policy is informative, deeper understanding requires sharper insights into policy and program imperatives, as well as their underlying dynamics. This is particularly important when comparisons are being drawn. With this in mind, and following a description of current reform trends and leader development activity in each society, we frame our comparison of the three sites across eight important areas. These are: the linkage between LDPs and global and societal trends; coherence between LDPs and education reforms; the place of guiding frameworks; responsibility for provision; access to programs; contextual and cultural sensitivity; dominant pedagogies employed; and research into and evaluation of programs. These issues were selected to represent first, macro issues — or leader development as viewed from a systemic perspective — second, issues related to established requirements and frameworks and; third, more micro issues such as pedagogy within programs.

Within the above framework the chapter is divided into four main sections. The first section provides a sketch of the current state of educational reform in each of the societies. This provides the policy context within which school leaders work and, as such, frames much of the current thrust and shape of their formal development.

The second section overviews the current state of leader development in each society. These outlines are by necessity descriptive and aim to introduce leader development policy and activity only in the three dynamic settings. Aspects of leader development covered include an overview of relevant policy, values and actions, and an illustration of how some of these are translated into practice. Given the scope (across) and depth (within) of the societies addressed our coverage unavoidably skims over some important elements and leaves us open to claims of over-generalization. However, given that few previous writings have looked across the societies in this area our main aim is to provide a flavor of the recent state of affairs and then use this as the basis for initial analysis.

The third section identifies emerging patterns by comparing leader development across the three Chinese societies using the eight areas specified above. Patterns identified may comprise both similarities and differences across societies — the former are labeled convergent patterns and the latter divergent patterns. A convergent pattern, for example, is that formal leader development in all three societies tends to focus on principals or leaders expressing a desire to be principals, and largely neglect other levels of leadership. Societies diverge, for example, in terms of the overt influence of politics or ideology on the shape and content of leader development programs.

The final section draws on the preceding analysis to outline briefly three issues and general questions which may promote deeper understanding of leader development across the societies. One of these issues, for example, is that leader development policy and activity across the three societies are deeply rooted in ordered social relationships and connections. Our discussion of a very limited number of issues does not pretend to be comprehensive; in fact, we acknowledge that we only scratch the surface of this important area.

WHY THREE CHINESE SOCIETIES?

We decided to address leader development across three Chinese societies rather than a single society for three interrelated reasons. First, as far as we are aware no attempt has been made to examine either the history or current state of leader development across the sites. Although separated in recent history by stark political and economic divides the three societies share deeply embedded cultural structures and traditions, which include an immutable dedication to education. The three societies are also sites of dynamic and increasingly inter-related economic growth; and are being continually reshaped by and are shaping globalization. As such, it is important not only to better understand how long-term tradition influences leader development, but also how more recent trends have infiltrated and affected the mix.

Second, understanding of leader development internationally tends to be dominated by Anglo-American language, theory, practices and structures. Given that much of the little which is written, especially in Taiwan and China, is in Chinese, pulling this together in English may inform leader development internationally. Third, even though the societies themselves inhabit the same geographic neighborhood, for various reasons, they know little of what happens in terms of leader development next door.

Whereas we would have liked to broaden out comparison to other Asian societies, and to current trends in Western English-Speaking and non-English-Speaking countries this was not practical given the complexity across the three societies themselves. Scholars wishing to pursue such comparison in Asia and beyond are referred to Hallinger (2003); Murphy (2006), some of the excellent work coming out of the NCSL in the UK, and other chapters included in this volume.

GENERAL EDUCATION REFORM ACROSS THREE CHINESE SOCIETIES

Since the early 1980s, the three societies have faced massive social transition — economically, politically and educationally. In 1978, China moved to implement the *Reform and Opening* (*gaige kaifang*) policy to increase economic growth and counter the hangover effects of the Cultural Revolution. On the other side of the Taiwan Strait, with the abolition of Martial Law in 1987, Taiwan launched the *Open to Reform* (*jieyan kaifang*) policy and subsequently witnessed a series of revolutionary social changes geared toward democracy and pluralism. From the signing of the Sino-British Joint Declaration in 1984 to the change of sovereignty in 1997, Hong Kong, the long-time British colony faced its own series of economic, political, social and cultural challenges. In all three societies global and societal pressures converged (as they continue to) to pressure education systems and professionals, and these became manifest in wide-ranging education reforms. Although these adopted different forms across the societies they shared a number of major common themes: decentralization and deregulation, school-based management, quality education, curriculum reform, marketization and teacher professional development.

While our purpose is not to provide a comprehensive picture of education reform in the three societies, some understanding of the reform context is essential to locate leader development. This section briefly reviews some major reform trends to describe this basic context, and hence frame our discussion of leader development in China, Taiwan and HKSAR.

Education Reform in China

The major education reform initiatives in China over the past two decades can be grouped around four major interrelated themes. These are quality education, increased market involvement, decentralization and accountability.

The 1985 release of *The Decision on the Reform of the Educational Structure* (Chinese Communist Party (CCP), 1985) is generally recognized as the beginning of education reform in post-Maoist China. The key theme throughout the document was to improve the quality of education (*suzhi jiaoyu*); a theme which has endured and continues, in various forms, to underpin current reforms. As stated in the document itself, "throughout the reform of the education system, it is imperative to bear in mind that reform is for the fundamental purpose of turning every person into a man or woman of quality and cultivating more constructive members of society." (CCP, 1985; cited in Li, 2004a, p. 301). Quality rhetoric continued to broadly frame major policy goals throughout the 1990s and 2000s, as reflected in the National Ninth (1996–2000), Tenth (2001–2005) and Eleventh (2006–2010) Five-year Plans. According to then-Vice Premier Li Lanqing (2004), quality education emphasized cultivating students' innovative spirit and practical skills; and aimed to transform them into exemplary builders of socialism (i.e. well-developed morally, intellectually, physically and aesthetically). This quest for quality was apparent in a series of policies targeting, for example, a shift to student-centered classroom practice, a new curriculum catering to individual student needs and improved teacher and principal qualifications.

An equally influential reform trend was increased free market (*ziyou shichang*) involvement in the school sector. As Tang and Wu (2000) explained, the changes proposed for schools as well as the broader system were hindered by complicated resource constraints. In order to cope with these schools were forced to supplement central funds in whatever ways they could. Typical strategies included, for example, leasing school facilities to evening schools, attracting donations from local enterprises and charging higher fees for students who did not meet basic entry requirements (called 'school-choice students' (*zexiaosheng*)). Many such forms of fundraising are formally endorsed and regulated, if not openly supported, by the government. For example, in Shanghai, policy specifically stipulates the maximum number of 'school-choice students' (usually not exceeding 20 per cent per year cohort) each senior secondary/high school can enroll as well as the maximum fee each can be charged (Shanghai Education Commission, 2006).

Partly as a result of limited resources, inter-school competition has drastically increased. Schools are pressured to compete for 'exemplary school' classification, better students and teachers, more school-based research outputs and better academic performance on district, provincial and/or national unified examinations. With the implementation of the quality education scheme, schools not only have to ensure that they are academically outstanding, but also unique in other ways. For example, in their increasingly visible publicity documents many schools highlight achievements such as becoming a 'Mathematics Olympic Champion', or nurturing a famous Chinese orchestra.

As in other parts of the world, quality and market related reforms in China were inevitably accompanied by increased decentralization and accountabilities. Decentralization in China involved the redistribution of power and responsibility from the central government to local communities; and then further to the school level (Tang & Wu, 2000). A key factor in this rebalancing was adoption of the 'principal responsibility system' in schools. This attempted to reverse structures established during Mao's Chairmanship which posted a party secretary in each school and gave them considerable power in all aspects of school governance and ideology. The 'principal-responsibility system' repositioned the school principal rather than the party secretary as the nominal key leader in the school. The effects of this policy, when combined with those of the quality education scheme, granted principals more autonomy in terms of school-based curriculum, and teacher development, recruitment and promotion.

An integral aspect of decentralization is increased public accountability for academic performance and resource utilization. Chinese principals are now held more personally accountable for school performance than ever before. For example, a system recently established in Shanghai sorts principals into five grades (special-, first-, second-, third- and fourth-classes) and delineates twelve salary levels (Feng, 2003). Under this system, principals' pay is linked to both their qualifications and their school's performance.

In sum, after 20 years of reform, and even though the government remains the most important educational player, schools are no longer purely state agencies. To survive and excel within the evolving state-stipulated policy framework they must deal with oft-times overlapping and even conflicting state and local interests. Consequently, school leaders lead in a new political and social environment, deal with more complex power relations and educational goals and involve more diverse internal and external school stakeholders. This new situation calls for the continuous development of school leaders.

Educational Reform in Taiwan

The beginning of recent education reform in Taiwan can be roughly traced to the mid-1980s. At that time, the Taiwanese education system was highly politicized, tightly controlled by central authorities and run largely on authoritarian grounds. By the mid-1980s, however, large segments of the population began to criticize this state of affairs. Civic and public concerns about education continued to mount and eventually prompted a series of social movements calling for radical systemic restructuring of education (Pan & Yu, 1999; Shan & Chang, 2000). A landmark public demonstration in April 1994 by the League of Educational Reform (*jiaogai lianmeng*) pressured the government to accelerate the reform process (Shan & Chang, 2000; Pan, 2007). From 1994 onward Taiwan became awash with education reform.

A key reform tenet targeted a shift from central authoritarianism to more pluralistic and democratic structures — or increased levels of democratic participation. Subsequently, the Ministry of Education decentralized much of its regulatory power and authority to municipal and county bureaus of education, thus handing responsibility for a wide range of decision-making to local authorities. For example, the 1994 *Teacher Cultivation Law (shizi peiyufa)* broke the traditional monopoly held by the 15 Normal institutions to train teachers and allowed other qualified colleges and universities to establish 'Teacher Education Programs'. By 2005, 75 institutions were recognized as legitimate teacher training institutions (Chang, 2006). This has spawned a much wider range of more diversified programs and fierce competition for participants (Fwu & Wang, 2002). As a result of this competition, a number of program providers turned to school leader programs to differentiate themselves in the marketplace.

Sustained public pressure prompted the government toward further reform and in 1994 it established the *Review Committee on Educational Reform*. The Committee's recommendations marked a major shift in government policy and philosophy; these included: (1) to deregulate education; (2) to develop every student; (3) to reform the streaming system through examinations and increase upward mobility; (4) to improve educational quality; and (5) to build a lifelong learning society (Review Committee on Educational Reform of the Executive Yuen, 1996). All major recommendations were addressed by the Taiwanese Ministry of Education and operationalized in tandem with earlier reforms through the policy document Action Plan for Educational Reform (Chang, 2006; Wu, 2006). In all, twelve major policy measures were proposed to address the Committee's recommendations. Although wide ranging, two of the strongest reform themes reinforced the importance of decentralization and teacher development (Weng, 2003).

The 1995 *Teachers' Act* and 1999 *Educational Fundamental Act* established and built into law Teacher Review Committees and Associations of Teachers and of Parents. These bodies provided a legal foundation for teachers and parents to share decision-making with local government and school-level administrators. Included in this newly-allocated power was the right of teachers to be involved in the selection of principals and teachers. For example, the 1995 Act transferred the principal's power to hire teachers to a school-based search committee comprising administrators, teachers and parents; and granted teachers the right to form union-like associations with the power to negotiate their rights and obligations with administrators. The *Educational Fundamental Act* of 1999 further diluted the traditional power of the principal by legislating more parental involvement in internal decision-making processes thereby radically changing the principal selection and tenure mechanisms. Since 1999, principals are selected and contracted for four years by district-level committees composed of administrators, parents, teachers and other educational experts (Fwu & Wang, 2001; Pan, 2007).

Devolution-related reforms strongly promoted school based-management in Taiwan, thereby giving schools even more internal autonomy. Official recognition of the professional status of teachers led to more active participation across school life. Decentralization of governance functions was accompanied by wide ranging curriculum reform aimed specifically at improving the quality of education. For example, the Nine-year Curriculum Framework released in 2002 allowed 20 per cent of curriculum to be determined at the school level. All these reforms combined (as they still do) to redefine the working environment, job and expectations of school leaders. Decentralization of curriculum and governance was accompanied by a concomitant interest in teacher and leader development. Teacher quality and professional status were highlighted by the educational reforms as a key ingredient for improving the quality of education. The *Teachers' Act* and its later amendments require teachers to engage in continuous in-service professional development. For the purposes of the Act, principals are regarded as teachers.

To summarise, since the mid-1980s, education reform in Taiwan has pushed very strongly indeed toward democratizing education, mainly through devolving decision-making authority to local and school levels. There is little doubt that this has had significant effects on school leaders. Yang (2001) claims that the role of principals has become diverse and paradoxical as they are charged with control and responsibility for curriculum, personnel and budget, but are also expected to share decision-making power with parents, teachers and other community members. This new situation also called for the continuous professional development of school leaders.

Education Reform in the HKSAR[1]

Cheng (2000) describes recent education reforms in Hong Kong as arriving in two overlapping waves, roughly separated by the release of the *Education Commission Report No. 7* (ECR7) in 1997. The first wave, pre-1997, can be characterized as a top-down approach to reform, with an emphasis on increasing resource input. Post-1997 reforms targeted a school-based, bottom-up approach. Hong Kong now appears to be on the cusp of a new, more hybrid wave which uses a combination of the top-down and bottom-up approaches. One example of this is school-based management.

From 1984 to 1997, literally hundreds of policy recommendations were proposed by the Education Commission (EC), the pre-eminent education policy advisory body in Hong Kong (Cheng, 2003; Lo, 1997). Viewed together, the resultant policies covered a broad range of issues, including the medium of instruction, teacher education, the private school sector, special education, assessment and selection mechanisms, curriculum development, teaching and learning conditions, school management and school inspection (Cheng, 2000 & 2003). Although all impacted school leadership, perhaps the most influential was the School Management Initiative (SMI), which represented the Education Department's first attempt to target the school as the unit of change (Education and Manpower Branch & Education Department, 1991). The SMI provided a school-based management framework with clearer roles for principals, greater participation in decision making, more systematic planning and evaluation of school activities, and more flexibility in using resources (Dimmock & Walker, 1998).

Following the change of sovereignty in 1997, the new SAR Government confirmed its dedication to education reform. In his first policy address, the Chief Executive endorsed ECR7 and announced a comprehensive review of the education system. Associated policies moved HKSAR into a new era of school reform. In comparison to earlier reform efforts, the emphasis shifted to a very different theory of action for driving educational improvement. First, the reforms more deliberately focused on schools as the unit of change: they were concerned primarily with improving internal school conditions and the quality of student learning. Second, they recognized the uniqueness of individual schools and that this was accompanied by different needs and problems. Improvement strategies were based largely on the diagnosis of the needs within specific school-based contexts. Third, they involved melded organizational (school organization and culture) and classroom interventions (related to teaching and learning) to effect change in schools. Policies also promoted networking and the sharing of effective practice (Li, 2004a; Chiu & Chung, 2003).

Other reforms included major changes to approaches to learning and teaching and to a deeply entrenched examination system (Education Commission, 2000, 2000a). In order to make more room for the ideals incorporating new learning, the reforms also moved to fundamentally change the academic structure, admission system at different levels, and assessment mechanisms (especially the public examinations) (Education and Manpower Bureau, 2005). This package of reforms, particularly the more progressive approach to curriculum, pedagogy and assessment (Curriculum Development Council (CDC), 2001), poses a significant challenge to school leaders.

A related line of reform supporting the ideals of SMI and then ECR7 sought to improve school governance and management (Advisory Committee on School-based Management (ACSBM), 2000), school accountability (EMB, 2003, 2003a), and also the professional development of teachers and principals (Education Department 2002; Advisory Committee on Teacher Education and Qualifications (ACTEQ), 2003). These reform 'lines' are drastically altering the work lives of school practitioners and place increasing demands on leaders to improve their own and their school's performance.

Cased within the reforms, and particularly pertinent to implementation, was recognition across the three societies of the key role played by school leaders, and, at least to some extent, the importance of their preparation and development. We now turn specifically to this.

SCHOOL LEADER DEVELOPMENT ACROSS THREE CHINESE SOCIETIES

School Leader Development in China

Recognizing the importance of leader development within the broader reform environment, in 1989 the State Education Commission (SEC, renamed the Ministry of Education (MOE) in 1998) issued *Strengthening the Training for Principals of Elementary and Secondary Schools Nation-Wide*. The document stated: "Generally speaking, the performance of the elementary and secondary school principals cannot meet the demands of educational development and further reform, both in political and in professional aspects" (State Education Commission, 1989, p. 1). The policy thereby proposed a professional training scheme with attached certification for future and new principals (Feng, 2003). The central government further recognized the development needs of serving principals and suggested that some form of certification was necessary. These requirements were expressly stipulated in the MOE's *Training Regulations for School Principals* in 1999.

The basic aim of principal development policy was to facilitate the provision of quality education (Article 6) and to formulate detailed guidelines to steer development initiatives. All newly-appointed principals were to be certified through a series of development programs of not less than 300 contact hours prior to or within six months after taking office (Articles 6 & 20). It also stipulated that serving principals undergo not less than 240 hours of continuous development hours over a five-year cycle. If they failed to fulfill this requirement they would be given one year to 'make it up', or be 'dismissed' (Articles 6 & 20). In addition to induction and continuing training programs, the policy stipulated advanced training programs for 'backbone principals' (*gugan xiaozhang* — a title granted to principals considered the most outstanding (Article 6)). Subsequently, a *Professional Development Project for One Thousand Backbone Principals* (*qianming gugan xiaozhang yanxiu jihua*) was launched in 2000.

The past two decades have witnessed an expansion of program providers. During the 1980s, leader development was mainly conducted by a relatively small number of centralized teacher training schools, each catering to different levels. The *National Academy of Education Administration* (NAEA) was responsible for training provincial education bureau officials and other selected education leaders from across the nation; provincial Institutes of Education trained selected education leaders across the province; city-level Institutes of Education trained educational leaders under the city governance and the county-Level Teacher Training Schools were responsible for training local school leaders (UNDP Research Team, 1997). Normal universities in China, which are usually responsible for pre-service teacher training, did not participate in in-service school leader development until 1989 when the *National Training Centre for High School Principals* was established at East China Normal University in Shanghai, one of the best Normal universities in China. The center launched its first development program in April 1990. Ten years later, the *National Training Centre for Primary School Principals* was established at Beijing Normal University, also one of the top Normal universities in the country. These two centers run advanced programs for national 'backbone' principals. Backbone principals are selected at various levels, for example, at the school-, municipal- and national-levels. The two centers are responsible mainly for training national-level backbone principals. These principals are drawn from all provinces and are generally officially considered the best principals in China. Some comprehensive universities, such as Fudan and Peking, also participate in leader development, mainly through providing self-financed, part-time postgraduate certificate courses or workshops.

As well as the work done by university providers at the national level, local training institutions develop courses which address the more immediate local context (Feng, 2003), but still within the state-authorized framework. In 2001 The Ministry of Education issued two directives, called respectively the *Directive Teaching Plan for Principal Induction Training Program* and *Directive Teaching Plan for Principal Continuous Training Program* (Ministry of Education, 2001). These directives required local training institutions to design programs for principals that were: context-specific, target group specific, linked theory to practice, applicable to practical situations, needs-driven, and attentive to school outcomes (Walker, Hallinger & Qian, 2007). The directives outlined the basic modules each training program was to adopt. For example, they stipulated that 150 out of the 240 development hours were built around topics (ten hours for each) such as modern society and education, comparative education, education law and regulations, and quality education. Another 70 hours could be designed to meet local needs, and 20 hours allocated for school visits, seminars and/or case studies (Ministry of Education, 2001). The Ministry of Education (2002) also published a list of recommended textbooks for the use with the Tenth-Five Year (2001–2005) principal training programs. Thus, most induction and continuous training programs were (and are) provided in the form of lectures around pre-designated topics on a part-time basis.

The advanced training programs run by the two national centers are usually month-long, full-time intensive programs. An official notice sent recently by the National Training Centre for Primary School Principals (2006) explained that the program was built around three major purposes and seven specific aims. The first major purpose was to facilitate the implementation of two reform decisions: the *Decisions on Deepening Education Reform* and *Promoting Quality Education in an All-round Way* issued by the CCP and State Council in 1999, and the *Decision on Reform and Development of Basic Education* issued by the State Council in 2001. The second and third purposes were, respectively, to improve principals' ability to promote quality education and to develop a high-quality cadre of professional principals. By the end of the program, principals should:

a. know major decisions made at the 6th Plenary Session of the 16th Party Central Committee (October 2006);
b. be familiar with Proposals on *Further Reinforcing and Improving Moral Education in Schools* (2004);
c. understand the latest revisions to the *Compulsory Education Law*;

    d. understand the design of the eleventh National Five Year Plan (2006–2010);

    e. be familiar with current education policies, theories and local and international developments;

    f. understand the major issues of the New Curriculum Reform;

    g. understand recent management theories and improve their innovative spirit(translated from *Principal Development Net*, 2006).

Principals under 50 without previous advanced training are eligible for selection to the program, but places are strictly limited. Each province[2] in China is assigned two places and some Special Economic Zones (SEZs) are assigned one — so each month-long program enrolls around 68 principals and is funded by the Ministry of Education. As opposed to earlier training courses, the high profile program uses a range of methods, including: lectures by and discussion with senior education officials, experts and professors; experience sharing with peers from across the nation; school visits and essay writing. The center awards an advanced training certificate at promotion exercises. Given the strictly limited number of places, being selected to participate in these national programs is considered a great honor and marks those involved as being 'the best of the best'. Participants in these programs tend be selected from highly-visible elite schools. The elitist nature of the program, and the fact that it is state-driven, in many ways, sums up leader development practices in China.

School Leader Development in Taiwan

As in China, principal development in Taiwan is implemented at the district level within a centralized regulatory system. Unlike China, however, to be considered for the government-subsidized development courses required to apply for a principalship, leaders must qualify to sit and then pass an examination. The process runs like this: first, leaders who have reached a specified administrative level in school and rate well on other criteria may apply for selection to sit for the examination. Criteria include, for example, candidates 'service performance', personal, formal education level and outcomes of yearly evaluations. Performance in each category is awarded certain points and when the total of these reaches a certain level candidates are eligible to sit for the examination. The examination is set by local Bureaus of Education within central guidelines, and includes written (theoretical) and oral (analytic and experiential) components (requirements are in the *Regulation for Principals', Directors, and Teachers' Selection, Training and Moving* (amended in March 2, 2007). Regulations require that the training include topics such as professional literacy, gender equality and multi-cultural awareness.

Second, candidates who successfully pass the examination (at a certain level) are required to attend official government-subsidized pre-service training (*chuxun*). Third, if they successfully complete this course they are eligible to apply for certain principal positions when they become available. There are few formal development requirements after appointment, and, traditionally, minimal opportunities for those not eligible to mount the formal track.

In an effort to address this latter situation and tap increasing interest in leader development, in 2001, Taipei Municipal Bureau of Education commissioned National Taiwan Normal University (widely regarded as the best normal university in Taiwan) and Taipei Municipal Educational University to develop and run two additional leader development programs. The nine-month part-time programs were designed for leaders wishing to sit for the formal examination — in other words, before stage one of the process outlined above. These courses were aptly named principal 'cultivation' programs. These courses broke new ground in that they added non-mandatory opportunities for development before selection, required no examination, involved experienced principals as coaches, included regular clinical practice visits and provided (six) officially recognized credits toward the examination. Courses remained traditional in that program entry was still based on formal seniority and location. After selection as 'potential principals', candidates attend the Taipei In-service Teacher Training Centre for the eight-weeks of official training (*chuxun*) aimed specifically at principalship preparation. Given that this course is the most important centrally controlled element of school leader training in Taiwan, and is similar across districts, it is worth further description.

The official Taipei program caters for potential middle school principal candidates. Successful completion of the program certifies participants as qualified reserve principals (*houyong xiaozhang*) who may then be considered by principal selection committees when positions become available. Translated literally, the program promotes the ideal of 'Being healthy, caring, excellent and creative principals' (*jiankang youai, zhuoyue chuangxin*). It aims to help the aspiring principals: (1) cultivate professional capacity, a noble character (*gaoshang pingde*) and to become a healthy, 'sound' person committed to self-development and reflection; (2) stimulate team spirit and cooperation and enhance leadership and interpersonal communication skills; (3) become familiar with policies concerning educational quality and shaping of educational visions toward excellence, refinement, quality, and creativity; (4) make principals professionally capable and help them fully develop their educational ideas.

The program includes two basic components. First, the fixed or 'Unit' courses cover topics such as vision building, strategic piloting, effective administration, curriculum development, building a friendly school, resource integration, campus construction and pioneering. Second, the 'Belt' curriculum aims toward helping participants integrate learning, theory and practice. This includes development planning, problem-based learning (PBL), contextually relevant cases, mentoring by experienced principals, issue-based discussion and experience sharing.

Content is delivered mostly through traditional lecturing by invited speakers such as mayors, government officials, university professors, principals, legislators and judges. A form of PBL is practiced throughout the program and one day each week is reserved for clinical practice and school visits. In order to cultivate a supportive environment for peer learning, participants are required to live-in for three days a week with a full-time retired principal acting as a mentor. Collective group study aims to build peer alliances and deeper sharing. During the program, participants make presentations, write self-reflection papers and submit PBL reports as part of their final evaluation.

Although the 'examination' process for aspiring principals appears coherent, it has been criticized as too short-term, disconnected and overly prescribed by the central bureaucracy (Lin, 2002). The same basic process has been used for more than 20 years to prepare candidates for the principalship (Chen, 2004). In many cases, rather than having specialized programs for leaders they attend teacher professional development or teacher cultivation courses. There appear no other regulations specifically addressing school leader development.

Another possible influence of the 'qualifying' examination and related courses is that the process is so demanding in terms of required commitment that it may deflect policy commitment for leader development for all but aspiring principals. Presently there are very few requirements for serving school principals beyond general 'cover-all' legislation. Although in-service teacher training centers and other tertiary institutions offer some lectures and credit courses for this group, they tend to be irregular and bereft of a coherent structure.

Outside of Taipei City, newly established principal centers (attached to tertiary institutions) conduct nine-month part-time principal cultivation courses commissioned by central authorities (Lin, 2003). There are also opportunities for development provided within and outside of the government framework. Included among these are freely accessible school leader e-learning programs designed to build e-learning leadership communities (http://192.192.169.230/edu_pdr/index.htm). Also in an effort to assist leader development, Taipei Municipal University of Education has an impressive collection of freely available resources. Principals' Associations and other professional organizations organize seminars, workshops and peer sharing, but these are on an informal and irregular basis only.

School Leader Development in HKSAR[3]

This section mainly covers leader development in Hong Kong as organized around the recently implemented Education and Manpower Bureau (EMB) leader development framework.

Prior to 2000, leader preparation and development in Hong Kong followed an incoherent and scattered path. New principals were required to attend a basic short-term induction course focused almost exclusively on administrative matters. Other opportunities for potential, newly-appointed and serving principals were diffuse and organized on an ad hoc basis by the Education Department (ED),[4] different school sponsoring bodies (SSBs), higher education providers and their associated specialized centers, and some professional associations (Walker, 2004).

Things changed quite radically in 1999 when the then Chief Executive announced in his annual policy address that from 2000–2001, all newly appointed principals would need to complete certain requirements prior to appointment (HKSAR Government, 1999). This edict prompted a rush of program and policy activity in leader development and lead to the release of a consultation paper designed to reframe leader development (Task Group on Training and Development of School Heads, 1999). The paper recommended the establishment of a mandatory structure to guide principal preparation and development and set out a number of principles to guide its construction.

The consultation paper elicited considerable debate and various components were shifted, changed or discarded over about a two-year period and built into a second consultative document being released in 2002. In a slightly abridged form this document, entitled *The Continuing Professional Development for School Excellence* (Education Department, 2002a), came into formal effect in 2002. The framework underpinning the policy was drawn from *Key Qualities of the Principalship in Hong Kong* (Walker, Dimmock, Chan, Chan, Cheung, & Wong, 2002). The resultant programs were underpinned by these 'qualities' (standards) which were organized as clustered sets of values, knowledge, skills and attributes around six core areas of school leadership: Strategic Direction and Policy Environment; Teaching, Learning and Curriculum; Leader and Teacher Growth and Development; Staff and Resource Management; Quality Assurance and Management; and External Communication and Connection (Education Department 2002).

The policy constituted a substantial shift from the status quo in that it delineated levels of leader development, introduced mandatory requirements and a time-regulated structure including for principal certification, demanded that (at least) aspiring principals had to pay for their own certification, adopted a set of 'local' leadership beliefs and standards, encouraged school leaders to take responsibility for their own and their colleagues' learning, and aimed to significantly elevate the value of formal, non-university accredited development programs. The subsequent continuing professional development (CPD) programs (including the in-service program for newly appointed principals) were designed to encourage a continuous learning culture among principals (Education Department, 2002).

The principal development policy framework attempted to affect change through both cultural and structural pathways. The beliefs and major requirements are summarized below (Education Department, 2002a),

a. Principals are responsible for their own professional growth.
b. Principals have a mandate to be professionally up-to-date and to provide a role model for their own teaching staff in terms of CPD.
c. CPD enhances principals' professionalism and leadership for the benefit of students and student learning.
d. CPD builds on principals' individual strengths and is by nature developmental.
e. CPD opportunities need to be varied to reflect the needs of aspiring, newly appointed and experienced principals and be open to individual selection.
f. CPD embraces collegial input and support from the education sector as well as other professional sectors.

The major requirements were linked to different levels of leadership.

a. Aspiring principals (APs) (vice principals, department heads and senior teachers) must attain the *Certification for Principalship* (CFP), as well as complying with existing appointment conditions, before being considered for appointment as a principal. The certification remains in effect for five-years.
b. Newly appointed principals (NAPs) (principals in the first two years of their principalship) must participate in a four-part designated program; engage in CPD activities relevant to their personal and school needs; and present a professional portfolio to their governing boards annually.
c. Serving principals (SPs) (principals with more than two years of experience) must undertake CPD activities for at least 150 hours in a three-year cycle. This CPD covers three activity modes: (1) structured learning, (2) action learning and (3) service to education and the community (Education Department, 2002b).

Staged implementation and evaluation of selected program components (EMB, 2004) prompted adjustments and improvement while attempting to maintain the overall integrity of the framework. Wong (2005) studied the various factors affecting the impact of leadership training on new female secondary school principals and compared these with similar programs in England. At the time of the study, the designated program for newly appointed principals was mandatory in HKSAR. Wong reported that "it seems that all HKSAR respondents found the NAP program useful in providing them with a support system, which included a databank of information and a professional network with other principals, both new and experienced. By knowing that they were not alone and with the sharing of experiences and practices, the respondents felt more confident and were able to look at their roles with a wider perspective ..." and "...the NAPs found that the training was essential and had been useful in enhancing their confidence and in providing some kind of emotional support, though they vary in telling exactly what the impact was" (p. 15).

In response to shifting demands and initial, if somewhat unsophisticated evaluations, programs were adjusted to add additional professional and psychological support, increased contextualization, and the purposeful building of multi-layered communities of practice. In short, new changes aimed to further embed professional learning both in schools and within the principalship community. The first program designed to do this — named 'Blue Skies' — was implemented in 2005 (Walker & Quong, 2005). This program is illustrative of a new wave of programs which aim to better operationalize the EMB framework. As Walker and Dimmock (2006) explain, the new programs seek to shift the focus of leader development from a concentration on structures to one focusing on learning.

Before continuing an important caveat is worth repeating. It is not possible to include an account of all Leader Development Programs happening across the three sites; these are far too numerous, too scattered and, in many cases, undocumented. From what we do know, the need for better trained, more professional school leaders is presently emphasized across the three societies as reformers recognize that a new type of leadership is essential if worthwhile change is to have a chance of success. The reform of leader development, however, remains a work in progress; often because of political ramifications and the scope of the reforms themselves. This has lead to claims, in some cases, that it has not gone far enough, and in others, that it is too far removed from the intent of the reforms themselves. For example, while acknowledging the positive impact of recent reform in China, such as the 'Principal Responsibility System', Tang (2001) suggests this has stumbled at the implementation stage because it failed to include key functions such as teacher recruitment and school-based curriculum development.

CROSS-SOCIETAL LEADER DEVELOPMENT ISSUES

Leader development across the three societies is in many ways at a crossroads. Important progress has been made over the last 10 to 15 years in terms of establishing policy structures to promote principal preparation and development. Although school leader development has progressed substantially during this period there have been few concerted attempts to analyze what is happening in the societies individually, and none to compare them holistically. Based on the state of play as described above, this section attempts to summarize the current status of leader development across the three societies and in the process tease out where they diverge from and converge with each other in eight predetermined areas. It should be noted here that very little empirical research beyond localized program evaluations has been done in the area; part of the purpose of this chapter is to encourage such research. We do not presume to cover all related issues, but attempt to address some of the more important of these.

The issues are organized in the following way. First, they begin with 'macro issues', that is, leader development as viewed from a systemic perspective. These include the extent to which leader development across the societies is driven by a 'big P' political focus, and by a more general education reform agenda. Second level issues relate, for example, to established frameworks, certification and other structural features. Third level issues focus on the more micro development provision, such as pedagogy. Second, within the issues we attempt to identify where they converge, or exhibit similarities, and where they diverge from each other; and indicate the strength and/or details of how they differ.

The issues discussed are listed below. Although we selected and separated these for ease of communication it should be noted that they are unavoidably and closely linked to each other in an ongoing dynamic fashion. For example, the frameworks and pedagogies employed in or across programs are influenced and influence practitioner involvement, provider fit and evaluative mechanisms.

- The extent to which leader development policies are linked to broader societal or global influences.
- The extent to which leader development policies cohere with broader education reform agendas.
- The extent to which an explicit framework is in place to guide leader development programs.
- Responsibility for provision of leader development programs.

- The extent of discretion given to future principals to access pre-appointment programs.
- The contextual or cultural sensitivity of leader development programs.
- The dominant pedagogies used in leader development programs.
- Research into and evaluation of leader development programs.

A socio-political focus refers to the extent to which leader development policies are driven by broader (beyond education) socio-political and/or globalized influences. Leader development in all three societies reflects global influences and local political agendas. Multi-level leader development policies across the three societies reflect easily recognizable global trends, be they at different levels of intensity. Key trends such as decentralization, quality education and outcomes based education mirror trends common in developed and developing countries alike and are increasingly driven at a macro level by political-economic agendas. As such, education is held up as the key to building a competitive economy, one where workers are creative, flexible, innovative and knowledgeable. As schools have grown in importance in government eyes, so has the importance of school leadership.

Although moves toward marketization underpin broad moves to upgrade development, including leader development, across societies, the market itself in China remains more directly and explicitly regulated by the state. For example, educational policy continues to stress dedication to communist/socialist ideology across separate initiatives. Direct state intervention in Taiwan is less apparent, but nevertheless endures in more subtle forms. For example, the rhetoric of democracy and pluralism takes a high profile in government education development and training. In Hong Kong, at least at present, there is less direct state political intervention and shaping, perhaps because of its more established democratic traditions. Even this, however, has been challenged at certain levels over recent years.

Reform coherence refers to the extent to which the substance of leader development policies cohere with stated education reform agendas. A common criticism of leader development policy is that it has failed to connect adequately with the reforms principals are asked to implement. Reform coherence can be considered at two levels across the three societies; at a formal (stated) policy level and an informal (actual) level. The former refer to the linkage between LDPs and 'leadership life' in schools. Within these levels further differentiation can be made between rhetorical (political) coherence, intent (goal) coherence and implementation (content/process) coherence.

At both formal and informal rhetorical levels the shape of leader development policy across the three societies is tightly connected with broader political and educational reforms. For example, in China leader development policy notes specifically knowledge of 'new' curriculum reform, moral education reform and the 'current' education policy. Likewise, leader development policy in Hong Kong and Taiwan is replete with direct reference to recent education policies and broader political trends such as democratization and devolution.

In terms of policy intent, the stated goals of leader development policy across the societies appear less coherent with the more explicit stated goals of the major education reforms. For example, in China government policy states that the aim of principal development is to facilitate quality education and cultivate the 'building blocks' of socialism. In such cases the incoherence seems related to the inexact nature of the goals themselves; i.e. the actual substance of the goals themselves is unclear, thereby making connections hard to explicate and thus link to reality. This situation appears common across the three societies and may be because the policy goals themselves are contested, ambiguous and shifting. It is difficult for leader development policies and practices to support reform actualization if the aims of the reforms themselves are unclear or, in cases such as Hong Kong, constantly shifting. In other words, it is difficult to implement policy with fidelity if the targets are constantly moving. The bottom line here is that whereas there appears coherence at a broad level, poorly defined intent makes it difficult to connect reform and leader development.

At the more informal implementation level there appears modest connection between what is needed by leaders to make reforms work in schools and the substance of leader development programs — this is true across all three societies. For example, program content generally falls short of providing the skills, knowledge and most importantly the mindset needed to implement the instructional or curricular reforms necessary to improve student outcomes. This may be attributed to different reasons in different societies. These include what can be labeled as 'distraction' 'over-concentration' and/or 'over-crowdedness'. For example, in China, relevant knowledge and skills incorporated in leader development policy seem distracted by an over emphasis on ideological structures. In Taiwan there appears an over-concentration on technical/ managerial skills in some programs; and in Hong Kong, reforms have appeared at such a rapid rate that it is often difficult for policy implementers and leader developers to determine which are the most important.

The analysis indicates that although leader development policies cohere with the broader political and educational reforms at the rhetorical levels, there is a lack of coherence between the stated goals of education reform and leader development policies and the actual substance of leader development programs. One possible reason is that the goals of education reforms are contested and shifting. A further analysis indicates that policies adopted in these three Chinese societies, as in other regions of Asia, suggest a movement away from educational practices that are consistent with traditional cultural values and norms. In other words the rhetoric of the reform promotes more proactive, open, democratic, and participative principals. However, how to incorporate these values into leader development programs remains a huge challenge for leader developers as it challenges not only surface-level structures, but also more deeply held cultural traditional and norms.

The issue of coherence is a complex one. There is little doubt that the sentiment promoted rhetorically and in stated intent are closely aligned to each other, however, there appears much less connection between the formal substance of LDPs and between this and real life in schools. However despite continued disconnection at some levels between reform policy and leader development, the same malaise that typified leadership development agendas for so many years is no longer apparent.

Guiding Framework relates to the extent to which an explicit/professional framework is in place to guide leader development programs. For our purposes here a framework refers to the form and strength of structural requirements, certification and the leader levels incorporated. Structural requirements refer to the strength of the framework, including the level of content prescription and attached time requirements; certification includes requirements needed to apply for a principalship. Leadership levels refer to the career stages included in the framework.

Structural Requirements   Formal LDPs in all three societies dictate at least the title and shape of different formal courses. Only the HKSAR framework is underpinned by a locally-developed set of standards — known as Key Qualities. There, programs across the three levels of principalship are underpinned, at least formally, by the six core areas of leadership. The Chinese framework is underpinned by a set of general aims, common textbooks and brief course outlines. The Taiwanese framework can be classified as 'semi-clear' in that it depends on competition and an examination focus to provide guidance. However, decentralization in China and Taiwan, and tendering in HKSAR does encourage some local (provider, district or provincial) input and interpretation. All frameworks seem more concerned with formal, mechanistic requirements, such as time and level, rather than ongoing improvement. It is worth noting that pressures other than the formal mandatory requirements also serve as a driver for school leaders to peruse further development. For example, in Taiwan principals must reapply for their jobs every four years. Hence, although no formal requirement exists for the ongoing development of serving principals (as is in place in Hong Kong) 'hidden' pressure remains for these principals to continue learning.

Prescribed Time   All three societies prescribe to varying degrees minimum time and content requirements for formal pre-principal certification. HKSAR requirements for aspiring principals mandate a needs analysis exercise, a formal 72-hour course, and an action learning project. China requires 300 hours of formal face-to-face activity within national content and ideological guidelines, and using nationally recommended textbooks. In Taiwan, content is again framed, if more loosely, by central requirements and examinations. All three societies have requirements for serving principals, but these vary significantly. For example, China requires that all principals engage in 240 hours of professional development over a five-year period and earmarks a small number of elite principals for high level intensive training. HKSAR requires that Newly Appointed Principals fulfill minimum requirements and that serving principals (with more than two years experience) engage in 150-hours of development within three established domains. Taiwan is the least demanding in terms of requirements for serving principals by 'requesting' just 18 hours per year. Principal requirements are not differentiated by policy from requirements for teachers and are included as part of teacher professional development requirements.

Principalship Certification   To become a principal in all three societies requires formal certification. Likewise, certification is controlled, overseen and awarded by the government. Chinese universities are minimally involved in certificating courses or processes whereas similar institutions in HKSAR and Taiwan develop and run the courses through tender. Universities in HKSAR seem more heavily involved than those in Taiwan. In China and Taiwan, courses and certification processes are decentralized to the district or provincial level through directly established government institutions. In HKSAR, universities are in effect tendered agents of the state who develop and run programs for set periods of time according to government demands and monitoring mechanisms. Some programs are tendered for a one-year period only making it difficult to maintain consistency.

Levels of Leadership   Policy and programs in all three societies attempt to address different levels of leadership, or rather principalship, but do so to different degrees. Leader development policy in China predominantly targets new principals and serving principals. There is also special provision for experienced principals of elite schools. Taiwan policy concentrates almost exclusively on pre-service principal preparation and gives scant formal attention to serving principals or people interested in becoming principals who have not reached a certain hierarchical level (although teachers who qualify to become directors, approximately equivalent to vice-principals, do participate in a 6-week training course). Policy in HKSAR is alone in differentiating requirements for three levels of leadership: Aspiring, Newly-Appointed and Serving Principals. In none of the three societies is formal leader development extended to either teacher leaders or mid-level leaders, although in some cases these may be addressed by general teacher development policy.

Program provision refers to the agencies which run leader development programs and the input they have into these programs. In all three societies the government retains considerable control of leader development programs and involves outside agencies, predominantly universities or other institutes of higher learning at their leisure. For example, in Taiwan a number of institutes have established principal training centers in an attempt to win government money, or, in some cases, to run courses outside the formal framework. In HKSAR four universities or higher education institutes compete vigorously for government money to run programs. In China universities play even less of a role in provision. Even though the government has established national training centers in Beijing and Shanghai on university sites, they are affiliated more with the Ministry of Education than the universities themselves. As such, universities across the three societies can be seen more as agents of provision rather than professional entities driving program content, process and progress. There has been some criticism of the government monopoly of provision in China where only state-authorized development programs are fully supported financially and politically. Even though opportunities are emerging from outside of government frameworks these are often depicted by 'official' training institutions as profit-driven and ill-qualified (Chen, 2005). Thus, voices from official institutions have urged the government to issue new policies to sanction and license leader training organizations (Chen, 2005; Chu, 2005).

Program access refers to the extent of discretion given to future potential principals to access formal pre-appointment programs. Formal requirements diverge in terms of who can access pre-principal programs (and, by default, those for serving principals). Access pathways range from 'access through self-selection' in HKSAR, to 'access through seniority' in Taiwan, to 'access through seniority-plus-political-affiliation' in China. In all three societies it is compulsory for aspiring principals to gain some sort of accreditation to be eligible to become a principal.

In HKSAR anyone with an interest in becoming a principal can enroll in the Aspiring Principal course and therefore apply for a principalship (in reality, however, those with more experience are generally selected for the post). As a result HKSAR, at any given time, has a proportionally larger and more diverse pool of certified potential principals than the other two societies regardless of the number of principal vacancies. In both China and Taiwan, only candidates identified systemically as future principals have access to programs, and the number of candidates involved in these programs is linked to projected future principalship vacancies. In Taiwan, potential candidates must have reached a certain administrative level in the school to be eligible to sit for the qualifying exam and interview. Those who achieve the highest score must then complete a one-month intensive training program before they are allowed to go on a 'reserve list' for a principalship (decided at a district level). Such access, through scaling, rating and examination appears somewhat akin to the rigorous Imperial Examination in China and reflects traditional respect for layered hierarchy and seniority.

In China only those identified as potential principals (or who have recently become principals) have access to the 300-hour certification exercise. It is generally understood that future principals are active members of the CCP and are variously connected to officials or serving principals through established social networks. They have also demonstrated their willingness and ability to follow policy and the current party line. For example, access to high-level training 'backbone principal' courses usually symbolizes a high recognition of the principal's work. However, such recognition seems more likely to be given to principals from elite schools, while those from difficult schools have less opportunity (Chu, 2005). Opportunities are thus unevenly distributed on traditional grounds of status, seniority, political linkage and social networks.

An important issue in terms of access emerges here for aspiring and serving principals. The strategies implemented in both China and Taiwan revolve around the bureaucratically-framed identification of excellent leaders. For example, a major strategy in China is the identification and cultivation of 'excellent' serving practitioners. Part of this strategy is that they return to their provinces and 'share' what they have learned but, at this stage, we have little idea of whether this happens and, if it does, whether it has any effect. Different provinces and districts have somewhat similar structures which aim to give LDPs the flexibility to cater to more localized needs. Again, however, we are unsure how this is working. What we do know however is that seniority, status and connection appear very important across the societies, particularly in China and that any wide-scale development spread will be framed by this.

Cultural/contextual sensitivity refers to the extent to which Leader Development policy, programs and processes draw on indigenous knowledge and adhere to established social processes. Contextual sensitivity relates to whether local education agencies, for example at a city, provincial and district level have the discretion to adapt or adjust content and or processes to local features. Within the formalized frameworks, localized government providers in China have room to adjust some components to address specific local needs. Such discretion however is restricted by required reform-linked knowledge and political norms, and relatively standardized formal materials. For example, government officials are regularly invited to report on the latest policy development — this is considered an important part of all programs. In addition, 'textbooks' recommended by the Ministry of Education include volumes such as Deng Xiaoping's *Ideas on Education* (Ministry of Education, 2002). Aims and content are therefore mainly China-focused and draw little from 'outside' theory, beliefs and/or research findings; this is reinforced by the fact that the preponderance of materials are written in Chinese. As a result, the substance of programs concentrates on political issues, what is seen as contemporary management theory and technical skills. It may be suggested, therefore, that Chinese Leader Development programs would benefit from increased cross-societal fertilization.

On the other hand, societal culture also provides an important backdrop to, and influence on leader development programs. For example, just as East Asian teachers have developed culturally-adaptive ways of large-class teacher-centered teaching, most leader development programs, particularly those adopted in China, are built around lecturing and textbook learning. Furthermore, Chinese LDPs operate within a multi-layered centralized educational system. Within the system, both central and provincial governments maintain the right to largely determine the mode and content of development programs which in turn attempt to both motivate and control principals. For example, by granting very few principals the title of 'backbone principal' and sending those to prestigious higher-level programs (either provincial or national level), the state makes these principals eligible for further promotion, thus increasing their motivation. When they return from the 'backbone' program, they are held up as role-models for other principals and thus preserve ingrained status differentials.

In terms of content, HKSAR and Taiwan tend to be less overtly political and draw more heavily on overseas theory, values and research. In Taiwan content leans toward more technical aspects of leadership and management, whereas in Hong Kong it attempts a firmer balance between educative and technical substance. However, given its colonial roots and location as an international city, HKSAR appears to have developed a certain dependence on Western knowledge and literature, and has only recently attempted to incorporate local indigenous research and understanding into the substance of its programs. Given its size, HKSAR does not need to decentralize for local specificity. On the whole, contextual application in Hong Kong is not built purposefully into programs as in China or Taiwan, but is basically left to serendipity and individual provider preferences. Taiwan seems to lie somewhere between HKSAR and China in this regard, perhaps leaning a little more toward the former. It is similar to China, however, in that local districts have room to tailor some materials to local needs and most literature used is written in Chinese.

Pedagogy refers to the range of teaching/training methods used in LDPs, and includes practitioner involvement in instructional or other roles. Although there have been moves recently across the three societies to expand how they approach leader development, most LDPs remain predominantly classroom based. This is particularly so in China where formal lecturing is used overwhelmingly, although often in concert with visits to recognized, high performing schools. Taiwan also relies mainly on formal lecturing methods but is moving toward using Problem Based Learning (PBL), mentoring, case studies, peer discussion and school visits. At this stage the extent to which these have taken hold remains unclear. A number of programs and initiatives in Hong Kong have introduced different forms of mentoring, action learning, networked peer learning and other experiential learning methods. Although these have been actively pursued and promoted in certain programs and in a number of ways, evidence supporting their efficacy has yet to be produced.

LDPs in all three societies involve experienced practitioners in one role or another, normally under the title of mentor. This can be seen as an extension of naturally occurring relationships modeled on familial structures within traditional Chinese culture. Within such structures relationships are as much about social networking and connection as they are about professional issues. Thus mentoring as a process of simultaneous learning and networking is considered quite 'natural' in all three Chinese education systems, but inevitably reflects hierarchical status. The all important networking function not only facilitates transferring social capital among leaders but also breeds Chinese prototypes of hierarchically-constructed professional learning communities among Chinese school leaders.[5]

Relational structures take a number of different forms across the three societies' education systems. In Taiwan, pre-service programs include experienced respected principals or retired principals to mentor future principals. Experienced principals are also involved formally in Chinese programs but are used mainly to share their tacit knowledge in formal lectures and through small group discussion. Mentors or sponsors are used extensively in HKSAR programs for legitimization, learning and networking. As such, they exert a core influence on a number of recent programs where they work closely with beginning principals in schools over a 12-month period to form small (and hopefully enduring) networked learning communities. It is now a requirement in government tendered programs in HKSAR that experienced principals are involved in this capacity.

Program impact refers to the ways leader development programs are evaluated and researched. Evaluation of programs across the three societies appears to be relatively neglected. The form of evaluation conducted can largely be classified as program (or even policy fulfillment mechanisms) rather than program-impact evaluation. In other words it uses 'tick-the-box' participant feedback to gauge program effectiveness in terms of whether participants 'like' the program or 'found it useful', but rarely whether it makes a difference to practice in the schools. If LDPs do not make a difference to improving the readiness and effectiveness of new principals, or the exercise of leadership by serving principals in terms of changed practice and improved student learning and lives, their purpose and indeed existence may be questionable.

CONCLUSION

So far we have described and analyzed school leader development in and across three Chinese societies within eight areas. In doing so we have attempted to isolate a number of patterns of leadership development and link them to similarities or differences between the three societies. From these patterns a number of interrelated conclusions may be drawn. We suggest three of these below.

Whereas recent policy across the three societies has certainly highlighted the importance of school leader development and tightened formal structural requirements, it may be that these risk becoming more important than the raison d'etre for leader development itself. It seems important that policy makers and program providers consider more deeply the purpose, content and methodologies (quality) associated with effective development and move beyond bland mechanical requirements (quantity) such as how many hours are required and what textbooks should be used. Whereas the establishment of formal frameworks comprises an important first step, if policy remains at this level, programs may become little more than another bureaucratic hoop through which leaders must jump.

Firm bureaucratic and/or ideological control also raises questions about the type of leader development funded, promoted and so valued in a particular society. The fact that leader development across the three societies, to varying degrees, is predominantly statist in philosophy, is telling.

To avoid this scenario, policy makers and providers should shift their attention to areas such as: how leaders learn best; the metaphorical underpinnings of policy beliefs (organic or mechanistic); program ability to promote flexibility and self renewal; what is required to lead schools into the future; whether the frameworks and programs actually make a positive difference to leadership practice and student outcomes; program alignment with reform initiatives; current knowledge of 'good' leadership; and ways to balance bureaucratic and professional goals. The basic question here is: *What is the real purpose of leader development and what effect do we expect it to have in schools?*

Leader development policy and activity across the three societies are deeply rooted in ordered social relationships and connections. That this endures despite the very different recent socio-political histories clearly reflects the shared cultural traditions of the three Chinese societies. Seniority and the importance of ordered social relationships are apparent in a myriad of forms at all levels, from policy formation to program enactment. They also incorporate political, regional, personal and professional domains. Ordered personal and social relationships or guanxi remain an important facet of Chinese life and influence leader development in multiple ways. First, broadly understood relational norms and connections determine who should become a principal, and therefore, who is involved in leader development; including the order of this involvement. Second, it helps determine how different leaders are grouped for training and, importantly, whether connections endure beyond formal activities. Third, they influence the dynamics within programs, courses and other activities. This includes mentoring arrangements, peer discussions, school visits and acceptable teachers and teaching methodology.

Whether the widely understood formal and informal norms benefit or detract from effective leader development is in some ways irrelevant, since the status quo appears unlikely to change significantly in the foreseeable future. Although such norms may be usefully questioned, a more productive investigative avenue might be to look for ways to build policies and programs around an understanding of how relationships work and how these can be manipulated or harnessed for worthwhile leader development. For example, ordered mentoring and hierarchically structured learning networks may be purposefully built into programs; policy makers may more openly define cross-sector groupings; or programs may adapt methodologies, such as story or experience-based learning to suit cultural nuances. The basic question here is: *How can leader developers use engrained cultural traditions to further understand leader identities and mould meaningful learning opportunities?* However, as indicated in earlier analysis, given the extent of misalignment between engrained cultural traditions and imposed (often imported) reform policies, a further question is: *How can leader developers harness engrained cultural traditions but develop the kind of leaders who can promote the educational reforms in Chinese societies?*

School leaders themselves have been largely left 'out of the loop' in terms of what is needed and what constitutes effective leader development. There seems scant recognition of the value that school leaders themselves can bring to programs; this neglect endures despite increased symbolic recognition in many programs. Leader development programs may well become more relevant and thus effective if they connect more closely with school/leader lives, provide greater opportunities for a range of involvement by leaders themselves and target relevant educational outcomes. There may be a number of reasons why leaders are out of the loop. A first reason relates again to accepted relational boundaries — issues of hierarchy may well block increased practitioner involvement by making it unacceptable to ask for input from certain groups. A second reason may be the lack of worthwhile leadership/school improvement research available, or third, that policy makers and program providers remain too distant from what is happening in schools. Fourth, there may be a shortage of trust in practitioner perspectives, particularly by higher education providers.

Two major shortfalls related to missing practitioner voices are that programs may remain irrelevant to the lives and jobs of leaders, and that the dominant pedagogies employed remain content-heavy, instructor-centered and traditionally delivered. Policy makers and providers across the three societies' education systems may consider program relevance in tandem with ways to get practitioners more involved. For example, the place of process-based, rather than content-based approaches to leader development; the level of involvement offered to practitioners — from developing to conducting programs; balancing academic, political and practitioner perspectives; individualizing professional learning and locating more learning in the lives of school leaders. The basic question here is: *What do school leaders themselves believe they need to improve in their jobs and, what can they do in terms of leadership development to help make this happen?*

Of course there are many other issues; although important, those presented above are indicative only and leave fertile ground for further theoretical and empirical research. Given the dearth of research, some interrelated questions which may be usefully addressed are suggested below.

- Given that we know something about how LDPs work across the three societies why are they framed and shaped as they are? Are differences driven by cultural, political, and demographic factors or by a combination of factors?
- Given the inadequate state of evaluation into the programs themselves and their subsequent impact, how should evaluations in areas ranging from policy to pedagogy be framed by familiar Western or more indigenous frameworks?
- Given increasing (if minimal) knowledge about cultural/contextual/individual influences on learning styles how do potential and serving principals appear to learn best?
- Is there anything peculiarly 'Chinese' in the way leader development is run within and across the three societies? Answers to this question may be usefully framed by comparisons specifically with other Asian societies but also with other developing societies, and developed societies from which much of the current literature emanates.

Leader development has progressed remarkably quickly across all three Chinese societies, but our understanding of whether existing programs work and what else is needed remains in its infancy. The same can be said of the emerging polices and activities relating to leadership development in the three societies' education systems. More research is needed. That said, it is doubtful whether any society has worked out and implemented a perfect approach to leader development. In this chapter we have attempted to pull together some of what is known about school leadership development in three linked-yet-discrete settings — HKSAR, Taiwan and Mainland China — and suggested that this may act as a stimulus to encourage further understanding.

ACKNOWLEDGEMENTS

This project is supported by the Research Grants Council of Hong Kong through an Earmarked Grant (CUHK4619/05H). We wish to thank Professors Phillip Hallinger, Clive Dimmock and Lin Ming-Bih for their critique of an earlier draft of this chapter.

NOTES

1. For further information on the Hong Kong reform context see Cheng (2003 & 2005), Mok and Welch (2002), Morris and Scott (2003), and Walker (2003).
2. In Mainland China, there are 32 provincial districts: 4 municipal cities, 5 autonomous regions, and 23 provinces.
3. For a more comprehensive account of leader development in Hong Kong see Cheung & Walker (2006); Walker & Dimmock (2005) Walker & Kwong (2006).
4. The new Education and Manpower Bureau (EMB) was formed by the merger of the old Bureau and the Education Department (ED) on 1 January 2003. It was changed to Education Bureau (EDB) in 2007.
5. For further discussion of the influence of culture on mentoring structures and processes see, Lumby, Walker, Bryant, Bush, & Bjork (in press) and Walker (2007).

REFERENCES

Advisory Committee on School-based Management. (2000). *Transforming schools into dynamic and accountable professional learning communities–School-based management consultation document.* Hong Kong: Printing Department.

Advisory Committee on Teacher Education and Qualifications (ACTEQ). (2003). *Towards a learning profession – The teacher competencies framework (TCF) and the continuing professional development (CPD) of teachers.* Hong Kong: Printing Department.

CCP Central Committee. (1985) *Decisions of the Central Committee of the Chinese Communist Party on the Reform of the Educational System.* PRC: CCP Central Committee. (In Chinese)

Chang, F. C. (2006). The analysis of educational reform in Taiwan since 1994. *Educational Resources and Research Bimonthly,* 68, 221–240. (In Chinese)

Chen, B. S. (2004). *Policy implementation of principal selection and appointment.* Taibei: Guanxue Wenhua. (In Chinese)

Chen, Y. K. (2005). Principal professional development and quality assurance for principal training. *Educational Leadership Training and Research,* 1, 7–15. (In Chinese)

Cheng, Y. C. (2000). The characteristics of Hong Kong school principals' leadership: the influence of societal culture. *Asia Pacific Journal of Education,* 20(2), 68–86.

Cheng, Y. C. (2003). Trends in educational reform in the Asia-Pacific region. In J. P. Keeves & R. Watanabe (Eds.), *International handbook of educational research in the Asia-Pacific region,* pp. 3–16. Dordrecht, The Netherlands: Kluwer.

Cheng, Y. C. (2005). Globalization and educational reforms in Hong Kong: Paradigm shift. In J. Zaida, K. Freeman, M. Geo-JaJa, S. Majhanovich, V. Rust, & R. Zajda (Eds.). *The international handbook on globalization and education policy research,* pp.165–187. Dordrecht, The Netherlands: Springer.

Cheung, M. B., & Walker, A. (2006). Inner worlds and outer limits: The formation of beginning school principals in Hong Kong. *Journal of Educational Administration,* 44(4), 389–407.

Chiu, C. S., & Chung, Y. P. (2003). *The quality school project: Final report.* Hong Kong: Faculty of Education, The Chinese University of Hong Kong.

Chu, H, Q. (2005). Macro governance of principal training. *Educational Leadership Training and Research,* 1, 23–34. (In Chinese)

Curriculum Development Council. (2001). *Learning to learn: The way forward in curriculum development.* Hong Kong: Curriculum Development Council.

Dimmock, C., & Walker, A. (1998). Transforming Hong Kong's schools: Trends and emerging issues. *Journal of Educational Administration*, 36(5), 476–491.

Education and Manpower Branch, & Education Department. (1991). *The school management initiative: Setting the framework for quality in Hong Kong schools.* Hong Kong: Government Printer, Hong Kong.

Education and Manpower Bureau. (2003). *Enhancing school development and accountability through school self-evaluation and external school review.* [Education and Manpower Bureau Circular No.23/2003]. Hong Kong: Education and Manpower Bureau, HKSAR.

Education and Manpower Bureau. (2003a). *Enhancing school development and accountability through school self-evaluation and external school review: The use and reporting of key performance measures.* [Education and Manpower Bureau Circular No.269/2003]. Hong Kong: Education and Manpower Bureau, HKSAR.

Education and Manpower Bureau. (2004). *Report of the panel for the review of the designated programme for newly appointed principals.* Unpublished report, Hong Kong, Education and Manpower Bureau, HKSAR.

Education Commission. (2000a). *Learning for life, learning through life: Reform proposals for the education system in Hong Kong.* Hong Kong: Printing Department.

Education Commission. (2000b, September). *Reform proposals for the education system in Hong Kong.* Hong Kong: Printing Department.

Education Department. (2002, February & September). *Continuing professional development for school excellence consultation paper on continuing development of principals.* Hong Kong, Education Department, Hong Kong Government.

Education Department. (2002a). *Continuing professional development for school excellence – Consultation paper on continuing professional development of principals.* Hong Kong: Printing Department.

Education Department. (2002b). *Administration Circular No. 31/2002—Principals' continuing professional development.* Hong Kong: Education Department.

Feng, D. M. (2003). Principal training in the People's Republic of China: Retrospect and prospect. In P. Hallinger (Ed.), *Reshaping the Landscape of School Leadership Development: A Global Perspective*, pp. 205–216. Lisse, The Netherlands: Swets & Zeitilinger.

Fwu, B. J., & Wang, H. H. (2002). The social status of teachers in Taiwan. *Comparative Education*, 38(2), 211–224.

Fwu, B.J., & Wang, H. H. (March, 2001). *Principals at the crossroads: Profiles, preparation and role perceptions of secondary school principals in Taiwan.* Paper presented at the International Conference on School Leaders Preparation, Licensure, Certification, Selection, Evaluation and Professional Development, Taipei, Taiwan.

HKSAR Government. (1999). *Policy objectives.* Hong Kong: Printing Department.

Hallinger, P. (2003). (Ed.). *Reshaping the landscape of school leadership development: A global perspective.* The Netherlands: Swets & Zeitilinger.

Li, L. Q. (2004). *Education: For 1.3 Billion – Former Chinese Vice Premier Li Lanqing on 10 Years of Education Reform and Development.* Beijing: Foreign Language Teaching and Research Press.

Li, Y. Y. (2004a). Issues encountered by programme facilitators during comprehensive school reform: The first year of the Quality Schools Project in Hong Kong. *Educational Research Journal*, 19(1), 93–120.

Lin, M. D. (2002). *School leadership: Concepts and principal's professional careers.* Taibei: Higher education publishing. (In Chinese)

Lin, M. D. (2003). Professional development for principals in Taiwan: The status quo and future needs. In P. Hallinger (Ed.), *Reshaping the landscape of school leadership development: A global perspective*, pp. 191–204. Lisse, The Netherlands: Swets & Zeitilinger.

Lo, L. N. K. (1997). Policy change and educational development in Hong Kong. *American Asian Review*, 15(4), 325–370.

Lumby, J., Walker, A., Bryant, M., Bush, T., & Bjork, L. (in press). In M. Young, G. Crow, J. Murphy & R. Ogawa (Eds.). *The University Council of Educational Administration: Handbook on the education of school leaders.* Netherlands: Springer.

Ministry of Education. (2001). *The directive teaching plan for continuous principal training programs.* China: Ministry of Education.

Ministry of Education (2002). *Recommended textbooks for the Tenth National Five-Year principal training programs.* Taiwan: Ministry of Education.

Mok, J. K. H., & Welch, A. R. (2002). Economic rationalism, managerialism and structural reform in education. In J. K. H. Mok & D.K.K.Chan (Eds.), *Globalization and education: The quest for quality education in Hong Kong,* pp. 23–40. Hong Kong: Hong Kong University Press.

Morris, P., & Scott, I. (2003). Educational reform and policy implementation in Hong Kong. *Journal of Education Policy,* 18(1), 71–84.

Murphy, J. (2006). *Preparing school leaders: defining a research and action agenda.* Lanham MD: University Council for Educational Administration.

National Training Centre for Primary School Principals. (2006). *A Notice on holding the 18th, 19th, and 20th National Advanced Principal Development Course.* Available at: http://pdn.cea.bnu.edu.cn/training/newcls/200608.php (In Chinese)

Pan, H. L. (2007). School effectiveness and improvement in Taiwan. In T. Townsend (Ed). *International handbook of school effectiveness and improvement,* pp. 269–286. Lisse, The Netherlands: Swets & Zeitilinger

Pan, H. L., & Yu, C. (1999). Educational reforms and their impacts on school effectiveness and improvement in Taiwan, R.O.C. School *Effectiveness and Improvement,* 10(1), 72–85.

Review Committee on Educational Reform of the Executive Yuen. (1996). *Final consultation report for educational reform.* Taipei: Review Committee on Educational Reform of the Executive Yuen.

Shan, W. J., & Chang, C. C.(2000). Social change and educational development in Taiwan, 1945–1999. In T. Townsend & Y. C. Cheng (Eds). *Educational change and development in the Asia-Pacific region: Challenges for the future,* pp.185–206. Lisse: Swets & Zeitlinger.

Shanghai Education Commission. (2006). *On the enrolment work of senior secondary schools in 2007.* China: Shanghai Education Commission.

State Education Commission (1989). *On strengthening the training for principals of elementary and secondary schools nation-wide.* China: State Education Commission.

Tang, X., & Wu, X. (2000). Educational change and development in the People's Republic of China: Challenges for the future. In T. Townsend & Y. C. Cheng (Eds.), *Educational change and development in the Asia-Pacific region: Challenges for the future,* pp. 133–162. Lisse, The Netherlands: Swets & Zeitlinger.

Task Group on Training and Development of School Heads (1999). *Leadership Training Programme for Principals Consultation Document.* Hong Kong: Printing Department

UNDP Research Team (1997). A comparative study of Chinese and foreign principal training. *Journal of Jiangsu Institution of Education,* 2, 6–14. (In Chinese)

Walker, A. (2003). School leadership and management. In J. Keeves & R. Watanabe (Eds.), *The handbook of educational research in the Asia-Pacific region,* pp. 973–986. Dordrecht, The Netherlands: Kluwer.

Walker, A. (2004) Constitution and culture: Exploring the deep leadership structures of Hong Kong schools. *Discourse: Studies in the Cultural Politics of Education,* 25(1) 75–94.

Walker, A. (2007). Leading authentically at the crossroads of reform and culture. *Journal of Educational Change,* 8(3). 257–273.

Walker, A., & Dimmock, C. (2005). Developing leadership in context. In M. Coles & G. Southworth (Eds.), *Developing leadership: Creating the schools of tomorrow,* pp. 88–64. Milton Keyes: Open University Press.

Walker, A., & Dimmock, C. (2006). Preparing leaders, preparing learners: the Hong Kong experience. *School Leadership and Management,* 26(2), 125–147.

Walker, A., Hallinger, P., & Qian, H.Y. (2007). Leadership development for school effectiveness and improvement in East Asia. In T. Townsend (Ed.), *International handbook of school effectiveness and school improvement,* pp. 659–677. Dordrecht, The Netherlands: Springer.

Walker, A., & Kwong, K. S. C. (June, 2006). *School Management Training - COUNTRY REPORT: Hong Kong Special Administrative Region, People's Republic of China.* Oslo, Norway: University of Oslo.

Walker, A., & Quong, T. (2005). Blue skies: *A professional learning programme (package) for beginning principals in Hong Kong.* Hong Kong, Hong Kong Centre for the Development of Educational Leadership.

Walker, A., Dimmock, C., Chan, A., Chan, W. K., Cheung, M. B. & Wong Y. H. (2002). *Key qualities of the principalship in Hong Kong.* Hong Kong: Hong Kong Centre for the Development of Educational Leadership.

Weng, F. Y. (2003). Centralization and decentralization in educational governance. In K. H. Mok (Ed.), *Centralization and decentralization: Educational reforms and changing governance in Chinese societies,* pp. 39–58. Hong Kong: CERC of University of Hong Kong & Kluwer.

Wong, S. L. (2005). *Impact of leadership training on newly-appointed female principals in middle/secondary schools in England and Hong Kong.* Nottingham, National College for School Leadership.

Wu, C. S. (2006). Examination and improvement on educational reform in Taiwan: 1994–2006. *Bulletin of Educational Resources, 32,* 1–21. (In Chinese)

Yang, C. L. (2001, March). *The changing principalship and its implication for preparing selecting and evaluating principals.* Paper presented at the International Conference on School Leaders Preparation, Licensure, Certification, Selection, Evaluation and Professional Development, Taipei, Taiwan.

21

Professional Learning of School Leaders in Australia

Michelle Anderson, Elizabeth Kleinhenz, Bill Mulford and David Gurr

In Australia, the professional learning of school leaders has seldom mattered more. The importance of school leadership stems both from an increasing emphasis on improving schools and a foreshadowed crisis in attracting sufficient quality applicants to principal class positions.

There has long been an assumption that leadership matters to organizations, although the empirical and conceptual evidence for this is contested (Lakomski, 2005). Nevertheless, recent Australian research (Mulford, Silins and Leithwood, 2004) and major international reviews of research (Leithwood and Riehl, 2005; Leithwood, Seashore Louis, Anderson, and Wahslstrom, 2004; Leithwood, Day, Sammons, Harris and Hopkins, 2006) provide a powerful and persuasive case that principal leadership, and educational leadership more broadly conceived, are, after the impact of teachers, the second most important element in improving student learning, albeit that the effects are often indirect. Leadership development programs need to ensure that this knowledge base on successful school leadership is used to improve schools.

Overseas, and in Australia, there are many instances of difficulties in recruiting sufficient quality applicants for principal positions (Collins, 2006). Barty, Thompson, Blackmore and Sachs (2005), Carlin, d'Arbon, Dorman, Duignan and Neidhart (2003), and Lacey (2002), amongst others, have all highlighted actual and/or emerging difficulties in the Australian context. The picture is complex however, as there are not necessarily universal shortages, with school location, size of school, the presence of an incumbent principal, local educational policies, and social and generational changes important determiners of the attractiveness of a principal position (Collins, 2006). Nevertheless, it is clear that the preparation of future school leaders needs to be a priority, particularly given the likely retirement of most of the current school principals over the next five to ten years.

A key challenge for developers of school leadership programs is to identify those factors that are of central importance in the preparation of school leaders, including the capacity to take on a broad range of responsibilities and facilitate shared leadership and the relationship between leadership and student outcomes. Attention needs to be given to the recruitment and selection of school leaders who have the qualities and capacities that lead teachers and schools to improve student learning. Stakeholders have also drawn attention to the need to establish working conditions and support structures that will improve the retention of effective leaders.

Education in Australia is a complex interplay between various levels of government, public and private providers of schools and related services (including the professional learning of school leaders), and stakeholder groups. Australia has a Commonwealth Government that oversees six state and two territory governments. Constitutionally, school education is the responsibility of the six state and two territory governments, yet there is a vibrant and diverse non-government sector, largely funded by federal government grants and school fees. Approximately two thirds of students attend government schools, twenty percent Catholic schools, with the remainder attending an independent school (most of which have a religious affiliation).

Over the past 40 years there has been an increasing role for the federal government in the provision of school education. In terms of the professional learning of school leaders, there are many players. At the Commonwealth level, Teaching Australia – Australian Institute for Teaching and School Leadership is, amongst other things, charged by government with developing policy advice and providing a range of services related to school leadership development (e.g. provision of a seven-day residential program for principals titled *Leading Australia's Schools* and described in more detail later). It has been particularly active in discussions about leadership standards. At the State and Territory level, each government has large public school systems to service, with leadership development an increasing focus. In addition to award courses provided by universities, across Australia there are many service organizations focused on leadership development. Some providers represent key stakeholder groups (e.g. Australian Primary Principals Association, Australian Secondary Principals Association, Association of Heads of Independent Schools of Australia, Association of Principals of Catholic Secondary Schools of Australia, Australian Principals Associations Professional Development Council). Other providers are more broadly focused (e.g. Australian Council for Educational Leaders, Australian College of Educators). New groups continue to form with, for example, the research and publishing organization, the Australian Council for Educational Research, constructing a leadership centre in 2007. In summary, Australia has a complex and dynamic policy and program environment for the development of educational leaders.

This chapter explores issues relating to the structure, processes and effectiveness of existing school leadership preparation and development programs, recent initiatives that have been adopted, and the areas where more support appears to be needed.

PATHWAYS TO BECOMING A SCHOOL LEADER

Despite the number and variety of leadership learning programs available in Australia, a four-year teaching qualification and registration remain the only formal requirements for school leaders. Su, Gamage and Miniberg (2003) characterize the approach in Australia as an 'apprenticeship' model whereby teachers gradually gain experience on-the-job and move up the ranks to principalship.

Higher qualifications in leadership are not mandatory, although possession of such qualifications may well enhance applicants' prospects of gaining and retaining leadership positions. Many individuals who aspire to leadership positions in schools are choosing to avail themselves of higher degrees and other opportunities offered by different providers (e.g. The University of Melbourne and Monash University have recently established Master of School Leadership degrees in response to demand from individuals and the systems). Gamage and Ueyama (2004) found that 34 per cent of principals and deputy principals in 130 NSW schools across three school districts had Masters degrees in educational administration and management. Gurr, Drysdale and

Goode (2007) reported that of a sample of 206 Victorian principals, 44 per cent had a graduate certificate/diploma or a Masters in educational leadership, whilst 53 per cent of a sample of 131 Tasmanian principals reported having an educational administration qualification.

There are some specific requirements for becoming a school leader in some sectors. For example, in the Catholic system in Western Australia, school principals also require specific Religious Education Accreditation and, once appointed, must continue to work towards a Masters degree in either Theology or Religious Education. So, too, there are now examples of moves to formalize principal preparation in the States and Territories. Western Australia's Introductory Leadership program is one such example outlined later in this chapter.

Issues to do with succession planning are fuelling a need for better pathways and processes of support for prospective and established school leaders. Research by the Australian Catholic University and Right Angles Consulting for the Australian Principals Association's Professional Development Committee (APAPDC, 2004) suggests that few examples in Australia can be found of strategic succession planning processes for schools and systems. However, education systems recognize this as an issue and are developing strategies that focus on succession planning in the context of overarching planning for improvement and reform. The researchers highlight the work of the Sydney Catholic Education Office and South Australia's Centre for Leaders in Education as examples of moves towards better processes for leadership succession. The latter offers programs to self-identified teachers, coordinators, and assistant and deputy principals, and provides scholarships for teachers and leaders identified by District Superintendents to attend the *Preparing for the Principalship* program.

Figure 21.1 illustrates the type of framework now being developed to map school leaders' pathways and development in Australia. This example, presented in 2006 at the National School Leadership Invitational Conference, is from the Queensland government school system is similar to frameworks being used in other systems. It traces the 'leadership journey' from aspirations

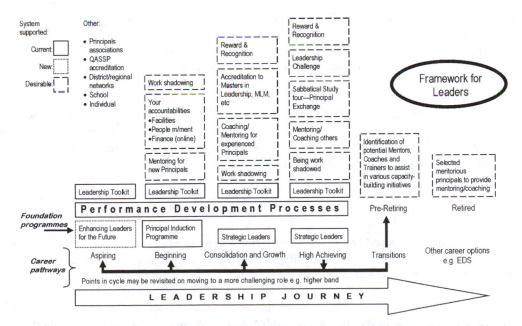

FIGURE 21.1 School leadership framework, Queensland's Department of Education and the Arts, March 2006, National School Leadership invitational conference.

through to beginning in leadership roles, consolidation and growth, high achievement in the role, and transitions to other roles, including preparation for retirement. Such continua are being developed to support the preparation and ongoing professional learning of school leaders by identifying the types of foundation programs and other activities needed at different stages of the career. While a number of the elements in Figure 21.1 are not yet implemented, their identification as part of a public strategy document is a promising development.

USING STANDARDS FRAMEWORKS TO GUIDE PROFESSIONAL LEARNING

The use of standards frameworks to guide the professional learning and development of school leaders is a notable development in recent years. Standards frameworks are starting to have a major role in helping school leaders to learn what it is that they need to know and be able to do in order to develop professionally. They provide leaders and aspiring leaders with a learning continuum that gives long-term direction to professional learning.

Ingvarson and Kleinhenz (2006) argue that a powerful way of using standards to support leaders' professional learning is to incorporate them into a standards based professional learning system that requires participants to gather, and present for assessment, evidence of having met the standards. While it might not be possible to argue that there is a strong school leadership profession in Australia currently, there is a widespread desire among members of principal associations to move in that direction. A standards based professional learning system operationalizes standards: that is, it indicates how a leader's performance will be assessed and what level of performance indicates that the standard has been attained. It has four components:

- profession-wide standards that describe the knowledge, skills, values and dispositions of school leaders;
- an infrastructure for professional learning that supports people as they gather evidence of meeting the standards;
- fair, valid, consistent and reliable assessment leading to certification; and
- recognition and reward, such as progression in a career structure or increased financial remuneration.

Ingvarson and Kleinhenz (2006) suggest the most effective sets of leadership standards are able to indicate not only what leaders should aim to achieve, and the kinds of professional learning needed to achieve it, but also the kind of evidence they would need to produce to show that the standards have been met. Currently, the latter aspect is not so well developed.

STANDARDS FOR SCHOOL LEADERSHIP IN AUSTRALIA

Although Australia has a good record in international comparisons of student performance, there are strong pressures to lift schooling quality and improve access (Anderson et al., 2008). Standards are seen by employing authorities and professional associations as one way to address this issue. Over the last 15 years or so, both have been active in developing standards.

Every Australian state and territory education system now has, or is in the process of developing, some form of standards or standards referenced framework for school leadership. Only a few of these efforts reflect a deep understanding of what standards are and what is involved in developing standards that are usable. As yet, most leadership standards in Australia would need further development before they could form the basis of a professional learning system for school leaders (Ingvarson and Anderson, 2007).

Recent sets of standards, however, do look more like profession-wide standards than the lists of competencies and elements of job descriptions which characterized many of the statements about leaders' work in the 1990s. The more recently developed standards are generally broader and deeper, and they reflect a more complex and comprehensive professional knowledge base.

There is evidence of States and Territories sharing their leadership frameworks and activities through bodies such as the Ministerial Council on Education, Employment and Training (MCEETYA), which has developed a Framework of Standards that integrates standards for teachers and school leaders. The Framework provides a key point of reference around which future collaborative work for the development of profession-wide standards could be organized and a 'common and recognizable reference point for professional engagement' (MCEETYA, 2003).

The majority of standards frameworks for school leadership in Australia have been developed predominantly by employers in conjunction with school leader professional associations and academics. Examples include, the empirically based NSW Department of Education and Training's *Professional Capability Framework* (Scott, 2003), Western Australia's *Performance Standards for School Leadership,* the *Leadership Framework for Lutheran Schools* (Lutheran Education Australia, 2005), and the *Leadership in Catholic Schools* framework developed by the Catholic Education Commission of Victoria (CECV).

The development of the CECV leadership framework is illustrative of the complexity and care involved in the development of leadership standards. In 2003 the CECV commissioned ACER to assist in the development of leadership standards. This initiative, funded by the Australian Government Quality Teaching Program (AGQTP), was influenced by two major trends: the growing recognition that new kinds of school leadership centered on successful student learning, are now needed in schools; and the movement towards standards-based professional learning and accountability. The main target group was those practicing teachers who aspired to senior leadership roles in schools. The standards were developed to validate the work of teachers who were already leading others to improve students' learning opportunities and outcomes. At the same time, they were intended for use as a 'road map' to guide the professional learning and development of aspiring leaders.

The standards cannot be described as fully 'profession-wide' in that they were developed for a particular group of leaders — those who work in Victorian Catholic schools. This is immediately apparent in the five 'key' leadership areas, which form the domains of these standards: the faith community; a vision for the whole school; teaching and learning; people and resources; and pastoral and community.

The developers of the standards faced the dilemma, common to all developers of standards for school leaders, of identifying and distinguishing between understandings about 'leadership' itself, and descriptions of what school leaders actually do. The standards attempt to bring these two together by setting out 'leadership actions' in the five key areas, and showing how every one of these actions is underpinned by all of five 'guiding conceptions' of leadership identified from the literature, chiefly from the work of Fullan (2001). These are: having a clear moral purpose; relationship building; understanding and managing change; knowledge creation and sharing; and ensuring coherence and alignment of structures. A website, *Leadership in Catholic Schools: Development Framework and Standards of Practice,* can be accessed at www.cecv.melb.catholic. edu.au.

Sets of school leadership standards have also been developed by school leaders' professional associations. A review of standards for school leadership in Australia highlighted the contribution of two professional associations (Ingvarson, Anderson, Gronn and Jackson, 2006). The Australian Council for Educational Leaders (ACEL; www.acel.org.au) developed a leadership standards framework in response to the establishment in 2005 of Teaching Australia (a Federal Government initiative providing nation-wide policy, research and programs on quality teaching and school leadership) and impetus this gave to developing ACEL positions on several important professional issues. The ACEL standards encompass seven professional elements:

- The leader in me
- The leader in shaping the future
- The leader and the learning organization
- The leader and collaborative learning communities
- The leader in a quality organization
- The leader and strategic resource management
- The leader advocating

Each element has a summary statement and detailed description of the required knowledge and qualities.

The APAPDC (www.apapdc.edu.au) has a set of five educational leadership propositions to describe the desirable characteristics of current and future educational leaders:

- Leadership starts from within
- Leadership is about influencing others
- Leadership develops a rich learning environment
- Leadership builds professionalism and management capability
- Leadership inspires leadership actions and aspirations in others

While standards frameworks in Australia may be developed and presented in different ways, overall there is a striking similarity in the core components, particularly the explicit focus on learning (e.g. Queensland's Department of Education and the Arts *Leadership Matters – leadership capabilities for education Queensland principals*, 2006, and South Australia's Centre for Leaders in Education, which has drawn on the APAPDC's five leadership propositions to underpin its *Leaders Learning Framework*, 2005). Renewed emphasis on learning has occurred because such outcomes as balancing the potentially competing objectives of quality, equity and efficiency are crucial, and the environment of learning is more complex.

Debate over the purposes and principles underpinning the standards frameworks for school leadership presents continuing challenges for developers. The standards can act as an important ethical and research-based frame of reference for, among other activities, professional leadership learning and development. This purpose of professional standards is important when considered alongside findings such as those of Duignan (2004, p. 40), who points out that, 'leaders in contemporary organizations require frames of reference that can assist them to manage situations of uncertainty, ambiguity and seeming contradictions and paradox.' School leaders are expected not only to manage schools well but to know how to develop their schools as organizations with the capacity to constantly review and improve their performance (Ingvarson and Anderson, 2007).

Developers of recently published school leadership standards acknowledge there is a need to review the standards, possibly every three to five years, to ensure their ongoing relevance and currency (e.g. Queensland Department of Education and the Arts, 2006).

THE PROVISION OF PROFESSIONAL LEARNING FOR SCHOOL LEADERS

Rapid change and the diversity of the Australian context of school leadership, present key challenges for the provision of professional learning. At a national level, there is no consistent or coordinated framework for providing professional learning for school leaders in Australia. The diversity of providers and program offerings for school leaders in Australia is, simultaneously, a valued characteristic of the Australian context, and an obstacle to greater coherence. The wide array of professional learning opportunities on offer can meet a diverse range of school leaders' needs in different settings and stages of career (e.g. see Ingvarson et al., 2006). Equally, however, diversity of provision and providers increases the complexities involved in ascertaining and quantifying levels of investment in professional learning, coordinating efforts, and drawing conclusions about impact.

Reconceptualizing what counts as quality school leadership has also forced the providers of professional learning to reconsider what counts as quality professional leadership learning and development. Consistent with a number of other reviews of literature on the critical features of quality professional leadership learning, from overseas (e.g. Davis et al., 2005), are Ingvarson, Meiers and Beavis' (2005) four evaluation studies of the AGQTP funded programs between 2001 to 2003. In total, data for these evaluations was gathered from 3,250 teachers who had participated in professional learning programs.

The evaluation team drew on a wide body of overseas and Australian research to identify a number of features of effective professional learning. These included (1) *content focus*, recognizing the importance of *what* was to be learned; (2) *active learning* engagement and reflection on learning; (3) provision of effective and timely *feedback* from a 'coach' or supporting peers; and (4) giving *follow up* support during the implementation phase of a professional learning program. The researchers concluded that 'effective integration of new skills requires programs to have a clear theoretical foundation supported by research, modeling in real settings, and opportunities to practice the new skills and receive feedback' (Ingvarson et al., 2005, p. 8).

These and other generic features of professional learning (e.g. that it should be organized around collaborative problem solving) are frequently identified in the literature as being essential to the development of effective school leaders. Space precludes including full descriptions of each of these features. However, collectively, they can be organized into categories about structure, content, methods and measures of success, which can be used to guide research, development and evaluation of professional learning offered by different providers. The remaining sections of this chapter use these categories to frame a discussion about professional learning offered by different school systems in Australia.

Current Structural Arrangements

Principal preparation and other school leadership programs reflect a variety of structures, collaborations, and institutional arrangements. At the state, territory and national levels, Australia has many providers of professional learning for school leaders. These include specially developed leadership centers such as the South Australian Centre for Leaders in Education (SACLE), the Western Australian Leadership Centre, and Queensland's Indigenous Education Leadership Institute, and the provision of postgraduate courses in educational leadership and administration in universities.

Nationally, professional association providers focused on educational leadership include the Australian Council for Educational Leaders (ACEL), which has membership from all educational sectors, and the APAPDC which is a construction of the main principal associations. Many other national professional associations have a broad membership base and offer a range of programs for different school personnel, some of which is focused on educational leadership. For example, the Australian Joint Council of Professional Teaching Associations (AJCPTA) and the Australian College of Educators (ACE) have organizational members in all States and Territories that provide leadership programs for teachers and current holders of leadership positions. The work of these associations provides an important alternative to government and university principal preparation programs. In many cases a feature of the programs offered is the close connection to experience of those leading schools.

The Australian Government has initiated a number of strategies aimed at supporting and improving school leader effectiveness, such as the AGQTP, which in 2007 is funding 12 activities that focused on building leadership capacity across the country. A prominent example is provided by the *Dare to Lead* project, which is run through the APAPDC.

Dare to Lead was conceived in 1999, when the presidents of the national principal associations agreed that school leaders needed to play a critical role in helping to remove the gap in educational outcomes between Indigenous students and other young Australians. Forums were held across Australia in 2000 and 2001, following which a coalition of school leaders formally signed up to tackle this issue in schools. By mid-2006 almost 4000 school leaders were members of the *Dare to Lead* coalition with participation voluntary and free. All schools on becoming members agree to engage in planning and implementation around the project's goals to support Indigenous students. These goals include: improving literacy performance levels in primary schools at Year 5 by at least ten per cent; and improving completion rates of recognized Year 12 courses. Access to regular professional learning, newsletters, website and subsidized resources (generated by school leaders and Indigenous educators) are all features of the support participants receive. Exemplary work in schools is profiled for various publications and peer presentations, and there are 'Excellence in Leadership' in Indigenous Education awards which showcase good practice.

Increasingly government education departments are constructing comprehensive leadership development programs, often in association with universities and other providers. In part the need for these programs is driven by a concern that there will not be enough qualified and appropriate people to fill the principal class positions that will become available over the next decade. For example, the Victorian Department of Education launched in 2006 a comprehensive professional development program for current and aspirant leaders, *Learning to Lead Effective Schools*. The program includes a suite of 19 separate offerings for aspirant leaders, assistant principals and principals, with some programs targeting such specified groups as female aspirant principals. This program is framed by the Victorian Department's *Developmental Learning Framework for School Leaders*. This framework, also launched in 2006, is based on Sergiovanni's five leadership forces (technical, human, educational, symbolic and cultural) and Hay Group research on leadership capabilities. Most programs are offered at no cost to participants and low cost to schools. The cost to schools is mostly in terms of time release of individual teachers and leaders. One program, the Master of School Leadership, provides sponsored places in degree programs offered by the University of Melbourne and Monash University. By the end of 2006, 240 aspirant and recently appointed principals had been sponsored, receiving half fee costs, plus up to ten days each for time release of individuals from schools.

Target Groups

While there is considerable emphasis being given to school leadership, and there is an increased investment in the ongoing development of school leaders, typically, the focus of professional learning for school leaders has been on principals or those aspiring to this role in schools. For example, of the 12 AGQTP funded programs, the most widely established are probably those for newly appointed principals (e.g. induction programs). More recently, attention is being paid to the provision of professional learning programs for prospective school leaders — especially aspirant principals. An example is the AGQTP NSW *Strengthening Leadership* for assistant principals and teachers who hold coordinator positions in primary and secondary schools.

However, rather than treating the principal class as a homogenous group, providers are now recognizing the need to develop programs which cater for the diversity of leaders in Australia and which target particular groups.

A number of school leadership programs specifically target women, who are currently under-represented among Australian school principals. An important example is the Victorian Department of Education's *Eleanor Davis* program which provides leadership development, mentoring and shadowing for women with high potential for future school principalship. Another is the program of activities organized by the Western Australian Leadership Centre as part of its Women in Leadership Strategy. These activities include opportunities for women to participate in a virtual learning website, networking, mentoring, study tours and focused professional learning.

Indigenous leadership is also a current key area of development in Australia. Amid growing concerns about the relatively low outcomes of Indigenous children, different providers are implementing leadership development activities. Examples include the aforementioned *Dare to Lead* project, and the newly offered *Stronger Smarter Principals Leadership Program* for current and aspiring school leaders serving Indigenous communities throughout Australia. This program is offered by The Indigenous Education Leadership Institute in Queensland, and includes an intensive week-long program and follow-up review and school mentoring support.

The Northern Territory Department of Employment, Education and Training has also embarked on an *Indigenous Leaders Network* project. By 2020, the Indigenous student population in the Northern Territory (NT) is projected to rise from 30 per cent to 50 per cent of all students. This projected increase in Indigenous student numbers has created a major impetus for recruiting and supporting more Indigenous school leaders. In response, the Northern Territory DEET has developed and delivered a number of leadership forums that specifically target Indigenous school leaders. The forums aim to impact on student learning in the NT, through bridging the home culture to school/agency culture divide by: enhancing participants' capacity to lead in bi-cultural educational contexts, and collectively advocating and working towards appropriate shifts in worksite cultures and practices. As a result of the forum discussions, recommendations for more bi-culturally competent workplaces were developed in 2006. These recommendations are informing a six-day bi-cultural leadership module phase for the Indigenous leader participants which will involve seminar sessions and shadowing a leader in another community school. The program developers envisage using the feedback from participants to develop a suite of pilot programs that will lead to the development of a bi-cultural leadership module for the NT more broadly.

As with many of the current wave of leadership learning developments in Australia, Indigenous leadership programs are still in their infancy. Specific research in Indigenous educational leadership is rare (d'Arbon, Frawley and Richardson, 2004). A promising development is the recent Australian Research Council funded longitudinal research project – *Linking Worlds: Strengthening the leadership capacity of Indigenous educational leaders in remote education settings*. d'Arbon et al. (2004) outline the key features of the research, which include the involvement of principals in the study's design, methodologies and decision making. A key aim of the research project will be to review and enhance current professional learning offered by different providers on the specific issue of Indigenous leadership in remote educational contexts.

Among Teaching Australia's activities is the *Leading Australia's Schools* program focused on mid-career principals. The program is intended for school principals who are in the formative years of their principalship and who are likely to make an on-going contribution for a considerable period. The program is nation-wide in its coverage and includes up to 80 principals per year in two cohorts. The intention is to develop a critical mass of high performing school leaders, who in turn can take on responsibility for school improvement at school and system levels. The first cohort commenced in June 2006. Developed and delivered by the Hay Group and the University of Melbourne, the program includes two face-to-face residential sessions, of five and two days respectively, and a field-based project. The themes guiding the course are: the nature and challenge of leadership; myself as leader; leading a learning organization; myself as a leader in education; and myself as a leader of the future. Participants also undertake a diagnostic analysis of their leadership qualities. Having completed the program, participants may apply for advanced standing of 25 points toward a 100 point Master of School Leadership at the University of Melbourne. The program is provided at no cost to participants.

The increasing emphasis on shared leadership models in schools has prompted the need for professional learning for leadership teams. The provision of professional learning for leadership teams is not a new concept, and there are examples from the 1990s (e.g. Berry, 1997). A range of programs for building the capacity of school teams is now either underway or in development in most state and territory school systems. In light of calls for a need to spread the leadership load in schools and to develop schools as professional learning communities, the professional learning of leadership teams seems set to increase in importance.

Support and Recognition for School Leaders

There is no consistent, coordinated state or national approach to the support and recognition of school leaders undertaking professional leadership learning activities. Information, such as details about the costs, resource programs and support for school leaders in their professional learning is not readily available in the public domain, although the relevant school system authorities are using such information in planning their programs. One form of support that appears to be in common use is the partial or full financial subsidy of the professional learning. As with the Victorian *Learning to Lead Effective Schools* program, generally, this kind of financial assistance is used to pay for attendance at the program or to pay for time release of individuals from schools.

There is a variety of award schemes for giving recognition to successful principals and other school leaders. These schemes are operated by a number of professional associations, such as the Australian Council for Educational Leaders, the Australian College of Educators and Teaching Australia's Australian Government National Awards for Quality Schooling (AGNAQS). In a number of States and Territories, an individual's participation in specific leadership programs is recognized through the award of a certificate in, for example, school leadership and management. Other leadership learning providers have negotiated for their programs to be recognized by universities, typically in the form of credit towards a higher qualification.

Support for school leaders in rural and remote areas is another significant issue, particularly the provision of preparation programs that take into account the social and cultural context of small schools (Wildy and Clarke, 2005). The large distances that separate many schools from professional learning providers is a feature of Australia and present a challenge for the provision of quality professional learning. Most school systems now have programs in place to assist the professional learning of principals and leadership teams of small schools.

Content of Professional Learning for School Leaders

As described earlier in this chapter, research clearly shows that *content* is a critical factor in any program of professional learning. Examination of content is a critical point of reference for what school leadership means and for the purposes it serves.

The content of school leaders' professional learning in Australia appears increasingly to be linked to how school leadership is conceived in standards frameworks. The various domains of leadership set out in standards frameworks indicate current emphases. These include a strong focus on enhancing learning for students and teachers. In most, if not all standards for school leaders, there is a particularly strong emphasis on creating the conditions for the learning of others in schools (e.g. NSW's *Leadership Capability Framework* explicitly encompasses the dimensions 'personal' and 'interpersonal').

Program content commonly includes areas such as financial management, human resources management, and school accountability and planning. Such components are particularly common in programs geared toward the preparation of aspirant principal leaders or induction into the principalship, such as the Western Australian Leadership Centre's Introductory School Leadership Program, which covers five modules spanning six days during school holidays. A school leader's role in finance, human resources management, curriculum development, and school planning and accountability are key areas of focus. The modules are organized so that aspirant principals can choose to attend one or more blocks of the program. Completion of each module helps participants gather evidence on their development in one or more domains of the Centre's Leadership Framework. For example, a candidate completing the module Leading Curriculum is able to gather evidence for the 'policy and direction' and 'teaching and learning' areas of the Leadership Framework. The Centre's focus is more on developing leadership and leadership potential than on operational management. A trained facilitator, usually an experienced school leader, and a content expert deliver each module. Rural Districts can seek approval from the Leadership Centre to deliver the modules. In collaboration with academics and school leaders, the Centre has developed scenario items grounded in schools contexts. Responses from prospective school leaders are used to assess the degree to which aspiring principals possess the attributes, values and knowledge identified in the Centre's Leadership Framework. Approximately 400 individuals each year had completed all five modules.

Another emerging important content area is that of information and communication technologies (ICT). In a recent study, published by Teaching Australia, Moyle (2006) showed how changing expectations and contexts of school leaders' work have implications for how they support the integration of ICT into teaching and learning, and the day-to-day running and accountability processes of the school. Moyle used 40 focus groups of educational leaders from all States and Territories and across sectors to review leadership learning with ICT. She reported that most of the focus groups' experience of professional learning in this area was school-based and often self-directed, in part because of the different starting points of individuals. It was not surprising then to find that participants noted the need for skills development prior to the understanding the possible uses of ICT in improving teaching and learning. Moyle's research showed how leaders can play a pivotal role in using ICT to help make the shift from teacher centered to learner centered learning. The importance of a whole school 'strategic focus' in integrating ICT into teaching and learning was emphasized, as was leading and establishing processes to create the conditions for effective, learner centered ICT use.

Moyle's (2006) review found that the breadth and depth of the changes required for effective integration of ICT into school learning programs made heavy demands on school leaders. These demands went well beyond knowledge of the technologies, and called for highly developed levels of pedagogical and curriculum skills. This finding has obvious significance for the development of professional learning programs for school leaders.

A number of Australian studies have investigated school leaders' perceptions of their professional learning and development and areas they see as priorities. Drawing on the findings from several research projects, mainly in Queensland, Dempster (2001) concludes that professional learning, 'requires a fine balance between learning what the system requires of individual school leaders and what practicing professionals require of themselves and their colleagues' (p. 20). Dempster's research suggests that, from the perspective of the participants, the former has tended to take precedence over the latter in what is commonly provided.

Methods of Professional Learning for School Leaders

Active modes of learning are becoming more prominent in leadership development programs. Examples of this form of learning include lengthy structured and mentor supported internships, induction programs, shadowing, problem-based simulations, case study tasks and journal and portfolio entries (e.g. see Cranston, Tromans and Reugebrink, 2004). These activities are intended to place the individual in as authentic a situation as possible, and to model effective leadership.

There is an increasing emphasis on mentoring, coaching and shadowing type programs and approaches to professional leadership learning (e.g. O'Mahony and Matthews, 2003). Use of these modes of learning are consistent with the earlier mentioned features of quality professional learning and calls from practitioners in such studies as Su, Gamage and Miniberg's (2003) study of 102 principals and deputy principals across three NSW school districts. In this study practitioners recommended they wanted, for example;

> …more mentoring by experienced site administrators, more emphasis on practical skills and realistic issues and problems that principals may face…[and] longer commitment to fieldwork. (p. 52)

Formal mentoring programs for principal development have been in existence in Australia since the 1990s but there are now more systematic attempts to better coordinate the design and provision of such programs (Hansford and Ehrich, 2006). Mentoring programs feature prominently within strategies to support and develop school leaders (e.g. see Figure 21.1). An example is the SAGE mentoring program that was operated by the Australian Principals Centre and Deakin University.

The SAGE program (supporting, accomplishing, guiding and enriching) is an accredited mentor training program that was developed in response to requests from a group of government school principals. Barnett and O'Mahony (2005) report that the program is underpinned by five elements of effective mentoring — teaching, sponsoring, encouraging, counseling and befriending. Mentors complete a learning styles inventory in order to increase their own awareness of how they learn. Over 750 principals, assistant principals and teachers throughout Australia have been trained through the SAGE program. In 2004–05 the program was applied to a beginning principal program, which involved 32 mentor pairs in 64 schools located in one Victorian government school region. The formal component of the program consists of three face-to-face sessions over a 12-month period, designed to complement the on-going contact between mentors and mentees.

Research generally reports that participants value leadership mentoring and coaching programs (e.g. see the review of 40 studies by Hansford and Ehrich, 2006, including five studies from Australia). Using interviews with a new district director and six of her principals in rural Queensland, Healy et al. (2001) found that well-led conversations via coaching can be an effective professional development strategy for learning, growth and change in educational leaders. The importance of developing trust in these conversations and of making hidden values and feelings overt was stressed.

A survey of 233 primary and 180 secondary school principals and deputy school principals in Western Australia (Harrison et al., 1998) found that school leaders were motivated by extended professional learning opportunities that enabled networking and the sharing of ideas and experiences among colleagues. The authors, however, noted differences between men and women in their preferences for modes of professional learning: for example, women rated peer coaching and work-shadowing higher than did men. Differences were also noted between rural and urban school leaders: rural school leaders rated conferences and peer-assisted learning such as mentoring and work shadowing more highly than did urban school leaders. The authors interpreted the latter finding as indicating that urban school leaders have more opportunities for informal interaction than their rural counterparts.

Determining the Success of Professional Learning Offerings

As yet there is little research evidence in Australia about how specific program components affect school leaders' development and performance on the job, or which attempt to assess the benefits relative to program costs. Such research gaps are not unique to Australia but reflect more general challenges in research on educational leadership internationally (e.g. Darling-Hammond et al., 2007; Davis et al., 2005).

The Leadership for Organisational Learning and Student Outcomes (LOLSO) research (Mulford, 2003; Silins and Mulford, 2002a & b, 2004; Silins, Mulford and Zarins, 2002) offers rare insight into the crucial role professional learning plays in both school and student learning. The LOLSO research involved 96 Australian secondary schools, including over 5,000 students and 3,700 teachers and their principals. It found that leadership that makes a difference is both position based (principal) and distributive (administrative team and teachers). But both are only indirectly related to student outcomes. Organizational learning (OL) is the important intervening variable between leadership and teacher work and then student outcomes. That is, leadership contributes to OL, which in turn influences what happens in the core business of the school — the teaching and learning. It influences the way students perceive teachers organize and conduct their instruction, and their educational interactions with, and expectations for, their students. OL involves three sequential development stages: trusting and collaborative climate; shared and monitored mission; and, taking initiatives and risks. Importantly, each of these developmental stages is supported by appropriate and ongoing professional development.

Ongoing research in Tasmania and Victoria as part of the eight country *International Successful School Principalship Project* has also identified relevant professional learning as a crucial contributor to one of four factors that make up school capacity building (similar to organizational learning) both for principals and teachers. While the principal personal characteristics (such as being professional, persistent and/or a planner) are not related to student literacy, numeracy or social outcomes, school capacity building is related, especially to student social outcomes. (Mulford, personal communication)

In a promising development, Victoria's Department of Education and Training has commissioned Roy Morgan Research to undertake a longitudinal evaluation of the government's leadership development initiatives, including accelerated development programs for high potential leaders; mentoring for new principals; coaching to enhance the capabilities of experienced principals and the development program for high performing principals. The evaluation is looking at the short-term and long-term impacts of the programs in a range of outcome areas. The Victorian Department will also undertake evaluations of other programs for school leadership teams, assistant principals and other aspiring leaders.

CONCLUSION: KEY ISSUES AND CHALLENGES

From a major review of school leadership development programs across eleven countries, including Australia, Hallinger (2003, p. 290) identified seven global issues critical for the preparation of school leaders in the future:

- Evolving from passive to active learning;
- Creating systemic solutions that connect training to practice;
- Crafting an appropriate role and tools for using performance standards;
- Creating effective transitions into the leadership role;
- Evaluating leadership preparation and development;
- Developing and validating an indigenous knowledge base across cultures;
- Creating a research and development role for universities.

These issues pose significant challenges for the provision and support of professional learning of prospective and established school leaders. Within the current state of play in Australia, attempts to tackle these types of issues are being made. However, it is too soon to tell whether efforts to address such issues will succeed. At a research level, there are significant gaps in knowledge. Despite the increasing emphasis on more on-the-job active professional learning methods, it is not yet clear how this is translating into more effective schooling. The relatively small scale and fragmented nature of much of the research and evaluation studies makes it difficult to develop knowledge and understanding of quality professional leadership learning. Effectiveness needs to be judged longitudinally, using a broad range of indicators including, but not limited to, the impact on student learning outcomes. The linkage between leadership preparation programs and career progression (e.g. aspiring, beginning, consolidation and growth, high achieving, transition) requires further interrogation. To this end, a number of contextual and implementation issues present particular challenges for Australian school leaders and professional learning providers.

Greater attention needs to be given to changes in education and the implications this has for the type of leaders needed, and therefore the type of leadership development. In particular, there has been relatively limited attention to learning activities designed to support models of shared leadership. Mulford (2003), for example, argues that to build on the preference for educators to learn from each other, there needs to be increased development of quality network learning communities, acting and/or shared leadership roles and apprenticeships and/or mentoring. Further research on succession planning programs and principal class selection processes are needed. Such research can help identify and clarify those approaches likely to enhance teacher aspirations to the principal class. It can help illuminate whether selection processes do reflect the new demands on school leaders (Mulford, 2003).

Increasingly, principals and the students they support are coming from diverse backgrounds. Added to this complexity are the diverse environments of school leaders' work in Australia. School size, poverty, home educational environment are among a range of factors that demand attention (Mulford, 2003). Provision of learning needs to account for this complexity and diversity. In Australia, the establishment of targeted leadership development programs (e.g. *Dare to Lead*) is an example of strategies being used by employers and professional associations to address this need.

The pressure on school leaders in an era of significant school-based responsibilities also has implications for the content and process of professional learning programs. Effective school leadership requires high-level intellectual and personal capabilities, and technical competencies. Striking an appropriate balance between developing these aspects, and meeting individual and school system needs, is a continuing challenge.

Resourcing leadership development opportunities remains problematic. There are at least two issues here, the first associated with encouraging schools and individuals to invest in leadership development, and the second with providing programs that are appropriate and affordable. Systemic programs that are provided at no cost or reduced cost, and which include provision for time release from schools for participants appear to be well attended Two noteworthy examples are the Victorian Department of Education sponsorship for the past three years of 80 places in Masters of School Leadership programs, and sponsorship by education systems and/or schools, of the full cost of 80 places each year for the past two years in the Teaching Australian residential program, *Leading Australia's Schools*. Both of these programs receive more applicants than there are places available.

Within this chapter, standards are a notable feature of the Australian school leadership landscape. In Australia, many attempts are being made, as elsewhere, to use standards to guide professional learning. The development and use of leadership standards frameworks can play a significant role in this regard so long as the frameworks draw on a strong evidence base, and are subject to on-going monitoring and evaluation of impact. In Australia, it is common to find sets of standards that do not go beyond the first step. That is, the set of standards attempt to define what leaders should know and be able to do. A key challenge is to find methods of professional learning that are effective in helping future leaders develop toward those standards and show that they have met them. To this end, Australia must act urgently if it wants well-prepared school leaders.

NOTE

This chapter draws extensively on Anderson, M. and Kleinhenz, E. (forthcoming) Professional learning of school leaders in Australia, Chapter 6 in M. Anderson, P. Gronn, L. Ingvarson, A. Jackson, E. Kleinhenz, P. McKenzie, B. Mulford and N. Thornton (20008). *OECD Improving School Leadership Activity: Australia Country Background Report* (Canberra: Department of Education, Science and Training). The contributions of the Department of Education, Employment and Workplace Relations (formerly the Department of Education, Science and Training), the project National Advisory Committee, and the individuals and organizations consulted for that report are gratefully acknowledged. The views in this chapter are those of the authors and not necessarily of any other organization or individual.

REFERENCES

Australian Principals Professional Development Council – APAPDC (2004) *Learn: Lead: Succeed — A resource to support the building of leadership in Australian schools,* Australian Principals Associations Professional Development Council (APAPDC).

Barty, K., Thompson, P., Blackmore, J. & Sachs, J. (2005) Unpacking the issues: Researching the shortage of school principals in two states in Australia, *The Australian Educational Researcher,* 32(3).

Barnett, B. & O'Mahony, G. (2005). Sage mentors: experienced principals sharing their wisdom, and getting a little guidance in return. *Teacher, Australian Council for Educational Research*, November, 46–48.

Berry, G. (1997). Leadership strategies for quality management in primary schools, *Leading & Managing*, 3(2), 97–122.

Carlin, P. d'Arbon, T., Dorman, J., Duignan, P. & Neidhart, H. (2003). Leadership succession for Catholic schools in Victoria, South Australia and Tasmania. *Leadership Succession Project (VSAT) Final Report*, April 2003.

Collins, R. (2006). The principal shortage and what we should be doing about it. *The Australian Educational Leader,* 4, 16–19.

Cranston, N., Tromans, C. & Reugebrink, M. (2004). Forgotten leaders: What do we know about the deputy principalship in secondary schools? *International Journal of Leadership in Education*, 7(3), 225–242.

d'Arbon, T., Frawley, J. & Richardson, N. (2004). Linking worlds: a project to research Indigenous educators as leaders in remote community school settings. Paper presented to AARE International Education Research Conference, 'Doing the public good', Melbourne Nov 29–Dec 2, 2004.

Darling-Hammond, L., LaPointe, M., Meyerson, D. & Orr, M. (2007). *Preparing school leaders for a changing world: Executive summary.* Stanford, CA: Standard University, Stanford Educational Leadership Institute.

Davis, S., Darling-Hammond, L., LaPointe, M. & Meyerson, D. (2005). *School Leadership Study: Developing Successful Principals*. Stanford Educational Leadership Institute, CA, Commissioned by The Wallace Foundation.

Dempster, N. (2001). The professional development of school principals: a fine balance. Professorial lecture, 24 May, Griffith University public lecture series, New South Wales, Australia.

Duignan, P. (2004). Forming capable leaders: from competencies to capabilities. *New Zealand Journal of Educational Leadership*, 19(2), 5–13.

Fullan, M. (2001). *Leading in a culture of change.* San Francisco: Jossey Bass.

Gamage, D. & Ueyama, T. (2004). Professional development perspectives of principals in Australia and Japan. *Educational Forum*, 69(1), 65–78.

Gurr, D., Drysdale, L. & Goode, H. (2007) Findings from the Survey Phase of the International Successful School Principalship Project: Principal demographics and principal perceptions of success. Paper presented at the American Educational Research Association conference, Chicago, April 2007.

Hallinger, P. (2003). School leadership preparation and development in global perspective: Future challenges and opportunities, in P. Hallinger (Ed.) *Reshaping the Landscape of School Leadership Development.* Lisse: Swets and Zeitlinger, 289–300.

Hansford, B. & Ehrich, L.C. (2006). The principalship: how significant is mentoring? *Journal of Educational Administration*, 44(1), 36–52.

Harrison B.T., Clarke, R., Hill, S. & Harvey, M. (1998) School leadership: The challenge of continuous professional education, *Leading & Managing*, 4(2) Winter, 83–98.

Healy, L., Ehrich, L.C., Hansford, B.C. & Stewart, D. (2001). Conversations: a means of learning, growth and change, *Journal of Educational Administration*, 39(4), 332–345.

Ingvarson, L. & Anderson, M. (2007). Standards for school leadership: Gateway to a stronger profession? Australian Council for Educational Research, Research conference 2007, *The Leadership Challenge: Improving learning in schools*, 12–14 August 2007, Melbourne, Victoria. Conference Proceedings: www.acer.edu.au

Ingvarson, L., Anderson, M., Gronn, P. & Jackson, A. (2006) Standards for School Leadership Project: A

Critical Review of Literature, Australian Council for Educational Research (ACER) commissioned review by Teaching Australia – Australian Institute for Teaching and School Leadership in 2005.

Ingvarson, L. & Kleinhenz, K. (2006). A standards-guided professional learning system. *Centre for Strategic Education Seminar Series paper No. 153.*

Ingvarson, L., Meiers, M. & Beavis, A. (2005). Factors affecting the impact of professional development programs on teachers' knowledge, practice, student outcomes & efficacy. *Education Policy Analysis Archives*, 13(10), 1–28.

Lacey, K. (2002). Factors that Impact on Principal-Level Leadership Aspirations. Unpublished doctoral thesis, the University of Melbourne.

Leithwood, K., Day, C., Sammons, P., Harris, A. & Hopkins, D. (2006). *Seven Strong Claims About Successful School Leadership*. Nottingham, National College of School Leadership.

Leithwood, K.& Riehl, C. (2005). What we know about successful school leadership. In W. Firestone & C. Riehl (Eds.), *A New Agenda: Directions for research on educational leadership*. New York, Teachers College Press, 22–47.

Leithwood, K., Seashore Louis, K.A., Anderson, S. & Wahlstrom, K. (2004). *How Leadership Influences Student Learning*. New York, The Wallace Foundation.

Lakomski, G. (2005). *Managing without Leadership*. Oxford, Elsevier.

Lutheran Education Australia (2005). *Leadership Framework for Lutheran Schools*, www.lea.org.au/show_file.asp?id=208&table=personnel

Ministerial Council on Education, Employment and Training (MCEETYA) (2003) *A national framework for professional standards for teaching*, Carlton, Victoria, MCEETYA.

Moyle, K. (2006). *Leadership and Learning with ICT: Voices from the Profession*. Teaching Australia - Australian Institute for Teaching and School Leadership.

Mulford, B. (2003). *School Leaders: Changing Roles and Impact on Teacher and School Effectiveness*. Paris, Education and Training Policy Division OECD.

Mulford, W., Silins, H. & Leithwood, K. (2004). *Educational Leadership for Organisational Learning and Improved Student Outcomes*. Dordrecht, Kluwer.

O'Mahony, G. & Matthews, R. (2003). Me and my shadow: How new leaders learn about leadership. *Leading and Managing*, 9(1), 52–63.

Queensland Department of Education and the Arts (2006). *Annual Statement of Expectations for Schools* Web: http://education.qld.gov.au/strategic/accountability/spaf.html

Scott, G. (2003) *Learning principals: Leadership capability and learning research in the New South Wales Department of Education and Training*, NSW, Department of Education and Training Professional Support and Curriculum Directorate, Sydney, NSW.

Silins, H. & Mulford, B. (2002a). Leadership and school results. K. Leithwood & P. Hallinger (Eds.),, *Second International Handbook of Educational Leadership and Administration*. Norwell, MA: Kluwer, 561–612.

Silins, H. & Mulford, B. (2002b). Schools as learning organisations: The case for system, teacher and student learning. *The Journal of Educational Administration*, 40(5), 425–446.

Silins, H. & Mulford, B. (2004). Schools as learning organisations: Effects on teacher leadership and student outcomes. *School Effectiveness and School Improvement,* 15(3-4), 443–466.

Silins, H., Mulford, B. & Zarins, S. (2002). Organisational learning and school change. *Educational Administration Quarterly*, 38(5), 613–642.

South Australian Centre for Leaders in Education (2005). *Leaders Learning Framework*. Department of Education and Children's Services, South Australia, accessed on 16 October 2007 http://www.sacle.edu.au/leaderframework.html

Su, Z., Gamage, D. & Miniberg, E. (2003). Professional preparation and development of school leaders in Australia and the USA. *International Education Journal*, 4(1), 42–59.

Wildy, H. & Clarke, S. (2005) Leading the small rural school: The case of the novice principal, *Leading & Managing*, 11(1), 43–56.

22

Leadership Development in Small Island States

Tony Bush, Marie-Therese Purvis and Linda Barallon

The purpose of this chapter is to assess the extent and nature of leadership preparation and development in small island states. The literature on this topic is very limited. Louisy (1999, p. xi) notes that interest in such states did not attract much attention until the 1960s and that literature on educational issues began to emerge much later. Crossley and Holmes (1999, p. 3) give credit to the Commonwealth Secretariat for placing the problems of small island states on the agenda.

The chapter will begin by defining small island states and will then discuss the major contextual factors affecting these educational systems. Subsequent sections will examine several major aspects of leadership development and the chapter will conclude with an overview, including recommendations for further research.

WHAT IS A SMALL ISLAND STATE?

There is no widely accepted definition of a small island state (Crowards 2002, p. 143) and some commentators (e.g. Ballantyne, 1998; ECDPM, 1998) argue that it is largely a political construct, reflected, for example, in membership of the Association of Small Island States (AOSIS). However, this body includes relatively large states, such as Cuba with 11 million people, and most writers tend to exclude such countries from their definitions. Crowards (2002) suggests that small island states may be defined with respect to land area or GDP, but most definitions focus on population.

Armstrong and Read (2003) use a population threshold of 3 million but the UN institutions prefer one million while the Commonwealth, and Holmes and Crossley (2004), choose 1.5 million. We accept the widely expressed view (Crowards 2002, Armstrong and Read 2003) that such definitions are arbitrary but have decided to follow the UN criterion and focus on states with fewer than one million people. This limit excludes certain important centers for leadership development, such as Hong Kong and Singapore, but allows a rare focus on other systems with a less well developed literature. The one million ceiling includes many Caribbean states, several islands in the Pacific and Indian oceans and the well developed Mediterranean islands of Cyprus and Malta.

CHARACTERISTICS OF SMALL ISLAND STATES

Small island states share a number of characteristics that mark them out as a distinctive category of nation. These are:

- Geographical isolation.
- Economic vulnerability
- Lack of HE provision
- Limited resources in the many small island 'developing' states.

Geographical Isolation

Many islands are remote from the main developed economies and this places them at a social and economic disadvantage compared to nations in the major continents. Armstrong and Read (2003, p. 108) note that 'the economic vulnerability of small island . . . states is compounded by their isolation, which raises transport and communication costs'. Ballantyne (1998) adds that, while isolation is a major attraction for tourists wishing to 'get away from it all', these countries are fragile and vulnerable. Briguglio and Galea (2004) say that remoteness creates 'peripherality', leading to marginalization from the main commercial centers. Campling and Rosalie (2006, p. 119), for example, note that the Seychelles is physically isolated, separated from East Africa by more than 1500km of ocean. The Cape Verde islands, off the coast of West Africa, also suffer the adverse consequences of their isolation from the mainland (IRIN 2003). Luteru and Teasdale (1993, p. 297) refer to 'the isolation of rural and outer island communities' in the South Pacific while Murray Thomas (1993, p. 233) adds that '[South Pacific] island peoples are spread sparsely across Oceania, separated from each other by wide expanses of sea'. Smith (2006) charts the decline of Easter Island and attributes this to its remoteness from other communities. It 'was completely isolated from any other community. There was no hope of rescue, no chance of escape' (p. 232). This isolation, particularly when combined with limited resources, makes it difficult for such small islands to provide appropriate development opportunities for school leaders.

Economic Vulnerability

Small island states are not necessarily poor, and in Cyprus, for example, 'the quality and standard of life are high' (Georgiou et al. 2001, p. 71). Read (2004, p. 365) claims that 'small size does not preclude sustained growth success in spite of the many challenges faced by small states'. However, Easterly and Kraay (2000, p. 2013) note their dependence on a small range of economic activities, 'making them more vulnerable to terms of trade shocks' than large states that can more easily diversify. Because of their narrow economic base, highly specific agricultural sectors and tourism, they are highly dependent upon external trade, particularly imports (Armstrong and Read, 2003), and have a limited ability to exploit economies of scale (Briguglio and Galea, 2004). UN and Commonwealth indices have confirmed the fragility and vulnerability of many small island states (ECDPM, 1998). This is particularly true of the many small island *developing* states (SIDS).

Campling and Rosalie (2006) apply much of this analysis to the Seychelles. They note that isolation makes the country internationally uncompetitive. Seychelles' key trading partners are geographically distant EU countries and high transport costs — both for canned tuna exports and the inflow of European tourists — act like a hidden tariff on trade. They add that such vulnerabilities have a significant potential impact on public expenditure, including education. 'Contemporary levels of social welfare spending are probably unsustainable' (Campling and Rosalie, 2006, p. 121).

Lack of Higher Education Provision

In most developed countries, leadership preparation is provided by universities. Many small island states either do not have their own higher education provision or lack the specific capability to plan and deliver programs to develop principals. Cyprus and Malta have their own universities but Scott (2001) notes that the development of higher education in other small island states has been limited by their vulnerable economies. The small countries in the Eastern Caribbean, for example, have neither a university campus nor the resources to send principals in sufficient numbers to be trained in Barbados, the nearest convenient centre (Scott, 2001), although the Sir Arthur Lewis Community College provides post-school education in St. Lucia (Crossley and Holmes 1999, p. 42). Where such countries are able to provide leadership training, it is often in collaboration with universities in other countries (Bush 2005; Scott 2001).

Limited Resources

Small island states often experience shortages of natural, financial and human resources. Scott (2001) notes the inadequate water supplies in many such countries while Armstrong and Read (2003, p. 104) state that 'their natural resources are likely to be limited and undiversified'. The 'very modest agricultural base' (IRIN, 2003) of the Cape Verde islands, for example, means that many children are hungry when they arrive at school. As a consequence, the key source of growth in small states is likely to be higher value-added activities using human capital intensively (Armstrong and Read, 2003, p. 104). Several commentators (e.g. Read, 2004, ECDPM, 1998) refer to the importance of human capacity as a driver for growth. Crossley and Holmes (2001, p. 401) add that investment in education and training will be a key strategy for nations seeking to reduce the 'knowledge gap' between small island states and the large developed economies.

Capacity development is, therefore, seen as 'the most critical need' (Binger, 2000, p. 1) for small island states, which often experience 'capacity bottle necks' (Binger, 2000, p. 4). Mauritius is one country that 'places a lot of faith in the power of education to contribute to the country's social and economic development' (Bunwaree, 2001, p. 257). A significant problem for professional development, however, is the limited pool of candidates available to develop for senior positions (Briguglio and Galea, 2004; Easterly and Kraay, 2000). Referring to the South Pacific, Murray Thomas (1993, p. 241) notes that 'the small size of the populations of many of the island states [results] in a constricted pool of talent from which to draw personnel'. Many successful small states have developed selective in-migration policies to overcome such domestic labor supply constraints (Read, 2004). The Seychelles, for example, deals with its shortage of secondary school teachers by appointing candidates from India, Kenya and Sri Lanka (Bush 2005). However, this further reduces the pool of potential school leaders as such migrant teachers are rarely considered for *senior* management posts.

Diversity, not Uniformity

Although small island states share several characteristics, notably their size and location, they are also a very diverse group of nations. They are located across the globe, notably in the Caribbean, the Indian Ocean, the Mediterranean and the Pacific Ocean. They have different levels of economic and social development, ranging from middle income countries, such as Cyprus and Malta, to very poor South Pacific nations. Luteru and Teasdale (1993, pp. 296–297) caution against simplistic 'one size fits all' solutions for the problems faced by small island states:

> One of the most striking, but least understood, features of the [Pacific Island Communities] is their diversity, not only between countries, but also within them. This diversity becomes apparent when one considers such factors as population, land area, ethnic composition, per capita income and resource endowment. By implication, this suggests that no solution or strategy to address the development problems of one country would necessarily have the same effect in others.

This argument is even more powerful when deployed to consider all small island states and not just those in the South Pacific.

LEADERSHIP SUCCESSION

Leadership succession relates to the several processes involved in ensuring a sufficient supply of suitably qualified leaders. Murray Thomas (1993, p. 240), referring to the South Pacific, encapsulates this in a question. 'Who decides what system will be used for recruiting, training and promoting educational personnel?'

In principle, there are two main strategies available to identify potential school leaders. First, those interested in such positions may be able to 'self nominate' by applying for available posts and submitting themselves to the (stated or implicit) selection criteria. This approach is typically used by education systems with a high degree of decentralization. The main limitation of this strategy is that insufficient well-qualified candidates may submit themselves for scrutiny. In England, for example, the imminent retirement of the post-war 'baby-boom' era of school principals has led to widespread concern that there may not be enough replacements, leading to a national 'succession planning' initiative, led by the National College for School Leadership (www.ncsl. org.uk). The second strategy, typically used by centralized systems, is a planned approach, leading to central determination of who should be considered for promotion. This approach may be criticized on grounds of equal opportunity. 'What influence do people's ethnic or cultural origins have on their chances of being recruited, trained and promoted?' (Murray Thomas, 1993, p. 240) Central planning reduces the 'chance' element and provides the potential for smooth leadership succession, but may lead to only 'acceptable' people being appointed and developed.

Gronn and Ribbins (2003) discuss this issue in respect of small island states. They refer to 'ascriptive' systems, which tend to emphasize the personal characteristics of individuals and usually reproduce a leadership cohort (often predominantly male) from a narrow social base. Cyprus is one small island that has adopted an approach that leads to the appointment of highly experienced, and usually male, principals (Pashiardis and Ribbins, 2003: Gronn and Ribbins, 2003). 'Discrimination against women teachers with regards to their promotion to leadership posts . . . should be considered unfair' (Georgiou et al., 2001, p. 81).

Bezzina (2002, p. 10), referring to Malta, notes that most of his interviewees 'were promoted to principalship on the basis of seniority', and adds that 'none of the principals regarded themselves as working to a career plan designed to [lead] to a principalship position'. This may be regarded as the inevitable consequence of top-down selection processes but it also reflects a reluctance to give up classroom teaching (Bezzina, 2002, p. 11).

Small island communities are often intimate in the sense that people in particular professional groups are very familiar with colleagues' strengths and development needs. Senior Ministry personnel usually know all their school leaders and are well placed to adopt a 'chess board' approach to leadership succession. In the Seychelles, for example, the Ministry decides who shall be nominated for places on its headship development program. As successful completion of this program is a requirement for headship, the Ministry effectively acts as a 'gatekeeper' to senior leadership by its control over who shall be trained (Bush, 2005). Barallon (in preparation), in a study of leadership development in the Seychelles, confirms that the senior management team (SMT) of the Ministry of Education 'has this daunting role to play' in identifying potential middle and senior leaders. The SMT members say that leaders are identified for senior posts based on:

- Performance appraisal
- Recommendations from immediate supervisors
- Academic qualifications
- Years of experience (Barallon, in preparation)

Barallon (in preparation) adds that such criteria are supplemented by more personal considerations. 'In practice, political affiliation is a contributing factor in the outcome of the identification process' (p. 5). Bezzina (2002, pp. 13–14) shows that such political discrimination previously applied in Malta, as one of his respondents explains:

> The posts of deputy principals were very difficult to get because of the political atmosphere . . . It was practically impossible if you had any connection with the Malta Union of Teachers (MUT) or if you were not particularly tied with the government party, then you wouldn't have any chance... to get the post...there were always a chosen few.

The scope for such political decisions is reduced if formal qualifications, or another form of specific preparation, are prerequisites for promotion to senior posts, as has been the case in Malta since 1994.

LEADERSHIP PREPARATION

The notion of preparation suggests a preconceived orientation towards career development, by the potential principals and/or system leaders. In several countries, e.g. Canada, England and the United States, aspiring principals must complete an approved qualification before being considered for appointment. This focuses the attention of ambitious teachers who know what is required to progress towards senior leadership.

In most small island states, there are no such formal requirements although potential principals in the Seychelles are expected to obtain the MA qualification offered in conjunction with the University of Warwick (Barallon in preparation; Bush 2005). Bezzina (2002, p. 11) states that, in Malta, 'all prospective principals need to be in possession of a diploma in educational administration and management or its equivalent', a requirement introduced in 1994. The need for preparation was taken seriously by most of his interviewees; 'you needed that kind of preparation and training and dialogue with your course colleagues' (p.12). Significantly, though, the participants in his study regard their leadership experience as equally, if not more, valuable. 'Most principals spoke of their period as deputy principals as crucial to their professional growth' (p. 12).

A more typical example is that of Cyprus, where 'few [aspirant principals] engaged in substantial and proactive preparation' (Pashiardis and Ribbins, 2003, p. 29). A few principals had taken short courses but they were skeptical of their value, describing them as too 'theoretical'. In practice, most had experienced an 'apprenticeship' model where they learned from working with 'good and supportive' (Pashiardis and Ribbins, 2003, p. 29)) principals. One female principal interviewed by Pashiardis and Ribbins (2003, p. 30) commented on the notion of preparation:

> In Cyprus, in education, there is really no such thing as preparing for the post.

This comment could be echoed in many other small island states, Georgiou et al. (2001, p. 80) point out that principals are not well prepared to tackle the many educational and social demands facing them in the 21st century. They add that successful school leaders should be prepared and 'have a clear vision of the school's destiny' (p. 82).

LEADERSHIP SELECTION

The recruitment and selection of school principals follows the 'succession' processes discussed above. Criteria are developed by senior personnel in the Ministry of Education or in related bodies, and may be explicit or implicit. In the Fiji islands, for example, principals are appointed by the Ministry of Education. Cardno and Howse's (2005, p. 38) summary of their job description illustrates the heavy expectations of school leaders in many small island states:

> The principal's role is unquestionably described as that of educational and professional leader who enhances staff and student performance and also undertakes teaching duties. In addition the principal is the chief executive of the school, is accountable to the Ministry and the Board [of Governors], responsible for staff performance and maintaining relationships with staff and with community, and required to operate within government policy and legislative requirements.

In highly centralized systems, the principal's role may be circumscribed by the strong control of decisions by central bodies, as Georgiou et al. (2001 pp. 76–77) show in respect of Cyprus:

> Principals have no responsibility with regard to the appointment of their staff, the selection of textbooks, the setting of examinations and the development of their own curricula because of the centralized system of education in Cyprus. In fact, Cypriot principals' main functions revolve around routine administrative matters.

Bezzina (2001) makes a similar point about Malta, referring to a 'dependency culture' (p.110) created, in part, by centralized decision-making. 'Those having executive powers need to break a long-standing behaviour pattern of their own, that of dictating what has to be done to all problems as they arise' (Bezzina, 2001, p. 111).

As previously noted, small states are characterized by a high level of personal knowledge of teachers and school leaders, leading to formal or informal judgments about staff readiness for senior posts such as that of principal. In Cyprus, for example, teachers are appointed, located, transferred and promoted by the Educational Service Commission (ESC), an independent five member body appointed by the President (Pashiardis and Ribbins, 2003, p. 14). The ESC supposedly has regard to three factors when choosing assistant principals and principals:

- Years of service
- Worth and excellence as a teacher
- Other diplomas, degrees or academic credentials

Pashiardis and Ribbins (2003, p. 15) conclude that, as candidates have much the same academic qualifications, and because almost everyone is rated as an excellent teacher, the only significant differentiation comes from years in service. This leads to most secondary principals being appointed when over 50 years old. The UNESCO national review of education on the island confirms that 'the principal criterion is age and seniority . . . competence in performing the work is scarcely taken into account' (Drake et al., 1997, pp. 56–58). The review concludes that 'the system establishes what can only be described as a "gerontology in education" (p. 58). The system also reinforces patriarchy with 68 percent of secondary principals being men, despite women being in the majority in the teaching profession (Pashiardis and Ribbins, 2003, p. 15).

Appointing older males is not an inevitable consequence of the selection process. As Gronn and Ribbins (2003, p. 91) point out, 'culturally grounded recruitment and selection regimes generate particular occupational profiles'. In the Seychelles, the dominance of women in most professional settings is reflected in the appointment of principals. A large majority of teachers and middle leaders are women, as are almost all the senior civil servants in the Ministry of Education. Because most of the potential candidates, and the Ministry selectors, are women, it is not surprising that women dominate headship, with 27 even of the 33 schools being led by women (Bush 2005). Despite this dominance, gender is not one of the eleven criteria outlined by Barallon's (in preparation, p. 8) respondents. These may be summarized as:

- Qualifications
- Experience
- Current position
- Perceived level of interest and commitment
- Formal and informal appraisal

However, Barallon (in preparation, p. 8) notes that 'those selection criteria of leaders have never been formalized and, in the past, most leaders have been appointed to such positions on the basis of being good practitioners in the classroom'. However, she adds that training for leadership is soon to become a requirement for new principals. Significantly, 'softer' criteria, such as values, are also important, as one SMT member shows:

> We need people from within, who know the system well through experience of working for the MoE, who share our vision and values. Such posts are reserved only for qualified locals and naturalised expatriates'. (Barallon, in preparation, p. 9)

Barallon (in preparation, p. 9) concludes that, in practice, all senior leaders are of Seychelles' nationality.

INDUCTION FOR LEADERSHIP

Induction is the process by which new incumbents become familiar with the context in which they are leading, including the school culture. Crow (2005) distinguishes between professional socialization (preparing to enter the profession) and organizational socialization (learning how to lead in a particular context). There is little evidence of formal induction in most educational systems, particularly those in developing countries (Bush and Oduro 2006). The literature on school leadership in small island states barely addresses this issue but Gronn and Ribbins' (2003, p. 86) note that few Cypriot principals 'found their formal induction to be satisfactory and soon they had to fall back on better-known examples of previous principals as their role models'. Cardno and Howse (2004) also note the need for induction courses for new principals in Fiji.

Barallon's (in preparation) study of leadership development in the Seychelles shows that her respondents regard induction and mentoring 'as an area of weakness'. While induction is expected to take place at school level for middle leaders, this is supposed to be done at Ministry level for principals. However, she adds that some senior leaders say that they have never been inducted. One-to-one support is given to newly appointed leaders 'on request' (p. 12), and networking is organized within school zones, but this falls short of a comprehensive induction program.

LEADERSHIP DEVELOPMENT

Leadership development is often the generic term used to describe any form of preparation or training for headship. In this section, we use it specifically to refer to activities undertaken *following* appointment as principal, i.e. in-service training. Such provision may be seen as complementary to pre-service preparation or as a substitute for it. In developing countries, including many small island states, pre-service preparation is rare and the limited resources are devoted to in-service support (Bush and Oduro, 2006). This has two main advantages:

- It has the potential to target the specific context-bound needs of principals, rather than just providing generic preparation.
- It makes good use of resources in that all participants are already principals whereas some aspirant principals may never reach that level.

Crossley and Holmes (1999 p. 24) stress the importance of providing support for leaders in remote island communities. They emphasize the value of exchanges, visits and attachments, information and networking, and technical meetings.

Cardno and Howse's (2004) review of secondary school principals in Fiji shows the breadth of development activities engaged in by their interviewees. These range from university degrees and diplomas to management workshops and various types of on-the-job support. Despite, or perhaps because of, this diversity, these principals complain that 'the nature of current training is ad hoc and the initiatives are not formalised' (p. 24). The Fijian interviews were asked to specify their management development needs and their responses were categorized into six broad themes:

- Inspiring and visioning change
- Interpersonal and people skills
- Capacity to delegate and empower others
- Managing uncertainty

- Capacity to develop networks
- Effective and efficient management and administration (Cardno and Howse, 2004, p. 25)

Billot's (2003) study of Tonga found that similar themes were identified by principals and the author concludes that principals 'saw a need for skills and competencies that supported teaching and learning, with effective management skills being of less importance' (Billot, 2003, p. 16).

Scott's (2001, p. 247) report of the Lakehead project in nine Eastern Caribbean nations sets out the intention 'to provide head teachers and senior education personnel with the skills and knowledge and the management and supervisory processes necessary for the effective running of the schools in the respective countries'. While they warn of the dangers of adopting Western paradigms, the structure and content of the modules, including management, leadership, resource planning, pastoral care and instruction, seem very similar to what Bush and Jackson (2002) have described as an international curriculum for school leadership development.

In the Seychelles, the MA program presented by the University of Warwick was originally intended to be an 'in-service' program for practicing heads. Subsequently, it has developed into a pre-service course for potential new principals. The Ministry has also introduced a local upgrading program, the Advanced Diploma in Educational Leadership (ADEL), intended to prepare participants for entry to the master's program. This is essentially an 'in-service' course for existing middle leaders who are likely to progress to senior leadership in due course (Barallon, in preparation; Bush, 2005).

Bezzina (2001, p. 117) refers to the importance of lifelong learning for leaders and notes the particular value of development for principals who were not 'adequately trained, prepared or exposed' before taking up their posts.

CONCLUSION

Small Island states share several characteristics that combine to make it difficult for them to develop school leaders. They are often isolated and have fragile economies. They have little or no higher education provision and often have limited resources. However, there is also considerable diversity within the sector, not least in terms of size and economic development. Such differences make it difficult, even dangerous, to reach overarching conclusions. As Murray Thomas (1993, p. 246) indicates, 'cultural analysis . . . has been the missing link' in assessing the needs of small island states.

There are similar problems in proposing solutions derived from very different contexts, usually those from advanced countries in the West. As Watson (2001, p. 29) suggests, 'educational policies cannot easily be transplanted from one national and social context to another'. Bush, Qiang and Fang (1998, p. 137) add that 'all theories and interpretations of practice must be "grounded" in the specific context'. These cautions suggest that arguing for specific forms of leadership development should be avoided unless they are based firmly on local needs and cultural imperatives.

In most small island states, successful teaching experience has usually been regarded as the main criterion for promotion to senior positions and little attention has been given to specific preparation for principals. In many of these countries, system leaders know the teachers and school leaders personally and this often means an absence of formal selection processes, with due attention to equal opportunities, that characterize procedures in most of the larger developed countries. Personal considerations such as perceived shared values, and political affiliation, co-exist with the limited formal criteria, often confined to professional experience. These lead to senior people with the perceived 'right' qualities being appointed as principals.

Preparation for leadership, before or after appointment, is often limited although both Malta and the Seychelles do require a formal qualification. Many leaders rely on an 'apprenticeship' model, where they learn the job from their principals while carrying out a more junior post, such as deputy principal. This can work well if the role model is competent, but it does not 'widen the lens' to allow aspirants to understand and experience alternative approaches. In any case, its effectiveness is random, depending on the quality of the leadership experience on offer in the aspirant's school. Even where this is good, it means that new leaders are likely to replicate previous practice rather than developing their own approach based on wider learning.

Notions of lifelong learning are gaining ground and are increasingly being applied to professional development in small island states (e.g. Crossley and Holmes 1999, p. 62). This requirement applies just as readily to school leaders as it does to teachers and other education professionals. The 'ideal' model would provide for pre-appointment preparation of potential leaders, thorough induction for newly appointed principals, and ongoing support and development opportunities for experienced leaders. In practice, however, limited financial and human resources mean that little of this can be achieved in many small island developing countries, even if such processes are deemed to be important for the particular national context. The model shown in Figure 22.1 is an attempt to adapt perceived 'best practice' to the realities facing many small island states.

TABLE 22.1
A Model for Leadership Preparation in Small Island States (Adapted from Bush and Oduro 2006)

Component	Western Countries	Africa	Small Island States (current)	Small Island States (proposed)
Budgets	Good	Very limited	Often limited	Limited but to be augmented by donors
Preparation capacity	Good	Very limited	Often limited	Develop through a 'train the trainers' program
Nature of preparation	Variable but increasingly pre-service	Limited and usually in-service	Variable but often limited	Coherent in-service provision
Qualification	Variable but often leading to a professional or academic qualification	Usually no accreditation	Variable but often no accreditation	Certificate in school leadership
Funding	Government or candidate funding	Very limited, ad hoc and episodic	Variable but often limited	Long-term government or donor funding
Appointment	Based on formal qualifications	Based on teaching experience plus political or cultural factors	Usually based on teaching experience plus political or cultural factors	Based on teaching experience and leadership potential assessed by trained principals
Induction	Often linked to further preparation and may include mentoring	Little formal induction	Little formal induction	To include in-service preparation, networking and mentoring

Towards a Model for Leadership Preparation in Small Island States

Bush and Oduro (2006) propose a normative model for leadership preparation in Africa and contrast it with current practice, and with the approach in many Western countries. Table 22.1 adapts this model to show practice and possible developments in small island states.

Table 22.1 is underpinned by the twin assumption that schools are more likely to be effective if they have good leadership and that leaders are 'made not born'. Specific preparation is required if teachers, learners and communities are to have the schools they need and deserve. There are dangers in prescribing one approach to meet the needs of such diverse societies but there are sufficient commonalities to justify a tentative model. Because these states often have limited financial and human resources, and often have no higher education provision, the model suggests that the main focus should be on in-service preparation delivered partly be practicing school principals. An alternative is to develop a partnership model where governments link with an external provider (Barallon, in preparation; Scott, 2001), funded either by donors or the host government. This model should be customized to the specific context and needs of this diverse category of state but the key element is that there should be a systematic and determined focus on the development of leaders. Good leadership is an essential requirement for successful schools and this is too important to be left to chance.

Towards a Research Agenda

The preparation of this chapter has been hampered by the lack of literature on this theme and, in particular, by the very limited research on leadership preparation and development in most small island states. To address this problem we recommend that two types of research be undertaken:

Carefully structured empirical enquiries into development practice in individual states. These investigations may address one or more of the main sub-themes; leadership succession, preparation, selection, induction and in-service development.

Comparative studies of practice in two or more countries. These should adopt a common enquiry framework to facilitate meaningful cross-country judgments about one or more of the sub-themes indicated above.

Given the limited financial and human resources available in many small island states, the research is likely to require donor funding and to be led by leading international researchers with a specialist interest in this topic. The outcomes of such a program of research would include capacity building for emerging researchers as well as enhanced knowledge and understanding of leadership development practice within and across small island states.

REFERENCES

Armstrong, H. and Read, R. (2003), The determinants of economic growth in small states, *The Round Table*, 368, 99–124.

Ballantyne, P. (1998), *Small Islands, Big Issues*, Maastricht, One World News Service.

Barallon, L. (in preparation), Leadership Development in the Seychelles, Mahe.

Bezzina, C. (2001), From administering to managing and leading: The case of Malta, in Pashiardis, P. (Ed.), *International Perspectives on Educational Leadership*, Hong Kong, University of Hong Kong, pp. 106–124.

Bezzina, C. (2002), The making of secondary school principals: Some perspectives from the island of Malta, *International Studies in Educational Administration*, 30(2), 2–16.

Billot, J. (2003), A Case Study of School Principals in Tonga, Auckland, *Commonwealth Council for Educational Administration and Management*.

Binger, A. (2000), Capacity Development Initiative, Country Capacity Development Needs and Priorities: Report for Small Island Developing States, GEF-UNDP.

Briguglio, L. and Galea, W. (2004), *Updating and Augmenting the Economic Vulnerability Index,* Malta, University of Malta.

Bunwaree, S. (2001), The marginal in the miracle: human capital in the Mauritius, *International Journal of Educational Development,* 21, 257–271.

Bush, T. (2005), School Leadership in the 21st Century: Seychelles and International Perspectives, Keynote presentation to the Seychelles Education Conference, Mahe, May

Bush, T. and Jackson, D. (2002), Preparation for School Leadership: International Perspectives, *Educational Management and Administration*, 30(4), 417–429.

Bush, T. and Oduro, G. (2006), New Principals in Africa: Preparation, Induction and Practice, *Journal of Educational Administration*, 44(4): 359–375.

Bush, T., Qiang, H. and Fang, J. (1998), Educational management in China: An overview, *Compare*, 28(2), 133–140.

Campling, L. and Rosalie, M. (2006), Sustaining social development in a small island developing state? The case of Seychelles, *Sustainable Development,* 14, 115–125.

Cardno, C. and Howse, J. (2004), A Study of the Secondary School Principals' Role, Workload and Management Development Needs in the Fiji Islands, Auckland, *Commonwealth Council for Educational Administration and Management*.

Cardno, C. and Howse, J. (2005), The role and management development needs of secondary principals in Tonga and the Fiji Islands, *International Studies in Educational Administration*, 33(3), 36–47.

Crossley, M. and Holmes, K. (1999), *Educational Development in the Small States of the Commonwealth: Retrospect and Prospect,* London, Commonwealth Secretariat.

Crossley, M. and Holmes, K. (2001), Challenges for educational research: international development, partnerships and capacity building in small states, *Oxford Review of Education*, 27(3), 401–406.

Crow, G. (2005), Complexity and the beginning principal in the United States: Perspectives on Socialisation, *Journal of Educational Administration*, 44(4), 310–325.

Crowards, T. (2002), Defining the category of "small" states, *Journal of International Development*, 14, 143–179.

Drake, P., Pair, C., Ross, K., Postlethwaite, T. and Ziogas, G. (1997), *Appraisal Study on the Cyprus Educational System*, Paris, International Institute for Educational Planning.

Easterly, W. and Kraay, A. (2000), Small states, small problems? Income, growth and volatility in small states, *World Development*, 28(11), 2013–2027.

ECDPM (1998), What Place for Small Island States in a Successor Lome Agreement? (Lome Negotiating Agreement Brief No. 2), Maastricht, EDCPM.

Georgiou, M., Papayianni, O., Savvides, I. and Pashiardis, P. (2001), Educational leadership as a paradox: The case of Cyprus, in Pashiardis, P. (Ed.), *International Perspectives on Educational Leadership*, Hong Kong, University of Hong Kong, pp. 70–92.

Gronn, P. and Ribbins, P. (2003), The making of secondary school principals on selected small islands, *International Studies in Educational Administration*, 31(2), 13–34.

Holmes, K. and Crossley, M. (2004), Whose knowledge, whose values? The contribution of local knowledge to education policy processes: a case study of research development initiatives in the small state of Saint Lucia, *Compare,* 34(2), 197–214.

IRIN (2003), *Cape Verde: Feeding for the Future*, UN Office for the Coordination of Human Affairs.

Louisy, H. (1999), Preface, in Crossley, M. and Holmes, K. (1999), *Educational Development in the Small States of the Commonwealth: Retrospect and Prospect*, London, Commonwealth Secretariat.

Luteru, P. and Teasdale, G. (1993), Aid and education in the South Pacific: The context for development, *Comparative Education*, 29(3), 293–306.

Murray Thomas, R. (1993), Education in the South Pacific: The context for development, *Comparative Education*, 29(3), 233–247.

Pashiardis, P. and Ribbins, P. (2003), On Cyprus: The making of secondary school principals, *International Studies in Educational Administration*, 31(2), 13–34.

Read, R. (2004), The implications of increasing globalisation and regionalism for economic growth of small island states, *World Development*, 32(2), 365–378.

Scott, F. (2001), Developing human resources for effective school management in small Caribbean states, *International Journal of Educational Development*, 21, 245–256.

Smith, R. (2006), When is an island not an island?, *Journal of Developing Societies*, 22(3), 227–233.

Watson, K. (2001), Comparative educational research: The need for reconceptualisation and fresh insights, in Watson, K. (Ed.), *Doing Comparative Research: Issues and Problems,* Oxford, Symposium Books, pp. 23–42.

23

Epilogue

Jacky Lumby, Petros Pashiardis and Gary Crow

SO WHERE HAVE WE GOT TO?

Editing this volume has been a journey where the endeavor to help others learn overlays considerable learning of our own. As we have discovered, the term 'international handbook' can be interpreted in very many different ways. Some focus on the word international, and assume that the volume will include reference to most, or even all, parts of the world. No doubt there will be those who skim the table of contents and note that there is no chapter related to their corner of the globe. We were aware at the commencement of the project that such global inclusiveness is not possible. We are now even more certain, having received the contributions of authors which evidence the extensive, expansive and rich variation of leadership and its development, even within each nation state, let alone across the world. A handbook is not an encyclopedia, and 'international' has always signified to us a state of mind, not a travelogue.

The term 'handbook' has similar connotations for some, raising expectations of an all encompassing tour of current practice and research. Such an aim can never be achieved in any absolute sense. Nevertheless, we feel the volume represents an extensive review of the state of the art of leadership development in primary and secondary educational contexts, sufficient to allow judgment of major themes, trends, and the extent of the field's research based knowledge and understanding. What we know and how we know it emerges from the multiplicity of ontological, epistemological and axiological positions of the authors. The third question which follows, raised by Peter Ribbins in his chapter, is what should be done? The handbook contains a rich array of ideas in response to this question, both in terms of the advances in the practice of leadership preparation and development and further research which may be needed.

Reflecting on our process of editing, what then justifies the title international handbook? Primarily, it is the rich diversity of content which, though it allows dipping in to consider just one perspective or a single context, also provides an opportunity for the reader to adopt integrative, intercultural, interdisciplinary, and comparative perspectives, as defined in our introduction, thereby supporting heightened sensitivity to context and knowledge of global trends (Paige & Mestenhauser, 1999).

In this epilogue we take a final brief look at the handbook's major themes: the nature and importance of leadership, and consequently its preparation and development. We also reflect on trends in practice and the research issues which result.

LEADERSHIP AND ITS DEVELOPMENT

In his chapter, Begley provides an analysis of the meta-purposes of leadership. However, the difference the detail at the micro level makes leaps out from even a cursory skim of chapters. The impact of, for example, faith and philosophy, of culture, of the perspective of each gender, render leadership a profoundly various and variously perceived human activity. Despite the lack of accord on what leadership is and particularly how it is most effectively enacted, many authors attest to the growing attention to leadership by educational policy makers and the wide agreement on the need for school leaders who exhibit the capacity to improve the quality of teaching, learning and wider community outcomes. Consequently, it is not surprising that leadership preparation and development have also become major areas of concern. Many countries have given increasing consideration to providing appropriate training and professional development opportunities to aspiring and existing school leaders.

Huber's chapter uses his 2004 study to reveal a number of patterns or tendencies in school leadership development around the world. A trend appears to be the growing recognition that schools are not static organizations that require administration, but learning organizations in need of continuous development. His findings indicate the persistence of programs aimed at improving the individual school leader's competencies while other models are emerging, focused on enhancing the collective leadership capacity of the whole school. If whole school development is the aim, then the target group widens, potentially including not only staff, but also parents and members of the local and political communities. However, only a few programs appear to be designed with more than the individual leader, and particularly the principal, in mind. While some strands of leadership theorizing may think teams and communities, formal and informal development persistently thinks individual. Hierarchy and charisma, largely set aside within Anglophone leadership theory, remain deeply embedded in many preparation and development programs throughout the world. However, the content of the handbook also makes clear that hierarchy matters considerably in many cultures and that there are multiple ways of thinking about leadership, and therefore its preparation. For example, Macpherson and Tofighian lead us to an understanding of the profound implications of Middle Eastern faiths and philosophy, challenging the primacy of Anglophone theory, and particularly its grounding in rationality.

A second trend is an international tendency to move away from standardized programs for all participants in a specific time frame. Instead, leadership development is increasingly conceptualized as a continuous, life-long process responding to different career stages and customized to the needs of leaders and their schools. Professional development is shifting to modularized, multi-phase designs with an emphasis on leading and improving schools, rather than just managing and maintaining them. It follows that school leaders are expected to initiate, support and sustain continuous change and improvement for the benefit of all students.

In this context, while some development remains traditional in purpose and method, other programs are moving away from administrative and legal aspects to incorporate or strengthen communication and cooperation, using a wider range of modes of learning and delivery. Problem-based learning, project work, internships, shadowing, coaching and mentoring involve participants in cooperative problem solving processes.

A third trend is the politicization of leadership development, at least in some settings. Due to the added attention from policy makers of school leadership development and the shortage in some areas of school leaders, there is a tendency to view leadership development in a more contested and political way. Calls for greater variety in the sources of leadership development as well as calls for the assessment of leadership development programs and initiatives are two examples of this politicization. The rise of non-governmental organizations as major sources of leadership preparation has increased the variety of leadership providers as well as the contested view of what is considered appropriate preparation pedagogy, curriculum, and models. In addition, the neo-conservative swing of governments in some countries has increased the pressure on traditional leadership preparation and development providers and emphasized calls for the assessment of leadership preparation. While this assessment is long overdue, the purpose is not always politically neutral. These factors suggest that the future of leadership development is likely to continue to be politically charged. Whether this will enhance or hinder the investigation and debate around leadership development is still to be seen.

RESEARCHING LEADERSHIP PREPARATION AND DEVELOPMENT

In our introduction, we envisioned research and scholarship as a world effort to solve problems which are both locally specific and globally present (Heck, 1998). We outlined some of the barriers identified by Heck over a decade ago: an absence of a universal leadership paradigm, a disproportionate focus on the principal alone and insufficiently sophisticated and rigorous methods (Heck, 1996). In their chapter Leithwood and Levin describe the advances made but also the numerous persisting issues. They depict the way forward as predicated on a greater degree of contact and cooperation between researchers to allow more 'cumulative and replicative research'. In their view, more of the same is unlikely to bring significant advances in how we understand the efficacy of development. As editors reflecting on the handbook chapters as a whole, we agree. The challenges in achieving contact and cooperation are considerable, but the volume gives signs of some progress. The dominance of Anglophone theory and practice is subject to a rising tide of objection. While many chapters draw on single country or small scale research, larger cross nation and cross cultural studies are also evident. Paradigms of leadership which recognize the significance of culture, emotion or of faith signal dissatisfaction with the limitations of rational approaches. Experimentation and evaluation of experimentation in development processes is breaking the hold of traditional course based approaches. There is also evidence of a lack of movement. The focus on the principal seems relatively unshaken as yet, despite the growth in emphasis on variations of distributed, dispersed, democratic and community construction of leadership. Equity is far from achieved, for women and people of color particularly. The volume celebrates the distance we have come, but also identifies the road yet to be traveled. Our hope as editors is that the handbook will provide a resource and inspiration for the many scholars, policy makers and practitioners committed to the road.

REFERENCES

Heck, R. (1996). Leadership and Culture: Conceptual and methodological issues in comparing models across cultural settings. *Journal of Educational Administration*, *34*(5), 74–97.

Heck, R. H. (1998). Conceptual and methodological issues in investigating principal leadership across cultures, *Peabody Journal of Education*, *73*(2), 51–80.

Paige, R. M. & Mestenhauser, J. A. (1999). Internationalizing Educational Administration, *Educational Administration Quarterly*, *35*(4), 500–517.

INDEX

A

Accountability
    in China, 413
    in context of principal evaluations, 271, 273
    as dominant meta-value, 38
    effects of demands of principalship, 276
    emphasis on school administrator, 265
    in Europe, 348
    in Mexico, 316
    and principal evaluations, 264
    and summative evaluations, 265
    in three Chinese-speaking societies, 412
    training in Australia, 445
Accountability pressures, 1
Adab, 404, 405
Administration
    de-emphasis on, 169–170
    as focus in Hong Kong, 420
Administrator internship placements, 98
Adult learning, 151
Aesthetic purposes, of education, 21–22
Affection, role in early learning, 146–147
Affirmative action, 114
    failure to alleviate gender inequities, 130
    unresolved gender inequities with, 120
Africa
    Anglophone and Francophone traditions, 367, 368
    centralization of school curricula, 376
    characteristics, roles and contexts of school leaders, 374–376
    colonial education heritage, 368
    colonialization legacy, 367
    culture of violence effects on schools, 378–379
    current research, 376
    democratization of school management, 375
    dilemmas in school leadership, 377–379
    dropout rates, 377
    funding problems for schools, 377
    gender issues in education, 379
    leadership curriculum examples, 205
    missionary education, 368
    Nigerian curriculum, 205
    parent inaccessibility, 378

    primary education dilemmas, 377
    progress in school leadership development, 376
    school leadership development in, 367, 368–374
    sociopolitical context, 367–368
    South African curriculum, 205–206
    teacher salary dilemmas, 378
    textbook shortages, 378
    traditional Islamic education, 368
    traditional precolonial education, 367–368
    tribe, clan, and religion influences, 375
Al-Farabi, 399, 400
Andragogy, 151
Animus anima, 148
Arenas of influence, 31–32
Argentina, 325
    crisis in public schools, 328
    mutual distrust between administration and school system, 337
    resistance to autonomy process, 330
    school leaders' work in, 336
    social and political context, 325
    "taxi" teachers phenomenon, 330
Ashland University (Ohio/U.S.), 220
Assessment centers
    calls for, 467
    in England, 182–183
Attachment behavior, 147, 159
    applicability to adult learning, 150
Attachment styles, 147
Attribution theory, 149
Australasia
    Australian curricula, 209
    leadership curriculum examples, 209
    New Zealand leadership curricula, 209
    University of Wollongong curriculum, 209–210
Australia
    advertising and marketing, 191
    assessment issues, 438, 441, 447
    career pathways, 436–438
    Coaching for Experienced Principals program, 250
    commonalities with U.S. entrepreneurial programs, 224
    content of leadership learning, 445–446